Clinician's Guide to Bipolar Disorder

Clinician's Guide to Bipolar Disorder

Editor: Francisco Watkins

AMERICAN
MEDICAL PUBLISHERS
www.americanmedicalpublishers.com

AMERICAN
MEDICAL PUBLISHERS
www.americanmedicalpublishers.com

Cataloging-in-Publication Data

Clinician's guide to bipolar disorder / edited by Francisco Watkins.
p. cm.
Includes bibliographical references and index.
ISBN 979-8-88740-013-6
1. Manic-depressive illness. 2. Manic-depressive illness--Treatment. 3. Cognitive neuroscience.
4. Depression, Mental. 5. Mania. I. Watkins, Francisco.
RC516 .C55 2023
616.895--dc23

American Medical Publishers,
41 Flatbush Avenue,
1st Floor, New York,
NY 11217, USA

ISBN 979-8-88740-013-6 (Hardback)

Contents

Preface

Bipolar disorder refers to the mental health condition and chronic mood disorder that involves abrupt changes in behavior, mood, thought processes and energy levels. Cyclothymic disorder, bipolar I disorder and bipolar II disorder are the three primary types of bipolar disorders. A few of the prominent symptoms of bipolar disorder are erratic changes in behavior and mood, which can cause serious distress and difficulty in daily life. Other significant symptoms include an extremely low or elevated mood. The risk factors of bipolar disorder include significant levels of trauma or stress, certain medical conditions, family history of bipolar disorder, and alcohol or drug addiction. It can be diagnosed through a variety of methods including mood charting, physical examinations, psychiatric evaluations, etc. The treatment of bipolar disorder includes a variety of therapies, such as self-management techniques, psychotherapy, beneficial lifestyle behaviors, and medications. This book aims to understand the clinical perspectives of bipolar disorders. It presents researches and studies performed by experts across the globe. The book is appropriate for students seeking detailed information in this area as well as for experts.

Various studies have approached the subject by analyzing it with a single perspective, but the present book provides diverse methodologies and techniques to address this field. This book contains theories and applications needed for understanding the subject from different perspectives. The aim is to keep the readers informed about the progresses in the field; therefore, the contributions were carefully examined to compile novel researches by specialists from across the globe.

Indeed, the job of the editor is the most crucial and challenging in compiling all chapters into a single book. In the end, I would extend my sincere thanks to the chapter authors for their profound work. I am also thankful for the support provided by my family and colleagues during the compilation of this book.

Editor

1

C-reactive protein concentration in bipolar disorder: association with genetic variants

Ann-Kristin Evers[1], Julia Veeh[1], Rhiannon McNeill[1,2], Andreas Reif[1†] and Sarah Kittel-Schneider[1,2*†]

Abstract

Background: Several recent studies have investigated the role of C-reactive protein (CRP) in bipolar disorder (BD), but few studies have directly investigated the interaction between *CRP* genetic variants and peripheral CRP concentration across different phases of BD. In this study, we aimed to replicate previous findings that demonstrated altered CRP levels in BD, and to investigate whether there is an association of peripheral protein expression with genetic variants in the *CRP* gene.

Methods: 221 patients were included in the study, of which 183 (all episodes, 46 not medicated, 174 medicated) were genotyped for *CRP* single-nucleotide polymorphisms (SNPs) shown to influence peripheral CRP protein expression (rs1800947, rs2808630, rs1417938, rs1205).

Results: There were no differences in CRP levels associated with the genotypes, only regarding the rs1205 SNP there were significantly different CRP protein expression between the genotypes when taking body mass index, age, BD polarity, subtype and leukocyte number into account. However, we could show significantly elevated CRP protein expression in manic patients compared to euthymic and depressed patients, independent from genotype. Medication was found to have no effect on CRP protein expression.

Conclusions: These results indicate that low grade inflammation might play a role in mania and might be rather a state than a trait marker of bipolar disorder.

Keywords: Bipolar disorder, Genotype, C-reactive protein, Biomarker, Inflammation

Background

Bipolar disorder (BD) is primarily a periodic disease that has a global burden (Ferrari et al. 2016). It is characterized by the occurrence of (hypo-)manic and depressive episodes, and in a number of patients these mood states increase in frequency and severity over time, as well as decreasing responsiveness to treatment and that can result in a chronic course (Gildengers et al. 2014). The pathogenesis of BD is still relatively unknown. According to current findings, it is a multifactorial disease (Pitchot et al. 2012). BD is among the psychiatric disorders with the highest heritability, which is estimated at about 80% (Craddock and Jones 1999). However, developmental and environmental risk factors are additionally thought to play a role in the pathogenesis of the disorder (Landgraf et al. 2014).

There is increasing evidence that neuro-inflammation may play a role in the molecular pathomechanisms of BD (Muneer 2016). Increased levels of the inflammatory marker C-reactive protein (CRP) have been reported in BD in comparison to healthy controls (Bai et al. 2014; Chang and Chen 2017; Dargél et al. 2015). Elevated CRP levels have also been associated with an increased level of all-cause mortality in BD (Hayes et al. 2015). BD has been linked to metabolic and immunologic dysregulations (Berk et al. 2013; Leboyer et al. 2016; Modabbernia et al. 2013; Munkholm et al. 2013), and in BD patients, there appears to be a high comorbidity with somatic diseases such as cardiovascular disease, diabetes mellitus and autoimmune thyroiditis (Benros et al. 2013; Chakrabarti

*Correspondence: kittel_s@ukw.de
†Andreas Reif and Sarah Kittel-Schneider contributed equally to this work
[2] Department of Psychiatry, Psychosomatic Medicine and Psychotherapy, University Hospital, University of Würzburg, Margarete-Höppel-Platz 1, 97080 Würzburg, Germany
Full list of author information is available at the end of the article

2011; Rosenblat et al. 2017). In support of this, mortality due to cardiovascular disease has been reported as doubled in BD patients (Osby et al. 2001). Taken together, it has therefore been suggested that there are inflammatory subgroups in BD, and possibly also in other psychiatric disorders (Osimo et al. 2018). This would place these types of mood disorder in an inflammatory disease cluster, together with e.g. cardiovascular disease and obesity, in a "diseasesome" network (Midic et al. 2009; Perrino et al. 2017). Delineating this cluster, for example with the help of biomarkers, might pinpoint a group of patients which could be responsive to treatment options targeting the inflammasome.

The potential role and the direction of causality of CRP in the pathogenesis of BD is currently unclear. It has been hypothesized that stress can trigger an increase in CRP expression, which in turn leads to increased permeability of the blood–brain barrier. This consequently permits easier diffusion across the barrier for certain molecules, such as pro-inflammatory cytokines or auto-antibodies, which could cause multiple abnormalities in the brain (Hsuchou et al. 2012). CRP levels may act as a mood state marker in BD (Dargél et al. 2015; Jacoby et al. 2016; Wysokinski et al. 2015), and high levels of CRP may also represent an early warning sign for the onset of manic symptoms in depressed patients (Becking et al. 2013). Studies in the general population suggest that elevated CRP levels may even be predictive for the onset of BD (Wium-Andersen et al. 2016), and high levels of CRP are significantly correlated with BD disease severity (Dickerson et al. 2007; Lee et al. 2013). However, there are also negative findings regarding an association of CRP and BD, which may be partly due to the immunosuppressive actions of mood stabilizing medication (Dickerson et al. 2015; Haarman et al. 2014). Furthermore, it is not known what may trigger CRP production in BD patients. External stressors might activate the hypothalamus–pituitary–adrenal (HPA) axis, leading to increased secretion of cortisol and adrenergic hormones and an according change in immunological processes. However as elevated CRP levels are only found in a subgroup of BD patients, genetic susceptibility might pay a role. In support of this, several genetic polymorphisms in the CRP and other genes have been shown to influence peripheral CRP levels in different cohorts of psychiatric and non-psychiatric patients, as well as the general population (Carlson et al. 2005; Halder et al. 2010; Pankow et al. 2001; Prins et al. 2016; Reiner et al. 2012).

The first aim of the present cross-sectional study was to determine whether *CRP* genotype influences peripheral CRP concentration in BD patients. Patients were genotyped for the previously published functional *CRP* single nucleotide polymorphisms (SNPs) rs1800947 (Halder et al. 2010), rs1417938 (Henderson et al. 2015; Martínez-Calatrava et al. 2007), rs1205 (Halder et al. 2010; Flores-Alfaro et al. 2012) and rs2808630 (Kittel-Schneider et al. 2018). We then investigated a possible association of current polarity, bipolar subtype, medication and several other variables with serum CRP concentration.

Methods

Participants

A naturalistic sample of 221 BD patients in all mood phases (depressed, manic, mixed, euthymic) were recruited from 2009 to 2014 who were treated as inpatients at the Department of Psychiatry, Psychosomatic Medicine and Psychotherapy, University Hospital Würzburg, Würzburg, Germany. The patients were all of Caucasian origin and mostly from the lower Franconian area. The patients were diagnosed according to DSM-IV criteria independently by two specialists (SKS and AR). Information about smoking status, BMI, medication, CRP values, renal function and leukocyte values was obtained from the clinical routine data during the inpatient treatment. Blood for CRP analysis was drawn of the majority of the patients when the patients were admitted, only in few cases (the euthymic cases) blood was taken for CRP levels when the patients were discharged. A detailed description of sample characteristics and demographic data is presented in Table 1. Inclusion criteria were a diagnosis of bipolar disorder as primary psychiatric diagnosis and age $\geq$ 18 years. Exclusion criteria were severe somatic disorders (severe cardiovascular disease, severe neurological diseases, acute or chronic infections, carcinomas and autoimmune diseases) and organic affective disorders. Written informed consent was obtained from all participants before study evaluation. The authors assert that all procedures contributing to this work comply with the ethical standards of the relevant national and institutional committees on human experimentation and with the Helsinki Declaration of 1975, as revised in 2008. The ethics committee of the University of Würzburg approved the study.

Genotyping

183/221 participants gave approval for genetic testing. DNA was isolated from ethylenediaminetetraacetic acid (EDTA)-monovettes using the de-salting method (Miller et al. 1988) and DNA concentration and quality was assessed by spectrophotometric measurement (Infinite® 200 PRO, *Tecan Group Ltd., Männedorf, Switzerland*). Competitive Allele Specific Polymerase Chain Reaction (KASP) assay (He et al. 2014) was performed according to manufacturer's instructions (LGC Genomics, *Berlin, Germany*) to genotype previously published SNPs in the *CRP* gene (rs1800947, rs1417938, rs1205

Table 1 Sample characteristics and demographic data of bipolar patients

		n	Ratio
Sex (male/female)		86/135	0.64
Cigarettes (smoker/non-smoker)		100/103	0.97
	n	**M**	**SD**
Age at sampling (years)	221	49.6	15.10
BMI (kg/m^2)	139	28.2	6.01
Leukocytes (1000/µl)	204	6.6	3.77
MDRD (ml/min/1.73 m^2)	206	86.7	23.58
Medication			**N**
Lithium only MS			9
Anticonvulsant only MS			5
Antipsychotic only MS			16
Combination Li + antidepressant			14
Combination Li + antipsychotic			15
Combination Li + antidepressant + antipsychotic			28
Combination Li + anticonvulsant + antidepressant			6
Combination Li + anticonvulsant + antipsychotic			8
Combination Li + anticonvulsant + antidepressant + antipsychotic			6
Combination anticonvulsant + antidepressant			9
Combination anticonvulsant + antipsychotic			14
Combination antidepressant + antipsychotic			31
Combination anticonvulsant + antidepressant + antipschotic			14
No mood stabilizer			46
Only antidepressants			16
No psychotropic medication			30
Medication not available			1
Subtype			**N**
Bipolar I/Bipolar II/Bipolar III/not specified			108/85/5/23
Polarity at sampling			**N**
Euthymic			7
Depressed			123
Manic (including hypomanic and mixed states)			89
Illness duration (in years)			18.14 ± 12.5
Number of depressed episodes			9.67 ± 18.55
Number of manic episodes			1.75 ± 7.97
Number mixed episodes			7.06 ± 16.85
Number of all previous episodes			17.51 ± 35.91

BMI body mass index, *MDRD* Modification of Diet in Renal Disease, *MS* mood stabilizer, *Li* lithium

and one tagSNP rs2808630). The SNPs were selected due to previously published studies in different study population which showed that those common variants might influence the CRP protein levels [rs1800947 (Halder et al. 2010), rs1417938 (Henderson et al. 2015; Martínez-Calatrava et al. 2007), rs1205 (Halder et al. 2010; Flores-Alfaro et al. 2012) and rs2808630 (Kittel-Schneider et al. 2018)].

5 to 50 ng/µl of DNA was tested in a 384-well plate by Wet DNA method. Fluorescent signal from the two FRET (fluorescence resonance energy transfer) cassettes [frequency- and amplitude modulation (FAM) and hexachlorocyclopentadiene (HEX)] was detected with a LightCycler® 480 (F. Hoffmann-La Roche Ltd., *Basel, Switzerland*). In order to confirm the genotyping quality, we analyzed samples in duplicates as internal controls

on each plate, including negative water controls. As an external control, two additional samples whose genotypes were already known were also included on each plate, confirming the genotyping quality over all measurements. Genotype frequencies of all tested *CRP* SNPs were consistent with the Hardy–Weinberg equilibrium. Recently, rs17460165, rs17860481 and rs52802864 SNPs have been merged into one SNP, rs1800947. However, C and G alleles are the most common alleles in the European population, therefore it did not appear necessary to genotype for other newly described alleles (see http://www.ensembl.org/Homo_sapiens/Variation/Sequence?db=core;r=1:159713148-159714148;v=rs1800947;vdb=variation;vf=1229971).

CRP serum levels

CRP serum levels were measured in routine blood parameter checks when patients were hospitalized. Serum CRP was measured with the cobas® system (cobas® Integra 800, cobas® 6000, cobas® 8000, *Roche Diagnostics, Indianapolis, USA*) according to manufacturer's instructions. This system measures human CRP by agglutination with latex particles which are coated with anti-CRP-antibodies. The amount of agglutination is then measured by turbidimetry at 552 nm. The normal range of CRP with this method is given between 0.0 and 0.5 mg/dl.

Statistical analysis

Statistical analyses were conducted with SPSS (Statistical Package for the Social Sciences for Windows, version 24, IBM Corp., Armonk, New York). CRP levels were not normally distributed, as revealed by testing with the Kolmogorov–Smirnov and Shapiro–Wilk tests (both $p<0.001$). Therefore non-parametric tests were conducted to determine whether genotype differences could be seen in CRP expression (Kruskal–Wallis test, Mann–Whitney U-test). When the number of patients was large enough in the subgroup analysis, for example regarding the episodes, ANOVA and ANCOVA were also performed. For those SNPs whose subgroups were large enough, we additionally conducted exploratory ANOVA and ANCOVA analysis including several covariates. Correlation of CRP with metric variables was tested by Spearman's test. The level of significance was corrected for multiple comparison with Bonferroni correction (4 tested SNPs for the main hypothesis, $p \leq 0.05/4$) and set at $p \leq 0.013$.

Results

Association of confounders with CRP levels

CRP serum levels in the whole sample were significantly positively correlated with body mass index (Spearman's correlation $r=0.359$, $p<0.0001$), age (Spearman's correlation $r=0.186$, $p=0.005$) and leukocyte numbers (Spearman's correlation, $r=0.253$, $p<0.0001$). Renal function as measured by Modification of Diet in Renal Disease (MDRD) value were not significantly correlated with CRP levels. Even though nominally increased CRP values were observed in male patients ($n=86$, $M=0.4280$ mg/dl, *SD* 0.90729) compared to female patients ($n=135$, $M=0.3805$ mg/dl, *SD* 0.05137), the difference was not statistically significant [t (219) $= -0.470$, $p=0.639$]. The same applies to the nominally increased CRP for smokers ($n=100$, $M=0.446$ mg/dl, *SD* 0.85207) compared to non-smokers ($n=103$, $M=0.3670$ mg/dl, *SD* 0.65085). CRP levels were not significantly different between patients taking lithium and patients taking other medication (lithium group n = 86 vs. non-lithium group n = 135, Mann–Whitney-U-test, $p=0.512$).

The BD group as a whole had a mean CRP concentration of 0.40 ml/*dl* (±0.73 mg/dl SD; 95% CI 0.30 to 0.50), with significantly elevated CRP levels during manic episodes after correction for multiple comparison [ANOVA, F (2, 216) $=5.888$, $p=0.003$] (see Fig. 1) compared to euthymic and depressed episodes. Manic patients had a mean CRP level concentration of 0.60 mg/dl (±1.05 mg/dl *SD*, with a range between 0.01 mg/dl and 5.90 mg/dl), while euthymic patients had a mean concentration of 0.20 mg/dl (±0.22 mg/dl *SD*, with a range between 0.03 mg/dl and 0.68 mg/dl) and depressed patients had a mean concentration of 0.27 mg/dl (±0.34 mg/dl *SD*, with a range between 0.01 mg/dl and 1.99 mg/dl) (see Fig. 1). Significant differences were additionally found relating to the subtypes of BD. Patients classified as bipolar subtype I ($n=108$, $M=0.5340$ mg/dl, *SD* 0.07176) had significantly elevated CRP levels [t (139, 792) $=2.717$, $p=0.007$] in

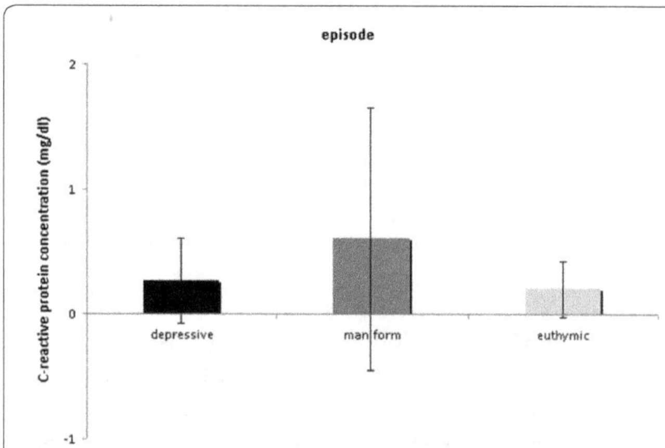

Fig. 1 Measured levels of C-reactive protein levels in bipolar patients in different episodes. Manic patients (n = 89) showed significantly higher C-reactive protein levels as compared to euthymic (n = 7) and depressed patients (n = 123) (ANOVA, $p=0.003$). C-reactive protein levels are given as mean values ± standard deviation

comparison to bipolar subtype II ($n=85$, $M=0.2601$ mg/dl, *SD* 0.34693), BD III and BD NOS. However, because there were significantly more manic episode patients in the BD I group (Chi-Square test, $p=0.005$), an exploratory ANCOVA was calculated including episode as a covariate. The result was then no longer significant after correction for multiple comparison (ANCOVA, CRP concentration differences between BD I, BD II, BD III and BD NOS, $p=0.032$). Duration of illness was significantly positively correlated with CRP levels (Spearman's correlation $r=0.212$, $p=0.004$).

Association of genetic variation in the CRP gene with serum CRP concentration

We assessed if there were differences between the genotypes of four SNPs (rs1800947, rs1417938, rs1205 and rs2808630) in CRP levels (Table 2). No significant differences in CRP levels were detected between different genotypes using non parametric Kruskal–Wallis analysis. However, exploratory ANCOVA analysis using body mass index, leukocyte number, age, current polarity and bipolar subtype as covariables revealed significant differences between the genotypes in the rs1205 SNP, which remained marginally significant even after correcting for multiple comparison [ANCOVA, F (2, 710) = 1.023, $p=0.013$]. No significant differences were found for any of the other SNPs. However, there was a trend for increased CRP expression in the minor AA carriers of the rs1417938 SNP, for decreased CRP levels in the minor allele carriers of rs2808630 and rs1800947 SNPs (Table 2). The distribution of all genotypes, call rates and minor allel frequency is given in Additional file 1: Table S1.

Additionally, we evaluated if there was a different distribution of the genotypes between the different current episodes, which was not the case (Chi Square-test, every $p \geq 0.5$, see Additional file 2: Table S2a–d).

Discussion

We were able to replicate previous findings of increased CRP levels in BD patients suffering from a manic episode as compared to euthymic and depressed patients (Horsdal et al. 2017; Wysokinski et al. 2015). This finding is also supported by a previous meta-analysis (Fernandes et al. 2016). However, inconsistent findings have been reported, finding either no CRP level differences between episodes or also elevated CRP levels between in depressed vs. euthymic patients (Balukova et al. 2016; Jacoby et al. 2016; Tsai et al. 2014). Furthermore, a previous meta-analysis has shown significantly elevated CRP levels in manic but also in euthymic patients compared to depressed patients with BD (Dargél et al. 2015). Taken together, those results point to an inflammatory component in BD and the results of our own and previous studies suggest that elevated CRP levels might rather be a state than a trait marker of BD (Dargél et al. 2015). However, it has to be considered, that most studies are investigating medicated patients and medication might have an effect on CRP concentration. But it has been published that increased CRP levels could be measured during the manic episode of BD I patients, in this sample only in medication-free patients (Uyanik et al. 2015). Even though the anti-inflammatory effects of lithium could be demonstrated in earlier studies (Beurel and Jope 2014; Fond et al. 2014), lithium (among other drugs) did not have a significant effect on CRP concentration in our

Table 2 Genotype distribution and C-reactive protein concentration in bipolar patients

rs1800947	**GG**	**CG**	**CC**
n	140	17	2
CRP [mg/dl]	0.39 ± 0.73 SD	0.19 ± 0.23 SD	0.25 ± 0.10 SD
rs1417938	**TT**	**AT**	**AA**
n	89	75	15
CRP [mg/dl]	0.42 ± 0.88 SD	0.36 ± 0.52 SD	0.32 ± 0.27 SD
rs1205	**CC**	**CT**	**TT**
n	87	69	25
CRP [mg/dl]	0.41 ± 0.71 SD	0.32 ± 0.44 SD	0.43 ± 1.18 SD
rs2808630	**TT**	**CT**	**CC**
n	83	80	10
CRP [mg/dl]	0.37 ± 0.71 SD	0.35 ± 0.54 SD	0.82 ± 1.55 SD

Genotype distribution of the 4 investigated SNPs in the whole sample is displayed as well as mean CRP concentration ± SD

CRP C-reactive protein, *n* number, *SD* standard deviation

study which is consistent with a previous meta-analysis (Dargél et al. 2015).

As already shown, we also found an association between CRP level and body mass index (Bai et al. 2015; Marshe et al. 2017), and between CRP levels and patient's age (Avramopoulos et al. 2015; Wysokinski et al. 2015). Contrary to Horsdal et al. (2017), we were able to confirm a correlation between raised CRP levels and the white blood cell count, as documented in an earlier study (Tsai et al. 2014). However, we found only nominal but no significantly elevated CRP in the smokers vs. non-smokers in our study, in previous studies smoking significantly influenced CRP levels (Bai et al. 2015; Huang et al. 2013).

Although we could find an association between CRP concentration and mood episode, the directionality of this association cannot be positively inferred. Thus, the links between inflammation and this psychiatric disorder remain unclear and may be bi-directional. Further studies should investigate the relationship between CRP concentration and the progression of BD, and BD's potential role as an epiphenomenon of low-grade inflammation. Another explanation might be that increased CRP is due to activation of the stress axis in manic episodes because of the general increase in activity (psychomotor activity, lack of sleep, etc.). Additionally, we found a significant correlation of increased CRP levels with longer duration of the illness which could be interpreted as a sign of neuronal progression of the course of BD over the life span.

Regarding the question if CRP levels could be used as biomarker for early detection of emerging episodes in bipolar disorder or a prognostic biomarker for the course of the disorder of the life span including the development of somatic comorbidities, there are several issues that need to be addressed in future studies. The CRP level differences in the manic patients compared to the euthymic as well in our study as in previous studies are very small even if they are significantly different (Dargél et al. 2015; Uyanik et al. 2015). Therefore it is difficult to define a cut-off CRP level that could be used as an early detection for emerging manic episodes in the individual patient as well as use this as a prognostic marker for a more severe course or development of comorbid somatic diseases. It might prove more fruitful to develop composite-biomarkers for personalized early detection or prognosis by the integration of CRP and potentially other protein markers and genetic, imaging and neuropsychological data. However, to define inflammatory subgroups that might benefit from add-on inflammatory therapeutics might be possible using only slightly elevated CRP levels (Müller 2019; Soczynska et al. 2009).

In our study, there were hints that there are differences between the rs1205 SNP genotypes in our sample of bipolar patients regarding CRP levels. In a recent study investigating late life depression, female rs1205 TT carriers displayed significantly more depressed symptoms but had lower CRP levels than the other genotypes, while the AA carriers of female rs1417938 were associated with a decreased risk of depression and had slightly elevated CRP levels (Ancelin et al. 2015). In contrast to our findings, a lower concentration of CRP was reported in men with greater odds of having clinically significant depression, but only in patients with the rs1205 minor AA genotype (Almeida et al. 2009). Similarly, the major allele CC of the rs1205 SNP was strongly associated with adolescent emotional problems and metabolic syndrome (Gaysina et al. 2011).

Minor rs1205 allele (TT) carriers, who showed in our study featuring significantly increased CRP levels, might also be at elevated risk for somatic disorders, especially including cardiovascular and metabolic diseases. Homozygous variant-type (TT) carriers of rs1205 had a threefold increased risk for heart valve reoperation and elevated CRP levels compared to ancestral allele carriers (Lee et al. 2016; Wypasek et al. 2015). Peric and collaborators also reported a trend toward higher maximum transvalvular gradient in carriers of T alleles in the rs1205 SNP, suggesting that the T allele could be a potential marker concerning severe and heavily calcified aortic stenosis (Peric et al. 2013). The susceptibility and severity of community-acquired pneumonia was additionally associated with the frequency of the *CRP* rs1205 TT genotype (Chou et al. 2016). In the future, follow-up studies would be of high interest to investigate if those BD patients of our sample with CRP risk variants and/or elevated CRP might be at an increased risk for cardiovascular disease.

The remarkable overlap between psycho-immuno-endocrinologic mechanisms in BD and cardiometabolic illnesses, as well as other chronic inflammatory diseases, may be due to common genetic variants. It is of note that the rare recessive genotype rs1800947 CC of the CRP gene was recently found to have a significant influence on CRP concentration, mortality and depressive symptoms in chronic heart failure patients; the highest risk CC carriers had the highest hs-CRP levels (Kittel-Schneider et al. 2018). In comparison, our study revealed a trend of decreased CRP levels for rs1800947 CC carriers in BD patients which is in line with previous findings in the Health 2000 Study (Kettunen et al. 2011) as well as in other previous studies (Carlson et al. 2005; Miller et al. 2005; Zee and Ridker 2002). The reason for the contrasting results is unclear and indicated that genetic influences might lead to differential effects in different disorders.

Conclusions

In summary, we could add to the evidence that a part of the variance of CRP expression in serum could be explained by functional variants in the CRP gene. However, the direction and effect of those genetic variants seem to vary in different somatic and psychiatric disorders, as well as in the healthy general population. However, the differences between CRP levels between BD patients in a manic episode vs. depressed and euthymic patients were much more pronounced than the genotype effect. Further studies are therefore needed to confirm these current findings, and to determine whether CRP might be indeed more useful as an early detection or prognostic marker in BD or at least used as a part of a composite-biomarker, or might be suitable as a biomarker for distinguishing inflammatory subgroups.

Significant outcomes

CRP protein levels were significantly increased in bipolar manic patients.

BMI, age and leukocyte levels were positively correlated with CRP protein levels.

Duration of illness was positively correlated with CRP protein levels.

Strengths and limitations

The results of our study have some limitations. Firstly, the peripheral CRP level within the blood may also be influenced by further external factors which we did not take into account. Not only may the covariates considered by the present study (such as smoking or body mass index) play a role, but other parameters such as physical activity, an unhealthy lifestyle or stress may also influence CRP concentration. We were unable to include these other possible covariates in this study. Secondly, even though we excluded patients from the study who demonstrably suffered from current infections or carcinomas, it is possible that undiagnosed illnesses may have affected CRP levels. Thirdly, longitudinal data from different timepoints would have been more informative in the search for trait- or state biomarkers and inflammatory subtypes. Finally, the validity of the genetic results is limited by the relatively low number of patients.

The strength of the study is that we investigated a naturalistic sample of bipolar patients in all episodes and we could take several variables that might influence CRP levels into account because the information was available. Furthermore, this sample consisted of a relatively homogenous origin so that influences on CRP levels and differences in CRP genetic variants due to the origin of the patients are reduced.

Supplementary information

Additional file 1: Table S1. Distribution of genotypes of all tested SNPs.

Additional file 2: Table S2. a. Distribution of rs2808630 genotypes with regard to current episode. b. Distribution of rs1417938 genotypes with regard to current episode. c. Distribution of rs1205 genotypes with regard to current episode. d Distribution of rs1800947 genotypes with regard to current episode.

Abbreviations

BD: bipolar disorder; CRP: C-reactive protein; SNPs: single nucleotide polymorphisms; MDD: major depressive disorder; BMI: body mass index; MDRD: Modification of Diet in Renal Disease; MS: mood stabilizer; Li: lithium; HPA axis: hypothalamus–pituitary–adrenal axis; KASP: Competitive Allele Specific Polymerase Chain Reaction; EDTA: ethylenediaminetetraacetic acid; FRET: fluorescence resonance energy transfer; FAM: frequency- and amplitude modulation; HEX: hexachlorocyclopentadiene.

Acknowledgements

We thank Theresia Töpner for the technical support in the genotyping and the patients for participating in this study.

Authors' contributions

AKE, JV, SKS acquired and analyzed the data and drafted the article. RMcN and AR interpreted the data and revised the draft. AR and SKS contributed equally. All authors read and approved the final manuscript.

Author details

[1] Department of Psychiatry, Psychosomatic Medicine and Psychotherapy, University Hospital Frankfurt, Goethe University, Frankfurt Am Main, Germany. [2] Department of Psychiatry, Psychosomatic Medicine and Psychotherapy, University Hospital, University of Würzburg, Margarete-Höppel-Platz 1, 97080 Würzburg, Germany.

References

Almeida OP, Norman PE, Allcock R, van Bockxmeer F, Hankey GJ, Jamrozik K, Flicker L. Polymorphisms of the CRP gene inhibit inflammatory response and increase susceptibility to depression: the Health in Men Study. Int J Epidemiol. 2009;38:1049–59. https://doi.org/10.1093/ije/dyp199.

Ancelin M-L, Farré A, Carrière I, Ritchie K, Chaudieu I, Ryan J. C-reactive protein gene variants: independent association with late-life depression and circulating protein levels. Transl Psychiatry. 2015;5:e499. https://doi.org/10.1038/tp.2014.145.

Avramopoulos D, Pearce BD, McGrath J, Wolyniec P, Wang R, Eckart N, Hatzimanolis A, Goes FS, Nestadt G, Mulle J, et al. Infection and inflammation in schizophrenia and bipolar disorder: a genome wide study for interactions with genetic variation. PLoS ONE. 2015;10:e0116696. https://doi.org/10.1371/journal.pone.0116696.

Bai Y-M, Su T-P, Tsai S-J, Wen-Fei C, Li C-T, Pei-Chi T, Mu-Hong C. Comparison of inflammatory cytokine levels among type I/type II and manic/hypomanic/euthymic/depressive states of bipolar disorder. J Affect Disord. 2014;166:187–92. https://doi.org/10.1016/j.jad.2014.05.009.

Bai Y-M, Su T-P, Li C-T, Tsai S-J, Chen M-H, Tu P-C, Chiou W-F. Comparison of pro-inflammatory cytokines among patients with bipolar disorder and unipolar depression and normal controls. Bipolar Disord. 2015;17:269–77. https://doi.org/10.1111/bdi.12259.

Balukova SM, Haarman BCM, Riemersma-Van der Lek RF, Schoevers RA. Does CRP predict outcome in bipolar disorder in regular outpatient care? Int J Bipolar Disord. 2016;4:14. https://doi.org/10.1186/s40345-016-0055-3.

Becking K, Boschloo L, Vogelzangs N, Haarman BCM, Riemersma-van der Lek R, Penninx BWJH, Schoevers RA. The association between immune activation and manic symptoms in patients with a depressive disorder. Transl Psychiatry. 2013;3:e314. https://doi.org/10.1038/tp.2013.87.

Benros ME, Waltoft BL, Nordentoft M, Ostergaard SD, Eaton WW, Krogh J, Mortensen PB. Autoimmune diseases and severe infections as risk factors for mood disorders: a nationwide study. JAMA Psychiatry. 2013;70:812–20. https://doi.org/10.1001/jamapsychiatry.2013.1111.

Berk M, Williams LJ, Jacka FN, O'Neil A, Pasco JA, Moylan S, Allen NB, Stuart AL, Hayley AC, Byrne ML, et al. So depression is an inflammatory disease, but where does the inflammation come from? BMC Med. 2013;11:200. https://doi.org/10.1186/1741-7015-11-200.

Beurel E, Jope RS. Inflammation and lithium: clues to mechanisms contributing to suicide-linked traits. Transl Psychiatry. 2014;4:e488. https://doi.org/10.1038/tp.2014.129.

Carlson CS, Aldred SF, Lee PK, Tracy RP, Schwartz SM, Rieder M, Liu K, Williams OD, Iribarren C, Lewis EC, et al. Polymorphisms within the C-reactive protein (CRP) promoter region are associated with plasma CRP levels. Am J Hum Genet. 2005;77:64–77. https://doi.org/10.1086/431366.

Chakrabarti S. Thyroid functions and bipolar affective disorder. J Thyroid Res. 2011;2011:306367. https://doi.org/10.4061/2011/306367.

Chang HH, Chen PS. C-reactive protein as a differential biomarker of bipolar versus unipolar depression: response. World J Biol Psychiatry. 2017;18:73–4. https://doi.org/10.1080/15622975.2016.1208845.

Chou S-C, Ko H-W, Lin Y-C. CRP/IL-6/IL-10 single-nucleotide polymorphisms correlate with the susceptibility and severity of community-aquired pneumonia. Genet Test Mol Biomarkers. 2016;20:732–40. https://doi.org/10.1089/gtmb.2016.0156.

Craddock N, Jones I. Genetics of bipolar disorder. J Med Genet. 1999;36:585–94.

Dargél AA, Godin O, Kapczinski F, Kupfer DJ, Leboyer M. C-reactive protein alterations in bipolar disorder: a meta-analysis. J Clin Psychiatry. 2015;76:142–50. https://doi.org/10.4088/JCP.14r09007.

Dickerson F, Stallings C, Origoni A, Boronow J, Yolken R. Elevated serum levels of C-reactive protein are associated with mania symptoms in outpatients with bipolar disorder. Prog Neuropsychopharmacol Biol Psychiatry. 2007;31:952–5. https://doi.org/10.1016/j.pnpbp.2007.02.018.

Dickerson F, Katsafanas E, Schweinfurth LAB, Savage CLG, Stallings C, Origoni A, Khushalani S, Lillehoj E, Yolken R. Immune alterations in acute bipolar depression. Acta Psychiatr Scand. 2015;132:204–10. https://doi.org/10.1111/acps.12451.

ensembl.org. Hinxton: European Molecular Biology Laboratory´s European Bioinformatics Institute. http://www.ensembl.org/Homo_sapiens/Variation/Sequence?db=core;r=1:159713148-159714148;v=rs1800947;vdb=variation;vf=1229971. Accessed 18 Aug 2018.

Fernandes BS, Steiner J, Molendijk ML, Dodd S, Nardin P, Gonçalves C-A, Jacka F, Köhler CA, Karmakar C, Carvalho AF, et al. C-reactive protein concentrations across the mood spectrum in bipolar disorder: a systematic review and meta-analysis. Lancet Psychiatry. 2016;3:1147–56. https://doi.org/10.1016/S2215-0366(16)30370-4.

Ferrari AJ, Stockings E, Khoo J-P, Erskine HE, Degenhardt L, Vos T, Whiteford HA. The prevalence and burden of bipolar disorder: findings from the Global Burden of Disease Study 2013. Bipolar Disord. 2016;18:440–50. https://doi.org/10.1111/bdi.12423.

Flores-Alfaro E, Fernández-Tilapa G, Salazar-Martínez E, Cruz M, Illades-Aguiar B, Parra-Rojas I. Common variants in the CRP gene are associated with serum C-reactive protein levels and body mass index in healthy individuals in Mexico. Genet Mol Res. 2012;11:2258–67. https://doi.org/10.4238/2012.May.14.5.

Fond G, Hamdani N, Kapczinski F, Boukouaci W, Drancourt N, Dargel A, Oliveira J, Le Guen E, Marlinge E, Tamouza R, et al. Effectiveness and tolerance of anti-inflammatory drugs' add-on therapy in major mental disorders: a systematic qualitative review. Acta Psychiatr Scand. 2014;129:163–79. https://doi.org/10.1111/acps.12211.

Gaysina D, Pierce M, Richards M, Hotopf M, Kuh D, Hardy R. Association between adolescent emotional problems and metabolic syndrome: the modifying effect of C-reactive protein gene (CRP) polymorphisms. Brain Behav Immun. 2011;25:750–8. https://doi.org/10.1016/j.bbi.2011.01.019.

Gildengers AG, Chung K-H, Huang S-H, Begley A, Aizenstein HJ, Tsai S-Y. Neuroprogressive effects of lifetime illness duration in older adults with bipolar disorder. Bipolar Disord. 2014;16:617–23. https://doi.org/10.1111/bdi.12204.

Haarman BCM, Riemersma-Van der Lek RF, Burger H, Netkova M, Drexhage RC, Bootsman F, Mesman E, Hillegers MH, Spijker AT, Hoencamp E, et al. Relationship between clinical features and inflammation-related monocyte gene expression in bipolar disorder—towards a better understanding of psychoimmunological interactions. Bipolar Disord. 2014;16:137–50. https://doi.org/10.1111/bdi.12142.

Halder I, Marsland AL, Cheong J, Muldoon MF, Ferrell RE, Manuck SB. Polymorphisms in the CRP gene moderate an association between depressive symptoms and circulating levels of C-reactive protein. Brain Behav Immun. 2010;24:160–7. https://doi.org/10.1016/j.bbi.2009.09.014.

Hayes JF, Miles J, Walters K, King M, Osborn DPJ. A systematic review and meta-analysis of premature mortality in bipolar affective disorder. Acta Psychiatr Scand. 2015;131:417–25. https://doi.org/10.1111/acps.12408.

He C, Holme J, Anthony J. SNP genotyping: the KASP assay. Methods Mol Biol. 2014;1145:75–86. https://doi.org/10.1007/978-1-4939-0446-4_7.

Henderson P, Kennedy NA, van Limbergen JE, Cameron FL, Satsangi J, Russell RK, Wilson DC. Serum C-reactive protein and CRP genotype in pediatric inflammatory bowel disease: influence on phenotype, natural history, and response to therapy. Inflamm Bowel Dis. 2015;21:596–605. https://doi.org/10.1097/MIB.0000000000000296.

Horsdal HT, Köhler-Forsberg O, Benros ME, Gasse C. C-reactive protein and white blood cell levels in schizophrenia, bipolar disorders and depression—associations with mortality and psychiatric outcomes: a population-based study. Eur Psychiatry. 2017;44:164–72. https://doi.org/10.1016/j.eurpsy.2017.04.012.

Hsuchou H, Kastin AJ, Mishra PK, Pan W. C-reactive protein increases BBB permeability: implications for obesity and neuroinflammation. Cell Physiol Biochem. 2012;30:1109–19. https://doi.org/10.1159/000343302.

Huang C-C, Chung C-M, Leu H-B, Lin T-H, Hung S-I, Wu T-C, Huang P-H, Lin S-J, Pan W-H, Chen J-W. Genetic variation in C-reactive protein in ethnic Chinese population in Taiwan. Eur J Clin Invest. 2013;43:449–56. https://doi.org/10.1111/eci.12067.

Jacoby AS, Munkholm K, Vinberg M, Pedersen BK, Kessing LV. Cytokines, brain-derived neurotrophic factor and C-reactive protein in bipolar I disorder—results from a prospective study. J Affect Disord. 2016;197:167–74. https://doi.org/10.1016/j.jad.2016.03.040.

Kettunen T, Eklund C, Kähönen M, Jula A, Päivä H, Lyytikäinen L-P, Hurme M, Lehtimäki T. Polymorphism in the C-reactive protein (CRP) gene affects CRP levels in plasma and one early marker of atherosclerosis in men: the Health 2000 Survey. Scand J Clin Lab Invest. 2011;71:353–61. https://doi.org/10.3109/00365513.2011.568123.

Kittel-Schneider S, Kaspar M, Berliner D, Weber H, Deckert J, Ertl G, Störk S, Angermann C, Reif A. CRP genetic variants are associated with mortality and depressive symptoms in chronic heart failure patients. Brain Behav Immun. 2018;71:133–41. https://doi.org/10.1016/j.bbi.2018.04.002.

Landgraf D, McCarthy MJ, Welsh DK. Circadian clock and stress interactions in the molecular biology of psychiatric disorders. Curr Psychiatry Rep. 2014;16:483. https://doi.org/10.1007/s11920-014-0483-7.

Leboyer M, Oliveira J, Tamouza R, Groc L. Is it time for immunopsychiatry in psychotic disorders? Psychopharmacology. 2016;233:1651–60. https://doi.org/10.1007/s00213-016-4266-1.

Lee S-Y, Chen S-L, Chang Y-H, Chen PS, Huang S-Y, Tzeng N-S, Wang Y-S, Wang L-J, Lee IH, Wang T-Y, et al. Inflammation's association with metabolic profiles before and after a twelve-week clinical trial in drug-naïve patients with bipolar II disorder. PLoS ONE. 2013;8:e66847. https://doi.org/10.1371/journal.pone.0066847.

Lee KE, Kim JH, Chung JE, Lee GY, Cho YJ, Chang BC, Gwak HS. Association of inflammatory gene polymorphisms with mechanical heart valve reoperation. Springerplus. 2016;5:937. https://doi.org/10.1186/s40064-016-2566-x.

Marshe VS, Pira S, Mantere O, Bosche B, Looper KJ, Herrmann N, Müller DJ, Rej S. C-reactive protein and cardiovascular risk in bipolar disorder patients: a systematic review. Prog Neuropsychopharmacol Biol Psychiatry. 2017;79:442–51. https://doi.org/10.1016/j.pnpbp.2017.07.026.

Martínez-Calatrava MJ, González-Sánchez JL, Martínez-Larrad MT, Pérez-Barba M, Serrano-Ríos M. Common haplotypes of the C-reactive protein gene

and circulating leptin levels influence the interindividual variability in serum C-reactive protein levels. The Segovia study. Thromb Haemost. 2007;98:1088–95.
Midic U, Oldfield CJ, Dunker AK, Obradovic Z, Uversky VN. Unfoldomics of human genetic diseases: illustrative examples of ordered and intrinsically disordered members of the human diseasome. Protein Pept Lett. 2009;16:1533–47.
Miller SA, Dykes DD, Polesky HF. A simple salting out procedure for extracting DNA from human nucleated cells. Nucleic Acids Res. 1988;16:1215.
Miller DT, Zee RYL, Suk Danik J, Kozlowski P, Chasman DI, Lazarus R, Cook NR, Ridker PM, Kwiatkowski DJ. Association of common CRP gene variants with CRP levels and cardiovascular events. Ann Hum Genet. 2005;69:623–38. https://doi.org/10.1111/j.1529-8817.2005.00210.x.
Modabbernia A, Taslimi S, Brietzke E, Ashrafi M. Cytokine alterations in bipolar disorder: a meta-analysis of 30 studies. Biol Psychiatry. 2013;74:15–25. https://doi.org/10.1016/j.biopsych.2013.01.007.
Müller N. COX-2 inhibitors, aspirin, and other potential anti-inflammatory treatments for psychiatric disorders. Front Psychiatry. 2019;10:375. https://doi.org/10.3389/fpsyt.2019.00375.
Muneer A. Bipolar disorder: role of Inflammation and the development of disease biomarkers. Psychiatry Investig. 2016;13:18–33. https://doi.org/10.4306/pi.2016.13.1.18.
Munkholm K, Braüner JV, Kessing LV, Vinberg M. Cytokines in bipolar disorder vs healthy control subjects: a systematic review and meta-analysis. J Psychiatr Res. 2013;47:1119–33. https://doi.org/10.1016/j.jpsychires.2013.05.018.
Osby U, Brandt L, Correia N, Ekbom A, Sparén P. Excess mortality in bipolar and unipolar disorder in Sweden. Arch Gen Psychiatry. 2001;58:844–50.
Osimo EF, Cardinal RN, Jones PB, Khandaker GM. Prevalence and correlates of low-grade systemic inflammation in adult psychiatric inpatients: an electronic health record-based study. Psychoneuroendocrinology. 2018;91:226–34. https://doi.org/10.1016/j.psyneuen.2018.02.031.
Pankow JS, Folsom AR, Cushman M, Borecki IB, Hopkins PN, Eckfeldt JH, Tracy RP. Familial and genetic determinants of systemic markers of inflammation: the NHLBI family heart study. Atherosclerosis. 2001;154:681–9.
Peric D, Potaczek D, Wypasek E, Undas A. Association of the +1846 c>t (rs1205) polymorphism of the C-reactive protein gene with the severity of calcification and mean transvalvular gradient in aortic valve stenosis. Eur Heart J. 2013;34:P3914–P3914. https://doi.org/10.1093/eurheartj/eht309.P3914.
Perrino C, Barabási A-L, Condorelli G, Davidson SM, de Windt L, Dimmeler S, Engel FB, Hausenloy DJ, Hill JA, van Laake LW, et al. Epigenomic and transcriptomic approaches in the post-genomic era: path to novel targets for diagnosis and therapy of the ischaemic heart? Position Paper of the European Society of Cardiology Working Group on Cellular Biology of the Heart. Cardiovasc Res. 2017;113:725–36. https://doi.org/10.1093/cvr//cvx070.
Pitchot W, Scantamburlo G, Ansseau M, Souery D. Le trouble bipolaire: une affection bien complexe. Rev Med Liege. 2012;67:366–73.
Prins BP, Abbasi A, Wong A, Vaez A, Nolte I, Franceschini N, Stuart PE, Guterriez Achury J, Mistry V, Bradfield JP, et al. Investigating the causal relationship of C-reactive protein with 32 complex somatic and psychiatric outcomes: a large-scale cross-consortium mendelian randomization study. PLoS Med. 2016;13:e1001976. https://doi.org/10.1371/journal.pmed.1001976.
Reiner AP, Beleza S, Franceschini N, Auer PL, Robinson JG, Kooperberg C, Peters U, Tang H. Genome-wide association and population genetic analysis of C-reactive protein in African American and Hispanic American women. Am J Hum Genet. 2012;91:502–12. https://doi.org/10.1016/j.ajhg.2012.07.023.
Rosenblat JD, McIntyre RS. Bipolar disorder and immune dysfunction: epidemiological findings, proposed pathophysiology and clinical implications. Brain Sci. 2017. https://doi.org/10.3390/brainsci7110144.
Soczynska JK, Kennedy SH, Goldstein BI, Lachowski A, Woldeyohannes HO, McIntyre RS. The effect of tumor necrosis factor antagonists on mood and mental health-associated quality of life: novel hypothesis-driven treatments for bipolar depression? Neurotoxicology. 2009;30:497–521. https://doi.org/10.1016/j.neuro.2009.03.004
Tsai S-Y, Chung K-H, Huang S-H, Chen P-H, Lee H-C, Kuo C-J. Persistent inflammation and its relationship to leptin and insulin in phases of bipolar disorder from acute depression to full remission. Bipolar Disord. 2014;16:800–8. https://doi.org/10.1111/bdi.12240.
Uyanik V, Tuglu C, Gorgulu Y, Kunduracilar H, Uyanik MS. Assessment of cytokine levels and hs-CRP in bipolar I disorder before and after treatment. Psychiatry Res. 2015;228:386–92. https://doi.org/10.1016/j.psychres.2015.05.078.
Wium-Andersen MK, Ørsted DD, Nordestgaard BG. Elevated C-reactive protein and late-onset bipolar disorder in 78 809 individuals from the general population. Br J Psychiatry. 2016;208:138–45. https://doi.org/10.1192/bjp.bp.114.150870.
Wypasek E, Potaczek DP, Undas A. Association of the C-reactive protein gene (CRP) rs1205 C>T polymorphism with aortic valve calcification in patients with aortic stenosis. Int J Mol Sci. 2015;16:23745–59. https://doi.org/10.3390/ijms161023745.
Wysokiński A, Margulska A, Strzelecki D, Kłoszewska I. Levels of C-reactive protein (CRP) in patients with schizophrenia, unipolar depression and bipolar disorder. Nord J Psychiatry. 2015;69:346–53. https://doi.org/10.3109/08039488.2014.984755.
Zee RYL, Ridker PM. Polymorphism in the human C-reactive protein (CRP) gene, plasma concentrations of CRP, and the risk of future arterial thrombosis. Atherosclerosis. 2002;162:217–9.

2

The existential crisis of bipolar II disorder

Michael Gitlin[1*] and Gin S. Malhi[2,3]

Abstract

The issue of categorical vs. dimensional classification of bipolar disorder continues to generate controversy as it has for generations. Despite the evidence that no psychiatric disorder has discrete boundaries separating pathological and nonpathological states, and within a disorder, no clear differences separate subtypes-which would suggest a more dimensional approach-there are valid reasons to continue with our current categorical system, which distinguishes bipolar I from bipolar II disorder. Complicating the issue, a number of interested constituencies, including patients and their families, clinicians, scientists/researchers, and governmental agencies and insurance companies have different interests and needs in this controversy. This paper reviews both the advantages and disadvantages of continuing the bipolar I/bipolar II split vs. redefining bipolar disorder as one unified diagnosis. Even with one unified diagnosis, other aspects of psychopathology can be used to further describe and classify the disorder. These include both predominant polarity and categorizing symptoms by ACE-activity, cognition and energy. As a field, we must decide whether changing our current classification before we have a defining biology and genetic profile of bipolar disorder is worth the disruption in our current diagnostic system.

Keywords: Bipolar I, Bipolar II, Diagnosis, Nomenclature

Background

Until 25 years ago, bipolar II disorder was the Pinocchio of psychiatric disorders-long recognized and referred to- but not a "real disorder". Finally, in 1994, bipolar II disorder was finally given formal recognition in the Diagnostic and Statistical Manual of Mental Disorders (DSM-IV) (American Psychiatric Association 1994). This recognition has continued in all subsequent DSMs with notably little modification of its definition. Thus, as we settled into the new millennium it seemed as if bipolar II disorder had sufficiently matured and achieved full diagnostic status and was now on par with other major mood disorders such as major depression and bipolar I disorder. Indeed, a decade ago it was even deemed worthy of an entire book (Parker 2012). At the same time, its prevalence seemed to be increasing with estimates of an expanded definition (i.e., bipolar spectrum) up to 4.5% in one study and, with definitional modification, 10.9% in others (Merikangas et al. 2011; Angst et al. 2003). Surely, its status was assured.

And yet, in the last few years, a debate has arisen as to the validity and utility of bipolar II as a diagnostic category. Some authors have suggested its elimination (hence, the existential crisis) (Malhi et al. 2019a, b) while others support its continued inclusion in our diagnostic systems (Ha et al. 2019; Nierenberg 2019; Ostacher 2017; Post 2018, 2019; Schaffer 2018; Vieta 2019). In a field as imprecise as ours, it is not surprising that these debates occur. As always, there is at least some merit to both sides of the debate. This paper will summarize both sides of this discussion, highlighting the not always congruent needs of clinicians, patients, researchers and others and the role that this distinction plays in the debate.

History

As reviewed by Shorter (2012), the classification of mood disorders has a long history with a continued evolution over thousands of years. Although much of the effort prior to the last four decades was to conceptualize and elucidate the relationship between excited states and depressive states, there was frequent acknowledgment

*Correspondence: MGitlin@mednet.ucla.edu
[1] Department of Psychiatry, Geffen School of Medicine at UCLA, Los Angeles, USA
Full list of author information is available at the end of the article

about the dimensional nature of mood pathology. More recently, formally defining a subset of manic-depressive illness in which the patient never has marked excited states and at worse they are relatively mild, was first declared by the Research Diagnostic Criteria (Spitzer et al. 1978) in which the term bipolar II first appears. Remarkably, it took 16 more years for DSM to agree that the distinction between bipolar I and bipolar II was worthy of official recognition and include it in its 4th revision.

Core conceptual issue

As many observers have noted, the core issue in evaluating the merits of bipolar II as a distinct disorder is the creation of a categorical system (such as the DSM or ICD) for what are clearly dimensional forms of psychopathology. This is a problem for all psychiatric diagnoses to some extent and there is no evidence that *any* psychiatric disorder has discrete boundaries that demarcate the disorder either from other psychiatric disorders or normal nonpathological variations of mood, cognition, personality features and so on. This concept is implicitly acknowledged in the multicluster (A, B and C) approach in DSMs in which there was more overlap between some personality disorders (within clusters) than others (across clusters). Dimensional thinking in psychopathology has also given rise to the more colloquial description of spectrum disorders-depressive spectrum disorders, obsessive–compulsive spectrum disorders and, of course, bipolar spectrum disorders. The awkward 'fit' of dimensional pathology and measurement into boundary-driven categories is also true for many, but not all, nonpsychiatric disorders. As examples, the boundaries of hypertension and "mild" diabetes create categories out of dimensional measurements, with the definition of pathology shifting over time similar to what is seen in the diagnostic systems for psychiatric disorders. More generally, still, the same can be said for obesity and anorexia nervosa—both of which are subject to cultural factors.

For bipolar II disorder, the purely dimensional approach would be to conceptualize bipolar disorder as one diagnostic entity with variation in the expression of the disorder across individuals (Malhi et al. 2016). In contrast, the categorical approach, currently expressed in our major diagnostic systems, is predicated on the assumption that although there are sufficient similarities to warrant grouping of the disorders there are also sufficient and important distinctions between bipolar disorders (bipolar I vs. bipolar II) to justify the different names/labels (see below for a more detailed discussion of the merits of each of these approaches). As the most egregious example in psychiatry, providing different diagnostic terms and different diagnostic codes to major depression and dysthymic disorder (as occurs in both the DSM and ICD systems) suggests to clinicians, especially those in training, that these are separate disorders even though the preponderance of the evidence suggests that they are one depressive disorder with differences in course. In this way, our diagnostic systems shape clinicians' thinking, some times in ways that are clinically simply wrong.

The use of diagnostic categories and systems

A key question that governs the dimensional/categorical distinction in difficult contexts is: for whom are diagnostic categories composed? In other words, who needs or uses them? It would seem that four groups have a stake in this: (1) patients and their families; (2) clinicians; (3) scientists/clinical researchers; and (4) governmental agencies, insurance companies and the legal profession—all have differing needs, make different uses of the diagnoses and require different applications from a diagnostic system.

The first group that has an interest in this issue are patients and their families. As Porter (1997) reminded us, among the central roles that physicians have been tasked with for millennia is giving semantic shape—a label, a diagnosis—to patients' suffering due to illness. For this purpose, describing a disorder in dimensional terms simply does not suffice for most patients and their families. A term, a categorical diagnosis: "You have a disorder called X" is what is specifically asked for and needed. Does it help patients and their families to distinguish between bipolar I and II disorders vs. combining them within the term "bipolar disorder"? The recent controversy over the decision for DSM-5 to eliminate Asperger's syndrome as a separate disorder from autism and subsume it under autism spectrum disorders is another example of that controversy (see below for more discussion on this point).

The second group that is clearly invested in diagnosis is clinicians. They have a different set of needs from a diagnostic system as compared to patients and their families. For clinicians, a useful diagnostic system would conform (at least somewhat) with the clinical realities that they see (face validity), be simple enough to use without extraordinary training, provide them with a reliable and widely accepted language for communication and perhaps most importantly have clear prognostic and/or treatment implications. Given these multiple and specific needs, it is difficult (although not impossible) for clinicians to adapt to changes in the diagnostic system. Familiarity and expertise with a recognized system of classification means that there is inevitably significant inertia to change.

The third group, scientists/researchers, rely on diagnostic systems for different purposes than the other three groups. Scientists/researchers have the goals of:

(1) elucidating how psychopathology expresses itself in different categories, i.e. to have an accurate representation of how nature is "carved at the joints". This would require a set of biological and genetic studies to distinguish between related disorders based on scientific data, not somewhat arbitrary decisions by committees. (2) Accurate diagnostic classification based on biology would then lead to more targeted treatment algorithms that employ science/pathology based diagnoses. Analogies in medicine abound but maybe the best example is the distinction of different types of cancer even within the same general name, e.g., breast cancer, based on underlying biology-estrogen positive tumors are treated differently than are estrogen-negative cancers.

A fourth group-government agencies and insurance companies-comprise an interested group in only some countries, most glaringly, the United States. Here, the purpose of diagnoses may be to define psychopathological entities that justify treatment that will then be paid for by governmental or commercial insurances. In the United States, new medications are approved by the Food and Drug Adminstration (FDA) for the treatment of one or more specific disorders. If a medication is approved for treatment of bipolar I disorder but not bipolar II disorder, insurance payors may refuse to pay for treatment for the second (in this case, bipolar II) disorder. Clearly, having one more broadly defined category of bipolar disorder would obviate this problem.

Lumping vs. splitting: advantages and disadvantages

Each approach-combining bipolar I and II into one disorder vs. keeping them separate solves different problems. Table 1 presents the advantages of each of these two approaches.

Table 1 Advantages of *merging* bipolar I and II disorder vs. maintaining distinction

Advantages of merging
1. Conforms to clinical dimensional reality. Truer reflection of clinical picture of illness
2. Promotes greater consistency in treatment approaches
3. Encourages more coherence in bipolar spectrum thinking and research—accommodates mixed states and allows for differential clinical expression of bipolar disorder
Advantages of maintaining distinction
1. Consistent with lack of evidence to support change
2. Less disruptive to patients and families
3. Acknowledges differences in clinical characteristics
a. Dominance of depression in bipolar II disorder
b. Differential susceptibility to switching
c. Greater functional impairment in bipolar I disorder due to destructive nature of manic states

The advantages of a unified diagnosis

1. Conforms to clinical dimensional reality: The most important and core advantage of a unified single diagnosis is that it is more accurate. It is true—i.e. it reflects the dimensional reality of bipolar disorder. In practical terms it also obviates the need for the nonspecific and loosely applied 4-day and 7-day time criteria that are used to define hypomania/mania respectively, and furthermore subsumes the 'fix' that DSM-5 has concocted and slipped into its conditions for further study section—namely, 'short-duration hypomania'—inadvertently acknowledging perhaps the inexactness of its extant definitions. The current formulation of short-duration hypomania in DSM-5 alongside hypomania and mania is confusing because it clearly points to the real-world cut-off between normalcy and manic symptoms as being closer to 2 days as opposed to 4.

   Empirically, it is clear that the intensity and severity of excited states exists on a continuum. One can colloquially describe patients as having "bipolar 1.5" if their excited states are either on the more severe end of hypomania or the milder end of mania, but would it not be both more accurate and simpler to describe this state using the language of severity as one would for any other disorder in medicine-e.g., a milder or a more severe flareup of an autoimmune disorder, for example, or to simply capture the duration by describing how long the symptoms have lasted?

   Combining bipolar I and II disorders (and implicitly, hypomania and mania) also reflects the lack of any biological characteristics that consistently distinguish between these two disorders as currently defined (Vieta and Suppes 2008). Genetically, although some studies have shown that the two subtypes of bipolar breed true; i.e., in the families of bipolar I patients, one sees more bipolar I relatives and only some bipolar II patients, whereas in the families of bipolar II patients, there are a greater number of bipolar II patients with a relative paucity of bipolar Is (Rice et al. 1987 and others), we can simply conceptualize this as reflecting the genetic contribution towards illness severity, similar to the genetic contribution towards cycling frequency (Fisfalen et al. 2005).
2. Conceptually, one unified bipolar disorder would also encourage and allow an overarching set of treatment principles. Of course, the nuances of treating bipolar patients with milder manic states may differ from that in treating more severe bipolar patients. Secondary analyses of studies could then examine potential

predictors of treatment response based on severity (e.g., such as the potential risk of a treatment emergent affective switch-TEAS) in order to guide clinicians. Here too, this would be analogous to different treatment approaches of more vs. less severe autoimmune flareups.

3. Having one unified bipolar diagnosis with the inherent understanding of a disorder with dimensional elements would also encourage a more coherent discussion of bipolar spectrum disorders. Currently, with the bipolar I/bipolar II categorical distinction, a mood syndrome characterized by depressive states as well as excited/energized states that do not meet criteria for hypomania are vaguely described as bipolar spectrum disorders. Although a unified bipolar diagnosis would still require some (admittedly arbitrary) boundaries, simply acknowledging the dimensional expressions of bipolar disorder would encourage thinking about spectrum presentations more easily. For example, it would also allow cyclothymia to be included within the bipolar diagnosis, thereby eliminating another rather arbitrary distinction within the current bipolar diagnoses and perhaps limit the likelihood of non-sensical variants such as short-duration cyclothymia (Malhi and Bell 2019). Continuity would also mean that manic number of days could be captured, and other patterns such as mixed states could be included alongside the two extremes of mania and depression.

   One of the key problems in practice is that although the idea of dimensionality is increasingly being accepted, it is still limited mainly to mood, which has maintained primacy when considering mood disorders—perhaps understandably given their name. But in reality, depressive and bipolar disorders, or in traditional terms manic-depressive illnesses, are often an admixture of symptoms that don't neatly fall into DSM categories of major depression or mania. The current DSM fix for this—namely, mixed features has been justifiably criticized and instead an alternative conception that draws on Weygandt's and Kraepelin's concepts regarding mixed states has been proposed. In this model three domains of symptoms have been posited—activity, cognition and emotion (Malhi et al. 2018) with mood subsumed by the latter. Apart from accommodating mixed states as has been described in detail elsewhere (Malhi et al. 2019c), this allows for an appreciation of why bipolar I and II may sometimes appear to be so different (see Fig. 1). Here it is postulated that the pathophysiology that drives mania (*Manic Drive*) differentially affects symptoms within different domains because of their intrinsic properties. Individual symptoms can be regarded as having their own inherent 'elasticity' that stems from the nature of the disturbance that causes them, and so when these processes are impacted upon this is reflected in the displacement of the system and creation of various symptoms. The differing properties underpinning each symptom/group of symptoms then leads to the extent to which a symptom is expressed—in other words its severity. In this way a distinction can be seen between Bipolar I in which every system is 'maxed out' and stretched to the limit, and bipolar II, in which because some symptoms are more susceptible than others a different pattern of expression is formed and this creates a seemingly different picture—when in fact the constituents are the same (see Fig. 1).

The advantages of continuing the bipolar I vs. II split

In contrast, there are a different set of reasons for continuing the separation of bipolar I vs. bipolar II disorders some of which provide a different set of advantages.

1. First, why should we merge the two subtypes until we have the biological and genetic data justifying the unity of the two disorders? One day, biological and genetic studies may provide a more scientific basis for distinguishing subtypes of bipolar disorder (or not). That day has not yet arrived. As noted above, the two subtypes breed true in family studies. Should that not be enough to continue the split for now?
2. As noted above, altering diagnostic systems (especially without the biological data not currently available to justify these changes) would burden patients and families. Bipolar II disorder is often seen as a more palatable diagnosis compared to bipolar I disorder. Would bipolar II patients reject the notion of having a bipolar diagnosis because they do not identify with others who have full blown manias?

   Additionally, important clinical characteristics distinguish bipolar I and II disorders. First, depression dominates bipolar II disorder far more than it does bipolar I disorder in both the percentage of time spent in depression and the ratio of depressive to manic/hypomanic times (Judd et al. 2002, 2003). Second, switch rates associated with antidepressants are twice as high with bipolar I vs II disorders (Bond et al. 2008). Consistent with this, when bipolar I patients switch into excited states, they develop full mania 45% of the time and hypomania 55% of the time whereas bipolar II patients who have a TEAS develop a hypomania 95% of the time (Bond et al. 2008). These data suggest that there is a different clinical profile for bipolar II disorder and that it has a different susceptibility to the induction of mania and

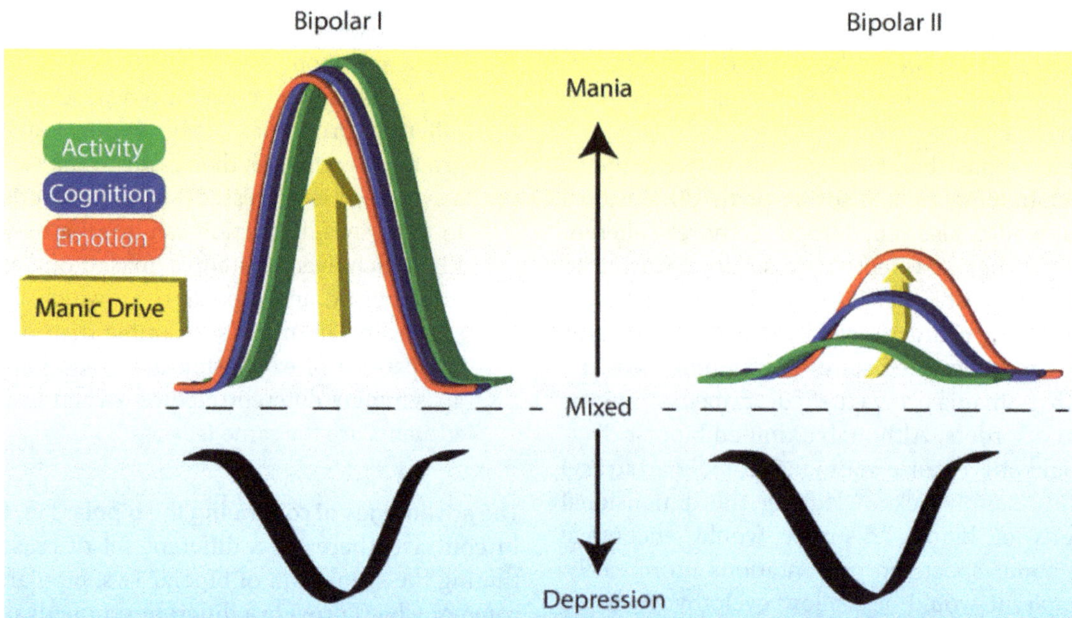

Fig. 1 ACE Model of mania. This schematic shows how manic drive, perhaps through differential action on different symptomatic domains can create a seemingly separate phenotype when in fact the difference in manifestation is largely because of the inherent properties of different neurocognitive schema and neural systems within the brain. In florid mania, manic drive (shown in yellow) is so extreme that irrespective of the inherent rigidity of various domains, they are all extended (akin to elastic bands) to the same extent. And so, activity, cognition and emotion are all impacted equally and symptoms from each of these domains are evident. However, when manic drive is more modest, those domains that are inherently more pliant are impacted first and hence why there is separation between emotion, cognition and activity. Emotion, by its very nature is more malleable and variable, whereas cognition succumbs more slowly, and activity is the most hard-wired and therefore requires significant manic drive before it is impacted. The figure also shows that lesser degrees of variation and more subtle changes lead to a more mixed presentation in which features of both mania and depression exist alongside each other, by virtue of belonging to independent domains (ACE). This schematic then explains how 'bipolar II' and other putative subtypes could perhaps be created and yet have the same underlying mechanisms and therefore, in essence, remain the same illness

that as a consequence, optimal treatment algorithms may differ between bipolar I and bipolar II patients. Thus, from a practical perspective keeping the distinction would perhaps help clinicians assess risk/benefit ratios more accurately.

Furthermore, given the inherently and definitionally greater functional impairment in mania vs. hypomania, distinguishing bipolar I from bipolar II disorders would concretize for clinicians the need to think more carefully about excited states in those labelled bipolar I disorder. This would include both the above mentioned risks with antidepressants [overblown as they might be (Gitlin 2018)], but also the need to more aggressively treat emerging excited/energized states in those with bipolar I disorder, since they are capable of accelerating into a far more destructive state than those with bipolar II disorder.

Alternative options for classifying bipolar disorder

The proper classification of mood disorders in general, and in particular, bipolar disorder has been a longstanding conundrum. As is currently the case, in the absence of the basic scientific data that would allow a more biologically based classification system, interested observers can only suggest improvements on our current, somewhat arbitrary system. With that caveat, there may be other methods of classifying bipolar disorder.

An example of an alternate method of classifying bipolar disorder utilizes predominant polarity as the central factor, initially described by Angst (1978) and revisited and updated more recently by others (Popovic et al. 2012; Carvalho et al. 2014). Predominant polarity (PP) reflects the relative number and severity of manic vs. depressive episodes within individual patients, defined by at least twice as many episodes of one pole vs. the other (Colom et al. 2006). Patients may be mania predominant, depression predominant or neither, when neither pole dominates the clinical course. Rates of PP differ markedly across different populations but, in general, depressive PP patients outnumber manic PP patients (Pal 2019).

As reviewed elsewhere (Malhi et al. 2019a), other criteria that may also be used to characterize bipolar disorder include duration of episodes and severity of functional impairment. Whether these characteristics can be used to create meaningful diagnostic categories is not clear and perhaps that can be used in the manner that *specifiers* are currently used in DSM-5. The ACE model mentioned previously allows for a transdiagnostic classification of mood disorders—combining depressive and bipolar disorders, including mixed states and allowing for links to anxiety and even psychosis.

Conceptual and societal consequences of diagnostic categories

Until we have a biological/genetic basis for our mood classification system, our diagnoses will remain tentative at best, based on somewhat arbitrary criteria of severity and/or duration and hence not always clinically useful in terms of prognosticating outcomes or determining optimal therapies. Nonetheless, for now, the question is whether the distinction between bipolar I and bipolar II disorder is clinically useful and should be continued or changed. To address this it is perhaps useful to consider an existing example—the merging of autism and Asperger's syndrome in DSM-5 into autism spectrum disorder (ASD). This is a critical example of where two disorders have been merged into one broader dimensional category. In that circumstance, the framers of DSM-5 felt that the conceptual unity of autism as a disorder that could be expressed on a continuum outweighed the somewhat arbitrary distinction between Asperger's as a mild autism spectrum disorder from more classic autism. It is important to note that at times, diagnostic categories become important issues of identity to both patients and their families. This was certainly the case with ASD where there were objections among patients and families about using the term associated with the more severe disorder and patients protesting that "I don't have autism; I have Asperger's." Similarly, perhaps for many patients there is a risk that they would reject the notion of having 'bipolar disorder' because their excited so called 'manic' states are not as severe as mania and as such they can identify with bipolar II (the milder, and putatively somewhat different form of the illness) but cannot identify with the label 'bipolar disorder" as it connotes a more severe, more destructive, mania characterized often by psychotic symptoms.

Nonetheless, classification systems do indeed shape as well as reflect clinicians' and patients' thinking. Over time, measured in years, not decades, we would all get accustomed to the new diagnostic categories. Reviewing history once again, the emergence of the DSM-III with its new terminology and diagnostic categories is a good example. At first, there were legitimate objections to the somewhat arbitrary nature of the new categories. (e.g., "why would we eliminate anxiety neurosis?" or "What is the relationship of dysthymic disorder to the types of patients we have been seeing in psychoanalytic psychotherapy?"). But gradually the field has accepted these new terms and diagnostic categories have continued to refine the classificatory criteria in subsequent DSMs. Furthermore, the new generation of mental health professionals who grew up with DSM-III and beyond, predictably accepted this system and over time it has become integral to our lexicon and thinking. Thus, perhaps if we merged bipolar I and II into one category with other specifiers (such as predominant polarity), and utilized a model that didn't assign so much emphasis to mood such as ACE, then after an initial period of adjustment in which there would no doubt be some voicing concerns, objections and even predictions of catastrophic consequences—these would, over time, diminish and give way to gradual acceptance.

Conclusion

It is our opinion that, from a conceptual viewpoint, eliminating bipolar II disorder would be the most intellectually honest. The question is whether it is worth the work of this change now or whether it would be wiser to wait for the anticipated genetic studies over the coming years and decades until we have a more biologically informed classification system.

Acknowledgements
None.

Authors' contributions
Both authors contributed equally to the writing. Both authors read and approved the final manuscript.

Author details
[1] Department of Psychiatry, Geffen School of Medicine at UCLA, Los Angeles, USA. [2] CADE Clinic, Department of Psychiatry, Royal North Shore Hospital, St Leonards, USA. [3] Discipline of Psychiatry, Faculty of Medicine and Health, The University of Sydney, Sydney, Australia.

References

American Psychiatric Association. Diagnostic and statistical manual of mental disorders. 4th ed. Washington (DC): American Psychological Association; 1994.

Angst J. The course of affective disorders. II. Typology of bipolar manic-depressive illness. Arch Gen Psychiatr. 1978;226(1):65–73.

Angst J, Gamma A, Benazi F, et al. Toward a re-definition of subthreshold bipolarity: epidemiology and proposed criteria for bipolar-II, minor bipolar disorders and hypomania. J Affect Disord. 2003;73:133–46.

Bond DJ, Noronha MM, Kauer-Sant'Anna M, et al. Antidepressant-associated mood elevation in bipolar Ii disorder compared with bipolar I disorder and major depressive disorder: a systematic review and meta-analysis. J Clin Psychol. 2008;69:1589–601.

Carvalho AF, McIntyre RS, Dimelis D, et al. Predominant polarity as a course specifier for bipolar disorder: a systematic review. J Affect Disord. 2014;163:56–64.

Colom F, Vieta E, Daban C, Pacchiarotti I, Sanchez-Moreno J. Clinical and therapeutic implications of predominant polarity in bipolar disorder. J Affect Disord. 2006;93:13–7.
Fisfalen ME, Schulze TG, DePaulo JR Jr, et al. Familial variation in episode frequency in bipolar affective disorder. Am J Psychiatry. 2005;167(7):1266–72.
Gitlin MJ. Antidepressants in bipolar depression: an enduring controversy. Int J Bipolar Dis. 2018. https://doi.org/10.1186/s40345-018-0133-9.
Ha K, Ha TH, Hong KS. Bipolar I and bipolar II: it's time for something new for a better understanding and classification of bipolar disorders. Can J Psychiatry. 2019;64(8):548–9.
Judd LL, Akiskal HS, Schettler PJ, et al. The long-term natural history of the weekly symptomatic status of bipolar I disorder. Arch Gen Psych. 2002;59:530–7.
Judd LL, Akiskal HS, Schettler PJ, et al. A prospective investigation of the natural history of the long-term weekly symptomatic status of bipolar II disorder. Arch Gen Psychol. 2003;60:261–9.
Malhi GS, Bell E. Fake views: cyclothymia—a dithering disorder? Aust NZJ Psychiatry. 2019. https://doi.org/10.1177/0004867419867764.
Malhi GS, Byrow Y, Boyce P, et al. Why the hype about subtype? Bipolar I, bipolar II—it's simply bipolar, through and through! Aust NZJ Psychiatry. 2016;50(4):303–6.
Malhi G, Fritz K, Elangovan P, Irwin L. Mixed states: modelling and management. CNS Drugs. 2019a;33(4):301–13.
Malhi G, Irwin L, Hamilton A, Morris G, Boyce P, Mulder R, Porter R. Modelling mood disorders: an ACE solution? Bipolar Disord. 2018;20(Suppl 2):4–16.
Malhi GS, Irwin L, Outhred T. Counting the days from bipolar II to bipolar true! Acta Psychiatr Scand. 2019b;139:211–3.
Malhi GS, Outhred T, Irwin L. Bipolar II is a myth. Can J Psychiatry. 2019c;64(8):531–6.
Merikangas KR, Jin R, He JP, et al. Prevalence and correlates of bipolar spectrum disorder in the world mental health survey initiative. Arch Gen Psychiatry. 2011;68(3):241–51.
Nierenberg AA. Bipolar II disorder is NOT a myth. Can J Psychiatry. 2019;64(8):537–40.
Ostacher MJ. Bipolar II should only exist if we can actually study treatments of it otherwise, what purpose does it serve? Bipolar Disord. 2017;20:395–6.
Pal A. Predominant polarity in bipolar affective disorder: a scoping review of its relationship with clinical variables and its implications. Indian J Psychol Med. 2019;41:9–17.
Parker G. Bipolar II disorder: modelling, measuring, and managing. Cambridge: Cambridge University Press; 2012.
Popovic D, Reinares M, Goikolea JM, et al. Polarity index of pharmacological agents used for maintenance treatment of bipolar disorder. Eur Neuropsychopharmacol. 2012;22:339–46.
Porter R. The greatest benefit to mankind. New York: Norton & Co.; 1997.
Post RM. Bipolar II: comments on its validity and utility. Bipolar Disord. 2018;20:280–1.
Post RM. Bipolar II disorder: not so sure it is time for something new. Can J Psychiatry. 2019;64(8):544–7.
Rice J, Reich T, Andreasen NC, et al. The familial transmission of bipolar illness. Arch Gen Psych. 1987;44:441–7.
Schaffer A. Why bipolar II disorder does not deserve its status as the overlooked middle child. Bipolar Disord. 2018;20:397–8.
Shorter E. Bipolar disorder in historical perspective. Bipolar II disorder modelling, measuring, and managing. 2nd ed. Cambridge: Cambridge University Press; 2012. p. 1–9.
Spitzer RL, Endicott J, Robins E. Research diagnostic criteria: rationale and reliability. Arch Gen Psych. 1978;35:773–82.
Vieta E, Suppes T. Bipolar II disorder: arguments for and against a distinct diagnostic entity. Bipolar Disord. 2008;10(1 Pt 2):163–78.
Vieta E. Bipolar II disorder: frequent, valid, and reliable. Can J Psychiatry. 2019;64(8):541–3.

3

Potential pharmacogenomic targets in bipolar disorder: considerations for current testing and the development of decision support tools to individualize treatment selection

Alfredo B. Cuéllar-Barboza[1,2], Susan L. McElroy[3], Marin Veldic[1], Balwinder Singh[1], Simon Kung[2], Francisco Romo-Nava[3], Nicolas A. Nunez[2], Alejandra Cabello-Arreola[2], Brandon J. Coombes[4], Miguel Prieto[5], Hannah K. Betcher[2], Katherine M. Moore[2], Stacey J. Winham[4], Joanna M. Biernacka[1,4] and Mark A. Frye[1,2*]

Abstract

Background: Treatment in bipolar disorder (BD) is commonly applied as a multimodal therapy based on decision algorithms that lack an integrative understanding of molecular mechanisms or a biomarker associated clinical outcome measure. Pharmacogenetics/genomics study the individual genetic variation associated with drug response. This selective review of pharmacogenomics and pharmacogenomic testing (PGT) in BD will focus on candidate genes and genome wide association studies of pharmacokinetic drug metabolism and pharmacodynamic drug response/adverse event, and the potential role of decision support tools that incorporate multiple genotype/phenotype drug recommendations.

Main body: We searched PubMed from January 2013 to May 2019, to identify studies reporting on BD and pharmacogenetics, pharmacogenomics and PGT. Studies were selected considering their contribution to the field. We summarize our findings in: targeted candidate genes of pharmacokinetic and pharmacodynamic pathways, genome-wide association studies and, PGT platforms, related to BD treatment. This field has grown from studies of metabolizing enzymes (i.e., pharmacokinetics) and drug transporters (i.e., pharmacodynamics), to untargeted investigations across the entire genome with the potential to merge genomic data with additional biological information.

Conclusions: The complexity of BD genetics and, the heterogeneity in BD drug-related phenotypes, are important considerations for the design and interpretation of BD PGT. The clinical applicability of PGT in psychiatry is in its infancy and is far from reaching the robust impact it has in other medical disciplines. Nonetheless, promising findings are discovered with increasing frequency with remarkable relevance in neuroscience, pharmacology and biology.

Keywords: Pharmacogenomic testing, Bipolar disorder, Pharmacogenetics

Background

Bipolar Disorder (BD) is a complex chronic mood disorder where patient's lives are variably associated with episodic recurrence (Angst and Sellaro 2000; Judd and Akiskal 2003), psychosocial and functional disability (Tohen et al. 2000; Zarate et al. 2000), and substantial

*Correspondence: mfrye@mayo.edu
[2] Department of Psychiatry and Psychology, Mayo Clinic, 200 First Street SW, Rochester, MN 55905, USA
Full list of author information is available at the end of the article

morbidity and mortality especially in the depressive phase of illness (Frye 2011). While there have been advances in disease classification of illness subtype (i.e., BD-I, BD-II), symptom specifier (i.e., anxious distress, mixed features, rapid cycling, peripartum onset), and increasing recognition of high rates of comorbidity, the illness remains highly heterogeneous within patient groups and within a single patient's longitudinal course of illness (Malhi et al. 2018). Moreover, the Diagnostic and Statistical Manual of Mental Disorders (DSM-5) classification is not defined by an underlying pathophysiology and as such, limits the current understanding of neurobiological mechanisms of differential illness presentation and development of biomarkers of disease burden (Frey et al. 2013; Harrison et al. 2018).

There is no greater psychotropic pharmacopoeia in psychiatry than that of BD. Treatment selection with lithium, mood stabilizing anticonvulsants, mood stabilizing atypical antipsychotics, typical antipsychotics, unimodal antidepressants, and benzodiazepines, most commonly as a multimodal therapy, will be based on a number of factors including: clinical evidence base, phase of illness and symptom severity, BD-I vs BD-II subtype, level of cyclicity, and additional mental health and medical diagnoses that may impact efficacy and/or side effect burden. Molecular drug mechanisms of action, biomarkers of treatment response or adverse events, are not part of any clinical decision algorithm in BD. Oftentimes, polypharmacotherapy is necessary to achieve remission (Frye et al. 2000). However, multimodal drug therapy is challenging given the potential for pharmacokinetic drug–drug interactions and cumulative side effect burden. Developing biomarkers to individualize treatment in hopes of increasing rates of remission, tolerability, and adherence or mitigate serious drug related adverse event risk would represent a paradigm shift in current clinical practice models for both prescribers and patients.

Pharmacogenetics/genomics study the individual genetic variation associated with drug response. This field has grown from studies of metabolizing enzymes (i.e., pharmacokinetics) and drug transporters (i.e., pharmacodynamics), to untargeted investigations across the entire genome with the potential to merge genomic data with additional biological information (Weinshilboum and Wang 2017). Additional focus on a patient's individual biology, vs solely broad Food and Drug Administration (FDA) indication labeling, may facilitate patient care with the "right drug, right dose, right time" (Bielinski et al. 2014). There are early pharmacogenomic studies in most treatment classes in BD (Pisanu et al. 2018b). This is of special importance in BD, where early intervention can have a positive impact in the progression of the disease (Post 2018).

For this selective review of pharmacogenomics in BD we searched PubMed from January 2013 to May 2019, to identify studies reporting on BD and pharmacogenetics, pharmacogenomics and pharmacogenomic testing (PGT). The authors selected studies based on their contribution to the field. We focus on candidate genes and genome wide association studies (GWAS) of pharmacokinetic drug metabolism and pharmacodynamic drug response/adverse event, and the potential role of decision support tools (DST) that incorporate multiple genotype/phenotype drug recommendations. The Clinical Pharmacogenomics Implementation Consortium (CPIC) (Relling and Klein 2011), was established as a joint effort between PharmGKB and the Pharmacogenomics Research Network (PGRN) to develop peer-reviewed guidelines for implementation of PGT, will be reviewed to illustrate early examples of clinical practice recommendations.

Targeted candidate genes in pharmacokinetic drug metabolism

The Cytochrome P450 (CYP) superfamily of proteins (2D6, 2C9, 2C19, 3A4) is one of the most important enzymatic classes responsible for phase I drug-metabolism, and thus, relevant to most of psychiatric medication's metabolism and bioactivation (Spina and de Leon 2015). The notable exception, given its lack of metabolism is lithium. Early efforts in pharmacogenetics were, in part, dedicated to CYP genotyping/metabolic phenotyping with the goal of operationally defining phenotype classes that would be associated with response and side effects. These CYP phenotypic classifications [i.e., poor, intermediate, extensive (normal), and ultra-rapid] are the most common application of commercial PGT in psychiatry (Eum et al. 2016), however, no standardized model prevails to date (Gaedigk et al. 2017). It is important to acknowledge that race and ethnicity are important sources of variability between populations in allele composition and frequency of CYP genes. Inter-individual variability is even larger than that observed between ancestries producing large ranges of CYP activity among individuals. Moreover, CYP genes are strongly influenced by complex environmental factors that cannot be accounted by current PGT (McGraw et al. 2018). Nonetheless, the poor metabolizer phenotype and use of antidepressants has been the focus of a number of forensic cases of possible drug related fatality (i.e., 2D6), has driven a number of FDA drug label revisions (i.e., 2D6, 2C19) related to arrhythmia risk, and has been speculated, given black box warning for antidepressants in young adults, as a possible mechanism of treatment emergent suicidal ideation and antidepressant induced mania (AIM), both phenomena often identified early in the course of treatment [reviewed by (Nassan et al.

2016)]. Table 1 summarizes the evidence on pharmacokinetic PGT by drug class. Comprehensive sources on CYP PGT in psychiatry (Spina and de Leon 2015; Eum et al. 2016; Solomon et al. 2019) and *CYP2D6* genetic variation considerations (Nofziger et al. 2020) are reviewed elsewhere.

CYP2D6

CYP2D6 is the most involved CYP isoform in psychiatric drug metabolism, and hundreds of *CYP2D6* polymorphisms and copy number variations have been identified, many of which have unknown effects (McGraw et al. 2018). Multiple antidepressants and antipsychotics of different classes are its substrates, and CYP2D6 is inhibited strongly by fluoxetine, paroxetine, perphenazine and thioridazine. A recent study by Gaedgik et al. (2017) analyzed 177 reports of a world-wide population compromised of approximately 60,000 unrelated subjects and categorized them in metabolism phenotypes according to genotype meeting CPIC guidelines. Europeans represented most of the genotyped population (36%) and also had the greatest proportion of poor metabolizers (average, 5.4%), while Asians, Oceanians, and Middle Eastern populations, showed rates lower or equal to 1%. Ultra-rapid metabolizers were most represented in Oceanian (21.2%), Ashkenazi Jewish (11.5%), and Middle Eastern (11.2%) populations, with the lowest proportion in subjects from East Asia (1.4%). In spite of such efforts, the great genotypic variation in *CYP2D6* confers confounding effects to the actual metabolism phenotype observed in individuals, and clinical studies may not always reflect an accurate prediction of treatment response, tolerability, or even pharmacokinetic parameters. It is also important to note that most of these clinical studies are non-prospective, have great heterogeneity in design, often have low subject numbers and do not control for environmental or drug–drug interactions (Eum et al. 2016).

Fifteen antipsychotics are major or minor substrates of CYP2D6 including most options for BD treatment, with quetiapine (CYP3A4, CYP3A5) and ziprasidone (CYP1A2, CYP3A4) as notable exceptions (Eum et al. 2016). There is variability in the magnitude of change in 2D6 poor-metabolizers' antipsychotic serum concentrations and/or half-life for primary CYP2D6 antipsychotic substrates [i.e., 1.7X increase in aripiprazole serum concentration (Hendset et al. 2007), 2X increase and 7X increase in half-life of aripiprazole and risperidone respectively (Eum et al. 2016)]. A recent large retrospective cohort of *CYP2D6* genotyped subjects treated with either risperidone (N = 1288) or aripiprazole (N = 1334) found statistically significant decreased metabolic ratios (i.e. metabolite/parent drug) for both drugs in poor and intermediate metabolizers; while greater metabolic ratios for ultra-rapid metabolizers, were only statistically significant for risperidone (Jukic et al. 2019). Moreover, poor and intermediate metabolizers showed increased risperidone and aripiprazole active moiety. These two drugs seem to present the greatest caution in 2D6 poor-metabolizer dosing; for further information on *CYP2D6* and dosing precautions see Table 1.

A meta-analysis found no association between *CYP2D6* genotyping and psychosis treatment efficacy in schizophrenia (Fleeman et al. 2011; Muller et al. 2012) however, it is important to point out that the authors found great variability of methodology and outcomes. The same study found, when including only prospective studies, a positive association between genotype, quantified only as mutant (i.e., not normal) vs wild type (i.e., normal), and tardive dyskinesia (Fleeman et al. 2011). In the retrospective study mentioned above, Jukic et al., found dose reductions from clinicians in both risperidone (19%) and aripiprazole (15%) poor metabolizers, however, only risperidone poor and ultra-rapid metabolizers show significantly higher switching to other antipsychotic agents; with no metabolizing phenotype showing greater switch to other agents in the aripiprazole group (Jukic et al. 2019). Performing prospective studies in BD will be of paramount importance before reaching more applicable clinical interpretations of *CYP2D6* genotyping and antipsychotic prescription.

Studies associating *CYP2D6* genotype and antidepressant pharmacokinetics and treatment response have been mostly performed in major depression. In patients treated with escitalopram (Ng et al. 2013; Hodgson et al. 2014, 2015), venlafaxine (Ng et al. 2013; Taranu et al. 2017) and nortriptyline (Hodgson et al. 2014, 2015), there was no association between metabolizing phenotype of CYP2D6 and response to these agents. The sole exception is the Lobello et al. (2010) study, which reviewed four placebo-controlled studies (n = 464) where 2D6 poor metabolizers, in comparison to extensive metabolizers, had significantly higher levels of serum parent compound venlafaxine, lower levels of active metabolite O-desmethylvenlafaxine, reduced baseline to endpoint change in depression scores, and significantly lower rates of treatment response and remission.

There is limited evidence that CYP2D6 poor-metabolizers were more likely to discontinue antidepressants (Berard et al. 2017). Antidepressant induced mania (AIM) has been reported in 3 bipolar depressed patients with a 2D6 poor metabolizer phenotype when prescribed 2D6 metabolized antidepressants (Sanchez-Iglesias et al. 2016). Similar to antipsychotics, *CYP2D6* genotyping does not have a clear role in clinical decision for antidepressant prescription in bipolar patients, further

Table 1 Potential content of commercial PGT+

Gene*	Drug-class	Use in bipolar disorder	Trial on BD population	CPIC level of evidence	FDA label
CYP2D6	Second-Generation Antipsychotics (SGAs)	Positive association of CYP2D6 genotype and tardive dyskinesia (Fleeman et al. 2011)	No	Not included	No
	SGAs	Positive association of CYP2D6 genotype and weight gain (Fleeman et al. 2011)	No	Not included	No
	Aripiprazole	Changes in serum concentrations in poor metabolizers (Hendset et al. 2007)	No	B	Actionable
	Risperidone	Changes in serum concentrations in poor metabolizers (Eum et al. 2016)	No	B	Informative
	Tricyclic Antidepressants	Association of changes in serum concentrations with metabolizer phenotype (Hicks et al. 2017)	No	A, Guideline	Informative
	Selective Serotonin Reuptake Inhibitors (SSRIs)	Association of changes in serum concentrations with metabolizer phenotype (Hicks et al. 2015)	No	C-D, Guideline	Informative
		Antidepressant induced mania (AIM) in 3 poor metabolizer bipolar patients (Sanchez-Iglesias et al. 2016)	Yes (mixed)	Not included	No
CYP2C19	Tricyclic Antidepressants	Association of changes in serum concentrations with metabolizer phenotype (Hicks et al. 2017)	No	A, Guideline	No
	Citalopram, Escitalopram	Association of changes in serum concentrations with metabolizer phenotype (Hicks et al. 2015)	No	A, Guideline	Actionable
	Escitalopram	A retrospective study of 2087 gentoyped patients showed that poor and ultrarapid CYP2C19 metabolizers seem to predict greater switching from escitalopram to another agent (Jukic et al. 2018)	Multiple Diagnosis	Not included	No
	Sertraline	Association of changes in serum concentrations with metabolizer phenotype (Hicks et al. 2015)	No	B, Guideline	No
HLA-B	Carbamazepine	There is a strong recommendation by the CPIC of not to use carbamazepine in carbamazepine naive patients, with HLA-B*15:02 positive subjects given a "Greater risk of carbamazepine-induced SJS/TEN". Proceed with caution in HLA-B*15:02 negative subjects, depending on HLA-A*31:01 genotype; there may be an average risk in negative vs. Higher risk in positive alleles (Phillips et al. 2018) HLA-B variants have been associated with carbamazepine induced agranulocytosis/granulocytopenia in European populations (Goldstein et al. 2014)	No	A	Actionable

Table 1 (continued)

Gene*	Drug-class	Use in bipolar disorder	Trial on BD population	CPIC level of evidence	FDA label
CYP2C9	Valproate	The loss-of-function alleles, CYP2C9*2 or CYP2C9*3, display significant reduction in valproate metabolism in children; furthermore, low CYP2C9 expression in patients with CYP2C9*1/*1 genotype also leads to a decrease in valproate metabolizing capacity (Monostory et al. 2019)	No	No	No
GRIK4	Citalopram	Initial modest association observed in the STAR*D trial (Paddock et al. 2007). Meta-analysis results showed that the C allele appeared more frequently than the T allele in responders to treatment (OR: 1.22; 95% CI 1.035–1.445; z = 2.36; p = 0.018) (Kawaguchi and Glatt 2014)	No	Level D	No
	Haloperidol	Early and modest evidence of association with antimanic effect of haloperidol in BD (Drago et al. 2013)	Yes	No	No
DRD2	Aripiprazole, Risperidone	C/C homozygotes improved in positive symptoms more than the T carriers during 12 weeks of treatment with aripiprazole or risperidone, C/C homozygotes developed more akathisia during treatment with aripiprazole, rolactin elevation in males treated with risperidone, in that C/C homozygotes had lower elevation of prolactin compared to the T carriers (Zhang et al. 2015)	First-episode psychosis	C (Risperidone)	No
	Antipsychotics	A meta-analysis of 698 schizophrenia patients, found that Del allele carrier of the -141C Ins/Del polymorphism, were significantly associated with poorer antipsychotic drug response, compared to the Ins/Ins genotype, OR = .65, p = 0.03 (Zhang et al. 2010)	No	C (Risperidone)	
SLC6A4	Antidepressants	A meta-analysis of 1034 bipolar patients and antidepressant remission rates reported reduced anti-depressive remission rates in S-carriers of the serotonin transporter promoter polymorphism (OR = 0.64, p = .006, I2 = 0.0%) (Rao et al. 2019)	Yes	Not included	No
		A 6-study (453 bipolar patients) meta-analysis demonstrated a marginally significant evidence of association of the S allele with AIM (OR = 1.35; 95% CI 0.99–1.85; P = 0.059) (Frye et al. 2015)	Yes	Not included	No

Table 1 (continued)

Gene*	Drug-class	Use in bipolar disorder	Trial on BD population	CPIC level of evidence	FDA label
EPHX1	Carbamazepine	Carriers of the SCN1A IVS5-91GA variant or of EPHX1 c.337TC variant presented significantly lower levels of plasma CBZ compared to carriers of the common alleles (0.71 ± 0.28 vs 1.11 ± 0.69 μgmL per mgKg for SCN1A IVS5-91 AA vs GG and 0.76 ± 0.16 vs 0.94 ± 0.49 μgmL per mgKg for EPHX1 c.337 CC vs TT; P0.05 for both) (Daci et al. 2015)	No	D	No
HLA-A	Carbamazepine	Due to "Greater risk of carbamazepine-induced SJS/TEN" by CPIC, proceed with caution in HLA-B*15:02 negative subjects, depending on HLA-A*31:01 genotype; there may be an average risk in negative vs. Higher risk in positive alleles (Phillips et al. 2018)	No	A	Actionable
HTR2A	Antidepressants	A meta-analysis found association of greater antidepressant response in major depressive disorder, for the dominant models of rs6313 5HTR2A-T > C polymorphism (OR = 1.62; 95% CI 1.21–2.18; P = 0.008) and rs7997012G > A (OR = 1.92; 95% CI 1.02–3.61; P = 0.044) (Lin et al. 2014)	No	D	No
HTR2C	Clozapine, Olanzapine, Risperidone	A meta-analysis found significant association betwen the C allele of the HTR2C rs1414334:C > G polymorphism (OR = 2.44; 95%CI [1.48, 4.00]; P = 0.0004; I2 = 0), the HTR2C -697 G/C polymorphism (OR = 1.54; 95%CI [0.99, 2.40]; P = 0.05; I2 = 0), and olanzapine/clozapine/risperidone-induced metabolic syndrome (Ma et al. 2014)	No	D	No
OPRM1	Naltrexone	Several trials have found an association between the A118G rs1799971 polymorphism and naltrexone response (Patriquin et al. 2015), review	No	C/D	No
ABCB1	Antidepressants	Multiple genetic variants have been explored. Mixed evidence of association with less dose for remission, response, time to remission and remission in treatment of unipolar depression with antidepressants. The majority of evidence found associations with side effects and tolerability. (For a comprehensive review see (Bruckl and Uhr 2016)	No	A/B	No
COMT	SSRIs	Significant association between rs13306278 and remission (P = 0.038) in 1914 depressed patients from STAR*D genotyped for COMT (Ji et al. 2012)	No	C	No

Table 1 (continued)

Gene*	Drug-class	Use in bipolar disorder	Trial on BD population	CPIC level of evidence	FDA label
CYP3A5	Alprazolam	In a study of 19 healthy volunteers, CYP3A5 non-expressors had a lower alprazolam clearance compared carriers of the CYP3A5*1/*1 and CYP3A5*1/*3 alleles (Park et al. 2006)	No	C	No
UGT1A4	Lamotrigine	A meta-analysis found no associations between concentration to dose ratio (CDR) values and different polymorphisms of UGT1A4. The non-pediatric population showed a non-significant trend of association between UGT1A4 142T > G WT and higher CDR (Kim and Kim 2019)	No	D	No

*The genetic variants genotyped in PGT for each gene are many times unknown, thus interpretation must be done with caution

**These recommendations follow the CPIC Guidelines

studies, especially regarding the AIM risk warrant further exploration.

CYP2C19

Highly polymorphic-but significantly less than *CYP2D6*, *CYP2C19* is mainly involved in the metabolism of tricyclic and selective serotonin reuptake inhibitors (SSRI) antidepressants, and benzodiazepines. Its genotype status influences the concentrations of amitriptyline and imipramine, and precautions are suggested for poor metabolizers (Hicks et al. 2015, 2017). Citalopram, escitalopram and sertraline show higher serum concentrations in CYP2C19 poor metabolizers, however, in contrast with the above, the wide therapeutic window of these drugs suggest that their effects may be more difficult to simply categorize by their metabolic phenotype (Spina and de Leon 2015). Nonetheless, a recent study by Jukic et al. (Jukic et al. 2018) in more than two-thousand Europeans with multiple psychiatric diagnosis, genotyped for *CYP2C19* and medicated with escitalopram, showed that both poor and ultra-rapid *CYP2C19* metabolizers predicted greater switching from escitalopram to another antidepressant. In this same study, *CYP2C19* poor metabolizers showed greater odds of having lower than threshold therapeutic levels compared to extensive metabolizers; while this makes sense for ultra-rapid metabolizers, this is counterintuitive to poor metabolizer pharmacokinetics and may represent reduced treatment adherence (Jukic et al. 2018). In contrast, Fabbri and colleagues (Fabbri et al. 2018) found in a meta-analysis that *CYP2C19* poor-metabolizers had higher side-effects compared to extensive metabolizers at weeks 2–4, however, also showed higher symptom improvement and remission in major depression when treated with citalopram or escitalopram. A 10-year retrospective cohort found that *CYP2C19* poor metabolizers were more frequently observed in bipolar (9.8%) vs. unipolar subjects (0.6%, $p=0.003$) (Veldic et al. 2019). The apparent impact of *CYP2C19* genotype in treatment response to citalopram and escitalopram in depression, together with the observations of differences in *CYP2C19* pharmacogenetics of bipolar depressed patients, warrants further exploration.

CYP2C9

CYP2C9 shows similar polymorphic variation to *CYP2C19*, but its role in the biotransformation of psychotropic drugs is minor (Spina and de Leon 2015). Of relevance, the secondary role it has in adult valproate metabolism seems to become clinically crucial in children, where it is responsible for most of this drug's metabolism. Thus, its genotyping is recommended by some experts in this population (Monostory et al. 2019). CYP2C9 also modifies fluoxetine's CYP2D6 metabolism but with an unknown clinical impact (Llerena et al. 2004).

Other pharmacokinetic genes such as *ABCB1* and *UGT1A4* are mentioned in Table 1.

Ethnic, environmental and drug–drug interaction variables also provide an enormous source of variability to the final metabolic phenotype expressed by the patient. Thus, bioinformatic tools based on systems biology will likely be needed in order to generate more intuitive models and clinical decision tools, based on pharmacokinetic PGT (McGraw et al. 2018).

Targeted candidate genes in pharmacodynamic drug response/adverse event

Pharmacodynamic pharmacogenetic candidate gene studies of most bipolar drug classes have been performed, with genetic variants selected mechanistically from neurotransmission, gene transcription, neuroplasticity, intracellular messenger cascades, and other pathways. However, our drug mechanism of action understanding is incomplete and limits hypothesis-driven design of candidate gene studies and their interpretation; moreover, current PGT may potentiate the intrinsic risk for false positive discoveries (Farrell et al. 2015). Nonetheless, we discuss the findings from such candidate gene studies so that clinicians who are faced with PGT DST, understand how the genetic variants included in these platforms were selected and why they should be careful with their interpretation.

Lithium

Lithium is the gold-standard mood stabilizing agent, with an extensive clinical evidence database for acute mania, bipolar depression, maintenance treatment (Bauer and Gitlin 2016), and suicidality prevention (Cipriani et al. 2013; Song et al. 2017). Clinical markers of response suggest that distinct patient groups may be more responsive to lithium (Grof et al. 1993; Post et al. 2016) suggesting a possible familial trait suggestive of genetic transmission (Grof et al. 1993, 2002, 2009). Lithium has been the most extensively studied of BD medications at the pharmacogenetic level and comprehensive reviews are available covering this topic (Alda 2015; Pisanu et al. 2016; Budde et al. 2017; Pickard 2017; Serretti 2017; Pisanu et al. 2018b).

Lithium mechanism of action involves multiple molecular mechanisms (Li et al. 2012). Thus, pharmacogenomic studies based on candidate genes have focused in genes implicated in many of these pathways. Neurotransmission genes for instance, largely based in monoamines—many of which are included in PGT—did not prompt any sufficiently robust associations of lithium treatment response (Budde et al. 2017; Pisanu et al. 2018b). Also included in PGT, the genetic single nucleotide polymorphism (SNP) rs6265, Val66Met, of *BDNF*, largely used to study neuroplasticity, showed mixed results (Michelon et al. 2006; Dmitrzak-Weglarz et al. 2008, Drago et al. 2010; Wang et al. 2012). GSK-3β is inhibited by lithium and, it is involved in neurogenesis, plasticity, and transcription through the Wnt canonical signaling pathway (Valvezan and Klein 2012). However, no robust evidence was found or replicated for *GSK3B* genetic variants (Michelon et al. 2006; Szczepankiewicz et al. 2006; Sathur Raghuraman et al. 2018); nor in other variants involved in genetic transcription, neuronal survival and plasticity, as SNPs in the CREB family (Mamdani et al. 2008) in association to lithium treatment response. Similarly, other variants related to inositol metabolism, involved in lithium's mechanism of action, did not resulted in strong replicable results (Pisanu et al. 2016).

Lithium renal adverse events are an important though rare concern in BD treatment (Shine et al. 2015). To better inform lithium safety, a pharmacogenetic study of urinary concentration phenotypes were assessed in a group of 78 BD patients receiving lithium for a mean of 16 ± 9 years; in association with the *GSK3B*-50 C/T polymorphism, the authors found a statistically significant, though very modest association, not subjected to multiple testing correction, between the C-allele and kidney function, encouraging larger studies to better ascertain the potential role of *GSK3B* in informing lithium renal toxicity (Rybakowski et al. 2013).

Valproic acid

Valproic acid (VPA) is recommended in the treatment of bipolar mania, depression and maintenance (Grunze et al. 2013, 2018; Yatham et al. 2018). Sodium channel blockade is one of VPA's proposed mechanisms of action. Genetic variation in the *SCN* family genes, specifically SCN2A, which encodes of the sodium channel (Haug et al. 2001), has shown mixed evidence of association with VPA response (Haerian et al. 2013; Li et al. 2016); it is important to reference that these studies were conducted in epilepsy patients and anticonvulsant and mood stabilization therapeutic mechanisms of action may differ. Included in PGT, *CACNA1C* and other calcium channel coding genes have been tested for VPA efficacy, but they prompted negative results (Lv et al. 2015), again, these studies were conducted in epilepsy patients. In bipolar populations, VPA response showed a positive association with XBP1-116 C/G polymorphism, but replication is needed (Kim et al. 2009). *GNB3* variants have also been associated with metabolic abnormalities in cross-over (Chang et al. 2010) and prospective studies (Chen et al. 2017) of BD patients treated with VPA.

Carbamazepine and lamotrigine

Although rare, serious dermatologic adverse events are observed with antiepileptic mood-stabilizers. Carriers of the HLA-B*15:02 allele in Asian population, specifically of Han Chinese descent, are at risk of developing severe hypersensitivity reactions in association with carbamazepine, lamotrigine, and phenytoin treatment (Bloch et al. 2014); moreover, the FDA recommends PGT in patients of Asian ancestry for this specific variation before initiating carbamazepine treatment (Drozda et al. 2018). The generalizability to other anticonvulsants or other racial ethnic groups in BD has not been investigated.

Atypical antipsychotics

Weight-gain and other metabolic dysfunction is a major concern in BD treatment, especially regarding second-generation antipsychotics (SGAs) and mood-stabilizers. A recent meta-analysis of the genetic risk of anti-psychotics, predominantly SGAs-induced weight gain, explored 38 SNPS from 20 different genes in 6 independent samples (N = 6770) with predominant Caucasian and Asian ancestry (Zhang et al. 2016). 13 SNPs from 9 genes, namely *ADRA2A, ADRB3, BDNF, DRD2, GNB3, HTR2C, INSIG2, MC4R* and *SNAP25* showed statistically significant associations with antipsychotic-related weight gain (P-values < 0.05–0.001), while SNPs in *ADRA2A, DRD2, HTR2C,* and *MC4R* had the largest effect sizes (Hedges' g's = 0.30–0.80, ORs = 1.47–1.96 (Zhang et al. 2016). Important limitations to this meta-analysis include important heterogeneity, from selected antipsychotic agents, previous exposure to antipsychotics, time of exposure; also, the lack of multiple testing analysis. As with most genetic association studies, further functional analysis of these SNPs is needed before reaching a complete understanding of their actual biological impact on the mentioned genes or else. *ADR2A, BDNF,* and *DRD2* are included in most PGT commercial assays, however, the variants included in these tools are most of the time proprietary and thus it is unknown whether they test for the SNPs found in Zhang et al.'s study. Other efforts in understanding weight gain, specifically in BD, secondary to SGAs or mood stabilizers in 486 Systematic Treatment Enhancement Program for Bipolar Disorder subjects that did not identify significant candidate genes of weight gain liability (Creta et al. 2015).

Antidepressants

Clinical recommendations have been developed to address antidepressant use in bipolar depression hopefully reducing "the striking incongruity" between the widespread use of antidepressants in BD and the limited evidence that supports their use (Pacchiarotti et al. 2013). One concern of antidepressant use in BD is risk of AIM. A meta-analysis of controlled trials of antidepressants in bipolar depression reported a 12.5% rate of treatment emergent mania (Tondo et al. 2010). While there are clinical factors identified with AIM (Frye et al. 2006, Goldberg et al. 2007), there is increasing investigation of genetic markers in this drug related adverse event. The most studied genetic association for AIM has involved the serotonin transporter gene (*SLC6A4*), that encodes the protein in charge of serotonin synaptic reuptake, and the variants involved in its genetic expression. There are predominantly 2 well-known polymorphisms: (5-HTTLPR) with long (L) and short (S) allele variants and a second intron variable number of tandem repeats (VNTR). 5-HTTLPR association to AIM has been studied with meta-analysis showing conflicting information (Daray et al. 2010; Biernacka et al. 2012). A more recent meta-analysis combining the Mayo Clinic Bipolar Biobank with 5 prior AIM studies, provided marginal evidence of association for the S-allele of 5-HTTLPR with AIM ($p = 0.059$). On the other hand, haplotype analysis including SNP rs25531 (A/G), and the intron 2 VNTR (9, 10, 12 repeat alleles) showed that the L-A-10 haplotype was associated with a reduced risk of AIM ($p = 0.012$) (Frye et al. 2015). *SLC6A4* variation is included in PGT commercial testing, however, before using it to inform AD prescription in BD, further exploration of the relationship between *SLC6A4* variation and risk of AIM is needed. For instance, intron 2 VNTR and other SNPs with an impact in *SLC6A4* expression, need to be employed in risk calculation, rather than focusing exclusively on the promoter long/short variant (Frye et al. 2015).

GWAS of drug response/adverse event

GWAS employ an agnostic or untargeted approach and do not rely on mechanistic hypothesis. They have prompted the most promising results regarding genetic markers of treatment response in BD.

Lithium

Most pharmacogenetic GWAS of BD have largely focused in Lithium. Initial efforts showed promising SNPs of risk, but they did not reach genome-wide significance of $p \leq 5 \times 10^{-8}$ (Perlis et al. 2009; Squassina et al. 2011). The first genome-wide significant finding associated with lithium response, assessed by retrospective Alda scales, was achieved with a relatively small population (N = 294) of Han Chinese BD-I patients, and was replicated in an independent population (N = 100) (Chen et al. 2014). A robust association was observed for rs17026688 ($p = 5.5 \times 10^{-37}$) and rs17026651 ($p = 2.52 \times 10^{-37}$), variants in strong linkage disequilibrium (LD) in the *GADL1* gene, and replicated ($p = 9.19 \times 10^{-15}$ for each SNP). Moreover, they showed a 93% sensitivity in predicting lithium response (Chen et al. 2014). *GADL1* encodes a protein similar to GABA metabolism enzymes, suggesting biological plausibility of this finding. Furthermore, the effect-size of the association for the T-allele carriers and lithium response was enormous: 88.5 [95% confidence interval 41.4–198.0] (Chen et al. 2014). A study of this variant in a candidate gene study of Han Chinese patients additionally suggested a significant association with less recurrence and thus as a potential marker of lithium maintenance treatment (Chen et al. 2016). *GADL1* SNPs were not further replicated outside of this initial work (Hou et al. 2014; Ikeda et al. 2014; Cruceanu et al. 2015; Kotambail et al. 2015), however, Asian ancestry replications included both Han Chinese and Japanese populations (Hou et al. 2014) and Japanese-only populations (Ikeda et al. 2014). Moreover, the phenotype in the Chen et al., original study was narrower than further replications (Chen et al. 2014). An analysis of gene expression found no activity of *GADL1* in post mortem brain studies from individuals with BD (Birnbaum et al. 2014). The authors of this expression analysis hypothesized that, given the greater expression of *GADL1* in the kidney and its involvement in renal function (Liu et al. 2012), *GADL1* association to treatment response may be rather due to a renal function phenotype (Birnbaum et al. 2014).This is an important lesson in pharmacogenetics, showing the difficulty in interpreting and replicating even the most promising pharmacogenetic variants. Given its original and strong association with lithium response but further limitations in biological interpretation and replication, *GADL1* variants should be regarded with caution as potential pharmacogenetic markers of BD.

The largest pharmacogenetic consortium of lithium, the International Consortium on Lithium Genetics (ConLiGen), performed a GWAS in 2563 "bipolar spectrum" patients—mainly bipolar 1—from 22 participating sites, and showed a genome-wide significant association with a group of SNPs in a single region of chromosome 21 (Hou et al. 2016). This region has two genes that code non-coding RNAs, which in turn could be involved in gene expression (Hou et al. 2016), however, the actual functional effect of these variants is yet to be fully investigated. Interestingly, a prospective sample (N=73) showed association with this region and lower relapse rates in 2-year follow-up (Hou et al. 2016). Replication, biological and clinical interpretation of this finding remains to be elucidated. Similar findings were found by the same group, showing an inverse relationship between lithium response and schizophrenia polygenic risk (Amare et al. 2018). Moreover, a cross-trait meta-GWAS found 15 genetic variants that may have overlapping effects on lithium treatment response and susceptibility to SCZ; bioinformatic analysis of these variants suggested the involvement of the HLA antigen complex and inflammatory cytokines (Amare et al. 2018). HLA members are included in some commercial PGT, however, their role in establishing lithium response is not yet validated. A GWAS performed in bipolar 1, 2, not specified and schizoaffective disorder, patients from Sweden and the United Kingdom with subjective (N=2698) and objective (N=1176) measures of treatment response, showed no genome wide significant results comparing lithium response between BD patients. However, when compared to healthy controls, a variant from imputation, prompted a validated genome-wide significant result in rs116323614 ($p=2.74\times10^{-8}$), located in *SESTD1*. The later gene seems to be involved in phospholipid synthesis, which are potential lithium targets (Song et al. 2016). The biological and clinical relevance of this association remains to be determined. Not only should they be regarded with caution in PGT but, to our knowledge, none of these variants are available for PGT commercials assays to date.

Clozapine

Clozapine is a SGA used in treatment resistant BD patients (Frye et al. 1998). In spite of its evident clinical benefit, clozapine use is limited due to clozapine-induced agranulocytosis/granulocytopenia (CIAG). Significant pharmacogenetic studied have explored this phenomenon, as recently reviewed by Numata et al. (2018). Several GWAS have been conducted, an initial effort by Goldstein et al., on 161 CIAG cases and 1196 controls of European descent, found genome-wide associations for variants in *HLA-DQB1* and in *HLA-B* (Goldstein et al. 2014). In meta-analysis, only the HLA-DQB1 variant showed a nominally significant independent replication for a variant in HLA-DQB1 (OR=15.6, P=0.015, positive predictive value=35.1), while a novel variant in rs149104283, an intronic transcript of *SLCO1B3* and *SLCO1B7*, was associated with CIAG (OR=4.32, $P=1.79\times10^{-8}$) (Legge et al. 2017), but was not replicated in a Japanese sample (Saito et al. 2017). A GWAS in Japanese samples including 50 cases of CIAG vs. 2905 controls, identified rs1800625 in the HLA region, particularly an association of HLA-B*59:01 with CIAG (Saito et al. 2016).

Dermatologic severe reactions to mood stabilizers and CIAG genetic risk, are for now better understood in Asian ancestries, thus limiting the use of PGT to this population.

No prospective trials have followed PGT and safety/tolerability phenotypes. Interestingly, a retrospective survey associating efficacy and tolerability in MD and BD patients with PGT, observed accordance between side effect tolerability phenotype and the 15 evaluated genes (70.6%), however, this latter association was not significant (p=0.71) (Tonozzi et al. 2018).

Potential role of DST that incorporate multiple genotype/phenotype drug recommendations

A number of commercially available platforms have been developed that rapidly assess pharmacokinetic and pharmacodynamic variation and develop a proprietary DST or algorithm to individualize treatment selection.

A narrative review by Bousman and Hopwood (Bousman and Hopwood 2016) found 22 commercial companies offering PGT to five countries most prevalent in the USA (n = 13), followed by Australia and Canada (both n = 3). The majority of these platforms have focused on antidepressants in major depressive disorder primarily and antipsychotics in schizophrenia secondarily. Many of the pharmacogenetics candidate genes identified in response or adverse studies are commercially available as part of a DST. The extent of existing literature or clinical evidence base reviewed to assign a specific genotype a phenotypic pharmacokinetic (i.e., poor metabolizer) or pharmacodynamic (i.e., short form vs long form serotonin transporter) classification for each drug of the DST is proprietary. There is early work to suggest that different commercial products vary substantially, both in laboratory analysis of genotype and subsequent phenotypic classification (Bousman and Dunlop 2018).

There are early uncontrolled observations investigating the efficacy of PGT. Tonnozi et al. (2018) reported PGT of 15 genes (specific variants not reported) in 352 patients with major depression and BD. They reported that more than 60% of the self-reported retrospective treatment response and phenotype outcomes agreed (p = 0.001) and more than 70% of the reported side effect tolerability and phenotype outcome agreed, but this latter association was not significant. The retrospective nature of this association is a clear limitation. Prospective studies of DST have been compared to treatment as usual (TAU).

The Genomics Used to Improve Depression Decisions (GUIDED) trial is the largest study to date that randomized 1167 patients with major depression TAU vs genotype guided care. The primary outcome measure, baseline to endpoint in the Hamilton Depression Rating Scale, showed no significant difference between treatment groups, but secondary outcomes of treatment response and remission rates were statistically significant higher in in guided care vs TAU, though it is not clear if multiple testing was accounted for (Greden et al. 2019). Furthermore, patients randomized to guided care who switched from non-concordant treatment to concordant treatment, defined as agreement between DST recommendation and actual treatment selected, in comparison to those who stayed on non-concordant treatment, achieved a significant reduction in depressive symptoms and higher rates of response and remission. A recent meta-analysis of 5 studies, including Greden et al. (2019), reported that patients randomized to genotype guided care (n = 887) were 1.71 (95% CI 1.17–2.48, p = 0.005) times more likely to achieve remission than those patients randomized to TAU (Bousman et al. 2019). While the field continues to investigate these DST and attempt consensus as to their clinical utility, none of these studies have systematically investigated antidepressants or antipsychotics in BD. A small retrospective study of 30 BD-I and BD-II patients reported a similar observation to Greden et al. (2019) that as treatment concordance rates increased (i.e., genotype guided recommendation and actual treatment selected) from 13% at baseline and 40% at 3-month follow up, symptom severity as measured by the Clinical Global Impression—severity measure decreased (Ielmini et al. 2018). The bipolar pharamacopoiea would clearly advance where clinical treatment could be more individualized in reducing the risk:benefit ratio of antidepressants (i.e., AIM: depression efficacy) and atypical antipsychotics (tardive dyskinesia or cardiometabolics: depression efficacy).

There are two important examples of commissions dedicated to the evaluation of PGT in all medicine specialties. The Evaluation of Genomic Applications in Practice and Prevention (EGAPP) working group, part of the Centers of Disease Control and Prevention, developed a systematic process for evaluating genetic and PGT; they reviewed the utility of CYP450 PGT in major depression SSRI prescription more than 10 years ago and concluded, based on criteria of analytical validity, clinical validity, clinical usefulness, among other ethical/social aspects, that more research was needed before the benefit of PGT could be determined (E.o.G.A.i.P.a.P.E.W. Evaluation of Genomic Applications in Practice and Prevention (EGAPP) Working Group 2007). Concern was raised that important evidence from smaller pharmacogenetic trials and meta-analysis were not included that may have excluded important safety considerations related to CYP2D6 genotyping (Mrazek 2010). Commissioned by the National Health Service, the UK Genetic Testing Network (UKGTN) uses similar-to EGAPP but more extended criteria, to determine the benefit of PGT (UKGTN 2019b). Unfortunately, only dementia PGT is part of the psychiatry-related reports generated by this organization (UKGTN 2019a, b). However, using UKGTN modified criteria, Bousman and Hopwood (Bousman and Hopwood 2016) developed levels of evidence for pharmacogenetic testing variants available in commercial tests. Related to antidepressant therapy, a number of important development considerations were reviewed including: (1) 53% of the 46 tested genes had only preliminary or low supporting evidence (20% met criteria for the highest level), (2) only 60% of *CYP2D6* and *CYP2C19* metabolism-related variants were included in the commercial tests, (3) SNPs included per gene were not always reported in the commercial test, (4) limited availability of drug–drug and drug–gene interaction tools, and (5) not accounting for additional environmental effects and ancestry.

PGT also needs to be cost-effective and studies on willingness-to-pay show patient's preference for PGT, in order to avoid trial-and-error prescriptions, medication changes and adverse events, is significant (Herbild et al. 2008, 2009). Early first investigations of PGT in mood and anxiety disorders appears promising. In a health claims dataset propensity-score, matched 6-month, case–control analysis, individuals with a mood/anxiety disorder (14.8% bipolar) who received PGT (n = 817), in comparison to similar mood/anxiety disorder individuals who did not receive PGT testing (n = 2745), recorded 40% fewer emergency room visits and 58% fewer inpatient all cause hospitalizations (Perlis et al. 2018). While overall 6-month number of psychotropic medications did not differ, overall costs were estimated to be nearly $2000 lower in the PGT group.

Conclusions

DST based on the pharmacogenomics evidence base for BD are significantly underdeveloped in comparison to antidepressants for major depressive disorder and antipsychotics for schizophrenia. PGT commercial assays provide a few robust clinical applications for safety concerns raised by BD treatment, especially in cutaneous side effects of mood-stabilizers in Asian populations. Other potential uses in BD are mostly limited to metabolic phenotype associated variants. However, in comparison to genetic variation associated with adverse event or quantifiable biological process (i.e., rash, QTc prolongation), the bar to establish pharmacogenomic efficacy is significantly higher and to date, the evidence base for treatment recommendations is significantly less (Ahmed et al. 2018). It is important to note that most of these commercial assays vary in content—which may be not fully disclosed—of the genetic tests provided. Moreover, they may provide limited interpretation tools.

It is possible, but yet not investigated, that pharmacogenetic phenotyping in BD may differ by disease phase (e.g., mania, depression, maintenance), clinical components or subphenotypes (e.g., rapid cycling, obesity, binge eating), presence/absence and composition of multimodal drug therapy, environmental influences that magnify or mitigate genetic variation, and overall illness staging (at-risk, first episode, chronic illness with loss of euthymia and functional baseline).

The complexity of BD genetics and, the heterogeneity in BD drug-related phenotypes, are important considerations for the design and interpretation of BD PGT. As BD genetic risk is better understood by additional GWAS and functional genomic studies, the underlying neurobiology of the illness will provide better guidance for genomic testing of pharmacotherapy interventions. Furthermore, risk calculating tools would need to go beyond PGT, and include other important markers of risk, namely clinical risk factors, neuroimaging findings, among others; to better achieve precision medicine in BD (Perlis 2016).

The fast growing consortiums and GWAS studies on lithium response seem one of the most promising avenues for BD pharmacogenomics. Variants in *GADL1* and genes coding non-coding RNAs have been associated with this phenotype. However, these studies have thus far taught us important lessons, such as the one on Chen et al., *GADL1* study. In spite of showing genome-wide associations and large effect sizes, further investigation on *GADL1* did not support its association with lithium response. Moreover, functional studies seem to suggest that the *GADL1* SNPs associated with lithium response, do not have an effect on its genetic expression at the brain level. This is a remarkable reminder of the caution needed when interpreting pharmacogenetic studies, a precaution that is even more crucial before PGT reaches clinical implementation. It is also important to bear in mind that genetics are only a step in the complex "omic" levels that may explain the heritability of a given phenotype. Thus, PGT in BD need to be complemented with epigenetics, gene expression, proteomic, etc., and tested in cellular models such as the ones, for example, provided by induced pluripotent stem cells. Relevant examples of genomic tool integration in BD are emerging. Pisanu et al. (2018a) integrated GWAS lithium response findings in cellular lines, measured their effect on gene expression and, integrating these technologies, they found a potential target in a zinc-finger protein coding gene. Induced pluripotent stem cell lines have revealed hyperexcitability phenotypes in BD neurons that are reversed in lithium response patients (Mertens et al. 2015), underscored the importance of GSK3-β and other Wnt signaling members in the BD neuronal cell-lines (Madison et al. 2015), and elicited a promising new "pathway of lithium response", that governs the phosphorylation of *CRMP2*, which seems to be indirectly modulating GSK3-β (Tobe et al. 2017). The implementation of in silico and machine-learning technologies, will also be crucial in integrating these findings to design intuitive models that help us mimic the biological complexity of genetic–phenotypic interactions.

The clinical applicability of PGT in psychiatry is in its infancy (Stern et al. 2018) and is far from reaching the robust impact it has for instance, in other medical disciplines such as oncology. Nonetheless, promising findings in pharmacogenomic markers of efficacy are discovered with increasing frequency, especially for lithium. Over the last 10 years, pharmacogenetics and other pharmacogenomic technologies have evolved significantly, promising results of remarkable relevance in neuroscience, pharmacology and biology. Their ultimate goal of generating precision medicine in BD, may be a reality not so far in our future.

Abbreviations

BD: Bipolar disorder; DSM-5: Diagnostic and Statistical Manual of Mental Disorders; FDA: Food and Drug Administration; CPIC: Clinical Pharmacogenomics Implementation Consortium; PGRN: Pharmacogenomics Research Network; PGT: Pharmacogenomic testing; CYP: Cytochrome P450; VPA: Valproic acid; SGA: Second-generation antipsychotics; AIM: Antidepressant induced mania; SSRI: Selective serotonin reuptake inhibitors; SNP: Single nucleotide polymorphism; *SLC6A4*: Serotonin transporter gene; GWAS: Genome wide association studies; ConLiGen: Consortium on Lithium Genetics; CIAG: Clozapine-induced agranulocytosis; DST: Decision Support Tool; TAU: Treatment as usual; GUIDED: The Genomics Used to Improve Depression Decisions; EGAPP: The Evaluation of Genomic Applications in Practice and Prevention; UKGTN: UK Genetic Testing Network.

Acknowledgements

Not applicable.

Authors' contributions

ABCB and MAF conceived the idea, selected the studies, and wrote the original draft of the manuscript. All of the authors contributed with writing and revising the different versions of the manuscript. The final version of the manuscript was accepted by all authors before submission. All authors read and approved the final manuscript.

Competing interests

AB Cuellar-Barboza reports no financial relationships with commercial interests. SL McElroy has been a consultant to or member of the scientific advisory boards of Allergan, Avanir, Bracket, F. Hoffmann-La Roche Ltd., Mitsubishi Tanabe Pharma America, Myriad, Opiant, Shire, and Sunovion. She has been a principal or co-investigator on studies sponsored by Allergan, Avanir, Azevan, Brainsway, Marriott Foundation, Medibio, Myriad, Neurocrine, Novo Nordisk, Shire, and Sunovion. She is also an inventor on United States Patent No. 6,323,236 B2, Use of Sulfamate Derivatives for Treating Impulse Control Disorders, and along with the patent's assignee, University of Cincinnati, Cincinnati, Ohio, has received payments from Johnson & Johnson, which has exclusive rights under the patent. M Veldic reports no financial relationships with commercial interests. B Singh received research time support from Medibio, unrelated to the current study. S Kung reports no financial relationships with commercial interests. F Romo-Nava reports no financial relationships with commercial interests. N Nuñez reports no financial relationships with commercial interests. A Cabello-Arreola reports no financial relationships with commercial interests. B Coombes reports no financial relationships with commercial interests. M Prieto reports no financial relationships with commercial interests. HK Betcher reports no financial relationships with commercial interests. KM Moore reports no financial relationships with commercial interests. SJ Winham reports no financial relationships with commercial interests. JM Biernacka reports no financial relationships with commercial interests. MA Frye reports Grant Support from Assurex Health, Mayo Foundation, Medibio. Consultant (Mayo) - Actify Neurotherapies, Allergan, Intra-Cellular Therapies, Inc., Janssen, Myriad, Neuralstem Inc.,Takeda, Teva Pharmaceuticals. He reports CME/Travel/Honoraria from the American Physician Institute, CME Outfitters, Global Academy for Medical Education. Mayo Clinic has a financial interest in AssureRX and OneOme and the technology referenced in this publication.

Author details

[1] Department of Psychiatry, University Hospital, Universidad Autonoma de Nuevo Leon, Monterrey, Mexico. [2] Department of Psychiatry and Psychology, Mayo Clinic, 200 First Street SW, Rochester, MN 55905, USA. [3] Lindner Center of HOPE and Department of Psychiatry, University of Cincinnati, Cincinnati, OH, USA. [4] Department of Health Sciences Research, Mayo Clinic, Rochester, USA. [5] Department of Psychiatry, Universidad de los Andes, Santiago, Chile.

References

Ahmed AT, Weinshilboum R, Frye MA. Benefits of and barriers to pharmacogenomics-guided treatment for major depressive disorder. Clin Pharmacol Ther. 2018;103(5):767–9.

Alda M. Lithium in the treatment of bipolar disorder: pharmacology and pharmacogenetics. Mol Psychiatry. 2015;20(6):661–70.

Amare AT, Schubert KO, Hou L, Clark SR, Papiol S, Heilbronner U, Degenhardt F, Tekola-Ayele F, Hsu YH, Shekhtman T, Adli M, Akula N, Akiyama K, Ardau R, Arias B, Aubry JM, Backlund L, Bhattacharjee AK, Bellivier F, Benabarre A, Bengesser S, Biernacka JM, Birner A, Brichant-Petitjean C, Cervantes P, Chen HC, Chillotti C, Cichon S, Cruceanu C, Czerski PM, Dalkner N, Dayer A, Del Zompo M, DePaulo JR, Etain B, Falkai P, Forstner AJ, Frisen L, Frye MA, Fullerton JM, Gard S, Garnham JS, Goes FS, Grigoroiu-Serbanescu M, Grof P, Hashimoto R, Hauser J, Herms S, Hoffmann P, Hofmann A, Jamain S, Jimenez E, Kahn JP, Kassem L, Kuo PH, Kato T, Kelsoe J, Kittel-Schneider S, Kliwicki S, Konig B, Kusumi I, Laje G, Landen M, Lavebratt C, Leboyer M, Leckband SG, Tortorella A, Manchia M, Martinsson L, McCarthy MJ, McElroy S, Colom F, Mitjans M, Mondimore FM, Monteleone P, Nievergelt CM, Nothen MM, Novak T, O'Donovan C, Ozaki N, Osby U, Pfennig A, Potash JB, Reif A, Reininghaus E, Rouleau GA, Rybakowski JK, Schalling M, Schofield PR, Schweizer BW, Severino G, Shilling PD, Shimoda K, Simhandl C, Slaney CM, Squassina A, Stamm T, Stopkova P, Maj M, Turecki G, Vieta E, Volkert J, Witt S, Wright A, Zandi PP, Mitchell PB, Bauer M, Alda M, Rietschel M, McMahon FJ, Schulze TG, Baune BT. Association of polygenic score for schizophrenia and HLA antigen and inflammation genes with response to lithium in bipolar affective disorder: a genome-wide association study. JAMA Psychiatry. 2018;75(1):65–74.

Angst J, Sellaro R. Historical perspectives and natural history of bipolar disorder. Biol Psychiatry. 2000;48(6):445–57.

Bauer M, Gitlin MJ. The essential guide to lithium treatment. New York: Springer; 2016.

Berard A, Gaedigk A, Sheehy O, Chambers C, Roth M, Bozzo P, Johnson D, Kao K, Lavigne S, Wolfe L, Quinn D, Dieter K, Zhao JP. Association between CYP2D6 genotypes and the risk of antidepressant discontinuation, dosage modification and the occurrence of maternal depression during pregnancy. Front Pharmacol. 2017;8:402.

Bielinski SJ, Olson JE, Pathak J, Weinshilboum RM, Wang L, Lyke KJ, Ryu E, Targonski PV, Van Norstrand MD, Hathcock MA, Takahashi PY, McCormick JB, Johnson KJ, Maschke KJ, Rohrer Vitek CR, Ellingson MS, Wieben ED, Farrugia G, Morrisette JA, Kruckeberg KJ, Bruflat JK, Peterson LM, Blommel JH, Skierka JM, Ferber MJ, Black JL, Baudhuin LM, Klee EW, Ross JL, Veldhuizen TL, Schultz CG, Caraballo PJ, Freimuth RR, Chute CG, Kullo IJ. Preemptive genotyping for personalized medicine: design of the right drug, right dose, right time-using genomic data to individualize treatment protocol. Mayo Clin Proc. 2014;89(1):25–33.

Biernacka JM, McElroy SL, Crow S, Sharp A, Benitez J, Veldic M, Kung S, Cunningham JM, Post RM, Mrazek D, Frye MA. Pharmacogenomics of antidepressant induced mania: a review and meta-analysis of the serotonin transporter gene (5HTTLPR) association. J Affect Disord. 2012;136(1–2):e21–9.

Birnbaum R, Shin JH, Weinberger D. Variant GADL1 and response to lithium in bipolar I disorder. N Engl J Med. 2014;370(19):1855–6.

Bloch KM, Sills GJ, Pirmohamed M, Alfirevic A. Pharmacogenetics of antiepileptic drug-induced hypersensitivity. Pharmacogenomics. 2014;15(6):857–68.

Bousman CA, Dunlop BW. Genotype, phenotype, and medication recommendation agreement among commercial pharmacogenetic-based decision support tools. Pharmacogenomics J. 2018;18(5):613–22.

Bousman CA, Hopwood M. Commercial pharmacogenetic-based decision-support tools in psychiatry. Lancet Psychiatry. 2016;3(6):585–90.

Bousman CA, Arandjelovic K, Mancuso SG, Eyre HA, Dunlop BW. Pharmacogenetic tests and depressive symptom remission: a meta-analysis of randomized controlled trials. Pharmacogenomics. 2019;20(1):37–47.

Bruckl TM, Uhr M. ABCB1 genotyping in the treatment of depression. Pharmacogenomics. 2016;17(18):2039–69.

Budde M, Degner D, Brockmoller J, Schulze TG. Pharmacogenomic aspects of bipolar disorder: an update. Eur Neuropsychopharmacol. 2017;27(6):599–609.

Chang HH, Gean PW, Chou CH, Yang YK, Tsai HC, Lu RB, Chen PS. C825T polymorphism of the GNB3 gene on valproate-related metabolic abnormalities in bipolar disorder patients. J Clin Psychopharmacol. 2010;30(5):512–7.

Chen CH, Lee CS, Lee MT, Ouyang WC, Chen CC, Chong MY, Wu JY, Tan HK, Lee YC, Chuo LJ, Chiu NY, Tsang HY, Chang TJ, Lung FW, Chiu CH, Chang CH, Chen YS, Hou YM, Chen CC, Lai TJ, Tung CL, Chen CY, Lane HY, Su TP, Feng J, Lin JJ, Chang CJ, Teng PR, Liu CY, Chen CK, Liu IC, Chen JJ, Lu T, Fan CC, Wu CK, Li CF, Wang KH, Wu LS, Peng HL, Chang CP, Lu LS, Chen YT, Cheng AT. Variant GADL1 and response to lithium therapy in bipolar I disorder. N Engl J Med. 2014;370(2):119–28.

Chen CK, Lee CS, Chen HY, Wu LS, Chang JC, Liu CY, Cheng AT. GADL1 variant and medication adherence in predicting response to lithium maintenance treatment in bipolar I disorder. BJPsych Open. 2016;2(5):301–6.

Chen PS, Chang HH, Huang CC, Lee CC, Lee SY, Chen SL, Huang SY, Yang YK, Lu RB. A longitudinal study of the association between the GNB3 C825T polymorphism and metabolic disturbance in bipolar II patients treated with valproate. Pharmacogenomics J. 2017;17(2):155–61.

Cipriani A, Hawton K, Stockton S, Geddes JR. Lithium in the prevention of suicide in mood disorders: updated systematic review and meta-analysis. BMJ. 2013;346:f3646.

Creta E, Fabbri C, Serretti A. Genetics of second-generation antipsychotic and mood stabilizer-induced weight gain in bipolar disorder: common and specific effects of key regulators of fat-mass homoeostasis genes. Pharmacogenet Genomics. 2015;25(7):354–62.

Cruceanu C, Alda M, Dion PA, Turecki G, Rouleau GA. No evidence for GADL1 variation as a bipolar disorder susceptibility factor in a Caucasian lithium-responsive cohort. Am J Psychiatry. 2015;172(1):94–5.

Daci A, Beretta G, Vllasaliu D, Shala A, Govori V, Norata GD, Krasniqi S. Polymorphic variants of SCN1A and EPHX1 influence plasma carbamazepine concentration, metabolism and pharmacoresistance in a population of Kosovar Albanian epileptic patients. PLoS ONE. 2015;10(11):e0142408.

Daray FM, Thommi SB, Ghaemi SN. The pharmacogenetics of antidepressant-induced mania: a systematic review and meta-analysis. Bipolar Disord. 2010;12(7):702–6.

Dmitrzak-Weglarz M, Rybakowski JK, Suwalska A, Skibinska M, Leszczynska-Rodziewicz A, Szczepankiewicz A, Hauser J. Association studies of the BDNF and the NTRK2 gene polymorphisms with prophylactic lithium response in bipolar patients. Pharmacogenomics. 2008;9(11):1595–603.

Drago A, Serretti A, Smith R, Huezo-Diaz P, Malitas P, Albani D, Ronchi DD, Pae CU, Aitchison KJ. No association between genetic markers in BDNF gene and lithium prophylaxis in a Greek sample. Int J Psychiatry Clin Pract. 2010;14(2):154–7.

Drago A, Giegling I, Schafer M, Hartmann AM, Friedl M, Konte B, Moller HJ, De Ronchi D, Stassen HH, Serretti A, Rujescu D. AKAP13, CACNA1, GRIK4 and GRIA1 genetic variations may be associated with haloperidol efficacy during acute treatment. Eur Neuropsychopharmacol. 2013;23(8):887–94.

Drozda K, Pacanowski MA, Grimstein C, Zineh I. Pharmacogenetic labeling of FDA-Approved drugs: a regulatory retrospective. JACC Basic Transl Sci. 2018;3(4):545–9.

E.o.G.A.i.P.a.P.E.W. Evaluation of Genomic Applications in Practice and Prevention (EGAPP) Working Group. Recommendations from the EGAPP Working Group: testing for cytochrome P450 polymorphisms in adults with nonpsychotic depression treated with selective serotonin reuptake inhibitors. Genet Med. 2007;9(12):819–25.

Eum S, Lee AM, Bishop JR. Pharmacogenetic tests for antipsychotic medications: clinical implications and considerations. Dialogues Clin Neurosci. 2016;18(3):323–37.

Fabbri C, Tansey KE, Perlis RH, Hauser J, Henigsberg N, Maier W, Mors O, Placentino A, Rietschel M, Souery D, Breen G, Curtis C, Lee SH, Newhouse S, Patel H, O'Donovan M, Lewis G, Jenkins G, Weinshilboum RM, Farmer A, Aitchison KJ, Craig I, McGuffin P, Schruers K, Biernacka JM, Uher R, Lewis CM. Effect of cytochrome CYP2C19 metabolizing activity on antidepressant response and side effects: meta-analysis of data from genome-wide association studies. Eur Neuropsychopharmacol. 2018;28(8):945–54.

Farrell MS, Werge T, Sklar P, Owen MJ, Ophoff RA, O'Donovan MC, Corvin A, Cichon S, Sullivan PF. Evaluating historical candidate genes for schizophrenia. Mol Psychiatry. 2015;20(5):555–62.

Fleeman N, Dundar Y, Dickson R, Jorgensen A, Pushpakom S, McLeod C, Pirmohamed M, Walley T. Cytochrome P450 testing for prescribing antipsychotics in adults with schizophrenia: systematic review and meta-analyses. Pharmacogenomics J. 2011;11(1):1–14.

Frey BN, Andreazza AC, Houenou J, Jamain S, Goldstein BI, Frye MA, Leboyer M, Berk M, Malhi GS, Lopez-Jaramillo C, Taylor VH, Dodd S, Frangou S, Hall GB, Fernandes BS, Kauer-Sant'Anna M, Yatham LN, Kapczinski F, Young LT. Biomarkers in bipolar disorder: a positional paper from the International Society for Bipolar Disorders Biomarkers Task Force. Aust N Z J Psychiatry. 2013;47(4):321–32.

Frye MA. Clinical practice. Bipolar disorder—a focus on depression. N Engl J Med. 2011;364(1):51–9.

Frye MA, Ketter TA, Altshuler LL, Denicoff K, Dunn RT, Kimbrell TA, Cora-Locatelli G, Post RM. Clozapine in bipolar disorder: treatment implications for other atypical antipsychotics. J Affect Disord. 1998;48(2–3):91–104.

Frye MA, Ketter TA, Leverich GS, Huggins T, Lantz C, Denicoff KD, Post RM. The increasing use of polypharmacotherapy for refractory mood disorders: 22 years of study. J Clin Psychiatry. 2000;61(1):9–15.

Frye MA, Yatham LN, Calabrese JR, Bowden CL, Ketter TA, Suppes T, Adams BE, Thompson TR. Incidence and time course of subsyndromal symptoms in patients with bipolar I disorder: an evaluation of 2 placebo-controlled maintenance trials. J Clin Psychiatry. 2006;67(11):1721–8.

Frye MA, McElroy SL, Prieto ML, Harper KL, Walker DL, Kung S, Chauhan M, Crow S, Sutor B, Galardy CW, Veldic M, Palmer BA, Geske JR, Fuentes M, Cuellar-Barboza AB, Seymour LR, Mori N, Biernacka JM. Clinical risk factors and serotonin transporter gene variants associated with antidepressant-induced mania. J Clin Psychiatry. 2015;76(2):174–80.

Gaedigk A, Sangkuhl K, Whirl-Carrillo M, Klein T, Leeder JS. Prediction of CYP2D6 phenotype from genotype across world populations. Genet Med. 2017;19(1):69–76.

Goldberg JF, Perlis RH, Ghaemi SN, Calabrese JR, Bowden CL, Wisniewski S, Miklowitz DJ, Sachs GS, Thase ME. Adjunctive antidepressant use and symptomatic recovery among bipolar depressed patients with concomitant manic symptoms: findings from the STEP-BD. Am J Psychiatry. 2007;164(9):1348–55.

Goldstein JI, Jarskog LF, Hilliard C, Alfirevic A, Duncan L, Fourches D, Huang H, Lek M, Neale BM, Ripke S, Shianna K, Szatkiewicz JP, Tropsha A, van den Oord EJ, Cascorbi I, Dettling M, Gazit E, Goff DC, Holden AL, Kelly DL, Malhotra AK, Nielsen J, Pirmohamed M, Rujescu D, Werge T, Levy DL, Josiassen RC, Kennedy JL, Lieberman JA, Daly MJ, Sullivan PF. Clozapine-induced agranulocytosis is associated with rare HLA-DQB1 and HLA-B alleles. Nat Commun. 2014;5:4757.

Greden JF, Parikh SV, Rothschild AJ, Thase ME, Dunlop BW, DeBattista C, Conway CR, Forester BP, Mondimore FM, Shelton RC, Macaluso M, Li J, Brown K, Gilbert A, Burns L, Jablonski MR, Dechairo B. Impact of pharmacogenomics on clinical outcomes in major depressive disorder in the GUIDED trial: a large, patient- and rater-blinded, randomized, controlled study. J Psychiatr Res. 2019;111:59–67.

Grof P, Alda M, Grof E, Fox D, Cameron P. The challenge of predicting response to stabilising lithium treatment. The importance of patient selection. Br J Psychiatry. 1993;163(Suppl21):16–9.

Grof P, Duffy A, Cavazzoni P, Grof E, Garnham J, MacDougall M, O'Donovan C, Alda M. Is response to prophylactic lithium a familial trait? J Clin Psychiatry. 2002;63(10):942–7.

Grof P, Duffy A, Alda M, Hajek T. Lithium response across generations. Acta Psychiatr Scand. 2009;120(5):378–85.

Grunze H, Vieta E, Goodwin GM, Bowden C, Licht RW, Moller HJ, Kasper S. The World Federation of Societies of Biological Psychiatry (WFSBP) guidelines for the biological treatment of bipolar disorders: update 2012 on the long-term treatment of bipolar disorder. World J Biol Psychiatry. 2013;14(3):154–219.

Grunze H, Vieta E, Goodwin GM, Bowden C, Licht RW, Azorin JM, Yatham L, Mosolov S, Moller HJ, Kasper S. The World Federation of Societies of Biological Psychiatry (WFSBP) Guidelines for the Biological Treatment of Bipolar Disorders: acute and long-term treatment of mixed states in bipolar disorder. World J Biol Psychiatry. 2018;19(1):2–58.

Haerian BS, Baum L, Kwan P, Tan HJ, Raymond AA, Mohamed Z. SCN1A, SCN2A and SCN3A gene polymorphisms and responsiveness to antiepileptic drugs: a multicenter cohort study and meta-analysis. Pharmacogenomics. 2013;14(10):1153–66.

Harrison PJ, Geddes JR, Tunbridge EM. The Emerging Neurobiology of Bipolar Disorder. Trends Neurosci. 2018;41(1):18–30.

Haug K, Hallmann K, Rebstock J, Dullinger J, Muth S, Haverkamp F, Pfeiffer H, Rau B, Elger CE, Propping P, Heils A. The voltage-gated sodium channel gene SCN2A and idiopathic generalized epilepsy. Epilepsy Res. 2001;47(3):243–6.

Hendset M, Hermann M, Lunde H, Refsum H, Molden E. Impact of the CYP2D6 genotype on steady-state serum concentrations of aripiprazole and dehydroaripiprazole. Eur J Clin Pharmacol. 2007;63(12):1147–51.

Herbild L, Gyrd-Hansen D, Bech M. Patient preferences for pharmacogenetic screening in depression. Int J Technol Assess Health Care. 2008;24(1):96–103.

Herbild L, Bech M, Gyrd-Hansen D. Estimating the Danish populations' preferences for pharmacogenetic testing using a discrete choice experiment. The case of treating depression. Value Health. 2009;12(4):560–7.

Hicks JK, Bishop JR, Sangkuhl K, Muller DJ, Ji Y, Leckband SG, Leeder JS, Graham RL, Chiulli DL, LLerena A, Skaar TC, Scott SA, Stingl JC, Klein TE, Caudle KE, Gaedigk A, C. Clinical Pharmacogenetics Implementation. Clinical Pharmacogenetics Implementation Consortium (CPIC) guideline for CYP2D6 and CYP2C19 genotypes and dosing of selective serotonin reuptake inhibitors. Clin Pharmacol Ther. 2015;98(2):127–34.

Hicks JK, Sangkuhl K, Swen JJ, Ellingrod VL, Muller DJ, Shimoda K, Bishop JR, Kharasch ED, Skaar TC, Gaedigk A, Dunnenberger HM, Klein TE, Caudle KE, Stingl JC. Clinical pharmacogenetics implementation consortium guideline (CPIC) for CYP2D6 and CYP2C19 genotypes and dosing of tricyclic antidepressants: 2016 update. Clin Pharmacol Ther. 2017;102(1):37–44.

Hodgson K, Tansey K, Dernovsek MZ, Hauser J, Henigsberg N, Maier W, Mors O, Placentino A, Rietschel M, Souery D, Smith R, Craig IW, Farmer AE, Aitchison KJ, Belsey S, Davis OS, Uher R, McGuffin P. Genetic differences in cytochrome P450 enzymes and antidepressant treatment response. J Psychopharmacol. 2014;28(2):133–41.

Hodgson K, Tansey KE, Uher R, Dernovsek MZ, Mors O, Hauser J, Souery D, Maier W, Henigsberg N, Rietschel M, Placentino A, Craig IW, Aitchison KJ, Farmer AE, Dobson RJ, McGuffin P. Exploring the role of drug-metabolising enzymes in antidepressant side effects. Psychopharmacology. 2015;232(14):2609–17.

Hou L, Heilbronner U, Rietschel M, Kato T, Kuo PH, McMahon FJ, Schulze TG. Variant GADL1 and response to lithium in bipolar I disorder. N Engl J Med. 2014;370(19):1857–9.

Hou L, Heilbronner U, Degenhardt F, Adli M, Akiyama K, Akula N, Ardau R, Arias B, Backlund L, Banzato CEM, Benabarre A, Bengesser S, Bhattacharjee AK, Biernacka JM, Birner A, Brichant-Petitjean C, Bui ET, Cervantes P, Chen GB, Chen HC, Chillotti C, Cichon S, Clark SR, Colom F, Cousins DA, Cruceanu C, Czerski PM, Dantas CR, Dayer A, Etain B, Falkai P, Forstner AJ, Frisen L, Fullerton JM, Gard S, Garnham JS, Goes FS, Grof P, Gruber O, Hashimoto R, Hauser J, Herms S, Hoffmann P, Hofmann A, Jamain S, Jimenez E, Kahn JP, Kassem L, Kittel-Schneider S, Kliwicki S, Konig B, Kusumi I, Lackner N, Laje G, Landen M, Lavebratt C, Leboyer M, Leckband SG, Jaramillo CAL, MacQueen G, Manchia M, Martinsson L, Mattheisen M, McCarthy MJ, McElroy SL, Mitjans M, Mondimore FM, Monteleone P, Nievergelt CM, Nothen MM, Osby U, Ozaki N, Perlis RH, Pfennig A, Reich-Erkelenz D, Rouleau GA, Schofield PR, Schubert KO, Schweizer BW, Seemuller F, Severino G, Shekhtman T, Shilling PD, Shimoda K, Simhandl C, Slaney CM, Smoller JW, Squassina A, Stamm T, Stopkova P, Tighe SK, Tortorella A, Turecki G, Volkert J, Witt S, Wright A, Young LT, Zandi PP, Potash JB, DePaulo JR, Bauer M, Reininghaus EZ, Novak T, Aubry JM, Maj M, Baune BT, Mitchell PB, Vieta E, Frye MA, Rybakowski JK, Kuo PH, Kato T, Grigoroiu-Serbanescu M, Reif A, Del Zompo M, Bellivier F, Schalling M, Wray NR, Kelsoe JR, Alda M, Rietschel M, McMahon FJ, Schulze TG. Genetic variants associated with response to lithium treatment in bipolar disorder: a genome-wide association study. Lancet. 2016;387(10023):1085–93.

Ielmini M, Poloni N, Caselli I, Espadaler J, Tuson M, Grecchi A, Callegari C. The utility of pharmacogenetic testing to support the treatment of bipolar disorder. Pharmgenomics Pers Med. 2018;11:35–42.

Ikeda M, Kondo K, Iwata N. Variant GADL1 and response to lithium in bipolar I disorder. N Engl J Med. 2014;370(19):1856–7.

Ji Y, Biernacka J, Snyder K, Drews M, Pelleymounter LL, Colby C, Wang L, Mrazek DA, Weinshilboum RM. Catechol O methyltransferase pharmacogenomics and selective serotonin reuptake inhibitor response. Pharmacogenomics J. 2012;12(1):78–85.

Judd LL, Akiskal HS. Depressive episodes and symptoms dominate the longitudinal course of bipolar disorder. Curr Psychiatry Rep. 2003;5(6):417–8.

Jukic MM, Haslemo T, Molden E, Ingelman-Sundberg M. Impact of CYP2C19 genotype on escitalopram exposure and therapeutic failure: a retrospective study based on 2087 patients. Am J Psychiatry. 2018;175(5):463–70.

Jukic MM, Smith RL, Haslemo T, Molden E, Ingelman-Sundberg M. Effect of CYP2D6 genotype on exposure and efficacy of risperidone and aripiprazole: a retrospective, cohort study. Lancet Psychiatry. 2019;6(5):418–26.

Kawaguchi DM, Glatt SJ. GRIK4 polymorphism and its association with antidepressant response in depressed patients: a meta-analysis. Pharmacogenomics. 2014;15(11):1451–9.

Kim SC, Kim MG. Meta-analysis of the influence of UGT genetic polymorphisms on lamotrigine concentration. Basic Clin Pharmacol Toxicol. 2019;124(2):163–9.

Kim B, Kim CY, Lee MJ, Joo YH. Preliminary evidence on the association between XBP1-116C/G polymorphism and response to prophylactic treatment with valproate in bipolar disorders. Psychiatry Res. 2009;168(3):209–12.

Kotambail A, Mathur A, Bhat SM, Rai PS, Sharma PS, Satyamoorthy K. GADL1 gene polymorphisms and lithium response in bipolar I disorder: lack of association from an Indian population. Psychiatr Genet. 2015;25(1):39–40.

Legge SE, Hamshere ML, Ripke S, Pardinas AF, Goldstein JI, Rees E, Richards AL, Leonenko G, Jorskog LF, Chambert KD, Collier DA, Genovese G, Giegling I, Holmans P, Jonasdottir A, Kirov G, McCarroll SA, MacCabe JH, Mantripragada K, Moran JL, Neale BM, Stefansson H, Rujescu D, Daly MJ, Sullivan PF, Owen MJ, O'Donovan MC, Walters JTR. Genome-wide common and rare variant analysis provides novel insights into clozapine-associated neutropenia. Mol Psychiatry. 2017;22(10):1502–8.

Li X, Frye MA, Shelton RC. Review of pharmacological treatment in mood disorders and future directions for drug development. Neuropsychopharmacology. 2012;37(1):77–101.

Li X, Zhang J, Wu X, Yan H, Zhang Y, He RH, Tang YJ, He YJ, Tan D, Mao XY, Yin JY, Liu ZQ, Zhou HH, Liu J. Polymorphisms of ABAT, SCN2A and ALDH5A1 may affect valproic acid responses in the treatment of epilepsy in Chinese. Pharmacogenomics. 2016;17(18):2007–14.

Lin JY, Jiang MY, Kan ZM, Chu Y. Influence of 5-HTR2A genetic polymorphisms on the efficacy of antidepressants in the treatment of major depressive disorder: a meta-analysis. J Affect Disord. 2014;168:430–8.

Liu P, Ge X, Ding H, Jiang H, Christensen BM, Li J. Role of glutamate decarboxylase-like protein 1 (GADL1) in taurine biosynthesis. J Biol Chem. 2012;287(49):40898–906.

Llerena A, Dorado ALP, Berecz R, Gonzalez AP, Penas LEM. Effect of CYP2D6 and CYP2C9 genotypes on fluoxetine and norfluoxetine plasma concentrations during steady-state conditions. Eur J Clin Pharmacol. 2004;59(12):869–73.

Lobello KW, Preskorn SH, Guico-Pabia CJ, Jiang Q, Paul J, Nichols AI, Patroneva A, Ninan PT. Cytochrome P450 2D6 phenotype predicts antidepressant efficacy of venlafaxine: a secondary analysis of 4 studies in major depressive disorder. J Clin Psychiatry. 2010;71(11):1482–7.

Lv N, Qu J, Long H, Zhou L, Cao Y, Long L, Liu Z, Xiao B. Association study between polymorphisms in the CACNA1A, CACNA1C, and CACNA1H genes and drug-resistant epilepsy in the Chinese Han population. Seizure. 2015;30:64–9.

Ma X, Maimaitirexiati T, Zhang R, Gui X, Zhang W, Xu G, Hu G. HTR2C polymorphisms, olanzapine-induced weight gain and antipsychotic-induced metabolic syndrome in schizophrenia patients: a meta-analysis. Int J Psychiatry Clin Pract. 2014;18(4):229–42.

Madison JM, Zhou F, Nigam A, Hussain A, Barker DD, Nehme R, van der Ven K, Hsu J, Wolf P, Fleishman M, O'Dushlaine C, Rose S, Chambert K, Lau FH, Ahfeldt T, Rueckert EH, Sheridan SD, Fass DM, Nemesh J, Mullen TE, Daheron L, McCarroll S, Sklar P, Perlis RH, Haggarty SJ. Characterization of bipolar disorder patient-specific induced pluripotent stem cells from a family reveals neurodevelopmental and mRNA expression abnormalities. Mol Psychiatry. 2015;20(6):703–17.

Malhi GS, Irwin L, Hamilton A, Morris G, Boyce P, Mulder R, Porter RJ. Modelling mood disorders: an ACE solution? Bipolar Disord. 2018;20(Suppl 2):4–16.

Mamdani F, Alda M, Grof P, Young LT, Rouleau G, Turecki G. Lithium response and genetic variation in the CREB family of genes. Am J Med Genet B Neuropsychiatr Genet. 2008;147b(4):500–4.

McGraw J, Gerhardt A, Morris TC. Opportunities and obstacles in genotypic prediction of cytochrome P450 phenotypes. Expert Opin Drug Metab Toxicol. 2018;14(7):659–61.

Mertens J, Wang QW, Kim Y, Yu DX, Pham S, Yang B, Zheng Y, Diffenderfer KE, Zhang J, Soltani S, Eames T, Schafer ST, Boyer L, Marchetto MC, Nurnberger JI, Calabrese JR, Odegaard KJ, McCarthy MJ, Zandi PP, Alda M, Nievergelt CM, Mi S, Brennand KJ, Kelsoe JR, Gage FH, Yao J. Differential responses to lithium in hyperexcitable neurons from patients with bipolar disorder. Nature. 2015;527(7576):95–9.

Michelon L, Meira-Lima I, Cordeiro Q, Miguita K, Breen G, Collier D, Vallada H. Association study of the INPP1, 5HTT, BDNF, AP-2beta and GSK-3beta GENE variants and restrospectively scored response to lithium prophylaxis in bipolar disorder. Neurosci Lett. 2006;403(3):288–93.

Monostory K, Nagy A, Toth K, Budi T, Kiss A, Deri M, Csukly G. Relevance of CYP2C9 function in valproate therapy. Curr Neuropharmacol. 2019;17(1):99–106.

Mrazek D. Psychiatric pharmacogenomics. New York: Oxford University Press; 2010.

Muller DJ, Brandl EJ, Hwang R, Tiwari AK, Sturgess JE, Zai CC, Lieberman JA, Kennedy JL, Richter MA. The AmpliChip(R) CYP450 test and response to treatment in schizophrenia and obsessive compulsive disorder: a pilot study and focus on cases with abnormal CYP2D6 drug metabolism. Genet Test Mol Biomarkers. 2012;16(8):897–903.

Nassan M, Nicholson WT, Elliott MA, Rohrer Vitek CR, Black JL, Frye MA. Pharmacokinetic pharmacogenetic prescribing guidelines for antidepressants: a template for psychiatric precision medicine. Mayo Clin Proc. 2016;91(7):897–907.

Ng C, Sarris J, Singh A, Bousman C, Byron K, Peh LH, Smith DJ, Tan CH, Schweitzer I. Pharmacogenetic polymorphisms and response to escitalopram and venlafaxine over 8 weeks in major depression. Hum Psychopharmacol. 2013;28(5):516–22.

Nofziger C, Turner AJ, Sangkuhl K, Whirl-Carrillo M, Agundez JAG, Black JL, Dunnenberger HM, Ruano G, Kennedy MA, Phillips MS, Hachad H, Klein TE, Gaedigk A. PharmVar GeneFocus: CYP2D6. Clin Pharmacol Ther. 2020;107(1):154–70.

Numata S, Umehara H, Ohmori T, Hashimoto R. Clozapine pharmacogenetic studies in schizophrenia: efficacy and agranulocytosis. Front Pharmacol. 2018;9:1049.

Pacchiarotti I, Bond DJ, Baldessarini RJ, Nolen WA, Grunze H, Licht RW, Post RM, Berk M, Goodwin GM, Sachs GS, Tondo L, Findling RL, Youngstrom EA, Tohen M, Undurraga J, Gonzalez-Pinto A, Goldberg JF, Yildiz A, Altshuler LL, Calabrese JR, Mitchell PB, Thase ME, Koukopoulos A, Colom F, Frye MA, Malhi GS, Fountoulakis KN, Vazquez G, Perlis RH, Ketter TA, Cassidy F, Akiskal H, Azorin JM, Valenti M, Mazzei DH, Lafer B, Kato T, Mazzarini L, Martinez-Aran A, Parker G, Souery D, Ozerdem A, McElroy SL, Girardi P, Bauer M, Yatham LN, Zarate CA, Nierenberg AA, Birmaher B, Kanba S, El-Mallakh RS, Serretti A, Rihmer Z, Young AH, Kotzalidis GD, MacQueen GM, Bowden CL, Ghaemi SN, Lopez-Jaramillo C, Rybakowski J, Ha K, Perugi G, Kasper S, Amsterdam JD, Hirschfeld RM, Kapczinski F, Vieta E. The International Society for Bipolar Disorders (ISBD) task force report on antidepressant use in bipolar disorders. Am J Psychiatry. 2013;170(11):1249–62.

Paddock S, Laje G, Charney D, Rush AJ, Wilson AF, Sorant AJM, Lipsky R, Wisniewski SR, Manji H, McMahon FJ. Association of GRIK4 with outcome of antidepressant treatment in the STAR*D cohort. Am J Psychiatry. 2007;164(8):1181–8.

Park JY, Kim KA, Park PW, Lee OJ, Kang DK, Shon JH, Liu KH, Shin JG. Effect of CYP3A5*3 genotype on the pharmacokinetics and pharmacodynamics of alprazolam in healthy subjects. Clin Pharmacol Ther. 2006;79(6):590–9.

Patriquin MA, Bauer IE, Soares JC, Graham DP, Nielsen DA. Addiction pharmacogenetics: a systematic review of the genetic variation of the dopaminergic system. Psychiatr Genet. 2015;25(5):181–93.

Perlis RH. Abandoning personalization to get to precision in the pharmacotherapy of depression. World Psychiatry. 2016;15(3):228–35.

Perlis RH, Smoller JW, Ferreira MA, McQuillin A, Bass N, Lawrence J, Sachs GS, Nimgaonkar V, Scolnick EM, Gurling H, Sklar P, Purcell S. A genomewide association study of response to lithium for prevention of recurrence in bipolar disorder. Am J Psychiatry. 2009;166(6):718–25.

Perlis RH, Mehta R, Edwards AM, Tiwari A, Imbens GW. Pharmacogenetic testing among patients with mood and anxiety disorders is associated with decreased utilization and cost: a propensity-score matched study. Depress Anxiety. 2018;35(10):946–52.

Phillips EJ, Sukasem C, Whirl-Carrillo M, Muller DJ, Dunnenberger HM, Chantratita W, Goldspiel B, Chen YT, Carleton BC, George AL Jr, Mushiroda T, Klein T, Gammal RS, Pirmohamed M. Clinical pharmacogenetics implementation consortium guideline for HLA genotype and use of carbamazepine and oxcarbazepine: 2017 update. Clin Pharmacol Ther. 2018;103(4):574–81.

Pickard BS. Genomics of lithium action and response. Neurotherapeutics. 2017;14(3):582–7.

Pisanu C, Melis C, Squassina A. Lithium pharmacogenetics: where do we stand? Drug Dev Res 2016;77(7):368–73.

Pisanu C, Congiu D, Costa M, Chillotti C, Ardau R, Severino G, Angius A, Heilbronner U, Hou L, McMahon FJ, Schulze TG, Del Zompo M, Squassina A. Convergent analysis of genome-wide genotyping and transcriptomic data suggests association of zinc finger genes with lithium response in bipolar disorder. Am J Med Genet B Neuropsychiatr Genet. 2018a;177(7):658–64.

Pisanu C, Heilbronner U, Squassina A. The role of pharmacogenomics in bipolar disorder: moving towards precision medicine. Mol Diagn Ther. 2018b;22(4):409–20.

Post RM. Preventing the malignant transformation of bipolar disorder. JAMA. 2018;319(12):1197–8.

Post RM, Leverich GS, Kupka R, Keck PE Jr, McElroy SL, Altshuler LL, Frye MA, Rowe M, Grunze H, Suppes T, Nolen WA. Clinical correlates of sustained response to individual drugs used in naturalistic treatment of patients with bipolar disorder. Compr Psychiatry. 2016;66:146–56.

Rao S, Han X, Shi M, Siu CO, Waye MMY, Liu G, Wing YK. Associations of the serotonin transporter promoter polymorphism (5-HTTLPR) with bipolar disorder and treatment response: a systematic review and meta-analysis. Prog Neuropsychopharmacol Biol Psychiatry. 2019;89:214–26.

Relling MV, Klein TE. CPIC: clinical pharmacogenetics implementation consortium of the pharmacogenomics research network. Clin Pharmacol Ther. 2011;89(3):464–7.

Rybakowski JK, Abramowicz M, Szczepankiewicz A, Michalak M, Hauser J, Czekalski S. The association of glycogen synthase kinase-3beta (GSK-3beta) gene polymorphism with kidney function in long-term lithium-treated bipolar patients. Int J Bipolar Disord. 2013;1:8.

Saito T, Ikeda M, Mushiroda T, Ozeki T, Kondo K, Shimasaki A, Kawase K, Hashimoto S, Yamamori H, Yasuda Y, Fujimoto M, Ohi K, Takeda M, Kamatani Y, Numata S, Ohmori T, Ueno S, Makinodan M, Nishihata Y, Kubota M, Kimura T, Kanahara N, Hashimoto N, Fujita K, Nemoto K, Fukao T, Suwa T, Noda T, Yada Y, Takaki M, Kida N, Otsuru T, Murakami M, Takahashi A, Kubo M, Hashimoto R, Iwata N. Pharmacogenomic study of clozapine-induced agranulocytosis/granulocytopenia in a Japanese population. Biol Psychiatry. 2016;80(8):636–42.

Saito T, Ikeda M, Hashimoto R, Iwata N, Yamamori H, Yasuda Y, Fujimoto M, Kondo K, Shimasaki A, Kawase K, Miyata M, Mushiroda T, Ozeki T, Kubo M, Fujita K, Kida N, Nakai M, Otsuru T, Fukuji Y, Murakami M, Mizuno K, Shiratsuchi T, Numata S, Ohmori T, Ueno SI, Yada Y, Tanaka S, Kishi Y, Takaki M, Mamoto A, Taniguchi N, Sawa Y, Watanabe H, Noda T, Amano Y, Kimura T, Fukao T, Suwa T, Murai T, Kubota M, Ueda K, Tabuse H, Kanahara N, Kawai N, Nemoto K, Makinodan M, Nishihata Y, Hashimoto N, Kusumi I, Fujii Y, Miyata R, Hirakawa K, Ozaki N. Transethnic replication study to assess the association between clozapine-induced agranulocytosis/granulocytopenia and genes at 12p12.2 in a Japanese population. Biol Psychiatry. 2017;82(1):e9–10.

Sanchez-Iglesias S, Garcia-Solaesa V, Garcia-Berrocal B, Sanchez-Martin A, Lorenzo-Romo C, Martin-Pinto T, Gaedigk A, Gonzalez-Buitrago JM, Isidoro-Garcia M. Role of pharmacogenetics in improving the safety of psychiatric care by predicting the potential risks of Mania in CYP2D6 poor metabolizers diagnosed with bipolar disorder. Medicine (Baltimore). 2016;95(6):e2473.

Sathur Raghuraman B, Paul P, Nadella RK, Kapur V, Purushottam M, Jain S, Kannan R, Del Zompo M, Viswanath B. GSK-3b 50 T/C polymorphism in bipolar disorder and its relationship with clinical phenotypes and treatment response. J Affect Disord. 2018;241:433–5.

Serretti A. Genetics and pharmacogenetics of mood disorders. Psychiatr Pol. 2017;51(2):197–203.

Shine B, McKnight RF, Leaver L, Geddes JR. Long-term effects of lithium on renal, thyroid, and parathyroid function: a retrospective analysis of laboratory data. Lancet. 2015;386(9992):461–8.

Solomon HV, Cates KW, Li KJ. Does obtaining CYP2D6 and CYP2C19 pharmacogenetic testing predict antidepressant response or adverse drug reactions? Psychiatry Res. 2019;271:604–13.

Song J, Bergen SE, Di Florio A, Karlsson R, Charney A, Ruderfer DM, Stahl EA, Chambert KD, Moran JL, Gordon-Smith K, Forty L, Green EK, Jones I, Jones L, Scolnick EM, Sklar P, Smoller JW, Lichtenstein P, Hultman C, Craddock N, Landen M, Smoller JW, Perlis RH, Lee PH, Castro VM, Hoffnagle AG, Sklar P, Stahl EA, Purcell SM, Ruderfer DM, Charney AW, Roussos P, Michele Pato CP, Medeiros H, Sobel J, Craddock N, Jones I, Forty L, Florio AD, Green E, Jones L, Gordon-Smith K, Landen M, Hultman C, Jureus A, Bergen S, McCarroll S, Moran J, Smoller JW, Chambert K, Belliveau RA. Genome-wide association study identifies SESTD1 as a novel risk gene for lithium-responsive bipolar disorder. Mol Psychiatry. 2016;21(9):1290–7.

Song J, Sjolander A, Joas E, Bergen SE, Runeson B, Larsson H, Landen M, Lichtenstein P. Suicidal behavior during lithium and valproate treatment: a within-individual 8-year prospective study of 50,000 patients with bipolar disorder. Am J Psychiatry. 2017;174(8):795–802.

Spina E, de Leon J. Clinical applications of CYP genotyping in psychiatry. J Neural Transm (Vienna). 2015;122(1):5–28.

Squassina A, Manchia M, Borg J, Congiu D, Costa M, Georgitsi M, Chillotti C, Ardau R, Mitropoulos K, Severino G, Del Zompo M, Patrinos GP. Evidence for association of an ACCN1 gene variant with response to lithium treatment in Sardinian patients with bipolar disorder. Pharmacogenomics. 2011;12(11):1559–69.

Stern S, Linker S, Vadodaria KC, Marchetto MC, Gage FH. Prediction of response to drug therapy in psychiatric disorders. Open Biol. 2018;8(5):180031.

Szczepankiewicz A, Rybakowski JK, Suwalska A, Skibinska M, Leszczynska-Rodziewicz A, Dmitrzak-Weglarz M, Czerski PM, Hauser J. Association study of the glycogen synthase kinase-3beta gene polymorphism with prophylactic lithium response in bipolar patients. World J Biol Psychiatry. 2006;7(3):158–61.

Taranu A, Colle R, Gressier F, El Asmar K, Becquemont L, Corruble E, Verstuyft C. Should a routine genotyping of CYP2D6 and CYP2C19 genetic polymorphisms be recommended to predict venlafaxine efficacy in depressed patients treated in psychiatric settings? Pharmacogenomics. 2017;18(7):639–50.

Tobe BTD, Crain AM, Winquist AM, Calabrese B, Makihara H, Zhao WN, Lalonde J, Nakamura H, Konopaske G, Sidor M, Pernia CD, Yamashita N, Wada M, Inoue Y, Nakamura F, Sheridan SD, Logan RW, Brandel M, Wu D, Hunsberger J, Dorsett L, Duerr C, Basa RCB, McCarthy MJ, Udeshi ND, Mertins P, Carr SA, Rouleau GA, Mastrangelo L, Li J, Gutierrez GJ, Brill LM, Venizelos N, Chen G, Nye JS, Manji H, Price JH, McClung CA, Akiskal HS, Alda M, Chuang DM, Coyle JT, Liu Y, Teng YD, Ohshima T, Mikoshiba K, Sidman RL, Halpain S, Haggarty SJ, Goshima Y, Snyder EY. Probing the lithium-response pathway in hiPSCs implicates the phosphoregulatory set-point for a cytoskeletal modulator in bipolar pathogenesis. Proc Natl Acad Sci USA. 2017;114(22):E4462–e4471.

Tohen M, Hennen J, Zarate CM Jr, Baldessarini RJ, Strakowski SM, Stoll AL, Faedda GL, Suppes T, Gebre-Medhin P, Cohen BM. Two-year syndromal and functional recovery in 219 cases of first-episode major affective disorder with psychotic features. Am J Psychiatry. 2000;157(2):220–8.

Tondo L, Vazquez G, Baldessarini RJ. Mania associated with antidepressant treatment: comprehensive meta-analytic review. Acta Psychiatr Scand. 2010;121(6):404–14.

Tonozzi TR, Braunstein GD, Kammesheidt A, Curran C, Golshan S, Kelsoe J. Pharmacogenetic profile and major depressive and/or bipolar disorder treatment: a retrospective, cross-sectional study. Pharmacogenomics. 2018;19(15):1169–79.

UKGTN. 2019a. Report_Gene_Test_Recommendations_CSAG_SEPT17_amend_353.pdf.

UKGTN. UK Genetic Testing Network. 2019b.

Valvezan AJ, Klein PS. GSK-3 and Wnt signaling in neurogenesis and bipolar disorder. Front Mol Neurosci. 2012;5:1.

Veldic M, Ahmed AT, Blacker CJ, Geske JR, Biernacka JM, Borreggine KL, Moore KM, Prieto ML, Vande Voort JL, Croarkin PE, Hoberg AA, Kung S, Alarcon RD, Keeth N, Singh B, Bobo WV, Frye MA. Cytochrome P450 2C19 poor metabolizer phenotype in treatment resistant depression: treatment and diagnostic implications. Front Pharmacol. 2019;10:83.

Wang Z, Li Z, Chen J, Huang J, Yuan C, Hong W, Yu S, Fang Y. Association of BDNF gene polymorphism with bipolar disorders in Han Chinese population. Genes Brain Behav. 2012;11(5):524–8.

Weinshilboum RM, Wang L. Pharmacogenomics: precision medicine and drug response. Mayo Clin Proc. 2017;92(11):1711–22.

Yatham LN, Kennedy SH, Parikh SV, Schaffer A, Bond DJ, Frey BN, Sharma V, Goldstein BI, Rej S, Beaulieu S, Alda M, MacQueen G, Milev RV, Ravindran A, O'Donovan C, McIntosh D, Lam RW, Vazquez G, Kapczinski F, McIntyre RS, Kozicky J, Kanba S, Lafer B, Suppes T, Calabrese JR, Vieta E, Malhi G, Post RM, Berk M. Canadian Network for Mood and Anxiety Treatments (CANMAT) and International Society for Bipolar Disorders (ISBD) 2018 guidelines for the management of patients with bipolar disorder. Bipolar Disord. 2018;20(2):97–170.

Zarate CA Jr, Tohen M, Land M, Cavanagh S. Functional impairment and cognition in bipolar disorder. Psychiatr Q. 2000;71(4):309–29.

Zhang JP, Lencz T, Malhotra AK. D2 receptor genetic variation and clinical response to antipsychotic drug treatment: a meta-analysis. Am J Psychiatry. 2010;167(7):763–72.

Zhang JP, Robinson DG, Gallego JA, John M, Yu J, Addington J, Tohen M, Kane JM, Malhotra AK, Lencz T. Association of a schizophrenia risk variant at the DRD2 locus with antipsychotic treatment response in first-episode psychosis. Schizophr Bull. 2015;41(6):1248–55.

Zhang JP, Lencz T, Zhang RX, Nitta M, Maayan L, John M, Robinson DG, Fleischhacker WW, Kahn RS, Ophoff RA, Kane JM, Malhotra AK, Correll CU. Pharmacogenetic associations of antipsychotic drug-related weight gain: a systematic review and meta-analysis. Schizophr Bull. 2016;42(6):1418–37.

4

Evaluating endophenotypes for bipolar disorder

Riccardo Guglielmo[1,2], Kamilla Woznica Miskowiak[3] and Gregor Hasler[1*]

Abstract

Background: Phenotypic heterogeneity is a major impediment to the elucidation of the neurobiology and genetics of bipolar disorder. Endophenotype could help in reducing heterogeneity by defining biological traits that are more direct expressions of gene effects. The aim of this review is to examine the recent literature on clinical, epidemiological, neurobiological, and genetic findings and to select and evaluate candidate endophenotypes for bipolar disorder. Evaluating putative endophenotype could be helpful in better understanding the neurobiology of bipolar disorder by improving the definition of bipolar-related phenotypes in genetic studies. In this manner, research on endophenotypes could be useful to improve psychopathological diagnostics in the long-run by dissecting psychiatric macro phenotypes into biologically valid components.

Main body: The associations among the psychopathological and biological endophenotypes are discussed with respect to specificity, temporal stability, heritability, familiarity, and clinical and biological plausibility. Numerous findings regarding brain function, brain structure, neuropsychology and altered neurochemical pathways in patients with bipolar disorder and their relatives deserve further investigation. Overall, major findings suggest a developmental origin of this disorder as all the candidate endophenotypes that we have been able to select are present both in the early stages of the disorder as well as in subjects at risk.

Conclusions: Among the stronger candidate endophenotypes, we suggest circadian rhythm instability, dysmodulation of emotion and reward, altered neuroimmune state, attention and executive dysfunctions, anterior cingulate cortex thickness and early white matter abnormalities. In particular, early white matter abnormalities could be the result of a vulnerable brain on which new stressors are added in young adulthood which favours the onset of the disorder. Possible pathways that lead to a vulnerable brain are discussed starting from the data about molecular and imaging endophenotypes of bipolar disorder.

Keywords: Bipolar disorder, Endophenotype, Neuroinflammation, Neuroimaging, Cognition

Background

The diagnosis of Bipolar Disorder (BD) is based on clusters of symptoms and characteristics of clinical course that do not necessarily describe homogenous disorders but that rather reflect final common pathways of different pathophysiological processes involving genetic and environmental contributors. In addition, the boundaries between BD and schizophrenia and between BD and recurrent major depression are not as distinct as assumed in the past. Specifically, heterogeneity implicit in the current classification schema is a reason for the limited success of clinical studies, at the levels of treatment, neurobiology, and genetics. In contrast to other branches of medicine, psychiatry suffers from a diagnostic and classification system that is not based on pathophysiology and etiology, being dependent on nosological tradition, expert consensus, psychometric reliability, and clinical utility. Dissecting

*Correspondence: gregor.hasler@unifr.ch
[1] Psychiatry Research Unit, Fribourg Network for Mental Health (RFSM), University of Fribourg, Chemin du Cardinal-Journet 3, 1752 Villars-sur-Glâne, Switzerland
Full list of author information is available at the end of the article

psychiatric macro phenotypes into biologically valid components presumes the ability to make diagnosis more certain, more specific, and more amenable to tailored treatment. In this context, research on endophenotypes finds its value as it has the merit to reduce heterogeneity by defining biological traits that are more direct expressions of gene effects. Moreover, the search of endophenotypes has a prevention potential because they can be used to identify individuals who are at risk of developing a mental disorder. Naturally, endophenotypes could contribute to a clinically useful reclassification that will improve the treatment of mental disorders.

For reminding, the term "endophenotype" was described as an internal, intermediate phenotype (i.e., not obvious to the unaided eye) that fills the gap in the causal chain between genes and distal diseases (Gottesman and Gould 2003) and therefore might help to resolve questions about etiology. The endophenotype concept assumes that the number of genes involved in the variations of endophenotypes representing more elementary phenomena (as opposed to the behavioural macros found in the DSM) and is less than the number involved in producing the full disease (Gottesman and Gould 2003). Endophenotypes provide a means for identifying the "upstream" traits underlying clinical phenotypes, as well as the "downstream" biological consequences of genes (Hasler et al. 2006).

The evaluation of a candidate endophenotype is generally based on the endophenotype criteria concept developed by Gottesman and Gould (2003). However, taking into account the increasing recognition of the importance of epigenetic transformations and developmental factors in the expression of psychiatric phenotypes (Gottesman and Hanson 2005; Hasler et al. 2005), the criterion "state independence" might be particularly difficult to achieve for candidate endophenotypes. Therefore, Hasler et al. (2006) proposed to slightly modify this criterion, emphasizing the role of time and age. Below are the modified criteria:

1. An endophenotype is associated with illness, in the general population.
2. An endophenotype is heritable.
3. An endophenotype is state independent (i.e. manifests in an individual whether or not illness is active) but age-normed and might need to be elicited by a challenge.
4. Within families, endophenotype and illness co-segregate (i.e. the endophenotype is more prevalent among the ill relatives of ill probands compared with the healthy relatives of the ill probands).
5. An endophenotype identified in probands is found in their unaffected relatives at a higher rate than in the general population.

Apart from the above criteria, disease specificity and clinical and biological plausibility have also been discussed as evaluation criteria for endophenotypes (Tsuang et al. 1993), to relate phenotypic definitions to clinically relevant outcomes, to enhance the elucidation of clinically relevant pathophysiological mechanisms (Lavori et al. 2002), and to increase prior probability of utility in genetic studies (Freimer and Sabatti 2003, 2004).

It is important to emphasize that endophenotypes are heritable quantitative measurable biological traits that reflect genetically relevant aspects of the heterogeneous pathophysiology of the disease. As such, endophenotypes are clearly different from diagnostic biomarkers that are evaluated by measures of sensitivity and specificity. This is because it cannot be assumed that the current definitions of psychiatric diseases are biologically valid. Further, a biomarker is not necessarily embedded in the genotype and behavior/psychopathology pathway of a disease as it is the case of an endophenotype.

A number of putative endophenotypes have been proposed for BD, including executive dysfunction, learning and memory impairments, cognitive changes after tryptophan depletion, circadian rhythm instability, dysmodulation of reward and motivation, functional and structural brain abnormalities, sensitivity to psychostimulants and cholinergic sensitivity (Hasler et al. 2006). Unfortunately, few studies systematically assess the criteria needed for a measure to be considered an endophenotype. In this context, well-designed twin, family, and prospective studies evaluating candidate endophenotypes for BD, are still scarce. In twin studies, broader and dimensional diagnostic definitions (e.g., schizophrenia spectrum) might provide higher heritability estimates than narrow diagnostic definitions (e.g., pure schizophrenia). Likewise, in longitudinal studies, broader diagnostic categories (mood disorders spectrum) showed greater stability over time than narrow diagnostic definitions (e.g., pure BD) (Hasler et al. 2006). Thus, relatively broad endophenotypes (brain function endophenotypes, e.g., cognitive performance) might be the most heritable and most appropriate for genetic studies (Hasler et al. 2006) and some authors proposed to relax the disorder-specificity requirement of endophenotypes giving more attention to neurocircuitry activity instead of behaviors as starting points in searches for endophenotypes (Beauchaine and Constantino 2017).

Finally, the National Institute of Mental Health has launched the Research Domain Criteria project (RDoC) in 2009 to explore basic dimensions of functioning that span the full range of human behavior from normal to abnormal. The primary goal of this project is to develop a classification system for mental health disorders that is dimensional (rather than categorical) and that links to neurobiological systems. Endophenotypes could be of great importance in this context. In fact, as they are close to the genes, they could help to identify the genetic basis of core symptom domains of mental disorders. Specifically, they could provide more construct-valid indicators of the six major domains including in the RDoC framework. Moreover, since endophenotypes cut across traditional disorder boundaries, they are consistent with the transdiagnostic approach and emphasis in RDoC on identifying etiological processes that underlie multiple conditions (Miller and Rockstroh 2013).

Here, we presented systematic review articles and meta-analyses, or recent research articles when analytical articles were not available. Our priority was given to longitudinal twin, family, and association studies when available. We did not include endophenotypes that were primarily examined in major depression (e.g., return of depressive symptoms after tryptophan and catecholamine depletion, increased stress sensitivity, or dysfunctions of the hypothalamic–pituitary–adrenal axis). In addition to the specificity criterion, we selected putative endophenotypes on the basis of empirical studies in euthymic patients and in unaffected subjects at substantially increased risk for BD.

In this review, we will present majors advances in the field of BD endophenotypes research by proposing the putative BD endophenotypes that best fill the endophenotype criteria. In Fig. 1, we have also enclosed and divided all the main results into molecular, cognitive and imaging endophenotypes. In this manner, we link key neuroanatomical and neurochemical abnormalities to candidate genes and to key behavioural components of BD.

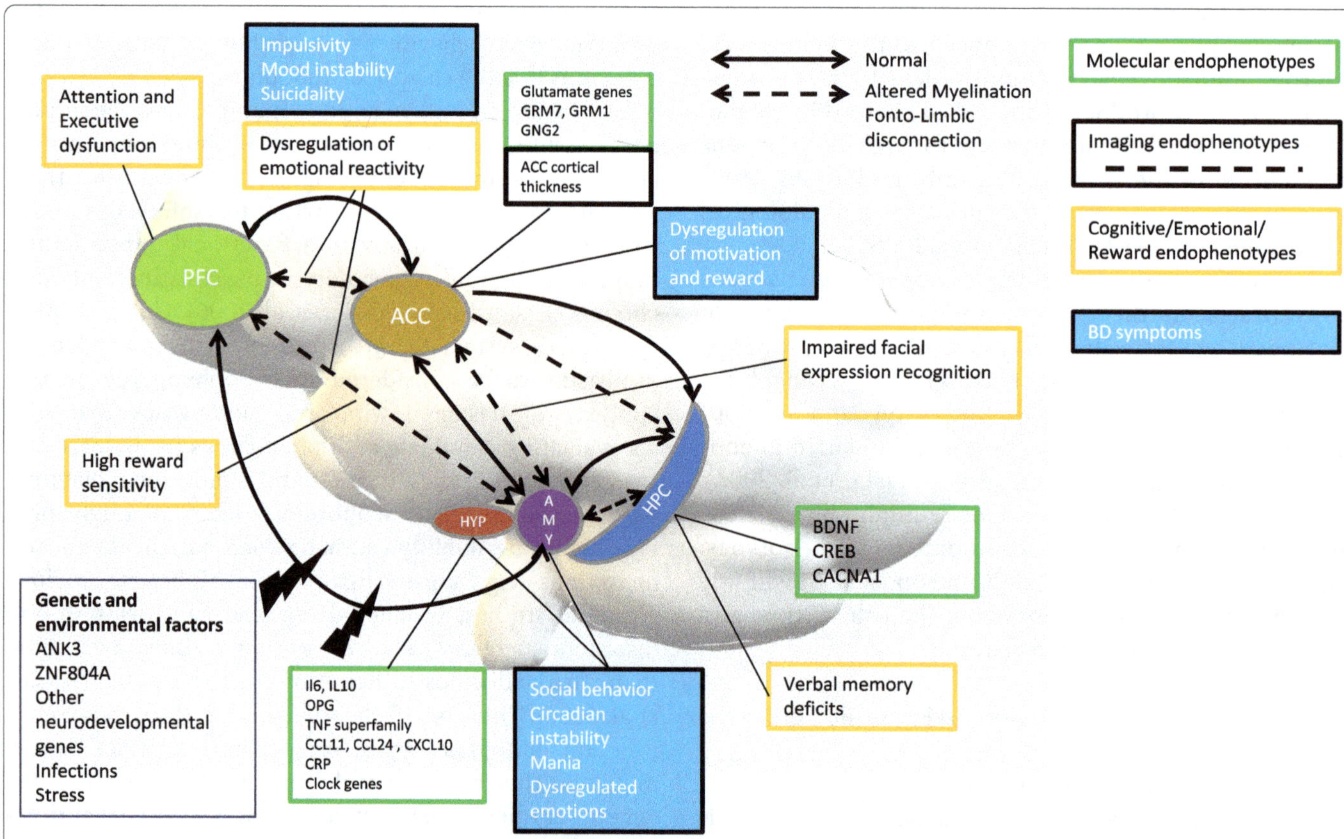

Fig. 1 Putative endophenotypes for bipolar disorder. Heuristic model to link the putative endophenotypes (molecular, imaging and cognitive) to distal phenotypes like BD symptoms. Major findings in endophenotype research suggest a developmental origin of BD. This figure shows as the interplay between environmental risk factors like stress and infections, and the genetic susceptibility of different systems like immune, circadian and glutamatergic systems could shape a vulnerable brain on which new stressors are added in young adulthood which favours the onset and the progression of the disorder. *ACC* anterior cingulate cortex, Calcium Voltage-Gated Channel Subunit Alpha1, *ANK3* Ankyrin 3, *AMY* amygdala, *BDNF* Brain Derived Neurotrophic Factor, *CACNA1* Calcium Voltage-Gated Channel Subunit Alpha1, *CCL11* C-C Motif Chemokine Ligand 11, *CCL24* C-C Motif Chemokine Ligand 24, *CXCL10* C-X-C Motif Chemokine Ligand 10, *CRP* C-Reactive Protein, *CREB* CREB Binding Protein, *GRM1* Glutamate Metabotropic Receptor 1, *GRM7* Glutamate Metabotropic Receptor 7, *GNG2* G Protein Subunit Gamma 2, *HPC* hippocampus, *HYP* hypothalamus, *IL6* Interleukin 6, *IL10* Interleukin 10, *OPG* Osteoprotegerin, *PFC* prefrontal cortex, *TNF* Tumor Necrosis Factor, *ZNF804A* Zinc Finger Protein 804A

Molecular endophenotypes

Altered neuroimmune state

A large body of evidence supports the association between an altered neuroimmune state and BD, although it remains unclear if this reflects a trait or state marker of illness activity or both. The rationale stems from the so-called "sickness behavior," an interplay between inflammatory states and social and behavioural changes, which includes mood changes, social withdrawal and heightened sensitivity to both positive and negative social stimuli to help an individual to determine which persons might be supportive and which individuals will not and should be avoided, in order to better recruit help and care to facilitate recovery from sickness (Shattuck and Muehlenbein 2016; Dantzer et al. 2008; Eisenberger et al. 2017). Moreover, patients with mood disorders show comorbidities with autoimmune pathologies and subjects suffering of autoimmune diseases present an increased risk of developing BD (Rosenblat and McIntyre 2017; Cremaschi et al. 2017). There is also preliminary pre-clinical evidence suggesting that traditional mood stabilizers modulate neuroinflammation and contrasting clinical results about the action of mood stabilizers on inflammation (Kang et al. 2012; Zhang et al. 2012; Nassar and Azab 2014) as well as some evidence exists about the adjunctive use of drugs with anti-inflammatory properties (i.e. acetylsalicylic, celecoxib and omega-3 fatty acids) for managing BD, in particular bipolar depression (Muneer 2016).

High concentrations of pro-inflammatory cytokines and low concentrations of anti-inflammatory cytokines were reported (Brietzke et al. 2009b) respectively when BD patients in manic and depressive phases are compared to normal controls with a return to normality in the euthymic phase. These illness-related fluctuations suggest that inflammation is a state dependent trait of the acute episodes rather than a trait marker of BD (Cetin et al. 2012).

On the other hand, we have some evidence for an altered neuroimmune state even in euthymic BD patients relative to healthy controls. In particular, euthymic BD patients have been found to display elevated plasma levels of IL-6, osteoprotegerin (OPG) (Hope et al. 2011) and serum levels of IL-10 (Hsu et al. 2014). Euthymic patients have also been found to have elevated levels of tumour necrosis factor [TNF] superfamily molecules, including TNF-like weak inducer of apoptosis [TWEAK] and soluble TNF receptor type 1 [sTNFR1] (Barbosa et al. 2017). Additional evidence indicates increased serum chemokine levels, including CXCL-10, and elevated plasma levels of CCL11, CCL24 and CXCL10 in euthymic patients. In contrast, reduced serum levels of CCL24, and CXCL8 have been found (Brietzke et al. 2009a; Barbosa et al. 2013). Taken together these findings are suggestive of imbalance of cytokines rather than a simple increase. Finally, we have some evidence of abnormally elevated levels of C-reactive protein (CRP) in all phase of BD with a substantial increase during a manic episode and moderate increase in depressive and euthymic phases (Dargel et al. 2015; Fernandes et al. 2016; Evers et al. 2019). Consistent with the research findings on peripheral inflammatory markers, studies using positron emission tomography (PET), revealed increased microglia activation in the brain in euthymic BD patients. Specifically, microglia showed significantly increased activation in the right but not in the left hippocampus of BD patients compared to healthy controls (Haarman et al. 2014). In a subsequent study, an in vivo positive relation was found between microglial activation and neuronal integrity corresponding to a differentiated microglial function where some microglia induce apoptosis while others stimulate neurogenesis (Haarman et al. 2014, 2016). Investigations of the CSF of euthymic BD patients and healthy controls show increased levels of monocyte chemoattractant protein-1 [MCP-1] and chitinase-3-like protein 1 [YKL-40] (Jakobsson et al. 2015), as well as elevated levels of IL-8 and IL-1β (Isgren et al. 2015; Soderlund et al. 2011) in BD. These findings of central inflammatory markers in BD along with the findings about peripheral altered neuroimmune state support the neuroinflammatory hypothesis of BD.

Variance in the inflammatory response seems to be associated with genetic variance in healthy subjects given a strong impact of genetic heritability on inflammatory molecules. A comprehensive study of cytokine production in healthy subjects showed that host genetics plays a significant role in inter-individual variability of cytokine production in response to different types of stimuli with particularly high genetic influence on monocyte derived cytokines, including the IL-1β/IL-6 pathway. In addition, the authors identified 17 new genome-wide significant loci (QTLs) that influence cytokine production, finding biological pathways that contain cytokine QTLs map to pattern recognition receptors (TLR1-6-10 cluster), cytokine and complement inhibitors, and the kallikrein system (Li et al. 2016). Li et al. concluded that monocyte-derived cQTLs are associated to a susceptibility to infections, while Tcell-derived cQTLs overlap with loci associated to autoimmune diseases (Li et al. 2016). The high genetic heritability of inflammatory response is also supported by studies in twins subjects (Wessel et al. 2007; Roederer et al. 2015; Brodin et al. 2015).

There is growing evidence for co-segregation of altered neuroimmune state in families at risk for BD. Significantly increased IL-6 and Brain-derived neurotrophic factor (BDNF) protein levels were found in BD offspring compared to controls (Duffy et al. 2014). The highest levels of both markers were found in those High-Risk (HR) offspring in early clinical stages of the illness compared to later clinical stages. In addition, the genotype of HR individuals influenced the association between risk status and clinical stage of illness development for gene expression. In the early stage of illness development, HR offspring with *BDNF VAL/VAL* genotype had higher mRNA expression levels than HR offspring who were MET carriers (Duffy et al. 2014). These data were not replicated in other studies, possibly due to differences in patients 'clinical disease stages in sample sizes (Nery et al. 2016; Sanjay et al. 2017). In addition, body mass index (BMI) may have a moderating effect. In fact HR offspring are likely to exhibit elevations in BDNF as a function of increasing weight and moreover a BMI by BDNF interaction in nucleus accumbens (NAc) volume has been found (Mansur et al. 2017).

Neuro-immune-developmental hypothesis

The above preliminary evidence for differences in candidate immune and neurotrophic markers over the clinical stages of illness has been confirmed by a temporally dynamic changes of the immune states in offspring of BD patients from adolescence through adulthood in follow-up studies. In comparison to healthy controls, BD offspring showed increased proinflammatory state during adolescence, an anti-inflammatory state during young adulthood and a virtually normalized immune state in adulthood. A background of reduced numbers of circulating CD3+ and CD3+CD4+ T cells is continuously presents, suggesting a partial T cell defect leading to a deregulated immune system (Snijders et al. 2017). In particular, BD offspring showed increased inflammatory gene expression in monocytes, high serum PTX3 levels, but normal CCL2 levels during adolescence. In young adulthood, monocyte activation remained in a lesser degree with serum PTX3 levels remained high, and signs of monocyte migration became apparent through increased CCL2 levels. Finally at adulthood, circulating monocytes lost their activation state, but CCL2 levels remained increased suggesting a stronger migrating activity of these monocytes to the tissues (Mesman et al. 2015). These results were replicated in another study that showed a high inflammatory state in adolescent BD offspring found reduced numbers of Tregs with high expression of pro-inflammatory genes in monocytes. The same studies demonstrated a reduced numbers of T cells capable of producing the proinflammatory cytokines IFN-γ and IL-17 during young adulthood. Finally a stabilisation of these states at adulthood was reported with a reduced expression of pro-inflammatory genes in monocytes (Snijders et al. 2016). Of note, these temporal dynamic changes of the immune state seem to differentiate BD from major depressive disorder (MDD) as some studies suggested that MDD patients share with BD patients an early partial T cell defect but as opposed to BD this immunogical signature becomes more prominent with increasing age, also including an increased immune activation (Grosse et al. 2016).

The finding of a proinflammatory state during adolescence is of particular importance, as the brain is involved in major plastic changes and it is highly vulnerable during this developmental period. Interestingly, an imaging study of youth at risk for BD found altered development of white matter (WM) in the at risk population compared to healthy controls in the corpus callosum and temporal associative tracts, suggesting once again that early altered myelination during development could play a role in the pathophysiology of BD (Versace et al. 2010).

We can therefore conclude that different data support biological and clinical plausibility of an altered neuroimmune state as endophenotype in BD. Cytokines and other inflammatory molecules may pass or act in the CNS at least by 3 different pathways: the "humoral pathway", which involves cytokine passage through leaky regions in the blood–brain barrier [BBB], "neural pathway", which involves bind to peripheral afferent nerve fibres such as the vagus nerve, thus stimulating ascending catecholaminergic fibres in the brain, and recently the "cellular pathway", which involves the trafficking of activated immune cells, typically monocytes, to the brain vasculature and parenchyma has been proposed (Miller and Raison 2016). Inflammatory alterations occur in BD patients as well as in their unaffected relatives (URs) significantly more than in healthy controls either peripherally or centrally in the nervous system and this inflammatory condition can produce negative effects on brain structure and ultimately behavior, especially by early modification of WM structure. In fact, in BD patients it has been shown that WM structure alterations mostly located in the anterior part of the brain, are linked to cytokines levels and T cells percentage (Benedetti et al. 2016; Magioncalda et al. 2018) as well as to the tryptophan degradation cascade, i.e. the increased levels of cytokines reduce the tryptophan-derived serotonin, increasing the production of tryptophan catabolites, which impact on the neurotoxicity (Poletti et al. 2018). Moreover, BD and in general mood disorders have been characterized by accelerated aging. Studies have reported elevated levels of circulating inflammatory cytokines in mood disorders and shorter telomere length, suggestive of accelerating aging (Lindqvist et al. 2015). Consequently, a "telomere-inflammation network" has been proposed to explain a complex interplay between altered inflammatory–immune responses and telomere dynamics in the etiopathogenesis of these disorders. Inflammation and telomere shortening show a bidirectional association: a pro-inflammatory state seems to contribute to aging and telomere dysfunction, and telomere attrition is able to induce low-grade inflammation (Squassina et al. 2019). In line with this, patients with mood disorders show comorbidities with aging-related diseases, such as cardiovascular and respiratory diseases, diabetes, hypertension and cognitive decline which are also characterized by an inflammatory state, that in turn could lead to telomere shortening.

The above findings suggest that an altered neuroimmune state could be a candidate endophenotype for BD and in particular it speaks about a neuro-immune-developmental pathogenesis of BD. In particular, an early pro-inflammatory state either during pregnancy (Allswede et al. 2020) or adolescence (Mesman et al. 2015; Snijders et al. 2017) may perturb the fetal and young brain development shaping brain structures and in particular WM, followed by a virtually normalized immune state at adulthood with a background of continuously low-grade inflammation responsible of shortening telomere length and accelerated aging, leading to the characteristics symptoms of BD.

Circadian rhythm instability

Clinical features of BD, such as diurnal variation in mood, early morning awakening, and cyclicity and seasonality of recurrences, have led to speculation that dysregulation of circadian rhythm might be a central mechanism in the pathophysiology of BD. Disturbance of the sleep–wake cycle was found to be the most common prodrome of mania (Jackson et al. 2003; Wehr et al. 1987); experimentally induced sleep deprivation is associated with the onset of hypomania or mania in a considerable portion of patients; and antimanic drugs were shown to stabilize circadian rhythms (Klemfuss 1992; Klemfuss and Kripke 1995).

Twin research in healthy individuals provided evidence for the heritability of circadian clinical characteristics (Dauvilliers et al. 2005) and for a genetic control of the human circadian clock (Linkowski et al. 1993), sleep architecture variables [the amount of slow wave and rapid eye movement (REM) sleep (Linkowski 1999)] and polysomnography profiles during non-REM sleep (De Gennaro et al. 2008). A mutation in a human clock gene, *hPER2*, has been specifically associated with a familial variant of human sleep behavior (Toh et al. 2001), and a polymorphism in the human *CLOCK* gene has been associated with circadian mood fluctuation and illness recurrence in BD (Benedetti et al. 2003).

Findings are conflicting with regard to whereas abnormalities in the circadian rhythm are state independent. Some evidence indicates that the circadian rhythm in euthymic BD patients is persistently unstable (Jones et al. 2005) and can be aggravated with environmental influences, such as weather conditions and seasonal changes (Hakkarainen et al. 2003). Indeed, euthymic BD patients, compared with healthy controls, display trait-like alterations in several circadian features such as sleep time and time in bed, sleep onset latency, melatonin secretion and periods of being awake after sleep onset (Ng et al. 2015; Dallaspezia and Benedetti 2009). In addition, in a systematic analysis of circadian rhythm activity in pedigrees segregating severe BD (BP-I), Pagani et al. (2016) showed that euthymic BD patients slept longer and woke up later compared to their URs. The authors also provided evidence for a genome-wide significant linkage for interdaily stability, a measure of day-to-day variability of the waveform of activity, near chromosome 12pter. Interestingly, in this genomic region some genes could influence circadian rhythm, including the histone lysine demethylase JARID1a (*KMD5A*) and calcium channel subunit 1C (*CACNA1C*). In contrast, a subsequent study that extended this pedigree and included independent control subjects found no sleep disturbance difference between BD patients, URs and controls, after adjustments for current mood symptoms. This could suggest that state characteristics play a role in circadian abnormalities in BD (Verkooijen et al. 2017).

As for the chronotype, there are some suggestions of a link between BD and evening chronotype, particularly the depressive aspects of BD (Wood et al. 2009). Nevertheless one longitudinal study showed no difference between eveningness and mood state in BD, suggesting that chronotype is independent of mood state and thus a trait marker of the disorder (Seleem et al. 2015).

Lithium, which has been shown to modify the phase and period of circadian rhythms in a variety of species, ranging from unicellular organism and insects to mice and even humans, is a glycogen synthase kinase 3 (*GSK-3*) inhibitor (Gould et al. 2004). Martinek et al. (2001) identified the *Drosophila* orthologue of *GSK-3*, *SHAGGY* , as a component of the circadian cycles. Overexpression of *SHAGGY* lengthened the *Drosophila* free-running circadian cycle. Additionally, a decrease in *SHAGGY* activity resulted in an increase in circadian period length (Martinek et al. 2001), the effect (increase in circadian period) that has been noted in numerous species, including *Drosophila*, after treatment with lithium (Klemfuss 1992; Padiath et al. 2004). Conversely, another study reported that the inhibitors of *GSK-3β* shortened the circadian period of mammalian cells instead of lengthening it (Hirota et al. 2008).

Taken together, these data suggest that the effect of lithium on circadian cycles (Gould and Manji 2002) mediates some of its therapeutic actions in BD, supporting the hypothesis that circadian rhythm instability is etiologically associated with BD and a candidate endophenotype. Finally, preliminary evidence suggests that genetic factors involved in the regulation of the human circadian clock might represent vulnerability factors of BD. Specifically, *GSK3-β* (Benedetti et al. 2004) as well as *CLOCK* (Benedetti et al. 2003; Kripke et al. 2009), *PER3* and *ARNTL* (Nievergelt et al. 2006), *TIMELESS* (Mansour et al. 2005), and *NR1D1 ROR* (Lai et al. 2015) genes all have demonstrated modest associations with BD, supporting a polygenetic heritability.

Imaging endophenotypes

Early-onset white matter abnormalities

White matter abnormalities (WMA) are abnormalities in the brain that are seen as bright foci on T2-weighted MRI scans. Most recent techniques include diffusion tensor imaging (DTI) and voxel-based morphometry (VBM). DTI draws maps of the diffusion pattern of water molecules, allowing the detection of microstructural details of normal or altered anatomy of a given region. One of the most used measures of WM DTI studies is fractional anisotropy (FA) which describes the directional selectivity of the random diffusion of water molecules with higher FA values (maximum value is 1.0) are observed along heavily myelinated WM tracts (Kochunov et al. 2012). Voxel-based morphometry (VBM), is an automated MRI technique typically uses T1-weighted volumetric MRI scans and essentially performs statistical tests across all voxels (volumetric picture elements) in the image to identify volume differences between groups (Whitwell 2009). Several studies showed widespread WM disruption in adults BD patients as well as in at-risk subjects.

Evidence of early WMA comes from studies on patients with a first episode BD. A meta-analytic study on this matter found reduced intracranial and WM total volumes in first-episode mania in particular in regions subserving emotional regulation, reward processing and cognitive function (Vita et al. 2009). Several studies have continuously reported decreased fractional anisotropy (FA) in WM tracts connecting circuits implicated in the impaired emotion regulation and reward processing in BD such as prefrontal cortex (PFC) regions with the ventral striatum and amygdala (Schneider et al. 2012). These findings were confirmed by a more recent meta-analysis that found significant total WM volume reduction in first episode BD patients compared to controls. The authors also found some common brain abnormalities present in first-episode schizophrenia or BD with a significant overlap but whole grey matter volume deficits and lateral ventricular enlargement appear to be more prominent in first-episode schizophrenia whereas WM volume reduction seems more prominent in BD (De Peri et al. 2012).

DTI based research has contributed to the notion of structural dysconnectivity between limbic and prefrontal regions in BD. By using DTI techniques, WMA in euthymic BD patients were found in cingulum bundle (Emsell et al. 2013), limbic-striatal, callosal and prefrontal regions (Benedetti et al. 2011b; Emsell et al. 2013; Leow et al. 2013) and in the anterior limb of the internal capsule, anterior thalamic radiation, inferior longitudinal fasciculus, corona radiata, superior longitudinal fasciculus, and uncinate fasciculus (Benedetti et al. 2011a, b; Chaddock et al. 2009). Meta-analyses confirmed the presence of WMA in patients with BD, with the risk of WMA being more than threefold higher in patients with BD than in healthy control populations (Altshuler et al. 1995; Videbech 1997). In particular, DTI meta-analyses studies in BD have shown fractional anisotropy (FA) reduction in clusters located in both anterior and posterior WM areas (Nortje et al. 2013; Vederine et al. 2011), T2 weighted images meta-analytics studies shown increased rates of deep WM hyperintensities (WMH) in BD (Kempton et al. 2008; Beyer et al. 2009), one meta-analysis of voxel based morphometry (VBM) studies shown lower WM concentrations in the left inferior longitudinal fasciculus, left superior corona radiata, and left posterior cingulum (Ganzola and Duchesne 2017). A large and recent meta-analytic study using coordinates, T-maps, and individual MRI data confirmed decreased WM volume in the posterior corpus callosum extending to WM in the posterior cingulate cortex not associated with clinical variables. This suggests that the observed WM decrease is state independent and could be a trait marker of the disease (Pezzoli et al. 2018). Finally, a recent mega-and meta-analysis of the largest DTI dataset of patients with BD, collected via the ENIGMA network, found widespread WMA in BD. Specifically, altered WM connectivity within the corpus callosum and the cingulum were strongly associated with BD diagnosis, suggesting a global profile of illness-related microstructural abnormalities (Favre et al. 2019). However, the findings are not disorder-specific since similar alterations were found in schizophrenia and MDD (Kelly et al. 2018; Wise et al. 2016). Of note, studies suggested that decreased fronto-temporal white matter FA could be applied to differentiate between BD and MDD (Favre et al. 2019; Kelly et al. 2018; Benedetti et al. 2011a; Chen et al. 2016).

WMA as a putative BD endophenotype may have clinical implications. WMA were found to be predictive of lithium and antidepressant response in BD patients (Kato et al. 2000; Bollettini et al. 2015). On the other hand, lithium intake has been associated with neuroprotective effects on WM (Abramovic et al. 2018). In particular, higher FA associated with lithium use could reflect a direct influence of lithium on water diffusion or a beneficial effect on myelination as an increase in axial diffusivity has been linked to the duration of lithium treatment, and influenced by gene variants affecting *GSK-3* via the Wnt/β-catenin and the Akt/CREB pathways (Benedetti et al. 2013; Meffre et al. 2015). Thus, it has been suggested that lithium treatment could counteract the WMA associated with BD (Benedetti et al. 2013).

Findings from twin, family, and association studies have revealed that much of the variability in WM tracts across multiple DTI measures is influenced by genetic factors (Chiang et al. 2011; Jahanshad et al. 2013; Hatton et al. 2018; Lee et al. 2017; Vuoksimaa et al. 2017) and heritability estimates were high in bilateral WM tracts and the corpus callosum (Vuoksimaa et al. 2017). In contrast to genetic influences, shared environmental influences were non-significant for either global or tract-specific influences (Gustavson et al. 2019).

Regarding co-segregation of WMA with the genetic risk of BD, there is compelling evidence that are more frequent in URs compared to controls. Widespread FA reductions and significant lower FA values have been found in BD patients and their URs respect to healthy control subjects particularly in corpus callosum, the dorsal part of the right cingulum bundle, the hippocampal part of the cingulum bundle bilaterally, and the uncinate fasciculus (Sprooten et al. 2013, 2016; Mahapatra et al. 2017; Linke et al. 2020). Of note, a 2-year follow-up study identified similar trajectories of FA reductions for controls and high-risk young adults and failed to find differences in FA among URs of BD patients and healthy controls, suggesting that difference in WM integrity could occur in earlier childhood and be a necessary but not sufficient condition to develop future BD (Ganzola et al. 2017). Another possible explication of the negative results of this follow-up study is that evidence indicates that in individuals at-risk for BD, WMA has been found in specifically brain regions (i.e. superior corona radiata (SCR)/corticospinal tract (CST) and the body of the corpus callosum) whereas changes in other WM tracts seem to be a disease state marker (Linke et al. 2020).

The aetiology of WMA identified in BD is unknown; however, several lines of evidence indicate a potential neurodevelopmental origin, as findings of WMA in individuals at-risk, as well as in early onset BD patients, support the potential involvement of neurodevelopmental mechanisms (i.e. early altered myelination) in the pathophysiology of BD. In support of this hypothesis, genetic studies suggest an involvement of key neurodevelopmental genes as risk factors for WMA in BD (Gurung and Prata 2015). In particular, polymorphisms in *ANK3* that is involved in neurogenesis and in maintaining axonal structure on brain integrity, and in *ZNF804A*, which encodes a zinc finger protein, involved in neurodevelopment and myelin transcription have been associated with BD, and abnormal WM integrity in BD (Squarcina et al. 2017; Gurung and Prata 2015).

Taken together, the data mentioned above suggest WMA and fronto-limbic disconnection as one of the most reliable endophenotype of BD, mediating the relationship between the underlying genetic vulnerability and the clinical expression. WMA in BD may lead to impaired connectivity between cortical and subcortical regions which may have downstream effects leading to core psychopathological features of this disorder, such as impulsivity, processing of emotions and reward, cognitive performance and disrupted night sleep.

Anterior cingulate cortex and glutamatergic abnormalities

The anterior cingulate cortex (ACC) is the frontal part of the cingulate cortex, with connections to both the limbic system and the prefrontal cortex. The ACC can be divided into two sub regions. The perigenual ACC (pACC) is responsible for processing emotions and regulating the endocrine and autonomic responses to emotions. The dorsal ACC (dACC), also known as the midcingulate cortex, is responsible for cognitive processing, specifically reward-based decision making (Jumah and Dossani 2020).

Lesions of the ventral ACC impair the ability of the autonomic system to respond to emotional stimuli, an inability to experience emotion related to concepts, and inability to use information regarding the probability of aversive social consequences versus reward in guiding social behavior (Damasio et al. 1990). Lesions of the dorsal ACC are associated with attentional deficits and impaired performance on tasks requiring controlled processing (Ochsner et al. 2001).

Volume reductions in the ACC located ventral (subgenual) and anterior (pregenual) to the genu of the corpus callosum have been implicated by numerous studies of mood disorders (Drevets et al. 1997; Harrison et al. 2018; Foland-Ross et al. 2011; Elvsashagen et al. 2013; Lyoo et al. 2006). Specifically, a volume reduction in the left subgenual ACC has been associated with familial MDD and BD by magnetic resonance imaging (MRI) morphometric measures (Drevets et al. 1997) and by post-mortem neuropathological studies, which have shown glial reduction in the corresponding grey matter (Harrison et al. 2018). These findings of volume reduction of ACC are supported by other magnetic resonance imaging studies of the ACC in BD patients which have found reduced cortical thickness in the left anterior cingulate region independent of acute symptoms, suggesting state-independence (Foland-Ross et al. 2011; Elvsashagen et al. 2013; Lyoo et al. 2006).

This reduction in volume exists early in the illness across MDD and BD (Botteron et al. 2002; Hirayasu et al. 1999) but seems to become more pronounced during illness progression, according to preliminary evidence in twins discordant for MDD (Botteron et al. 1999). A volumetric MRI study found reduced subgenual PFC volume in subjects at high familial risk for BD (Drevets 2004). Consistently, another volumetric MRI study comparing URs of patients with BD or schizophrenia showed that anterior ACC abnormalities were specifically associated with genetic risk of BD (McDonald et al. 2004). However, most recent studies on ACC volume and ACC cortical thickness failed to show any significant abnormalities in ACC in URs of BD compared to HC (Hanford et al. 2016; Roberts et al. 2016; Sugranyes et al. 2017; Yalin et al. 2019; Hajek et al. 2008, 2010) with the exception of one study (Sanches et al. 2019). This discrepancy is likely due to small sample size and the presence of lifetime MDD diagnosis in the first-degree relatives of BD of the latter study.

The mechanisms underlying these structural ACC changes remain unclear. However, glutamate may be relevant in BD (Vieta et al. 2018). In particular, the ACC contains abundant concentrations of glucocorticoid receptors that play a major role in attenuating the glucocorticoid response to stress (Diorio et al. 1993). In addition, psychosocial stress enhancement glutamate release and may lead to glutamatergic toxicity (Musazzi et al. 2011).

There is considerable evidence for a high heritability of cortical thickness (Blokland et al. 2012) stress response and cerebral glutamate levels (Legind et al. 2019). Both stress response and glutamate levels have a neurotoxic effect through increases neuronal intracellular calcium levels leading to neuronal cell death or damage (Kritis et al. 2015). Moreover, animal studies found an important role of the Metabotropic glutamate receptor 7 (*GRM7*) in early cortical development. For example, *Grm7* knockdown increases neural progenitor cell (NPC) proliferation, decreases terminal mitosis and neuronal differentiation, leading to abnormal neuronal morphology by interacting with CREB and Yes-associated protein (YAP). Overexpression of *Grm7* along with *Creb* knockdown, or *Yap* knockdown have shown to ameliorate these defects in neurogenesis (Xia et al. 2015). These findings may be relevant for BD since *GRM7* polymorphisms have been associated with the disorder (Noroozi et al. 2019).

Reduced cortical thickness along with glutamatergic abnormalities found in BD and URs bring together the endophenotype criteria of state independent and heritability. This putative endophenotype is not specific for BD; similar abnormalities were also found in MDD and schizophrenia. However, magnetic resonance spectroscopy studies have found disorder-specific changes of the central glutamate system. In BD, Glutamate–Glutamine (Glx) has found to be increased in all mood states (Yuksel and Ongur 2010). In contrast, reduced prefrontal and subcortical GLx has appeared as a consistent finding in MDD. Given the limited reliability and validity of symptom-based diagnostic methods to differentiate between unipolar and bipolar depression, glutamate-related imaging measures have the potential to significantly improve precision and neurobiological validity of mood disorder subtyping.

Taken together, a possible explanation for reduced cortical thickness in BD is a dynamic interplay between the genetic factors influencing brain morphology (i.e. glutamatergic and glucocorticoid system) and environmental factors (i.e. stress) starting from fetal development.

Cortical thickness of Subgenual Anterior Cingulate Cortex (sgACC) is a putative neuroimaging endophenotype for BD because it fills all the endophenotype criteria and it talks about a developmental hypothesis of BD as it could be the result of the underlying susceptibility genes and environmental factors during life acting on the fragility of the cortical structure leading to the clinical expression of BD. Thinning of grey matter of sgACC worth more research as a putative endophenotype of BD as it represents one of the main finding of neuropathological studies with the absence of any contradictory reports up to now (Harrison et al. 2018).

Cognitive, emotional and reward processing endophenotypes

Attention and executive functions

Comparative neuropsychological studies in severe psychiatric disorders showed that cognitive impairments in BD patients were similar to those of patients with schizophrenia or MDD with the differences being predominantly quantitative rather than qualitative (Daban et al. 2006; Zaninotto et al. 2015, 2016). In particular executive dysfunction is a key contributor to psychosocial disability, poor occupational functioning and lower quality of life in BD (Goswami et al. 2006; Fountoulakis et al. 2017; Drakopoulos et al. 2020). Executive functions is an umbrella term covering several functions involved in general-purpose control mechanisms, such as planning, inhibition and mental flexibility. Nevertheless, numerous studies and meta-analysis have shown deficits of executive functions across all phase of illness, including euthymia (Kurtz and Gerraty 2009; Bortolato et al. 2015; Bourne et al. 2013; Bora and Pantelis 2015). Specifically, a recent meta-analysis found deficits across set-shifting, inhibition, planning, verbal fluency, working memory, and sustained attention in euthymic BD patients compared to controls (Dickinson et al. 2017).

Individual differences in executive functions are almost entirely genetic in origin as reported by a multivariate twin study of three executive functions (inhibiting dominant responses, updating working memory representations, and shifting attention between task sets) which found that executive functions are influenced by a highly heritable (99%) common factor that goes beyond general intelligence or perceptual speed (Friedman et al. 2008). A highly heritable aspect of executive functions is executive attention, a process that involves dopamine-rich frontal areas including the anterior cingulate (Fan et al. 2001; Swan and Carmelli 2002). In keeping with this, recent results suggest that the dopamine transporter gene (*SLC6A3*) polymorphism influences attentional processes (Kuc et al. 2020). Specifically, individuals with the *9R allele* of the Dopamine transporter gene (*SLC6A3*), when compared to those *10R*, were characterized by less efficient orienting processes and poorer attentional switching (Kuc et al. 2020). Of note, *SLC6A3* polymorphisms have been associated with BD by several studies (Pinsonneault et al. 2011; Greenwood et al. 2006; Douglas et al. 2016). It has been suggested that prefrontal DA and dopaminergic system-related genes play a dominant role in modulating top-down but not bottom-up attention (Schneider et al. 2015). Consistent with this, deficient top-down regulatory mechanisms during anticipation of reward and excessive emotion regulation during anticipation of losses is an important feature of BD patients as shown by fronto-limbic disconnection during reward anticipation in BD (Vai et al. 2019).

Regarding co-segregation of this putative endophenotype, there is compelling evidence that URs of BD patients show reduced executive functions including, executive control (Ferrier et al. 2004; Sepede et al. 2012), sustained attention (Brotman et al. 2009), abstract problem-solving, working memory, interference control (Doyle et al. 2009; Kim et al. 2015), set-shifting (Antila et al. 2007) and response inhibition (Frangou et al. 2005), compared to healthy controls. Consistent with this, meta-analytic evidence indicated worse performance in URs in all cognitive domains studied, including executive functions. Although the effect sizes were small ($d < 0.5$), they were significantly different from healthy controls for executive function (Arts et al. 2008). This is particularly true for speed dependent measure of executive functions (Bora 2017), a possible marker of abnormality of WM structure as speed of information processing relying on the efficiency of the whole brain network of cortical fibres connections (Wen et al. 2011). Interestingly, some evidence shows that a state of elevated inflammation that in turn led to elevated glutamatergic neurotransmission correlate with poor processing speed (Haroon et al. 2016), implying an interaction between inflammation, increased brain glutamate levels and cognitive impairments in BD subjects.

Learning and memory

Among cognitive functions, verbal memory deficits were consistently found in BD. Deficits of verbal learning and memory was found in euthymic bipolar patients (Bourne et al. 2013) providing evidence for the state independence of this dysfunction. Verbal learning deficits during the euthymic phase are associated with work disability and poorer clinical and functional outcomes (Burdick et al. 2010; Vieta et al. 2018), representing a major contributor to the overall burden of disability.

Unaffected twins of BD patients also showed reduced short-term and long-term verbal learning and memory (Gourovitch et al. 1999). This corroborates with deficits in verbal long-delay free recall and verbal recognition in URS of BD patients (Sobczak et al. 2002, 2003; Keri et al. 2001). However, evidence from meta-analysis studies in URs is conflicting. Indeed, some studies showed significant deficits in verbal memory (Arts et al. 2008; Bora and Ozerdem 2017; Bora et al. 2009), whereas a recent meta-analysis found no difference in verbal learning and memory between URs of probands with BD and controls (Bora 2017).

In healthy subjects, verbal learning and memory were found to have a particularly high heritability with a genetic component explaining 56% of total variance found in a twin study on memory functions. In particular, this study demonstrated that monozygotic intraclass correlation was significantly larger than the dizygotic correlation for verbal learning and memory but not for response discrimination, learning strategy, and recognition (Swan et al. 1999).

Neurobiological mechanisms that are potentially involved in the synaptic plasticity required for learning and memory include glutamatergic neurotransmission (Bannerman et al. 1995) and changes in gene expression brought about by neurotrophic factors, such as cyclic adenosine monophosphate response element binding protein (CREB) and BDNF (Bourtchuladze et al. 1994; Egan et al. 2003).

The presence of verbal learning and memory deficits in BD patients as well as in first-episode patients and HR subjects, suggest that these deficits are already evident early in BD and that these neurodevelopmental abnormalities have genetic underpinnings.

Dysregulation of emotion and reward

Individuals with BD are characterized by a dysregulation of the reward system. Heightened incentive motivation and compulsiveness toward reinforced behaviors are characteristic symptoms of the manic phase of BD, whereas loss of interest, lack of reactivity to positive events, and anhedonia are core features of the depressive phase of the disorder. First evidence of a dysregulation of the dopamine reward system came from observations that dopamine agonists induce mania-like behaviour in healthy individuals (Jacobs and Silverstone 1986). Euphoria has been related to amphetamine-induced dopamine release in human ventral striatum (Drevets et al. 2001). Enhanced rewarding effects of psychostimulants in patients with affective illness and induction of mania in individuals with BD has been proposed as a trait-like dysfunction of the dopaminergic system associated with impairment of the brain reward function (Tremblay et al. 2002; Hasler et al. 2006).

Evidence of the heritability of reward abnormalities includes a functional polymorphism of the *COMT* gene that has been associated with the individual variation in the brain response to dopaminergic challenge (Mattay et al. 2003).

Many studies investigating the dysregulation of the behavioural activation system (BAS) and found that individuals along the bipolar spectrum exhibit higher BAS sensitivity than controls even in a euthymic state (Alloy et al. 2008). A prospective study also found that adolescents with no prior history of BD who exhibited an ambitious goal-striving cognitive style at baseline had a greater likelihood and shorter time to first lifetime onset of BD than those without this cognitive style (Alloy et al. 2012). These findings suggest that the high reward sensitivity may be independent of mood state and a potential reward-related endophenotype (Hasler et al. 2006).

Neuroimaging findings point to dysregulation of ventral striatum and mesial prefrontal cortex functions in BD. Increased metabolism in the striatum in both depressed and manic BD patients have been found (Mah et al. 2007; Blumberg et al. 2000), suggesting that elevated metabolic activity in the striatum may be a state-independent illness marker. Interestingly, an fMRI study found a greater ventral striatal and right-sided orbitofrontal (OFC) activity during anticipation, but not outcome, of monetary reward, in euthymic BD patients relative to healthy controls. Interestingly, there was no difference in neural activation between bipolar I and healthy control subjects during anticipation or receipt of monetary loss, suggesting specificity for reward-related fronto-striatal activity as putative trait-like endophenotype in BD (Nusslock et al. 2012; Macoveanu et al. 2020).

Dysmodulation of reward and emotion processing and emotion regulation, including failure to down-regulate emotional reactivity to positive stimuli, may represent a specific endophenotype of BD given evidence of co-segregation of these traits in families at risk for BD. Behavioural studies have found that BD patients and URs compared to healthy controls showed a reduced ability to modulate risk taking in the face of certain types of stressors (Hidiroglu et al. 2013) and increased trait impulsivity and impulsive decision-making (Wessa et al. 2015).

Fronto-limbic disconnection during emotion and reward processing is a putative neuroimaging endophenotype for BD as it could mediate the relationship between the underlying susceptibility genes and the clinical expression of BD (Vai et al. 2014, 2019). Imaging studies have linked the behavioural features to WM integrity in cortico-limbic connectivity with possible deficient top-down regulatory mechanisms during anticipation of reward and deficient emotion regulation during anticipation of losses. In the reward circuitry, youth offspring of parents with BD exhibit altered patterns of frontal activation and ventrolateral prefrontal cortex-striatal functional connectivity than offspring of non-bipolar parents and of healthy parents (Manelis et al. 2016). High-risk offspring had weaker functional connectivity between the pregenual cingulate and the right ventrolateral prefrontal cortex while anticipating rewards than did low-risk offspring, but had a stronger connectivity between these regions while anticipating losses (Singh et al. 2014). These studies joint to aberrant prefrontal activations and connectivity during reward processing in URs.

Compared to health comparison subjects, BD patients and URs showed increased activity of the orbitofrontal cortex and the amygdala, related to heightened sensitivity to reward and deficient prediction error signal (Linke et al. 2012) and in particular WMA coupled with a significant increased number of errors during set shifting and increased risk taking (Linke et al. 2013; Saricicek et al. 2016). This suggests that an altered myelination during development plays a role in the pathophysiology of BD (Caetano et al. 2008).

Impaired facial expression recognition

Impairments in affective cognition are increasingly recognized as part of the neurocognitive profile and possible treatment targets in BD. Affective cognition may partially reflect neurocognitive functioning in social contexts and moderate the association between neurocognitive impairments and socio-occupational difficulties in BD.

State- and trait-related affective cognitive impairments in BD have been observed across the three phases of the illness and the most consistent findings were trait-related difficulties in facial emotion recognition (Miskowiak et al. 2019). Specifically, a recent systematic review by the International Society of Bipolar Disorder (ISBD) targeting cognition task force, identified global or selective facial emotion recognition deficits in 77% of studies of remitted patients and in 71% of studies of symptomatic BD patients (Miskowiak et al. 2019). Both remitted and symptomatic patients showed difficulties in facial emotion recognition indicating that this may be a trait-related impairment in BD.

At the same manner, URs exhibit abnormalities at the behavioural and neural levels of emotion processing and regulation, including deficits in the recognition of emotional faces. Several studies showed consistent non-specific deficits in the recognition of facial displays of emotion in URs [for a review see Miskowiak et al. (2017)]. These facial expression recognition problems in URs have been shown to be accompanied by aberrant frontal and/or limbic activation. Unaffected youths have been shown to exhibit decreased amygdala and inferior frontal gyrus response to angry facial expressions (Brotman et al. 2014) and exaggerated amygdala response to fearful (but not happy) faces (Dima et al. 2016; Olsavsky et al. 2012). In contrast, a study of adult URs showed exaggerated amygdala response to happy (but not fearful) faces coupled with increased mPFC reactivity to both happy and fearful faces (Surguladze et al. 2010).

Taken together, there is consistent evidence for aberrant fronto-limbic activity to emotional faces in URs. The discrepancy in the direction the activity changes may be due to different experimental paradigms across studies (i.e., passive viewing vs. task-directed processing of faces), or could indicate age-related differences in individuals at familial risk for BD (Miskowiak et al. 2017).

Notably, a pivotal study including 196 adolescent twins (47 monozygotic and 51 dizygotic pairs) provides the first evidence for heritability of neuroelectric indicators of face emotional processing and suggests that event-related brain potentials (ERPs) components sensitive to emotional expressions can potentially serve as endophenotypes (Anokhin et al. 2010). In particular, the amplitude of the ERP components N240 and P300 showed heritability to emotional response to happy, fearful and neutral faces. This study showed that a substantial proportion of the observed individual variation in these ERP responses can be attributed to genetic factors (36–64% for N240 and 42–62% for P300 components, respectively) (Anokhin et al. 2010).

Perspectives

Bipolar disorder molecular-related endophenotypes like alteration of the neuroimmune state (Fig. 1, Table 1) showed good evidence regarding endophenotype criteria. Major advances in biological and genetic studies have allowed going beyond the monoamine hypothesis of mood disorders making them more systematic disorders. If on one hand serotonin and dopamine systems retain

Table 1 Evaluation of putative endophenotypes for bipolar disorder

Endophenotype	Associated with BD	Heritability	State-independence	Co-segregation	Familial association	Total
Imaging endophenotypes						
White matters abnormalities	+++	+++	+	+	+++	11
Acc cortical thickness	+++	+	+	+	+	7
Cognitive, emotional and reward processing endophenotypes						
Attention and executive dysfunctions	+++	+++	+	++	+	10
Dysregulation of emotion and reward	+++	+	++	+	+	8
Learning and memory	+++	+	+	±	+	6.5
Impaired facial expression recognition	+	+	+	+	+	5
Molecular endophenotypes						
CCL11	+	+	±	+	+	4.5
sTNFR1	+	−	+++	0	0	4
CCL24	++	0	++	−	−	4
CXCL10	++	−	++	0	0	4
BDNF	+	+	±	±	−	3
CRP	+	+	±	±	−	3
TWEAK	++	0	+	0	0	3
IL-10	±	+	±	−	−	2
OPG	+	−	±	0	0	1.5

− one or more studies did not support this finding (with no positive studies), or the majority of studies do not support this finding; ± equal number of studies support this finding and do not support this finding; + at least one study supports this finding and no studies do not support this finding, or the majority of studies support this finding; ++ two or more studies support this finding, and no studies do not support this finding; +++ three or more studies support this finding, and no studies do not support this finding; 0, data not available

Scores: − 0; ± 0.5; + 1

their importance for symptoms like mood instability, modulation of reward and motivation, cognition, other biological systems have become increasingly important.

To date, we can assert that we have substantial data about a putative role of an altered neuroimmune state in BD. Research in recent years has elucidated that BD is characterized by an imbalance of inflammatory molecules rather than a simple elevation or reduction of these. Specifically, research on offspring of BD patients suggests that BD could be characterized by a temporal dynamic changes of the immune state: increased proinflammatory state during adolescence, an anti-inflammatory state during young adulthood and a virtually normalized immune state at adulthood suggesting a partial T cell defect i.e. reduced numbers of CD3+ T cells and CD3+CD4+ T helper cells, leading to the deregulated immune system. A neuro-immune-developmental hypothesis of BD could be invoked as an early proinflammatory state either during pregnancy (Allswede et al. 2020) or adolescence (Mesman et al. 2015; Snijders et al. 2017) may perturb the fetal and young brain development shaping brain structures and in particular WM, followed by a virtually normalized immune state at adulthood with a background of continuously low-grade inflammation responsible of shortening telomere length and accelerated aging, leading to the characteristics symptoms of BD.

Because manipulation of the circadian rhythm such as light therapy, phase advance treatment and sleep deprivation can have antidepressant efficacy, circadian abnormalities have been hypothesized to be etiologically associated with affective disorders. Research into circadian rhythm endophenotypes in BD has allowed discovering some genetic factors involved in the regulation of the human circadian clock as vulnerability factors of BD. However, it is not clear if circadian rhythm abnormalities are a trait or state marker of this disorder. In this sense, growing evidence suggests evening chronotype as a putative endophenotype of BD but it warrants further investigation.

Imaging-related endophenotypes (Fig. 1, Table 1) are among those that have received more attention in recent years, thanks to technological advances in the field of neuroimaging. In particular DTI and VBM techniques have allowed confirming early WMA in BD patients and subjects at risk, allowing corroborating the structural dysconnectivity amongst limbic and prefrontal regions as one of the major candidate endophenotypes of BD, mediating the relationship between the underlying genetic vulnerability and the clinical expression of this disorder. The presence of similar pattern of structural dysconnectivity in other major psychiatric disorders like schizophrenia and MDD, confirm that an underlying genetic vulnerability is partially shared among psychotic disorders and mood disorders. However preliminary evidence suggests that WMA and structural dysconnectivity could follow different trajectories in these disorders. In particular studies on untreated first episode BD and schizophrenia suggest that BD patients had decreased FA in cingulum, internal capsule, posterior corpus callosum, tapetum, and occipital WM including posterior thalamic radiation and inferior longitudinal fasciculus/inferior fronto-occipital fasciculus compared to schizophrenic patients. This data suggest that WMA may be intrinsic to BD rather than schizophrenia pathophysiology (Lu et al. 2011). Compared to MDD, studies suggested that decreased fronto-temporal WM FA could be applied to differentiate between BD and MDD (Favre et al. 2019; Kelly et al. 2018; Benedetti et al. 2011a; Chen et al. 2016) and that BD was associated with a greater reduced WM integrity in the left posterior cingulum compared to MDD (Wise et al. 2016).

Targeting the glutamatergic system is one of the last frontier of pharmacological treatment of resistant depression, as esketamine was granted FDA approval in 2019 for MDD and evidence exists for ketamine in bipolar depression (Zarate et al. 2012). Glutamate seems primarily involved in cortical development and it is one of the major players of cortical thickness found in BD patients. The biological role of glutamate in BD could be mediated by interactions between glutamate genetic load (i.e. glutamate genes polymorphisms), hypercortisolemia, stress-induced reduction in neurotrophic factors, and stress-induced reduction in neurogenesis.

BD cognitive-related endophenotypes (Fig. 1, Table 1) have received intensive interest because of their negative impact on quality of life and socio-occupational outcome. In particular, executive dysfunction and verbal memory deficits could be considered as putative endophenotypes of BD. However, evidence suggests that impairments in BD patients were similar to those of schizophrenic or MDD subjects and the differences between these disorders are predominantly quantitative rather than qualitative. It thus seems that BD, MDD and schizophrenia shared a common neurobiological background underlies cognitive deficits making it difficult to research specific genetic mechanisms of BD.

The search for the endophenotypes of BD and more generally of mental disorders remains of considerable importance. In fact, it has implications for the etiology of the disorder, diagnosis and clinical implications. With regards to BD, it is possible to postulate a possible developmental etiology of this disorder. In particular, the latest finding of the research about endophenotypes shows some anomalies already present at the beginning of the disorder and also in young people at risk, confirming this hypothesis. Specifically, early WMA play a central role in the pathophysiology of BD. It is possible to postulate that starting from the fetal period the interplay between environmental risk factors like stress and infections, and the genetic susceptibility of different systems like immune, circadian and glutamatergic systems among others, shape a vulnerable brain. Early WMA could be the result of this vulnerable brain on which new stressors are added in young adulthood which favour the onset of the disorder as the brain does not have the appropriate resilience to resist.

In the long run, the discovery and systematic evaluation of BD endophenotypes, along with identification of specific environmental risk factors, will provide the basis of a new classification system. Such a classification system, based on etiology and pathophysiology, is needed because the improvement of the phenotypic definition of BD will likely facilitate the identification of vulnerability genes and possibly the development of better preventive strategies and treatments.

Research on endophenotypes over the past 30 years has been fruitful, but numerous domains of study deserve further investigation. Animal models and experimental clinical research have to focus on the interplay between genetic and environmental risk factors during development by studying specific brain maturation trajectories. In this sense, a promising field of the research is the relationship between circadian and immune systems to modulate brain maturation in response to external factors such as infection. In fact, several evidences suggest the integration of clock genes, particularly *Bmal1* into the immune control circuitry, allowing organisms to prepare and respond to daily changes in the external environment (Oishi et al. 2017; Nguyen et al. 2013; Early et al. 2018).

BMAL1 has been linked to BD (Mansour et al. 2006; Nievergelt et al. 2006). It has been shown that *BMAL1* has anti-inflammatory properties in normal conditions, as it rhythmically binds to the promoter regions of *CCL2* and *CCL8*, suppressing their transcription (Nguyen et al. 2013) and his deletion facilitate accumulation of reactive oxygen species and the proinflammatory cytokine, IL-1β (Early et al. 2018). Moreover growing evidence indicates that chemokines and cytokines are key player of normal and pathological brain development (Meyer et al. 2009). The response of the innate immune system to external threats is dependent on time of day. Therefore, a stimulating research objective will be to establish whether the shaping of a brain vulnerable to the development of BD is due to the timing of the interaction between immune and circadian systems genetic load (i.e. polymorphisms) and environmental risk factors.

Conclusion

The aim of this narrative review was to use a sensitive literature search to provide an integrative synopsis of the topic. Limitations of this strategy include the non-systematic approach of this review selecting a combination of original research, meta-analyses and reviews as sources of information.

Main results of this overview confirm fronto-limbic dissociation linked to WMA as an established imaging endophenotype in BD.

Research about molecular endophenotypes shows a pivotal role of pathways linked to inflammation, circadian, glutamatergic and calcium systems in the pathophysiology and symptoms manifestation of BD. However the lack of studies on co-segregation and particularly familial association in unaffected relatives, do not allow to drawn definitive conclusions.

Findings about cognitive/reward/emotional endophenotypes link BD particularly with attention and executive dysfunction as well as altered reward processing rather than with learning and memory dysfunctions. Impaired facial expression recognition is an interesting and promising field of research, but more investigations are needed.

Even if research about bipolar endophenotypes has been fruitful in the last years, more efforts are needed to perform longitudinal familial studies to better understand possible trajectories of co-segregation and familial associations and to help guide future research. In this context, the definition of endophenotypes in a way that takes developmental and environmental factors into account to detect vulnerability genes is an exciting model for epidemiological research in BD.

Acknowledgements
Not applicable.

Authors' contributions
All authors met criteria for authorship. All authors read and approved the final manuscript.

Author details
[1]Psychiatry Research Unit, Fribourg Network for Mental Health (RFSM), University of Fribourg, Chemin du Cardinal-Journet 3, 1752 Villars-sur-Glâne, Switzerland. [2]Department of Neuroscience, Institute of Psychiatry, Catholic University Medical School, Largo Francesco Vito 1, 00168 Rome, Italy. [3]Copenhagen Affective Disorder Research Centre (CADIC), Psychiatric Centre Copenhagen, Copenhagen University Hospital, Rigshospitalet, Copenhagen, Denmark.

References

Abramovic L, Boks MPM, Vreeker A, Verkooijen S, van Bergen AH, Ophoff RA, Kahn RS, van Haren NEM. White matter disruptions in patients with bipolar disorder. Eur Neuropsychopharmacol. 2018;28:743–51.

Alloy LB, Abramson LY, Walshaw PD, Cogswell A, Grandin LD, Hughes ME, Iacoviello BM, Whitehouse WG, Urosevic S, Nusslock R, Hogan ME. Behavioral approach system and behavioral inhibition system sensitivities and bipolar spectrum disorders: prospective prediction of bipolar mood episodes. Bipolar Disord. 2008;10:310–22.

Alloy LB, Bender RE, Whitehouse WG, Wagner CA, Liu RT, Grant DA, Jager-Hyman S, Molz A, Choi JY, Harmon-Jones E, Abramson LY. High behavioral approach system (BAS) sensitivity, reward responsiveness, and goal-striving predict first onset of bipolar spectrum disorders: a prospective behavioral high-risk design. J Abnorm Psychol. 2012;121:339–51.

Allswede DM, Yolken RH, Buka SL, Cannon TD. Cytokine concentrations throughout pregnancy and risk for psychosis in adult offspring: a longitudinal case-control study. Lancet Psychiatry. 2020;7:254–61.

Altshuler LL, Curran JG, Hauser P, Mintz J, Denicoff K, Post R. T2 hyperintensities in bipolar disorder: magnetic resonance imaging comparison and literature meta-analysis. Am J Psychiatry. 1995;152:1139–44.

Anokhin AP, Golosheykin S, Heath AC. Heritability of individual differences in cortical processing of facial affect. Behav Genet. 2010;40:178–85.

Antila M, Tuulio-Henriksson A, Kieseppa T, Eerola M, Partonen T, Lonnqvist J. Cognitive functioning in patients with familial bipolar I disorder and their unaffected relatives. Psychol Med. 2007;37:679–87.

Arts B, Jabben N, Krabbendam L, van Os J. Meta-analyses of cognitive functioning in euthymic bipolar patients and their first-degree relatives. Psychol Med. 2008;38:771–85.

Bannerman DM, Good MA, Butcher SP, Ramsay M, Morris RG. Distinct components of spatial learning revealed by prior training and NMDA receptor blockade. Nature. 1995;378:182–6.

Barbosa IG, Rocha NP, Bauer ME, de Miranda AS, Huguet RB, Reis HJ, Zunszain PA, Horowitz MA, Pariante CM, Teixeira AL. Chemokines in bipolar disorder: trait or state? Eur Arch Psychiatry Clin Neurosci. 2013;263:159–65.

Barbosa IG, Vaz GN, Rocha NP, Machado-Vieira R, Ventura MRD, Huguet RB, Bauer ME, Berk M, Teixeira AL. Plasma levels of tumor necrosis factor superfamily molecules are increased in bipolar disorder. Clin Psychopharmacol Neurosci. 2017;15:269–75.

Beauchaine TP, Constantino JN. Redefining the endophenotype concept to accommodate transdiagnostic vulnerabilities and etiological complexity. Biomark Med. 2017;11:769–80.

Benedetti F, Serretti A, Colombo C, Barbini B, Lorenzi C, Campori E, Smeraldi E. Influence of CLOCK gene polymorphism on circadian mood fluctuation and illness recurrence in bipolar depression. Am J Med Genet B Neuropsychiatr Genet. 2003;123B:23–6.

Benedetti F, Bernasconi A, Lorenzi C, Pontiggia A, Serretti A, Colombo C, Smeraldi E. A single nucleotide polymorphism in glycogen synthase kinase 3-beta promoter gene influences onset of illness in patients affected by bipolar disorder. Neurosci Lett. 2004;355:37–40.

Benedetti F, Absinta M, Rocca MA, Radaelli D, Poletti S, Bernasconi A, Dallaspezia S, Pagani E, Falini A, Copetti M, Colombo C, Comi G, Smeraldi E, Filippi M. Tract-specific white matter structural disruption in patients with bipolar disorder. Bipolar Disord. 2011a;13:414–24.

Benedetti F, Yeh PH, Bellani M, Radaelli D, Nicoletti MA, Poletti S, Falini A, Dallaspezia S, Colombo C, Scotti G, Smeraldi E, Soares JC, Brambilla P. Disruption of white matter integrity in bipolar depression as a possible structural marker of illness. Biol Psychiatry. 2011b;69:309–17.

Benedetti F, Bollettini I, Barberi I, Radaelli D, Poletti S, Locatelli C, Pirovano A, Lorenzi C, Falini A, Colombo C, Smeraldi E. Lithium and GSK3-beta promoter gene variants influence white matter microstructure in bipolar disorder. Neuropsychopharmacology. 2013;38:313–27.

Benedetti F, Poletti S, Hoogenboezem TA, Mazza E, Ambree O, de Wit H, Wijkhuijs AJ, Locatelli C, Bollettini I, Colombo C, Arolt V, Drexhage HA. Inflammatory cytokines influence measures of white matter integrity in bipolar disorder. J Affect Disord. 2016;202:1–9.

Beyer JL, Young R, Kuchibhatla M, Krishnan KR. Hyperintense MRI lesions in bipolar disorder: a meta-analysis and review. Int Rev Psychiatry. 2009;21:394–409.

Blokland GA, de Zubicaray GI, McMahon KL, Wright MJ. Genetic and environmental influences on neuroimaging phenotypes: a meta-analytical perspective on twin imaging studies. Twin Res Hum Genet. 2012;15:351–71.

Blumberg HP, Stern E, Martinez D, Ricketts S, de Asis J, White T, Epstein J, McBride PA, Eidelberg D, Kocsis JH, Silbersweig DA. Increased anterior cingulate and caudate activity in bipolar mania. Biol Psychiatry. 2000;48:1045–52.

Bollettini I, Poletti S, Locatelli C, Vai B, Smeraldi E, Colombo C, Benedetti F. Disruption of white matter integrity marks poor antidepressant response in bipolar disorder. J Affect Disord. 2015;174:233–40.

Bora E. A comparative meta-analysis of neurocognition in first-degree relatives of patients with schizophrenia and bipolar disorder. Eur Psychiatry. 2017;45:121–8.

Bora E, Ozerdem A. A meta-analysis of neurocognition in youth with familial high risk for bipolar disorder. Eur Psychiatry. 2017;44:17–23.

Bora E, Pantelis C. Meta-analysis of cognitive impairment in first-episode bipolar disorder: comparison with first-episode schizophrenia and healthy controls. Schizophr Bull. 2015;41:1095–104.

Bora E, Yucel M, Pantelis C. Cognitive endophenotypes of bipolar disorder: a meta-analysis of neuropsychological deficits in euthymic patients and their first-degree relatives. J Affect Disord. 2009;113:1–20.

Bortolato B, Miskowiak KW, Kohler CA, Vieta E, Carvalho AF. Cognitive dysfunction in bipolar disorder and schizophrenia: a systematic review of meta-analyses. Neuropsychiatr Dis Treat. 2015;11:3111–25.

Botteron KN, Heath AC, Price A, Sternhell KE, Singer TM. An epidemiological twin study of prefrontal neuromorphometry in early onset depression. Biol Psychiatry. 1999;45:59S.

Botteron KN, Raichle ME, Drevets WC, Heath AC, Todd RD. Volumetric reduction in left subgenual prefrontal cortex in early onset depression. Biol Psychiatry. 2002;51:342–4.

Bourne C, Aydemir O, Balanza-Martinez V, Bora E, Brissos S, Cavanagh JT, Clark L, Cubukcuoglu Z, Dias VV, Dittmann S, Ferrier IN, Fleck DE, Frangou S, Gallagher P, Jones L, Kieseppa T, Martinez-Aran A, Melle I, Moore PB, Mur M, Pfennig A, Raust A, Senturk V, Simonsen C, Smith DJ, Bio DS, Soeiro-De-souza MG, Stoddart SD, Sundet K, Szoke A, Thompson JM, Torrent C, Zalla T, Craddock N, Andreassen OA, Leboyer M, Vieta E, Bauer M, Worhunsky PD, Tzagarakis C, Rogers RD, Geddes JR, Goodwin GM. Neuropsychological testing of cognitive impairment in euthymic bipolar disorder: an individual patient data meta-analysis. Acta Psychiatr Scand. 2013;128:149–62.

Bourtchuladze R, Frenguelli B, Blendy J, Cioffi D, Schutz G, Silva AJ. Deficient long-term memory in mice with a targeted mutation of the cAMP-responsive element-binding protein. Cell. 1994;79:59–68.

Brietzke E, Kauer-Sant'anna M, Teixeira AL, Kapczinski F. Abnormalities in serum chemokine levels in euthymic patients with bipolar disorder. Brain Behav Immun. 2009a;23:1079–82.

Brietzke E, Stertz L, Fernandes BS, Kauer-Sant'anna M, Mascarenhas M, Escosteguy Vargas A, Chies JA, Kapczinski F. Comparison of cytokine levels in depressed, manic and euthymic patients with bipolar disorder. J Affect Disord. 2009b;116:214–7.

Brodin P, Jojic V, Gao T, Bhattacharya S, Angel CJ, Furman D, Shen-Orr S, Dekker CL, Swan GE, Butte AJ, Maecker HT, Davis MM. Variation in the human immune system is largely driven by non-heritable influences. Cell. 2015;160:37–47.

Brotman MA, Rooney MH, Skup M, Pine DS, Leibenluft E. Increased intrasubject variability in response time in youths with bipolar disorder and at-risk family members. J Am Acad Child Adolesc Psychiatry. 2009;48:628–35.

Brotman MA, Deveney CM, Thomas LA, Hinton KE, Yi JY, Pine DS, Leibenluft E. Parametric modulation of neural activity during face emotion

processing in unaffected youth at familial risk for bipolar disorder. Bipolar Disord. 2014;16:756–63.
Burdick KE, Goldberg JF, Harrow M. Neurocognitive dysfunction and psychosocial outcome in patients with bipolar I disorder at 15-year follow-up. Acta Psychiatr Scand. 2010;122:499–506.
Caetano SC, Silveira CM, Kaur S, Nicoletti M, Hatch JP, Brambilla P, Sassi R, Axelson D, Keshavan MS, Ryan ND, Birmaher B, Soares JC. Abnormal corpus callosum myelination in pediatric bipolar patients. J Affect Disord. 2008;108:297–301.
Cetin T, Guloksuz S, Cetin EA, Gazioglu SB, Deniz G, Oral ET, van Os J. Plasma concentrations of soluble cytokine receptors in euthymic bipolar patients with and without subsyndromal symptoms. BMC Psychiatry. 2012;12:158.
Chaddock CA, Barker GJ, Marshall N, Schulze K, Hall MH, Fern A, Walshe M, Bramon E, Chitnis XA, Murray R, McDonald C. White matter microstructural impairments and genetic liability to familial bipolar I disorder. Br J Psychiatry. 2009;194:527–34.
Chen G, Hu X, Li L, Huang X, Lui S, Kuang W, Ai H, Bi F, Gu Z, Gong Q. Disorganization of white matter architecture in major depressive disorder: a meta-analysis of diffusion tensor imaging with tract-based spatial statistics. Sci Rep. 2016;6:21825.
Chiang MC, McMahon KL, de Zubicaray GI, Martin NG, Hickie I, Toga AW, Wright MJ, Thompson PM. Genetics of white matter development: a DTI study of 705 twins and their siblings aged 12 to 29. Neuroimage. 2011;54:2308–17.
Cremaschi L, Kardell M, Johansson V, Isgren A, Sellgren CM, Altamura AC, Hultman CM, Landen M. Prevalences of autoimmune diseases in schizophrenia, bipolar I and II disorder, and controls. Psychiatry Res. 2017;258:9–14.
Daban C, Martinez-Aran A, Torrent C, Tabares-Seisdedos R, Balanza-Martinez V, Salazar-Fraile J, Selva-Vera G, Vieta E. Specificity of cognitive deficits in bipolar disorder versus schizophrenia. A systematic review. Psychother Psychosom. 2006;75:72–84.
Dallaspezia S, Benedetti F. Melatonin, circadian rhythms, and the clock genes in bipolar disorder. Curr Psychiatry Rep. 2009;11:488–93.
Damasio AR, Tranel D, Damasio H. Individuals with sociopathic behavior caused by frontal damage fail to respond autonomically to social stimuli. Behav Brain Res. 1990;41:81–94.
Dantzer R, O'Connor JC, Freund GG, Johnson RW, Kelley KW. From inflammation to sickness and depression: when the immune system subjugates the brain. Nat Rev Neurosci. 2008;9:46–56.
Dargel AA, Godin O, Kapczinski F, Kupfer DJ, Leboyer M. C-reactive protein alterations in bipolar disorder: a meta-analysis. J Clin Psychiatry. 2015;76:142–50.
Dauvilliers Y, Maret S, Tafti M. Genetics of normal and pathological sleep in humans. Sleep Med Rev. 2005;9:91–100.
de Gennaro L, Marzano C, Fratello F, Moroni F, Pellicciari MC, Ferlazzo F, Costa S, Couyoumdjian A, Curcio G, Sforza E, Malafosse A, Finelli LA, Pasqualetti P, Ferrara M, Bertini M, Rossini PM. The electroencephalographic fingerprint of sleep is genetically determined: a twin study. Ann Neurol. 2008;64:455–60.
de Peri L, Crescini A, Deste G, Fusar-Poli P, Sacchetti E, Vita A. Brain structural abnormalities at the onset of schizophrenia and bipolar disorder: a meta-analysis of controlled magnetic resonance imaging studies. Curr Pharm Des. 2012;18:486–94.
Dickinson T, Becerra R, Coombes J. Executive functioning deficits among adults with bipolar disorder (types I and II): a systematic review and meta-analysis. J Affect Disord. 2017;218:407–27.
Dima D, Roberts RE, Frangou S. Connectomic markers of disease expression, genetic risk and resilience in bipolar disorder. Transl Psychiatry. 2016;6:e706.
Diorio D, Viau V, Meaney MJ. The role of the medial prefrontal cortex (cingulate gyrus) in the regulation of hypothalamic-pituitary-adrenal responses to stress. J Neurosci. 1993;13:3839–47.
Douglas LN, McGuire AB, Manzardo AM, Butler MG. High-resolution chromosome ideogram representation of recognized genes for bipolar disorder. Gene. 2016;586:136–47.
Doyle AE, Wozniak J, Wilens TE, Henin A, Seidman LJ, Petty C, Fried R, Gross LM, Faraone SV, Biederman J. Neurocognitive impairment in unaffected siblings of youth with bipolar disorder. Psychol Med. 2009;39:1253–63.
Drakopoulos J, Sparding T, Clements C, Palsson E, Landen M. Executive functioning but not IQ or illness severity predicts occupational status in bipolar disorder. Int J Bipolar Disord. 2020;8:7.
Drevets WC, Price JL, Simpson JR, Todd RD, Reich T, Vannier M, Raichle ME. Subgenual prefrontal cortex abnormalities in mood disorders. Nature. 1997;386:824–7.
Drevets WC, Gautier C, Price JC, Kupfer DJ, Kinahan PE, Grace AA, Price JL, Mathis CA. Amphetamine-induced dopamine release in human ventral striatum correlates with euphoria. Biol Psychiatry. 2001;49:81–96.
Drevets WC, Ryan N, Bogers W, Birmaher B, Axelson D, Dahl RE. Subgenual prefrontal cortex volume decreased in healthy humans at high familial risk for mood disorders. Soc Neurosci Abstr. 2004;799:18.
Duffy A, Horrocks J, Doucette S, Keown-Stoneman C, Grof P, Andreazza A, Young LT. Immunological and neurotrophic markers of risk status and illness development in high-risk youth: understanding the neurobiological underpinnings of bipolar disorder. Int J Bipolar Disord. 2014;2:29.
Early JO, Menon D, Wyse CA, Cervantes-Silva MP, Zaslona Z, Carroll RG, Palsson-Mcdermott EM, Angiari S, Ryan DG, Corcoran SE, Timmons G, Geiger SS, Fitzpatrick DJ, O'Connell D, Xavier RJ, Hokamp K, O'Neill LAJ, Curtis AM. Circadian clock protein BMAL1 regulates IL-1beta in macrophages via NRF2. Proc Natl Acad Sci USA. 2018;115:E8460–8.
Egan MF, Kojima M, Callicott JH, Goldberg TE, Kolachana BS, Bertolino A, Zaitsev E, Gold B, Goldman D, Dean M, Lu B, Weinberger DR. The BDNF val66met polymorphism affects activity-dependent secretion of BDNF and human memory and hippocampal function. Cell. 2003;112:257–69.
Eisenberger NI, Moieni M, Inagaki TK, Muscatell KA, Irwin MR. In sickness and in health: the co-regulation of inflammation and social behavior. Neuropsychopharmacology. 2017;42:242–53.
Elvsashagen T, Westlye LT, Boen E, Hol PK, Andreassen OA, Boye B, Malt UF. Bipolar II disorder is associated with thinning of prefrontal and temporal cortices involved in affect regulation. Bipolar Disord. 2013;15:855–64.
Emsell L, Leemans A, Langan C, van Hecke W, Barker GJ, McCarthy P, Jeurissen B, Sijbers J, Sunaert S, Cannon DM, McDonald C. Limbic and callosal white matter changes in euthymic bipolar I disorder: an advanced diffusion magnetic resonance imaging tractography study. Biol Psychiatry. 2013;73:194–201.
Evers AK, Veeh J, McNeill R, Reif A, Kittel-Schneider S. C-reactive protein concentration in bipolar disorder: association with genetic variants. Int J Bipolar Disord. 2019;7:26.
Fan J, Wu Y, Fossella JA, Posner MI. Assessing the heritability of attentional networks. BMC Neurosci. 2001;2:14.
Favre P, Pauling M, Stout J, Hozer F, Sarrazin S, Abe C, Alda M, Alloza C, Alonso-Lana S, Andreassen OA, Baune BT, Benedetti F, Busatto GF, Canales-Rodriguez EJ, Caseras X, Chaim-Avancini TM, Ching CRK, Dannlowski U, Deppe M, Eyler LT, Fatjo-Vilas M, Foley SF, Grotegerd D, Hajek T, Haukvik UK, Howells FM, Jahanshad N, Kugel H, Lagerberg TV, Lawrie SM, Linke JO, McIntosh A, Melloni EMT, Mitchell PB, Polosan M, Pomarol-Clotet E, Repple J, Roberts G, Roos A, Rosa PGP, Salvador R, Sarro S, Schofield PR, Serpa MH, Sim K, Stein DJ, Sussmann JE, Temmingh HS, Thompson PM, Verdolini N, Vieta E, Wessa M, Whalley HC, Zanetti MV, Leboyer M, Mangin JF, Henry C, Duchesnay E, Houenou J, the ENIGMA Bipolar Disorder Working Group. Widespread white matter microstructural abnormalities in bipolar disorder: evidence from mega- and meta-analyses across 3033 individuals. Neuropsychopharmacology. 2019;44:2285–93.
Fernandes BS, Steiner J, Molendijk ML, Dodd S, Nardin P, Goncalves CA, Jacka F, Kohler CA, Karmakar C, Carvalho AF, Berk M. C-reactive protein concentrations across the mood spectrum in bipolar disorder: a systematic review and meta-analysis. Lancet Psychiatry. 2016;3:1147–56.
Ferrier IN, Chowdhury R, Thompson JM, Watson S, Young AH. Neurocognitive function in unaffected first-degree relatives of patients with bipolar disorder: a preliminary report. Bipolar Disord. 2004;6:319–22.
Foland-Ross LC, Thompson PM, Sugar CA, Madsen SK, Shen JK, Penfold C, Ahlf K, Rasser PE, Fischer J, Yang Y, Townsend J, Bookheimer SY, Altshuler LL. Investigation of cortical thickness abnormalities in lithium-free adults with bipolar I disorder using cortical pattern matching. Am J Psychiatry. 2011;168:530–9.
Fountoulakis KN, Vieta E, Young A, Yatham L, Grunze H, Blier P, Moeller HJ, Kasper S. The International College of Neuropsychopharmacology (CINP) treatment guidelines for bipolar disorder in adults (CINP-BD-2017), Part 4: unmet needs in the treatment of bipolar disorder

and recommendations for future research. Int J Neuropsychopharmacol. 2017;20:196–205.
Frangou S, Haldane M, Roddy D, Kumari V. Evidence for deficit in tasks of ventral, but not dorsal, prefrontal executive function as an endophenotypic marker for bipolar disorder. Biol Psychiatry. 2005;58:838–9.
Freimer N, Sabatti C. The human phenome project. Nat Genet. 2003;34:15–21.
Freimer N, Sabatti C. The use of pedigree, sib-pair and association studies of common diseases for genetic mapping and epidemiology. Nat Genet. 2004;36:1045–51.
Friedman NP, Miyake A, Young SE, Defries JC, Corley RP, Hewitt JK. Individual differences in executive functions are almost entirely genetic in origin. J Exp Psychol Gen. 2008;137:201–25.
Ganzola R, Duchesne S. Voxel-based morphometry meta-analysis of gray and white matter finds significant areas of differences in bipolar patients from healthy controls. Bipolar Disord. 2017;19:74–83.
Ganzola R, Nickson T, Bastin ME, Giles S, Macdonald A, Sussmann J, McIntosh AM, Whalley HC, Duchesne S. Longitudinal differences in white matter integrity in youth at high familial risk for bipolar disorder. Bipolar Disord. 2017;19:158–67.
Goswami U, Sharma A, Khastigir U, Ferrier IN, Young AH, Gallagher P, Thompson JM, Moore PB. Neuropsychological dysfunction, soft neurological signs and social disability in euthymic patients with bipolar disorder. Br J Psychiatry. 2006;188:366–73.
Gottesman II, Gould TD. The endophenotype concept in psychiatry: etymology and strategic intentions. Am J Psychiatry. 2003;160:636–45.
Gottesman II, Hanson DR. Human development: biological and genetic processes. Annu Rev Psychol. 2005;56:263–86.
Gould TD, Manji HK. The Wnt signaling pathway in bipolar disorder. Neuroscientist. 2002;8:497–511.
Gould TD, Chen G, Manji HK. In vivo evidence in the brain for lithium inhibition of glycogen synthase kinase-3. Neuropsychopharmacology. 2004;29:32–8.
Gourovitch ML, Torrey EF, Gold JM, Randolph C, Weinberger DR, Goldberg TE. Neuropsychological performance of monozygotic twins discordant for bipolar disorder. Biol Psychiatry. 1999;45:639–46.
Greenwood TA, Schork NJ, Eskin E, Kelsoe JR. Identification of additional variants within the human dopamine transporter gene provides further evidence for an association with bipolar disorder in two independent samples. Mol Psychiatry. 2006;11(125–133):115.
Grosse L, Hoogenboezem T, Ambree O, Bellingrath S, Jorgens S, de Wit HJ, Wijkhuijs AM, Arolt V, Drexhage HA. Deficiencies of the T and natural killer cell system in major depressive disorder: T regulatory cell defects are associated with inflammatory monocyte activation. Brain Behav Immun. 2016;54:38–44.
Gurung R, Prata DP. What is the impact of genome-wide supported risk variants for schizophrenia and bipolar disorder on brain structure and function? A systematic review. Psychol Med. 2015;45:2461–80.
Gustavson DE, Hatton SN, Elman JA, Panizzon MS, Franz CE, Hagler DJ Jr, Fennema-Notestine C, Eyler LT, Mcevoy LK, Neale MC, Gillespie N, Dale AM, Lyons MJ, Kremen WS. Predominantly global genetic influences on individual white matter tract microstructure. Neuroimage. 2019;184:871–80.
Haarman BC, Riemersma-Van der Lek RF, de Groot JC, Ruhe HG, Klein HC, Zandstra TE, Burger H, Schoevers RA, de Vries EF, Drexhage HA, Nolen WA, Doorduin J. Neuroinflammation in bipolar disorder—a [(11) C]-(R)-PK11195 positron emission tomography study. Brain Behav Immun. 2014;40:219–25.
Haarman BC, Burger H, Doorduin J, Renken RJ, Sibeijn-Kuiper AJ, Marsman JB, de Vries EF, de Groot JC, Drexhage HA, Mendes R, Nolen WA, Riemersma-Van der Lek RF. Volume, metabolites and neuroinflammation of the hippocampus in bipolar disorder—a combined magnetic resonance imaging and positron emission tomography study. Brain Behav Immun. 2016;56:21–33.
Hajek T, Gunde E, Bernier D, Slaney C, Propper L, Grof P, Macqueen G, Duffy A, Alda M. Subgenual cingulate volumes in affected and unaffected offspring of bipolar parents. J Affect Disord. 2008;108:263–9.
Hajek T, Novak T, Kopecek M, Gunde E, Alda M, Hoschl C. Subgenual cingulate volumes in offspring of bipolar parents and in sporadic bipolar patients. Eur Arch Psychiatry Clin Neurosci. 2010;260:297–304.
Hakkarainen R, Johansson C, Kieseppa T, Partonen T, Koskenvuo M, Kaprio J, Lonnqvist J. Seasonal changes, sleep length and circadian preference among twins with bipolar disorder. BMC Psychiatry. 2003;3:6.
Hanford LC, Sassi RB, Minuzzi L, Hall GB. Cortical thickness in symptomatic and asymptomatic bipolar offspring. Psychiatry Res Neuroimaging. 2016;251:26–33.
Haroon E, Fleischer CC, Felger JC, Chen X, Woolwine BJ, Patel T, Hu XP, Miller AH. Conceptual convergence: increased inflammation is associated with increased basal ganglia glutamate in patients with major depression. Mol Psychiatry. 2016;21:1351–7.
Harrison PJ, Colbourne L, Harrison CH. The neuropathology of bipolar disorder: systematic review and meta-analysis. Mol Psychiatry. 2018;25(8):1787–808.
Hasler G, Pine DS, Kleinbaum DG, Gamma A, Luckenbaugh D, Ajdacic V, Eich D, Rossler W, Angst J. Depressive symptoms during childhood and adult obesity: the Zurich cohort study. Mol Psychiatry. 2005;10:842–50.
Hasler G, Drevets WC, Gould TD, Gottesman II, Manji HK. Toward constructing an endophenotype strategy for bipolar disorders. Biol Psychiatry. 2006;60:93–105.
Hatton SN, Panizzon MS, Vuoksimaa E, Hagler DJ, Fennema-Notestine C, Rinker D, Eyler LT, Franz CE, Lyons MJ, Neale MC, Tsuang MT, Dale AM, Kremen WS. Genetic relatedness of axial and radial diffusivity indices of cerebral white matter microstructure in late middle age. Hum Brain Mapp. 2018;39:2235–45.
Hidiroglu C, Demirci Esen O, Tunca Z, Neslihan Gurz Yalcin S, Lombardo L, Glahn DC, Ozerdem A. Can risk-taking be an endophenotype for bipolar disorder? A study on patients with bipolar disorder type I and their first-degree relatives. J Int Neuropsychol Soc. 2013;19:474–82.
Hirayasu Y, Shenton ME, Salisbury DF, Kwon JS, Wible CG, Fischer IA, Yurgelun-Todd D, Zarate C, Kikinis R, Jolesz FA, McCarley RW. Subgenual cingulate cortex volume in first-episode psychosis. Am J Psychiatry. 1999;156:1091–3.
Hirota T, Lewis WG, Liu AC, Lee JW, Schultz PG, Kay SA. A chemical biology approach reveals period shortening of the mammalian circadian clock by specific inhibition of GSK-3beta. Proc Natl Acad Sci USA. 2008;105:20746–51.
Hope S, Dieset I, Agartz I, Steen NE, Ueland T, Melle I, Aukrust P, Andreassen OA. Affective symptoms are associated with markers of inflammation and immune activation in bipolar disorders but not in schizophrenia. J Psychiatr Res. 2011;45:1608–16.
Hsu JW, Lirng JF, Wang SJ, Lin CL, Yang KC, Liao MH, Chou YH. Association of thalamic serotonin transporter and interleukin-10 in bipolar I disorder: a SPECT study. Bipolar Disord. 2014;16:241–8.
Isgren A, Jakobsson J, Palsson E, Ekman CJ, Johansson AG, Sellgren C, Blennow K, Zetterberg H, Landen M. Increased cerebrospinal fluid interleukin-8 in bipolar disorder patients associated with lithium and antipsychotic treatment. Brain Behav Immun. 2015;43:198–204.
Jackson A, Cavanagh J, Scott J. A systematic review of manic and depressive prodromes. J Affect Disord. 2003;74:209–17.
Jacobs D, Silverstone T. Dextroamphetamine-induced arousal in human subjects as a model for mania. Psychol Med. 1986;16:323–9.
Jahanshad N, Kochunov PV, Sprooten E, Mandl RC, Nichols TE, Almasy L, Blangero J, Brouwer RM, Curran JE, de Zubicaray GI, Duggirala R, Fox PT, Hong LE, Landman BA, Martin NG, McMahon KL, Medland SE, Mitchell BD, Olvera RL, Peterson CP, Starr JM, Sussmann JE, Toga AW, Wardlaw JM, Wright MJ, Hulshoff Pol HE, Bastin ME, McIntosh AM, Deary IJ, Thompson PM, Glahn DC. Multi-site genetic analysis of diffusion images and voxelwise heritability analysis: a pilot project of the ENIGMA-DTI working group. Neuroimage. 2013;81:455–69.
Jakobsson J, Bjerke M, Sahebi S, Isgren A, Ekman CJ, Sellgren C, Olsson B, Zetterberg H, Blennow K, Palsson E, Landen M. Monocyte and microglial activation in patients with mood-stabilized bipolar disorder. J Psychiatry Neurosci. 2015;40:250–8.
Jones SH, Hare DJ, Evershed K. Actigraphic assessment of circadian activity and sleep patterns in bipolar disorder. Bipolar Disord. 2005;7:176–86.
Jumah FR, Dossani RH. Neuroanatomy, cingulate cortex. StatPearls, Treasure Island (FL); 2020.
Kang K, Kim YJ, Kim YH, Roh JN, Nam JM, Kim PY, Ryu WS, Lee SH, Yoon BW. Lithium pretreatment reduces brain injury after intracerebral hemorrhage in rats. Neurol Res. 2012;34:447–54.

Kato T, Fujii K, Kamiya A, Kato N. White matter hyperintensity detected by magnetic resonance imaging and lithium response in bipolar disorder: a preliminary observation. Psychiatry Clin Neurosci. 2000;54:117–20.

Kelly S, Jahanshad N, Zalesky A, Kochunov P, Agartz I, Alloza C, Andreassen OA, Arango C, Banaj N, Bouix S, Bousman CA, Brouwer RM, Bruggemann J, Bustillo J, Cahn W, Calhoun V, Cannon D, Carr V, Catts S, Chen J, Chen JX, Chen X, Chiapponi C, Cho KK, Ciullo V, Corvin AS, Crespo-Facorro B, Cropley V, de Rossi P, Diaz-Caneja CM, Dickie EW, Ehrlich S, Fan FM, Faskowitz J, Fatouros-Bergman H, Flyckt L, Ford JM, Fouche JP, Fukunaga M, Gill M, Glahn DC, Gollub R, Goudzwaard ED, Guo H, Gur RE, Gur RC, Gurholt TP, Hashimoto R, Hatton SN, Henskens FA, Hibar DP, Hickie IB, Hong LE, Horacek J, Howells FM, Hulshoff Pol HE, Hyde CL, Isaev D, Jablensky A, Jansen PR, Janssen J, Jonsson EG, Jung LA, Kahn RS, Kikinis Z, Liu K, Klauser P, Knochel C, Kubicki M, Lagopoulos J, Langen C, Lawrie S, Lenroot RK, Lim KO, Lopez-Jaramillo C, Lyall A, Magnotta V, Mandl RCW, Mathalon DH, McCarley RW, McCarthy-Jones S, McDonald C, McEwen S, McIntosh A, Melicher T, Mesholam-Gately RI, Michie PT, Mowry B, Mueller BA, Newell DT, O'Donnell P, Oertel-Knochel V, Oestreich L, Paciga SA, Pantelis C, Pasternak O, Pearlson G, Pellicano GR, Pereira A, Pineda Zapata J, et al. Widespread white matter microstructural differences in schizophrenia across 4322 individuals: results from the ENIGMA Schizophrenia DTI Working Group. Mol Psychiatry. 2018;23:1261–9.

Kempton MJ, Geddes JR, Ettinger U, Williams SC, Grasby PM. Meta-analysis, database, and meta-regression of 98 structural imaging studies in bipolar disorder. Arch Gen Psychiatry. 2008;65:1017–32.

Keri S, Kelemen O, Benedek G, Janka Z. Different trait markers for schizophrenia and bipolar disorder: a neurocognitive approach. Psychol Med. 2001;31:915–22.

Kim D, Kim JW, Koo TH, Yun HR, Won SH. Shared and distinct neurocognitive endophenotypes of schizophrenia and psychotic bipolar disorder. Clin Psychopharmacol Neurosci. 2015;13:94–102.

Klemfuss H. Rhythms and the pharmacology of lithium. Pharmacol Ther. 1992;56:53–78.

Klemfuss H, Kripke DF. Antimanic drugs stabilize hamster circadian rhythms. Psychiatry Res. 1995;57:215–22.

Kochunov P, Williamson DE, Lancaster J, Fox P, Cornell J, Blangero J, Glahn DC. Fractional anisotropy of water diffusion in cerebral white matter across the lifespan. Neurobiol Aging. 2012;33:9–20.

Kripke DF, Nievergelt CM, Joo E, Shekhtman T, Kelsoe JR. Circadian polymorphisms associated with affective disorders. J Circadian Rhythms. 2009;7:2.

Kritis AA, Stamoula EG, Paniskaki KA, Vavilis TD. Researching glutamate-induced cytotoxicity in different cell lines: a comparative/collective analysis/study. Front Cell Neurosci. 2015;9:91.

Kuc K, Bielecki M, Racicka-Pawlukiewicz E, Czerwinski MB, Cybulska-Klosowicz A. The SLC6A3 gene polymorphism is related to the development of attentional functions but not to ADHD. Sci Rep. 2020;10:6176.

Kurtz MM, Gerraty RT. A meta-analytic investigation of neurocognitive deficits in bipolar illness: profile and effects of clinical state. Neuropsychology. 2009;23:551–62.

Lai YC, Kao CF, Lu ML, Chen HC, Chen PY, Chen CH, Shen WW, Wu JY, Lu RB, Kuo PH. Investigation of associations between NR1D1, RORA and RORB genes and bipolar disorder. PLoS ONE. 2015;10:e0121245.

Lavori PW, Krause-Steinrauf H, Brophy M, Buxbaum J, Cockroft J, Cox DR, Fiore L, Greely HT, Greenberg H, Holmes EW, Nelson LM, Sugarman J. Principles, organization, and operation of a DNA bank for clinical trials: a Department of Veterans Affairs cooperative study. Control Clin Trials. 2002;23:222–39.

Lee SJ, Steiner RJ, Yu Y, Short SJ, Neale MC, Styner MA, Zhu H, Gilmore JH. Common and heritable components of white matter microstructure predict cognitive function at 1 and 2 y. Proc Natl Acad Sci USA. 2017;114:148–53.

Legind CS, Broberg BV, Mandl RCW, Brouwer R, Anhoj SJ, Hilker R, Jensen MH, McGuire P, Pol HH, Fagerlund B, Rostrup E, Glenthoj BY. Heritability of cerebral glutamate levels and their association with schizophrenia spectrum disorders: a (1)[*H*]-spectroscopy twin study. Neuropsychopharmacology. 2019;44:581–9.

Leow A, Ajilore O, Zhan L, Arienzo D, Gadelkarim J, Zhang A, Moody T, van Horn J, Feusner J, Kumar A, Thompson P, Altshuler L. Impaired inter-hemispheric integration in bipolar disorder revealed with brain network analyses. Biol Psychiatry. 2013;73:183–93.

Li Y, Oosting M, Smeekens SP, Jaeger M, Aguirre-Gamboa R, Le KTT, Deelen P, Ricano-Ponce I, Schoffelen T, Jansen AFM, Swertz MA, Withoff S, van de Vosse E, van Deuren M, van de Veerdonk F, Zhernakova A, van der Meer JWM, Xavier RJ, Franke L, Joosten LAB, Wijmenga C, Kumar V, Netea MG. A functional genomics approach to understand variation in cytokine production in humans. Cell. 2016;167:1099.e14-1110.e14.

Lindqvist D, Epel ES, Mellon SH, Penninx BW, Revesz D, Verhoeven JE, Reus VI, Lin J, Mahan L, Hough CM, Rosser R, Bersani FS, Blackburn EH, Wolkowitz OM. Psychiatric disorders and leukocyte telomere length: underlying mechanisms linking mental illness with cellular aging. Neurosci Biobehav Rev. 2015;55:333–64.

Linke J, King AV, Rietschel M, Strohmaier J, Hennerici M, Gass A, Meyer-Lindenberg A, Wessa M. Increased medial orbitofrontal and amygdala activation: evidence for a systems-level endophenotype of bipolar I disorder. Am J Psychiatry. 2012;169:316–25.

Linke J, King AV, Poupon C, Hennerici MG, Gass A, Wessa M. Impaired anatomical connectivity and related executive functions: differentiating vulnerability and disease marker in bipolar disorder. Biol Psychiatry. 2013;74:908–16.

Linke JO, Stavish C, Adleman NE, Sarlls J, Towbin KE, Leibenluft E, Brotman MA. White matter microstructure in youth with and at risk for bipolar disorder. Bipolar Disord. 2020;22:163–73.

Linkowski P. EEG sleep patterns in twins. J Sleep Res. 1999;8(Suppl 1):11–3.

Linkowski P, van Onderbergen A, Kerkhofs M, Bosson D, Mendlewicz J, van Cauter E. Twin study of the 24-h cortisol profile: evidence for genetic control of the human circadian clock. Am J Physiol. 1993;264:E173–81.

Lu LH, Zhou XJ, Keedy SK, Reilly JL, Sweeney JA. White matter microstructure in untreated first episode bipolar disorder with psychosis: comparison with schizophrenia. Bipolar Disord. 2011;13:604–13.

Lyoo IK, Sung YH, Dager SR, Friedman SD, Lee JY, Kim SJ, Kim N, Dunner DL, Renshaw PF. Regional cerebral cortical thinning in bipolar disorder. Bipolar Disord. 2006;8:65–74.

Macoveanu J, Kjaerstad HL, Chase HW, Frangou S, Knudsen GM, Vinberg M, Kessing LV, Miskowiak KW. Abnormal prefrontal cortex processing of reward prediction errors in recently diagnosed patients with bipolar disorder and their unaffected relatives. Bipolar Disord. 2020;22(8):849–59.

Magioncalda P, Martino M, Tardito S, Sterlini B, Conio B, Marozzi V, Adavastro G, Capobianco L, Russo D, Parodi A, Kalli F, Nasi G, Altosole T, Piaggio N, Northoff G, Fenoglio D, Inglese M, Filaci G, Amore M. White matter microstructure alterations correlate with terminally differentiated CD8+ effector T cell depletion in the peripheral blood in mania: combined DTI and immunological investigation in the different phases of bipolar disorder. Brain Behav Immun. 2018;73:192–204.

Mah L, Zarate CA Jr, Singh J, Duan YF, Luckenbaugh DA, Manji HK, Drevets WC. Regional cerebral glucose metabolic abnormalities in bipolar II depression. Biol Psychiatry. 2007;61:765–75.

Mahapatra A, Khandelwal SK, Sharan P, Garg A, Mishra NK. Diffusion tensor imaging tractography study in bipolar disorder patients compared to first-degree relatives and healthy controls. Psychiatry Clin Neurosci. 2017;71:706–15.

Manelis A, Ladouceur CD, Graur S, Monk K, Bonar LK, Hickey MB, Dwojak AC, Axelson D, Goldstein BI, Goldstein TR, Bebko G, Bertocci MA, Gill MK, Birmaher B, Phillips ML. Altered functioning of reward circuitry in youth offspring of parents with bipolar disorder. Psychol Med. 2016;46:197–208.

Mansour HA, Monk TH, Nimgaonkar VL. Circadian genes and bipolar disorder. Ann Med. 2005;37:196–205.

Mansour HA, Wood J, Logue T, Chowdari KV, Dayal M, Kupfer DJ, Monk TH, Devlin B, Nimgaonkar VL. Association study of eight circadian genes with bipolar I disorder, schizoaffective disorder and schizophrenia. Genes Brain Behav. 2006;5:150–7.

Mansur RB, Brietzke E, McIntyre RS, Cao B, Lee Y, Japiassu L, Chen K, Lu R, Lu W, Li T, Xu G, Lin K. BDNF and BMI effects on brain structures of bipolar offspring: results from the global mood and brain science initiative. Acta Psychiatr Scand. 2017;136:607–14.

Martinek S, Inonog S, Manoukian AS, Young MW. A role for the segment polarity gene shaggy/GSK-3 in the Drosophila circadian clock. Cell. 2001;105:769–79.

Mattay VS, Goldberg TE, Fera F, Hariri AR, Tessitore A, Egan MF, Kolachana B, Callicott JH, Weinberger DR. Catechol *O*-methyltransferase val158-met genotype and individual variation in the brain response to amphetamine. Proc Natl Acad Sci USA. 2003;100:6186–91.

McDonald C, Bullmore ET, Sham PC, Chitnis X, Wickham H, Bramon E, Murray RM. Association of genetic risks for schizophrenia and bipolar disorder with specific and generic brain structural endophenotypes. Arch Gen Psychiatry. 2004;61:974–84.

Meffre D, Massaad C, Grenier J. Lithium chloride stimulates PLP and MBP expression in oligodendrocytes via Wnt/beta-catenin and Akt/CREB pathways. Neuroscience. 2015;284:962–71.

Mesman E, Hillegers MH, Ambree O, Arolt V, Nolen WA, Drexhage HA. Monocyte activation, brain-derived neurotrophic factor (BDNF), and S100B in bipolar offspring: a follow-up study from adolescence into adulthood. Bipolar Disord. 2015;17:39–49.

Meyer U, Feldon J, Yee BK. A review of the fetal brain cytokine imbalance hypothesis of schizophrenia. Schizophr Bull. 2009;35:959–72.

Miller GA, Rockstroh B. Endophenotypes in psychopathology research: where do we stand? Annu Rev Clin Psychol. 2013;9:177–213.

Miller AH, Raison CL. The role of inflammation in depression: from evolutionary imperative to modern treatment target. Nat Rev Immunol. 2016;16:22–34.

Miskowiak KW, Kjaerstad HL, Meluken I, Petersen JZ, Maciel BR, Kohler CA, Vinberg M, Kessing LV, Carvalho AF. The search for neuroimaging and cognitive endophenotypes: a critical systematic review of studies involving unaffected first-degree relatives of individuals with bipolar disorder. Neurosci Biobehav Rev. 2017;73:1–22.

Miskowiak KW, Seeberg I, Kjaerstad HL, Burdick KE, Martinez-Aran A, Del Mar-bonnin C, Bowie CR, Carvalho AF, Gallagher P, Hasler G, Lafer B, Lopez-Jaramillo C, Sumiyoshi T, McIntyre RS, Schaffer A, Porter RJ, Purdon S, Torres IJ, Yatham LN, Young AH, Kessing LV, van Rheenen TE, Vieta E. Affective cognition in bipolar disorder: a systematic review by the ISBD targeting cognition task force. Bipolar Disord. 2019;21:686–719.

Muneer A. Bipolar disorder: role of inflammation and the development of disease biomarkers. Psychiatry Investig. 2016;13:18–33.

Musazzi L, Racagni G, Popoli M. Stress, glucocorticoids and glutamate release: effects of antidepressant drugs. Neurochem Int. 2011;59:138–49.

Nassar A, Azab AN. Effects of lithium on inflammation. ACS Chem Neurosci. 2014;5:451–8.

Nery FG, Gigante AD, Amaral JA, Fernandes FB, Berutti M, Almeida KM, Stertz L, Bristot G, Kapczinski F, Lafer B. Serum BDNF levels in unaffected first-degree relatives of patients with bipolar disorder. Braz J Psychiatry. 2016;38:197–200.

Ng TH, Chung KF, Ho FY, Yeung WF, Yung KP, Lam TH. Sleep-wake disturbance in interepisode bipolar disorder and high-risk individuals: a systematic review and meta-analysis. Sleep Med Rev. 2015;20:46–58.

Nguyen KD, Fentress SJ, Qiu Y, Yun K, Cox JS, Chawla A. Circadian gene Bmal1 regulates diurnal oscillations of Ly6C(hi) inflammatory monocytes. Science. 2013;341:1483–8.

Nievergelt CM, Kripke DF, Barrett TB, Burg E, Remick RA, Sadovnick AD, Mcelroy SL, Keck PE Jr, Schork NJ, Kelsoe JR. Suggestive evidence for association of the circadian genes PERIOD3 and ARNTL with bipolar disorder. Am J Med Genet B Neuropsychiatr Genet. 2006;141B:234–41.

Noroozi R, Taheri M, Omrani MD, Ghafouri-Fard S. Glutamate receptor metabotropic 7 (GRM7) gene polymorphisms in mood disorders and attention deficit hyperactive disorder. Neurochem Int. 2019;129:104483.

Nortje G, Stein DJ, Radua J, Mataix-Cols D, Horn N. Systematic review and voxel-based meta-analysis of diffusion tensor imaging studies in bipolar disorder. J Affect Disord. 2013;150:192–200.

Nusslock R, Almeida JR, Forbes EE, Versace A, Frank E, Labarbara EJ, Klein CR, Phillips ML. Waiting to win: elevated striatal and orbitofrontal cortical activity during reward anticipation in euthymic bipolar disorder adults. Bipolar Disord. 2012;14:249–60.

Ochsner KN, Kosslyn SM, Cosgrove GR, Cassem EH, Price BH, Nierenberg AA, Rauch SL. Deficits in visual cognition and attention following bilateral anterior cingulotomy. Neuropsychologia. 2001;39:219–30.

Oishi Y, Hayashi S, Isagawa T, Oshima M, Iwama A, Shimba S, Okamura H, Manabe I. Bmal1 regulates inflammatory responses in macrophages by modulating enhancer RNA transcription. Sci Rep. 2017;7:7086.

Olsavsky AK, Brotman MA, Rutenberg JG, Muhrer EJ, Deveney CM, Fromm SJ, Towbin K, Pine DS, Leibenluft E. Amygdala hyperactivation during face emotion processing in unaffected youth at risk for bipolar disorder. J Am Acad Child Adolesc Psychiatry. 2012;51:294–303.

Padiath QS, Paranjpe D, Jain S, Sharma VK. Glycogen synthase kinase 3beta as a likely target for the action of lithium on circadian clocks. Chronobiol Int. 2004;21:43–55.

Pagani L, St Clair PA, Teshiba TM, Service SK, Fears SC, Araya C, Araya X, Bejarano J, Ramirez M, Castrillon G, Gomez-Makhinson J, Lopez MC, Montoya G, Montoya CP, Aldana I, Navarro L, Freimer DG, Safaie B, Keung LW, Greenspan K, Chou K, Escobar JI, Ospina-Duque J, Kremeyer B, Ruiz-Linares A, Cantor RM, Lopez-Jaramillo C, Macaya G, Molina J, Reus VI, Sabatti C, Bearden CE, Takahashi JS, Freimer NB. Genetic contributions to circadian activity rhythm and sleep pattern phenotypes in pedigrees segregating for severe bipolar disorder. Proc Natl Acad Sci USA. 2016;113:E754–61.

Pezzoli S, Emsell L, Yip SW, Dima D, Giannakopoulos P, Zarei M, Tognin S, Arnone D, James A, Haller S, Frangou S, Goodwin GM, McDonald C, Kempton MJ. Meta-analysis of regional white matter volume in bipolar disorder with replication in an independent sample using coordinates, T-maps, and individual MRI data. Neurosci Biobehav Rev. 2018;84:162–70.

Pinsonneault JK, Han DD, Burdick KE, Kataki M, Bertolino A, Malhotra AK, Gu HH, Sadee W. Dopamine transporter gene variant affecting expression in human brain is associated with bipolar disorder. Neuropsychopharmacology. 2011;36:1644–55.

Poletti S, Myint AM, Schuetze G, Bollettini I, Mazza E, Grillitsch D, Locatelli C, Schwarz M, Colombo C, Benedetti F. Kynurenine pathway and white matter microstructure in bipolar disorder. Eur Arch Psychiatry Clin Neurosci. 2018;268:157–68.

Roberts G, Lenroot R, Frankland A, Yeung PK, Gale N, Wright A, Lau P, Levy F, Wen W, Mitchell PB. Abnormalities in left inferior frontal gyral thickness and parahippocampal gyral volume in young people at high genetic risk for bipolar disorder. Psychol Med. 2016;46:2083–96.

Roederer M, Quaye L, Mangino M, Beddall MH, Mahnke Y, Chattopadhyay P, Tosi I, Napolitano L, Terranova Barberio M, Menni C, Villanova F, di Meglio P, Spector TD, Nestle FO. The genetic architecture of the human immune system: a bioresource for autoimmunity and disease pathogenesis. Cell. 2015;161:387–403.

Rosenblat JD, McIntyre RS. Bipolar disorder and immune dysfunction: epidemiological findings, proposed pathophysiology and clinical implications. Brain Sci. 2017;7:144.

Sanches M, Amorim E, Mwangi B, Zunta-Soares GB, Soares JC. Smaller left anterior cingulate cortex in non-bipolar relatives of patients with bipolar disorder. Braz J Psychiatry. 2019;41:254–6.

Sanjay TN, Shivakumar V, Subbanna M, Biradar SU, Muralidharan K, Venkatasubramanian G. Plasma interleukin-6 in remitted early bipolar I disorder and subjects at high-risk for bipolar disorder. Asian J Psychiatr. 2017;30:212–3.

Saricicek A, Zorlu N, Yalin N, Hidiroglu C, Cavusoglu B, Ceylan D, Ada E, Tunca Z, Ozerdem A. Abnormal white matter integrity as a structural endophenotype for bipolar disorder. Psychol Med. 2016;46:1547–58.

Schneider MR, Delbello MP, McNamara RK, Strakowski SM, Adler CM. Neuroprogression in bipolar disorder. Bipolar Disord. 2012;14:356–74.

Schneider KK, Schote AB, Meyer J, Frings C. Genes of the dopaminergic system selectively modulate top-down but not bottom-up attention. Cogn Affect Behav Neurosci. 2015;15:104–16.

Seleem MA, Merranko JA, Goldstein TR, Goldstein BI, Axelson DA, Brent DA, Nimgaonkar VL, Diler RS, Sakolsky DJ, Kupfer DJ, Birmaher B. The longitudinal course of sleep timing and circadian preferences in adults with bipolar disorder. Bipolar Disord. 2015;17:392–402.

Sepede G, de Berardis D, Campanella D, Perrucci MG, Ferretti A, Serroni N, Moschetta FS, del Gratta C, Salerno RM, Ferro FM, di Giannantonio M, Onofrj M, Romani GL, Gambi F. Impaired sustained attention in euthymic bipolar disorder patients and non-affected relatives: an fMRI study. Bipolar Disord. 2012;14:764–79.

Shattuck EC, Muehlenbein MP. Towards an integrative picture of human sickness behavior. Brain Behav Immun. 2016;57:255–62.

Singh MK, Kelley RG, Howe ME, Reiss AL, Gotlib IH, Chang KD. Reward processing in healthy offspring of parents with bipolar disorder. JAMA Psychiat. 2014;71:1148–56.

Snijders G, Schiweck C, Mesman E, Grosse L, de Wit H, Nolen WA, Drexhage HA, Hillegers MHJ. A dynamic course of T cell defects in individuals at risk for mood disorders. Brain Behav Immun. 2016;58:11–7.

Snijders G, Mesman E, de Wit H, Wijkhuijs A, Nolen WA, Drexhage HA, Hillegers MHJ. Immune dysregulation in offspring of a bipolar parent. Altered serum levels of immune growth factors at adolescent age. Brain Behav Immun. 2017;64:116–23.

Sobczak S, Riedel WJ, Booij I, Aan Het Rot M, Deutz NE, Honig A. Cognition following acute tryptophan depletion: difference between first-degree relatives of bipolar disorder patients and matched healthy control volunteers. Psychol Med. 2002;32:503–15.

Sobczak S, Honig A, Schmitt JA, Riedel WJ. Pronounced cognitive deficits following an intravenous L-tryptophan challenge in first-degree relatives of bipolar patients compared to healthy controls. Neuropsychopharmacology. 2003;28:711–9.

Soderlund J, Olsson SK, Samuelsson M, Walther-Jallow L, Johansson C, Erhardt S, Landen M, Engberg G. Elevation of cerebrospinal fluid interleukin-1ss in bipolar disorder. J Psychiatry Neurosci. 2011;36:114–8.

Sprooten E, Fleming KM, Thomson PA, Bastin ME, Whalley HC, Hall J, Sussmann JE, McKirdy J, Blackwood D, Lawrie SM, McIntosh AM. White matter integrity as an intermediate phenotype: exploratory genome-wide association analysis in individuals at high risk of bipolar disorder. Psychiatry Res. 2013;206:223–31.

Sprooten E, Barrett J, McKay DR, Knowles EE, Mathias SR, Winkler AM, Brumbaugh MS, Landau S, Cyr L, Kochunov P, Glahn DC. A comprehensive tractography study of patients with bipolar disorder and their unaffected siblings. Hum Brain Mapp. 2016;37:3474–85.

Squarcina L, Houenou J, Altamura AC, Soares J, Brambilla P. Association of increased genotypes risk for bipolar disorder with brain white matter integrity investigated with tract-based spatial statistics: special section on "translational and neuroscience studies in affective disorders". Section Editor, Maria Nobile MD, PhD. This section of JAD focuses on the relevance of translational and neuroscience studies in providing a better understanding of the neural basis of affective disorders. The main aim is to briefly summarise relevant research findings in clinical neuroscience with particular regards to specific innovative topics in mood and anxiety disorders. J Affect Disord. 2017;221:312–7.

Squassina A, Pisanu C, Vanni R. Mood disorders, accelerated aging, and inflammation: is the link hidden in telomeres? Cells. 2019;8:52.

Sugranyes G, Sole-Padulles C, de la Serna E, Borras R, Romero S, Sanchez-Gistau V, Garcia-Rizo C, Goikolea JM, Bargallo N, Moreno D, Baeza I, Castro-Fornieles J. Cortical morphology characteristics of young offspring of patients with schizophrenia or bipolar disorder. J Am Acad Child Adolesc Psychiatry. 2017;56:79–88.

Surguladze SA, Marshall N, Schulze K, Hall MH, Walshe M, Bramon E, Phillips ML, Murray RM, McDonald C. Exaggerated neural response to emotional faces in patients with bipolar disorder and their first-degree relatives. Neuroimage. 2010;53:58–64.

Swan GE, Carmelli D. Evidence for genetic mediation of executive control: a study of aging male twins. J Gerontol B Psychol Sci Soc Sci. 2002;57:P133–43.

Swan GE, Reed T, Jack LM, Miller BL, Markee T, Wolf PA, Decarli C, Carmelli D. Differential genetic influence for components of memory in aging adult twins. Arch Neurol. 1999;56:1127–32.

Toh KL, Jones CR, He Y, Eide EJ, Hinz WA, Virshup DM, Ptacek LJ, Fu YH. An hPer2 phosphorylation site mutation in familial advanced sleep phase syndrome. Science. 2001;291:1040–3.

Tremblay LK, Naranjo CA, Cardenas L, Herrmann N, Busto UE. Probing brain reward system function in major depressive disorder: altered response to dextroamphetamine. Arch Gen Psychiatry. 2002;59:409–16.

Tsuang MT, Faraone SV, Lyons MJ. Identification of the phenotype in psychiatric genetics. Eur Arch Psychiatry Clin Neurosci. 1993;243:131–42.

Vai B, Bollettini I, Benedetti F. Corticolimbic connectivity as a possible biomarker for bipolar disorder. Expert Rev Neurother. 2014;14:631–50.

Vai B, Bertocchi C, Benedetti F. Cortico-limbic connectivity as a possible biomarker for bipolar disorder: where are we now? Expert Rev Neurother. 2019;19:159–72.

Vederine FE, Wessa M, Leboyer M, Houenou J. A meta-analysis of whole-brain diffusion tensor imaging studies in bipolar disorder. Prog Neuropsychopharmacol Biol Psychiatry. 2011;35:1820–6.

Verkooijen S, van Bergen AH, Knapen SE, Vreeker A, Abramovic L, Pagani L, Jung Y, Riemersma-Van der Lek R, Schoevers RA, Takahashi JS, Kahn RS, Boks MPM, Ophoff RA. An actigraphy study investigating sleep in bipolar I patients, unaffected siblings and controls. J Affect Disord. 2017;208:248–54.

Versace A, Ladouceur CD, Romero S, Birmaher B, Axelson DA, Kupfer DJ, Phillips ML. Altered development of white matter in youth at high familial risk for bipolar disorder: a diffusion tensor imaging study. J Am Acad Child Adolesc Psychiatry. 2010;49:1249–59, 1259.e1.

Videbech P. MRI findings in patients with affective disorder: a meta-analysis. Acta Psychiatr Scand. 1997;96:157–68.

Vieta E, Berk M, Schulze TG, Carvalho AF, Suppes T, Calabrese JR, Gao K, Miskowiak KW, Grande I. Bipolar disorders. Nat Rev Dis Prim. 2018;4:18008.

Vita A, de Peri L, Sacchetti E. Gray matter, white matter, brain, and intracranial volumes in first-episode bipolar disorder: a meta-analysis of magnetic resonance imaging studies. Bipolar Disord. 2009;11:807–14.

Vuoksimaa E, Panizzon MS, Hagler DJ Jr, Hatton SN, Fennema-Notestine C, Rinker D, Eyler LT, Franz CE, Lyons MJ, Neale MC, Tsuang MT, Dale AM, Kremen WS. Heritability of white matter microstructure in late middle age: a twin study of tract-based fractional anisotropy and absolute diffusivity indices. Hum Brain Mapp. 2017;38:2026–36.

Wehr TA, Sack DA, Rosenthal NE. Sleep reduction as a final common pathway in the genesis of mania. Am J Psychiatry. 1987;144:201–4.

Wen W, Zhu W, He Y, Kochan NA, Reppermund S, Slavin MJ, Brodaty H, Crawford J, Xia A, Sachdev P. Discrete neuroanatomical networks are associated with specific cognitive abilities in old age. J Neurosci. 2011;31:1204–12.

Wessa M, Kollmann B, Linke J, Schonfelder S, Kanske P. Increased impulsivity as a vulnerability marker for bipolar disorder: evidence from self-report and experimental measures in two high-risk populations. J Affect Disord. 2015;178:18–24.

Wessel J, Moratorio G, Rao F, Mahata M, Zhang L, Greene W, Rana BK, Kennedy BP, Khandrika S, Huang P, Lillie EO, Shih PA, Smith DW, Wen G, Hamilton BA, Ziegler MG, Witztum JL, Schork NJ, Schmid-Schonbein GW, O'Connor DT. C-reactive protein, an 'intermediate phenotype' for inflammation: human twin studies reveal heritability, association with blood pressure and the metabolic syndrome, and the influence of common polymorphism at catecholaminergic/beta-adrenergic pathway loci. J Hypertens. 2007;25:329–43.

Whitwell JL. Voxel-based morphometry: an automated technique for assessing structural changes in the brain. J Neurosci. 2009;29:9661–4.

Wise T, Radua J, Nortje G, Cleare AJ, Young AH, Arnone D. Voxel-based meta-analytical evidence of structural disconnectivity in major depression and bipolar disorder. Biol Psychiatry. 2016;79:293–302.

Wood J, Birmaher B, Axelson D, Ehmann M, Kalas C, Monk K, Turkin S, Kupfer DJ, Brent D, Monk TH, Nimgainkar VL. Replicable differences in preferred circadian phase between bipolar disorder patients and control individuals. Psychiatry Res. 2009;166:201–9.

Xia W, Liu Y, Jiao J. GRM7 regulates embryonic neurogenesis via CREB and YAP. Stem Cell Reports. 2015;4:795–810.

Yalin N, Saricicek A, Hidiroglu C, Zugman A, Direk N, Ada E, Cavusoglu B, Er A, Isik G, Ceylan D, Tunca Z, Kempton MJ, Ozerdem A. Cortical thickness and surface area as an endophenotype in bipolar disorder type I patients and their first-degree relatives. Neuroimage Clin. 2019;22:101695.

Yuksel C, Ongur D. Magnetic resonance spectroscopy studies of glutamate-related abnormalities in mood disorders. Biol Psychiatry. 2010;68:785–94.

Zaninotto L, Guglielmo R, Calati R, Ioime L, Camardese G, Janiri L, Bria P, Serretti A. Cognitive markers of psychotic unipolar depression: a meta-analytic study. J Affect Disord. 2015;174:580–8.

Zaninotto L, Solmi M, Veronese N, Guglielmo R, Ioime L, Camardese G, Serretti A. A meta-analysis of cognitive performance in melancholic versus non-melancholic unipolar depression. J Affect Disord. 2016;201:15–24.

Zarate CA Jr, Brutsche NE, Ibrahim L, Franco-Chaves J, Diazgranados N, Cravchik A, Selter J, Marquardt CA, Liberty V, Luckenbaugh DA. Replication of ketamine's antidepressant efficacy in bipolar depression: a randomized controlled add-on trial. Biol Psychiatry. 2012;71:939–46.

Zhang Z, Zhang ZY, Wu Y, Schluesener HJ. Valproic acid ameliorates inflammation in experimental autoimmune encephalomyelitis rats. Neuroscience. 2012;221:140–50.

5

Characterization of affective lability across subgroups of psychosis spectrum disorders

Margrethe Collier Høegh[1*], Ingrid Melle[1], Sofie R. Aminoff[1,2], Beathe Haatveit[1], Stine Holmstul Olsen[1], Idun B. Huflåtten[1], Torill Ueland[1,3] and Trine Vik Lagerberg[1]

Abstract

Background: Affective lability is elevated and associated with increased clinical burden in psychosis spectrum disorders. The extent to which the level, structure and dispersion of affective lability varies between the specific disorders included in the psychosis spectrum is however unclear. To have potential value as a treatment target, further characterization of affective lability in these populations is necessary. The main aim of our study was to investigate differences in the architecture of affective lability in different psychosis spectrum disorders, and if putative differences remained when we controlled for current symptom status.

Methods: Affective lability was measured with The Affective Lability Scale Short Form (ALS-SF) in participants with schizophrenia (SZ, n = 76), bipolar I disorder (BD-I, n = 105), bipolar II disorder (BD-II, n = 68) and a mixed psychosis-affective group (MP, n = 48). Multiple analyses of covariance were conducted to compare the ALS-SF total and subdimension scores of the diagnostic groups, correcting for current psychotic, affective and anxiety symptoms, substance use and sex. Double generalized linear models were performed to compare the dispersion of affective lability in the different groups.

Results: Overall group differences in affective lability remained significant after adjusting for covariates ($p = .001$). BD-II had higher affective lability compared to SZ and BD-I ($p = .004$), with no significant differences between SZ and BD-I. There were no significant differences in the contributions of ALS-SF dimensions to the total affective lability or in dispersion of affective lability between the groups.

Conclusions: This study provides the construct of affective lability in psychosis spectrum disorders with more granular details that may have implications for research and clinical care. It demonstrates that despite overlap in core symptom profiles, BD-I is more similar to SZ than it is to BD-II concerning affective lability and the BD groups should consequently be studied apart. Further, affective lability appears to be characterized by fluctuations between depressive- and other affective states across different psychosis spectrum disorders, indicating that affective lability may be related to internalizing problems in these disorders. Finally, although the level varies between groups, affective lability is evenly spread and not driven by extremes across psychosis spectrum disorders and should be assessed irrespective of diagnosis.

*Correspondence: m.c.hoegh@medisin.uio.no
[1] CoE NORMENT, Norwegian Centre for Mental Disorders Research, Division of Mental Health and Addiction, University of Oslo and Oslo University Hospital, Building 49, Ullevål sykehus, Nydalen, PO Box 4956, 0424 Oslo, Norway
Full list of author information is available at the end of the article

Keywords: Affective lability, Bipolar disorders, Schizophrenia, Psychosis spectrum, The Affective Lability Scale-Short Form (ALS-SF)

Background

Affective lability, the propensity to experience rapid, unpredictable and excessive changes in affective states (Zwicker et al. 2019), is a central and common feature of affective instability that is associated with negative outcomes across psychiatric disorders (Patel et al. 2015; Marwaha et al. 2013a, 2014a, 2018; Broome et al. 2015a,b; McDonald et al. 2020). As a consequence, affective lability and other elements of affective instability are gradually becoming recognized as dimensional and transdiagnostic constructs in line with the Research Domain Criteria (RDoC) project of The National Institute of Mental Health (NIMH) (Broome et al. 2015b; Insel et al. 2010; Fernandez et al. 2016).

Due to the considerable overlap in the symptomatology and etiology of schizophrenia and bipolar disorder, the Kraepelinian dichotomy is increasingly being questioned (Craddock and Owen 2010; Pearlson 2015). Consequently, investigating the full spectrum of these disorders—referred to as psychosis spectrum disorders—is recommended when exploring both biomarkers and clinical features (Guloksuz and Os 2018). Still, studies investigating affective lability thus far have focused on bipolar disorder (BD), which is likely to be due to the fluctuations in affective states inherently tied to a BD diagnosis. Affective lability has been found to be both a trait- and a state-dependent factor in individuals with bipolar I (BD-I) and bipolar II (BD-II) disorders. It is present in periods of euthymia (Henry et al. 2008), early in the course of illness (Aminoff et al. 2012), in all polarities of the illness episodes (Henry et al. 2003; Gershon and Eidelman 2015; Faurholt-Jepsen et al. 2015; Verdolini et al. 2019), as well as in non-affected relatives (Hafeman et al. 2016; Birmaher et al. 2013). Due to its associations with adverse clinical correlates such as alcohol use disorders (AUD) (Lagerberg et al. 2017), suicidality (Aas et al. 2017; Ducasse et al. 2017), anxiety disorders (Aas et al. 2017), cardiometabolic risk (Dargel et al. 2018) and inflammation (Dargel et al. 2017), there is mounting evidence that affective lability may be a relevant therapeutic target in BD.

In schizophrenia (SZ), there has previously been limited emphasis on the prevalence and correlates of affective lability, despite indications that it can be a prominent facet of psychotic experiences (Patel et al. 2015; Marwaha et al. 2014b). Indeed, in our recently published study investigating affective lability across psychotic disorders, we found that affective lability was markedly elevated in individuals with SZ and BD compared to healthy controls, with equally high elevations in both groups (Høegh et al. 2020). Also, affective lability was significantly and independently associated with higher levels of positive psychotic- and depressive symptoms in SZ, and with higher levels of AUD and depressive symptoms in BD. This suggests that affective lability adds to the total illness burden across psychosis spectrum disorders. The findings highlight that increased awareness of affective lability in both research and clinical care is warranted.

To further elucidate the mechanisms of affective lability and its potential value as a treatment target consistent with personalized approaches to psychiatry, it is of interest to explore how and if affective lability varies between the specific disorders included in the psychosis spectrum. In line with this, a few previous studies with relatively small samples, as well as two larger studies, have found higher affective lability in individuals with BD-II compared with BD-I (Faurholt-Jepsen et al. 2015, 2019; O'Donnell et al. 2018; Marwaha et al. 2016). Knowledge about the expression of affective lability in SZ and how this expression overlaps with the broader psychosis spectrum, however, is scarce. Also, it is unclear if there are certain types of lability in affect that are more prominent in the different psychosis spectrum disorders. The presence of anxiety, for example, has been found to be high in both individuals with BD and SZ (Karpov et al. 2016; Achim et al. 2011), but to which extent it is part of the composition of affective lability in the various disorders is not known. For potential intervention efforts to be as targeted as possible, more precise knowledge about which affects that appear to be involved in the lability in the different diagnostic subgroups is needed.

Using the same sample as in our previous study (Høegh et al. 2020) together with newly added participants, we are now able to further explore affective lability measured by The Affective Lability Scale Short Form (ALS-SF) across specific psychosis spectrum disorders. These include SZ, BD-I, BD-II in addition to a mixed "psychosis-affective" (MP) group including schizoaffective disorder and psychotic disorders not otherwise specified (psychosis NOS) with prominent mood symptoms. Here, we aim to investigate if these groups exhibit differences in the architecture of affective lability that could aid further characterization of this phenomenon in psychosis spectrum disorders. We also aim to investigate whether putative differences in affective lability between the diagnostic groups are primarily mediated by differences in their current symptomatology. Finally, we explore potential variations in affective lability within the diagnostic categories in the psychosis spectrum, i.e. between individuals with the same type of disorder, by examining the within-group dispersion of ALS-SF scores, and whether this differs between the diagnostic groups. Such an investigation has, to our knowledge, yet to be conducted in this population and will highlight whether affective lability appears to be driven by subgroups with extreme scores or is more evenly spread within and across the different diagnostic groups.

Accordingly, we seek to investigate affective lability in four diagnostic groups within the psychosis spectrum: SZ, BD-I, BD-II and MP, and more specifically to:

1. Investigate (a) if there are differences in the total- and subdimension scores of ALS-SF between the groups, (b) if potential differences remain after controlling for current symptoms, and (c) which of the ALS-SF subdimensions contribute most to the total affective lability score in each of the diagnostic groups.
2. Investigate the dispersion of the ALS-SF scores within each diagnostic category and if there are differences in dispersion between the diagnostic groups.

Material and methods

Design

The current study is part of the larger Thematically Organized Psychosis (TOP) study at the Norwegian Center for Mental Disorders Research (NORMENT) in Oslo, Norway. Recruitment to the TOP study has been ongoing since 2003 and potential participants are referred via psychiatric inpatient and outpatient units, including specialized psychosis units as well as community teams, in a catchment area that is comprised of all the major hospitals in Oslo. As such, the overall representability of the sample is considered to be very good. The participants are given thorough information about the voluntary nature of the study and the possibility to withdraw at any time. The participants included in the study have to meet diagnostic criteria for a Diagnostic and Statistical Manual of Mental Disorders 4th Edition (DSM-IV) diagnosis of schizophrenia- or bipolar spectrum disorder and provide informed consent. Both individuals with established diagnoses and individuals who are diagnosed for the first time are included in the study. Further inclusion criteria are intelligence quotient (IQ) above 70, no prior history of severe head trauma and sufficient understanding of a Scandinavian language (Ringen et al. 2008).

Participants

The sample for the current study was comprised of two hundred and ninety-seven participants with psychosis spectrum disorders from the TOP study, and only participants who had completed the ALS-SF were included. The ALS-SF was originally introduced in a TOP study sub-protocol for participants with first episode mania, and a few years later included in the main protocol (i.e. to patients with other diagnoses than BD-I). It was mainly presented for participants with low levels of current affective symptoms. The diagnostic grouping in the current study was as follows: SZ (including schizophreniform [n=14]) n=76, BD-I n=105, BD-II=68 and MP (including psychosis NOS [n=32] and schizoaffective disorder [n=16]) n=48. The rationale for combining psychosis NOS and schizoaffective disorder into one "mixed" group was that these categories typically include patients with both psychotic- and affective symptoms that are diagnostically more heterogeneous than the other groups (Santelmann et al. 2015, 2016; Widing et al. 2020). Of the present sample, n=222 were used in our previous study investigating affective lability across the psychosis spectrum (Høegh et al. 2020), and are now re-analyzed along with the newly added participants to shed light on putative differences in affective lability between the specific psychotic disorders.

Clinical assessments

The diagnoses in the study were established by the Structured Clinical Interview for DSM-IV axis I disorders (SCID-1), modules A-E (First et al. 1995) which was carried out by trained medical doctors, psychiatrists or clinical psychologists. In the TOP study, diagnostic reliability is assessed with regular intervals and Cohen's kappa for diagnosis in the range between 0.92 and 0.99 has been found across different assessment teams. To assess current symptom state, the positive subscale of the Positive and Negative Syndrome Scale [PANSS (Kay et al. 1987)] was used for positive psychotic symptoms, and the depression item (G6) and the anxiety item (G2) in the general scale of the PANSS were used for depressive- and anxiety symptoms, respectively. PANSS G6 and PANSS G2 were chosen because they were the only measures of depression and anxiety that were collected at the same time point as the ALS-SF for all participants. The rating for G6 is based on the answer to one initial question ("how has your mood been in the past week, mostly good or mostly bad?") followed by 1–11 follow-up questions concerning the extent of the depressive state and its behavioral consequences. For G2, the rating is based on the same algorithm; one initial question ("have you been feeling worried or nervous in the past week?") and then

1 to 6 follow-up questions depending on the response to the first question. The Young Mania Rating Scale [YMRS (Young et al. 1978)] was used to assess manic symptoms. The Alcohol Use Disorders Identification Test [AUDIT (Saunders et al. 1993)] was used to evaluate the degree of harmful alcohol consumption, and drug related problems were measured with the Drug Use Disorders Identification Test [DUDIT (Berman et al. 2005)]. Duration of illness was estimated based on the age of onset of the first SCID-verified episode of psychosis for SZ and MP, and the first SCID-verified affective episode for BD-I and BD-II.

The Affective Lability Scale Short Form (ALS-SF)

To measure affective lability, we used the ALS-SF (Oliver and Simons 2004). The ALS-SF captures the total level of affective lability reported by an individual, but also subdimensions of affective lability covering oscillations between three subdomains: anxiety-depression, depression-elation and anger and normal mood. Thus, the scale provides an indication of whether affective lability is predominantly driven by specific- or a combination of affects. The ALS-SF has been found to have good psychometric properties (Aas et al. 2015; Look et al. 2010) and is widely used across different clinical populations. The 18 items of the scale are rated on a four-point Likert scale ranging from 0 ("very uncharacteristic of me") to 3 ("very characteristic of me") and yields a total score of affective lability as well as scores for the three subdomains. There are no validated cut-off scores for evaluating the severity of affective lability, but in our previous study we found mean ALS-SF total and subscale scores in the range of 0.17–0.39 for healthy controls, 0.85–1.33 for individuals with BD, and 0.69–1.34 for individuals with SZ (Høegh et al. 2020). This corresponds well with what has been found in at least one similar study (Marwaha et al. 2018).

Statistical analyses

Descriptive statistics, including means with standard deviations or frequencies with percentages where relevant, were used to investigate demographical and clinical characteristics of the different diagnostic groups. The groups were then compared using one-way between-groups analyses of variance (ANOVA) and chi-square tests. The Tukey's honestly significant difference (HSD) test was used for post-hoc comparisons where appropriate. To investigate group differences in the level of affective lability as measured by scores on the total- and subdimensions of the ALS-SF, a one-way between-groups multivariate analysis of variance (MANOVA) was conducted with Bonferroni post-hoc tests. A multiple analysis of covariance (MANCOVA) was then carried out to investigate if statistically significant group differences in affective lability remained significant when current symptom and substance use status were entered as covariates. The variables which were significantly associated with diagnostic group and/or with the ALS-SF domains in bivariate correlation analyses were entered as covariates. The selected covariates were as follows: current level of positive psychotic symptoms (PANSS P), manic symptoms (YMRS), depression (PANSS G6), anxiety (PANSS G2), alcohol use (AUDIT) and drug use (DUDIT) (see Table 1 for correlation coefficients). In addition to the symptom and substance use variables, sex was entered as a covariate as there was a significant difference in the number of females in the different groups and previous research has indicated that affective lability is higher in females in general (Marwaha et al. 2013b; Winkler et al. 2004). Age, which has also been found to be associated with affective lability previously (Broome et al. 2015b), was not associated with the diagnostic groups or with the ALS-SF scores in our sample and therefore not included in further analyses. Effect sizes were calculated by partial eta squared. To investigate which of the ALS-SF subdimensions contributed the most to the total affective lability, a one-way repeated measures ANOVA was performed for each group. The Statistical Package for the Social Sciences (SPSS Inc., Chicago, IL, version 26) was used for all statistical analyses and a significance level of $p \leq 0.05$ (two-tailed tests) was employed. For aim 2, ALS-SF scores for all dimensions for each diagnostic group were plotted into the Graphpad Prism tool (GraphPad Software, La Jolla California USA, version 8.0 for Windows) and converted into violin plots to illustrate score distributions. To further investigate variability in the ALS-SF scores, double generalized linear models (DGLM, $Y \sim Dx, \sim Dx$) were carried out using R (R core team 2017) to test if the ALS-SF score dispersions were significantly different between groups (for more detailed information see Additional file 1).

Table 1 Bivariate correlation analyses

	PANSS P	PANSS G2	PANSS G6	AUDIT	DUDIT	YMRS	SEX
ALS-SF total	$r_s=0.174$**	$r_s=0.381$**	$r_s=0.305$**	$r_s=0.153$**	$r_s=0.227$**	$r_s=0.282$**	$r_s=0.136$*

ALS-SF affective lability scale short form, *PANSS P* positive and negative syndrome scale positive subscale, *PANSS G2* positive and negative syndrome scale anxiety item, *PANSS G6* positive and negative syndrome scale depression item, *AUDIT* the alcohol use disorders identification test, *DUDIT* the drug use disorders identification test, *YMRS* young mania rating scale. *$p<0.05$, **$p<0.001$

Results

Demographics and clinical characteristics of the sample

Demographic and clinical characteristics for SZ, BD-I, BD-II and MP are presented in Table 2. A statistically significant difference in sex between the groups was found, with fewer women in the SZ group compared to remaining groups. There were also significantly more women in the BD-II compared to the BD-I group. In addition, the duration of illness between the groups was significantly different; the BD-I and BD-II groups had been ill longer than the SZ and MP groups ($p < 0.001$ and $p < 0.05$, respectively). Regarding clinical features, there were statistically significant differences between the groups for PANSS total, PANSS P, YMRS, G2 anxiety and AUDIT (see Table 2).

Affective lability in the diagnostic groups: total and subdimension scores

The mean scores for the ALS-SF dimensions for the different diagnostic groups are presented in Fig. 1. The MANOVA showed that there was a statistically significant difference in affective lability between the groups for all of the ALS dimensions: ALS-total $F = 8.446$, $df = 3$, $p < 0.001$; ALS anxiety-depression $F = 9.298$, $df = 3$, $p < 0.001$; ALS depression-elation $F = 7.281$, $p < 0.001$ and ALS anger $F = 4.252$, $p = 0.006$. Effect sizes were moderate; partial $eta^2 = 0.080$, 0.087, 0.069 and 0.042, respectively.

Post-hoc analyses with Bonferroni revealed that the BD-II group had significantly higher affective lability scores compared to all of the other groups for the ALS total ($p < 0.05$) and depression-elation ($p < 0.05$) dimensions. For the ALS anxiety-depression dimension, the scores for the BD-II group were significantly higher than those of the BD-I and SZ groups ($p < 0.001$ for both), but not the MP group ($p = 0.060$). Finally, the BD-II group had significantly higher scores compared to the SZ group ($p = 0.006$) and the MP group ($p = 0.042$) groups, but not the BD-I group ($p = 0.089$) on the anger dimension. There were no significant differences in the scores for the SZ and BD-I groups on any dimension ($p = 1.000$).

Results from multivariate analyses

The overall differences in affective lability between the groups remained statistically significant also after adjusting for the effects of sex, current symptom- and substance use status: ALS total $F = 5.305$, $df = 3$, $p = 0.001$; ALS anxiety-depression $F = 6.139$, $df = 3$, $p < 001$; ALS depression-elation $F = 4.432$, $df = 3$, $p = 0.005$ and ALS anger $F = 4.184$, $df = 3$, $p = 0.006$. Again, the effect sizes were moderate with partial eta^2 of 0.057, 0.067, 0.048 and 0.046. Post-hoc group comparisons with Bonferroni showed that the difference in AL between BD-II versus SZ and BD-I remained statistically significant for the ALS total ($p = 0.004$ for both SZ and BD-I), anxiety-depression (SZ $p = 0.038$, BD-I $p = 0.001$) and depression-elation dimensions (SZ $p = 0.031$, BD-I $p = 0.006$). The difference between BD-II and SZ on the anger domain also remained statistically significant ($p = 0.004$). The difference between the MP group and the BD-II group no longer remained statistically significant for the total-, depression-elation- and anger domains after adjusting for covariates.

Contributions of the ALS-SF subdimensions to the total score

In all of the diagnostic groups, the one-way repeated measures ANOVAs with Bonferroni post-hoc tests showed that the anxiety-depression and depression-elation dimensions contributed most to the total affective lability, with no significant differences in the level of scores between these dimensions in any group ($p = 1.000$ for SZ and BD-I, $p = 0.225$ for BD-II, $p = 0.814$ for MP). Across the board, the anger dimension was found to contribute significantly less to the total score compared to the anxiety-depression and depression-elation dimensions ($p < 0.001$).

Dispersion of affective lability scores within and between the diagnostic groups

The score distributions for all dimensions of the ALS-SF for the four diagnostic groups are shown in Fig. 2a–d. The median score is illustrated by a vertical straight line. The double generalized linear models found no significant differences ($p > 0.05$) in the score dispersions between any of the groups in any of the domains, indicating that despite differences in mean ALS-SF scores between groups, the dispersion in the scores was the same (for more information see Additional file 1).

Discussion

The construct of affective lability refers to the propensity to experience rapid, unpredictable and excessive changes in affective states (Zwicker et al. 2019). The main aim of the current study was to investigate differences in affective lability between different psychosis spectrum disorders. Our results show that individuals with BD-II had markedly elevated levels of total- and subdimension affective lability compared to BD-I and SZ, even when correcting for sex, the level of current symptoms and substance use. Affective lability in the MP group, on the other hand, was not significantly different from BD-II nor SZ or BD-I when the covariates were taken into account. There were no statistically significant differences between individuals with BD-I and SZ for any ALS-SF dimension and these two groups

Table 2 Demographics and clinical characteristics

	SZ (*n* = *76*)	BD-I (*n* = *105*)	BD-II (*n* = *68*)	MP (*n* = *48*)	Statistics	*P*-value
	Mean (SD)	Mean (SD)	Mean (SD)	Mean (SD)		
Age, years	29.8 (9.2)	31.6 (11.2)	29.4 (9.2)	29.5 (8.3)	F = 0.971, df = 3	0.407
Female sex, n (%)	27 (35.5)	56 (53.3)	47 (69.1)	27 (56.3)	X^2 = 16.608, df = 3	*0.001* SZ < all, BD-II > BD-1
Education, years	14.3 (3.1)	15.0 (2.9)	16.0 (2.8)	14.6 (3.1)	F = 1.950, df = 3	0.122
Duration of illness, years	4.1 (6.2)	9.9 (9.8)	13.1 (8.7)	6.1 (7.2)	F = 15.785, df = 3	*0.000* BD-I and BD-II > SZ, MP
PANSS—total	56.2 (15.6)	42.1(8.4)	43.0 (8.2)	53.8 (14.2)	F = 30.356, df = 3	*0.000* SZ, MP > BD-I, BD-II
PANSS—P	12.8 (4.8)	9.0 (2.5)	9.1 (2.6)	12.1 (3.8)	F = 28.431, df = 3	*0.000* SZ, MP > BD-I, BD-II
Depression (PANSS item G6)	2.3 (1.2)	2.3 (1.4)	2.7 (1.4)	2.4 (1.3)	F = 2.167, df = 3	0.092
Anxiety (PANSS item G2)	2.8 (1.2)	2.7 (1.3)	3.3 (1.4)	2.5 (1.2)	F = 3.599, df = 3	*0.014* BD-II > BD-I, MP
YMRS—total	3.5 (4.2)	2.3 (3.4)	3.0 (4.2)	1.7 (2.3)	F = 2.699, df = 3	*0.046**
AUDIT total	5.1 (4.9)	8.1 (7.1)	8.5 (6.4)	5.3 (5.1)	F = 5.648, df = 3	*0.001* SZ < BD-I, BD-II; MP < BD-II
DUDIT total	*3.1 (6.9)*	*3.6 (7.1)*	*2.8 (5.6)*	*3.2 (7.1)*	*F = 0.237, df = 3*	*0.871*

Statistically significant group differences are highlighted in italic

SZ schizophrenia, *BD* bipolar disorder, *MP* mixed psychosis, *PANSS* positive and negative syndrome scale, *YMRS* young mania rating scale, *AUDIT* the alcohol use disorders identification test, *DUDIT* drug use disorders identification test

*Post-hoc tests were non-significant

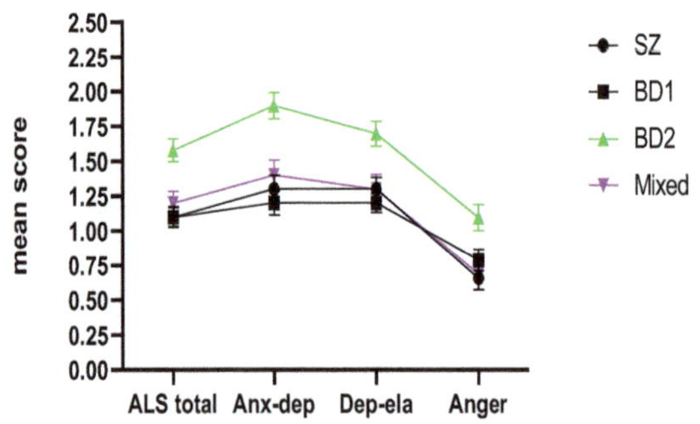

Fig. 1 ALS-SF mean and SEM scores. *SEM* standard error of the mean, *SZ* schizophrenia, *BD* bipolar disorder, *ALS-SF* affective lability scale short form, *anx-dep* anxiety-depression domain, *dep-ela* depression-elation domain

had very similar score patterns throughout. This suggests that despite the overlap in core affective symptom profiles of BD-I and BD-II, the BD-I group is more similar to SZ than it is to BD-II concerning levels of affective lability. Further, since we controlled for current symptoms, our findings imply that there are some trait-like differences between the disorders with respect to affective lability, where elevated affective lability is perhaps more inherently tied to BD-II compared to the other psychosis spectrum disorders.

Given that individuals with BD-II are more similar to healthy controls when it comes to neurobiology, genetics and cognition compared to BD-I and SZ (MacQueen et al. 2005), one can speculate if the high affective lability is based in environmental or clinical risk factors specific to BD-II. For instance, childhood trauma has been found to be associated with affective lability (Aas et al. 2014), but the prevalence rates of trauma are reported to be at the same level in individuals with BD-I and BD-II (Palmier-Claus et al. 2016; Janiri et al. 2015). The presence of comorbid Attention-Deficit/Hyperactivity Disorder (ADHD) and anxiety disorders is also likely to increase affective lability (Broome et al. 2015a; Aas et al. 2017), but again the rates are at the same level in BD-I versus BD-II (Pataki and Carlson 2013; Bennett et al. 2019; Brus et al. 2014; Pavlova et al. 2015). It is perhaps more plausible that the elevation in affective lability

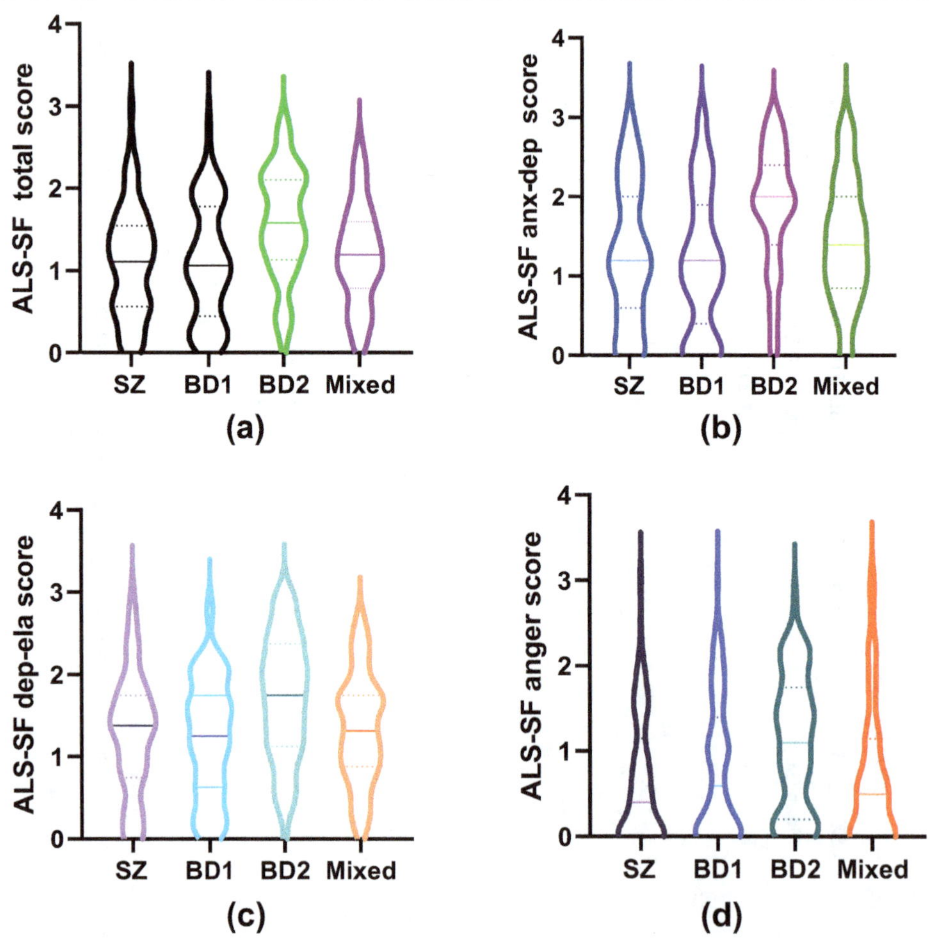

Fig. 2 a–d ALS-SF score distribution: **a** ALS-SF total score, **b** anxiety-depression dimension, **c** depression-elation dimension, **d** anger dimension. *SZ* schizophrenia, *BD* bipolar disorder, *ALS-SF* affective lability scale short form, *anx-dep* anxiety-depression dimension, *dep-ela* depression-elation domain

observed in individuals with BD-II is associated with more frequent and severe borderline personality traits (Saunders et al. 2020) and/or higher rates of depressive episodes and symptoms (Karanti et al. 2020), but this needs to be investigated further. In addition, affective lability, anxiety disorders, borderline personality disorders and BD-II appear to be more prevalent in women compared to men, and there may be some interrelationships here that are worthwhile looking into in future research. Regardless of origin, it seems important to investigate the BD groups separately with regards to affective lability. When it comes to the similarities between individuals with BD-I and SZ, this may not be surprising at least from a genetic point of view, given the established overlap between BD-I and SZ (Tamminga et al. 2013; Tesli et al. 2014). It is, however, important to keep in mind that both individuals with BD-I and SZ also present with higher affective lability rates than healthy controls (Høegh et al. 2020).

With respect to the architecture of affective lability, oscillations between anxiety-depression and depression-elation were the most typical for all groups. In our previous study, we found significant associations between affective lability and current depression in both SZ and BDs (Høegh et al. 2020). We now extend these findings to show that even when controlling for the level of depressive symptoms, significant between-group differences in affective lability persist. Somewhat surprisingly, we found that fluctuations between depression and elation were also prevalent, even in individuals with SZ, along with fluctuations involving anxiety. This is in line with the dimensional perspective of psychosis that has been found in previous research showing a large degree of symptomatic overlap between disorders (Os and Kapur 2009). The mean scores of the SZ, BD-I and MP groups on the anger dimension were low (0.66, 0.79 and 0.69, respectively). Although the anger score for the BD-II group was higher (1.08), it is still comparatively low relative to the BD-II scores for the other dimensions. Collectively, this is an indication that affective lability is related to more internalizing versus externalizing problems and behaviors in psychotic disorders, which is different from the pattern found in for example borderline personality disorder where rapid shifts involving anger appear to be more characteristic (Henry et al. 2001; Koenigsberg et al. 2002).

To our knowledge, the dispersion of ALS-SF scores in the different psychosis spectrum disorders has not previously been investigated. The violin plots showing the full distributions of the data confirm that the scores seem to be relatively evenly dispersed in all groups, i.e. the scores are not clustered around the minimum or maximum but rather around the median score. Hence, the level of affective lability in the groups does not appear to result primarily from the presence of subgroups of patients with extreme scores, but to represent the typical score pattern for each disorder. Visually, the shape of the distribution of scores in the BD-II group stands out, especially for the anxiety-depression dimension. Yet, the statistical analyses revealed no significant differences between the groups with regards to dispersion. This indicates that although the level varies between groups, affective lability is evenly spread and not driven by extremes across psychosis spectrum disorders and should be routinely assessed irrespective of diagnosis.

Limitations and strengths

The present study must be interpreted in light of some limitations. The cross-sectional nature of the study implies that we cannot make causal attributions about the association between diagnostic group and affective lability. In addition, data on comorbid anxiety disorders, personality disorders and ADHD are lacking, and the measures used for anxiety and depressive symptoms are based on a scale primarily developed for assessing psychotic symptoms. Hence, the possibility that current symptoms still could have influenced the association between affective lability and diagnostic group cannot be ruled out completely. However, we believe that the likelihood of this is limited due to the relatively low levels of anxiety and depressive symptoms. Further, the risk of recall- and response bias cannot be ruled out as the ALS-SF is a self-report instrument. The study also has several strengths; it has a large, diagnostically well-characterized sample covering the psychosis spectrum, and uses a multidimensional assessment scale of affective lability that provides a richer insight and understanding of the construct.

Conclusions

Our results illustrate that affective lability is more prominent in individuals with BD-II compared to SZ and BD-I, and that this is not explained by differences between the groups in sex, levels of affective-, psychotic- or anxiety symptoms or severity of substance use. BD-II thus appears to be a particularly vulnerable diagnostic group with respect to affective lability. No differences in affective lability were found between individuals with BD-I and SZ. The results further add information about the structure of affective lability in these disorders emphasizing the significance of fluctuations between depressive- and other affective states. The findings also show that there is an even dispersion of affective lability scores within each diagnostic group, and that the dispersion also appears to be largely equivalent across groups. Overall, the study provides the concept of affective lability in psychotic disorders with more granularity by showing differences and similarities between diagnostic groups that may have implications for both research and clinical practice.

Abbreviations

ALS-SF: Affective Lability Scale Short Form; SZ: Schizophrenia; BD: Bipolar disorder; RDoC: Research Domain Criteria; NIMH: The National Institute of Mental Health;

AUD: Alcohol Use Disorder; MP: Mixed Psychosis group; Psychosis NOS: Psychosis Not Otherwise Specified; TOP: Thematically Organized Psychosis Study; NORMENT: Norwegian Center for Mental Disorders Research; DSM-IV: Diagnostic and Statistical Manual of Mental Disorders 4th Edition; SCID: Structured Clinical Interview for DSM-IV; PANSS: Positive and Negative Syndrome Scale; YMRS: Young Mania Rating Scale; AUDIT: Alcohol Use Disorders Identification Test; DUDIT: Drug Use Disorders Identification Test; ANOVA: Analysis of Variance; HSD: Honestly Significant Difference test; MANOVA: Multivariate Analysis of Variance; MANCOVA: Multivariate Analysis of Covariance; SPSS: Statistical Package for the Social Sciences; DGLM: Double Generalized Linear Models; ADHD: Attention-Deficit/Hyperactivity Disorder.

Supplementary Information

Additional file 1: Double Generalized Linear Models.

Acknowledgements
The authors would like to extend a sincere thank you to all the participants in the TOP study for their time and effort. We would also like to thank everyone at NORMENT.

Authors' contributions
MCH and TVL designed the study. MCH conducted the data analyses and drafted the manuscript. TVL contributed with data analyses and -interpretation and with revising the paper. IM initiated the study and together with TU provided input concerning data analyses and interpretation of results. BH conducted the double generalized linear model analyses. SRA, MCH, SHO and IBH collected data. All authors were involved in critically reviewing the manuscript. All authors read and approved the final manuscript.

Author details
[1]CoE NORMENT, Norwegian Centre for Mental Disorders Research, Division of Mental Health and Addiction, University of Oslo and Oslo University Hospital, Building 49, Ullevål sykehus, Nydalen, PO Box 4956, 0424 Oslo, Norway. [2]Division of Mental Health and Addiction, Oslo University Hospital, Oslo, Norway. [3]Department of Psychology, University of Oslo, Oslo, Norway.

References
Aas M, Aminoff SR, Vik Lagerberg T, Etain B, Agartz I, Andreassen OA, et al. Affective lability in patients with bipolar disorders is associated with high levels of childhood trauma. Psychiatry Res. 2014;218(1–2):252–5.

Aas M, Pedersen G, Henry C, Bjella T, Bellivier F, Leboyer M, et al. Psychometric properties of the affective lability scale (54 and 18-item version) in patients with bipolar disorder, first-degree relatives, and healthy controls. J Affect Disord. 2015;172:375–80.

Aas M, Henry C, Bellivier F, Lajnef M, Gard S, Kahn JP, et al. Affective lability mediates the association between childhood trauma and suicide attempts, mixed episodes and co-morbid anxiety disorders in bipolar disorders. Psychol Med. 2017;47(5):902–12.

Achim AM, Maziade M, Raymond E, Olivier D, Merette C, Roy MA. How prevalent are anxiety disorders in schizophrenia? A meta-analysis and critical review on a significant association. Schizophr Bull. 2011;37(4):811–21.

Aminoff SR, Jensen J, Lagerberg TV, Hellvin T, Sundet K, Andreassen OA, et al. An association between affective lability and executive functioning in bipolar disorder. Psychiatry Res. 2012;198(1):58–61.

Bennett F, Hodgetts S, Close A, Frye M, Grunze H, Keck P, et al. Predictors of psychosocial outcome of bipolar disorder: data from the Stanley Foundation Bipolar Network. Int J Bipolar Disord. 2019;7(1):28.

Berman AH, Bergman H, Palmstierna T, Schlyter F. Evaluation of the drug use disorders identification test (DUDIT) in criminal justice and detoxification settings and in a Swedish population sample. Eur Addict Res. 2005;11(1):22–31.

Birmaher B, Goldstein BI, Axelson DA, Monk K, Hickey MB, Fan J, et al. Mood lability among offspring of parents with bipolar disorder and community controls. Bipolar Disord. 2013;15(3):253–63.

Broome MR, He Z, Iftikhar M, Eyden J, Marwaha S. Neurobiological and behavioural studies of affective instability in clinical populations: a systematic review. Neurosci Biobehav Rev. 2015a;51:243–54.

Broome MR, Saunders KE, Harrison PJ, Marwaha S. Mood instability: significance, definition and measurement. Br J Psychiatry. 2015b;207(4):283–5.

Brus MJ, Solanto MV, Goldberg JF. Adult ADHD vs. bipolar disorder in the DSM-5 era: a challenging differentiation for clinicians. J Psychiatr Pract. 2014;20(6):428–37.

Craddock N, Owen MJ. The Kraepelinian dichotomy—going, going…but still not gone. Br J Psychiatry. 2010;196(2):92–5.

Dargel AA, Godin O, Etain B, Hirakata V, Azorin JM, M'Bailara K, et al. Emotional reactivity, functioning, and C-reactive protein alterations in remitted bipolar patients: clinical relevance of a dimensional approach. Aust N Z J Psychiatry. 2017;51(8):788–98.

Dargel AA, Roussel F, Volant S, Etain B, Grant R, Azorin JM, et al. Emotional hyper-reactivity and cardiometabolic risk in remitted bipolar patients: a machine learning approach. Acta Psychiatr Scand. 2018;138:348.

Ducasse D, Jaussent I, Guillaume S, Azorin JM, Bellivier F, Belzeaux R, et al. Affect lability predicts occurrence of suicidal ideation in bipolar patients: a two-year prospective study. Acta Psychiatr Scand. 2017;135(5):460–9.

Faurholt-Jepsen M, Ritz C, Frost M, Mikkelsen RL, Margrethe Christensen E, Bardram J, et al. Mood instability in bipolar disorder type I versus type II-continuous daily electronic self-monitoring of illness activity using smartphones. J Affect Disord. 2015;186:342–9.

Faurholt-Jepsen M, Frost M, Busk J, Christensen EM, Bardram JE, Vinberg M, et al. Differences in mood instability in patients with bipolar disorder type I and II: a smartphone-based study. Int J Bipolar Disord. 2019;7(1):5.

Fernandez KC, Jazaieri H, Gross JJ. Emotion regulation: a transdiagnostic perspective on a new RDoC domain. Cognit Ther Res. 2016;40(3):426–40.

First MB, Spitzer RL, Gibbon M, Williams JBW. Structured clinical interview for DSM-IV axis I disorders: patient edition (SCID-P), version 2; 1995.

Gershon A, Eidelman P. Inter-episode affective intensity and instability: predictors of depression and functional impairment in bipolar disorder. J Behav Ther Exp Psychiatry. 2015;46:14–8.

Guloksuz S, van Os J. The slow death of the concept of schizophrenia and the painful birth of the psychosis spectrum. Psychol Med. 2018;48(2):229–44.

Hafeman DM, Merranko J, Axelson D, Goldstein BI, Goldstein T, Monk K, et al. Toward the definition of a bipolar prodrome: dimensional predictors of bipolar spectrum disorders in at-risk youths. Am J Psychiatry. 2016;173(7):695–704.

Henry C, Mitropoulou V, New AS, Koenigsberg HW, Silverman J, Siever LJ. Affective instability and impulsivity in borderline personality and bipolar II disorders: similarities and differences. J Psychiatr Res. 2001;35(6):307–12.

Henry C, Swendsen J, Van den Bulke D, Sorbara F, Demotes-Mainard J, Leboyer M. Emotional hyper-reactivity as a fundamental mood characteristic of manic and mixed states. Eur Psychiatry. 2003;18(3):124–8.

Henry C, Van den Bulke D, Bellivier F, Roy I, Swendsen J, M'Bailara K, et al. Affective lability and affect intensity as core dimensions of bipolar disorders during euthymic period. Psychiatry Res. 2008;159(1–2):1–6.

Høegh MC, Melle I, Aminoff SR, Laskemoen JF, Büchmann CB, Ueland T, et al. Affective lability across psychosis spectrum disorders. Eur Psychiatry. 2020;63(1):e53.

Insel T, Cuthbert B, Garvey M, Heinssen R, Pine DS, Quinn K, et al. Research domain criteria (RDoC): toward a new classification framework for research on mental disorders. Am J Psychiatry. 2010;167(7):748–51.

Janiri D, Sani G, Danese E, Simonetti A, Ambrosi E, Angeletti G, et al. Childhood traumatic experiences of patients with bipolar disorder type I and type II. J Affect Disord. 2015;175:92–7.

Karanti A, Kardell M, Joas E, Runeson B, Palsson E, Landen M. Characteristics of bipolar I and II disorder: a study of 8766 individuals. Bipolar Disord. 2020;22(4):392–400.

Karpov B, Joffe G, Aaltonen K, Suvisaari J, Baryshnikov I, Naatanen P, et al. Anxiety symptoms in a major mood and schizophrenia spectrum disorders. Eur Psychiatry. 2016;37:1–7.

Kay SR, Fiszbein A, Opler LA. The positive and negative syndrome scale (PANSS) for schizophrenia. Schizophr Bull. 1987;13(2):261–76.

Koenigsberg HW, Harvey PD, Mitropoulou V, Schmeidler J, New AS, Goodman M, et al. Characterizing affective instability in borderline personality disorder. Am J Psychiatry. 2002;159(5):784–8.

Lagerberg TV, Aminoff SR, Aas M, Bjella T, Henry C, Leboyer M, et al. Alcohol use disorders are associated with increased affective lability in bipolar disorder. J Affect Disord. 2017;208:316–24.

Look AE, Flory JD, Harvey PD, Siever LJ. Psychometric properties of a short form of the affective lability scale (ALS-18). Pers Individ Dif. 2010;49(3):187–91.

MacQueen GM, Hajek T, Alda M. The phenotypes of bipolar disorder: relevance for genetic investigations. Mol Psychiatry. 2005;10(9):811–26.

Marwaha S, Parsons N, Broome M. Mood instability, mental illness and suicidal ideas: results from a household survey. Soc Psychiatry Psychiatr Epidemiol. 2013a;48(9):1431–7.

Marwaha S, Parsons N, Flanagan S, Broome M. The prevalence and clinical associations of mood instability in adults living in England: results from the adult psychiatric morbidity survey 2007. Psychiatry Res. 2013b;205(3):262–8.

Marwaha S, He Z, Broome M, Singh SP, Scott J, Eyden J, et al. How is affective instability defined and measured? A systematic review. Psychol Med. 2014a;44(9):1793–808.

Marwaha S, Broome MR, Bebbington PE, Kuipers E, Freeman D. Mood instability and psychosis: analyses of British national survey data. Schizophr Bull. 2014b;40(2):269–77.

Marwaha S, Gordon-Smith K, Broome M, Briley PM, Perry A, Forty L, et al. Affective instability, childhood trauma and major affective disorders. J Affect Disord. 2016;190:764–71.

Marwaha S, Price C, Scott J, Weich S, Cairns A, Dale J, et al. Affective instability in those with and without mental disorders: a case control study. J Affect Disord. 2018;241:492–8.

McDonald K, Smith T, Broadbent M, Patel R, Geddes JR, Saunders KEA. Prevalence and incidence of clinical outcomes in patients presenting to secondary mental health care with mood instability and sleep disturbance. Eur Psychiatry. 2020;63(1):e59.

O'Donnell LA, Ellis AJ, Van de Loo MM, Stange JP, Axelson DA, Kowatch RA, et al. Mood instability as a predictor of clinical and functional outcomes in adolescents with bipolar I and bipolar II disorder. J Affect Disord. 2018;236:199–206.

Oliver MNI, Simons JS. The affective lability scales: development of a short-form measure. Pers Indiv Differ. 2004;37(6):1279–88.

Palmier-Claus JE, Berry K, Bucci S, Mansell W, Varese F. Relationship between childhood adversity and bipolar affective disorder: systematic review and meta-analysis. Br J Psychiatry. 2016;209(6):454–9.

Pataki C, Carlson GA. The comorbidity of ADHD and bipolar disorder: any less confusion? Curr Psychiatry Rep. 2013;15(7):372.

Patel R, Lloyd T, Jackson R, Ball M, Shetty H, Broadbent M, et al. Mood instability is a common feature of mental health disorders and is associated with poor clinical outcomes. BMJ Open. 2015;5(5):e007504.

Pavlova B, Perlis RH, Alda M, Uher R. Lifetime prevalence of anxiety disorders in people with bipolar disorder: a systematic review and meta-analysis. Lancet Psychiatry. 2015;2(8):710–7.

Pearlson GD. Etiologic, phenomenologic, and endophenotypic overlap of schizophrenia and bipolar disorder. Annu Rev Clin Psychol. 2015;11(1):251–81.

Ringen PA, Melle I, Birkenaes AB, Engh JA, Faerden A, Jónsdóttir H, et al. Illicit drug use in patients with psychotic disorders compared with that in the general population: a cross-sectional study. Acta Psychiatr Scand. 2008;117(2):133–8.

Santelmann H, Franklin J, Busshoff J, Baethge C. Test-retest reliability of schizoaffective disorder compared with schizophrenia, bipolar disorder, and unipolar depression—a systematic review and meta-analysis. Bipolar Disord. 2015;17(7):753–68.

Santelmann H, Franklin J, Busshoff J, Baethge C. Interrater reliability of schizoaffective disorder compared with schizophrenia, bipolar disorder, and unipolar depression—a systematic review and meta-analysis. Schizophr Res. 2016;176(2–3):357–63.

Saunders JB, Aasland OG, Babor TF, de la Fuente JR, Grant M. Development of the alcohol use disorders identification test (AUDIT): WHO collaborative project on early detection of persons with harmful alcohol consumption-II. Addiction. 1993;88(6):791–804.

Saunders KEA, Jones T, Perry A, Di Florio A, Craddock N, Jones I, et al. The influence of borderline personality traits on clinical outcomes in bipolar disorder. Bipolar Disord. 2020;23:368.

Tamminga CA, Ivleva EI, Keshavan MS, Pearlson GD, Clementz BA, Witte B, et al. Clinical phenotypes of psychosis in the bipolar-schizophrenia network on intermediate phenotypes (B-SNIP). Am J Psychiatry. 2013;170(11):1263–74.

Tesli M, Espeseth T, Bettella F, Mattingsdal M, Aas M, Melle I, et al. Polygenic risk score and the psychosis continuum model. Acta Psychiatr Scand. 2014;130(4):311–7.

Van Os J, Kapur S. Schizophrenia. The Lance. 2009;374(9690):635–45.

Verdolini N, Menculini G, Perugi G, Murru A, Samalin L, Angst J, Azorin JM, Bowden C, Mosolov S, Young AH, Barbuti M, Popovic D, Vieta E, Pacchiarotti I, for the BRIDGE-II-MIX Study Group. Sultans of swing: a reappraisal of the intertwined association between affective lability and mood reactivity in a post hoc analysis of the BRIDGE-II-MIX study. J Clin Psychiatry. 2019;80(2):17m12082.

Widing L, Simonsen C, Flaaten CB, Haatveit B, Vik RK, Wold KF, Åsbø G, Ueland T, Melle I. Symptom profiles in psychotic disorder not otherwise specified. Front Psychiatry. 2020.

Winkler D, Pjrek E, Heiden A, Wiesegger G, Klein N, Konstantinidis A, et al. Gender differences in the psychopathology of depressed inpatients. Eur Arch Psychiatry Clin Neurosci. 2004;254(4):209–14.

Young RC, Biggs JT, Ziegler VE, Meyer DA. A rating scale for mania: reliability, validity and sensitivity. Br J Psychiatry. 1978;133:429–35.

Zwicker A, Drobinin V, MacKenzie LE, Howes Vallis E, Patterson VC, Cumby J, et al. Affective lability in offspring of parents with major depressive disorder, bipo lar disorder and schizophrenia. Eur Child Adolesc Psychiatry. 2019;29:445–51.

6

Diagnostic stability in children and adolescents with bipolar disorder, a nationwide register-based study

Mathilde Frahm Laursen[1,2,7*], Rasmus W. Licht[1,2], Christoph U. Correll[3,4,5,6], Tobias Kallehauge[1], Ann-Eva Christensen[1], Maria Rodrigo-Domingo[1] and René Ernst Nielsen[1,2]

Abstract

Background: Diagnostic stability of bipolar disorder (BD) in children and adolescents, beyond the first contact has been investigated sparsely. The aim of this study was to investigate the diagnostic stability of BD in children and adolescents using over two decades of nationwide register-based data, and to examine factors associated with change from BD to schizophrenia (ICD-10: F20.x), schizoaffective disorder (ICD-10: F25.x) or other primary psychotic disorders (ICD-10 F23.x–24.x and F28.x–29.x).

Methods: Danish register-based data for all incident BD patients diagnosed prior to age 18 years, between January 1st 1995 and December 31st 2014 (N = 519). We graphically illustrated diagnostic change at different follow-up times and studied variables associated with diagnostic change after 3-year follow-up using Poisson regression with robust standard error estimates.

Results: The diagnosis of incident BD was relatively stable. The diagnosis did not change for 93% of those followed for at least 6 months, and remained unchanged for 86% and 73% of those followed at least 3 years and 10 years, respectively. In patients followed for at least 3 years after index BD (N = 478), the risk of diagnostic change was 61% higher in males versus females. The risk of diagnostic change for patients diagnosed during hospitalization was 74% higher compared to patients diagnosed at outpatient clinics/emergency rooms. The risk of diagnostic change for patients abusing substances other than alcohol and cannabis was 173% higher compared to patients not abusing such substances. The risk of diagnostic change for patients previously diagnosed with schizophrenia or related diagnosis was 257% higher compared to patients not having been diagnosed with such diagnosis previously, while the risk of diagnostic change in offspring of parents with schizophrenia or related diagnosis was 126% higher compared to patients who did not have parents diagnosed with such disorders.

Conclusion: Overall, the stability of the BD diagnosis in the Danish nationwide healthcare registers was high. Factors associated with risk of diagnostic change within 3 years of the initial diagnosis were being male, diagnosis given during hospitalization, substance abuse other than alcohol and cannabis, and a prior diagnosis of schizophrenia or related diagnosis in the patient or in their parents.

Keywords: Bipolar disorder, Child, Adolescent, Early-onset, Diagnostic stability

*Correspondence: mafro@rn.dk
[7] Unit for Psychiatric Research, Department of Psychiatry, Aalborg University Hospital, Mølleparkvej 10, 9000 Aalborg, Denmark
Full list of author information is available at the end of the article

Background

When following patients with bipolar disorder (BD) longitudinally, a diagnostic change might indicate either a progression of illness course or a prior lack of diagnostic precision. For example, it has been shown that primary psychotic disorders, i.e., psychotic non-affective disorders, like schizophrenia (SCZ), can have an illness trajectory that develops over a substantial period of time (Salvatore et al. 2012; Bromet et al. 2011).

In the study by Fenning et al. diagnostic stability was defined as the degree to which the original diagnosis is confirmed at follow-up (1994), and in some studies the diagnostic stability has been ascertained by measuring the positive predictive value of the onset-diagnosis compared to the follow-up-diagnosis (Amin et al. 1999). Several studies have estimated the diagnostic stability of adult-onset BD (Fennig et al. 1994; Amin et al. 1999; Marneros et al. 1991; Chen et al. 1998). A register-based study of adults diagnosed with BD during the first psychiatric contact [median age at first contact = 49.0 years (quartiles: 25.1–62.8)] with up to 9 years follow-up, showed that 31.2% had changed diagnosis during follow-up at the 10th contact, with the majority (12.9%) changing to SCZ, schizotypal disorder, and delusional disorders (Kessing 2005). The authors further showed that the stability of the incident BD diagnosis among adults ranged from 85.4% at second contact to 68.8% at the 10th contact, however, information on time related to the contacts was not provided.

In children and adolescents with bipolar disorder, called early-onset BD (EOBD), the diagnostic validity of EOBD has been called into question (Blader and Carlson 2007; Moreno et al. 2007). Despite this debate about EOBD, the stability of single manic episode and BD diagnoses has only been investigated sparsely in youth. Geller et al. (2000) found in 2000 that 85.7% of their cohort of children and adolescents diagnosed with BD as per DSM-IV (American Psychiatric Association 2000) (mean age at baseline was = 10.9 ± 2.7 years) continued to have that diagnosis at the 6-months follow-up, however, the authors did not conduct long-time follow-up. In a register-based study from 2014 by Kessing et al. (2015) the authors showed that 144 children and adolescents aged up to 19 years [median age at first contact = 17.4 years (quartiles: 16.3–18.2)] who were diagnosed with BD at first contact had a diagnostic stability of 76–83% from first to fifth contact, mean follow-up of 1.31 years (quartiles: 0.65–2.48 years). However, in addition to the scarcity of data about the diagnostic stability of BD in patients below age 18 years, detailed and longitudinal information about the change from BD to SCZ, schizoaffective disorder and other primary psychotic disorders are currently missing in this age group.

Thus, the aim of this study was to investigate the degree of diagnostic change in register-defined BD and to explore potential factors for such change in patients below age 18 years.

Methods

Design

This was a Danish nationwide register-based cohort study of BD included in the period January 1st, 1995 to December 31st, 2014 followed until April 28th, 2017. Potential factors for a diagnostic change within 3 years of index BD diagnosis were investigated. The contact leading to the first ever BD diagnosis is in the text referred to as the index.

Sample

The cohort consisted of children and adolescents with a first ever diagnosis of a single hypomanic episode, a single manic episode or BD (ICD-10: F30.x–F31.x) (World Health Organization 1992) during the age of 5–17 years who were registered in the Danish National Patient Register (NPR) (Lynge et al. 2011).

Registers utilized

The Civil Registration System uses a ten digit unique person identification number (CPR-number) assigned to all Danish citizens upon birth or immigration that allows linking data from different registries (Pedersen 2011). The Civil Registration System contains information on family relationships, and whether the person had emigrated, was missing, or had died at the end of the study period. The Danish Psychiatric Central Research Register (DPCRR) (Mors et al. 2011) contains information on all psychiatric contacts in Denmark from 1969 and onward. The Danish National Patient Register (NPR) (Lynge et al. 2011) contains information from 1977 and onward concerning every contact with any type of hospital in Denmark, including psychiatric hospitals from 1995.

Measures

Outcomes

The main outcome was diagnostic change from BD to any of the following ICD-10 diagnoses: schizophrenia (F20.x), schizoaffective disorder (F25.x) and other primary psychotic disorders (F23.x–24.x and F28.x–29.x) investigated at six different time-points.

The secondary outcome was potential risk factors associated with diagnostic change from BD to schizophrenia (ICD-10: F20.x), schizoaffective disorder (ICD-10: F25.x), or other primary psychotic disorders (ICD-10: F23.x–24.x and F28.x–29.x) for patients followed at least 3 years after index. Patients who received a different diagnosis (i.e. ICD-10: F20.x, 23.x–25.x and 28–29.x) during follow-up are referred to as the *group with diagnostic change,* while those who did not are referred to as the *group with unchanged BD.*

Procedure

We identified all patients receiving a first ever BD diagnosis and computed their follow-up time after index. We investigated the proportion of remaining patients with a stable BD diagnosis as well as those changing to SCZ, schizoaffective disorder (SA), and other primary psychotic disorders (psychosis not otherwise specified, PNOS) at 6 months, 1 year, 2 years, 3 years, 5 years, and 10 years from index. When relevant, we also present the percentage of patients changing between diagnostic groups (e.g. from PNOS to SCZ). The study sample diminished over time due to administrative censoring.

We described the entire sample at baseline, and investigated potential factors for diagnostic change 3 years after index among the demographic and clinical factors described in the section below. Utilizing anonymized healthcare register-data prohibited us from publishing data in which single patients could be identified, therefore variables or frequency strata containing information on less than four patients and aggregated data based on less than five patients are not shown.

We did not specifically investigate if patients had another diagnostic change back to BD again, after an initial diagnostic change from BD to SCZ, SA and PNOS, nor did we investigate if they had been given other comorbid psychiatric diagnoses in the study period after the initial diagnostic change, as this was not within the scope of the study.

Demographic and clinical factors

Sex

Sex was defined according to the CPR register (Pedersen 2011).

Psychiatric family history

History of psychiatric disorders in the parents was retrieved from the NPR and the DPCRR (Mors et al. 2011) and categorized into: (1) schizophrenia or related diagnoses (ICD-8: 295, 297, 298 excl. 298.0 and 298.1, 299 (World Health Organization 1967) and ICD-10: F20.x–F29.x (World Health Organization 1992), (2) Affective disorders (ICD-8: 296, 298.0, 298.1, 300.4 (World Health Organization 1967) and ICD-10: F30.x–F39.x (World Health Organization 1992), (3) Substance abuse [ICD-8: 291, 294.3, 303, 304 (World Health Organization 1967) and ICD-10: F.10.x–F19.x (World Health Organization 1992)], (4) Other psychiatric disorders (ICD-8: 291 to 315 (excluding the above mentioned) (World Health Organization 1967) and ICD-10: Fxx.x (excluding the above mentioned) (World Health Organization 1992) and [ICD-8: E950–E959, E980–E989 (World Health Organization 1967) and ICD-10: X60–X84, Y10–Y34 (World Health Organization 1992)]. The parents were followed from start of register until 1 year after the EOBD diagnosis of the child.

Age at first bipolar-spectrum diagnosis

Age at the index diagnosis was computed based on the date of birth and the date of first single hypomanic episode, single manic episode or first BD (ICD-10 F30.x/F31.x) (World Health Organization 1992), retrieving the diagnosis from the NPR (Lynge et al. 2011). Age at first bipolar-spectrum diagnosis was further dichotomized into EOBD: < 13 vs ≥ 13 years of age.

Age at first psychiatric contact

Data on age at first psychiatric contact were retrieved from the DPCRR (Mors et al. 2011) and the NPR (Lynge et al. 2011).

Psychiatric contacts were defined as being registered with a primary diagnosis of any psychiatric disorder [ICD-8: 291–315 (World Health Organization 1967) and ICD-10: Fxx.x (World Health Organization 1992)], or intentional self-harm acts [ICD-8: E950–E959, E980–E989 (World Health Organization 1967) and ICD-10: X60–X84, Y10–Y34 (World Health Organization 1992)].

Latest psychiatric diagnosis prior to BD diagnosis

Data on psychiatric contacts were retrieved from the NPR (Lynge et al. 2011) and the DPCRR (World Health Organization 1967) and categorized into: (1) schizophrenia or related diagnoses (ICD-8: 295, 297, 298 excl. 298.0 and 298.1, 299 (World Health Organization 1967) and ICD-10: F20.x–F29.x (World Health Organization 1992), (2) Affective disorders [ICD-8: 296, 298.0, 298.1, 300.4 (World Health Organization 1967) and ICD-10: F30.x–F39.x (World Health Organization 1992), (3) Substance abuse (ICD-8: 291, 294.3, 303, 304 (World Health Organization 1967)] and ICD-10: F.10.x–F19.x (World Health Organization 1992), (4) Other psychiatric disorders (ICD-8: 291 to 315 (excluding the above mentioned) (World Health Organization 1967) and ICD-10: Fxx.x (excluding the above mentioned) (World Health Organization 1992) and [ICD-8: E950–E959, E980–E989 (World Health Organization 1967) and ICD-10: X60–X84, Y10–Y34 (World Health Organization 1992)].

Substance abuse

Information on substance abuse was retrieved from the DPCRR (Mors et al. 2011) and the NPR (Lynge et al. 2011) and coded into two separate dichotomous variables with the possible levels of yes and no. The first variable was substance abuse of any type before or at time of first manic episode or first BD diagnosis, including alcohol (ICD-8: 291 and 303 (World Health Organization 1967) and ICD-10: F10.x) (World Health Organization 1992), cannabis (ICD-8 304.5 (World Health Organization 1967) and ICD-10: F12.x) (World Health Organization 1992), or substances other than alcohol or cannabis [ICD-8: 294.3, 304 excl. 304.5 (World Health Organization 1967) and ICD-10: F11.x, F13.x–F19.x] (World Health Organization 1992). The second variable was abuse of substances other than alcohol or cannabis (ICD-8: 294.3, 304 excl. 304.5 (World Health Organization 1967) and ICD-10: F11.x, F13.x–F19.x) (World Health Organization 1992) before or at time of first manic episode or first BD diagnosis.

Diagnostic setting

Data on first ever BD diagnosis were retrieved from the NPR (Lynge et al. 2011) and sub-divided into: (1) diagnosed during hospitalization or (2) diagnosed at outpatient clinic or in the emergency room (ER).

Period of diagnosis

The year of diagnosis was retrieved from the NPR (Lynge et al. 2011) and classified into two periods: (1) First BD diagnosis between January 1st 1995 and December 31st 2004, or (2) First ever BD diagnosis between January 1st 2005 and December 31st 2014, since the number of patients newly diagnosed with BD has increased substantially since 2005.

Psychotic BD diagnosis

When the first ever BD diagnosis was registered as psychotic BD (ICD-10: F30.2, F31.2 and F31.5) (World Health Organization 1992), dichotomized into yes/no.

Statistical analysis

Demographic and clinical data were described using total numbers and percentages or means and standard deviations, where appropriate.

The percentage of patients with a stable BD diagnosis and those changing to other diagnoses was illustrated graphically at different time-points. A sensitivity analysis was conducted excluding patients diagnosed with SCZ prior to first BD diagnosis.

Poisson regressions with robust standard errors were used to calculate the relative risk (Zou 2004) for diagnostic change between the groups of sex, abuse of alcohol and cannabis or other substances, diagnostic setting, psychotic BD diagnosis, year of diagnosis, latest psychiatric diagnosis prior to BD, psychiatric family history, respectively, as well as for an increase of one in the continuous variables age at first ever BD diagnosis, and age at first psychiatric contact, respectively. Results with $p<0.05$ were considered statistically significant.

Statistical analyses were performed with Stata 15 (StataCorp. 2017. Stata Statistical Software: Release 15. College Station, TX: StataCorp LLC).

Results

Baseline demographic and clinical characteristics for all children and adolescents with a first ever BD diagnosis between 1995 and 2014 (N = 519) as well as for those followed at least 3 years (N = 478) are present in Table 1. A lag of 1.5 years between the first psychiatric contact and first ever BD diagnosis was shown as well as only 7% of the sample being below age 13 years at time of first BD diagnosis (Table 1).

Diagnostic stability

Altogether, 519 patients received a first ever BD diagnosis during the study period. Within 6 months of the index diagnosis, 3% had changed diagnosis to SCZ, 1% to SA, and 3% to PNOS. The percentages that changed diagnosis at 1, 2, 3, and 5 years were similar, but were slightly higher for those followed at least 10 years (see Fig. 1).

Figure 1 shows transitions from BD to the specific diagnoses of SCZ, SA or PNOS after 6 months, 1, 2, 3, 5 and 10 years. Results show that only a minor proportion changed from PNOS or SA to SCZ over time, and almost none changed diagnosis from PNOS to SA. Furthermore, diagnostic change from BD to SA or PNOS was relatively rare. Diagnostic change from BD to PNOS was at most 6%, being 4% or less at all time-points for conversions from BD to SA. Most of the patients who changed diagnosis from BD did so to SCZ, and after 10 years of follow-up, 17% of the available sample (n = 169) had changed diagnosis to SCZ. Still, the majority (73%) of the patients with initial BD diagnoses did not change diagnosis even 10 years after the index BD diagnosis.

Our sensitivity analyses showed that excluding patients diagnosed with SCZ prior to the first ever BD diagnosis did not change percentages presented in Fig. 1 substantially (data not shown).

Altogether, 478 patients (92.1% of the original sample) were followed for at least 3 years. Of those patients, 86% continued to have an BD diagnosis whereas 14% had changed diagnosis to SCZ, SA or PNOS (Fig. 1). Forty-one patients were followed for less than < 3 years and had a mean ± SD follow-up time of 2.39 ± 0.74 years. Of those, 11 children and adolescents changed diagnosis from BD to SCZ, SA or PNOS.

Factors associated with diagnostic change

Table 2 presents the number and percentages for the examined factors in the group with an unchanged BD diagnosis and in the group with a diagnostic change at 3 years follow-up, as well as the RR of a diagnostic change.

Table 1 Characteristics of bipolar disorder (BD) in children and adolescents between 1995 and 2014

Variables	Total population included		Total population with 3-year follow-up	
	N	%	N	%
Children and adolescents with BD	519	100	478	92
Sex (females)	299	58	274	57
Family history of psychiatric disorders	162	32	–[a]	–[a]
Family history of bipolar disorder	57	11	–[a]	–[a]
Substance abuse total	53	10	48	10
Substance abuse, other than alcohol and cannabis	25	5	23	5
Diagnostic setting				
Inpatient	201	39	188	39
Outpatient	318	61	290	61
Psychotic BD at index	92	18	90	19
Index BD prior to 2005	131	25	130	27
Index BD < 13 years	36	7	32	7
Latest psychiatric diagnosis prior to BD				
Schizophrenia or related diagnosis	93	18	86	18
Affective disorders	130	25	117	24
Substance abuse	40	8	37	8
Other psychiatric disorders	286	55	263	55
Information about parents				
Schizophrenia or related diagnosis	44	9	–[a]	–[a]
Affective disorders	111	22	–[a]	–[a]
Substance abuse	77	15	–[a]	–[a]
Other psychiatric disorders	9	2	–[a]	–[a]
Variables	**Mean**	**SD**	**Mean**	**SD**
Age at first ever BD	15.9	2.1	15.9	2.1
Age at first psychiatric contact	14.4	3.6	14.3	3.6

[a] Numbers could not be reported in order to comply with the data protection rules set by Statistics Denmark in order to avoid allowing identification of individual patients in cells containing ≤ 5 patients

In patients followed for at least 3 years after index BD (N = 478), males had a RR = 1.61 (95% CI (1.03; 2.53), p = 0.038) for a diagnostic change compared to females. Patients diagnosed during hospitalization had a RR = 1.74 (95% CI 1.11; 2.73), p = 0.015) for a diagnostic change compared to patients diagnosed at outpatient clinics/ER. Patients abusing substances other than alcohol and cannabis had a RR = 2.73 (95% CI (1.48; 5.02) p = 0.001) for a diagnostic change compared to patients not abusing such substances. Patients previously diagnosed with SCZ or related disorder had a RR = 3.57 (95% CI (2.33; 5.47), p < 0.001) for a changing diagnosis, compared to patients who had not been diagnosed with SCZ previously. Patients whose parents had previously been diagnosed with a SCZ or a related diagnosis had a RR = 2.26 (95% CI (1.32; 3.90) p = 0.003) for a diagnostic change compared to patients without parents with SCZ or a related diagnosis (Table 2).

Discussion

Our investigation of the long-term diagnostic stability of BD according to the Danish registers showed that among patients with follow-up information 93% of the diagnoses were stable after 6 months, 90% after 1 year, 86% after 2 and 3 years, 83% after 5 years, and 73% after 10 years, respectively.

The stability of BD in the Danish registers was investigated previously by Kessing et al. (2015), who in the period from 1994 to 2012 in a cohort of 354 children and adolescents (age 0–19 years) found that, at their second psychiatric contact, 79.6% out of 98 patients continued to have a BD diagnosis and at fifth contact 77.3% out of 22 patients with follow-up information still had the BD diagnosis. The results by Kessing et al. (2015) resemble the findings in the current study although the time intervals between visits are not reported by Kessing et al. (2015) and we only know that the total follow-up time

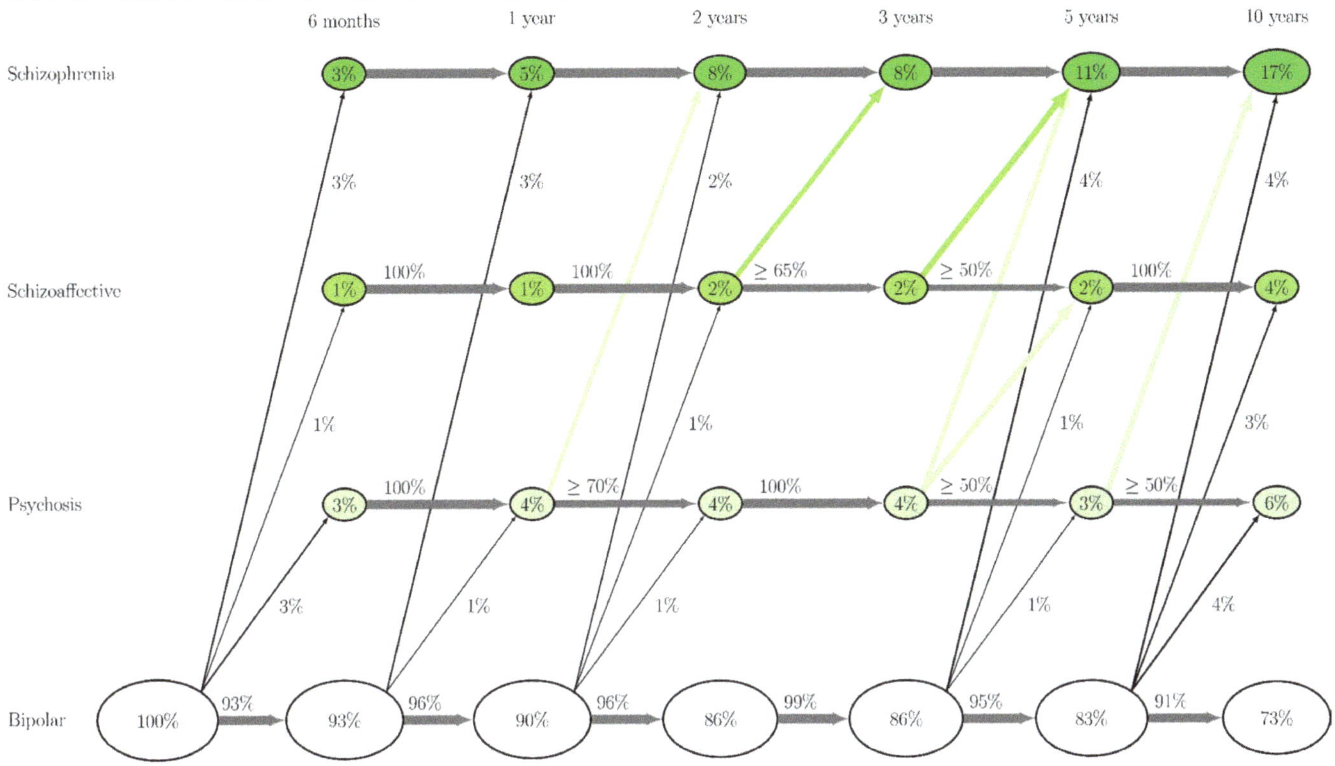

Fig. 1 Percentages of patients who changed diagnosis and patients continuing to have the diagnosis latest given to them. Percentages are computed using the number of patients available in the sample at each time point (N = 519 at baseline, N = 478 at 3 years follow-up, N = 169 at 10 years follow-up). The sum of the percentages in the ovals for each time point is 100%, as is the sum of the arrow percentages (both horizontal and rightwards), except for rounding errors. Arrows representing less than four patients are depicted as green arrows without percentages if originating from Psychosis (PNOS) or Schizoaffective (SA) groups, or not represented at all if originating from Bipolar (BD) group

was longer than 2.5 years for only 25% of the sample. Therefore, a direct comparison between the results from our study with the results of the second, third and fourth visits in the study by Kessing et al. (2015) were not possible, although both studies present supporting evidence of high diagnostic stability of the BD diagnosis in the Danish registers.

Furthermore, Kessing et al. found that 3.1% at the second contact, increasing to 4.6% at the fifth contact, had changed diagnostically to SCZ or a related diagnosis (ICD-10 F20.x–29.x). However, that study did not investigate the proportions who changed from BD to SCZ specifically. Therefore, the findings in the current study demonstrating that 3% had changed diagnosis to SCZ after 6 months and 17% after 10 years cannot be directly compared to findings by Kessing et al. (2015).

The risk of diagnostic change was significantly higher for (1) males than females, (2) in-patients compared to outpatients and patients diagnosed in the ER, (3) patients who were using substances other than alcohol and cannabis, (4) patients diagnosed with a SCZ or related diagnosis before index BD, and (5) patients with parents who had been previously diagnosed with a SCZ or related diagnosis. Diagnostic change might have been a consequence of illness progression with patients fulfilling the diagnostic criteria for ICD-10 BD at time of first ever BD diagnosis, and with a further progression in the psychopathology later on, leading to the diagnostic shift to PNOS, SA or SCZ seen at later contacts. The findings could also be a results of patients being misdiagnosed with BD in the first place due to an overlap of symptoms (Murray et al. 2004). However, notably, psychotic BD was not a significant factor for a diagnostic shift to SCZ or a related disorder. Nevertheless, affective disturbances have been shown to be a part of the SCZ prodrome (Cornblatt et al. 2003) and, as such, symptoms of a SCZ prodrome could potentially be misdiagnosed as BD. Why males had a higher risk for changing diagnosis than females at the 3 year follow-up is unclear, but could be ascribed to the fact that males develop SCZ at an earlier age than females (Usall et al. 2002). Indeed, males might have fulfilled diagnostic criteria for BD at baseline, but due to illness progression, a substantial proportion would have fulfilled diagnostic criteria for a SCZ or related diagnosis 3 years after first BD diagnosis.

Table 2 Bipolar disorder (BD) in children and adolescents with and without diagnostic change after 3 years of follow-up (N = 478)

	Group with unchanged BD (N = 412) N (%)	Group with diagnostic change (N = 66) N (%)	RR (95% CI)	*p* value
Sex				0.038
Female	244 (89.1%)	30 (10.9%)		
Male	168 (82.4%)	36 (17.6%)	1.61 (1.03; 2.53)	
Family history of psychiatric disorder				0.310
No	–[a] (87%)	–[a] (13%)		
Yes	–[a] (84%)	–[a] (16%)	1.27 (0.80; 2.03)	
Family history of BD				0.629
No	–[a] (86%)	–[a] (14%)		
Yes	–[a] (88%)	–[a] (12%)	0.82 (0.37; 1.18)	
Substance abuse (total)				0.286
No	373 (86.7%)	57 (13.3%)		
Yes	39 (81.3%)	9 (18.8%)	1.41 (0.75; 2.68)	
Substance abuse of other than alcohol and cannabis				0.001
No	397 (87.3%)	58 (12.7%)		
Yes	15 (65.2%)	8 (34.8%)	2.73 (1.48; 5.02)	
Diagnostic setting				0.015
Outpatient or ER	259 (89.3%)	31 (10.7%)		
Inpatient	153 (81.4%)	35 (18.6%)	1.74 (1.11; 2.73)	
Psychotic BD at index				0.055
No	340 (87.6%)	48 (12.4%)		
Yes	72 (80.0%)	18 (20.0%)	1.62 (0.99; 2.64)	
Index BD prior to 2005				0.988
No	300 (86.2%)	48 (13.8%)		
Yes	112 (86.2%)	18 (13.8%)	1.00 (0.61; 1.66)	
Index BD < 13 years				
No	384 (86.1%)	62 (13.9%)		
Yes	> 27 (–%)[1]	< 5 (–%)[1]	–[a]	–[a]
Latest psychiatric diagnosis prior to BD				
Schizophrenia or related diagnosis				< 0.0001
No	355 (90.6%)	37 (9.4%)		
Yes	57 (66.3%)	29 (33.7%)	3.57 (2.33; 5.47)	
Affective disorders				0.568
No	313 (86.7%)	48 (13.3%)		
Yes	99 (84.6%)	18 (15.4%)	1.16 (0.70; 1.91)	
Substance abuse				0.655
No	381 (86.4%)	60 (13.6%)		
Yes	31 (83.8%)	6 (16.2%)	1.19 (0.55; 2.57)	
Other psychiatric disorders				0.134
No	191 (88.8%)	24 (11.2%)		
Yes	221 (84.0%)	42 (16.0%)	1.43 (0.90; 2.29)	
Information about parents (N = 473)				
Schizophrenia or related diagnosis				0.003
No	–[a] (88%)	–[a] (12%)		
Yes	–[a] (72%)	–[a] (28%)	2.26 (1.32; 3.90)	
Affective disorders				0.680
No	–[a] (87%)	–[a] (13%)		

Table 2 (continued)

	Group with unchanged BD (N=412) N (%)	Group with diagnostic change (N=66) N (%)	RR (95% CI)	*p* value
Yes	–[a] (85%)	–[a] (15%)	1.12 (0.66; 1.91)	
Substance abuse				0.928
No	–[a] (86%)	–[a] (14%)		
Yes	–[a] (86%)	–[a] (14%)	1.03 (0.55; 1.92)	
Other psychiatric disorders				0.438
No	–[a] (86%)	–[a] (14%)		
Yes	–[a] (>55%)	–[a] (<45%)	1.64 (0.47; 5.68)	
	Mean (SD)	**Mean (SD)**	**RR (95% CI)**	**p-value**
Age at first ever BD diagnosis (N=478)	15.9 (2.1)	16.0 (2.1)	1.01 (0.91; 1.13)	0.857
Age at first psychiatric contact (N=478)	14.4 (3.5)	14.0 (4.3)	0.98 (0.92; 1.04)	0.465

[a] The exact numbers could not be reported in order to comply with the data protection rules set by Statistics Denmark in order to avoid allowing identification of individual patients in cells containing ≤ 5 patients

Lastly, BD can be more difficult to diagnose in children and adolescents than in adults, as reflected in two similar studies using different age groups by Kessing et al. (2005, 2015) who found that only 40.7% of children and adolescents got a diagnosis of mania or BD at first in- or outpatient contact in contrast to 56.2% of adults. In the current study the vast majority of the sample was diagnosed with an incident BD registry diagnosis between 13 and 18 years of age, making the study mostly comparable to other studies investigating BD in adolescents. However, future studies should focus of identifying symptoms that overlap, characteristics with the highest specificity for a diagnostically stable BD, or a diagnostically stable SCZ disorder diagnosis, and predictors of diagnostic change from BD to SCZ.

Strengths and limitations

The results of this study need to be interpreted in light of several limitations. First, we investigated only false positives, but not false negatives, i.e., to what degree patients are misdiagnosed and there is a substantial delay between the actual illness onset and the diagnosis of BD in children and adolescents. Second, we only investigated if patients with BD had diagnostic change to a SCZ, SA or PNOS, but we did not investigate all diagnoses given subsequently. It is possible to receive another BD diagnosis after a SCZ, SA or PNOS diagnosis, but we considered this as unlikely and therefore we did not investigate this issue. In a study by Laursen et al. (2019), using the Danish registers, it was found that only 2.3% of children and adolescents below age 18 years changed diagnosis from SCZ to BD during the study period (1995–2014). Third, we did not investigate comorbidities. After receiving a BD diagnosis, patients might later on be referred to psychiatric care primarily due to an ICD-10 F4.x diagnosis, e.g. anxiety (Faedda et al. 2014; Duffy et al. 2016), however, such conditions are frequently comorbid with BD, for which reason, BD would still be present. Fourth, we included single hypomanic episode and single manic episode as part of BD since we believed that a single hypomanic episode or a single manic episode will most likely be followed by another mood episode (Kessing 2005; Goodwin 2002). Fifth, there is a possibility of underreporting of the true incidence of BD because a proportion of BD might be misdiagnosed with e.g. major depression (Lish et al. 1994; Hirschfeld et al. 2003). Furthermore, the registry reflects clinical practice and is influenced by referral to hospital-based psychiatry as well as diagnostic culture. Sixth, we were unable to ascertain the true sensitivity as well as specificity of the BD diagnosis in the register because there is no information about the false and true negatives. Finally, results may not fully generalize to other countries, regions and health care systems, which is why similar studies are needed in other areas of the world. In the current study only few changed diagnostic group to PNOS and SA, thus, it was not possible to analyze whether factors associated with increased risk of diagnostic change would differ in those groups, compared to what was shown in Table 2. Lastly, in the current dataset we do not have SES data available and as such we were unable to investigate the effects thereof on diagnostic change.

Despite these limitations, this study has also several strengths. First, we used population-based nationwide registers and, since public healthcare in Denmark is free of charge, we included all patients diagnosed with BD without exclusion based on socioeconomic status or geographical location, as is the case in some insurance database healthcare studies. Second, the study had minimal loss to follow-up owing to the mandatory reporting of all data on in-patients and out-patients to the Danish health care registers. Third, we have been able to follow the majority of patients for at least 3 years after index and a quite large proportion for up to 10 years, which to our knowledge is the longest follow-up period investigating the diagnostic stability of BD.

Conclusion

The diagnosis of the BD in the Danish registers is relatively stable. The risk for diagnostic change from BD to SCZ, SA, or PNOS 3 years after first ever BD diagnosis are higher for males, inpatients, patients who had a SCZ or related diagnosis prior to first ever BD diagnosis, patients using substances other than alcohol and cannabis, and for patients whose parents had received a SCZ or related diagnosis. These risk factors should be considered and used in the screening and diagnostic practice as well as when following patients with BD longitudinally.

Abbreviations

Diagnoses-related

EOBD: Early-onset bipolar disorder; BD: Bipolar disorder; SA: Schizoaffective disorder; SCZ: Schizophrenia; PNOS: Psychosis not otherwise specified (other primary psychotic disorders).

Regarding statistics

SD: Standard deviations; RR: Relative risk.

Regarding the registers used

DPCRR: Danish Psychiatric Central Research Register; NPR: National Patient Register; CPR: Central Person Register (Civil registration System).

General

ER: Emergency room.

Acknowledgements

Thanks to Martin Kamp Dalgaard, B.Sc., for helping with presenting data graphically.

Authors' contributions

MFL, REN, MRD drafted the manuscript. TK, MRD, AC analyzed the patient data. MFL, REN, AC, MRD interpreted the data. REN, RWL, AC, MRD, CUC revised the manuscript. All authors read and approved the final manuscript.

Competing interests

MF. Laursen has reported no biomedical financial interests or potential conflicts of interest. M. Rodrigo-Domingo has reported no biomedical financial interests or potential conflicts of interest. A-E. Christensen has reported no biomedical financial interests or potential conflicts of interest. T. Kallehauge has reported no biomedical financial interests or potential conflicts of interest. R.W. Licht has received research grant from Glaxo Smith Kline, honoraria for lecturing from Pfizer, Glaxo Smith Kline, Eli Lilly, Astra-Zeneca, Bristol-Myers Squibb, Janssen Cilag, Lundbeck, Otsuka, Servier and honoraria from advisory board activity from Glaxo Smith Kline, Eli Lilly, Astra-Zeneca, Bristol-Myers Squibb, Janssen Cilag, and Sunovion. C.U. Correll has been a consultant and/or advisor to or has received honoraria from: Alkermes, Allergan, Angelini, Boehringer-Ingelheim, Gerson Lehrman Group, Indivior, IntraCellular Therapies, Janssen/J&J, LB Pharma, Lundbeck, Medavante, Medscape, Merck, Neurocrine, Noven, Otsuka, Pfizer, ROVI, Servier, Sunovion, Supernus, Takeda, and Teva. He has provided expert testimony for Bristol-Myers Squibb, Janssen, and Otsuka. He served on a Data Safety Monitoring Board for Boehringer-Ingelheim, Lundbeck, ROVI, Supernus, and Teva. He received royalties from UpToDate and grant support from Janssen and Takeda. He is also a shareholder of LB Pharma. R.E. Nielsen has received research grants from H. Lundbeck and Otsuka Pharmaceuticals for clinical trials, received speaking fees from Bristol-Myers Squibb, Astra Zeneca, Janssen & Cilag, Lundbeck, Servier, Otsuka Pharmaceuticals, and Eli Lilly and has acted as advisor to Astra Zeneca, Eli Lilly, Lundbeck, Otsuka Pharmaceuticals, Takeda, and Medivir.

Author details

[1] Psychiatry, Aalborg University Hospital, Aalborg, Denmark. [2] Department of Clinical Medicine, Aalborg University, Aalborg, Denmark. [3] Department of Psychiatry, The Zucker Hillside Hospital, Northwell Health, 75-59 263rd Street, Glen Oaks, New York City, NY, USA. [4] Department of Psychiatry and Molecular Medicine, Donald and Barbara Zucker School of Medicine at Hofstra/Northwell, Hempstead, NY, USA. [5] Center for Psychiatric Neuroscience, The Feinstein Institute for Medical Research, Manhasset, NY, USA. [6] Department of Child and Adolescent Psychiatry, Charité Universitätsmedizin, Berlin, Germany. [7] Unit for Psychiatric Research, Department of Psychiatry, Aalborg University Hospital, Mølleparkvej 10, 9000 Aalborg, Denmark.

References

American Psychiatric Association. Diagnostic and statistical manual of mental disorders: DSM-IV-TR. Washington DC: American Psychiatric Association; 2000.

Amin S, Singh SP, Brewin J, Jones PB, Medley I, Harrison G. Diagnostic stability of first-episode psychosis. Comparison of ICD-10 and DSM-III-R systems. Br J Psychiatry. 1999;175:537–43.

Blader JC, Carlson GA. Increased rates of bipolar disorder diagnoses among U.S. child, adolescent, and adult inpatients, 1996–2004. Biol Psychiatry. 2007;62(2):107–14.

Bromet EJ, Kotov R, Fochtmann LJ, et al. Diagnostic shifts during the decade following first admission for psychosis. Am J Psychiatry. 2011;168(11):1186–94. https://doi.org/10.1176/appi.ajp.2011.11010048.

Chen YR, Swann AC, Johnson BA. Stability of diagnosis in bipolar disorder. J Nerv Ment Dis. 1998;186(1):17–23.

Cornblatt BA, Lencz T, Smith CW, Correu CU, Auther AM, Nakayama E. The schizophrenia prodrome revisited: a neurodevelopmental perspective. Schizophr Bull. 2003;29(4):633–51.

Duffy A, Jones S, Goodday S, Bentall R. Candidate risks indicators for bipolar disorder: early intervention opportunities in high-risk youth. Int J Neuropsychopharmacol. 2016;19(1):pyv071. https://doi.org/10.1093/ijnp/pyv071.

Faedda GL, Serra G, Marangoni C, et al. Clinical risk factors for bipolar disorders: a systematic review of prospective studies. J Affect Disord. 2014;168:314–21. https://doi.org/10.1016/j.jad.2014.07.013.

Fennig S, Kovasznay B, Rich C, et al. Six-month stability of psychiatric diagnoses in first-admission patients with psychosis. Am J Psychiatry. 1994;151(8):1200–8. https://doi.org/10.1176/ajp.151.8.1200.

Geller B, Zimerman B, Williams M, et al. Six-month stability and outcome of a prepubertal and early adolescent bipolar disorder phenotype. J Child Adolesc Psychopharmacol. 2000;10(3):165–73. https://doi.org/10.1089/10445460050167278.

Goodwin G. Hypomania: what's in a name? Br J Psychiatry. 2002;181(02):94–5. https://doi.org/10.1017/S000712500016177X.

Hirschfeld RMA, Lewis L, Vornik LA. Perceptions and impact of bipolar disorder: how far have we really come? Results of the national depressive and manic-depressive association 2000 survey of individuals with bipolar disorder. J Clin Psychiatry. 2003;64(2):161–74.

Kessing LV. Diagnostic stability in bipolar disorder in clinical practise as according to ICD-10. J Affect Disord. 2005;85(3):293–9.

Kessing LV, Vradi E, Kragh Andersen P. Diagnostic stability in pediatric bipolar disorder. J Affect Disord. 2015;172C:417–21.

Laursen M, Valentin JB, Licht RW, Correll CU, Nielsen RE. Longitudinal outcomes in pediatric- and adult-onset bipolar patients compared to healthy and schizophrenia controls. Bipolar Disord. 2019. https://doi.org/10.1111/bdi.12793.

Lish JD, Dime-Meenan S, Whybrow PC, Price RA, Hirschfeld RM. The National Depressive and Manic-depressive Association (DMDA) survey of bipolar members. J Affect Disord. 1994;31(4):281–94.

Lynge E, Sandegaard JL, Rebolj M. The Danish National Patient Register. Scand J Public Health. 2011;39(7 Suppl):30–3. https://doi.org/10.1177/14034 94811401482.

Marneros A, Deister A, Rohde A. Stability of diagnoses in affective, schizoaffective and schizophrenic disorders Cross-sectional versus longitudinal diagnosis. Eur Arch Psychiatry Clin Neurosci. 1991;241(3):187–92.

Moreno C, Laje G, Blanco C, Jiang H, Schmidt AB, Olfson M. National trends in the outpatient diagnosis and treatment of bipolar disorder in youth. Arch Gen Psychiatry. 2007;64(9):1032–9.

Mors O, Perto GP, Mortensen PB. The Danish Psychiatric Central Research Register. Scand J Public Health. 2011;39(7 Suppl):54–7. https://doi.org/10.1177/1403494810395825.

Murray RM, Sham P, Van Os J, Zanelli J, Cannon M, McDonald C. A developmental model for similarities and dissimilarities between schizophrenia and bipolar disorder. Schizophr Res. 2004;71(2–3):405–16. https://doi.org/10.1016/j.schres.2004.03.002.

Pedersen CB. The Danish Civil Registration System. Scand J Public Health. 2011;39(7 Suppl):22–5. https://doi.org/10.1177/1403494810387965.

Salvatore P, Baldessarini RJ, Tohen M, et al. McLean-harvard international first-episode project: two-year stability of ICD-10 diagnoses in 500 first-episode psychotic disorder patients. J Clin Psychiatry. 2012;72(2):183–93. https://doi.org/10.4088/JCP.09m05311yel.

Usall J, Haro JM, Ochoa S, Marquez M, Araya S. Influence of gender on social outcome in schizophrenia. Acta Psychiatr Scand. 2002;106(5):337–42. https://doi.org/10.1034/j.1600-0447.2002.01351.x.

World Health Organization. International classification of diseases (ICD-8). Geneva: Switzerland; 1967.

World Health Organization. International statistical classification of diseases and related health problems, 10th revision (ICD-10). Geneva: Switzerland; 1992.

World Health Organization. ICD-10 Classifications of Mental and Behavioural Disorder: Clinical Descriptions and Diagnostic Guidelines. Vol F00–F99. Geneva; 1992.

Zou G. A modified poisson regression approach to prospective studies with binary data. Am J Epidemiol. 2004;159(7):702–6. https://doi.org/10.1093/aje/kwh090.

7

Defining phenotypes of long-term lithium and valproate response, including combination therapy: a modified application of the Alda scale in patients with bipolar disorders

Jinyoung Lee[1], Ji Hyun Baek[1*†], Dongbin Lee[1], Sung Woo Ahn[1], So-Yung Yang[1,2], Yujin Choi[3], Yong Chun Bahk[1] and Kyung Sue Hong[1*†]

Abstract

Background: When evaluating the long-term treatment response to mood stabilizers using the Alda scale, mood stabilizer combination therapy is typically considered a confounding factor, and patients receiving combination therapy are excluded from the analysis. However, this may result in bias if those under combination therapy are worse treatment responders. This study aims to explore whether the Alda scale is applicable to patients taking lithium and valproate combination therapy. We compared long-term treatment response in patients receiving monotherapy and combination therapy of the two drugs, and investigated clinical correlates of the responses to each drug.

Methods: The study subjects consisted of 102 patients with bipolar I (BD-I) or bipolar II (BD-II) disorder who had been undergoing maintenance treatment with lithium and/or valproate for more than 2 years at a single specialized bipolar disorder clinic. Long-term treatment response was measured using the Alda scale and compared among the lithium monotherapy group, the valproate monotherapy group, and the mood stabilizer combination group. Clinical correlates of long-term treatment response were evaluated in lithium users and valproate users separately.

Results: There were no significant differences in terms of baseline illness characteristics among groups. The combination group showed the worst treatment response for all the response measurements applied. This group also had the higher rate of 'poor responder' with a statistically significant difference compared to valproate group. Older age at onset and (hypo)manic episode at onset showed significant positive associations with total Alda score in lithium users, while comorbid anxiety disorders, obsessive–compulsive disorder and mixed episode showed significant negative associations in valproate users.

Conclusions: The combination group had poorer long-term treatment response but did not show distinct clinical characteristics compared to the monotherapy groups. When exploring the long-term effects of mood stabilizers, excluding patients undergoing combination treatment could result in bias because they may represent a poor response group. The long-term treatment responses of lithium and valproate had different clinical correlates.

Keywords: Bipolar disorder, Long-term treatment response, Lithium, Valproate, Alda scale, Clinical correlates

*Correspondence: jihyunbaek@skku.edu; hongks@skku.edu
†Ji Hyun Baek and Kyung Sue Hong contributed equally to this article as co-corresponding authors
[1] Department of Psychiatry, Sungkyunkwan University School of Medicine, Samsung Medical Center, Seoul, Republic of Korea
Full list of author information is available at the end of the article

Background

Almost all patients with bipolar disorder (BD) require maintenance pharmacotherapy to prevent subsequent episodes, complications, and residual disabilities even after acute episodes (Grunze et al. 2018; Yatham et al.

2018). Lithium and valproate are commonly used for maintenance treatment of BD, and several newer drugs have been added to the list of first-line recommendations (Miura et al. 2014; Goodwin et al. 2016; Yatham et al. 2018). However, the clinical and biological correlates of long-term treatment response to individual mood stabilizers are not well-defined (Pisanu et al. 2018).

In the last decade, the feasibility of large-scale pharmacogenomic studies has rapidly increased, and the international Consortium on Lithium Genetics (ConLiGen) and other groups have tried to identify the genetic basis of responsiveness to mood stabilizers (Manchia et al. 2013; Rybakowski 2013; Hou et al. 2016; Zhu et al. 2017). Considering the recurrent and biphasic course of BD, exploration of the genetic and clinical factors associated with maintenance therapy requires long-term observation. Therefore, retrospective measurement in naturalistic clinical settings is inevitable. In addition, the need to incorporate clinical correlates into pharmacogenetic analyses has been recognized (Lin et al. 2018).

The most widely adopted measurement tool for long-term treatment response to mood stabilizers in BD is the Alda scale (Manchia et al. 2013). It retrospectively measures global treatment outcome (A score) and several confounding factors that affect treatment outcome (B score). The total score is a composite score acquired by subtracting B from A (Grof et al. 2002). Recently, it has been suggested that the Alda scale requires modification. Scott et al. (Scott et al. 2017, 2019) proposed a validity issue regarding use of a single scoring system for the B score for multiple heterogenous aspects of confounders. They suggested a machine-learning approch to overcome this problem. Other researchers used global outcome scores (A score) in subjects with comparable conditions in terms of confounding factors, i.e., among low B scorers (Lee et al. 2011; Chen et al. 2016; Hou et al. 2016). In addition, whether the effects of the numbers and frequencies of previous episodes before starting the index medication (reflected in B1 and B2) need to be controlled as confounding factors or included as target candidates of outcome predictors depends on the study purpose and design. If the study aims to explore predictors or correlates of drug response, the previous course needs to be included in the analysis as a main independent variable. In that case, the response measurement system of the Alda scale needs to be modified.

Another important issue to be considered when assessing the long-term response to mood stabilizers is the enrollment of patients who are treated with mood stabilizer combination therapy. Until recently, most pharmacological studies measuring long-term treatment response to specific mood stabilizers recruited patients undergoing monotherapy (Gyulai et al. 2003; Pfennig et al. 2010; Manchia et al. 2013; Sportiche et al. 2017). In clinical practice, however, concomitant use of more than one mood stabilizer happens frequently, especially in patients with poor treatment response (Baek et al. 2014). Therefore, excluding those patients might generate a skewed distribution of subjects in terms of drug response, which results in a decrease in statistical power in clinical and biomarker studies. In a previous study by some of the present authors (Ahn et al. 2017), we tried to identify clinical correlates of long-term mood stabilizer response in patients taking lithium and/or valproate. In that study, we used the Alda scale and treated the lithium and valproate combination as a single index medication, and identified overall response correlates for the two drugs.

This study aimed to compare long-term treatment response among groups of patients treated with lithium and valproate. In measuring treatment response using the Alda scale, we included patients receiving mood stabilizer combination therapy and intended to explore whether the Alda scale is applicable in subjects under mood stabilizer combination therapy. We also explored the clinical correlates of the response to each drug.

Methods

Subjects

Patients who met DSM-IV criteria for bipolar I (BD-I) or bipolar II (BD-II) disorder and who had received treatment with lithium and/or valproate for more than 2 years between March 2009 and September 2017 at the Bipolar Disorder Clinic of Samsung Medical Center, a tertiary-care university-affiliated hospital, were included in the study. Two drugs, lithium and valproate, were the index medications for the study, and users of both drugs were included in the sample population. The lithium and valproate combination group included patients who had received combination therapy for more than 2 years. The best treatment was provided to each patient based on treatment guidelines (Grunze et al. 2013; Yatham et al. 2018), clinicians' experience, and patients' special concerns regarding adverse effects of the drug. We limited the age range of the subjects to between 18 and 55 years because older patients with bipolar disorder could have distinct clinical courses and treatment responses (Sajatovic et al. 2015). Those who showed evidence of neurologic disorders or general medical conditions related to mental symptoms were excluded. A total of 102 patients who met the above criteria and agreed to participate were enrolled in the study. All subjects had previously participated in the authors' clinical and genetic studies (Baek et al. 2011, 2016, 2019; Yang et al. 2015; Ahn et al. 2017), and 80 of them were involved in the previous study on long-term response to mood stabilizers

(Ahn et al. 2017). This study was approved by the Institutional Review Board of Samsung Medical Center.

Assessment of clinical characteristics

Comprehensive disease characteristics had been evaluated in previous studies described elsewhere (Baek et al. 2011, 2016, 2019; Yang et al. 2015; Ahn et al. 2017). Each evaluation was carried out by a direct interview using the revised version of the Korean version of the Diagnostic Interview for Genetic Studies (Joo et al. 2004) or the Structured Clinical Interview for DSM-IV Axis I Disorders (SCID). Basic demographic and clinical characteristics, clinical course of BD, and manifested symptoms of manic and depressive episodes on a lifetime basis were evaluated (Table 1).

Frequent experience of episodes was defined as having mood episodes, either depressive or (hypo)manic episodes, more than once per year after illness onset; we defined experience of the frequent episode based on frequency of the episode > 25%ile of the total patient sample calculated from our previous study with larger sample sizes (Baek et al. 2019). The polarity of onset was defined as the type of the first episode, where 0 denoted depressive and 1 denoted (hypo)manic. Rapid cycling and mixed episodes were defined following the DSM-IV-TR criteria. We measured seasonality using the Seasonal Pattern Assessment Questionnaire (SPAQ) (Rosenthal et al. 1987). We defined seasonality as having SPAQ-defined subsyndromal or syndromal seasonal affective disorder. Psychotic symptoms were defined as the experience of psychotic symptoms at least once in the patient's lifetime. Details of symptoms during the most severe (hypo)manic or depressive episode were evaluated using the definition of each symptom criterion in the DSM (Association, AP 2013).

Assessment of treatment response

Long-term response to treatment was evaluated through retrospective reviews of clinical records. When possible, additional information was obtained directly from the patients during their visits to the outpatient department. Assessments were performed using the Alda scale (Grof et al. 2002) and the overall section of item III of the CGI-BP (CGI-BP-III-O) (Spearing et al. 1997) at the same time. Treatment response in the combination group was evaluated based on the period when the patients received combination therapy.

The Alda scale consists of two rating sections. The Alda A score measures the degree of improvement during the course of treatment, from 0 to 10. The Alda B score evaluates confounding factors that affect the outcome independently of the medication (Criterion B) (Grof et al. 2002). The B1 and B2 parameters measure the number and frequency of previous episodes, while B3 and B4 measure whether subjects received medication for a sufficient period of time and were adequately compliant. B5 assesses the usage of additional medications to improve symptoms. The total Alda score ranges from 0 to 10 and is obtained by subtracting score B from score A. A higher Alda score indicates a better response to treatment. Additionally, we classified participants into two response groups ('good/moderate responders' vs. 'poor responders'). The best-fit theoretical model of two component with the cut-off point at a total score of 4.5 was set by frequentist mixture analysis in our previous study (Ahn et al. 2017). Therefore, a total score 5 or higher was defined as a good/moderate response and a score of 4 or lower was defined as a poor response.

The CGI-BP-III-O measures the degree of symptom improvement from the worst phase of illness prior to the initiation of the index medication; it ranges from 1 (very much improved) to 4 (no change) to 7 (very much worse).

Two research psychiatrists and the clinician who treated each patient (KSH, JHB, SWA, S-YY, and JL) independently reviewed the hospital records and had meetings to determine the consensus score on the treatment response.

Statistical analysis

We divided the subjects into three groups, the lithium monotherapy group (lithium group), the valproate monotherapy group (valproate group), and the lithium and valproate combination group (combination group), in order to compare participants' baseline characteristics and long-term treatment response. Comparisons of demographic and clinical variables and treatment response between the three medication groups were performed using the chi-square test (or Fisher's exact test) for categorical variables and analysis of variance (ANOVA) for continuous variables. Post-hoc analyses were done using the Bonferroni method for categorical variables and Tukey's test for continuous variables. The Pearson correlation coefficient was calculated to measure the correlation between the scores of treatment response measures.

We conducted simple regression analyses to explore the clinical correlates of the long-term treatment response to each drug. We performed these analyses excluding the combination group. The Alda total score was entered as a dependent variable, and each clinical factor was separately entered as an independent variable.

Probability (p) values less than 0.05 were considered statistically significant. All statistical analyses were done with IBM SPSS version 25.0.

Table 1 Comparison of baseline characteristics between medication groups

Demographic and illness characteristics	Lithium, (n=29)[1]	Valproate (n=56)[2]	Combination, (n=17)[3]	Group difference	
				Statistic	p-value
Sex [male, n (%)]	11 (37.9)	17 (30.4)	7 (41.2)	$\chi^2=0.913$	0.686
Age (current) [years, mean (SD)]	34.2 (9.2)	31.6 (8.65)	30.6 (8.3)	F=1.113	0.332
Education [years, mean (SD)]	15.3 (2.3)	15.0 (2.0)	14.6 (1.7)	F=0.617	0.542
Diagnosis [BD-I, n (%)]	28 (96.6)	44 (78.6)	15 (88.2)	FE	0.063
Age at onset [years, mean (SD)]	24.9 (9.3)	22.0 (7.1)	23.8 (8.4)	F=1.362	0.261
Polarity at first episode [(hypo) manic, n (%)]	15 (51.7)	23 (41.1)	11 (48.0)	$\chi^2=3.139$	0.208
Pre-index-medication illness duration [years, mean (SD)][a]	7.8 (5.8)	8.3 (6.6)	7.1 (4.5)	F=0.239	0.788
Frequency of episodes [frequent, n (%)]					
Total episodes	6 (20.7)	14 (25.0)	4 (23.5)	$\chi^2=0.197$	0.906
Major depressive episodes	5 (17.2)	10 (17.9)	4 (23.5)	$\chi^2=0.328$	0.849
(Hypo)manic episodes	6 (20.7)	15 (26.8)	5 (29.4)	$\chi^2=0.539$	0.764
Family history of psychiatric disorders [present, n (%)]	18 (62.1)	34 (60.7)	9 (61.0)	$\chi^2=0.414$	0.813
Family history of mood disorders [present, n (%)]	12 (41.4)	21 (37.5)	6 (35.3)	$\chi^2=0.196$	0.906
Any anxiety disorder [present, n (%)]	5 (17.2)	13 (23.2)	1 (5.9)	$\chi^2=2.636$	0.268
Obsessive–compulsive disorder [present, n (%)]	5 (17.2)	10 (17.9)	1 (5.9)	FE	0.465
Seasonality [present, n (%)]	4 (13.8)	21 (21.4)	4 (23.5)	$\chi^2=1.541$	0.819
Rapid cycling [present, n (%)]	1 (3.4)	3 (5.4)	0 (0.0)	FE	1.000
Psychotic symptoms [present, n (%)]	26 (89.7)	41 (73.2)	13 (76.5)	$\chi^2=3.099$	0.212
Mixed episodes	8 (27.6)	13 (23.6)	3 (17.6)	$\chi^2=0.585$	0.746
Symptoms of (hypo)manic episodes	**Present, n (%)**	**Present, n (%)**	**Present, n (%)**	**χ^2**	**p-value**
Elevated mood	25 (86.2)	39 (69.6)	14 (82.4)	3.306	0.192
Irritability	12 (41.4)	24 (42.9)	8 (47.1)	0.145	0.930
Grandiosity	23 (79.3)	36 (64.3)	11 (64.7)	2.149	0.341
Decreased sleep need	27 (93.1)	41 (73.2)	16 (94.1)	7.143	0.028[b]
Talkativeness	23 (79.3)	47 (83.9)	13 (76.5)	0.592	0.744
Flight of idea	24 (82.8)	39 (70.9)	12 (70.6)	1.539	0.463
Distractibility	27 (93.1)	44 (78.6)	15 (88.2)	FE	0.186
Hyperactivity	27 (93.1)	49 (87.5)	16 (94.1)	FE	0.732
Excessive involvement in activity	22 (75.9)	36 (64.3)	71 (69.6)	1.664	0.435
Delusion	20 (69.0)	28 (50.0)	12 (70.6)	4.003	0.135
Hallucination	6 (20.7)	16 (29.1)	6 (35.3)	1.254	0.534
Symptoms of depressive episodes	**Present, n (%)**	**Present, n (%)**	**Present, n (%)**	**χ^2**	**p-value**
Depressed mood	24 (82.8)	45 (80.4)	10 (13.2)	4.116	0.128
Decreased interest	23 (79.3)	42 (75.0)	10 (58.8)	2.449	0.294
Appetite change					
No appetite change	13 (44.8)	25 (44.6)	9 (52.9)	0.387	0.824
Decreased appetite	12 (41.4)	21 (37.5)	5 (29.4)	0.660	0.719
Increased appetite	2 (6.9)	5 (8.9)	1 (5.9)	FE	1.000
Insomnia	19 (65.5)	40 (71.4)	7 (41.2)	5.238	0.073
Hypersomnia	8 (27.6)	16 (28.6)	3 (17.6)	0.826	0.662
Agitation	8 (27.6)	15 (26.8)	5 (29.4)	0.046	0.977
Retardation	12 (41.4)	22 (39.3)	3 (17.6)	3.098	0.212
Fatigue or loss of energy	23 (79.3)	40 (71.4)	10 (58.8)	2.212	0.331
Guilty feeling or worthlessness	17 (58.6)	28 (50.0)	50 (49.0)	3.707	0.157
Indecisiveness (concentration)	23 (79.3)	41 (73.2)	10 (58.8)	2.286	0.319
Suicidal ideation	15 (51.7)	31 (55.4)	8 (47.1)	0.385	0.825
Delusion	8 (27.6)	15 (26.8)	6 (35.3)	0.478	0.787

Table 1 (continued)

Symptoms of depressive episodes	Present, n (%)	Present, n (%)	Present, n (%)	χ^2	p-value
Hallucination	3 (10.3)	9 (16.1)	2 (11.8)	FE	0.923

SD, standard deviation; BP-I, bipolar I disorder; FE, Fisher's exact test

[a] Duration from the illness onset to starting the index medications

[b] Significant difference in lithium vs. valproate group: p = 0.033; in valproate vs. combination group: p = 0.047; post-hoc analysis was conducted using Bonferroni's method

[1] Lithium monotherapy group

[2] Valproate monotherapy group

[3] Lithium and valproate combination group

Results

Baseline characteristics of the study subjects

Among all 102 subjects, 29 (28.4%) received lithium, 56 (54.9%) received valproate, and 17 (16.7%) received both lithium and valproate (combination group). Eighty-seven (85.3%) had BD-I and fifteen (14.7%) had BD-II. The mean duration of medication was 95.4 months (standard deviation: 70.9, range: 24–192). All subjects had received the index medication for two or more years (B3 = 0), and most of them showed adequate compliance, i.e., B4 = 0 or 1 in 90.2% of the subjects. Table 1 shows the detailed baseline characteristics of the participants. No significant differences were observed among the groups in terms of sociodemographic and disease characteristics including psychiatric comorbid conditions, seasonality, presence of psychotic symptoms, and mixed episodes. Of the manic symptoms measured, decreased need for sleep was more frequently observed in the valproate group compared to the lithium group (post-hoc p = 0.033) and the combination group (post-hoc p = 0.047). No significant differences were observed among groups regarding depressive symptoms.

Comparison of treatment response among the three medication groups

Significant differences of treatment response were observed among the three medication groups for all the response measurements, and the combination group showed the worst response (Table 2).

The combination group showed a greater CGI-BP-III-O score compared to the lithium group (post-hoc p = 0.019), and the valproate group (post-hoc

Table 2 Comparison of treatment responses between medication groups

	Lithium, (n = 29)[1]	Valproate, (n = 56)[2]	Combination, (n = 17)[3]	Statistic	*p*	Post-hoc analysis[a]		
						[1]vs.[2]	[1]vs.[3]	[2]vs.[3]
Patients total (N = 102)								
Alda A [mean (SD)]	6.4 (2.0)	7.1 (1.7)	5.5 (1.4)	F = 6.631	0.002	0.134	0.200	0.002
Alda C [mean (SD)]	2.9 (2.4)	4.1 (2.3)	1.5 (1.7)	F = 9.736	< 0.001	0.038	0.133	< 0.001
Poor responder [n (%)]	21 (72.4)	34 (60.7)	16 (94.1)	FE	0.022	0.495	0.260	0.023
CGI-BP-III-O [mean (SD)]	2.1 (1.0)	2.0 (0.9)	2.9 (1.0)	F = 5.816	0.004	0.919	0.019	0.003
	Lithium, (n = 28)[1]	**Valproate, (n = 44)[2]**	**Combination, (n = 15)[3]**	**Statistic**	***p***	**Post-hoc analysis[a]**		
						[1]vs.[2]	[1]vs.[3]	[2]vs.[3]
Bipolar I disorder (N = 87)								
Alda A [mean (SD)]	6.4 (2.0)	7.2 (1.4)	5.5 (1.9)	F = 5.822	0.004	0.139	0.246	0.004
Alda C [mean (SD)]	2.8 (2.4)	4.1 (2.3)	1.6 (1.8)	F = 7.799	0.001	0.047	0.228	0.001
Poor responder [n (%)]	21 (75.0)	26 (59.1)	14 (93.3)	FE	0.034	0.310	0.410	0.033
CGI-BP-III-O [mean (SD)]	2.0 (0.7)	1.7 (0.7)	2.2 (0.6)	F = 3.042	0.053	–	–	–

SD, standard deviation; Alda A, A score of the Alda scale (Grof et al. 2002); Alda C, total score of the Alda scale (Grof et al. 2002); CGI-BP-III-O, item III of the Clinical Global Impressions scale for use in bipolar illness, overall (Spearing et al. 1997); FE, Fisher's exact test

[a] Post-hoc analysis was conducted using Tukey's test

[1] Lithium monotherapy group

[2] Valproate monotherapy group

[3] Lithium and valproate combination group

p = 0.003). In addition, the combination group showed a lower Alda A score (post-hoc p = 0.002) and total score (post-hoc p < 0.001) in comparison with the valproate group. The valproate group showed a greater total Alda score compared to the lithium group (post-hoc p = 0.038). When classifying patients into two groups depending on the cut-off score set from our previous study (good/moderate responder vs. poor responder), the combination group had the highest rate of 'poor responder' with a statistically significant difference compared to the valproate group (post-hoc p = 0.023).

The three treatment outcome measures were highly correlated with one another (Additional file 1: Table S1).

Figure 1 illustrates the comparative distributions of the Alda scale scores between the combination group and the monotherapy groups. The combination group generally had lower Alda A and total scores compared to the monotherapy groups.

We additionally compared treatment response in the subset of subjects with BD-I (n = 87). These analyses showed similar results to those found in all subjects (Table 2). However, no significant difference was detected in terms of CGI-BP-III-O score.

Previous treatments of the combination group

We reviewed details of previous treatment histories of the combination group (Table 3). We explored if treatment regimens recommended for maintenance therapy in the CANMAT-ISBD guideline (Yatham et al. 2018) was administered on each patient. In three patients (patient number 1, 3, and 9 in Table 3), lithium and valproate combination therapy was tried as the second strategy (3/17 = 17.6%). In others, it was tried as the third or later treatment strategy (14/17 = 82.4%). Valproate and atypical antipsychotics combination therapy was the most commonly applied strategy (13/17 = 76.5%) before the current medications, followed by lithium and atypical antipsychotics combination therapy (10/17 = 58.8%). Antidepressant was tried in only one patient to alleviate obsessive compulsive symptoms (patient number 14 in Table 3).

Clinical correlates of treatment response for each drug

Table 4 and Additional file 1: Table S2 display the results of a simple regression analysis of total Alda score. In

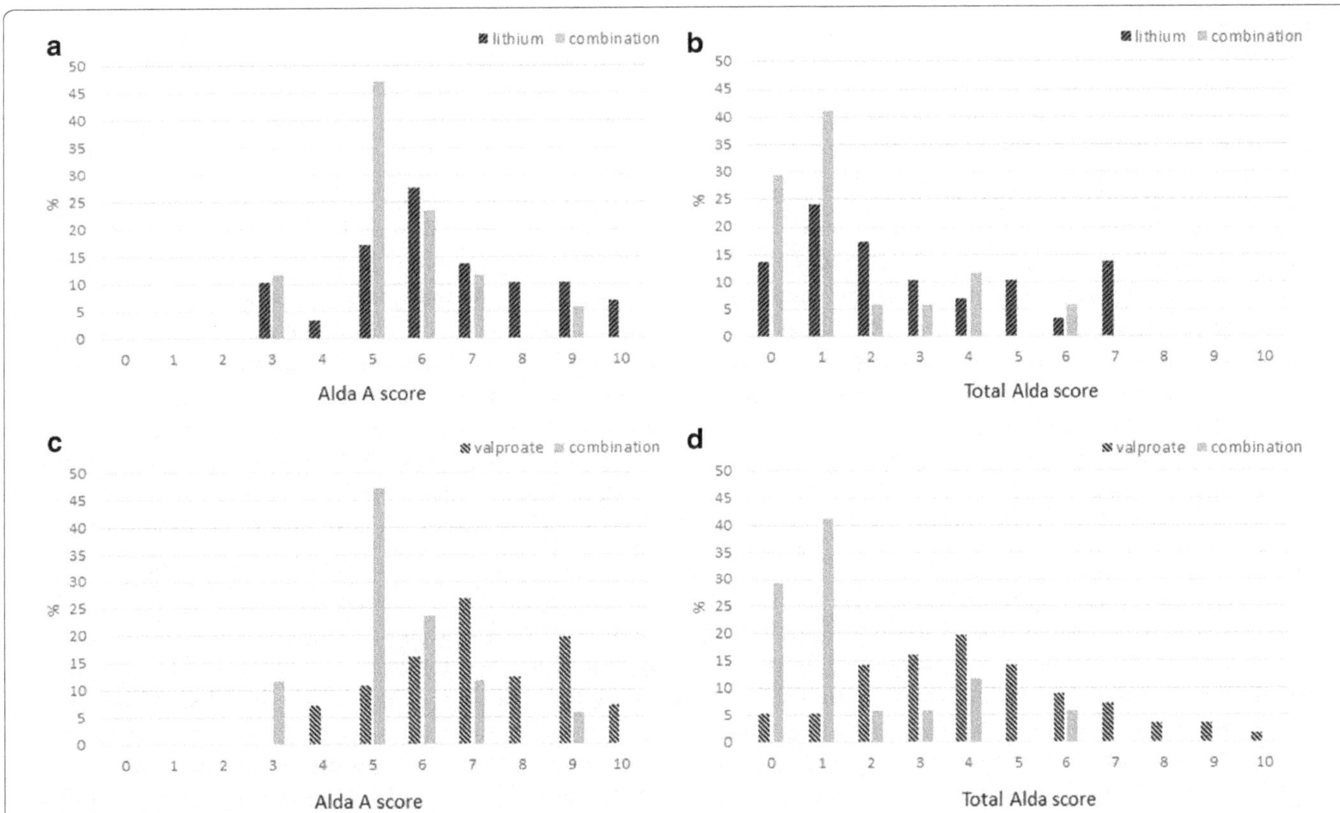

Fig. 1 Distribution of Alda scale scores in the monotherapy and combination groups. The x-axis illustrates the scores of the Alda and the y-axis illustrates percentage of patients in each group. **a** Alda A scores of the lithium users. **b** Total Alda scores of lithium users. **c** Alda A scores of valproate users. **d** Total Alda scores of valproate users

Table 3 Summary of previous and current medications for the maintenance therapy in the combination group

Case	Previous medication						Combination of LiVal	
	Lith[1]	Val[2]	Lamo[3]	AAP[4]	Lith + AAP[5]	Val + AAP[6]	Current medication	Order[a]
1	X	X	X	X	X	O	LiVal + AAP	Val → LiVal
2	X	X	X	O	X	O	LiVal + AAP	Val → LiVal
3	X	X	X	X	X	O	LiVal + AAP	Val → LiVal
4	X	X	X	O	X	O	LiVal + AAP	Val → LiVal
5	X	X	X	O	O	X	LiVal + AAP	Lith → LiVal
6	X	X	O	X	O	O	LiVal + AAP	Val → Lith → LiVal
7	X	X	X	O	O	X	LiVal + AAP	Lith → LiVal
8	X	X	X	X	O	O	LiVal + AAP	Lith → Val → LiVal
9	X	O	X	X	X	X	LiVal	Val → LiVal
10	X	X	X	X	O	O	LiVal + AAP	Lith → Val → LiVal
11	X	X	X	O	O	O	LiVal + AAP	Lith → Val → LiVal
12	O	O	X	O	O	O	LiVal + AAP	Val → Lival → Lith → LiVal
13	X	O	O	X	O	O	LiVal + AAP	Val → LiVal → Val → LiVal
14	X	O	X	O	X	O	LiVal + AAP	Val → LiVal
15	X	X	X	O	O	O	LiVal + AAP	Lith → LiVal
16	X	O	O	X	X	X	LiVal + Lamo	Val → LiVal
17	X	X	X	X	O	O	LiVal + AAP	Lith → Val → LiVal

Lith, lithium; Val, valproate; AAP, any atypical antipsychotic medication; LiVal, lithium and valproate combination; Lamo, lamotrigine

[a] The order in which lithium and valproate were administered

[1] Lithium monotherapy

[2] VALPROATE monotherapy

[3] Lamotrigine with or without lithium, valproate, and antipsychotics

[4] Atypical antipsychotics monotherapy

[5] Lithium with atypical antipsychotics

[6] Valproate with atypical antipsychotics

lithium users, older age at onset and (hypo) manic episode at onset showed significant positive associations with total Alda score. The presence of mixed episodes and comorbid anxiety disorders or obsessive–compulsive disorder showed a significant negative association with the total Alda score in valproate users (Table 4).

Among symptoms of depressive or manic episodes, increased appetite during depressive episodes was significantly associated with total Alda score in valproate users (Additional file 1: Table S2).

Discussion

In this study, we evaluated long-term response to maintenance treatment with specific mood stabilizers including subjects under mood stabilizer combination therapy. We observed that patients who received combination therapy showed poorer treatment response compared to those who received monotherapy. We also identified distinct clinical correlates of response to lithium and valproate.

The initial Alda scale (Grof et al. 2002) stated that the systematic use of antidepressants, antipsychotics, or additional mood stabilizers should be given a score of 2 on item B5 in order to suggest that the link between improvement and a specific treatment is less certain. However, in ConLiGen projects, item B5 was modified to allow the systematic use of antidepressant or antipsychotic medication only (Schulze et al. 2010). Thus, subjects under mood stabilizer combination therapy were excluded from the beginning. Furthermore, a recent study by Scott and colleagues (Scott et al. 2019) even suggested that subjects under combination therapy with antidepressant/ antipsychotics (high B5 scorers) need to be excluded at first. However, combination treatment for BD is quite pervasive and rapidly increasing (Greil et al. 2012; Baek et al. 2014; Fung et al. 2019). If we were to exclude all patients under combination treatment, a limited number of patients could be included in subjects.

Of combination treatment, the mood stabilizer combination strategy occupies a unique position in the treatment of BD. Lithium and valproate are both first-line treatment agents used for maintenance treatment of BD. But the combination of two first-line treatment agents is generally recommended when a patient does not show a satisfactory response to a single first-line agent (Yatham

Table 4 Clinical correlates of long-term treatment response in bipolar disorder patients: Results of simple regression analyses using the total Alda score as a dependent variable

Demographic and illness characteristics	Lithium (n=29)[1]			Valproate (n=56)[2]		
	Standardized beta	T	P	Standardized beta	T	P
Sex (female gender)	0.230	1.226	0.231	−0.161	−1.202	0.235
Age (current)	0.267	1.440	0.161	0.161	1.199	0.236
Education	−0.138	−0.712	0.483	0.142	1.056	0.296
Diagnosis (bipolar II disorder)	0.175	0.921	0.365	0.043	0.318	0.752
Age at onset	0.325	2.279	0.028	0.114	0.844	0.403
(Hypo)manic episode at onset	0.419	2.400	0.024	−0.068	−0.498	0.621
Pre-index-medication illness duration[a]	0.296	1.613	0.118	0.089	0.647	0.520
Frequency of episodes (frequent)						
Total	0.177	0.937	0.357	0.018	0.132	0.896
Major depressive	0.224	1.196	0.242	0.113	0.834	0.408
(Hypo)manic	−0.153	−0.807	0.427	−0.090	−0.665	0.509
Family history of psychiatric disorders	0.107	0.559	0.581	0.145	1.078	0.286
Family history of mood disorders	0.201	1.068	0.295	0.080	0.591	0.557
Any anxiety disorder	−0.209	−1.113	0.276	-0.475	−3.967	<0.001
Obsessive–compulsive disorder	-0.209	−1.113	0.276	-0.393	−3.145	0.003
Seasonality	−0.017	−0.072	0.944	0.221	1.377	0.177
Rapid cycling	0.338	1.865	0.073	−0.049	−0.362	0.719
Psychotic symptoms	−0.363	−2.022	0.053	−0.068	−0.498	0.621
Mixed episodes	−0.163	−0.859	0.398	−0.289	−2.196	0.033

[a] Duration from illness onset to start of the index medication

[1] Lithium monotherapy group

[2] Valproate monotherapy group

et al. 2018). Thus, patients given mood stabilizer combination treatment are more likely to be poor treatment responders. If we exclude all patients under mood stabilizer combination treatment, we will be disregarding the characteristics of many poor treatment responders in the analysis of pharmacological and pharmacogenetic factors.

In line with the preceding discussion, the combination group showed worse long-term treatment response compared to both monotherapy groups (Fig. 1 and Table 2). The mood stabilizer combination group had the lowest mean Alda A score, indicating that their low treatment response is not derived from high B scores associated with combination treatment. No significant difference was observed between the combination group and the monotherapy groups (either the lithium or the valproate group) in terms of baseline illness characteristics indicating that the difference in long-term treatment response is not derived from baseline illness characteristics. A few studies explored long-term treatment responses of combination therapy in comparison to mood stabilizer monotherapy. The BALANCE study (Geddes et al. 2010) compared the long-term treatment responses of mood stabilizer monotherapy and combination therapy; they reported greater decrease of recurrences in combination therapy. In that study, patients were randomly allocated into monotherapy vs. combination therapy groups. By contrast, in our study, the combination of lithium and valproate was chosen for individual patients through their treatment processes. Therefore, most of our subjects in the combination group had experienced trials of various other treatment regimens before the current medications, indicating inadequate responses to previous treatments including lithium and/or valproate monotherapies (Table 3). In another study, Musetti et al. (Musetti et al. 2018) compared monotherapy and combination therapy groups in a naturalistic setting as in the current study. In that study, current regimens of the combination group were chosen after some other trials including mood stabilizer monotherapy. As a result, combination group had greater episode frequency previously, and the reduction rate of recurrence was higher due to worse previous illness course. So in some way, the findings from the study by Musetti et al. corroborates with our study findings showing that poor treatment responders were allocated into combination therapy group.

Systematic meta-analysis and post-hoc analysis of randomized controlled trials found no significant differences between lithium and valproate in terms of long-term efficacy (Cipriani et al. 2013; Kang et al. 2020). In contrast, observational studies (Garnham et al. 2007; Kessing et al. 2018), a randomized open trial (Geddes et al. 2010) and a population-based cohort study (Hayes et al. 2016) reported the superiority of lithium as a monotherapy agent for maintenance treatment of BD. Our study did not find significant differences in terms of treatment response between lithium and valproate. It is also unknown whether there are distinct clinical correlates of treatment response depending on type of mood stabilizer. Considering that lithium and valproate have distinct neurobiological targets (Chiu et al. 2013), different clinical factors could contribute to the long-term response to each medication.

Prior studies on the clinical correlates of the long-term effects of mood stabilizers have more focused on lithium. A recent meta-analysis (Hui et al. 2019) reported that mania-depression-interval sequence (compared to depression-mania sequence), absence of rapid cycling, absence of psychotic symptoms, shorter pre-lithium illness duration, family history of bipolar disorder, and later illness onset were associated with better long-term treatment response to lithium. In our study, older age at onset and (hypo)manic episode at onset were significantly associated with long-term treatment response. Other factors that showed associations in the meta-analysis did not show significant associations in our study.

Regarding clinical correlates of valproate response, Gyulai et al. (Gyulai et al. 2003) reported that worse depression symptoms, rapid cycling, and comorbid alcohol use disorders were associated with the efficacy of valproate in a maintenance treatment. In addition, a study by Garnham et al. (Garnham et al. 2007) reported psychosis was associated with treatment response to valproate. In our study, comorbid anxiety disorder (Otto et al. 2006), obsessive–compulsive disorder (Shashidhara et al. 2015) and mixed episode (McIntyre et al. 2013; Young and Eberhard 2015), which are commonly known to be associated with poorer treatment responses, showed significant association with treatment response to valproate.

Several limitations of this study should be considered. First, the sample size is small. Subgroup analysis of BD-II patients could not be performed due to the limited sample size. For the same reason, evaluation of clinical correlates in the combination group was not possible. Second, this study measured treatment response retrospectively. However, as previously stated, retrospective evaluation is inevitable when evaluating long-term treatment response. We tried to carry out a comprehensive evaluation using diverse sources of information when determining long-term treatment response. Third, each patient's treatment strategy can be affected their treating physicians' preference. The clinicians' preference can indirectly impact on clinical correlates of the treatment responses of each drug. Finally, the participants were recruited from a single tertiary academic teaching hospital, it may be difficult to generalize the study's results.

Notwithstanding these limitations, this study has some strengths. As a naturalistic observational study, it may reflect the situation in real-world clinical practice. In addition, baseline disease characteristics were independently assessed in previous studies by the same authors before assessment of treatment response. Finally, even though the assessment of treatment response was retrospective, it was reliable, as the subjects were followed up for more than two years at a single institution.

Conclusions

In this study, we took a novel approach to evaluating long-term response to mood stabilizers. By applying the Alda scale with minor modifications, we measured the responses to lithium and valproate including subjects under combination therapy. The combination treatment group showed poor treatment outcomes. We identified several factors related to the long-term treatment response to each drug. Further efforts are warranted towards the development of measurement methods and study designs that can handle the effects of combination treatment in clinical and genetic studies of BD.

Supplementary information

Additional file 1: Table S1. Correlation between the evaluation tools of long-term treatment response. **Table S2.** Symptom profiles and long-term treatment response in bipolar disorder patients: Results of simple regression analyses using the total Alda score as a dependent variable.

Abbreviations

BD-I: Bipolar I disorder; BD-II: Bipolar II disorder; BD: Bipolar disorder; ConLiGen: Consortium on Lithium Genetics; SCID: Structured Clinical Interview for DSM-IV Axis I Disorders; SPAQ: Seasonal Pattern Assessment Questionnaire; CGI: Clinical Global Impressions; CGI-BP-III-O: Item III of the Clinical Global Impressions scale for use in bipolar illness, overall; Alda A: A score of the Alda scale; Alda C: Total score of the Alda scale; SD: Standard deviation; FE: Fisher's exact test; ANOVA: Analysis of variance.

Acknowledgements

None.

Authors' contributions

JL, JHB, DL, SWA, YC, SYY, KL, and KSH contributed to study design, data collection, and clinical rating. JL, JHB, and KSH wrote the manuscript. YC, SWA, SYY, and KSH contributed to data collection and management as well as patient chart reviews. JL and YCB undertook the statistical analysis. All authors read and approved the final manuscript.

Author details

[1] Department of Psychiatry, Sungkyunkwan University School of Medicine, Samsung Medical Center, Seoul, Republic of Korea. [2] Present Address: Department of Psychiatry, National Health Insurance Service, Ilsan Hospital, Goyang-si, Republic of Korea. [3] Center for Clinical Research, Samsung Biomedical Research Institute, Seoul, Republic of Korea.

References

Ahn SW, Baek JH, Yang SY, Kim Y, Cho Y, Choi Y, et al. Long-term response to mood stabilizer treatment and its clinical correlates in patients with bipolar disorders: a retrospective observational study. Int J Bipolar Disord. 2017;5:24.

Association, AP. Diagnostic and statistical manual of mental disorders (DSM-5®). ed. editor^editors.: American Psychiatric Pub; 2013. p.

Baek JH, Park DY, Choi J, Kim JS, Choi JS, Ha K, et al. Differences between bipolar I and bipolar II disorders in clinical features, comorbidity, and family history. J Affect Disord. 2011;131:59–67.

Baek JH, Ha K, Yatham LN, Chang JS, Ha TH, Jeon HJ, et al. Pattern of pharmacotherapy by episode types for patients with bipolar disorders and its concordance with treatment guidelines. J Clin Psychopharmacol. 2014;34:577–87.

Baek JH, Kim JS, Kim MJ, Ryu S, Lee K, Ha K, et al. Lifetime characteristics of evening-preference and irregular bed-rise time are associated with lifetime seasonal variation of mood and behavior: comparison between individuals with bipolar disorder and healthy controls. Behav Sleep Med. 2016;14:155–68.

Baek JH, Ha K, Kim Y, Cho YA, Yang SY, Choi Y, et al. Psychopathologic structure of bipolar disorders: exploring dimensional phenotypes, their relationships, and their associations with bipolar I and II disorders. Psychol Med. 2019;49:2177–85.

Chen CK, Lee CS, Chen HY, Wu LS, Chang JC, Liu CY, et al. GADL1 variant and medication adherence in predicting response to lithium maintenance treatment in bipolar I disorder. Br J Psych Open. 2016;2:301–6.

Chiu CT, Wang Z, Hunsberger JG, Chuang DM. Therapeutic potential of mood stabilizers lithium and valproic acid: beyond bipolar disorder. Pharmacol Rev. 2013;65:105–42.

Cipriani, A, Reid, K, Young, AH, Macritchie, K, Geddes, J. Valproic acid, valproate and divalproex in the maintenance treatment of bipolar disorder. Cochrane Database Syst Rev. 2013: Cd003196.

Garnham J, Munro A, Slaney C, Macdougall M, Passmore M, Duffy A, et al. Prophylactic treatment response in bipolar disorder: results of a naturalistic observation study. J Affect Disord. 2007;104:185–90.

Geddes JR, Goodwin GM, Rendell J, Azorin JM, Cipriani A, Ostacher MJ, et al. Lithium plus valproate combination therapy versus monotherapy for relapse prevention in bipolar I disorder (BALANCE): a randomised open-label trial. Lancet. 2010;375:385–95.

Goodwin GM, Haddad PM, Ferrier IN, Aronson JK, Barnes T, Cipriani A. et al. Evidence-based guidelines for treating bipolar disorder: revised third edition recommendations from the British Association for Psychopharmacology. J Psychopharmacol. 2016;30:495–553.

Grof P, Duffy A, Cavazzoni P, Grof E, Garnham J, MacDougall M, et al. Is response to prophylactic lithium a familial trait? J Clin Psychiatry. 2002;63:942–7.

Grunze H, Vieta E, Goodwin GM, Bowden C, Licht RW, Moller HJ, et al. The World Federation of Societies of Biological Psychiatry (WFSBP) guidelines for the biological treatment of bipolar disorders: update 2012 on the long-term treatment of bipolar disorder. World J Biol Psychiatry. 2013;14:154–21919.

Grunze H, Vieta E, Goodwin GM, Bowden C, Licht RW, Azorin JM, et al. The World Federation of Societies of Biological Psychiatry (WFSBP) Guidelines for the Biological Treatment of Bipolar Disorders: acute and long-term treatment of mixed states in bipolar disorder. World J Biol Psychiatry. 2018;19:2–58.

Gyulai L, Bowden CL, McElroy SL, Calabrese JR, Petty F, Swann AC, et al. Maintenance efficacy of divalproex in the prevention of bipolar depression. Neuropsychopharmacology. 2003;28:1374–82.

Hayes JF, Marston L, Walters K, Geddes JR, King M, Osborn DP. Lithium vs. valproate vs. olanzapine vs. quetiapine as maintenance monotherapy for bipolar disorder: a population-based UK cohort study using electronic health records. World Psychiatry. 2016;15:53–8.

Hou L, Heilbronner U, Degenhardt F, Adli M, Akiyama K, Akula N, et al. Genetic variants associated with response to lithium treatment in bipolar disorder: a genome-wide association study. Lancet. 2016;387:1085–93.

Hui TP, Kandola A, Shen L, Lewis G, Osborn DPJ, Geddes JR, et al. A systematic review and meta-analysis of clinical predictors of lithium response in bipolar disorder. Acta Psychiatr Scand. 2019;140:94–115.

Joo EJ, Joo YH, Hong JP, Hwang S, Maeng SJ, Han JH, et al. Korean version of the diagnostic interview for genetic studies: validity and reliability. Compr Psychiatry. 2004;45:225–9.

Kang MG, Qian H, Keramatian K, Chakrabarty T, Saraf G, Lam RW, et al. Lithium vs valproate in the maintenance treatment of bipolar I disorder: a post-hoc analysis of a randomized double-blind placebo-controlled trial. Aust N Z J Psychiatry. 2020;54:298–307.

Kessing, LV, Bauer, M, Nolen, WA, Severus, E, Goodwin, GM, Geddes, J. Effectiveness of maintenance therapy of lithium vs other mood stabilizers in monotherapy and in combinations: a systematic review of evidence from observational studies. Bipolar Disord. 2018.

Lee MT, Chen CH, Lee CS, Chen CC, Chong MY, Ouyang WC, et al. Genome-wide association study of bipolar I disorder in the Han Chinese population. Mol Psychiatry. 2011;16:548–56.

Lin E, Kuo PH, Liu YL, Yu YW, Yang AC, Tsai SJ. A deep learning approach for predicting antidepressant response in major depression using clinical and genetic biomarkers. Front Psychiatry. 2018;9:290.

Manchia M, Adli M, Akula N, Ardau R, Aubry JM, Backlund L, et al. Assessment of response to lithium maintenance treatment in bipolar disorder: a Consortium on Lithium Genetics (ConLiGen) Report. PLoS ONE. 2013;8:e65636.

McIntyre RS, Tohen M, Berk M, Zhao J, Weiller E. DSM-5 mixed specifier for manic episodes: evaluating the effect of depressive features on severity and treatment outcome using asenapine clinical trial data. J Affect Disord. 2013;150:378–83.

Miura T, Noma H, Furukawa TA, Mitsuyasu H, Tanaka S, Stockton S, et al. Comparative efficacy and tolerability of pharmacological treatments in the maintenance treatment of bipolar disorder: a systematic review and network meta-analysis. Lancet Psychiatry. 2014;1:351–9.

Musetti L, Tundo A, Benedetti A, Massimetti G, Cambiali E, Pergentini I, et al. Lithium, valproate, and carbamazepine prescribing patterns for long-term treatment of bipolar I and II disorders: a prospective study. Hum Psychopharmacol. 2018;33:e2676.

Otto MW, Simon NM, Wisniewski SR, Miklowitz DJ, Kogan JN, Reilly-Harrington NA, et al. Prospective 12-month course of bipolar disorder in out-patients with and without comorbid anxiety disorders. Br J Psychiatry. 2006;189:20–5.

Pfennig A, Schlattmann P, Alda M, Grof P, Glenn T, Muller-Oerlinghausen B, et al. Influence of atypical features on the quality of prophylactic effectiveness of long-term lithium treatment in bipolar disorders. Bipolar Disord. 2010;12:390–6.

Pisanu C, Heilbronner U, Squassina A. The role of pharmacogenomics in bipolar disorder: moving towards precision medicine. Mol Diagn Ther. 2018;22:409–20.

Rybakowski JK. Genetic influences on response to mood stabilizers in bipolar disorder: current status of knowledge. CNS Drugs. 2013;27:165–73.

Sajatovic M, Strejilevich SA, Gildengers AG, Dols A, Al Jurdi RK, Forester BP, et al. A report on older-age bipolar disorder from the International Society for Bipolar Disorders Task Force. Bipolar Disord. 2015;17:689–704.

Schulze TG, Alda M, Adli M, Akula N, Ardau R, Bui ET, et al. The International Consortium on Lithium Genetics (ConLiGen): an initiative by the NIMH and IGSLI to study the genetic basis of response to lithium treatment. Neuropsychobiology. 2010;62:72–8.

Scott J, Etain B, Manchia M, Brichant-Petitjean C, Geoffroy PA Schulze T, et al. An examination of the quality and performance of the Alda scale for classifying lithium response phenotypes. Bipolar Disord. 2019.

Scott J, Geoffroy PA, Sportiche S, Brichant-Petit-Jean C, Gard S, Kahn JP, et al. Cross-validation of clinical characteristics and treatment patterns associated with phenotypes for lithium response defined by the Alda scale. J Affect Disord. 2017;208:62–7.

Shashidhara M, Sushma BR, Viswanath B, Math SB, Janardhan Reddy YC. Comorbid obsessive compulsive disorder in patients with bipolar-I disorder. J Affect Disord. 2015;174:367–71.

Spearing MK, Post RM, Leverich GS, Brandt D, Nolen W. Modification of the Clinical Global Impressions (CGI) Scale for use in bipolar illness (BP): the CGI-BP. Psychiatry Res. 1997;73:159–71.

Sportiche S, Geoffroy PA, Brichant-Petitjean C, Gard S, Khan JP, Azorin JM, et al. Clinical factors associated with lithium response in bipolar disorders. Aust N Z J Psychiatry. 2017;51:524–30.

Yang SY, Huh IS, Baek JH, Cho EY, Choi MJ, Ryu S, et al. Association between ST8SIA2 and the Risk of schizophrenia and bipolar I disorder across diagnostic boundaries. PLoS ONE. 2015;10:e0139413.

Yatham LN, Kennedy SH, Parikh SV, Schaffer A, Bond DJ, Frey BN, et al. Canadian Network for Mood and Anxiety Treatments (CANMAT) and International Society for Bipolar Disorders (ISBD) 2018 guidelines for the management of patients with bipolar disorder. Bipolar Disord. 2018;20:97–170.

Young AH, Eberhard J. Evaluating depressive symptoms in mania: a naturalistic study of patients with bipolar disorder. Neuropsychiatr Dis Treat. 2015;11:1137–43.

Zhu MM, Li HL, Shi LH, Chen XP, Luo J, Zhang ZL. The pharmacogenomics of valproic acid. J Hum Genet. 2017;62:1009–144.

8

Regional lithium prescription rates and recurrence in bipolar disorder

Martin Sköld[1], Sindre Rolstad[2], Erik Joas[1], Mathias Kardell[1], Erik Pålsson[1], Guy M. Goodwin[3] and Mikael Landén[1,4*]

Abstract

Background: Lithium is the best documented maintenance treatment in bipolar disorder, but its use varies considerably across and within countries. It is not known whether regional differences in lithium prescription rates translate to differing regional outcomes.

Aims: To estimate associations between county specific lithium prescription rates and county specific recurrence odds of bipolar disorder in Sweden.

Method: Data from 14,616 patients with bipolar I disorder, bipolar II disorder, or bipolar disorder not otherwise specified were extracted from the Swedish national quality assurance register for bipolar disorders (BipoläR). Lithium prescription frequencies were calculated for 21 counties. Logistic regression analyses were run adjusted for confounders, with any type of recurrence as primary outcome, and incident elated and depressive episodes as secondary outcomes. Subsets of patients with bipolar I, II and not otherwise specified disorder were also analysed separately.

Results: Lithium prescription rates for populations with all bipolar subtypes ranged across counties from 37.7 to 84.9% (mean 52.4%). Higher regional prescription rates were significantly associated with lower rate of any type of recurrence. The association was stronger when bipolar I disorder was analysed separately.

Conclusions: The advantages for lithium use long acknowledged for bipolar I disorder are also seen for the rest of the bipolar spectrum. Results suggest that population level outcomes of bipolar disorder could be improved by increasing the number of patients using lithium.

Keywords: Bipolar disorder, Drug therapy, Lithium, Outcome assessment, Health care quality assessment

Background

Bipolar disorder (BD) is a severe psychiatric disorder associated with decreased quality of life, impaired functioning, increased risk of suicide, and stigma (Guilbert 2003; Judd et al. 2005; Crump et al. 2013). The disorder is associated with high societal costs due to the need for hospital care and loss of productivity in employment (Ekman et al. 2013). The lifetime prevalence for BD has been estimated to be composed of 0.6% for bipolar I disorder (BD I), 0.4% for bipolar II disorder (BD II), and 1.4% for subthreshold bipolar spectrum disorders (Merikangas et al. 2011).

Relapse prevention is the prime objective in long term management of BD due to the high risk of recurrence of manic, hypomanic, depressive, or mixed episodes. Thus, mood stabilising medication is recommended for BD patients to prevent such episodes and in most guidelines lithium is recommended as a first-line option for maintenance treatment in adult BD (Geddes and Miklowitz 2013; Goodwin et al. 2016; Fountoulakis et al. 2016; Grunze et al. 2013; Kendall et al. 2014; Yatham et al. 2018). Swedish national recommendations derive from international guidelines and holds lithium as the

*Correspondence: mikael.landen@gu.se
[1] Department of Psychiatry and Neurochemistry, Institute of Neuroscience and Physiology, Sahlgrenska Academy, University of Gothenburg, Blå Stråket 15, 413 45 Gothenburg, Sweden
Full list of author information is available at the end of the article

first-line option for long-term treatment (Adler et al. 2014). Lithium was first shown to be effective in mania in 1949 (Cade 1949) and has been known to prevent mood episodes in BD since the 1960s (Baastrup 1964; Hartigan 1963; Ferensztajn-Rochowiak et al. 2020). A meta-analysis of randomized controlled trials (RCT) with lithium maintenance treatment (n = 1580, seven trials) demonstrated significant relative risk reductions of 34% for any type of recurrent episodes, 48% for manic episodes, and 22% for depressive episodes (Severus et al. 2014).

However, guidelines also frequently suggest other drugs as first-line options for maintenance treatment: for example, the 2018 Canadian Network for Mood and Anxiety Treatments (CANMAT) guideline endorsed by the International Society for Bipolar Disorders (Yatham et al. 2018) lists six first-line options (lithium, quetiapine, divalproex, lamotrigine, asenapine, aripiprazole) along with two combination therapies (quetiapine + lithium/divalproex, aripiprazole + lithium/divalproex). This is despite a meta-analysis indicating that lithium was superior compared with alternative medication (Miura et al. 2014) and large observational studies showing that lithium more effectively prevents recurrences and hospitalization than valproate, lamotrigine and other mood stabilizers (Joas et al. 2017; Kessing et al. 2011, 2012). Moreover, lithium seems to have a specific anti-suicidal effect (Cipriani et al. 2013) not seen with, for example, valproate (Song et al. 2017). Lastly, there is little data from RCTs on the efficacy of lithium in BD II and BD not otherwise specified (NOS) populations (Goodwin et al. 2016; Yatham et al. 2018), so there is genuine uncertainty about lithium's value in a substantial number of patients within the bipolar spectrum.

The use of lithium has declined in Europe (Karanti et al. 2016) and the US (Blanco et al. 2002), which might be due to the regular blood-monitoring required, the awareness of adverse reactions/effects and the rise of heavily marketed alternatives. As a non-patented drug, lithium has not been marketed in a commercially conventional way. Whatever the reason, the use of lithium is often less than it should be at a time when mental health care providers are under pressure to improve outcomes by implementing evidence-based guidelines (Geddes and Miklowitz 2013; Goodwin et al. 2016; Fountoulakis et al. 2016; Grunze et al. 2013; Kendall et al. 2014; Yatham et al. 2018) and to use quality assurance programs to set goals for specific interventions. We propose that the proportion of patients treated with lithium is a potential quality indicator in BD management that is easy to measure. Quality assurance programs are concerned with populations rather than individual patients, but specifying the percentage of bipolar disorder patients that should be treated with lithium presents a challenge. This is because some individuals are likely to respond better to alternative treatment options despite lithium being the best treatment option for BD on average (Severus et al. 2014; Miura et al. 2014). Setting the goal that all BD patients should be treated with lithium would hinder personalised treatment and not yield optimal outcomes. On the other hand, if the proportion of lithium treated patients is too low, chances are that outcomes at a group level would improve by increasing the proportion of lithium treated patients.

The primary aim of this study was to investigate if outcomes in BD at a county level in Sweden are related to the prevalence of lithium prescriptions. Since it is currently not possible to set a target level for lithium use prevalence in a BD population because the optimal prevalence is unknown, the secondary aim was to investigate if a reasonable target for regional lithium prevalence can be determined.

Methods

Data source

Sweden has more than 100 health care quality registers that complement government-administered registries by collecting data on disease specific measures (Emilsson et al. 2015). The Swedish national quality register for bipolar disorders (BipoläR) was established in 2004 with the aim of improving the quality of care for BD patients in Sweden (BipoläR 2021). We used data from BipoläR because it contains more detailed information than the Swedish patient register where data is limited to international classification of diseases diagnoses: BipoläR contains information on, e.g., bipolar disorder subtype and psychiatric comorbidities, incident mood episodes managed in outpatient care, education, medication, and body mass index. In June 2016, the register contained more than 55,000 registrations of almost 20,000 unique patients (BipoläR 2021). Participation is voluntary for the clinician as well as the patients. Registering units include both private and public psychiatric outpatient health care units in Sweden (a total of 191 units were active in June 2016).

The quality register contains individualized data on bipolar subtype (BD I, II and NOS) and current comorbid psychiatric conditions according to Diagnostic and Statistical Manual of Mental Disorders-IV, interventions, and outcomes. The diagnoses are made in regular care and diagnostic assessments reflect clinical routine. This means that the use of structured diagnostic instruments varies across participating clinics but the mini-international neuropsychiatric interview is commonly used. During 2019, any form of structured diagnostic instrument had been used in 44% of new registrations in BipoläR. After the baseline registration, information about interventions and outcomes during the last 12 months is collected at annual follow-up examinations. At the annual follow-up, the number of depressive, manic, hypomanic, and mixed episodes are documented based on the patient interview and reviewing the past 12 months medical notes. This information is typically collected by the treating psychiatrist, or nurses trained in the diagnosis and treatment of bipolar disorder, who have access to all clinical data for the patient. Data are entered into a web-based application. Quality control is performed by data type restrictions and boundaries for registered values. Further, completeness and coverage of register data is checked annually. Diagnostic codes have also been benchmarked against medical records. Finally, the validity of the register has been assessed by comparing summary statistics to information in the national patient register and the Swedish prescribed drug register (BipoläR Årsrapport 2021).

Study population and measures

In the current study, we included patients diagnosed with BD I, BD II, or BD NOS. At the time of data extraction (June 2016), 19,948 patients were included in BipoläR, of whom 14,616 patients were diagnosed with BD I, BD II, or BD NOS and not excluded due to other missing data (Fig. 1). Of the 14,616 patients, a total of 5618 patients were diagnosed with BD I.

The following variables were extracted from BipoläR: BD subdiagnoses, psychiatric comorbidity, number of episodes during the past 12 months, current psychotropic drug treatment, age, sex, weight, height, and educational level. We used the most recent register entry for each patient regardless of year of entry.

Dichotomous variables were created for each type of episode that had occurred during the last 12 months prior to the last register entry. Psychiatric comorbidity was extracted both as any type of comorbidity, and as the following specific comorbidities: substance abuse or addiction, anxiety disorders, and personality disorders. Mood stabilizing drugs were in this study categorized as any mood stabilizer (lithium, lamotrigine, valproate, or carbamazepine), lithium, lamotrigine, valproate, and carbamazepine. Second generation antipsychotic drugs (e.g., olanzapine and quetiapine) might also qualify as mood stabilizers (Rybakowski 2018), but were here classified as neuroleptics because they are often used temporary to treat acute episodes and as needed rescue medication.

Items included in BipoläR have been subject to change over the years, some of which affected the choice of outcomes and variables for the present analyses. For example, in 2014 the variable concerning educational level was removed. Educational level is therefore presented for all study populations along with the number of missing data, but is not included in the regression analyses.

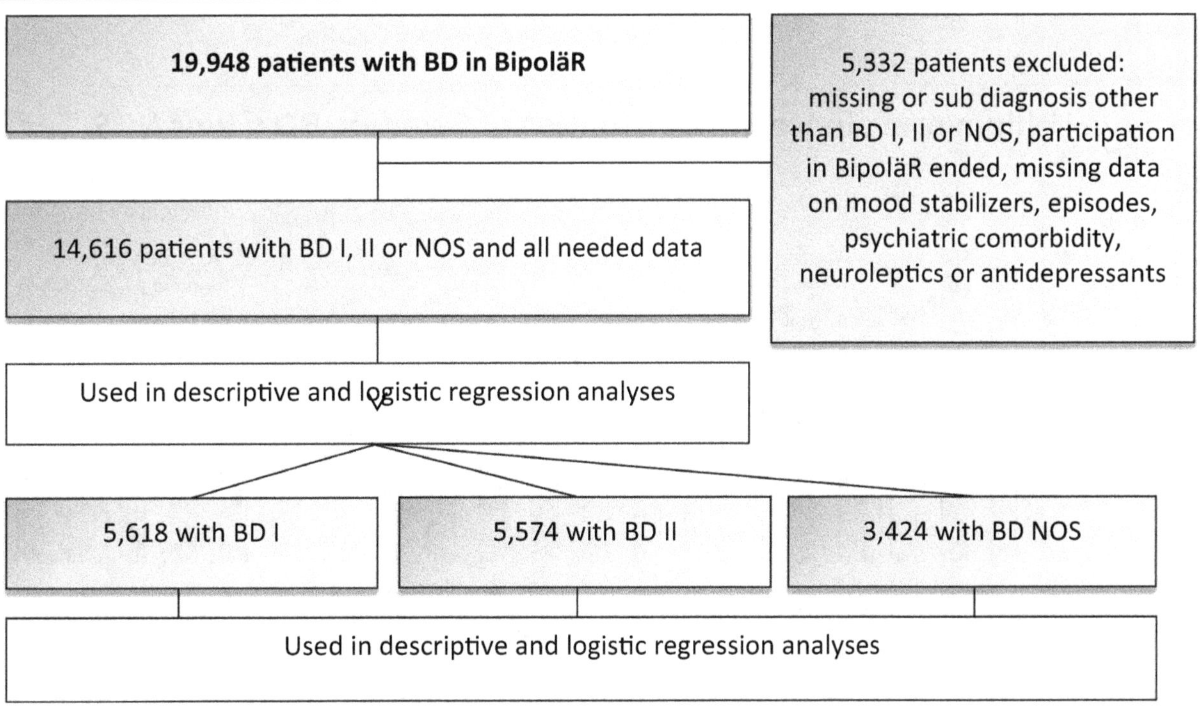

Fig. 1 Flowchart of inclusion and exclusion of study subjects

The analyses were conducted in two steps: we first analysed the 14,616 patients with BD I, BD II, or BD NOS. Secondly, as evidence for lithium in long-term prevention varies extensively between the subtypes (strongest for BD I) (Severus et al. 2014; Miura et al. 2014), separate analyses of the subsets of patients with BD I, BD II and BD NOS were carried out. The lithium prescription rate—defined as the proportion of bipolar disorder patients being on lithium at the time for annual follow-up—was calculated for each county. The prescription rate for the total population stratified by county is shown in Fig. 2. The same calculation of prescription rate was also made for the three subpopulations BD I, BD II and BD NOS. Further details on the prevalence of lithium use in the 21 Swedish counties and for the three subsets of patients can be found in the supplement.

Statistics

The primary outcome was any type of mood episode (coded 'yes' if at least one episode had occurred during the 12 months preceding the registration). Secondary outcomes were separate counts of depressive, manic, hypomanic, or mixed episode.

Logistic regression analyses conducted with relapse as the dependent variable and county lithium prevalence as the main independent variable were performed in two steps: (1) adjusted for age and sex; (2) also adjusted for psychiatric comorbidity (any type); two-sided testing was used for all analyses and the significance level was set to $p < 0.05$.

Results are presented with adjusted odds ratios (aOR) for a 10% point increase in lithium use prevalence, 95% confidence intervals (CI), *P*-values when applicable, and estimated (pseudo) R^2-values (Cox–Snell and Nagelkerke) for the different county groups. No problematic multicollinearities were found for the variables age, sex, psychiatric comorbidity (any type) and lithium prescription rate. IBM SPSS version 24 was used for all analyses.

It is possible that minor changes of lithium prescription rates might have occurred within counties during the study period, meaning that the number of relapses does not perfectly match county prescription rates by year. We therefore performed a sensitivity test where we calculated county lithium prevalences for the year 2015 only, and performed regression analyses for the combined population as well as for BD I group separately. These results are found in Additional file 1.

Results

Table 1 shows characteristics for the populations with BD I, BD II, BD NOS and the combined population. The average prescription rate of any mood stabiliser was > 80% for all the studied populations, with a 65% average lithium prescription rate in the BD I population. On average, 55% of the patients had at least one registered affective episode.

The lithium prevalence for the combined group ranged from 37.7 to 84.9% across the 21 counties of Sweden, with an average of 52.4%. The lithium prescription rate for each county is presented in Fig. 2. The lithium prevalence for the BD I group ranged from 48.6 to 93.5% across

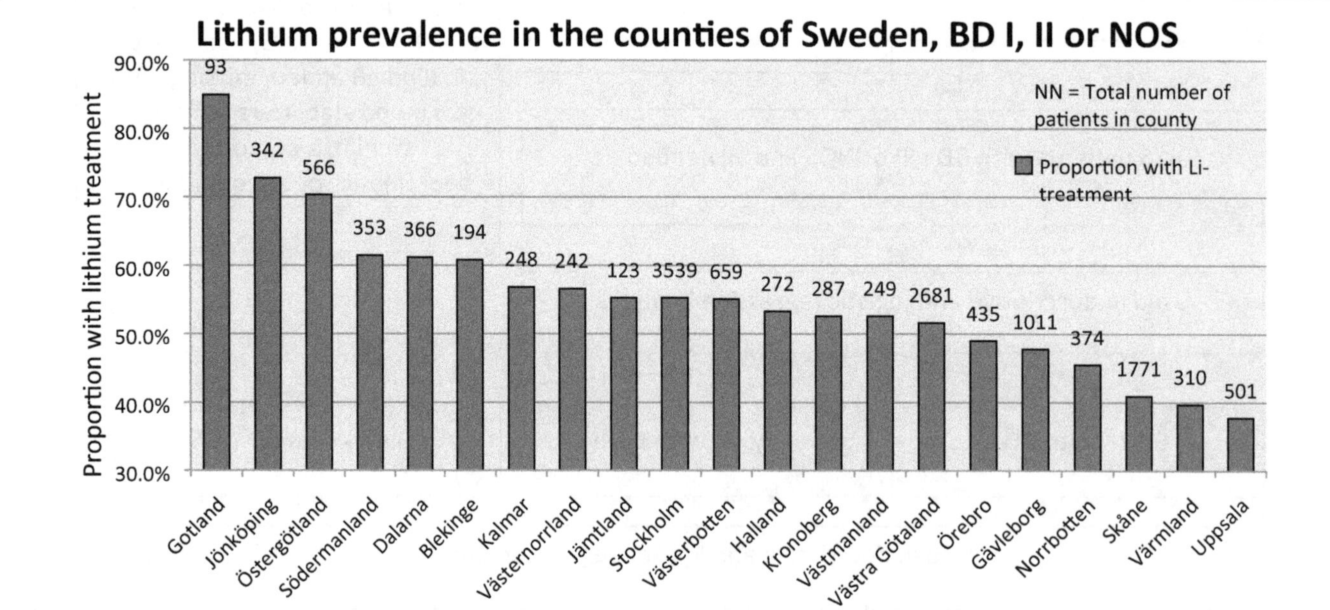

Fig. 2 County specific lithium prevalences. All BD patients

Table 1 Descriptive data for the study populations with BD I, BD II, BD NOS and the combined population

	BD I (n=5618)	BD II (n=5574)	NOS (n=3424)	Total (n=14,616)
Age years, mean (SD)	52.9 (15.8)	46.4 (16.0)	50.1 (16.4)	49.8 (16.3)
Gender (female), *n* (%)	3211 (57.2)	3799 (68.2)	2202 (64.3)	9212 (63.0)
Education, *n* (%)				
Less than high school	764 (13.6)	537 (9.6)	466 (13.6)	1767 (12.1)
Graduated high school	1158 (20.6)	992 (17.8)	633 (18.5)	2783 (19.0)
Graduated college or higher	1240 (22.1)	1102 (19.8)	560 (16.4)	2902 (19.9)
Missing data	2456 (43.7)	2943 (52.8)	1765 (51.5)	7164 (49.0)
BMI, mean (SD), missing	27.7 (5.4), 359	27.2 (5.7), 232	28.0 (5.7), 230	27.6 (5.6)
Psychiatric comorbidity, *n* (%)				
Any comorbidity	1137 (20.2)	1859 (33.4)	1178 (34.4)	4174 (28.6)
Substance abuse or addiction	226 (4.0)	196 (3.5)	140 (4.1)	562 (3.8)
Anxiety disorder	302 (5.4)	646 (11.6)	310 (9.1)	1258 (8.6)
Personality disorder	83 (1.5)	221 (4.0)	160 (4.7)	464 (3.2)
Mood stabilizers, *n* (%)				
Any mood stabilizers	4895 (87.1)	4610 (82.7)	2750 (80.3)	12255 (83.8)
Lithium	3664 (65.2)	2333 (41.9)	1667 (48.7)	7664 (52.4)
Lamotrigine	937 (16.7)	2242 (40.2)	924 (27.0)	4103 (28.1)
Valproate	712 (12.7)	382 (6.9)	275 (8.0)	1369 (9.4)
Carbamazepine	102 (1.8)	454 (0.8)	41 (1.2)	188 (1.3)
Neuroleptics, *n* (%)	2692 (47.9)	1837 (33.0)	1267 (37.0)	5796 (39.7)
Antidepressants, *n* (%)	1952 (34.7)	2920 (52.4)	1633 (47.7)	6505 (44.5)
Episode (at least one episode last 12 months), *n* (%), missing				
Any episode	2665 (47.4)	3614 (64.8)	1830 (53.4)	8109 (55.5)
Depressive episode	2041 (36.4), 11	3275 (58.8), 8	1603 (47.0), 12	6919 (47.4), 31
Manic episode	719 (12.9), 26	110 (2.0), 30	141 (4.1), 20	970 (6.7), 76
Hypomanic episode	1147(20.5), 20	1814 (32.6), 17	738 (21.7), 18	3699 (25.4), 55
Mixed episode	497 (8.9), 62	746 (13.4), 27	425 (12.5), 12	1668 (11.5), 101

counties, with an average of 65.2%. For the BD II and BD NOS groups, the lithium prevalence ranged from 27.0 to 77.8% (average 41.9%) and from 34.2 to 100% (average 48.7%), respectively. Percentages for each county are presented in Additional file 1.

The logistic regression analyses for the separate populations of BD I, BD II, BD NOS, as well as for the combined population are presented in Table 2. The regression analyses indicate that the odds of recurrence (any episode, depressive, and hypomanic) were higher in counties with higher lithium prevalence. This was observed at both steps of the analyses. For the aggregated population, the aOR (adjusted for age, sex and psychiatric comorbidity) for any type of episode was 0.84 (CI 0.80–0.88). The aOR can be interpreted as the decreased odds for a mood episode in the population when the lithium prescription rate is greater by 10% points. For the three subtypes, the odds ratio for relapse in any mood episode was significantly associated with lithium prevalence in all subtypes (BD I: aOR=0.78, 95% CI 0.70–0.87; BD II: aOR=0.90, 95% CI 0.84–0.96; BD NOS: aOR=0.82, 95% CI 0.74–0.90).

With respect to specific episodes (Table 2), higher lithium prevalence was associated with higher odds for relapse of depression in all subtypes. In BD I, higher lithium prevalence was also associated with higher odds for manic episodes. In BD II, higher lithium prevalence was also associated with higher odds for hypomanic episodes.

The results of the sensitivity analysis confined to the year 2015 corroborated the association found for the whole study period (Additional file 1).

Discussion

There were fewer relapses in BD in Swedish counties with high lithium prescription rate than in counties with low lithium prescription rates. The association was found in the whole BD population (BD I, BD II, or BD NOS) as well as in each subpopulation of BD I, BD II and BD NOS. For BD I, a 10% point greater lithium prevalence was associated with 20% reduction in odds of relapse. Given that almost half of patients suffered at least one relapse per year, an increase of odds at this scale means that increasing lithium prescription rates on a population

Table 2 Logistic regression analyses for the study populations with BD I, BD II, BD NOS and the combined population, adjusted for age, sex, and psychiatric comorbidity

Logistic regression analyses	n	aOR	CI, 95%	*P*	R^2
BD I					
Any episode	5618	0.78	0.70–0.87	< 0.001	0.06–0.08
Depressive episode	5607	0.81	0.72–0.90	< 0.001	0.05–0.07
Manic episode	5592	0.85	0.72–0.97	0.02	0.02–0.03
Hypomanic episode	5598	0.90	0.79–0.99	0.05	0.03–0.04
Mixed episode	5556	0.93	0.78–1.07		0.03–0.06
BD II					
Any episode	5574	0.90	0.84–0.96	0.001	0.07–0.1
Depressive episode	5566	0.93	0.87–0.99	0.02	0.06–0.08
Hypomanic episode	5557	0.87	0.80–0.93	< 0.001	0.06–0.09
Mixed episode	5547	0.96	0.87–1.04		0.03–0.06
BD NOS					
Any episode	3424	0.82	0.74–0.90	< 0.001	0.1–0.14
Depressive episode	3412	0.82	0.74–0.90	< 0.001	0.09–0.12
Hypomanic episode	3406	0.93	0.83–1.02		0.06–0.09
Mixed episode	3412	1.01	0.89–1.13		0.05–0.09
Total, all subpopulations					
Any episode	14,616	0.84	0.80–0.88	< 0.001	0.09–0.12
Depressive episode	14,585	0.87	0.83–0.92	< 0.001	0.08–0.10
Hypomanic episode	14,561	0.89	0.84–0.94	< 0.001	0.05–0.08
Mixed episode	14,515	0.94	0.88–1.01	0.097	0.04–0.07

Adjusted odds ratios (aOR) estimating differences for patients in counties with high lithium prevalence compared with counties with low lithium prevalence. The aOR can be interpreted as the decreased odds for a mood episode in the population when the lithium prescription rate is greater by 10% points

level has the potential to prevent a large number of relapses.

This study suggests that higher regional lithium use is associated with better regional outcomes even in a country with high average lithium use. As patients in counties with low lithium prevalence instead used other long-term medications to a greater degree, our findings also indicate that the beneficial effects of lithium cannot be fully rescued by using alternative treatments. The latter appears to conflict with the findings from a network meta-analysis by Miura et al. (2014) that suggested a general equivalence between a range of different treatments in relapse prevention studies. It should be noted, however, that almost all trials of neuroleptic drugs in BD have used an enriched RCT design that favours the study drug (Joas et al. 2017). Moreover, in RCTs typically conducted for regulatory submission, comprehensive exclusion criteria distort the study population, whereas we examined outcomes in a more heterogeneous population of BD patients.

The dataset is unusual in including BD II and BD NOS patients in substantial numbers. There are few RCTs of any plausible size that have included this population at all, especially over longer term follow-up. This is particularly true of trials that have included lithium as a treatment arm (Goodwin et al. 2016). Thus, the positive findings here are an important contribution to the existing literature and suggest that the advantages for lithium use long acknowledged for BD I patients are also seen over the rest of the bipolar spectrum.

We found no association between lithium prevalence and the recurrence rate of mixed episodes. It is possible that alternative treatments like valproate or carbamazepine have higher efficacy in atypical presentations (e.g., mixed episodes or dysphoric mania) (Cipriani et al. 2013; Fountoulakis et al. 2013). However, Joas et al. found lithium to be effective in preventing admission with a mixed episode (Joas et al. 2017). A possible explanation is that the study by Joas et al. included only hospitalizations, whereas our data also included milder relapses managed in outpatient settings. Another possible explanation is the low number of mixed episodes with ensuing low statistical power.

An intriguing corollary of these findings is that BD outcomes are likely different across countries depending on the use of lithium. Comparing outcomes in BD in relation to prescription rates of lithium across nations is challenging and requires comparable outcome data. But given the potential impact on public health, future studies should replicate these findings in the UK and other countries with data available in population. In a similar vein, the use of lithium in BD has declined in a majority of developed countries (Wolfsperger et al. 2007; Kessing et al. 2016; Karanti et al. 2016; Blanco et al. 2002; Rhee et al. 2020), even though there are examples of stable (Hayes et al. 2011) or even increasing (Castells et al. 2006) lithium prescription rates. A concerning possibility is that decreasing use of lithium has led to worse outcomes in BD. However, we are not aware of any previous study using our approach to study BD recurrence rate in relation to lithium prescription rates at a population level, let alone recurrences in relation to time trends in lithium use.

Strengths and limitations

A strength of this study is the real-world setting and the large number of patients included: 14,616 BD patients of whom 5618 had BD I, which is much higher than for any previous RCT or even meta-analysis (Severus et al. 2014; Miura et al. 2014) and provides strong statistical power. Moreover, as already indicated, BD II and BD NOS are rarely even included in clinical trials but are represented at an appropriate level here.

Among limitations to consider are first that the data source for the current study, BipoläR, only covers approximately 30% of the total Swedish bipolar population (BipoläR 2021). However, general trends observed in BipoläR, including a higher prevalence of bipolar disorder in women and secular trends in mood stabilizer treatment, are mirrored in the Swedish patient and prescribed drugs registers. This supports the assumption that observations from BipoläR are applicable to the total Swedish bipolar population. The study population was narrowed further mainly due to missing data. Even though the patients included in the current study thus comprise approximately 22% of the total Swedish bipolar population, there is a risk of selection bias. It is possible that the study has oversampled patients from well-functioning care providers as registering patients in BipoläR might be an indication of better care. Second, mood episodes were identified by clinicians who assessed the course during the last 12 months. In particular depressive episodes might be difficult to delineate as subsyndromal symptoms might linger for long time. Third, there are many other factors associated with specific counties that might impact outcomes, for instance psychiatric health care organization and culture, economic resources, and societal factors like unemployment rate, or educational level. Unfortunately, we were unable to control for potential differences in educational levels across the populations due to a change in the quality register BipoläR where this variable was removed. It is possible that a more well-functioning psychiatric health care system is the cause of both higher lithium prescription and less recurrences. Future studies should take into account other factors potentially reflecting quality of care that might confound the results. Fourth, patients who had changed their medical treatment during the last year were not excluded because the exact date when the change occurred is not known. This imposes a risk that recurrent episodes or their absence are a result of an older treatment regime rather than the current treatment. However, the latter can be seen as added noise that is more likely to diminish positive associations than to boost them. Fifth, we used data from patients' last registration during the study period 2004–2016. Even though the great majority of patient data were from the end of the study period and peaked during 2015, small changes of lithium prescription rates within counties during the study period means that the number of relapses does not perfectly match county prescription rates by year. We therefore conducted sensitivity analyses for year 2015 only, which corroborated the associations found for the whole period; see Additional file 1.

Conclusions

We provide evidence of an association between higher lithium prevalence rate and lower recurrence of illness at a regional level. Although no causal inference can be made directly from this study, it is compatible with results from prospective clinical trials and suggests that population outcomes across the bipolar spectrum (BD I, BD II, and BD NOS) might be improved by increasing the number of patients treated with lithium. Lithium prescription rate might hence serve as a quality indicator of BD care. Indeed, outcomes continued to improve with higher lithium prevalence despite the mean lithium prevalence for the population being 65.2% (BD I), which is much higher than in most other countries. Higher levels than this would be a worthwhile target in the quest to improve management of bipolar patients.

Abbreviations

aOR: Adjusted odds ratio; BD: Bipolar disorder; BDI: Bipolar I disorder; BD II: Bipolar II disorder; BipoläR: The Swedish national quality register for bipolar disorders; CANMAT: Canadian network for mood and anxiety treatments; NOS: Not otherwise specified; RCT: Randomized controlled trial.

Supplementary Information

Additional file1: Table S1. County specific lithium prevalences. All BD patients. **Table S2.** County specific lithium prevalences for BD I, BD II, and BD NOS. **Table S3.** Logistic regression analyses for patients with BD I, BD II, or BD NOS only year 2015. OR estimating differences for patients in counties with high lithium prevalence compared to counties with low lithium prevalence. Adjusted for age, sex and psychiatric comorbidity. **Table S4.** Logistic regression analyses for patients with BD I only year 2015. OR estimating differences for patients in counties with high lithium prevalence compared to counties with low lithium prevalence. Adjusted for age, sex and psychiatric comorbidity. **Figure S1.** Inclusion and exclusion flow chart.

Acknowledgements

We wish to thank clinicians and patients that contribute data to the Swedish National Quality Register for Bipolar Disorders: BipoläR.

Authors' contributions

MS analysis and interpretation of data, drafting of the manuscript; SR study design, interpretation of data, revision of the manuscript for important intellectual content; EJ analysis and interpretation of data, revision of the manuscript for important intellectual content; MK data acquisition, revision of the manuscript for important intellectual content; EP interpretation of data, revision of the manuscript for important intellectual content; GG study design, interpretation of data, revision of the manuscript for important intellectual content; ML conception of the study, study design, revision of the manuscript for important intellectual content. All authors read and approved the final manuscript.

Competing interests

All authors have completed the Unified Competing Interest form (available on request from the corresponding author) and declare: MS has nothing to disclose. SR has nothing to disclose. EJ has nothing to disclose. MK has nothing to disclose. EP has nothing to disclose. GG reports personal fees from Servier, personal fees from Lundbeck, personal fees from Medscape, personal fees from P1Vital, personal fees from Compass pathways, personal fees from Johnson&Johnson/Janssen, personal fees from Sage Therapeutics, personal fees from Novartis, outside the submitted work. ML reports grants from The Swedish Foundation for Strategic Research, grants from The Swedish Medical Research council, grants from The Swedish Federal Government under the LUA/ALF agreement, during the conduct of the study; personal fees from Lundbeck pharmaceuticals, outside the submitted work.

Author details
[1]Department of Psychiatry and Neurochemistry, Institute of Neuroscience and Physiology, Sahlgrenska Academy, University of Gothenburg, Blå Stråket 15, 413 45 Gothenburg, Sweden. [2]Department of Psychology, Faculty of Social Science, University of Gothenburg, Gothenburg, Sweden. [3]Department of Psychiatry, University of Oxford, Oxford, UK. [4]Department of Medical Epidemiology and Biostatistics, Karolinska Institutet, Stockholm, Sweden.

References

Adler M (ed), Häggström L, Jarbin H, Landén M, Liberg B, Mathé A, Rydén E, Svanborg C. Bipolär sjukdom: kliniska riktlinjer för utredning och behandling. Svenska Psykiatriska Föreningen; 2014. (trans: Bipolar disorder: Clinical guidelines for management and treatment, The Swedish Psychiatric Association). http://www.svenskpsykiatri.se/wp-content/uploads/2017/02/SPF-kliniska-riktlinjer-om-Bipol%C3%A4r-sjukdom.pdf.

BipoläR Årsrapport 2018. https://registercentrum.blob.core.windows.net/bipolar/r/Bipol-R-rsrapport-2018-BkxNjLjgZr.pdf. Accessed 12 Jan 2021.

Baastrup PC. The use of lithium in manic-depressive psychosis. Compr Psychiatry. 1964;5(6):396–408.

BipoläR—The Swedish national quality register for bipolar disorder. https://bipolar.registercentrum.se/in-english/bipolar-the-swedish-national-quality-register-for-bipolar-disorder/p/BySl1W2zb. Accessed 12 Jan 2021.

Blanco C, Laje G, Olfson M, Marcus SC, Pincus HA. Trends in the treatment of bipolar disorder by outpatient psychiatrists. Am J Psychiatry. 2002;159(6):1005–10.

Cade JF. Lithium salts in the treatment of psychotic excitement 1949. Bull World Health Organ. 2000;78(4):518–20.

Castells X, Vallano A, Rigau D, Perez J, Casas M, Capella D. Trends in lithium prescription in Spain from 1985 to 2003. J Affect Disord. 2006;91(2–3):273–6.

Cipriani A, Hawton K, Stockton S, Geddes JR. Lithium in the prevention of suicide in mood disorders: updated systematic review and meta-analysis. BMJ. 2013. https://doi.org/10.1136/bmj.f3646.

Crump C, Sundquist K, Winkleby MA, Sundquist J. Comorbidities and mortality in bipolar disorder: a Swedish national cohort study. JAMA Psychiat. 2013;70(9):931–9.

Ekman M, Granstrom O, Omerov S, Jacob J, Landen M. The societal cost of bipolar disorder in Sweden. Soc Psychiatry Psychiatr Epidemiol. 2013;48(10):1601–10.

Emilsson L, Lindahl B, Koster M, Lambe M, Ludvigsson JF. Review of 103 Swedish healthcare quality registries. J Intern Med. 2015;277(1):94–136.

Ferensztajn-Rochowiak E, ChBopocka-Wozniak M, Rybakowski JK. Ultra-long-term lithium therapy: all-important matters and a case of successful 50-year lithium treatment. Braz J Psychiatry. 2020. https://doi.org/10.1590/1516-4446-2020-1111.

Fountoulakis KN, Kontis D, Gonda X, Yatham LN. A systematic review of the evidence on the treatment of rapid cycling bipolar disorder. Bipolar Disord. 2013;15(2):115–37.

Fountoulakis KN, Grunze H, Vieta E, Young A, Yatham L, Blier P, et al. The International College of Neuro-Psychopharmacology (CINP) treatment guidelines for bipolar disorder in adults (CINP-BD-2017), part 3: the clinical guidelines. Int J Neuropsychopharmacol. 2016. https://doi.org/10.1093/ijnp/pyw109.

Geddes JR, Miklowitz DJ. Treatment of bipolar disorder. Lancet. 2013;381(9878):1672–82.

Goodwin GM, Haddad PM, Ferrier IN, Aronson JK, Barnes T, Cipriani A, et al. Evidence-based guidelines for treating bipolar disorder: revised third edition recommendations from the British Association for Psychopharmacology. J Psychopharmacol. 2016;30(6):495–553.

Grunze H, Vieta E, Goodwin GM, Bowden C, Licht RW, Moller HJ, et al. The World Federation of Societies of Biological Psychiatry (WFSBP) guidelines for the biological treatment of bipolar disorders: update 2012 on the long-term treatment of bipolar disorder. World J Biol Psychiatry Off J World Fed Soc Biol Psychiatry. 2013;14(3):154–219.

Guilbert JJ. The world health report 2002—reducing risks, promoting healthy life. Educ Health. 2003;16(2):230.

Hartigan GP. The use of lithium salts in affective disorders. Br J Psychiatry. 1963;109(463):810–4.

Hayes J, Prah P, Nazareth I, King M, Walters K, Petersen I, et al. Prescribing trends in bipolar disorder: cohort study in the United Kingdom THIN primary care database 1995–2009. PLoS ONE. 2011;6(12):e28725.

Joas E, Karanti A, Song J, Goodwin GM, Lichtenstein P, Landen M. Pharmacological treatment and risk of psychiatric hospital admission in bipolar disorder. Br J Psychiatry J Ment Sci. 2017;210(3):197–202.

Judd LL, Akiskal HS, Schettler PJ, Endicott J, Leon AC, Solomon DA, et al. Psychosocial disability in the course of bipolar I and II disorders: a prospective, comparative, longitudinal study. Arch Gen Psychiatry. 2005;62(12):1322–30.

Karanti A, Kardell M, Lundberg U, Landen M. Changes in mood stabilizer prescription patterns in bipolar disorder. J Affect Disord. 2016;195:50–6.

Kendall T, Morriss R, Mayo-Wilson E, Marcus E. Assessment and management of bipolar disorder: summary of updated NICE guidance. BMJ. 2014. https://doi.org/10.1136/bmj.g5673.

Kessing LV, Hellmund G, Geddes JR, Goodwin GM, Andersen PK, Valproate V. Lithium in the treatment of bipolar disorder in clinical practice: observational nationwide register-based cohort study. Br J Psychiatry J Ment Sci. 2011;199(1):57–63.

Kessing LV, Hellmund G, Andersen PK. An observational nationwide register based cohort study on lamotrigine versus lithium in bipolar disorder. J Psychopharmacol. 2012;26(5):644–52.

Kessing LV, Vradi E, Andersen PK. Nationwide and population-based prescription patterns in bipolar disorder. Bipolar Disord. 2016;18(2):174–82.

Merikangas KR, Jin R, He JP, Kessler RC, Lee S, Sampson NA, et al. Prevalence and correlates of bipolar spectrum disorder in the world mental health survey initiative. Arch Gen Psychiatry. 2011;68(3):241–51.

Miura T, Noma H, Furukawa TA, Mitsuyasu H, Tanaka S, Stockton S, et al. Comparative efficacy and tolerability of pharmacological treatments in the maintenance treatment of bipolar disorder: a systematic review and network meta-analysis. Lancet Psychiatry. 2014;1(5):351–9.

Rhee TG, Olfson M, Nierenberg AA, Wilkinson ST. 20-Year trends in the pharmacologic treatment of bipolar disorder by psychiatrists in outpatient care settings. Am J Psychiatry. 2020;177(8):706–15.

Rybakowski JK. Meaningful aspects of the term 'mood stabilizer.' Bipolar Disord. 2018;20(4):391–2.

Severus E, Taylor MJ, Sauer C, Pfennig A, Ritter P, Bauer M, et al. Lithium for prevention of mood episodes in bipolar disorders: systematic review and meta-analysis. Int J Bipolar Disord. 2014;2:15.

Song J, Sjölander A, Joas E, Bergen SE, Runeson B, Larsson H, et al. Suicidal behavior during lithium and valproate treatment: a within-individual 8-year prospective study of 50,000 patients with bipolar disorder. Am J Psychiatry. 2017;174(8):795–802.

Wolfsperger M, Greil W, Rossler W, Grohmann R. Pharmacological treatment of acute mania in psychiatric in-patients between 1994 and 2004. J Affect Disord. 2007;99(1–3):9–17.

Yatham LN, Kennedy SH, Parikh SV, Schaffer A, Bond DJ, Frey BN, et al. Canadian Network for Mood and Anxiety Treatments (CANMAT) and International Society for Bipolar Disorders (ISBD) 2018 guidelines for the management of patients with bipolar disorder. Bipolar Disord. 2018;20(2):97–170.

9

An integrative analysis of genome-wide association study and regulatory SNP annotation datasets identified candidate genes for bipolar disorder

Xin Qi[†], Yan Wen[†], Ping Li, Chujun Liang, Bolun Cheng, Mei Ma, Shiqiang Cheng, Lu Zhang, Li Liu, Om Prakash Kafle and Feng Zhang[*]

Abstract

Background: Bipolar disorder (BD) is a complex mood disorder. The genetic mechanism of BD remains largely unknown.

Methods: We conducted an integrative analysis of genome-wide association study (GWAS) and regulatory SNP (rSNP) annotation datasets, including transcription factor binding regions (TFBRs), chromatin interactive regions (CIRs), mature microRNA regions (miRNAs), long non-coding RNA regions (lncRNAs), topologically associated domains (TADs) and circular RNAs (circRNAs). Firstly, GWAS dataset 1 of BD (including 20,352 cases and 31,358 controls) and GWAS dataset 2 of BD (including 7481 BD patients and 9250 controls) were integrated with rSNP annotation database to obtain BD associated SNP regulatory elements and SNP regulatory element-target gene (E–G) pairs, respectively. Secondly, a comparative analysis of the two datasets results was conducted to identify the common rSNPs and also their target genes. Then, gene sets enrichment analysis (FUMA GWAS) and HumanNet-XC analysis were conducted to explore the functional relevance of identified target genes with BD.

Results: After the integrative analysis, we identified 52 TFBRs target genes, 44 TADs target genes, 55 CIRs target genes and 21 lncRNAs target genes for BD, such as *ITIH4* ($P_{dataset1}=6.68\times10^{-8}$, $P_{dataset2}=6.64\times10^{-7}$), *ITIH3* ($P_{dataset1}=1.09\times10^{-8}$, $P_{dataset2}=2.00\times10^{-7}$), *SYNE1* ($P_{dataset1}=1.80\times10^{-6}$, $P_{dataset2}=4.33\times10^{-9}$) and *OPRM1* ($P_{dataset1}=1.80\times10^{-6}$, $P_{dataset2}=4.33\times10^{-9}$).

Conclusion: We conducted a large-scale integrative analysis of GWAS and 6 common rSNP information datasets to explore the potential roles of rSNPs in the genetic mechanism of BD. We identified multiple candidate genes for BD, supporting the importance of rSNP in the development of BD.

Keywords: Bipolar disorder, Regulatory SNP, Genome-wide association studies

Background

Bipolar disorder (BD) is a common and often life-threatening mood disorder, which is characterized by recurrent manic, depressive or mixed states episodes (Judd et al. 2005). The prevalence of BD is more than 1%, and it is one of the important causes of disability among young adults (Merikangas et al. 2011; Alonso et al. 2010). BD can lead to cognitive and functional impairment and raised mortality, particularly death caused by suicide (Martinez-Aran et al. 2007). The suicide rate in BD patients is 20–30 times higher than in the general

*Correspondence: fzhxjtuqx@163.com
[†]Xin Qi and Yan Wen contributed equally to this work
Key Laboratory of Trace Elements and Endemic Diseases of National Health and Family Planning Commission, School of Public Health, Health Science Center, Xi'an Jiaotong University, No. 76 Yan Ta West Road, Xi'an 710061, People's Republic of China

populations (Pompili et al. 2013). BD brings heavy burdens to BD patients and society, including direct costs of treatment and indirect costs (Dilsaver 2011).

BD is a complex disorder with strong genetic factors (Mühleisen et al. 2014). The estimated heritability of BD ranged from 60 to 80% (Craddock and Forty 2006). Multiple genome-wide association studies (GWAS) of BD has been conducted. For instance, a large-scale GWAS of 7481 individuals with BD and 9250 controls identified a new susceptibility variant in *ODZ4* gene (Psychiatric et al. 2011). *TRANK1*, *LMAN2L* and *PTGFR* were also identified by GWAS as the candidate genes for BD (Chen et al. 2011). Although GWAS has successfully identified multiple susceptibility genes associated with BD, there is still a challenge to clarify the roles of genomic regulatory elements in the development of BD. Recent studies observed that the significant SNPs detected by GWAS were enriched in non-coding regulatory genomic loci, for instance, expression quantitative traits (eQTLs) (Vernot et al. 2012). However, limited efforts have been paid to explore the roles of genomic regulatory loci in the genetic mechanism of BD.

Regulatory single nucleotide polymorphisms (rSNPs) are a group of regulatory genomic loci, which can produce new regulatory elements, such as transcription factor binding regions (TFBRs) and chromatin interactive regions (CIRs) (Wu et al. 2009). SNPs involved in transcription factor binding sites (TFBSs) or that affect TF-DNA binding affinity were considered to be predominant rSNPs (Riva 2012). It is similar to the effect of SNPs on protein structure and function, and the functional effect of rSNPs has been widely studied in recent years (Munkhtulga et al. 2010). Previous studies found that rSNPs played a vital role in the molecular mechanism of complex diseases (Marco et al. 2006). For example, Marco et al. (2006) identified a gain-of-function rSNP in a non-coding region of alpha thalassemia, which could interfere the normal activation of the downstream alpha-like globin genes through producing new promoterlike element. Integrating GWAS dataset and rSNP annotation information has the potential to provide novel clues for clarifying the genetic mechanism of human complex diseases (Macintyre et al. 2010). For instance, Macintyre et al. (2010) identified 11 rSNPs with disrupted impact on TF binding site from disease- and trait-associated GWAS SNPs. The functional relevance of the 9 of 11 rSNPs had been reported by previous studies (Macintyre et al. 2010). The rSNPs (rs4150275 and rs17655) of *ERCC5* gene were also found to be associated with chronic obstructive pulmonary disease by combing GWAS and regulatory SNPs annotation information (Yeo et al. 2018).

To identify novel BD associated genetic loci, we performed an integrative analysis of GWAS and rSNP annotation database for BD. GWAS dataset 1 of BD and GWAS dataset 2 of BD were integrated with rSNP annotation database to obtain BD associated SNP regulatory elements and SNP regulatory element-target gene (E–G) pairs, respectively. Then, a comparative analysis of the two datasets results was conducted to identify the common rSNPs and their target genes. Additionally, the identified BD associated genes were subjected to enrichment analysis and HumanNet-XC analysis to explore the functional relevance of the identified genes with BD.

Materials and methods

GWAS dataset 1 of BD

A recent large-scale GWAS summary dataset of BD was driven from the Psychiatric Genomics Consortium (PGC) (Stahl et al. 2019). The detailed information of the dataset and analysis procedure can be found in this published study (Stahl et al. 2019). Briefly, 20,352 cases and 31,358 controls of European descent were included in this GWA study. A standardized quality control, imputation and analysis were performed in this published study according to the PGC "ricopili" pipeline (Stahl et al. 2019; Ripke S. Ricopili: a tool for visualizing regions of interest in select GWAS data sets 2014). The default criteria for retaining genotyped SNPs and subjects includes: SNP missingness < 0.05 (before sample removal) and SNP missingness < 0.02 (after sample removal); subject SNP missingness < 0.02; autosomal heterozygosity deviation ($|F_{het}| < 0.2$); difference in SNP missingness between cases and controls < 0.02; and SNP Hardy–Weinberg equilibrium ($P > 10^{-6}$ in controls or $P > 10^{-10}$ in cases). The software of IMPUTE2/SHAPEIT was used to perform genotype imputation (Howie et al. 2011; Delaneau et al. 2012). SNPs with imputation marker INFO score ≥ 0.6 and allele frequencies ≥ 0.01 and ≤ 0.99 were retained after imputation. Individual relatedness checks and principle component analysis (PCA) was also conducted in this study. After linkage disequilibrium (LD) pruning ($r^2 > 0.02$) and frequency filtering (minor allele frequency (MAF) > 0.05), 24,498 autosomal SNPs were finally retained and used to calculate the IBS (identity by state) matrix of relatedness checks. Individuals related to another (with pi_hat > 0.2) were detected and one member of each pair was removed at random after preferentially retaining cases over controls.

GWAS dataset 2 of BD

Another GWAS dataset of BD was driven from PGC (Psychiatric et al. 2011). The detailed information, including sample characteristics, experimental design and statistical analysis, was performed in the previous study (Psychiatric et al. 2011). In brief, this GWAS dataset contained 7481 subjects with BD and 9250 controls. SNP genotyping was performed using commercial platforms, such as Affymetrix 500 K, 5.0, 6.0 and Illumina HumanHap 500. Imputation was performed using BEAGLE 3.0 against the HapMap Phase 2 as Ref. (Browning and Browning 2007). After quality control, 2,415,422 autosomal SNPs with MAF ≥ 1% and imputation quality score $r^2 > 0.3$ were analyzed using logistic regression.

rSNP annotation dataset

The regulatory features of SNPs in human genome are annotated by the rSNPBase 3.1 database (http://rsnp3.psych.ac.cn/) (Guo and Wang 2018). rSNPBase 3.1 contains 119,630,196 rSNP annotation items, including human SNP-related regulatory elements as well as their target regulatory genes (Guo and Wang 2018). There are 6 common types of regulatory elements annotated by the rSNPBase 3.1, including transcription factor binding regions (TFBRs), chromatin interactive regions (CIRs), mature microRNA regions (miRNAs), long noncoding RNA regions (lncRNAs), topologically associated domains (TADs) and circular RNAs (circRNAs). They used genomic proximity to detect the relationship between the included regulatory elements and genes from Ensembl (GRCh37) (Aken et al. 2016).

Integrative analysis of GWAS and rSNP annotation information

To integrate the GWAS dataset of BD with the rSNP functional annotation information, the SNPs with GWAS P value < 10^{-5} were selected from GWAS dataset 1 and GWAS dataset 2, respectively. The selected SNPs were then annotated by rSNPBase 3.1 to obtain BD associated SNP regulatory elements as well as their target genes (including TFBRs, CIRs, miRNAs, lncRNAs and TADs). Then, a comparative analysis of the two datasets results was conducted to identify the common rSNPs and their target genes (except for circRNAs). A flowchart for this study was showed in Fig. 1.

Functional analysis of identified target genes

The gene sets enrichment analysis and HumanNet-XC analysis were conducted to explore the functional relevance of the target genes of identified rSNPs with BD. The gene sets enrichment analysis was implemented by FUMA GWAS (Functional Mapping and Annotation of Genome-Wide Association Studies, https://fuma.ctglab.nl/) (Watanabe et al. 2017). HumanNet-XC (Functional gene network extended by Co-citation) (http://www.inetbio.org/humannet/) were found to show the best performance in ranking disease-linked gene sets with minimal literature-dependent biases (Hwang et al. 2018). The gene-set analysis of HumanNet-XC were applied to the target genes of identified rSNP for exploring the disease-association with annotated disease genes from DisGeNET and DISEASES (Piñero et al. 2017; Pletscher-Frankild et al. 2015). The candidate genes for BD were selected according to their closeness to the guide genes, and the putative disease gene network was explored with an interactive network viewer (Hwang et al. 2018).

Results

BD associated rSNP and their target genes

GWAS dataset 1 study identified a group of rSNPs for BD, including 218 rSNP for TFBRs, 1200 rSNP for TADs, 624 rSNP for CIRs and 130 rSNP for lncRNAs, corresponding to 507, 362, 591 and 142 target regulatory genes, respectively (Additional file 1: Table S1). 1751 of these rSNPs had been demonstrated as eQTLs in the previous literature. For circRNA region, 2354 rSNPs were identified for BD. In GWAS dataset 2 study, we detected

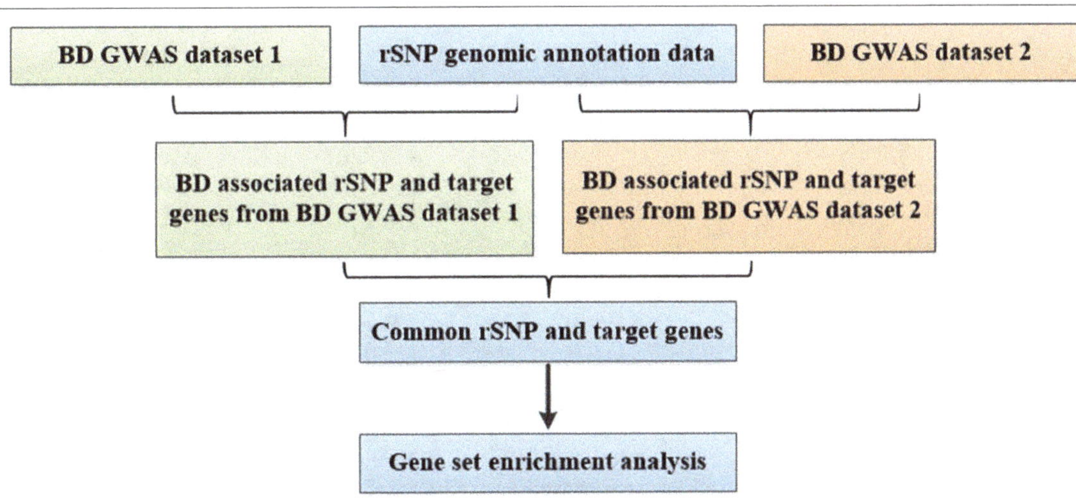

Fig. 1 Flowchart

24 rSNP for TFBRs, 192 rSNP for TADs, 54 rSNP for CIRs and 15 rSNPs for lncRNAs, corresponding to 77, 56, 71 and 21 target regulatory genes, respectively. Among these rSNPs, 200 rSNPs had been identified as eQTLs in published studies (Additional file 2: Table S2).

After comparing GWAS dataset 1 and GWAS dataset 2 study results, we identified 52 common target genes for TFBRs, 44 common target genes for TADs, 55 common target genes for CIRs and 21 common target genes for lncRNAs, respectively (Additional file 3: Table S3). Irrespective of different regulatory elements, 85 target regulatory genes of the identified rSNPs were found for BD, such as *ITIH4* ($P_{dataset1}=6.68\times10^{-8}$, $P_{dataset2}=6.64\times10^{-7}$), *ITIH3* ($P_{dataset1}=1.09\times10^{-8}$, $P_{dataset2}=2.00\times10^{-7}$), *SYNE1* ($P_{dataset1}=1.80\times10^{-6}$, $P_{dataset2}=4.33\times10^{-9}$), *OPRM1* ($P_{dataset1}=1.80\times10^{-6}$, $P_{dataset2}=4.33\times10^{-9}$) and *HDAC2* ($P_{dataset1}=6.58\times10^{-6}$, $P_{dataset2}=3.35\times10^{-8}$) (Additional file 3: Table S3). The top 20 genes were listed in Table 1.

Gene sets enrichment analysis

Additional file 4: Table S4 summarized the gene sets enrichment analysis results of 85 common target genes detected in the two datasets studies. We detected 5 significant immunologic signatures signals, such as GSE19401_PLN_VS_PEYERS_PATCH_FOLLICULAR_DC_UP (P value $=2.64\times10^{-6}$, adjusted $P=1.29\times10^{-2}$), GSE29618_BCELL_VS_PDC_DN (P value $=4.74\times10^{-5}$, adjusted $P=4.96\times10^{-2}$) and GSE43955_TH0_VS_TGFB_IL6_TH17_ACT_CD4_TCELL_10H_UP (P value $=4.97\times10^{-5}$, adjusted $P=4.96\times10^{-2}$).

HumanNet-XC disease gene prediction

HumanNet-XC tool was used to further explore the diseases closely related to the identified 85 target regulatory genes (Additional file 5: Figure S1). Among the 85 target regulatory genes, 53 genes were identified as guide genes and 2285 candidate genes within group connectivity of guide genes were found by HumanNet-XC (Additional file 6: Table S5, Additional file 7: Table S6). The results of annotated disease genes from DisGeNET and DISEASES were showed in Additional file 8: Table S7. Intriguingly, BD were found to be the most significant in the annotation genes from DisGeNET (P value $=7.41\times10^{-5}$).

Discussion

To explore the functional relevance of rSNP and their target genes in the pathogenesis of BD, we conducted an integrative analysis of GWAS and rSNPs annotation information. We identified a group of rSNP and their target genes for BD. Further functional analysis of the

Table 1 List of the top 20 common target genes shared by of BD GWAS dataset 1 and dataset 2

Gene	SNP-associated regulatory elements	BD GWAS dataset 1		BD GWAS dataset 2	
		SNP	$P_{dataset1}$	SNP	$P_{dataset2}$
IPCEF1	TADs	rs9371601	1.80×10^{-6}	rs9371601	4.33×10^{-9}
OPRM1	TADs	rs9371601	1.80×10^{-6}	rs9371601	4.33×10^{-9}
SYNE1	TADs	rs9371601	1.80×10^{-6}	rs9371601	4.33×10^{-9}
RGS17	TADs	rs215005	6.04×10^{-6}	rs214952	3.19×10^{-8}
TFB1M	TADs	rs215005	6.04×10^{-6}	rs214952	3.19×10^{-8}
CCDC170	TADs	rs9371601	1.80×10^{-6}	rs551900	3.35×10^{-8}
ENSG00000235652	TADs	rs548985	6.58×10^{-6}	rs551900	3.35×10^{-8}
HDAC2	TADs	rs548985	6.58×10^{-6}	rs551900	3.35×10^{-8}
KMT2D	CIRs	rs10783301	3.32×10^{-6}	rs10875914	8.27×10^{-8}
ENSG00000258101	CIRs, TFBRs	rs10459221	4.20×10^{-7}	rs10459232	8.81×10^{-8}
RHEBL1	CIRs, TFBRs	rs7969091	3.25×10^{-7}	rs7969091	8.91×10^{-8}
ENSG00000257346	CIRs, lncRNAs	rs11168839	2.89×10^{-6}	rs11168839	1.24×10^{-7}
PRKAG1	CIRs, TFBRs	rs2304275	1.45×10^{-6}	rs10875915	1.82×10^{-7}
ENSG00000257913	CIRs, TFBRs	rs2293445	6.51×10^{-6}	rs2293445	1.96×10^{-7}
VPRBP	TADs, CIRs, TFBRs	rs2302417	4.93×10^{-9}	rs736408	2.00×10^{-7}
ITIH3	TADs, CIRs, TFBRs	rs4481150	1.09×10^{-8}	rs736408	2.00×10^{-7}
ENSG00000272822	CIRs, TFBRs	rs1054442	3.27×10^{-6}	rs10783299	2.53×10^{-7}
RNU6-940P	CIRs, TFBRs	rs1054442	3.27×10^{-6}	rs10783299	2.53×10^{-7}
WNT1	CIRs, TFBRs	rs1054442	3.27×10^{-6}	rs10783299	2.53×10^{-7}
LMAN2L	TFBRs	rs72809838	6.47×10^{-9}	rs2271893	4.59×10^{-7}

TFBRs transcription factor binding regions, *CIRs* chromatin interactive regions, long *lncRNAs* non-coding RNAs regions, *TADs* topologically associated domains identified target genes support the importance of rSNPs in the genetic mechanism of BD.

Integrating BD GWAS and rSNP datasets observed association evidence between BD and the TADs and CIRs rSNPs of ITIH3, as well as the TFBRs and CIRs rSNP of ITIH4. ITIH4 has been confirmed to be a biomarker of neuroinflammation and neuroinflammation was involved in the development of BD (Yang et al. 2012; Najjar et al. 2013). Association analysis showed that rs2239547 (ITIH3/4-region) was significantly related with a history of suicide attempt in BD patients (Finseth et al. 2014). Besides, in a joint analysis of BD and schizophrenia, the ITIH3-ITIH4 region (rs2239547) reached genome-wide significance in the support for shared susceptibility (Ripke et al. 2011).

SYNE1 encodes spectrin repeat containing nuclear envelope protein 1, which is a part of a complex linking nucleoskeleton to cytoskeleton (Warren et al. 2005). The significant association between SYNE1 and BD have been observed in an samples of 1527 BD cases and 1579 controls, and a combined analysis of PGC-BD data ($P = 2.9 \times 10^{-8}$, OR = 1.104) (Green et al. 2013). Moreover, polymorphisms in SYNE1 conferred a greater risk of developing BD in the high genetic risk individuals (Gassó et al. 2016). Our study results suggested that the rSNP of SYNE1 may contributed to BD through TADs and TFBRs.

OPRM1 is a notable gene identified by this study. It has been demonstrated that OPRM1 was related to substance dependence and drug dependence (Glatt et al. 2007; Luo et al. 2003). The previous study showed that substance dependence had a close relationship with BD patients (Leventhal and Zimmerman 2010). Besides, a case–control study suggested that BD was significantly associated with a risk for substance use disorder and dependence, independent of psychiatric comorbidity (Wilens et al. 2008).

HDAC2 (histone deacetylase 2) is also identified for BD in our analysis. The inhibition of histone deacetylase had the effect on neuroprotective and neuroregenerative properties in animal models of brain diseases (Fischer et al. 2010). And the inhibition of histone deacetylase may supply a potential target in the treatment of BD (Machado-Vieira et al. 2011). In addition, it was found that HDAC2 were identified to be a risk gene for BD, and be involved in regulating early brain development (Xiang et al. 2017).

There are several issues need to be noted. First, the common 6 types of rSNP annotation information were collected from the rSNPBase 3.1. Some new regulatory elements are not included in the rSNPBase 3.1 database, for instance m6A (Harper et al. 1990). Second, a small part of subjects were overlapping between the two GWAS datasets of BD, which may affect the robust of our study results. Third, the functional annotation information of rSNP did not contain the biological effect of target genes in different tissue or cell types. Therefore, our rSNP analysis could not take tissue or cell types into account. Further studies are warranted to explore the roles of identified genes within different tissue and cell types. Forth, this study focused on the rSNP, which occupied a small part of whole genome. We think that using the genome-wide significance threshold (for example $P < 5.0 \times 10^{-8}$) is too strict and may miss bipolar disorder associated rSNPs. Therefore, we used the threshold of $P < 1.0 \times 10^{-5}$ in this study.

In conclusion, we conducted a large-scale integrative analysis of GWAS and 6 common rSNP information to explore the potential roles of rSNPs in the genetic mechanism of BD. We identified multiple rSNPs and candidate genes for BD. We hope that our study results are helpful for understanding the genetic mechanism of BD.

Supplementary information

Additional file 1: Table S1. rSNP functional annotation analysis results of BD GWAS dataset 1.

Additional file 2: Table S2. rSNP functional annotation analysis results of BD GWAS dataset 2.

Additional file 3: Table S3. List of the common target genes shared by BD GWAS dataset 1 and dataset 2.

Additional file 4: Table S4. FUMA gene set enrichment analysis results.

Additional file 5: Figure S1. Based on the 85 common target genes as guide genes, we used HumanNet-XC to predict network-based disease gene. The upper panel shows the interactive network viewer, and a group of guide genes (green nodes), which can be annotated by their neighbors as putative candidate genes (blue nodes). The local subnetwork of the first ranked candidate, ITIH4, and its neighbors were highlighted. DISEASES and DisGeNET, serving to validate the specific prediction result, already annotate the retrieved gene ITIH4 for Bipolar Disorder. The lower panel shows the guide genes, including the statistical significance of within group connectivity of guide genes, and the observed network performance for guide gene recovery reported as receiver operating characteristic curve (ROC) curves. The area under the receiver operating characteristic curve (AUROC) indicated the predictive HumanNet-XC networks performance for a disease, which was based on the efficiency of guide gene recovery.

Additional file 6: Table S5. List of the candidate genes identified by HumanNet-XC analysis.

Additional file 7: Table S6. List of the guide genes identified by HumanNet-XC analysis

Additional file 8: Table S7. HumanNet-XC gene-set analysis results.

Acknowledgements

This work was supported by the National Natural Scientific Foundation of China [81472925, 81673112, 81703177]; the Key projects of international cooperation among governments in scientific and technological innovation [2016YFE0119100]; the Natural Science Basic Research Plan in Shaanxi

Province of China [2017JZ024]; and the Fundamental Research Funds for the Central Universities.

Authors' contributions

XQ and YW drafted the manuscript. LZ designed the study. XQ, LZ, YW and PL performed the statistical analyses. CL, SC, MM and SC provided feasible advice on data analysis and drafting manuscript. All authors discussed the results and commented on the manuscript. All authors read and approved the final manuscript.

References

Aken BL, Ayling S, Barrell D, et al. The Ensembl gene annotation system. Database. 2016;2016:baw093.

Alonso J, Petukhova M, Vilagut G, et al. Days out of role due to common physical and mental conditions: results from the WHO World Mental Health surveys. Mol Psychiatry. 2010;16:1234.

Browning SR, Browning BL. Rapid and accurate haplotype phasing and missing-data inference for whole-genome association studies by use of localized haplotype clustering. Am J Hum Genet. 2007;81(5):1084–97.

Chen DT, Jiang X, Akula N, et al. Genome-wide association study meta-analysis of European and Asian-ancestry samples identifies three novel loci associated with bipolar disorder. Mol Psychiatry. 2011;18:195.

Craddock N, Forty L. Genetics of affective (mood) disorders. Eur J Hum Genet. 2006;14:660.

Delaneau O, Zagury J-F, Marchini J. Improved whole-chromosome phasing for disease and population genetic studies. Nat Methods. 2012;10:5.

Dilsaver SC. An estimate of the minimum economic burden of bipolar I and II disorders in the United States: 2009. J Affect Disord. 2011;129(1):79–83.

Finseth PI, Sønderby IE, Djurovic S, et al. Association analysis between suicidal behaviour and candidate genes of bipolar disorder and schizophrenia. J Affect Disord. 2014;163:110–4.

Fischer A, Sananbenesi F, Mungenast A, et al. Targeting the correct HDAC(s) to treat cognitive disorders. Trends Pharmacol Sci. 2010;31(12):605–17.

Gassó P, Sánchez-Gistau V, Mas S, et al. Association of CACNA1C and SYNE1 in offspring of patients with psychiatric disorders. Psychiatry Res. 2016;245:427–35.

Glatt SJ, Bousman C, Wang RS, et al. Evaluation of OPRM1 variants in heroin dependence by family-based association testing and meta-analysis. Drug Alcohol Depend. 2007;90(2–3):159–65.

Green EK, Grozeva D, Forty L, et al. Association at SYNE1 in both bipolar disorder and recurrent major depression. Mol Psychiatry. 2013;18(5):614–7.

Guo L, Wang J. rSNPBase 3.0: an updated database of SNP-related regulatory elements, element-gene pairs and SNP-based gene regulatory networks. Nucleic Acids Res. 2018;46(Database issue):D1111.

Harper JE, Miceli SM, Roberts RJ, et al. Sequence specificity of the human mRNA N6-adenosine methylase in vitro. Nucleic Acids Res. 1990;18(19):5735–41.

Howie B, Marchini J, Stephens M. Genotype imputation with thousands of genomes. G3 Genes Genomes Genet. 2011;1(6):457–70.

Hwang S, Kim CY, Yang S, et al. HumanNet v2: human gene networks for disease research. Nucleic Acids Res. 2018;47:D573–80.

Judd LL, Akiskal HS, Schettler PJ, et al. Psychosocial disability in the course of bipolar i and ii disorders: a prospective, comparative, longitudinal study. Arch Gen Psychiatry. 2005;62(12):1322–30.

Leventhal AM, Zimmerman M. The relative roles of bipolar disorder and psychomotor agitation in substance dependence. Psychol Addict Behav. 2010;24(2):360–5.

Logue MW, Baldwin C, Guffanti G, et al. A genome-wide association study of post-traumatic stress disorder identifies the retinoid-related orphan receptor alpha (RORA) gene as a significant risk locus. Mol Psychiatry. 2013;18(8):937–42.

Luo X, Kranzler HR, Zhao H, et al. Haplotypes at the OPRM1 locus are associated with susceptibility to substance dependence in European-Americans. Am J Med Genet B Neuropsychiatr Genet. 2003;120B(1):97–108.

Machado-Vieira R, Ibrahim L, Zarate CA Jr. Histone deacetylases and mood disorders: epigenetic programming in gene-environment interactions. CNS Neurosci Ther. 2011;17(6):699–704.

Macintyre G, Bailey J, Haviv I, et al. is-rSNP: a novel technique for in silico regulatory SNP detection. Bioinformatics. 2010;26(18):i524–30.

Marco DG, Vip V, Hughes JR, et al. A regulatory SNP causes a human genetic disease by creating a new transcriptional promoter. Science. 2006;312(5777):1215–7.

Martinez-Aran A, Vieta E, Torrent C, et al. Functional outcome in bipolar disorder: the role of clinical and cognitive factors. Bipolar Disord. 2007;9(1–2):103–13.

Merikangas KR, Jin R, He J, et al. Prevalence and correlates of bipolar spectrum disorder in the world mental health survey initiative. Arch Gen Psychiatry. 2011;68(3):241–51.

Mühleisen TW, Leber M, Schulze TG, et al. Genome-wide association study reveals two new risk loci for bipolar disorder. Nat Commun. 2014;5:3339.

Munkhtulga L, Nagashima S, Nakayama K, et al. Regulatory SNP in the RBP4 gene modified the expression in adipocytes and associated with BMI. Obesity. 2010;18(5):1006–14.

Najjar S, Pearlman DM, Alper K, et al. Neuroinflammation and psychiatric illness. J Neuroinflamm. 2013;10(1):816.

Piñero J, Bravo À, Queralt-Rosinach N, et al. DisGeNET: a comprehensive platform integrating information on human disease-associated genes and variants. Nucleic Acids Res. 2017;45(Database issue):D833–9.

Pletscher-Frankild S, Pallejà A, Tsafou K, et al. DISEASES: text mining and data integration of disease–gene associations. Methods. 2015;74:83–9.

Pompili M, Gonda X, Serafini G, et al. Epidemiology of suicide in bipolar disorders: a systematic review of the literature. Bipolar Disord. 2013;15(5):457–90.

Psychiatric GCBDWG, Sklar P, Ripke S, et al. Large-scale genome-wide association analysis of bipolar disorder identifies a new susceptibility locus near ODZ4. Nat Genet. 2011;43:977.

Ripke S. Ricopili: a tool for visualizing regions of interest in select GWAS data sets. 2014.

Ripke S, Sanders AR, Kendler KS, et al. Genome-wide association study identifies five new schizophrenia loci. Nat Genet. 2011;42(1):36–44.

Riva A. Large-scale computational identification of regulatory SNPs with rSNP-MAPPER. BMC Genom. 2012;13(4):S7.

Stahl EA, Breen G, Forstner AJ, et al. Genome-wide association study identifies 30 loci associated with bipolar disorder. Nat Genet. 2019;51(5):793–803.

Vernot B, Stergachis AB, Maurano MT, et al. Personal and population genomics of human regulatory variation. Genome Res. 2012;22(9):1689.

Warren DT, Qiuping Z, Weissberg PL, et al. Nesprins: intracellular scaffolds that maintain cell architecture and coordinate cell function? Expert Rev Mol Med. 2005;7(11):1–15.

Watanabe K, Taskesen E, van Bochoven A, et al. Functional mapping and annotation of genetic associations with FUMA. Nat Commun. 2017;8(1):1826.

Wilens TE, Biederman J, Adamson JJ, et al. Further evidence of an association between adolescent bipolar disorder with smoking and substance use disorders: a controlled study. Drug Alcohol Depend. 2008;95(3):188–98.

Wu L-C, Horng J-T, Chen Y-A. A computation to integrate the analysis of genetic variations occurring within regulatory elements and their possible effects. J Comput Biol. 2009;16(12):1731–47.

Xiang B, Liu K, Yu M, et al. Systematic genetic analyses of genome-wide association study data reveal an association between the key nucleosome remodeling and deacetylase complex and bipolar disorder development. Bipolar Disord. 2017;20(4):370–80.

Yang M-H, Yang Y-H, Lu C-Y, et al. Activity-dependent neuroprotector homeobox protein: a candidate protein identified in serum as diagnostic biomarker for Alzheimer's disease. J Proteom. 2012;75(12):3617–29.

Yeo J, Morales DA, Chen T, et al. RNAseq analysis of bronchial epithelial cells to identify COPD-associated genes and SNPs. BMC Pulm Med. 2018;18(1):42.

10

Transdiagnostic comparison of visual working memory capacity in bipolar disorder and schizophrenia

Catherine V. Barnes-Scheufler[1], Caroline Passow[1], Lara Rösler[1,2], Jutta S. Mayer[3], Viola Oertel[1], Sarah Kittel-Schneider[1,4], Silke Matura[1], Andreas Reif[1] and Robert A. Bittner[1,5*]

Abstract

Background: Impaired working memory is a core cognitive deficit in both bipolar disorder and schizophrenia. Its study might yield crucial insights into the underpinnings of both disorders on the cognitive and neurophysiological level. Visual working memory capacity is a particularly promising construct for such translational studies. However, it has not yet been investigated across the full spectrum of both disorders. The aim of our study was to compare the degree of reductions of visual working memory capacity in patients with bipolar disorder (PBD) and patients with schizophrenia (PSZ) using a paradigm well established in cognitive neuroscience.

Methods: 62 PBD, 64 PSZ, and 70 healthy controls (HC) completed a canonical visual change detection task. Participants had to encode the color of four circles and indicate after a short delay whether the color of one of the circles had changed or not. We estimated working memory capacity using Pashler's K.

Results: Working memory capacity was significantly reduced in both PBD and PSZ compared to HC. We observed a small effect size ($r = .202$) for the difference between HC and PBD and a medium effect size ($r = .370$) for the difference between HC and PSZ. Working memory capacity in PSZ was also significantly reduced compared to PBD with a small effect size ($r = .201$). Thus, PBD showed an intermediate level of impairment.

Conclusions: These findings provide evidence for a gradient of reduced working memory capacity in bipolar disorder and schizophrenia, with PSZ showing the strongest degree of impairment. This underscores the importance of disturbed information processing for both bipolar disorder and schizophrenia. Our results are compatible with the cognitive manifestation of a neurodevelopmental gradient affecting bipolar disorder to a lesser degree than schizophrenia. They also highlight the relevance of visual working memory capacity for the development of both behavior- and brain-based transdiagnostic biomarkers.

Keywords: Bipolar disorder, Schizophrenia, Cognitive dysfunction, Working memory capacity, Attention

Background

Cognitive impairment across a wide range of domains is a central common characteristic of both bipolar disorder and schizophrenia (Martínez-Arán et al. 2004; Kahn and Keefe 2013; Vöhringer et al. 2013; Bora and Pantelis 2015; Miskowiak et al. 2018). Consequently, both have been conceptualized as information processing disorders (Kahn and Keefe 2013; Bortolato et al. 2015). This paradigm supports the notion that transdiagnostic comparisons of crucial cognitive constructs are a central element of translational strategies to establish a psychiatric nosology based on the assessment of cognitive dimensions and the brain networks which give rise to them

*Correspondence: robert.bittner@med.uni-frankfurt.de
[1] Department of Psychiatry, Psychosomatic Medicine, and Psychotherapy, University Hospital Frankfurt, Goethe University, Heinrich-Hoffmann-Str. 10, 60528 Frankfurt am Main, Germany
Full list of author information is available at the end of the article

(Cuthbert 2014; Insel 2014). Ultimately, this should lead to the identification of neurobiologically distinct biotypes across diagnostic boundaries (Clementz et al. 2016) and the development of behavioral and brain-based biomarkers (Oertel-Knöchel et al. 2011). Furthermore, it might also facilitate a better understanding of the neurophysiological disturbances underlying impaired information processing and the development of more effective procognitive interventions.

The need for transdiagnostic studies is underscored by the substantial phenomenological and pathophysiological overlap of bipolar disorder and schizophrenia (Ivleva et al. 2010; Pearlson 2015). They have the highest amount of shared heritability among neuropsychiatric disorders (Anttila et al. 2018; Lee et al. 2019). Both are also regarded to different degrees as neurodevelopmental disorders (Bortolato et al. 2015; Pearlson 2015), possibly forming a neurodevelopmental continuum (Owen and O'Donovan 2017). This implies that risk factors disturbing brain development and cognition play a larger role in schizophrenia than in bipolar disorder. Interestingly, most studies have reported a gradient of cognitive impairment with patients with schizophrenia generally more affected than patients with bipolar disorder (Goldberg 1999; Schretlen et al. 2007; Ivleva et al. 2010; Lewandowski et al. 2011; Hill et al. 2013; Reilly and Sweeney 2014).

Working memory is universally regarded as a central cognitive domain for transdiagnostic studies of impaired information processing (Insel et al. 2010). It is a crucial determinant of essential cognitive functions such as language comprehension and reasoning (Baddeley 1992), as well as an important mediator of cognitive development and learning (Baddeley and Hitch 1974; Cowan 2014). Working memory dysfunction is a central cognitive deficit in both bipolar disorder and schizophrenia (Glahn et al. 2006; Barch and Smith 2008). It has been reported in a large number of behavioral studies in schizophrenia across all stages of illness (Lee and Park 2005; Barch and Smith 2008; Luck and Gold 2008; Fuller et al. 2009; Hahn et al. 2010; Anticevic et al. 2011b; Leonard et al. 2017; Mayer et al. 2018). Working memory impairment has also been demonstrated in bipolar disorder (Adler et al. 2004; Glahn et al. 2006; Thompson et al. 2007; Mayer and Park 2012; Jensen et al. 2016). While working memory deficits appear to be particularly pronounced in manic or depressive phases (Townsend et al. 2010), they persist during euthymic phases of the illness (Xu et al. 2012), at least in a sizable number of patients (Volkert et al. 2015). Direct comparisons between patients with bipolar I (BP-I) and bipolar II (BP-II) disorder indicate overall a similar degree of working memory impairment (Bora et al. 2011; Bora 2018). Additionally, there is evidence for a modestly greater degree of impairment in bipolar patients with a history of psychosis, compared to bipolar patients without a history of psychosis (Bora 2018).

One particularly relevant aspect of working memory is its limited capacity (Cowan 2001), which appears to constitute a core cognitive trait with high intra-individual stability over time (Kane and Engle 2002). Working memory capacity differs considerably between individuals and has strong links to high-level cognitive measures including global fluid intelligence, abstract reasoning, language abilities, mathematics, and overall scholastic performance (Daneman and Carpenter 1980; Cowan et al. 2005; Fukuda et al. 2010; Johnson, McMahon et al. 2013; Cowan 2014; Unsworth et al. 2014). Finding procognitive interventions which increase patients' working memory capacity should therefore also be a promising way to improve their general level of cognitive functioning (Johnson et al. 2013). Quantifying the degree to which working memory capacity is constrained across the schizo-bipolar spectrum is an important step toward this goal.

Based on the extensive body of work in the field of cognitive neuroscience (Luck and Vogel 2013), visual working memory capacity has been proposed as an especially suitable construct for this purpose (Barch et al. 2012). This is supported by its good construct validity and a number of specific properties. Visual working memory capacity correlates closely with measures of verbal working memory capacity but is less prone to chunking or rehearsal mechanisms (Luck and Vogel 1997; Cowan 2001), which could confound the estimation of pure working memory capacity. It has also been studied extensively using functional neuroimaging (Linden et al. 2003; Todd and Marois 2004; Vogel and Machizawa 2004). Conversely, spatial span paradigms are generally regarded as poorly suited for functional neuroimaging studies (Barch and Smith 2008). Additionally, paradigms assessing visual working memory capacity have good test–retest reliability (Xu et al. 2018; Dai et al. 2019) and have been employed successfully in animal studies (Wright et al. 2010).

Visual working memory capacity has been studied most commonly using change detection paradigms. Here, subjects have to remember one or more features such as color, location or orientation of an array of simple visual items. Subsequently, after a short delay interval they are shown a test array and have to make a judgment, whether the test array is identical or if a single item had changed. Healthy individuals are able to store information of about four objects at one time as integrated features (Luck and Vogel 1997; Wheeler and Treisman 2002). They are able to remember three to four items when required to encode a single feature such as color, or even two features of each item such as color and location.

Variations of the 'canonical' change detection paradigm have also been implemented (Feuerstahler et al. 2019). In change localization paradigms, subjects need to specify which item has changed. In partial-report change detection paradigms, the change decision during the test array is limited to a single item. In multiple change detection paradigms, more than one item might change during the test array.

Reduced visual working memory capacity has been observed in schizophrenia (Gold et al. 2010; Mayer et al. 2012; Hahn et al. 2018) and in bipolar disorder I with a history of psychosis (Gold et al. 2018). However, to our knowledge, no study has compared visual working memory capacity in cohorts of patients with schizophrenia and schizoaffective disorder (PSZ) and patients with bipolar disorder (PBD) representing the full spectrum of both disorders. The main goal of our study was to assess working memory capacity in PBD of all illness subtypes, as well as PSZ using a canonical change detection paradigm. We expected to observe a gradient of reduced working memory capacity with greater impairment in PSZ than in PBD.

Methods

Participants

We recruited 62 PBD (42 female, mean age 42.05, range: 20—61), and 64 PSZ (26 female, mean age 38.56, range: 20–57, n = 41 with schizophrenia and n = 23 with schizoaffective disorder) from psychiatric outpatient clinics in and around Frankfurt am Main, Germany. We established diagnoses of all patients according to DSM-5 criteria based on a clinical interview and careful chart review at a consensus diagnosis meeting chaired by one of the authors (R.A.B.). We pooled both patients diagnosed with schizophrenia and schizoaffective disorder because long-term diagnostic stability and inter-rater reliability of schizoaffective disorder is relatively poor (Maj et al. 2000).

The Positive and Negative Syndrome Scale (PANSS) was used to assess current psychopathology in PSZ (Kay et al. 1987). In order to establish euthymic mood state in PBD, participants were evaluated with the Young Mania Rating Scale (YMRS) and Montgomery-Åsberg Depression Rating Scale (MADRS) (Young et al. 1978; Montgomery and Åsberg 1979). Participants with YMRS values of ≥ 11 or MADRS values of ≥ 11 were excluded from our analysis.

70 matched healthy control subjects (HC), (44 female, mean age 38.61, range: 21–61) also participated. HC had no reported history of psychiatric illness, as well as no history in first-degree family members. They were recruited from the Frankfurt University campus and surrounding areas, as well as by online and printed advertisements. Current and past symptoms of psychiatric illness were ruled out using the German version of the Structural Clinical Interview SCID-I, from the Diagnostic and Statistical Manual, Version IV (Saß et al. 2003).

All participants reported no history of neurological illness and no drug use (excluding nicotine) within the past six months. All participants ranged in age from 20–61 years old. We matched subjects at the group level by conducting Kruskal–Wallis tests based on age ($H(2) = 3.902$, $p = 0.142$), and participants' years of education ($H(2) = 1.254$, $p = 0.534$), as well as parental years of education ($H(2) = 0.834$, $p = 0.659$).

We assessed handedness as a continuous variable using the Edinburgh Handedness Inventory (Oldfield 1971). We compared handedness scores between groups using a Kruskal–Wallis test and did not find a significant difference ($H(2) = 0.962$, p = 0.618).

The German Mehrfachwahl-Wortschatz-Intelligenz Test (MWT-B) (Lehrl et al. 2005) was administered to assess premorbid verbal intelligence.

Further socio-demographic information for all cohorts can be found in Table 1. Prior to signing the informed consent form, participants were informed of its contents by the investigator and what to do in the case of experiencing distress, and how to end participation in the study. The ethics committee of the University Hospital Frankfurt approved all study procedures.

Change detection task

We implemented a 'canonical' color change detection task (Fig. 1) on a personal computer using Presentation software in Version14.9 (www.neurobs.com). Stimuli were presented on a grey background (RGB values: 191, 191, 191) in a dimly lit room with a viewing distance of approximately 60 cm. Throughout the experiment, a black fixation cross was displayed at the center of the screen. Each trial began with the alert phase, during which the fixation cross turned to red for 500 ms. This was followed by a preparation phase of 500 ms. During the encoding phase a sample array of four colored circles was presented for 200 ms. Each circle had a visual angle of approximately 0.95°. These circles were spaced equally apart on an imaginary circle with 12 possible locations around the black fixation cross covering a visual angle of approximately 5.25°, and the minimum distance between two circles was 0.29°. Each circle had one of seven easily discriminable possible colors with the following RGB values: black (0, 0, 0), red (255, 0, 0), white (255, 255, 255), blue (0, 0, 255), green (0, 255, 0), yellow (255, 255, 0), and magenta (255, 0, 255), with no repetitions of colors within a trial. During the delay phase, the black fixation cross remained on the screen for

Table 1 Demographic and clinical characteristics of all groups

Group	n	Age (SD)	Gender	YOE (SD)	PYOE (SD)	IQ (SD)	DOI (SD)	Handed ness (SD)	YMRS (SD)	MADRS (SD)	PANSS Total (SD)	PANSS Positive (SD)	PANSS Negative (SD)
HC	70	38.61 (13.11)	62.86	16.27 (2.10)	14.91 (3.14)	116.03 (12.31)	–	64.50 (45.64)	–	–	–	–	–
PBD	62	42.05 (10.87)	67.74	16.34 (2.33)	14.67 (3.72)	117.84 (12.77)	13.57 (10.17)	71.87 (38.70)	1.66 (2.30)	3.23 (2.83)	–	–	–
BP-I	38	40.26 (10.77)	73.68	16.37 (2.03)	14.78 (3.68)	118.05 (14.50)	12.40 (9.37)	69.36 (41.86)	1.68 (2.20)	3.26 (3.00)	–	–	–
BP-II	24	44.88 (10.65)	58.33	16.29 (2.80)	14.50 (3.84)	117.50 (9.69)	15.42 (11.29)	75.83 (33.53)	1.63 (2.46)	3.17 (2.70)	–	–	–
HPS+	32	42.56 (9.60)	59.37	16.70 (1.75)	14.68 (3.74)	119.16 (13.29)	14.88 (10.34)	72.81 (34.47)	1.31 (1.87)	3.28 (2.91)	–	–	–
HPS-	30	41.50 (12.23)	76.67	15.97 (2.81)	14.67 (3.76)	116.43 (12.26)	12.17 (9.96)	70.86 (43.32)	2.03 (2.70)	3.17 (2.78)	–	–	–
PSZ	64	38.56 (10.30)	40.62	15.80 (2.75)	14.29 (3.73)	110.77 (13.35)	10.25 (9.22)	67.08 (44.64)	–	–	45.03 (10.35)	10.32 (3.61)	11.97 (4.21)
SZ	41	36.85 (9.57)	36.59	15.43 (2.85)	14.50 (3.78)	108.39 (11.37)	7.78 (7.41)	69.90 (38.83)	–	–	46.98 (10.53)	10.73 (4.01)	12.85 (4.34)
SZAFF	23	41.61 (11.07)	47.83	16.46 (2.48)	13.91 (3.72)	115.00 (15.69)	14.65 (10.57)	62.06 (54.08)	–	–	41.15 (9.02)	9.50 (2.54)	10.20 (3.38)
Main Group Differences	–	NS	HC > PSZ, PBD > PSZ	NS	NS	HC > PSZ, PBD > PSZ	NS	NS	–	–	–	–	–

Age reported as mean value (SD), gender as % female, YOE = mean years of education (SD), PYOE = mean value of highest reported years of education value from either parent (SD), IQ = mean value of premorbid IQ as measured by MWT-B (SD), DOI = duration of illness in years (SD), handedness as mean value measured by Edinburgh Handedness Inventory (SD); YMRS = Young Mania Rating Scale (SD), MADRS = Montgomery-Åsberg Depression Rating Scale (SD), and PANSS = Positive and Negative Syndrome Scale (SD) reported as total score and separate positive and negative subscales, NS = no significant effect

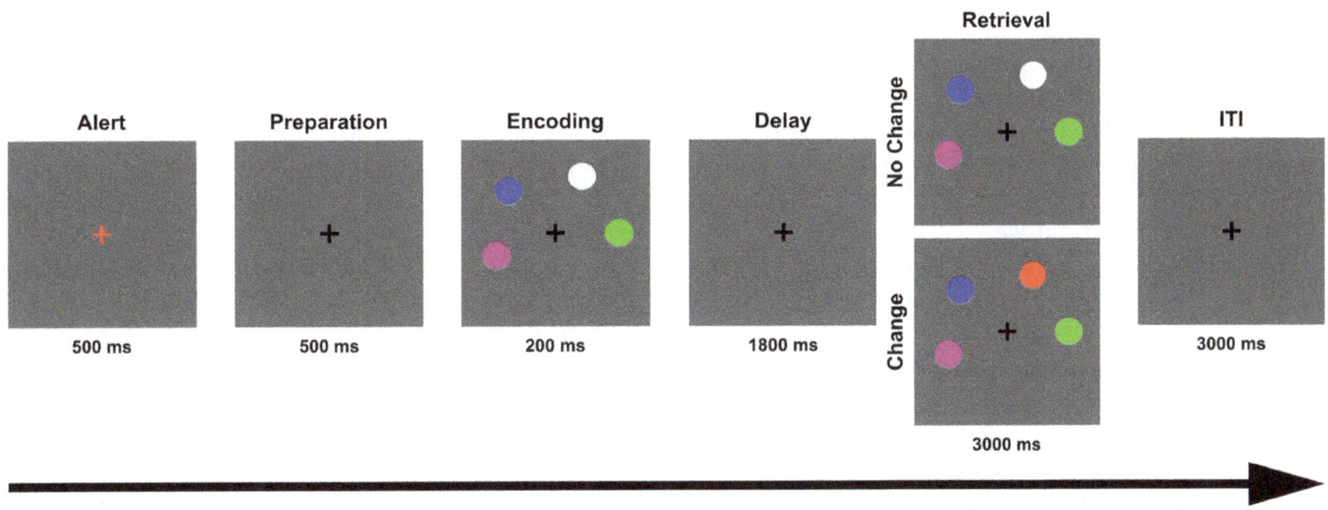

Fig. 1 The change detection task used to assess working memory capacity. Each trial began with the alert phase, during which the fixation cross turned to red for 500 ms. This was followed by a preparation phase of 500 ms. During the encoding phase a sample array of four colored circles was presented for 200 ms. During the delay phase, the black fixation cross remained on the screen for 1800 ms. The whole-display recognition test array followed, in which participants had a maximum duration of 3000 ms to decide if the test array was identical to the sample array presented in the encoding phase, or if one of the circles had changed color

1800 ms. A whole-display recognition test array followed, in which participants had a maximum duration of 3000 ms to decide if the test array was identical to the sample array presented in the encoding phase, or if one of the circles had changed color. Half of the trials were change trials (right mouse button), the other half no-change trials (left mouse button). In change trials, a randomly chosen circle changed its color. The total duration of each trial was 6000 ms followed by an inter-trial interval of 3000 ms. All participants received the same instructions prior to the beginning the task, and were asked to perform as accurately as possible, and to keep their eyes fixated constantly on the center of the screen. A total of 60 trials were tested in each participant, which required approximately nine minutes of testing time.

Medication scores

Patients were on stable medication for at least one month at the time of study. One PSZ and two PBD did not receive medication. Details of medication can be found in Table 2. We calculated olanzapine equivalence scores for antipsychotic medication (Gardner et al. 2010), and daily doses for mood stabilizers (lithium, valproate and lamotrigine) in both patient groups.

Calculation of working memory capacity

In order to quantify the amount of information participants stored in working memory by each participant, we calculated Pashler's *K*: $K = N \times ((H-FA) / (1-FA))$ (Pashler 1988). H is the hit rate (proportion of correct responses to change trials). FA is the false alarm rate (proportion of incorrect responses to no-change trials).

Table 2 Medication of patients with bipolar disorder and patients with schizophrenia

Group	FGA	SGA	FGA & SGA	OES (SD)	Lithium	Lithium Dose (SD)	Valproate	Valproate Dose (SD)	Lamotrigine	Lamotrigine Dose (SD)	Anti-depressants
HC	–	–		–	–	–	–	–	–	–	–
PBD	0	35	0	5.10 (6.78), 35	29	1078.62 (401.68)	10	1225.00 (454.15)	10	185.00 (57.98)	23
PSZ	1	62	5	17.72 (14.10), 62	3	750.00 (343.69)	2	350.00 (212.13)	0	–	14

Number of patients receiving the different medication classes at time of study. FGA = first-generation antipsychotics, SGA = second-generation antipsychotics. Olanzapine equivalence scores (OES) calculated according to Gardener et al. (2010), reported in mean (SD), and n of patients. Lithium, valproate and lamotrigine doses reported as n of patients and mean daily mg value (SD). Antidepressants reported as n of patients receiving this type of medication

N is the set size, which was always four. Our whole-display recognition paradigm required the use of Pashler's *K* as the appropriate estimate of working memory capacity (Rouder et al. 2011).We excluded datasets with accuracy at or below chance level of (50%) under the assumption that participants did not attend to the task, because they were thoroughly instructed and practiced the task with the experimenter. In total we excluded three PSZ; two had accuracies of 23%, and one 40%, one PBD with an accuracy of 23% and one HC with an accuracy of 47%.

Comparison of working memory capacity

The goal of our primary analysis was to assess group differences of working memory capacity. A Shapiro–Wilk test across all three groups revealed that our working memory capacity estimates did not follow a normal distribution ($W(196)=0.88$, $p<0.01$). Consequently, we used the non-parametric Kruskal–Wallis test for our primary planned analysis in order to detect working memory capacity differences across all three groups. We then conducted Mann–Whitney U tests for pairwise comparisons and calculated the effect size with $r=z/\sqrt{N}$. We interpreted effect sizes as follows: large effect size $r=0.5$, medium $r=0.3$, and small $r=0.1$ (Cohen 1988).

Investigation of possible demographic influences

Nominally higher, but not significantly different premorbid IQ values were recorded in PBD (mean = 117.84) than HC (mean = 116.03, $r=0.07$, $p=0.307$). Lower premorbid IQ was recorded in PSZ (mean = 110.77) compared to PBD ($r=0.26$, $p<0.001$) and HC ($r=0.20$, $p=0.006$). Gender was also not matched across participant groups ($\chi^2(2, 196)=10.91$, $p=0.004$). In order to control for the possible influences of group differences in premorbid IQ and gender on working memory capacity, we performed a one-way ANCOVA with the covariates premorbid IQ and gender. In order to test possible group differences in other demographic details including age, years of education, parental years of education, and handedness, we used Kruskal–Wallis tests.

Investigation of possible influences of psychopathology

We were also interested in the relationship between working memory capacity and clinical variables. To this end, we performed separate bivariate correlations in PBD and PSZ to examine the relationship between duration of illness, YMRS, MADRS, total PANSS scores, as well as the positive and negative subscales of PANSS with *K*.

Investigation of possible medication effects

There is evidence for an impact of antipsychotic medication (Reilly et al. 2006) and mood stabilizers (Khan et al. 2004; Senturk et al. 2007) on cognition, which might confound our analysis. We addressed this issue as follows.

We conducted a Mann–Whitney U test in order to investigate possible group differences in olanzapine equivalence scores for both patient groups. We also conducted Spearman's r bivariate correlations (r_s) to examine the relationship between working memory capacity and olanzapine equivalence scores in both PSZ and PBD.

In addition, we conducted another Mann–Whitney U test to check for a possible difference between PBD receiving antipsychotic medication at the time of the study and those PBD that were not receiving antipsychotic medication. We conducted additional Spearman's r bivariate correlations to examine the relationship between working memory capacity and daily lithium dose only in PBD because only three patients in the PSZ group received lithium treatment. Similarly, we only conducted Spearman's r bivariate correlations between working memory capacity and daily valproate and lamotrigine doses in PBD because only two patients in the PSZ group received valproate and none received lamotrigine.

Investigation of diagnostic subgroups

In order to evaluate possible working memory capacity differences in patient subgroups, we reviewed the pairwise comparisons of Mann–Whitney U tests of *K* in patients with (a) schizophrenia (SZ) versus schizoaffective disorder (SZAFF), (b) BP-I versus BP-II, and (c) bipolar with a history of psychotic symptoms (BP HPS+) versus bipolar without a history of psychotic symptoms (BP HPS-).

Results

Comparison of working memory capacity

Working memory capacity was highest in HC (Mean = 3.39, SD = 0.61) followed by PBD (Mean = 3.15, SD = 0.75) and then PSZ (Mean = 2.90, SD = 0.77). Our primary analysis revealed that *K* was significantly different across all three groups ($H(2)=19.43$, $p<0.001$). Pairwise group comparisons revealed a significant difference of *K* between PSZ and HC with a medium effect size ($r=0.370$, $p<0.001$) and between PBD and HC with a small effect size ($r=0.202$, $p=0.020$). There was also a significant reduction of working memory capacity in PSZ compared to PBD with a small effect size ($r=0.201$, $p=0.024$) (Table 3).

Investigation of possible demographic influences

In a one-way ANCOVA there was no significant relation of premorbid IQ, the covariate, to *K* across all groups ($F(1, 191)=0.19$, partial $\eta^2<0.01$, $p=0.661$). There was also no significant relation of gender, the covariate to

Table 3 Mean working memory (WM) capacity as estimated using Pashler's K (SD)

	WM Capacity mean (SD)	Group comparisons Effect size (*p*-value)								
		HC	PBD	BP-I	BP-II	BP HPS+	BP HPS-	PSZ	SZ	SZAFF
HC	3.39 (0.61)	–	0.202 (0.020)*	0.167 (0.082)	0.214 (0.038)*	0.216 (0.029)*	0.156 (0.120)	0.370 (<0.001)*	0.340 (<0.001)*	0.347 (<0.001)*
PBD	3.15 (0.75)	0.202 (0.020)*	–	–	–	–	–	0.201 (0.024)*	–	–
BP-I	3.22 (0.62)	0.167 (0.082)	–	–	0.104 (0.414)	–	–	–	0.211 (0.061)	0.290 (0.025)*
BP-II	3.03 (0.92)	0.214 (0.038)*	–	0.104 (0.414)	–	–	–	–	0.105 (0.395)	0.180 (0.217)
BP HPS+	3.19 (0.56)	0.216 (0.029)*	–	–	–	–	0.038 (0.767)	–	0.169 (0.148)	0.262 (0.052)
BP HPS-	3.10 (0.92)	0.156 (0.120)	–	–	–	0.038 (0.767)		–	0.171 (0.150)	0.233 (0.090)
PSZ	2.90 (0.77)	0.370 (<0.001)*	0.201 (0.024)*	–	–	–	–	–	–	–
SZ	2.89 (0.81)	0.340 (<0.001)*	–	0.211 (0.061)	0.105 (0.395)	0.169 (0.148)	0.171 (0.150)	–	–	-0.047 (0.705)
SZAFF	2.90 (0.70)	0.347 (<0.001)*	–	0.290 (0.025)*	0.180 (0.217)	0.262 (0.052)	0.233 (0.090)	–	-0.047 (0.705)	–

Results of Mann–Whitney U tests to test pairwise comparisons of working memory capacity estimated with Pashler's K and reported as effect size ($r=z/\sqrt{N}$) and *p*-value. HC = healthy controls, PBD = patients with bipolar disorder, BP-I = patients with bipolar type I, BP-II = bipolar patients with bipolar type II, BP HPS+ = bipolar patients with history of psychotic symptoms, BP HPS- = bipolar patients without history of psychotic symptoms, PSZ = patients with schizophrenia, SZ = patients with schizophrenia, SZAFF = patients with schizoaffective disorder. Statistical significance is indicated by *

K across all groups ($F(1, 191)=1.56$, partial $\eta^2<0.01$, $p=0.213$). A significant effect of group on K was still observed after controlling for both the effects of premorbid IQ and gender ($F(2, 191)=6.90$, partial $\eta^2=0.07$, $p=0.001$).

Investigation of possible psychopathological influences

There was no significant correlation between K and years of illness in either PBD ($r_s=-0.15$, $p=0.254$, $n=62$), or PSZ ($r_s<-0.01$, $p=0.961$, $n=64$). There was no significant correlation between K and scores on the YMRS ($r_s=0.10$, $p=0.449$), or MADRS ($r_s=-0.15$, $p=0.239$) in PBD. There was no significant correlation between K and total PANSS scores ($r_s=-0.15$, $p=0.242$), as well as PANSS positive ($r_s=-0.22$, $p=0.093$), and PANSS negative subscale ($r_s<0.01$, $p=0.947$) in PSZ.

Investigation of possible medication effects

We recorded higher olanzapine equivalence scores in PSZ ($Mdn=13.41$) compared to PBD ($Mdn=2.50$) ($U=626.50$, $z=-6.60$, $r=0.67$, $p<0.001$). Yet, we observed no significant correlation of K with olanzapine equivalence scores in either PSZ ($r_s=-0.16$, $p=0.202$, $n=62$), or PBD ($r_s=-0.14$, $p=0.285$, $n=35$). No significant difference was detected between K in PBD taking antipsychotic medication ($Mdn=3.31$) and those not taking antipsychotic medication ($Mdn=3.41$) ($U=427.00$, $z=-0.646$, $r=0.08$, $p=0.518$). Similarly, we observed no significant correlation between K and daily lithium dose in PBD ($r_s=-0.07$, $p=0.721$, $n=29$), as well as K and daily valproate dose ($r_s=-0.39$, $p=0.263$, $n=10$), and K and daily lamotrigine dose ($r_s=-0.51$, $p=0.136$, $n=10$) in PBD.

Investigation of diagnostic subgroups

Regarding our exploratory patient subgroup analyses, we observed no significant differences of K in any of the following Mann–Whitney U tests. This included the comparison of (a) schizophrenia (SZ) versus schizoaffective disorder (SZAFF) ($r=0.047$, $p=0.705$), (b) bipolar I (BP-I) versus bipolar II (BP-II) ($r=0.104$, $p=0.414$), and (c) bipolar with a history of psychotic symptoms (BP HPS+) versus bipolar without a history of psychotic symptoms (BP HPS-) ($r=0.038$, $p=0.767$) (Table 3). We consider these analyses exploratory as the sample sizes were relatively small, groups were not matched well and the effect sizes were all small.

Discussion

We investigated working memory capacity in bipolar disorder and schizophrenia compared to healthy controls in order to elucidate the degree of working memory impairment in these major psychiatric disorders. We observed a significant reduction in working memory capacity in PBD compared to HC and in PSZ compared to HC. Working memory capacity of PBD fell between PSZ and HC with a significant difference between both patient groups.

Our results indicate a gradient of reduced working memory capacity across the schizo-bipolar spectrum, with PSZ showing a stronger impairment with a medium effect size. By comparison, working memory capacity reduction in PBD was less pronounced with a small effect size. These findings match previous studies on working memory dysfunction in both disorders, which indicate a similar intermediate level of working memory impairment in PBD (Hamilton et al. 2009; Barch and Sheffield 2014). Our findings are also well in line with previous studies demonstrating a comparable gradient of impairment across a wide range of other cognitive domains (Goldberg 1999; Schretlen et al. 2007; Ivleva et al. 2010; Lewandowski et al. 2011; Hill et al. 2013; Reilly and Sweeney 2014).

Our three participant groups differed in their levels of premorbid IQ. We report significantly higher premorbid IQ in PBD and HC as compared to in PSZ, and no significant difference between PBD and HC. However, there is evidence, that premorbid intelligence scores tend to be lower in PSZ (Crawford et al. 1992; Khandaker et al. 2011), and supranormal in multiple measurements in PBD (Bora 2015). Nevertheless, we did not observe a significant influence of premorbid IQ on K, which is unsurprising considering we measured crystallized intelligence. In comparison, fluid intelligence seems to be correlated with working memory capacity (Fukuda et al. 2010).

Recently, a large multi-center study using both a change localization and a multiple change detection task reported an overall reduction of visual working memory capacity across psychotic disorders, i.e. schizophrenia, schizoaffective disorder and BP-I with a history of psychosis (Gold et al. 2018). The authors did not observe a significant difference between any of the three patient groups in either task. For the change localization task, visual working memory capacity was significantly lower in all three patient groups. Interestingly, for the multiple change detection task this reduction was most pronounced in patients with bipolar I disorder with a lifetime history of psychosis, with only a trend towards a significant reduction in patients with schizophrenia. These results indicate that visual working memory capacity reduction in BP-I with a lifetime history of psychosis is similar in magnitude to schizophrenia. However, it remains unclear, whether this similarity is attributable to the shared presence of psychosis, because the study did not include either BP-I without a lifetime history of psychosis or BP-II. In contrast to Gold et al., we observed an intermediate level of visual working memory capacity reduction in PBD. Several factors could account for this discrepancy. Firstly, we studied the full bipolar spectrum including BP-I without a history of psychosis and BP-II, rather than focusing only on the effect of psychotic illness across diagnostic categories. Interestingly, our exploratory subgroup analyses did not indicate a difference in visual working memory capacity between BP-I and BP-II. We also did not observe an effect of lifetime history of psychosis within the PBD group. However, these post-hoc findings need to be interpreted with caution due to the relatively small size of our subgroups.

There were also important differences in the paradigms employed. The number of possible changes might have influenced our results. Gold et al. observed a significant difference between healthy controls and all patient groups for their change localization task, which was a single change paradigm. By contrast, group differences were less pronounced in their multiple change detection paradigm with either zero, one, two, or five changes. Furthermore, we consistently maintained a set size of four objects, while Gold et al. used a set size of five objects. This difference might have affected results, because performance continues to decline as set size increases (Luck and Vogel 1997). This interpretation would also be in line with the notion, that deficits in PBD become more pronounced in tasks greatly exceeding their working memory capacity. It has been suggested, that a larger set size might have influenced subjects' strategies and minimized between-group differences (Gold et al. 2018). Conversely, there was some indication of a ceiling effect in the HC group in our data with 13 HC having a K of 4.0 compared to three PBD and two PSZ (Fig. 2). This implies, that our set size might have underestimated working memory capacity differences between HC and both PBD and PSZ. Using both set sizes within the same study might help to clarify this issue.

Our observation of a transdiagnostic reduction of working memory capacity across the schizo-bipolar spectrum raises the question, which cognitive mechanisms might be responsible. It has been proposed that the limits of working memory capacity are determined primarily by the amount of information which can be held in the focus of attention (Cowan 2001). Specifically, top-down attention appears to be crucial for the selection of information to be stored in working memory. The efficiency of this "gatekeeper" function has a substantial impact on working memory capacity (Vogel et al. 2005; Cowan and Morey 2006; McNab and Klingberg 2008). Thus, impaired attentional processes in patients might have contributed to our results. To our best knowledge, the potential impact of attentional dysfunction on working memory

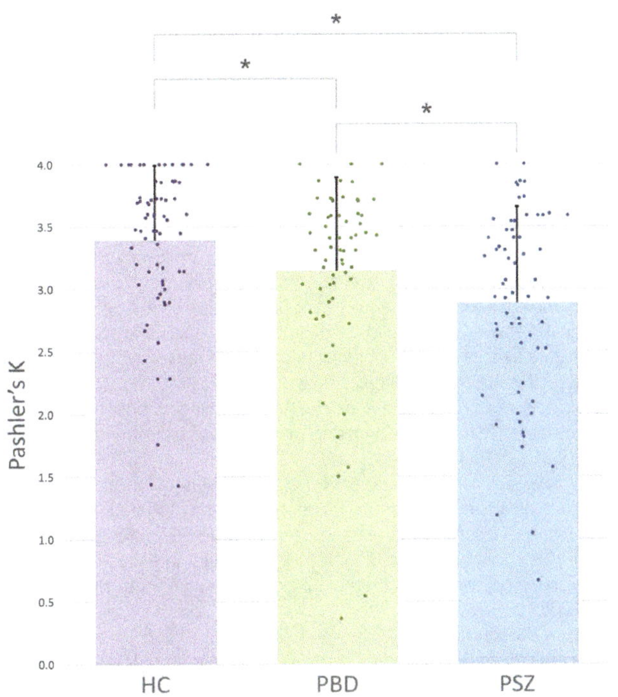

Fig. 2 Working memory capacity for all groups. Working memory capacity was estimated using Pashler's *K*. Bars indicate mean group average and scatter plot data indicates individual capacity estimates for healthy controls (HC) in purple, patients with bipolar disorder (PBD) in green, and patients with schizophrenia (PSZ) in blue. Error bars indicate standard deviation

impairment in bipolar disorder remains unknown. However, for schizophrenia there is experimental support for the presence of a selective impairment of top-down attentional control, which may disturb working memory encoding (Mayer et al. 2012). Furthermore, there is considerable evidence for a tendency in PSZ to show hyperfocusing of attention when processing visual information (Luck et al. 2019b). In the context of visual working memory, hyperfocusing might limit the amount of items which PSZ can focus on, thereby restricting the amount of information they can successfully encode (Leonard et al. 2013; Luck et al. 2019a).

This interpretation would also be compatible with a component-process model of working memory dysfunction in PSZ, which is based on converging behavioral and neuroimaging evidence for a primary impairment of working memory during the encoding stage (Tek et al. 2002; Hartman et al. 2003; Lee and Park 2005; Kim et al. 2006; Javitt et al. 2007; Fuller et al. 2009; Gold et al. 2010; Hahn et al. 2010; Anticevic et al. 2011a; Mayer et al. 2012).

Deficits during working memory encoding have been linked to impaired early-stage visual processing (Haenschel et al. 2007, 2009) as well as to disturbed interactions between prefrontal areas and visual areas closely involved in object processing (Bittner et al. 2015). So far it remains unclear, to which degree disturbances during the initial encoding of information contribute specifically to reduced working memory capacity in bipolar disorder and schizophrenia. Interestingly, there is evidence for differential mechanisms underlying working memory impairment in schizophrenia and bipolar disorder. While both groups were impaired in a spatial delayed response task, only patients with schizophrenia recorded more false memory responses by confidently responding that the information was correctly encoded even though it was not (Mayer and Park 2012).

Furthermore, there is evidence for an additional impairment of working memory maintenance in schizophrenia (Reilly et al. 2006; Stephane and Pellizzer 2007; Badcock et al. 2008), which could also contribute to reduced working memory capacity. Conversely, so far the presence of working memory maintenance deficits has not been investigated in patients with bipolar disorder. Future studies should try to elucidate the contribution of specific component processes to reduced working memory capacity across both disorders.

Importantly, two different models for working memory storage have been discussed. Originally, a discrete-slots model was proposed, where a specific number of items are stored up to capacity, and nothing is stored from the remaining items (Miller 1956; Luck and Vogel 1997; Cowan 2001). More recently, working memory capacity has been studied using a limited-resource model in which a dynamic precision resource spreads out across objects, such that a smaller amount of objects are encoded with higher precision (Bays and Husain 2008; Peters et al. 2018). While our paradigm was able to measure working memory capacity in a slot model, both the discrete-slot model and limited-resource model should be studied within the same patient groups.

It remains to be seen, whether the gradient of working memory capacity reduction is attributable to a comparable gradual manifestation of the same neurophysiological disturbances across diagnostic categories. Our findings also need to be reconciled with the disconnection hypothesis (Friston and Frith 1995), a parsimonious and well validated model for core cognitive and clinical features of schizophrenia that has also been recently applied to bipolar disorder (Perry et al. 2019). Functional neuroimaging studies are required to illuminate these issues.

Conclusion

To summarize, our data provide evidence for reduced visual working memory capacity in both bipolar disorder and schizophrenia. The observed gradient of cognitive dysfunction is compatible with the neurodevelopmental continuum model (Owen and O'Donovan 2017), which would place bipolar disorder between schizophrenia and healthy controls on a neurodevelopmental gradient, matching the degree and persistence of overall functional impairment in both disorders. This interpretation should be validated by investigating the transdiagnostic impact of genetic risk variants – especially CNVs – in genetic pathways regulating neurodevelopment on working memory capacity. However, there is also evidence for a contribution of additional pathophysiological factors such as inflammation (Bora 2019; Millett et al. 2019) to cognitive impairment in both disorders. Future studies should try to determine the specific contributions of such factors to reduced visual working memory capacity. Similarly, it remains an open question how shared and distinct genetic and environmental risk factors for either disorder might influence working memory capacity on the cognitive and neurophysiological level. Given their relevance for patients' functional capacity, future studies should also examine whether pro-cognitive interventions such as cognitive remediation could improve these deficits across diagnostic categories. Finally, our results highlight the utility of established constructs based on cognitive neuroscience for the investigation of impaired information processing in bipolar disorder similar to such endeavors in schizophrenia research (Barch and Smith 2008).

Abbreviations

PBD: Patients with bipolar disorder; PSZ: Patients with schizophrenia; HC: Healthy controls; YMRS: Young Mania Rating Scale; MADRS: Montgomery-Åsberg Depression Rating Scale; PANSS: The Positive and Negative Syndrome Scale; BP-I: Patients with bipolar I; BP-II: Patients with bipolar II; SZ: Patients with schizophrenia; SZAFF: Patients with schizoaffective disorder; BP HPS+: Bipolar with a history of psychotic symptoms; BP HPS-: Bipolar without a history of psychotic symptoms; *K*: Pashler's K; SCID-I: Structural Clinical Interview; SD: Standard deviation; YOE: Years of education; PYOE: Parental years of education; DOI: Duration of illness; MWT-B: German Mehrfachwahl-Wortschatz-Intelligenz Test.

Acknowledgements

The authors are grateful to Benjamin Peters and Meike Hettwer for helpful discussions, to Peter Hustedt, Michael Grube, Christoph Fehr, Martin Hambrecht for their support in recruiting patients, as well as to Lisa Goldschmidt, Tobias Lehmann, and Deliah Macht for help with data acquisition.

Authors' contributions

All authors made substantial contributions to the conception or design of the work, or the acquisition, analysis or interpretation of data. Authors RAB and LR designed the experiment. Authors CVB-S, CP and LR acquired the data. Authors CVB-S, CP, JSM, SM and RAB analyzed the data. Authors CVB-S and RAB undertook the literature searches and wrote the first draft of the manuscript. All authors contributed to and revised the manuscript. All authors read and approved the final manuscript.

Author details

[1] Department of Psychiatry, Psychosomatic Medicine, and Psychotherapy, University Hospital Frankfurt, Goethe University, Heinrich-Hoffmann-Str. 10, 60528 Frankfurt am Main, Germany. [2] Netherlands Institute for Neuroscience, Amsterdam, The Netherlands. [3] Department of Child and Adolescent Psychiatry, Psychosomatics and Psychotherapy, University Hospital Frankfurt, Goethe University, Frankfurt am Main, Germany. [4] Department of Psychiatry, Psychosomatic Medicine, and Psychotherapy, University Hospital Würzburg, Würzburg, Germany. [5] Ernst Strüngmann Institute for Neuroscience (ESI) in Cooperation with Max Planck Society, Frankfurt am Main, Germany.

References

Adler CM, Holland SK, Schmithorst V, Tuchfarber MJ, Strakowski SM. Changes in neuronal activation in patients with bipolar disorder during performance of a working memory task. Bipolar Disord. 2004;6(6):540–9.

Anticevic A, Repovs G, Barch DM. Working memory encoding and maintenance deficits in schizophrenia: neural evidence for activation and deactivation abnormalities. Schizophr Bull. 2011a;39(1):168–78.

Anticevic A, Repovs G, Corlett PR, Barch DM. Negative and nonemotional interference with visual working memory in schizophrenia. Biol Psychiatry. 2011b;70(12):1159–68.

Anttila V, Bulik-Sullivan B, Finucane HK, Walters RK, Bras J, Duncan L, Escott-Price V, Falcone GJ, Gormley P, Malik R. Analysis of shared heritability in common disorders of the brain. Science. 2018;360(6395):8757.

Badcock JC, Badcock DR, Read C, Jablensky A. Examining encoding imprecision in spatial working memory in schizophrenia. Schizophr Res. 2008;100(1–3):144–52.

Baddeley A. Working memory. Science. 1992;255(5044):556–9.

Baddeley AD, Hitch G. Working memory. Psychol Learning Motivat. 1974;8:47–89.

Barch DM, Moore H, Nee DE, Manoach DS, Luck SJ. CNTRICS imaging biomarkers selection: Working memory. Schizophr Bull. 2012;38(1):43–52.

Barch DM, Sheffield JM. Cognitive impairments in psychotic disorders: common mechanisms and measurement. World Psychiatry. 2014;13(3):224–32.

Barch DM, Smith E. The cognitive neuroscience of working memory: relevance to CNTRICS and schizophrenia. Biol Psychiatry. 2008;64(1):11–7.

Bays PM, Husain M. Dynamic shifts of limited working memory resources in human vision. Science. 2008;321(5890):851–4.

Bittner RA, Linden DE, Roebroeck A, Hartling F, Rotarska-Jagiela A, Maurer K, Goebel R, Singer W, Haenschel C. The when and where of working memory dysfunction in early-onset schizophrenia-a functional magnetic resonance imaging study. Cereb Cortex. 2015;25(9):2494–506.

Bora E. Developmental trajectory of cognitive impairment in bipolar disorder: comparison with schizophrenia. Eur Neuropsychopharmacol. 2015;25(2):158–68.

Bora E. Neurocognitive features in clinical subgroups of bipolar disorder: a meta-analysis. J Affect Disord. 2018;229:125–34.

Bora E. Peripheral inflammatory and neurotrophic biomarkers of cognitive impairment in schizophrenia: A meta-analysis. Psychol Med. 2019;49(12):1971–9.

Bora E, Pantelis C. Meta-analysis of cognitive impairment in first-episode bipolar disorder: comparison with first-episode schizophrenia and healthy controls. Schizophr Bull. 2015;41(5):1095–104.

Bora E, Yücel M, Pantelis C, Berk M. Meta-analytic review of neurocognition in bipolar II disorder. Acta Psychiatr Scand. 2011;123(3):165–74.

Bortolato B, Miskowiak KW, Köhler CA, Vieta E, Carvalho AF. Cognitive dysfunction in bipolar disorder and schizophrenia: a systematic review of meta-analyses. Neuropsychiatr Dis Treat. 2015;11:3111.

Clementz BA, Sweeney JA, Hamm JP, Ivleva EI, Ethridge LE, Pearlson GD, Keshavan MS, Tamminga CA. Identification of distinct psychosis biotypes using brain-based biomarkers. Am J Psychiatry. 2016;173(4):373–84.

Cohen J. Statistical power analysis. 1988.

Cowan N. The magical number 4 in short-term memory: a reconsideration of mental storage capacity. Behav Brain Sci. 2001;24(1):87–114.

Cowan N. Working memory underpins cognitive development, learning, and education. Educ Psychol Rev. 2014;26(2):197–223.

Cowan N, Elliott EM, Saults JS, Morey CC, Mattox S, Hismjatullina A, Conway AR. On the capacity of attention: Its estimation and its role in working memory and cognitive aptitudes. Cogn Psychol. 2005;51(1):42–100.

Cowan N, Morey CC. Visual working memory depends on attentional filtering. Trends Cogn Sci. 2006;10(4):139–41.

Crawford JR, Besson J, Bremner M, Ebmeier K, Cochrane R, Kirkwood K. Estimation of premorbid intelligence in schizophrenia. Br J Psychiatry. 1992;161(1):69–74.

Cuthbert BN. The RDoC framework: facilitating transition from ICD/DSM to dimensional approaches that integrate neuroscience and psychopathology. World Psychiatry. 2014;13(1):28–35.

Dai M, Li Y, Gan S, Du F. The reliability of estimating visual working memory capacity. Scientific reports. 2019;9(1):1–8.

Daneman M, Carpenter PA. Individual differences in working memory and reading. J Mem Lang. 1980;19(4):450.

Feuerstahler LM, Luck SJ, MacDonald A, Waller NG. A note on the identification of change detection task models to measure storage capacity and attention in visual working memory. Behav Res Methods. 2019;51(3):1360–70.

Friston KJ, Frith CD. Schizophrenia: a disconnection syndrome. Clin Neurosci. 1995;3(2):89–97.

Fukuda K, Vogel E, Mayr U, Awh E. Quantity, not quality: The relationship between fluid intelligence and working memory capacity. Psychon Bull Rev. 2010;17(5):673–9.

Fuller RL, Luck SJ, Braun EL, Robinson BM, McMahon RP, Gold JM. Impaired visual working memory consolidation in schizophrenia. Neuropsychology. 2009;23(1):71–80.

Gardner DM, Murphy AL, O'Donnell H, Centorrino F, Baldessarini RJ. International consensus study of antipsychotic dosing. Am J Psychiatry. 2010;167(6):686–93.

Glahn DC, Bearden CE, Cakir S, Barrett JA, Najt P, Serap Monkul E, Maples N, Velligan DI, Soares JC. Differential working memory impairment in bipolar disorder and schizophrenia: effects of lifetime history of psychosis. Bipolar Disord. 2006;8(2):117–23.

Gold JM, Barch DM, Feuerstahler LM, Carter CS, MacDonald AW 3rd, Ragland JD, Silverstein SM, Strauss ME, Luck SJ. Working Memory Impairment Across Psychotic disorders. Schizophr Bull. 2018;12:33.

Gold JM, Hahn B, Zhang WW, Robinson BM, Kappenman ES, Beck VM, Luck SJ. Reduced capacity but spared precision and maintenance of working memory representations in schizophrenia. Arch Gen Psychiatry. 2010;67(6):570–7.

Goldberg TE. Some fairly obvious distinctions between schizophrenia and bipolar disorder. Schizophr Res. 1999;39(2):127–32.

Haenschel C, Bittner RA, Haertling F, Rotarska-Jagiela A, Maurer K, Singer W, Linden DE. Contribution of impaired early-stage visual processing to working memory dysfunction in adolescents with schizophrenia: a study with event-related potentials and functional magnetic resonance imaging. Arch Gen Psychiatry. 2007;64(11):1229–40.

Haenschel C, Bittner RA, Waltz J, Haertling F, Wibral M, Singer W, Linden DE, Rodriguez E. Cortical oscillatory activity is critical for working memory as revealed by deficits in early-onset schizophrenia. J Neurosci. 2009;29(30):9481–9.

Hahn B, Robinson BM, Kaiser ST, Harvey AN, Beck VM, Leonard CJ, Kappenman ES, Luck SJ, Gold JM. Failure of schizophrenia patients to overcome salient distractors during working memory encoding. Biol Psychiatry. 2010;68(7):603–9.

Hahn B, Robinson BM, Leonard CJ, Luck SJ, Gold JM. Posterior parietal cortex dysfunction is central to working memory storage and broad cognitive deficits in schizophrenia. J Neurosci. 2018;34:8.

Hamilton LS, Altshuler LL, Townsend J, Bookheimer SY, Phillips OR, Fischer J, Woods RP, Mazziotta JC, Toga AW, Nuechterlein KH. Alterations in functional activation in euthymic bipolar disorder and schizophrenia during a working memory task. Hum Brain Mapp. 2009;30(12):3958–69.

Hartman M, Steketee MC, Silva S, Lanning K, McCann H. Working memory and schizophrenia: evidence for slowed encoding. Schizophr Res. 2003;59(2–3):99–113.

Hill SK, Reilly JL, Keefe RS, Gold JM, Bishop JR, Gershon ES, Tamminga CA, Pearlson GD, Keshavan MS, Sweeney JA. Neuropsychological impairments in schizophrenia and psychotic bipolar disorder: findings from the Bipolar-Schizophrenia Network on Intermediate Phenotypes (B-SNIP) study. Am J Psychiatry. 2013;170(11):1275–84.

Insel T, Cuthbert B, Garvey M, Heinssen R, Pine DS, Quinn K, Sanislow C, Wang P. Research domain criteria (RDoC): toward a new classification framework for research on mental disorders. Am Psychiatric Assoc. 2010;87:4567.

Insel TR. The NIMH research domain criteria (RDoC) project: precision medicine for psychiatry. Am J Psychiatry. 2014;171(4):395–7.

Ivleva EI, Morris DW, Moates AF, Suppes T, Thaker GK, Tamminga CA. Genetics and intermediate phenotypes of the schizophrenia–bipolar disorder boundary. Neurosci Biobehav Rev. 2010;34(6):897–921.

Javitt DC, Rabinowicz E, Silipo G, Dias EC. Encoding vs. retention: differential effects of cue manipulation on working memory performance in schizophrenia. Schizophr Res. 2007;91(1–3):159–68.

Jensen JH, Knorr U, Vinberg M, Kessing LV, Miskowiak KW. Discrete neurocognitive subgroups in fully or partially remitted bipolar disorder: associations with functional abilities. J Affect Disord. 2016;205:378–86.

Johnson MK, McMahon RP, Robinson BM, Harvey AN, Hahn B, Leonard CJ, Luck SJ, Gold JM. The relationship between working memory capacity and broad measures of cognitive ability in healthy adults and people with schizophrenia. Neuropsychology. 2013;27(2):220–9.

Kahn RS, Keefe RS. Schizophrenia is a cognitive illness: time for a change in focus. JAMA psychiatry. 2013;70(10):1107–12.

Kane MJ, Engle RW. The role of prefrontal cortex in working-memory capacity, executive attention, and general fluid intelligence: An individual-differences perspective. Psychon Bull Rev. 2002;9(4):637–71.

Kay SR, Fiszbein A, Opler LA. The positive and negative syndrome scale (PANSS) for schizophrenia. Schizophr Bull. 1987;13(2):261–76.

Khan A, Ginsberg LD, Asnis GM, Goodwin FK, Davis KH, Krishnan AA, Adams BE. Effect of lamotrigine on cognitive complaints in patients with bipolar I disorder. J Clin Psychiatry. 2004;65(11):1483–90.

Khandaker GM, Barnett JH, White IR, Jones PB. A quantitative meta-analysis of population-based studies of premorbid intelligence and schizophrenia. Schizophr Res. 2011;132(2–3):220–7.

Kim J, Park S, Shin Y-W, Lee KJ, Kwon JS. Self-initiated encoding facilitates object working memory in schizophrenia: implications for the etiology of working memory deficit. Schizophr Res. 2006;82(1):65–74.

Lee J, Park S. Working memory impairments in schizophrenia: a meta-analysis. J Abnorm Psychol. 2005;114(4):599.

Lee PH, Anttila V, Won H, Feng Y-CA, Rosenthal J, Zhu Z, Tucker-Drob EM, Nivard MG, Grotzinger AD, Posthuma D. Genomic relationships, novel loci, and pleiotropic mechanisms across eight psychiatric disorders. Cell. 2019;179(7):1469–82.

Lehrl S, Merz J, Burkhard G, Fischer B. Mehrfach-wortschatz-intelligenztest MWT-B. Balingen: Spitta Verlag; 2005.

Leonard CJ, Kaiser ST, Robinson BM, Kappenman ES, Hahn B, Gold JM, Luck SJ. Toward the neural mechanisms of reduced working memory capacity in schizophrenia. Cereb Cortex. 2013;23(7):1582–92.

Leonard CJ, Robinson BM, Hahn B, Luck SJ, Gold JM. Altered spatial profile of distraction in people with schizophrenia. J Abnorm Psychol. 2017;126(8):1077–86.

Lewandowski K, Cohen B, Öngur D. Evolution of neuropsychological dysfunction during the course of schizophrenia and bipolar disorder. Psychol Med. 2011;41(2):225–41.

Linden DE, Bittner RA, Muckli L, Waltz JA, Kriegeskorte N, Goebel R, Singer W, Munk MH. Cortical capacity constraints for visual working memory: dissociation of fMRI load effects in a fronto-parietal network. Neuroimage. 2003;20(3):1518–30.

Luck SJ, Gold JM. The construct of attention in schizophrenia. Biol Psychiatry. 2008;64(1):34–9.

Luck SJ, Vogel EK. Visual working memory capacity: from psychophysics and neurobiology to individual differences. Trends Cogn Sci. 2013;17(8):391–400.

Luck SJ, Hahn B, Leonard CJ, Gold JM. The hyperfocusing hypothesis: A new account of cognitive dysfunction in Schizophrenia. Schizophr Bull. 2019a;45(5):991–1000.

Luck SJ, Leonard CJ, Hahn B, Gold JM. Is Attentional Filtering Impaired in Schizophrenia? Schizophr Bull. 2019b;45(5):1001–11.

Luck SJ, Vogel EK. The capacity of visual working memory for features and conjunctions. Nature. 1997;390(6657):279–81.

Maj M, Pirozzi R, Formicola AM, Bartoli L, Bucci P. Reliability and validity of the DSM-IV diagnostic category of schizoaffective disorder: preliminary data. J Affect Disord. 2000;57(1–3):95–8.

Martínez-Arán A, Vieta E, Reinares M, Colom F, Torrent C, Sánchez-Moreno J, Benabarre A, Goikolea JM, Comes M, Salamero M. Cognitive function

across manic or hypomanic, depressed, and euthymic states in bipolar disorder. Am J Psychiatry. 2004;161(2):262–70.
Mayer JS, Fukuda K, Vogel EK, Park S. Impaired contingent attentional capture predicts reduced working memory capacity in schizophrenia. PLoS ONE. 2012;7(11):e48586.
Mayer JS, Park S. Working memory encoding and false memory in schizophrenia and bipolar disorder in a spatial delayed response task. J Abnorm Psychol. 2012;121(3):784.
Mayer JS, Stäblein M, Oertel-Knöchel V, Fiebach CJ. Functional Dissociation of Confident and Not-Confident Errors in the Spatial Delayed Response Task Demonstrates Impairments in Working Memory Encoding and Maintenance in Schizophrenia. Frontiers in psychiatry. 2018;9:202.
McNab F, Klingberg T. Prefrontal cortex and basal ganglia control access to working memory. Nat Neurosci. 2008;11(1):103.
Miller GA. The magical number seven, plus or minus two: Some limits on our capacity for processing information. Psychol Rev. 1956;63(2):81.
Millett C, Perez-Rodriguez M, Shanahan M, Larsen E, Yamamoto H, Bukowski C, Fichorova R, Burdick K. C-reactive protein is associated with cognitive performance in a large cohort of euthymic patients with bipolar disorder. Mol Psychiatry. 2019;22:1–10.
Miskowiak KW, Burdick K, Martinez-Aran A, Bonnin C, Bowie C, Carvalho A, Gallagher P, Lafer B, López-Jaramillo C, Sumiyoshi T. Assessing and addressing cognitive impairment in bipolar disorder: the International Society for Bipolar Disorders Targeting Cognition Task Force recommendations for clinicians. Bipolar Disord. 2018;20(3):184–94.
Montgomery SA, Åsberg M. A new depression scale designed to be sensitive to change. Br J Psychiatry. 1979;134(4):382–9.
Oertel-Knöchel V, Bittner RA, Knöchel C, Prvulovic D, Hampel H. Discovery and development of integrative biological markers for schizophrenia. Prog Neurobiol. 2011;95(4):686–702.
Oldfield RC. The assessment and analysis of handedness: the Edinburgh inventory. Neuropsychologia. 1971;9(1):97–113.
Owen MJ, O'Donovan MC. Schizophrenia and the neurodevelopmental continuum: evidence from genomics. World Psychiatry. 2017;16(3):227–35.
Pashler H. Familiarity and visual change detection. Percept Psychophys. 1988;44(4):369–78.
Pearlson GD. Etiologic, phenomenologic, and endophenotypic overlap of schizophrenia and bipolar disorder. Annu Rev Clin Psychol. 2015;11:251–81.
Perry A, Roberts G, Mitchell PB, Breakspear M. Connectomics of bipolar disorder: a critical review, and evidence for dynamic instabilities within interoceptive networks. Mol Psychiatry. 2019;24(9):1296–318.
Peters B, Rahm B, Czoschke S, Barnes C, Kaiser J, Bledowski C. Sequential whole report accesses different states in visual working memory. J Exp Psychol Learn Mem Cogn. 2018;44(4):588–603.
Reilly JL, Harris MS, Keshavan MS, Sweeney JA. Adverse effects of risperidone on spatial working memory in first-episode schizophrenia. Arch Gen Psychiatry. 2006;63(11):1189–97.
Reilly JL, Sweeney JA. Generalized and specific neurocognitive deficits in psychotic disorders: utility for evaluating pharmacological treatment effects and as intermediate phenotypes for gene discovery. Schizophr Bull. 2014;40(3):516–22.
Rouder JN, Morey RD, Morey CC, Cowan N. How to measure working memory capacity in the change detection paradigm. Psychon Bull Rev. 2011;18(2):324–30.
Saß H, Wittchen H-U, Zaudig M, Houben I. Dsm-iv-tr. Hogrefe, Göttingen: Diagnostische Kriterien; 2003.
Schretlen DJ, Cascella NG, Meyer SM, Kingery LR, Testa SM, Munro CA, Pulver AE, Rivkin P, Rao VA, Diaz-Asper CM. Neuropsychological functioning in bipolar disorder and schizophrenia. Biol Psychiatry. 2007;62(2):179–86.
Senturk V, Goker C, Bilgic A, Olmez S, Tugcu H, Oncu B, Cem Atbasoglu E. Impaired verbal memory and otherwise spared cognition in remitted bipolar patients on monotherapy with lithium or valproate. Bipolar Disord. 2007;9:136–44.
Stephane M, Pellizzer G. The dynamic architecture of working memory in schizophrenia. Schizophr Res. 2007;92(1–3):160–7.
Tek C, Gold J, Blaxton T, Wilk C, McMahon RP, Buchanan RW. Visual perceptual and working memory impairments in schizophrenia. Arch Gen Psychiatry. 2002;59(2):146–53.
Thompson JM, Gray JM, Hughes JH, Watson S, Young AH, Nicol Ferrier I. Impaired working memory monitoring in euthymic bipolar patients. Bipolar Disord. 2007;9(5):478–89.
Todd JJ, Marois R. Capacity limit of visual short-term memory in human posterior parietal cortex. Nature. 2004;428(6984):751.
Townsend J, Bookheimer SY, Foland-Ross LC, Sugar CA, Altshuler LL. fMRI abnormalities in dorsolateral prefrontal cortex during a working memory task in manic, euthymic and depressed bipolar subjects. Psychiatry Res Neuroimag. 2010;182(1):22–9.
Unsworth N, Fukuda K, Awh E, Vogel EK. Working memory and fluid intelligence: capacity, attention control, and secondary memory retrieval. Cogn Psychol. 2014;71:1–26.
Vogel EK, Machizawa MG. Neural activity predicts individual differences in visual working memory capacity. Nature. 2004;428(6984):748–51.
Vogel EK, McCollough AW, Machizawa MG. Neural measures reveal individual differences in controlling access to working memory. Nature. 2005;438(7067):500.
Vöhringer PA, Barroilhet S, Amerio A, Reale ML, Vergne D, Alvear KP, Ghaemi SN. Cognitive impairment in bipolar disorder and schizophrenia: a systematic review. Front Psychiatry. 2013;4:87.
Volkert J, Kopf J, Kazmaier J, Glaser F, Zierhut K, Schiele M, Kittel-Schneider S, Reif A. Evidence for cognitive subgroups in bipolar disorder and the influence of subclinical depression and sleep disturbances. Eur Neuropsychopharmacol. 2015;25(2):192–202.
Wheeler ME, Treisman AM. Binding in short-term visual memory. J Exp Psychol Gen. 2002;131(1):48.
Wright AA, Katz JS, Magnotti J, Elmore LC, Babb S. Testing pigeon memory in a change detection task. Psychon Bull Rev. 2010;17(2):243–9.
Xu G, Lin K, Rao D, Dang Y, Ouyang H, Guo Y, Ma J, Chen J. Neuropsychological performance in bipolar I, bipolar II and unipolar depression patients: a longitudinal, naturalistic study. J Affect Disord. 2012;136(3):328–39.
Xu Z, Adam K, Fang X, Vogel E. The reliability and stability of visual working memory capacity. Behav Res Methods. 2018;50(2):576–88.
Young RC, Biggs JT, Ziegler VE, Meyer DA. A rating scale for mania: reliability, validity and sensitivity. Br J Psychiatry. 1978;133(5):429–35.

11

Using density of antecedent events and trajectory path analysis to investigate family-correlated patterns of onset of bipolar I disorder: a comparison of cohorts from Europe and USA

Jan Scott[1,2], Florence Vorspan[2,3,4], Josephine Loftus[5], Frank Bellivier[2,3,4] and Bruno Etain[2,3,4*]

Abstract

Background: Major contributors to the global burden of bipolar disorders (BD) are the early age at onset (AAO) and the co-occurrence of non-mood disorders before and after the onset of BD. Using data from two independent cohorts from Europe and the USA, we investigated whether the trajectories of BD-I onset and patterns of psychiatric comorbidities differed in (a) individuals with or without a family history (FH) of BD, or (b) probands and parents who both had BD-I.

Methods: First, we estimated cumulative probabilities and AAO of comorbid mental disorders in familial and non-familial cases of BD-I (Europe, n = 573), and sex-matched proband-parent pairs of BD-I cases (USA, n = 194). Then we used time to onset analyses to compare overall AAO of BD-I and AAO according to onset polarity. Next, we examined associations between AAO and polarity of onset of BD-I according to individual experiences of comorbidities. This included analysis of the density of antecedent events (defined as the number of antecedent comorbidities per year of exposure to mental illness per individual) and time trend analysis of trajectory paths plotted for the subgroups included in each cohort (using R^2 goodness of fit analysis).

Results: Earlier AAO of BD-I was found in FH versus non-FH cases (log rank test = 7.63; p = 0.006) and in probands versus parents with BD-I (log rank test = 15.31; p = 0.001). In the European cohort, AAO of BD-I was significantly associated with factors such as: FH of BD (hazard ratio [HR]: 0.60), earlier AAO of first non-mood disorder (HR: 0.93) and greater number of comorbidities (HR: 0.74). In the USA cohort, probands with BD-I had an earlier AAO for depressive and manic episodes and AAO was also associated with e.g., number of comorbidities (HR: 0.65) and year of birth (HR: 2.44). Trajectory path analysis indicated significant differences in density of antecedents between subgroups within each cohort. However, the time trend R^2 analysis was significantly different for the European cohort only.

Conclusions: Estimating density of antecedent events and comparing trajectory plots for different BD subgroups are informative adjuncts to established statistical approaches and may offer additional insights that enhance understanding of the evolution of BD-I.

Keywords: Bipolar I disorder, Comorbidities, Trajectories, Antecedents, Cohorts, Family history

Background

Globally, bipolar disorders (BD) are ranked the sixth most burdensome disease in working age adults (Gore

*Correspondence: bruno.etain@inserm.fr
[2] Université de Paris, Paris, France
Full list of author information is available at the end of the article

et al. 2011). Key reasons for the substantial morbidity are that 75% of BD onsets occur at age < 30, and that BD is highly comorbid (Angst et al. 2002; Merikangas et al. 2007; Merikangas et al. 2008). These issues are amplified in individuals with a family history (FH) of BD who have an increased risk of developing BD, to experience an earlier age at onset (AAO) of BD, and to report high rates of mood and non-mood disorders during childhood and adolescence compared with control populations (e.g., Duffy et al. 2019; Hafeman et al. 2017; Lau et al. 2018). Emerging evidence confirms that many comorbidities occur before the first BD episode, i.e., they are antecedents of BD-onset not just complications of the disorder (e.g., Faedda et al. 2014; Hafeman et al. 2017; Carpenter et al. 2020).

For example, several meta-analyses report the lifetime rates of different psychiatric disorders in BD populations and some explore comorbidities in those at high risk of developing BD in the future (e.g., Lau et al. 2018; Pavlova et al. 2015; Messer et al. 2017). Whilst these confirm high rates of mood and non-mood disorders, the sequence of onset of the different comorbidities has only been examined consistently in prospective studies of offspring of parents with BD (e.g., Duffy et al. 2019; Mesman et al. 2013; Hafeman et al. 2017). The findings suggest that, for example, most anxiety disorders may occur earlier than mood problems and precede substance misuse (Lau et al. 2018).

However, many well-known offspring and youth cohort studies are still ongoing, and so large proportions of the research participants have not yet been followed through the entire peak age range for onset of BD (and/or for non-mood comorbidities) (e.g. Duffy et al. 2019; Lee et al. 2018; Koenders et al. 2020). Additionally, even though the study samples may be relatively large, the total number of BD cases is small in the offspring or controls (e.g. Duffy et al. 2019; Koenders et al. 2020). The potential consequence of this scenario is that these studies cannot yet fully account for the pattern of associations between comorbidities and being diagnosed with BD, nor any differences in comorbidity rates and the timing of onset of BD in familial and non-familial cases.

Studies of offspring and other cohorts have been undertaken over a number of decades, and have generated a number of other interesting observations. For example, when current and past research are examined side by side it appears that the AAO of BD may be decreasing (e.g., Golmard et al. 2016; Scott et al. 2018). Several explanations have been proposed for this phenomena. These include the possibility that a lower AAO of BD could be linked to increasing rates of psychiatric comorbidities and/or that it might be linked to higher familial loading and/or childhood adversity (e.g., Post et al. 2015). However, no study to date has determined how the pattern of onsets of comorbidities may be linked with AAO of BD in cases with or without a family history of BD. Likewise, very few studies have examined similarities in the evolution of BD in probands and parents, so it is not clear if there is concordance in the pattern of comorbidities across generations (Dierker et al. 1999).

Overall, our examination of previous research highlighted that gaps exist in the understanding of cumulative rates of and AAO of comorbidities observed in individuals who progress to a diagnosis of BD. Also, there are uncertainties regarding associations between the trajectories of comorbidities experienced (i.e., sequence and timing of onset of non-mood disorders) and their relationship to AAO of BD in subpopulations with different levels of premorbid risk (e.g. familial versus non-familial BD) (Carpenter et al. 2020). Further, we noted that many existing studies of comorbidity only focus on specific diagnoses or classes of diagnoses (such as anxiety disorders) without exploring whether other markers of illness burden (e.g., number and timing of onset of all the comorbidities experienced) are associated with polarity of onset or AAO of BD (Merikangas et al. 2017).

We decided to undertake a project to address some of these gaps but were mindful that there are several difficulties in undertaking research on trajectories of comorbidities in individuals with familial versus non-familial BD and/or between generations within the same family. The three most common problems identified in previous research were: the reliability of BD diagnoses; the quality of assessments of family history (FH); and the rigour of reporting of individual longitudinal psychiatric histories (Leckman et al. 1982; Wacholder et al. 1991; Duffy et al. 2011). To address these concerns, we used data from existing cohort studies that employed reliable and valid assessment tools and that were sufficiently similar methodologically to allow some cross-study conclusions to be drawn. We applied for access to two assembled cohorts of BD cases from which we extracted data on individuals who met recognized, international diagnostic criteria for BD-I (we chose to focus on this subtype, as the diagnosis of BD-I is the third most reliable diagnosis in psychiatry) (First 2016). Further, the cohort members: (i) were recruited to studies that paid specific attention to familiality, namely genetics studies in Europe (cases with/without a FH of BD) and the USA (proband-parent pairs of BD-I cases: PRB-PAR), (ii) were beyond the peak age range for risk of onset of BD-I (to allow us to carefully assess comorbidities that occur as antecedents versus consequences of BD-I onset), and (iii) the evaluations of best-estimate diagnoses and AAO of lifetime DSM IV comorbidities were undertaken using the same, well-established structured clinical interview assessment undertaken by trained researchers.

In this article, we investigate questions related to three themes-

(i) Patterns (type and AAO) of comorbid conditions in familial cases of BD-I and within-family correlation:

Do familial cases of BD-I (FH) demonstrate any differences in the type or AAO of lifetime comorbid mental disorders compared with non-familial cases (No FH; sometimes referred to as phenocopies or as 'sporadic 'BD cases)?

and

Do probands with BD-I demonstrate any differences in the type or AAO of lifetime comorbid mental disorders compared with their same-sex biological parent with BD (PRB-PAR pairs)?

(ii) Comorbid conditions and AAO of BD-I and AAO according to onset polarity:

In the two study cohorts (FH/No FH; PRB-PAR), is there any association between exposure to any comorbid mental disorder(s) and the AAO of BD-I and/or polarity of first episode of BD-I?

and

In each cohort, what are the similarities and differences in the overall pattern of comorbidities between subgroups?

(iii) Density of antecedent events and trajectory plots:

An additional goal of this project was to explore new ways of presenting comparative data that would be easy to interpret or understand (e.g., for patients and families, those outside academic settings). So, we explored—Is it possible to represent the pattern of comorbidities using novel metrics such as density of antecedent events (number of antecedent comorbidities per year of exposure to mental illness per individual) and plots of trajectory paths?

Do the estimates for antecedents and trajectories differ between subgroups included within each cohort?

Method

The project was approved by the French medical ethics committee (Comité de Protection des Personnes-IDRCB_AO1465_50_VI-Pitié Salpêtrière) and follows the Strengthening the Reporting of Observational Studies in Epidemiology guidelines (STROBE). Here, we summarize key elements of the methodology only, but Additional file 1: Appendix 1 includes further details of the protocol (including rationale for selection of datasets, statistical procedures, etc.) and separate STROBE checklists for each study cohort.

Sampling and data extraction

Assembled cohorts

Written informed consent was obtained from all participants and de-identified data on demographics and clinical phenotypes were extracted from a European genetics database study (data from France) and a genetic linkage study database provided by the NIMH Repository and Genomics Resource in the USA (permissions to use data from NRGR Bipolar Disorder distribution 12.0 was granted to Scott and colleagues; access ID number: 5c9874082337f). Additional file 1: Appendix 1 highlights similarities and differences in data collection and recording between Europe and the USA (Potash et al. 2007; Etain et al. 2012).

Familial and Non-Familial Cases: The European dataset comprised information about individuals meeting DSM-IV criteria for BD-I who were recruited via three French university-affiliated psychiatry departments between 1994 and 2008. Individuals aged > 18 were interviewed using the French version of the Diagnostic Interview for Genetic Studies (DIGS) and Family Interview for Genetic Studies (FIGS) (Maxwell 1992; Nurnberger et al. 1994).

Sex-Matched Proband-Parent Pairs (PRB-PAR): From datasets that included individuals with BD, we identified adults aged > 18 at baseline assessment who were recruited to USA-based genetics linkage studies between 1991 and 2003 and assessed using the DIGS. We extracted data on pairs of cases, comprising probands with a DSM-IV diagnosis of BD-I matched to their same sex biological parent with DSM-IV diagnosis of BD-I.

Illness trajectories

Clinical data collected using the DIGS allowed construction of individual patterns of exposure to comorbidities and illness trajectories. Information on comorbid disorders that fulfilled DSM-IV diagnostic criteria and the AAO of each full-threshold disorder experienced was recorded. We classified polarity of onset of BD-I as depressive (first mood episode met DSM-IV criteria for a major depressive episode) or manic (first mood episode met DSM-IV criteria for a manic and/or mixed episode). As in similar research, AAO were estimated from DIGS, case note and informant information (Egeland et al. 1987). Combining data from individual profiles allowed plots of illness trajectories for each subgroup to be generated (Thomas et al. 2009).

We further examined patterns of comorbidities by estimating the total number of comorbid conditions reported per individual (i.e., the combination of pre- and post-onset of BD), and the number of comorbid conditions that occurred prior to the onset of onset of BD-I per individual (Vaidyanathan et al. 2011). We then estimated the density of antecedent events, which represents the number of events per year of exposure to mental disorders prior to BD-I onset for each individual (where illness exposure is calculated as the time interval between AAO of the first DSM-IV diagnosis and AAO of the first episode of BD-I; and only comorbidities preceding BD onset are considered). As such, this variable encompasses several key elements regarding the nature, pattern and timing of comorbidities and offers a valuable proxy that we employed in our exploration of trajectory paths.

Statistical analysis

Analyses were undertaken using RStudio version 3.5.3, and SAS version 9.4. A priori we defined statistical significance as a p value of 0.05 or less.

Descriptive analysis

Categorical data regarding cumulative probabilities of DSM IV disorders were described using counts and percentages; continuous data regarding AAO of each diagnosis were described using medians with inter-quartile ranges (IQR). Basic characteristics were compared between subgroups using non-parametric univariate analyses (analyses for related samples were used for PRB-PAR).

Time to event (onset of BD-I) analysis

Kaplan Meier estimators tested subgroup differences in AAO of BD-I with statistical significance established using Mantel Haenszel log-rank tests. For the European cohort, we used an accelerated failure time (AFT) model to test effects of key covariates on the time to onset of BD-I (Wei 1992). An AFT model assumes that the effect of covariates (such as AAO of first comorbidity) may act multiplicatively with respect to the AAO of BD-I. The hazard ratio (HR) estimates, in effect, represent a time ratio with 95% confidence intervals (CI). As recommended, we employed generalized estimating equations (GEE) for analyses in PRB-PAR (Zeger et al. 1988). All these analyses included sex and year of birth as covariates.

Exploratory trajectory analysis

We used a time trend design to estimate longitudinal changes in health/illness status, with age representing the underlying time scale (Bailey et al. 2005; Thomas et al. 2009). Trend estimation was used to relate observations of interest (DSM IV diagnoses) to the time at which they occur (AAO). We first produced bubble plots to demonstrate the sequence and rates of comorbidities over time (using GraphPad Prism 8). The size of each bubble represents the cumulative probability of a DSM IV disorder occurring within a subgroup. The order in which the bubbles occur on the trajectory path represents the sequencing of onsets of each reported comorbidity. The location of the bubble on the y-axis identifies the median AAO of that disorder within the subgroup (the location of the bubbles on the x-axis approximates to the timing of onset of a disorder within the total course of illness) (Loftus et al. 2020).

Using the bubble plots, we then plotted a logistic trendline; this best-fitted curve line is recommended as the most appropriate option for analogous longitudinal data (Ho-Trieu and Tucker 1990; Thomas et al. 2009). The goodness of fit of the trajectory was estimated using the least square fitting process, where R^2 represents the fraction of the variance explained by the fitted trendline (R^2 range = 0–1; a value of one would indicate a perfect fit of data to the path of the trajectory curve) (Zheng 2000; Weisstein 2020). The R^2 for subgroups were compared statistically using a Z transformation (see Additional file 1: Appendix 1 for details). To further illuminate patterns represented in the bubble plots for each subgroup within each cohort, we analyzed differences in the number of antecedent comorbidities (without consideration of time frame) and in the density of antecedent events.

Results

For each cohort we show one table and one figure in the main text, with two additional tables and figures in the supplementary materials (Additional files 2, 3: Appendices 2 and 3). As the paper is primarily focused on trajectory paths and R^2 analyses, we only briefly report AFT and GEE findings.

Familial (FH) versus non-familial (no FH) BD-I cases

As shown in Table 1, the European cohort comprised 573 individuals; 322 were female (56.2%) and 209 (36.5%) had a confirmed FH of BD. The sample median AAO of BD-I was 22.0. Over half the cohort (N = 301; 52.5%) reported ≥ 1 comorbid DSM IV diagnosis (irrespective of mood disorder episodes) with a median AAO of the first full-threshold disorder of 18.0. The commonest non-mood comorbid condition was alcohol abuse (N = 124; 21.7%) and the rarest was OCD (N = 28; 5%). Social phobia had the youngest median AAO (15.0 years), whilst alcohol dependence had the oldest median AAO (28.5 years).

Comparison between subgroups demonstrated that about 61% of individuals with a FH and 57% without a FH (i.e., No FH group) reported a depressive polarity of onset of BD-I (Additional file 2: Table S1, Appendix 2). The median AAO was a statistically significant different for depressive onset polarity (FH: 20.0; No FH: 22.8; $p < 0.007$), but not for manic polarity of onset (FH: 22.0; No FH: 23.5). As shown in Additional file 2: Table S1,

Table 1 Characteristics of 573 individuals with BD-I (209 with a family history and 364 without a family history of BD)

	Cumulative probability		Median age at onset in years (interquartile range)
	Number	(%)[c]	
Females	322	56.2	
Family history of BD	209	36.5	
Age at onset of BD			22.0 (18.0, 30.5)
Duration of BD			16.0 (11.5, 25.3)
Lifetime comorbidities:			
≥ 1 comorbid mental disorder[a]	301	52.5	
Age at onset of first mental disorder[b]			18.0 (14.3, 25.5)
Social phobia	81	14.2	15.0 (11.5, 20.3)
Specific phobia	49	8.5	15.5 (10.3, 22.5)
Obsessive compulsive disorder	28	5.0	18.3 (14.0, 23.0)
Generalized anxiety disorder	45	7.9	20.8 (17.0, 27.5)
Agoraphobia	53	9.4	20.0 (15.3, 36.0)
Panic disorder	108	18.9	22.0 (17.5, 32.3)
Eating disorder	56	9.8	16.8 (14.0, 18.3)
Cannabis abuse	88	15.4	17.8 (17.0, 20.5)
Cannabis dependence	38	6.7	18.3 (16.5, 21.8)
Alcohol abuse	124	21.7	23.5 (18.3, 35.0)
Alcohol dependence	45	7.8	28.5 (21.3, 35.0)

[a] Comorbid mental disorder refers to any DSM IV diagnosed disorder that occurred (irrespective of BD-I mood episodes);

[b] First mental disorder refers to a clinical condition that met criteria for a full-threshold DSM IV diagnosis

[c] Denominator for comorbid disorders ranges from n = 549 to n = 573 (due to small number of sporadic missing values)

there were few differences in rates of specific comorbidities except for cannabis dependence (FH: 9.2%; No FH: 3.8%; $p<0.008$), and few differences in median AAO of comorbidities, except for agoraphobia (FH: 20.0; No FH: 26.5; $p<0.046$). However, Additional file 2: Table S2 shows that the FH group reported significantly more comorbidities in total (i.e., pre-and-post-onset of BD-I) and significantly more occurring prior to BD-I onset.

Time to event analysis showed that familial BD was associated with a significantly earlier AAO of BD-I (log rank test = 7.63; $p=0.006$). Analysis of AAO of BD-I according to polarity demonstrated that for manic onset, the best predictors of earlier AAO of mania was the presence of a FH of BD (HR: 0.60; 95% CI: 0.38, 0.94) and earlier AAO of first DSM IV diagnosis (HR: 0.97; 95% CI: 0.95, 0.99). For depressive polarity of onset, the best predictors of earlier AAO of BD-I were earlier AAO of first DSM IV diagnosis (HR: 0.93; 95% CI: 0.89, 0.98) and greater total number of comorbidities (HR: 0.74; 95% CI: 0.56, 0.95).

Figure 1 shows the bubble plots and best-fitted trajectory curves for the FH and No FH subgroups (separate plots that show depressive and manic polarities and mathematical formulae describing the trajectories are shown in Additional file 3: Fig. S1 in Appendix 3). As can be seen in Fig. 1, the trajectory curve for the FH subgroup looks flatter and the density of antecedents appears greater (and comorbidities cluster at an earlier age). These observations were confirmed by statistical analyses. The R^2 for the trajectory curves for the two subgroups were significantly different (FH: 0.88, 95% CI: 0.85, 0.91; No FH: 0.94, 95% CI: 0.92, 0.95; $Z=-2.98$; $p=0.01$). As shown in Additional file 2: Table S2, individuals with a FH reported significantly more antecedents compared with those with No FH (grouped medians: FH: 1.16; No FH: 0.47; $p<0.04$) and a significantly higher density of antecedents per individual (grouped medians: FH: 0.078; No FH: 0.051; $p<0.018$).

Proband-parent pairs

As shown in Table 2, the USA cohort comprised 184 individuals (92 PRB-PAR pairs); 100 individuals were female (54.3%). The median AAO of BD-I was 19.3 and median duration of BD-I at the time of interview assessment was 20.3 years. Over half the cohort (N = 95; 51.6%) reported ≥ 1 comorbid DSM IV mental disorder (irrespective of mood disorder episodes) with a median AAO of the first full-threshold disorder of 15.0 years. The commonest comorbid condition was AUD (N = 58; 31.5%) and the rarest was OCD (N = 6; 3.3%). Specific phobia had the earliest median AAO (9.0 years), whilst AUD had the latest median AAO (28.3 years).

Comparison between subgroups (Additional file 2: Table S3 in Appendix 2) demonstrated that 61% of both probands and parents reported depressive polarity of onset of BD-I. There were statistically significant differences in the median AAO of BD-I between PRB-PAR pairs for both depressive onset polarity (PRB: 17.3PAR: 23.0; $p<0.001$) and manic onset polarity (PRB: 20.0; PAR: 24.3; $p<0.001$). There were few differences regarding specific comorbidities, except for trends for OCD to be more common in PRB (PRB: 5.4%; PAR 1.1%; $p=0.067$) and the median AAO of AUD to be younger in PRB (PRB: 26.0; PR: 33.0; $p=0.052$).

Time to event analysis confirmed that PRB had a significantly earlier AAO of BD-I than PAR (log rank test = 15.31; $p=0.001$). Median AAO of BD-I in those with a manic onset was associated with number of comorbidities (HR: 0.65; 95% CI 0.44, 0.95) and year of birth (HR: 2.44; 95% CI: 1.58, 3.76), with later AAO of BD-I was associated with earlier year of birth. Median AAO in those with a depressive onset polarity was associated with the same two variables (HR for comorbidities:

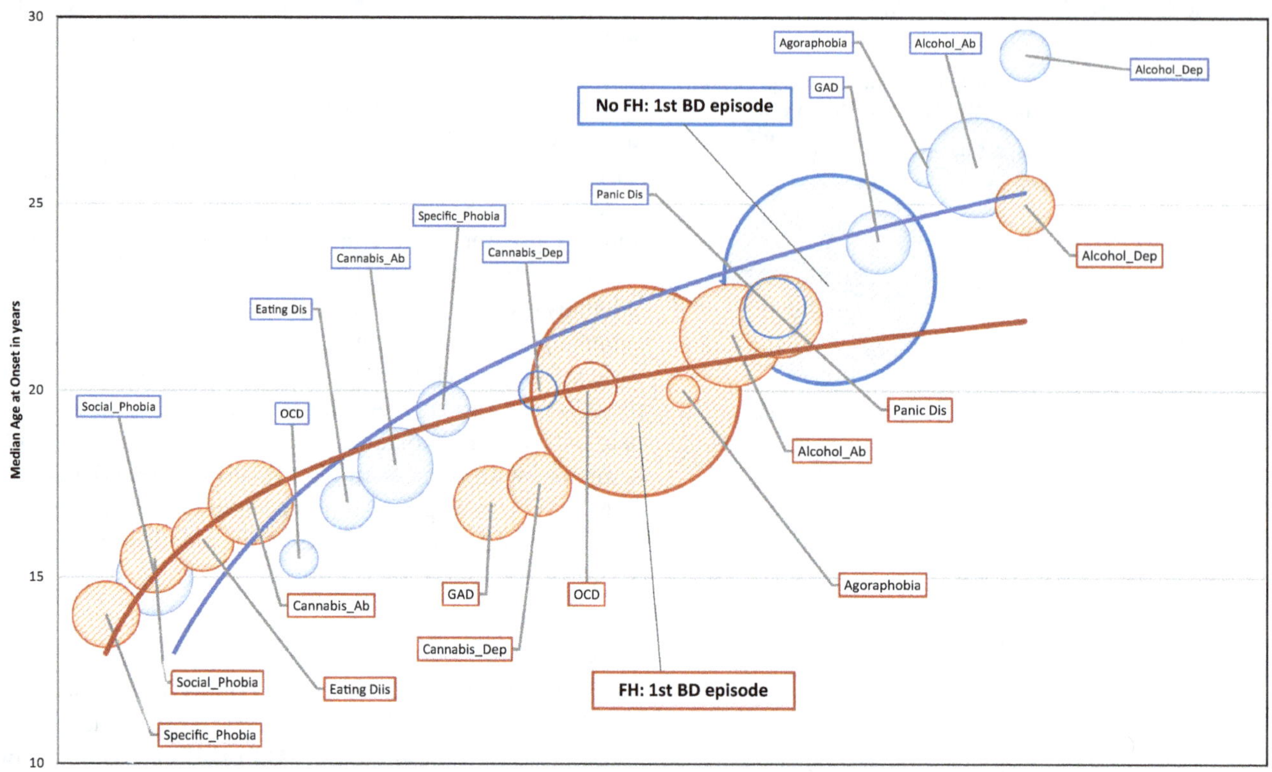

BD: Bipolar I Disorder; OCD: Obsessive Compulsive Disorder; GAD: Generalized Anxiety Disorder; Ab: Abuse; Dep: Dependence; Dis: Disorder; FH: Family History

FAMILY HISTORY (FH) NO FAMILY HISTORY (No FH)

Fig. 1 Trajectories of evolution of BD-I in groups with (FH) or without (no FH) a family history of Bipolar I Disorder (BD). In the bubble plot, the size of the bubble represents the proportion of the group who experience a particular disorder, the position of the bubble vertically gives the median AAO, whilst the position on the horizontal axis approximates to the timing of onset of a disorder in the interval between the onset of the first full threshold mental disorder and the onset of the last comorbidity. For example: in the FH subgroup, the median AAO of the first mental disorder (specific phobia) is about 13–14 years, whilst the median AAO of BD-I is about 20 years. The curve fits less well to the trajectory of comorbidities for the period post-onset of BD-I in the FH group. In the No FH group, the median AAO of the first mental disorder (social phobia) is about 14–15, whilst the median AAO of BD-I is about 22 years. In the No FH group, the curve fits less well to the trajectory path of those antecedent comorbidities with the earliest AAO. The bubbles for BD-I represent 100% in both subgroups. The location of that bubble for FH is lower on the vertical axis, indicating the disorder has an earlier AAO than in the 'No FH' group. Also, as can be observed, there appears to be a more obvious clustering of (relatively) early AAO antecedent comorbid disorders within a briefer time interval in the FH group, compared with the No FH group. There are a smaller number of between-group differences in the sequence and onset of different mental disorders

0.44; 95% CI: 0.29, 0.68; HR for year of birth: 1.29; 95% CI: 1.04, 1.58); sex was of borderline significance in this model (HR for male sex: 1.28; 95% CI: 0.94, 1.68). It was noted that PRB/PAR status was not a significant covariate in either model.

Figure 2 shows the bubble plots and best-fitted trajectory curves for the PRB and PAR subgroups (also see Additional file 3: Fig. S2 in Appendix 3). The path of the trajectory curves demonstrates similar AAO of the first mental disorder, but an earlier median AAO for BD-I for PRB compared with PAR. However, the R^2 for the trajectory curves for each subgroup were not significantly different (PRB: 0.90, 95% CI: 0.85, 0.93; PAR: 0.92, 95% CI: 0.88, 0.95; $Z=0.97$; $p=0.33$). As shown in Additional file 2: Table S4, PRB and PAR did not differ significantly in number of antecedents (grouped medians- PRB: 1.21; PAR: 0.96; $p=0.13$). However, as might be expected given the earlier AAO of BD, PRB had a significantly higher density of antecedents per individual (grouped medians- PRB: 0.088; PAR: 0.071; $p<0.04$).

Discussion

This study used a series of planned analyses to explore the relationships between psychiatric comorbidities occurring before and after the onset of BD-I in groups with different premorbid levels of risk. We found that few between-group differences were identified by basic summary estimates of cumulative probabilities or AAO of specific comorbidities (except e.g. for the prevalence

Table 2 Characteristics of 184 individuals with BD-I (92 sex-matched proband-parent pairs)

	Cumulative probability		Median age at onset in years (interquartile range)
	Number	(%)[c]	
Females	100	54.3	
Age at onset of BD			19 (15.3, 26.0)
Duration of BD			20.3 (10.3, 35.8)
Lifetime comorbidities:			
≥ 1 comorbid mental disorder[a]	95	51.6	
Age at onset of first mental disorder[b]			15.0 (10.5, 17.8)
Social phobia	9	5	14.5 (9.0, 20.3)
Specific phobia	14	7.5	9.0 (6.3, 13.8)
Obsessive compulsive disorder	6	3.3	17.5 (11.5, 28.0)
Generalized anxiety disorder	30	16.3	21.8 (17.0, 27.3)
Agoraphobia	12	6.5	17.8 (12.3, 28.0)
Panic disorder	33	18.0	23.0 (15.5, 32.3)
Eating disorder	11	6.0	17 (12.8, 22.5)
Substance use disorder	23	12.5	18.0 (15.8, 25.3)
Alcohol use disorder	58	31.5	28.3 (23.0, 37.5)

[a] Comorbid mental disorder refers to any DSM IV diagnosed disorder that occurred (irrespective of BD-I mood episodes);

[b] First mental disorder refers to a clinical condition that met criteria for a full-threshold DSM IV diagnosis

[c] Denominator for comorbid disorders ranges from n = 175 to n = 184 (due to small number of sporadic missing values)

of cannabis dependence in FH cases and the AAO of AUD in PRB cases). We formed the opinion that univariate analyses cannot tell the complete story of the interrelationship between comorbidities in BD. It was clear that more intriguing findings emerged when analyses are extended to consider the overall burden of comorbidities and whether the total exposure and/or timing of exposures to comorbidities is associated with AAO of BD. For example, we found that most FH and PRB cases experience ≥ 1 non-mood disorder prior to the onset of BD, and that the increased illness burden associated with all comorbidities appears to be due to incremental differences in the cumulative probability and/or AAO in these two subgroups compared with the other study groups. Furthermore, in the European cohort, AAO of the first DSM IV diagnosis was significantly associated with AAO of BD-I (irrespective of polarity), but only manic onset polarity was significantly associated with FH status. In contrast, in the USA cohort of PRB-PAR, AAO of BD-I was significantly associated with year of birth and burden of comorbidities irrespective of polarity of onset (and these covariates were more important than PRB-PAR status or AAO of first non-mood comorbidity). All of these findings were incorporated into the trajectory path analyses, which demonstrated that the density of antecedents was significantly higher in FH and PRB groups versus their comparators. However, the time trend R^2 analysis was significantly different for the subgroups in the European cohort only. The latter finding may indicate that there are more dissimilarities in the evolution of BD between FH and No FH subgroups than between PRB-PAR pairs.

Although the current design differs from prospective offspring and/or youth cohort studies (which include BD and non-BD cases), some of the novel elements of our methodology make it possible to expand on ideas reported in that previous work (e.g., Angst et al. 2002; Mesmen et al. 2013; Etain et al. 2017; Merikangas et al. 2017; Scott et al. 2018; Duffy et al. 2019; Carpenter et al. 2020). For example, previous findings have demonstrated that AAO of BD-I in those with a FH is significantly earlier than those without a FH, but the addition of trajectory curve plots allows us to show that it is the pattern in the FH group that deviates more from the projected or hypothetical path (the R^2 value indicates an inferior fit, or less predictable time trend curve for the FH compared with the No FH group). Likewise, in the PRB-PAR pairs, we showed that AAO of a first DSM IV disorder, sequence of comorbidities, number of antecedents are remarkably similar between offspring and parents. Whilst previous research has alluded to some concordance in comorbidities in PRB-PAR (Merikangas et al. 2017); to our knowledge, the current study is the first to demonstrate the similarities in these patterns and sequences using trajectory plots. As shown in Fig. 2, whilst the prevalence and AAO (size and location of bubbles), and trajectories (and R^2) are comparable in many respects, the plots highlight the significant decrease in AAO of BD-I in PRB compared to PAR. These observations about the nature of divergences between PRB and PAR are confirmed by the estimated magnitude of the density of antecedent events per individual (which is higher in PRB). Unfortunately, we cannot further explore the similarities in patterns of illness or significant differences in AAO of BD-I in PRB-PAR using the current dataset. However, other researchers have suggested that the potential role of exposure to childhood adversity, higher genetic load, genetic anticipation, or birth cohort effects are worthy of further examination (Post et al. 2015; Golmard et al. 2016; Post et al. 2016; Etain et al. 2017; Scott et al. 2018; Duffy et al. 2019).

We propose that the estimating the 'density of antecedent events' can offer useful insights into individual (time-dependent) differences in illness exposure, giving a degree of personalization to the trajectories reported. Of course, it might be argued that it is a derived variable employed as a proxy for individual

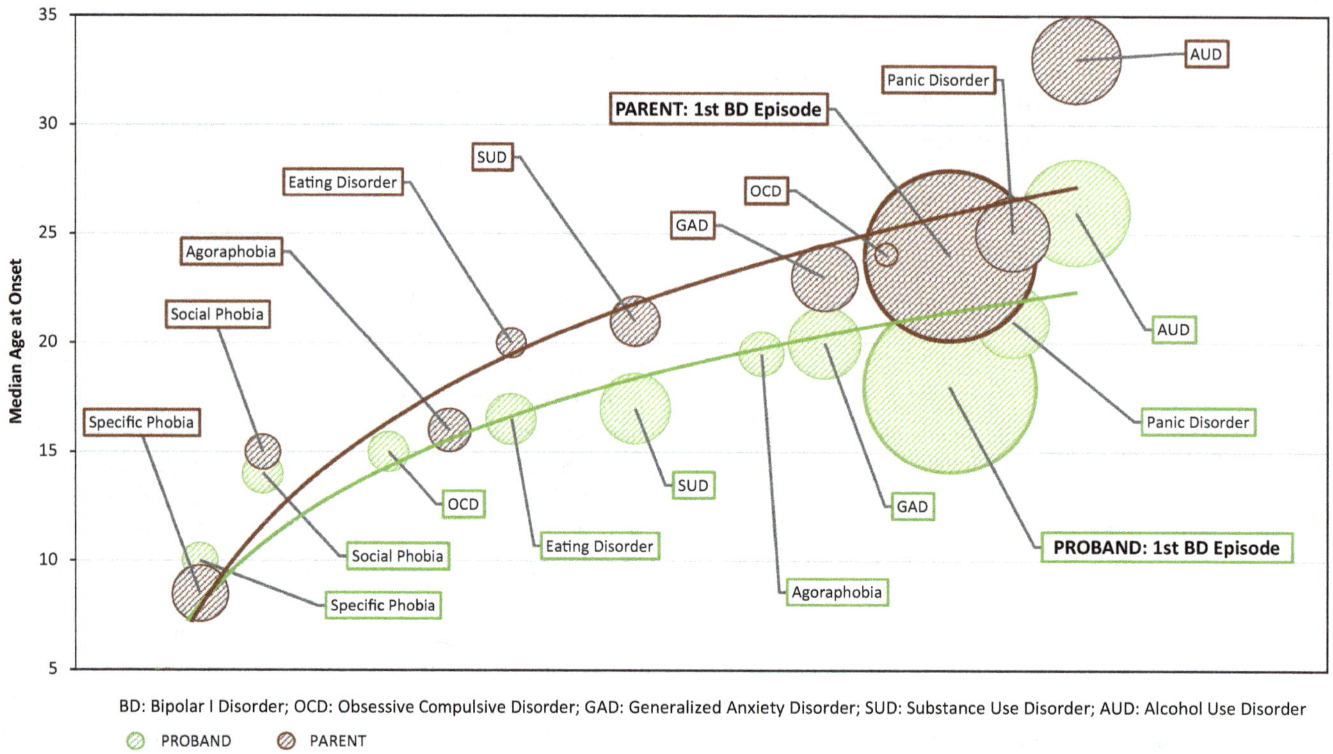

Fig. 2 Trajectories of evolution of BD-I in probands and parents. In the bubble plot, the size of the bubble represents the proportion of the group who experience a particular disorder, the position of the bubble vertically gives the median AAO, whilst the position on the horizontal axis approximates to the timing of onset of a disorder in the interval between the onset of the first full threshold mental disorder and the onset of the last comorbidity. It is notable that the median AAO of the first mental disorder (specific phobia) is similar in the Proband and Parent subgroups, and that the sequence of onset of disorders (except, e.g. OCD) is similar. The size of the bubbles is somewhat similar, but AAOs of comorbidities begin to occur earlier in the Proband subgroup, and median AAO of BD-I is clearly earlier than in the Parent subgroup. Both curves show the fit for the trajectory curve is less for comorbidities that occur post-onset of BD-I

experiences of comorbidities and primarily reflects rather than adds to the data represented within the trajectory plots. However, we suggest that the 'density of antecedent events' captures the important notion of 'counting people, not just disorders' and is advantageous for several reasons of which we highlight just two examples (Vaidyanathan et al. 2011; Merikangas et al. 2017). First, data from epidemiological studies indicates that, in a given population, the sequence of disorders occurring across childhood, adolescence and early adulthood has some predictability (i.e. phobia/anxiety problems are more common in childhood; eating disorders in adolescence; alcohol misuse occurs slightly later). However, the prevalence rates or AAO data do not necessarily clarify whether a large number of individuals experience one disorder during childhood or adolescence, etc., or whether a small group of individuals experience several disorders, with onsets beginning in childhood and continuing throughout adolescence, etc. (Kim-Cohen et al. 2003; Copeland et al. 2011). Developing knowledge about the different patterns of comorbidity and illness trajectories requires new approaches to reporting the core data. For example, in the current study we found that rates of comorbidities may vary between the different subgroups examined, but we also note that, even within the FH and PRB groups, there were some BD cases who did not report any non-mood comorbidities. So, we think that finding ways to express individualized estimates as well as group or sample estimates will help research into any links between AAO of severe mental disorders in subgroups that that experience several disorders over time (so-called multi-morbidity) compared with those that have limited exposure to comorbidities (Angst et al. 2002; Merikangas et al. 2017). Second, by estimating individual experiences of antecedents separately, analyses can raise awareness of different patterns and timing of onset of comorbidity. Investigators can then consider whether individuals who only experience post-BD onset comorbidities have different characteristics from other individuals with the same BD subtype. In the current study, using such estimates of comorbidities enabled us to demonstrate that FH cases and PRB cases had a higher density of antecedents per individual, which we propose is compatible with notions of lower resilience (with increased vulnerability to multi-morbidity) and earlier AAO of BD in some individuals, as suggested by other researchers in the field (Hafeman et al. 2017; Duffy et al. 2019).

Another aim of this study was to find clinically informative methods for describing the trajectories of comorbidities and onset of BD-I, and to explore alternative ways to offer visual representations of findings. We did consider approaches used by other investigators (e.g., multistate models) and other figurative representations of pathways to BD, such as Sanking plots or schematic representations (that do not incorporate subgroup data) (e.g., Caspi et al. 2020). We do not consider that our current approach is superior, but we think time trend and R^2 analyses have some merit. For example, this proved to be a pragmatic strategy for exploring complex data and the goodness of fit of trajectory models and graphically presenting the findings. Having made this observation, we accept that this exploratory approach is probably best be viewed as an adjunct rather than an alternative to established statistical analyses (such as time to event analyses, accelerated failure time model, generalized estimating equation, etc.).

We acknowledge several study limitations. Whilst the strict eligibility criteria for the original recruitment to the cohorts enhanced the reliability of data recordings, those criteria may reduce the clinical representativeness of our cases and the generalizability of findings. The data refer to assessments of retrospective events and, even though we applied the accepted, high-quality methodological strategies recommended for such studies, we know that recall bias may particularly affect AAO reporting and this could impact e.g., the validity of information regarding PRB and PAR. Also, there is increasing interest in subthreshold conditions, but these were not reported in the datasets obtained. However, the most important limitation is the relative lack of information regarding behavioural disorders. When the study cohorts were recruited, there was less awareness of the importance of associations between conditions such as ADHD and BD. (As noted in Additional file 1: Appendix 1, some of these conditions were assessed post-hoc, but the assessments employed meant we could not identify specific DSM IV diagnoses or AAO). Recent versions of the DIGS provide more detailed assessments of these conditions, but newer genetic datasets (such as those at NRGR) do not provide the detailed longitudinal information required to construct individual illness trajectories and/or had insufficient sample sizes. However, despite this study limitation, the AAO of first reported DSM IV disorders in the subgroups we studied are comparable to several other studies (Kim-Cohen et al. 2003; Golmard et al. 2016; Post et al. 2016; Etain et al. 2017; Lee et al. 2018; Caspi et al. 2020). Another obvious issue is that neither dataset included details about physical disorders (especially lacking information about AAO of any non-psychiatric problems). Given the known associations between physical disorders (such as cardio-respiratory and endocrine disorders) and BD, it would be of great interest to be able to incorporate medical conditions into the trajectory plots and density analyses to examine whether these also show any trends according to familial status or study location. Of course, these weaknesses highlight that replication and extension of the findings is required using independent datasets (Post et al. 2015; Golmard et al. 2016; Scott et al. 2018).

Conclusions

This study of illness trajectories suggests that these plots can, for example, be employed to indicate the real-time clustering of comorbidities more precisely in individuals with a confirmed diagnosis of BD-I who showed differing levels of premorbid vulnerability to developing this disorder. Further, the plots may indicate which comorbidities are more likely to be antecedents of BD and which occur post-onset of BD, etc. The shape of the curves allows observation of the relative differences in AAO of a first DSM IV disorder, the clustering of comorbidities within specific age ranges, the likely sequence of onsets of comorbidities, and any links between these phenomena and AAO of BD. We believe these plots summarize large amounts of data in a user-friendly manner and may stimulate discussions with lay groups and stakeholders about the evolution of BD. The use of metrics such as density of antecedent events, time trend analysis and trajectory plots alongside other recognized statistical models may also generate ideas regarding new avenues for research on trajectories of BD.

Note to readers: We encourage readers to also review the extensive appendices provided with this paper that include details of sample selection, methodology and other basic findings that could not be included within the main text.

Abbreviations

AAO: Age at onset; ADHD: Attention deficit hyperactivity disorder; AFT: Accelerated failure time; AUD: Alcohol use disorder; BD: Bipolar disorders; CI: Confidence interval; DSM: Diagnostic and statistical manual; DIGS: Diagnostic Interview for Genetic Studies; FH: Family history; FIGS: Family Interview for Genetic Studies; GEE: General estimating equations; HR: Hazard ratio; IQR: Inter-quartile ranges; NRGR: National Institute of Mental Health Repository and Genomics Resource; OCD: Obsessive compulsive disorder; PAR: Parent; PRB: Proband; STROBE: Strengthening the Reporting of Observational Studies in Epidemiology.

Supplementary Information

Additional file 1: Appendix 1: STROBE checklists and additional details of methodology.

Additional file 2: Appendix 2: Table S1. Comparison of rates and age at onset for each comorbidity and polarity of onset of BD-I in individuals with a family history of BD (n=209) or without a family history of BD (n=364). **Table S2.** Comparison of patterns of comorbidities in individuals with a family history or without a family history of BD. **Table S3**. Comparison of rates and age at onset for each comorbidity and polarity of onset of BD-I in probands (n=92) and their sex-matched parents (n=92). **Table S4**. Comparison of patterns of comorbidities in probands and parents.

Additional file 3: Appendix 3: **Figure S1**. Trajectory paths for FH and non-FH. **Figure S2**. Trajectory plots for Probands and Parents.

Acknowledgements

We thank the families who have participated in and contributed to the studies undertaken in France and the USA. We acknowledge the work undertaken by colleagues in Paris, Nancy and Bordeaux in assembling and assessing the French cohort. The authors wish to thank the NIMH Repository and Genomics Resource (NRGR; Bipolar Disorder distribution 12.0) and declare that NRGR provided access to the Bipolar Disorder Biomaterials and Clinical Data (access confirmation reference: application by Scott et al. (2018); ID number-5c9874082337f).

Authors' contributions

JS and BE designed the study. JS and FB applied for access to USA datasets. JS, BE and FB undertook and/or critically reviewed analyses. JS drafted the manuscript, all authors contributed to redrafting. All authors read and approved the final version of the submitted manuscript.

Funding

No specific funding was obtained for the development of this manuscript. NRGR request acknowledgement of the following (as a requisite for data use. For the USA cohort, data used were extracted from projects that participated in the National Institute of Mental Health (NIMH) Bipolar Disorder Genetics Initiative. From 1999 to 2003, the Principal Investigators and Co-Investigators were: Indiana University, Indianapolis, IN, R01 MH59545, John Nurnberger, M.D., Ph.D., Marvin J. Miller, M.D., Elizabeth S. Bowman, M.D., N. Leela Rau, M.D., P. Ryan Moe, M.D., Nalini Samavedy,M.D., Rif El-Mallakh,M.D. (at University of Louisville), Husseini Manji, M.D. (at Wayne State University), Debra A. Glitz, M.D. (at Wayne State University), Eric T. Meyer, M.S., Carrie Smiley, R.N., Tatiana Foroud, Ph.D., Leah Flury, M.S., Danielle M. Dick, Ph.D., Howard Edenberg, Ph.D.; Washington University, St. Louis, MO, R01 MH059534, John Rice, Ph.D, Theodore Reich, M.D., Allison Goate, Ph.D., Laura Bierut, M.D.; Johns Hopkins University, Baltimore, MD, R01 MH59533, Melvin McInnis M.D., J. Raymond DePaulo, Jr., M.D., Dean F. MacKinnon, M.D., Francis M. Mondimore, M.D., James B. Potash, M.D., Peter P. Zandi, Ph.D, Dimitrios Avramopoulos, and Jennifer Payne; University of Pennsylvania, PA, R01 MH59553, Wade Berrettini M.D.,Ph.D.; University of California at Irvine, CA, R01 MH60068, William Byerley M.D., and Mark Vawter M.D.; University of Iowa, IA, R01 MH059548, William Coryell M.D., and Raymond Crowe M.D.; University of Chicago, IL, R01 MH59535, Elliot Gershon, M.D., Judith Badner Ph.D., Francis McMahon M.D., Chunyu Liu Ph.D., Alan Sanders M.D., Maria Caserta, Steven Dinwiddie M.D., Tu Nguyen, Donna Harakal; University of California at San Diego, CA, R01 MH59567, John Kelsoe, M.D., Rebecca McKinney, B.A.; Rush University, IL, R01 MH059556, William Scheftner M.D., Howard M. Kravitz, D.O., M.P.H., Diana Marta, B.S., Annette Vaughn-Brown, MSN, RN, and Laurie Bederow, MA; NIMH Intramural Research Program, Bethesda, MD, 1Z01MH002810-01, Francis J. McMahon, M.D., Layla Kassem, PsyD, Sevilla Detera-Wadleigh, Ph.D, Lisa Austin, Ph.D, Dennis L. Murphy, M.D. From 2003 to 2007, the Principal Investigators and Co-Investigators were: Indiana University, Indianapolis, IN, R01 MH59545, John Nurnberger, M.D., Ph.D., Marvin J. Miller, M.D., Elizabeth S. Bowman, M.D., N. Leela Rau, M.D., P. Ryan Moe, M.D., Nalini Samavedy, M.D., Rif El-Mallakh, M.D. (at University of Louisville), Husseini Manji, M.D. (at Johnson and Johnson), Debra A. Glitz, M.D. (at Wayne State University), Eric T. Meyer, Ph.D., M.S. (at Oxford University, UK), Carrie Smiley, R.N., Tatiana Foroud, Ph.D., Leah Flury, M.S., Danielle M. Dick, Ph.D (at Virginia Commonwealth University), Howard Edenberg, Ph.D.; Washington University, St. Louis, MO, R01 MH059534, John Rice, Ph.D, Theodore Reich, M.D., Allison Goate, Ph.D., Laura Bierut, M.D. K02 DA21237; Johns Hopkins University, Baltimore, M.D., R01 MH59533, Melvin McInnis, M.D., J. Raymond DePaulo, Jr., M.D., Dean F. MacKinnon, M.D., Francis M. Mondimore, M.D., James B. Potash, M.D., Peter P. Zandi, Ph.D, Dimitrios Avramopoulos, and Jennifer Payne; University of Pennsylvania, PA, R01 MH59553, Wade Berrettini, M.D., Ph.D.; University of California at San Francisco, CA, R01 MH60068, William Byerley, M.D., and Sophia Vinogradov, M.D.; University of Iowa, IA, R01 MH059548, William Coryell, M.D., and Raymond Crowe, M.D.; University of Chicago, IL, R01 MH59535, Elliot Gershon, M.D., Judith Badner, Ph.D., Francis McMahon, M.D., Chunyu Liu, Ph.D., Alan Sanders, M.D., Maria Caserta, Steven Dinwiddie, M.D., Tu Nguyen, Donna Harakal; University of California at San Diego, CA, R01 MH59567, John Kelsoe, M.D., Rebecca McKinney, B.A.; Rush University, IL, R01 MH059556, William Scheftner, M.D., Howard M. Kravitz, D.O., M.P.H., Diana Marta, B.S., Annette Vaughn-Brown, M.S.N., R.N., and Laurie Bederow, M.A.; NIMH Intramural Research Program, Bethesda, MD, 1Z01MH002810-01, Francis J. McMahon, M.D., Layla Kassem, Psy.D., Sevilla Detera-Wadleigh, Ph.D, Lisa Austin, Ph.D, Dennis L. Murphy, M.D.; Howard University, William B. Lawson, M.D., Ph.D., Evarista Nwulia, M.D., and Maria Hipolito, M.D. This work was supported by the NIH grants P50CA89392 from the National Cancer Institute and 5K02DA021237 from the National Institute of Drug Abuse.

Author details

[1]Institute of Neuroscience, Newcastle University, Newcastle upon Tyne, UK. [2]Université de Paris, Paris, France. [3]AP-HP, Département de Psychiatrie et de Médecine Addictologique, GH Saint-Louis-Lariboisière-Fernand-Widal, DMU Neurosciences Tête et Cou, Paris, France. [4]Inserm UMRS 1144, Université de Paris, Paris, France. [5]Centre Expert Trouble Bipolaire, Hospital Princesse Grace, Monaco, Monaco.

References

Angst J, Sellaro R, Merikangas K. Multimorbidity of psychiatric disorders as an indicator of clinical severity. Eur Arch Psychiatry Clin Neurosci. 2002;252(4):147–54.

Bailey L, Vardulaki K, Langham J, Chandramohan D. Introduction to epidemiology. Maidenhead: McGraw-Hill, Open University Press. 2005. pp 224.

Carpenter J, Scott J, Iorfino F, Crouse J, Ho N, Hermens D, et al. Predicting the emergence of full-threshold bipolar I, bipolar II and psychotic disorders in young people presenting to early intervention mental health services. Psychol Med. 2020;30:1–11 (**Epub ahead of print**).

Caspi A, Houts R, Ambler A, Danese A, Elliott M, Hariri A, et al. Longitudinal assessment of mental health disorders and comorbidities across 4 decades among participants in the Dunedin birth cohort study. JAMA Netw Open. 2020;3(4):e203221.

Copeland W, Shanahan L, Costello E, Angold A. Cumulative prevalence of psychiatric disorders by young adulthood: a prospective cohort analysis from the Great Smoky Mountains Study. J Am Acad Child Adolesc Psychiatry. 2011;50(3):252–61.

Dierker LC, Merikangas KR, Szatmari P. Influence of parental concordance for psychiatric disorders on psychopathology in offspring. J Am Acad Child Adolesc Psychiatry. 1999;38(3):280–8.

Duffy A, Doucette S, Lewitzka U, Alda M, Hajek T, Grof P. Findings from bipolar offspring studies: methodology matters. Early Interv Psychiatry. 2011;5(3):181–91.

Duffy A, Goodday S, Keown-Stoneman C, Grof P. The emergent course of bipolar disorder: observations over two decades from the Canadian high-risk offspring cohort. Am J Psychiatry. 2019;176(9):720–9.

Egeland J, Blumenthal R, Nee J, Sharpe L, Endicott J. Reliability and relationship of various ages of onset criteria for major affective disorder. J Affect Disord. 1987;12:159–65.

Etain B, Lajnef M, Bellivier F, Mathieu F, Raust A, Cochet B, et al. Clinical expression of bipolar disorder type I as a function of age and polarity at onset: convergent findings in samples from France and the United States. J Clin Psychiatry. 2012;73:e561-566.

Etain B, Lajnef M, Henry C, Aubin V, Azorin J, Bellivier F, et al. Childhood trauma, dimensions of psychopathology and the clinical expression of bipolar disorders: a pathway analysis. J Psychiatr Res. 2017;95:37–45.

Faedda G, Serra G, Marangoni C, Salvatore P, Sani G, Vázquez G, Tondo L, et al. Clinical risk factors for bipolar disorders: a systematic review of prospective studies. J Affect Disord. 2014;168:314–21.

First MB. The importance of developmental field trials in the revision of psychiatric classifications. Lancet Psychiatry. 2016;3(6):579–84.

Gore F, Bloem P, Patton G, Ferguson J, Joseph V, Coffey C, et al. Global burden of disease in young people aged 10–24 years: a systematic analysis. Lancet. 2011;377(9783):2093–102.

Golmard J, Scott J, Etain B, Preisig M, Aubry J, Henry C, et al. Using admixture analysis to examine birth-cohort effects on age at onset of bipolar disorder. Acta Psychiatr Scand. 2016;133(3):205–13.

Hafeman D, Merranko J, Goldstein T, Axelson D, Goldstein B, Monk K, et al. Assessment of a Person-level risk calculator to predict new-onset bipolar spectrum disorder in youth at familial risk. JAMA Psychiat. 2017;74(8):841–7.

Ho-Trieu N, Tucker J. Another note on the use of a logarithmic time trend. Rev Mar Agric Econ. 1990;58(1):89–90.

Kim-Cohen J, Caspi A, Moffitt T, Harrington H, Milne B, Poulton R. Prior juvenile diagnoses in adults with mental disorder: developmental follow-back of a prospective-longitudinal cohort. Arch Gen Psychiatry. 2003;60:709–17.

Koenders MA, Mesman E, Giltay EJ, Elzinga BM, Hillegers MHJ. Traumatic experiences, family functioning, and mood disorder development in bipolar offspring. Br J Clin Psychol. 2020;59(3):277–89.

Lau P, Hawes D, Hunt C, Frankland A, Roberts G, Mitchell P. Prevalence of psychopathology in bipolar high-risk offspring and siblings: a meta-analysis. Eur Child Adolesc Psychiatry. 2018;27(7):823–37.

Lee H, Kim J, Lee Y, Heo N, Shim S, Kwon Y. Differences in psychopathology between offspring of parents with bipolar I disorder and those with bipolar II disorder: a cross-sectional study. Psychiatry Investig. 2018;15(12):1135–43.

Lee RSC, Hermens DF, Naismith SL, Kaur M, Guastella AJ, Glozier N, Scott J, Scott EM, Hickie IB. Clinical, neurocognitive and demographic factors associated with functional impairment in the Australian Brain and Mind Youth Cohort Study (2008–2016). BMJ Open. 2018;8(12):e022659.

Leckman J, Sholomskas D, Thompson W, Belanger A, Weissman M. Best estimate of lifetime psychiatric diagnosis: a methodological study. Arch Gen Psychiatry. 1982;39:879–83.

Loftus J, Scott J, Vorspan F, Icick R, Henry C, Gard S, et al. Psychiatric comorbidities in bipolar disorders: an examination of the prevalence and chronology of onset according to sex and bipolar subtype. J Affect Disord. 2020;15(267):258–63.

Maxwell ME. Intramural Research Program NIMH. FIGS: Family Interview for Genetic Studies. Clinical Neurogenetic Branch; 1992. Washington: NIMH.

Merikangas K, Akiskal H, Angst J, Greenberg P, Hirschfeld R, Petukhova M, Kessler R. Lifetime and 12-month prevalence of bipolar spectrum disorder in the National Comorbidity Survey replication. Arch Gen Psychiatry. 2007;64(5):543–52.

Merikangas K, Herrell R, Swendsen J, Rossler W, Ajdacic-Gross V, Angst J. Specificity of bipolar spectrum conditions in the comorbidity of mood and substance use disorders: results from the Zurich cohort study. Arch Gen Psychiatry. 2008;65:47–52.

Merikangas K, Bromet E, Druss B. Future surveillance of mental disorders in the United States: count people, not disorders. JAMA Psychiat. 2017;74(5):431–2.

Mesman E, Nolen WA, Reichart CG, Wals M, Hillegers MH. The Dutch bipolar offspring study: 12-year follow-up. Am J Psychiatry. 2013;170(5):542–9.

Messer T, Lammers G, Müller-Siecheneder F, Schmidt RF, Latifi S. Substance abuse in patients with bipolar disorder: a systematic review and meta-analysis. Psychiatry Res. 2017;253:338–50.

Nurnberger J, Blehar M, Kaufmann C, York-Cooler C, Simpson S, Harkavy-Friedman J, et al. Diagnostic interview for genetic studies. Rationale, unique features, and training NIMH. Genetics Initiative. Arch Gen Psychiatry. 1994;51:849–59.

Pavlova B, Perlis RH, Alda M, Uher R. Lifetime prevalence of anxiety disorders in people with bipolar disorder: a systematic review and meta-analysis. Lancet Psychiatry. 2015;2(8):710–7.

Post R, Leverich G, Kupka R, Keck P, McElroy S, Altshuler L, et al. Increases in multiple psychiatric disorders in parents and grandparents of patients with bipolar disorder from the USA compared with The Netherlands and Germany. Psychiatr Genet. 2015;25(5):194–200.

Post R, Altshuler L, Kupka R, McElroy S, Frye M, Rowe M, et al. Age of onset of bipolar disorder: combined effect of childhood adversity and familial loading of psychiatric disorders. J Psychiatr Res. 2016;81:63–70.

Potash J, Toolan J, Steele J, Miller E, Pearl J, Zandi P, NIMH Genetics Initiative Bipolar Disorder Consortium, et al. The bipolar disorder phenome database: a resource for genetic studies. Am J Psych. 2007;164(8):1229–37.

Scott J, Etain B, Azorin JM, Bellivier F. Secular trends in the age at onset of bipolar I disorder—support for birth cohort effects from multi-centre clinical observational studies. Eur Psychiatry. 2018;52:61–7.

Thomas MS, Annaz D, Ansari D, Scerif G, Jarrold C, Karmiloff-Smith A. Using developmental trajectories to understand developmental disorders. J Speech Lang Hear Res. 2009;52(2):336–58.

Vaidyanathan U, Patrick C, Iacono W. Patterns of comorbidity among mental disorders: a person-centered approach. Compr Psychiatry. 2011;52(5):527–35.

Wacholder S, Mitchell G, Pee D. Selecting an efficient design for assessing exposure-disease relationships in an assembled cohort. Biometrics. 1991;47(1):63–76.

Wei L. The accelerated failure time model: a useful alternative to the Cox regression model in survival analysis. Stat Med. 1992;11(14–15):1871–9.

Weisstein E. Least squares fitting-logarithmic curves. Wolfram Web Resource. Accessed on April 10, 2021 at: http://mathworld.wolfram.com/LeastSquaresFittingLogarithmic.html.

Zeger S, Liang K, Albert P. Models for longitudinal data: a generalized estimating equation approach. Biometrics. 1988;44:1049–60.

Zheng B. Summarizing the goodness of fit on generalized models for longitudinal data. Stat Med. 2000;19:1265–75.

12

Sleep and physical activity in patients with newly diagnosed bipolar disorder in remission, their first-degree unaffected relatives and healthy controls

Nikolaj Folke la Cour Karottki[1], Klara Coello[1], Sharleny Stanislaus[1], Sigurd Melbye[1], Hanne Lie Kjærstad[1], Kimie Stefanie Ormstrup Sletved[1], Lars Vedel Kessing[1,2] and Maj Vinberg[1,2,3*]

Abstract

Background: Sleep disturbances are a central feature in bipolar disorder (BD) that often persist in remission and seem to be present also in unaffected first-degree relatives (UR) of patients with BD, presenting a possible risk factor for later onset of BD. However, it is unknown if these disturbances are associated with unhealthy life-style as reflected in low levels of physical activity. We investigated sleep disturbances and physical activity levels in patients with newly diagnosed BD in full or partial remission, their UR and healthy controls (HC).

Methods: Sleep patterns and physical activity were compared in 227 patients with newly diagnosed BD, 76 UR and 148 HC. The Pittsburgh Sleep Quality Index (PSQI) and the International Physical Activity Questionnaire (IPAQ) were used to assess sleep disturbances and physical activity, respectively.

Results: In sex- and age-adjusted analyses, patients with BD exhibited more sleep disturbances and lower physical activity compared with UR and HC, respectively. Unaffected relatives reported significantly longer sleep latency and a non-significant trend towards more overall sleep disturbances compared with HC.

Conclusions: Sleep disturbances and less physical activity are present in patients with newly diagnosed BD in partial or full remission. Individuals at familiar risk of BD reported longer sleep latency and similar physical activity compared with HC. Further prospective studies are needed to clarify whether these discrete sleep disturbances act as risk factor for later onset of BD and whether increased physical activity in high-risk individuals may act as a protective factor against development of psychiatric illness.

Keywords: Bipolar disorder, Sleep, Physical activity, Unaffected relatives

Background

Bipolar disorder (BD) is a recurrent mood disorder with episodes of depression and mania. It is often associated with functional disability, decreased quality of life and reduced life expectancy (Rosa et al. 2014; Kessing and Andersen 2017). The mean age of onset is mid to late twenties in Europe and the estimated lifetime prevalence is thought to be 1–2% (Pedersen et al. 2014; Post et al. 2008). A substantial hereditary component is seen in families of patients with BD with the approximate lifetime risk of BD in first-degree relatives being 5–10% and monozygotic co-twins 40–70% (Craddock and Sklar 2013; McGuffin et al. 2003). Studies show that up to 50% of first-degree relatives of patients with BD will develop a mood disorder or another psychiatric illness (Mesman

*Correspondence: maj.vinberg@regionh.dk
[1] Copenhagen Affective Disorders Research Centre (CADIC), Psychiatric Center Copenhagen, Department O, 6243, Rigshospitalet, Blegdamsvej 9, 2100 Copenhagen, Denmark
Full list of author information is available at the end of the article

et al. 2013; Duffy et al. 2015). However, knowledge of the specific factors that run cross generations is needed to tailor a more integrated preventive approach. Further, there is a latency of approximately 6 years from onset to initial treatment of BD (Dagani et al. 2017). Yet, early treatment seems to hinder a more severe progression of the disorder (Bender and Alloy 2011; Shapero et al. 2017; Kessing et al. 2014) and it is thus crucial to discover robust risk factors and valid biomarkers.

Central features in BD are circadian rhythm abnormalities including sleep disturbances (Gold and Sylvia 2016; Takaesu 2018) characterized by difficulty falling asleep, maintaining sleep and early morning awakening leading to dissatisfaction with sleep quantity and quality (Buysse et al. 2017). These changes in sleep pattern often persist after manic and depressive episodes and they further seem to be present in unaffected first-degree relatives (UR) of patients with BD as well, presenting a possible risk factor of developing BD (Keskin et al. 2018; Melo et al. 2016a; Ritter et al. 2015). Unaffected first-degree relatives of patients with BD might have a latent-stage or risk stage BD (Kapczinski et al. 2009, 2014; Berk et al. 2017) due to a possible shared biological underpinning. A systematic review including 30 studies and 5778 high-risk individuals (Melo et al. 2016a) showed more sleep disturbances and poor sleep quality in high-risk individuals cross-sectionally. Five prospective studies were also included (n = 3759), four of which investigated offspring of parents with BD (follow-up periods ranged from 4 to 16 years) and these revealed that poor sleep quality, trouble falling asleep, early morning awakening, night-time awakenings and inadequate sleep could be an indicator of later onset of BD (Melo et al. 2016a). This is in line with a recent review focusing on sleep alterations anticipating the onset of BD including 17 studies both prospective (n = 6) and retrospective (n = 11), concluding that sleep alterations also seem to appear long before the onset of BD. Nevertheless, sleep disturbances have not been investigated in newly diagnosed BD and their healthy first-degree relatives (Pancheri et al. 2019).

Physical activity is widely known to reduce risk of all-cause mortality, cardiovascular disease and cancer-related mortality compared to sedentary behaviour (Andersen et al. 2000; Kodama et al. 2009; Lear et al. 2017; Piercy et al. 2018) and sleep disturbances are associated with a risk of all-cause mortality and cardiovascular events (Yin et al. 2017). Bipolar disorder is associated with comorbid somatic disorders mainly cardiovascular disease, obesity and non-insulin dependent diabetes (Evans et al. 2005). Putative reasons for these conditions and the increased mortality observed in patients with BD (Correll et al. 2017) include a more sedentary lifestyle (Vancampfort et al. 2016; Kilbourne et al. 2007) as well as abnormal sleep patterns (Yin et al. 2017; Cappuccio et al. 2010). The increased cardiovascular risk seems further to be present in youth with BD (Goldstein et al. 2015) and in young adults with newly diagnosed bipolar disorder (Coello et al. 2019). Consequently, it is highly interesting to investigate physical activity and sleep patterns in BD and preceding BD by studying patients with newly diagnosed BD and their first-degree relatives.

Overall patients with BD and UR seem to express a disturbed sleep pattern, however, whether this is associated with an unhealthy life-style reflected in decreased physical activity has not previously been studied in patients newly diagnosed with BD and their UR.

This study aimed to investigate sleep disturbances (and patterns) and patterns of physical activity among patients with newly diagnosed BD in full or partial remission, UR and HC. We hypothesized that patients with BD in full or partial remission would report more sleep disturbances and less physical activity than HC and that the UR would show an intermediary pattern in both outcomes.

Materials and methods

Study design

The Copenhagen Affective Disorder Clinic is an outpatient clinic that covers the Copenhagen Capital region catchment area of 1.6 million inhabitants and offers service for patients with newly diagnosed BD. Patients referred to the Copenhagen Affective Disorder Clinic as newly diagnosed with BD or having a first episode of (hypo)mania were routinely invited to participate in the Bipolar Onset Study (BIO) (Kessing et al. 2017). In the present cross-sectional study, we compared self-reported sleep patterns and physical activity levels across the three groups (patients with BD, UR and HC). Participants were recruited from June 2015 to December 2018.

Patients with bipolar disorder

All patients with newly diagnosed BD included in the BIO study were recruited from the Copenhagen Affective Disorder Clinic, an outpatient clinic covering the entire catchment area of the Capital Region of Denmark. Inclusion criteria were newly diagnosis with an ICD-10 diagnosis of BD or single (hypo)manic episode and age 18–70.

Unaffected relatives

First-degree relatives, siblings or children, to the patients included in the BIO-study, were recruited after permission from patients with BD, aged 15–50 years, with no history of substance abuse, psychotic illness or mood disorders according to the ICD-10 diagnostic system (International Statistical Classification of Diseases and Related Health Problems 10th Revision (ICD-10)-WHO 2016) were invited to participate upon obtaining consent from the patients.

Healthy controls

Healthy control persons matched on sex and age to the participants with BD were recruited from the Blood Bank at Rigshospitalet, Copenhagen, Denmark. Exclusion criteria included a personal or first-degree relative with a history of psychiatric disorders requiring treatment.

Psychiatric assessment

Diagnoses were confirmed using the Schedules for Clinical Assessment in Neuropsychiatry (Wing et al. 1990) and clinical assessments using the Hamilton Depression Scale-17 items (HAMD-17) (Hamilton 1960) and the Young Mania Rating Scale (YMRS) (Young et al. 1978). Only patients in remission or partial remission defined as a score ≤ 14 at the HAMD-17 and ≤ 14 at the YMRS were included in the present study. All participants completed three self-reported questionnaires: the Pittsburgh Sleep Quality Index (PSQI), the International Physical Activity Questionnaire (IPAQ) and the Copenhagen City Heart Study (CCHS) physical activity questionnaire at the day of the assessment.

Physical assessment

Lightly dressed and without shoes, height and weight was measured using a stadiometer and a calibrated floor scale.

Questionnaires

The PSQI (Buysse et al. 1989) covers the last month and includes items such as duration of sleep, sleep latency, sleep disturbances, daytime dysfunction due to sleepiness, sleep efficiency, sleep medication and perceived quality of sleep. A higher score shows worse self-evaluated sleep, and a score of ≥ 5 implies poor sleep quality.

The IPAQ short form (Craig et al. 2003) reflects physical activity the preceding 7 days and is a questionnaire to address level of physical activity and sedentary behavior. The IPAQ provides information regarding time spent in four intensity levels: (1) vigorous-intensive activity, (2) moderate-intensity activity, (3) walking and (4) sedentary. Participants were asked to recall activity level for the past 7 days. Summary measures of overall self-reported physical activity are reported as a continuous variable metabolic equivalent task (MET minutes a week), representing the energy expended during the physical activity. Higher scores correspond to higher activity.

The score is an estimated value of MET-minutes, the kilocalories that a person weighing 60 kg would expend. We then calculated the corresponding MET-minutes for everyone's weight, using the following formula:

$$Total\ METminutes * \left(\frac{Weight}{60}\right).$$

In accordance with the guidelines for IPAQ scoring, we truncated values above 180 min/day and excluded values exceeding 16 h/day of activity (IPAQ Group 2005).

As a secondary measurement of physical activity, we included the CCHS (Aguib and Al Suwaidi 2015) physical activity questionnaire. The CCHS is a population study of more than 24.000 men and women in Denmark, of 20 years or older with a follow-up time of 35 years. The focus is on cardiovascular disease and its risk factors including exercise. In the physical activity questionnaire used in CCHS, participants indicate one of four categories best characterizing their level of activity, ranging from less than 2 h of low activity per week to more than 4 h of strenuous activity per week.

Statistical analyses

The descriptive data were first explored for normality and categorical data were analyzed using the Chi-squared test. Continuous data was analyzed either using Student's T-test (parametric) or Mann–Whitney U-test (nonparametric) for two independent groups. Continuous data was described as median and quartiles if the assumptions of normality were not met. Using a general linear mixed model in SPSS version 26, we compared sleep disturbances and physical activity levels across the three groups with familial relationship as random factor, accounting for the relationship between family-related individuals, and age and sex as covariates. To check for the influence of mood symptoms, we included HAMD-17 and YMRS scores and smoking (package years) as covariates in additional analyses. To avoid overcorrection, we excluded sleep items when adjusting the PSQI. The significance threshold was set at $p \leq 0.05$. Spearman's rank-order correlation for nonparametric data post hoc analyses were done between groups (patients with BD, UR and HC) to check for correlations between sleep, physical activity, age, BMI and education levels. Within the BD group, we further examined correlations with age of onset, time of untreated BD, number of episodes and medication use. Untreated BD was defined as time from first hypomanic, manic or mixed episode to time of diagnosis. Finally, we compared the physical activity levels between the three groups using the CCHS to investigate whether it would provide the same pattern as the IPAQ.

Ethical

The study protocol was approved by the Committee on Health Research Ethics of the Capital Region of Denmark (Protocol No. H-7-2014-007) and the Danish Data Protection Agency, Capital Region of Copenhagen

(RHP-2015-023). All participants provided written informed consent. The study complied with the Declaration of Helsinki principles (Seoul, October 2008).

Results

Demographic and clinical characteristics

We included 451 participants, 227 patients newly diagnosed with BD in full or partial remission, 78 UR and 148 HC. The clinical and demographic variables are shown in Table 1. The age distribution was similar in the BD and HC groups (median [interquartile range]: BD = 28 [24–36] years vs. HC = 27 [24–36] years), while the UR group was younger (26 [22–31] years, $p = 0.010$). There were no statistically significant differences in sex distribution between the three groups. Education attainment differed statistically significantly, with HC having 16 years [15–17] vs. patients with BD 15 years [12–17] ($p \leq 0.001$) of education. There were no statistically significant differences in BMI between the groups. Patients with BD had a median age of illness onset of 17 [14–22] years and the median duration of untreated BD was 3 [1–10] years.

As expected, HAMD-17 and YMRS scores were statistically significantly higher in the BD group compared with UR and HC ($p = 0.001$), and UR also had higher HAMD-17 scores (2 [0–3] vs. 1 [0–2], $p = 0.004$) than HC.

Table 1 Clinical and demographic variables in patients with bipolar disorder (BD), unaffected relatives (UR) and healthy controls (HC)

	BD[1]	UR[2]	HC[3]	p-value
Number (n)	227	76	148	
Age (years)	28 [24–36]	26 [22–31]	27 [24–36]	0.01^{1-2} 0.921^{1-3} 0.28^{2-3}
Sex (Female n (%))	135 (59.5%)	43 (56.6%)	89 (60.0%)	
Alcohol (units/week)	3 [0–7]	2 [1–7]	5 [2–8]	0.918^{1-2} 0.000^{1-3} 0.001^{2-3}
Smoking (package years)	1.9 [0–6.8]	0 [0–0.4]	0 [0–0]	0.000^{1-2} 0.000^{1-3} 0.132^{2-3}
Education (years)	15 [12–17]	15 [13–17]	16 [15–17]	0.165^{1-2} $<0.001^{1-3}$ 0.069^{2-3}
BMI (kg/m^2)	24.6 [22.2–27.2]	23.9 [21.5–26.4]	23.7 [22.1–26.2]	0.108^{1-2} 0.131^{1-3} 0.623^{2-3}
HAM-D17	7 [3–10]	2 [0–3]	1 [0–2]	0.000^{1-2} 0.000^{1-3} 0.004^{2-3}
YMRS	2 [0–5]	0 [0–2]	0 [0–2]	0.000^{1-2} 0.000^{1-3} 0.708^{2-3}
Age of onset (years)	17 [14–22]	–	–	–
Total affective episodes	12 [6–23]	–	–	–
Illness duration (years)	9 [5–15]	–	–	–
Untreated bipolar disorder (years)	3 [1–10]	–	–	–
Antiepileptics	110 (52.6%)	–	–	–
Antipsychotics	93 (44.9%)	–	–	–
Antidepressants	102 (49.0%)	–	–	–
Lithium	79 (38.0%)	–	–	–
Combination treatment	2 [1–3]	–	–	–

Continuous variables shown as median [interquartile range] and categorical values as n (%). p-values denoted as the groups between which the comparison is made. Age of onset is the age at the time of the first affective episode. Illness duration is defined as the duration between first affective episode and inclusion in the study. Untreated bipolar disorder: time from first hypomanic, manic or mixed episode to time of diagnosis

HAM-D17 Hamilton Rating Depression Scale, 17 items, *YMRS* Young Mania Rating Scale

[1] Patients with bipolar disorder (BD)

[2] Unaffected first-degree relatives (UR)

[3] Healthy control persons (HR)

Sleep

Patients with BD had a total PSQI median [interquartile range] of 8 [5–11], indicating sleep disturbances even when in remission and differed statistically significantly from the UR group (5 [3–7], $p \leq 0.001$) and the HC group (4 [3–6], $p \leq 0.001$), see Table 2. At item level, all the PSQI subitems significantly differed between BD and HC, see Table 2. The differences in PSQI score remained statistically significant also when adjusting for depressive and manic symptoms and when adding smoking as a covariate (results not presented in detail). Further, removing the patients with BD with HAMD17 or YMRS above seven, leaving 99 patients with BD, the results, concerning PSQI and the subitems remained almost the same (results not presented in details) except that the significant differences between patients with BD and the UR were no longer significant concerning sleep disturbances (p=0.185) and overall sleep quality (p=0.078).

The UR group trended towards a higher median PSQI score than the HC (5 [3–7] vs. 4 [3–6], p=0.115). Further analyses, comparing the PSQI subitems, revealed that the UR experienced longer sleep latency than HC (p=0.022), see Fig. 1. Further, UR reported lower perceived sleep quality (p=0.078) and shorter sleep duration (p=0.089) than HC, however only at trend levels, see Table 2.

Table 2 Pittsburgh Sleep Quality Index (PSQI) in patients with bipolar disorder (BD), unaffected relatives (UR) and healthy controls (HC)

	BD[1]	UR[2]	HC[3]	p-value
Total PSQI	8 [5–11]	5 [3–7]	4 [3–6]	$< 0.001^{1-2}$ $<0.001^{1-3}$ 0.115^{2-3}
Duration of sleep (4)	0.0 [0–1]	0.0 [0–1]	0.0 [0–1]	0.803^{1-2} 0.045^{1-3} 0.089^{2-3}
Sleep disturbances (5b – 5j)	1.0 [1–2]	1.0 [1–1]	1.0 [1–1]	$< 0.001^{1-2}$ $<0.001^{1-3}$ 0.332^{2-3}
Sleep latency (2 + 5a)	2.0 [1–3]	1.0 [1–2]	1.0 [0–1]	0.007^{1-2} $<0.001^{1-3}$ 0.022^{2-3}
Day dysfunction due to sleepiness (8 + 9)	1.0 [1–2]	1.0 [0–1]	1.0 [1–1]	$< 0.001^{1-2}$ $<0.001^{1-3}$ 0.364^{2-3}
Sleep efficiency	0.0 [0–1]	0.0 [0–1]	0.0 [0–1]	0.012^{1-2} $<0.001^{1-3}$ 0.126^{2-3}
Overall sleep quality (6)	1.0 [1–2]	1.0 [0–1.5]	1.0 [0–1]	0.003^{1-2} $<0.001^{1-3}$ 0.078^{2-3}
Needs meds to sleep (7)	1.0 [0–3]	0.0 [0–0]	0.0 [0–0]	$< 0.001^{1-2}$ $<0.001^{1-3}$ 0.730^{2-3}

PSQI item number is shown in parenthesis. Higher scores equal worse outcome. p-values are denoted as the group between which the comparison is made and calculated based on mean values, using a linear mixed model. Results written as median [interquartile range]. All analyses are adjusted for age and sex

[1] Patients with bipolar disorder (BD)

[2] Unaffected first-degree relatives (UR)

[3] Healthy control persons (HR)

Physical activity

As can be seen from Table 3, there was a significant difference between the BD and the HC group (2093.8 [980.1–3870.1] MET-minutes vs. 3040.0 [1755.4–5353.7] MET-minutes, p=0.020), and the UR group showed an intermediary, non-significant pattern compared to HC. The difference was mainly in the vigorous (p=0.038) and moderate activity ($p \leq 0.001$), with walking not differing between BD and HC (p=0.717, Fig. 2). While the UR group showed an intermediary pattern when looking at median values, they had the highest mean values (median: 2533.7 [936.5–5624.0], mean: 4147.2 CI95: [3367.9–4926.4]). Sedentary behavior was significantly higher in the HC group compared with the BD and UR group. After adjusting for HAMD-17 score, we found no statistically significant differences in IPAQ score between the groups (BD vs. HC: p=0.304, BD vs. UR: p=0.155, UR vs. HC: p=0.603) while the differences remained significant when adjusting for YMRS score (BD vs. HC: p=0.008, BD vs. UR: p=0.012, UR vs. HC p=0.689).

When removing all participants with HAMD17 and YMRS above 7, the difference between patients with BD and HC on total IPAQ were no longer statistically significant (p=0.43), neither were the subitems vigorous activity (p=0.350) and sedentary (p=0.137). However, the patients with BD still had significantly lower scores on moderate activity (p=0.044) and on the total Copenhagen City Hearth Study score (p=0.001).

Post-hoc analyses

In post hoc analyses, no significant correlations between sleep and exercise when looking at total scores were found. Comparing all subitems of the PSQI and the IPAQ there was a significantly significant statistical correlation between moderate physical activity and total PSQI score (rho = – 0.174, $p \leq 0.001$), so more physical activity was correlated with fewer sleep disturbances. Looking separately at patients with BD, a similar however not statistically significant correlation was found between total PSQI and IPAQ (rho = – 0.118, p=0.096). In the patient group, we further showed a positively significant correlation between HAMD-17 and PSQI (rho=0.412, $p \leq 0.001$) and a negatively significant correlation between HAMD17 and IPAQ (rho = – 0.243, $p \leq 0.001$), also when removing the sleep items. Finally, YMRS without sleep items had a significantly positively correlation

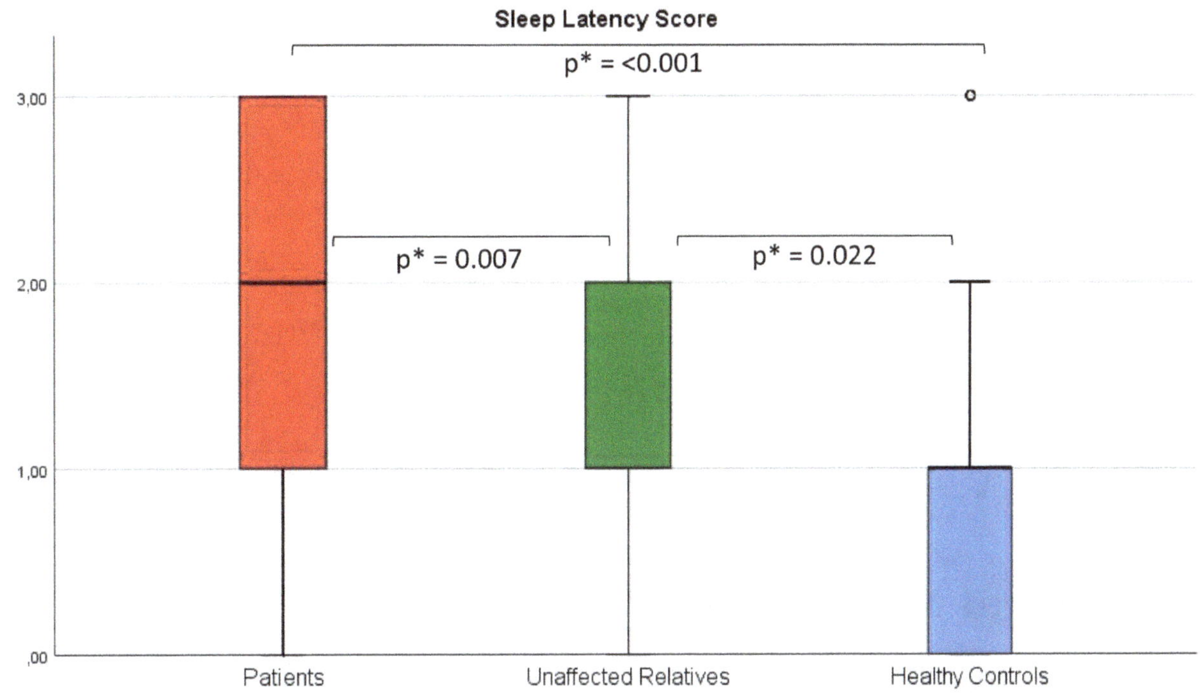

Fig. 1 Box plot of the subitem sleep latency from the Pittsburgh Sleep Quality Index in patients with bipolar disorder, their unaffected first-degree relatives and healthy controls. *Statistically significant at the 0.05 level

Table 3 International Physical Activity Questionnaire (IPAQ) and the physical activity questionnaire from the Copenhagen City Heart Study (CCHS) in patients with bipolar disorder (BD), unaffected relatives (UR) and healthy controls (HC)

	BD[1]	UR[2]	HC[3]	p-value
Vigorous activity (MET-minutes/week)	0 [0–1420]	443.3 [0.0–1781.0]	955.2 [0.0–2000.0]	0.187[1–2] 0.038[1–3] 0.747[2–3]
Moderate activity (MET-minutes/week)	336.6 [0.0–1012.0]	632.8 [70.8–1464.0]	1021.2 [449.4–1568.0]	0.008[1–2] < 0.001[1–3] 0.531[2–3]
Walking (MET-minutes/week)	603.4 [168.3–1582.4]	556.38 [79.1–1441.44]	656.7 [260.0–1568.0]	0.287[1–2] 0.717[1–3] 0.464[2–3]
Sedentary (minutes/day)	300.0 [60.0–480.0]	360 [157.5–480.0]	420.0 [300.0–540.0]	0.749[1–2] < 0.001[1–3] 0.020[2–3]
Total IPAQ exercise (MET-minutes/week)	2093.8 [980.1–3870.1]	2533.7 [936.5–5624.0]	3040.0 [1755.4–5353.7]	0.028[1–2] 0.020[1–3] 0.713[2–3]
Copenhagen city heart study	3 [2–3]	3 [3–3]	3 [3–3]	0.000[1–2] 0.000[1–3] 0.505[2–3]

Results written as median [interquartile range]. All analyses are adjusted for age and sex

MET metabolic equivalent of task, a measure for energy expenditure

[1] Patients with bipolar disorder (BD)

[2] Unaffected first-degree relatives (UR)

[3] Healthy control persons (HR)

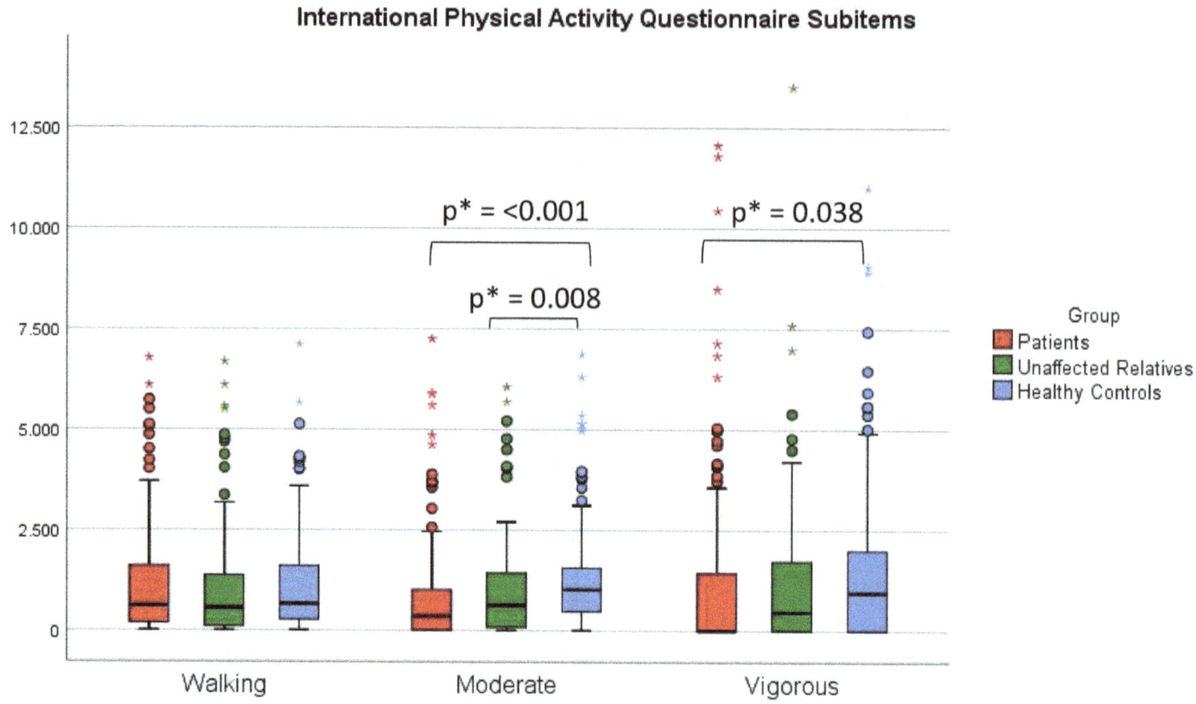

Fig. 2 Box plot of three subitems from the International Physical Activity Questionnaire, namely walking, moderate activity and vigorous activity patients with bipolar disorder, their unaffected first-degree relatives and healthy controls. *Statistically significant at the 0.05 level

with total PSQI score (rho = 0.213, p = 0.001), but not with IPAQ.

When investigating the group of patients with BD, we found that age of onset was statistically significantly correlated with total PSQI score (rho = −0.278, p = 0.0001), pointing towards more sleep disturbances the younger the age of onset. Time with untreated BD was significantly or near-significantly correlated to both PSQI (rho = 0.123, p = 0.081) and IPAQ (rho = 0.150, p = 0.033). The number of previous affective episodes correlated positively with both PSQI (rho = 0.185, p = 0.008) and IPAQ (rho = 0.141, p = 0.043) thus more episodes were correlated with more sleep disturbances and less physical activity.

Discussion

The present study reported data on sleep disturbances and levels of physical activity from a large sample of patients with newly diagnosed BD in remission or partial remission (n = 227), their UR (n = 76) and HC (n = 148). In accordance with our hypotheses, patients with newly diagnosed BD revealed more sleep disturbances and lower physical activity than the HC. This shows that at the time of diagnosis, patients with bipolar disorder experience sleep disturbances also when they are in partial or full remission. Further, in accordance with our hypothesis, activity levels and sleep disturbances in UR showed an intermediary pattern nonetheless, only the PSQI subitem "sleep latency" differed statistically significantly between UR and HC.

When looking at physical activity we initially found significant differences between BD and UR and between BD and HC, respectively. This was supported by similar differences in the results from the physical exercise questionnaire from the CCHS (Aguib and Al Suwaidi 2015). No differences were identified regarding UR vs. HC. The variance of IPAQ scores in the UR group was larger than among the HC and our lack of findings in this group could be due to the moderate number of participants in the UR group. After adjusting for subsyndromal mood symptoms, the statistically significant differences between patients with BD and HC was reduced to a trend level. This is in line with the statistically significant correlations seen between HAMD-17 and total PSQI and IPAQ scores, pointing towards the impact of having subsyndromal symptoms, thus more depressive symptoms seem to translate into less physical activity and more sleep disturbances. More physical activity seems to impact sleep in a beneficial manner and may be part of the reason why patients with BD exhibit more sleep disturbances.

Surprisingly, the BD group showed the lowest amount of sedentary behavior in contrast to what earlier studies have found (Vancampfort et al. 2016). A partial explanation could be due to actual absence from work or school (at the time of assessment) due to sick leave, in patients with BD. In accordance with prior observations (Kantomaa et al. 2016), we conducted a post hoc correlation analysis and saw a positive correlation between sedentary behavior and educational attainment (rho = 0.187, $p \leq 0.001$). Another explanation could be that the BD group underreported their sedentary behaviour, either due to unrealistic ideas about how much they sit or not wanting to reinforce the stigma of living with mental illness (Vancampfort et al. 2017). Thus, the lower reported sedentary behavior in the BD group may be due to inaccurate self-reporting of sedentary activity.

In post hoc correlation analyses we would have expected that more sleep disturbances would be correlated with less physical activity, but this was not the case when looking at total scores in the present sample. Interestingly, we found a negative correlation between moderate physical activity and total PSQI score, suggesting that moderate physical activity could be beneficial for sleep quality. Especially depressive episodes are thought to have beneficial effects from physical activity and this may also be the case for manic episodes, even though the area still lacks well-designed randomized controlled trials (Melo et al. 2016b). In our sample, patients with BD present with a low amount of moderate to vigorous activity, possibly accounting partially for their increased amount of sleep disturbances and their overall higher depression scores.

In a similar study, however not comprising newly diagnosed BD, including 107 patients with BD type I, 74 UR and 80 HC, UR reported longer sleep duration and later time of sleep than HC (Verkooijen et al. 2017). In their case, differences between groups were fully attributed to differences in mood symptoms, and group differences disappeared when adjusting for HAMD-17 and YMRS scores. As stated above, sleep latency remained statistically significantly longer among UR compared with HC in our study, when performing a similar adjustment. Looking at prospective studies of BD offspring four studies have been conducted and over all poor sleepers including those with insomnia predicted onset of BD (Pancheri et al. 2019).

When stating these differences in psychical activity and sleep patterns the impact of medication in the BD group must be considered, as most of the patients received medication at the time of the assessment (87.3%). The medication can unpredictably influence the results in the BD group. Many psychotropic drugs have either sedative or excitatory effects and may affect the amount of physical exercise and sleep. However, the UR group can be observed without the influence of medical treatment.

Sleep disturbances and physical activity in unaffected relatives

Judging from the hereditability of BD, we would expect around 30–40% of the UR to develop psychiatric illness. If sleep disturbances act as a risk marker for onset of psychiatric illness, we would expect a higher average on the PSQI within the UR group. Our results show that the UR had a trend ($p = 0.072$) towards reporting more overall sleep disturbances than the HC and reported significantly longer sleep latency, pointing towards that sleep disturbances seems to be a risk or even a trait factor. Two studies including prospective data on high-risk participants (Ritter et al. 2015; Levenson et al. 2015) showed that sleep disturbances seem to be a prognostic indicator of the development of BD in high-risk youth. However, more prospective studies are needed to establish discrete sleep disturbances as risk factor for later onset of BD. Physical activity seems as stated to reduce risk of all-cause mortality thus an increased physical activity in high-risk individuals may act as a protective factor against development of psychiatric illness. Here, the UR group exhibited an intermediary level of physical activity and it is not possible from the present cross-sectional design to pinpoint whether physical activity acts as a protective factor. Nevertheless, the results also point towards that physical exercise have a beneficial impact on sleep, which can be useful as a clinical advice.

Strengths

First, we recruited a relatively large sample of patients newly diagnosed with BD, their UR and HC. Second, our BD population is recruited from the Copenhagen Affective Disorder Clinic, covering the entire Capital Region of Denmark that offers treatment for patients with newly diagnosed BD. Despite this unique possibility to recruit patients with BD early in their illness course, our findings of illness duration (9 years) and untreated BD (3 years) shows the well-known diagnostic delay in accurately diagnosing BD (Baldessarini et al. 2007). Third, our study profited from high validity of the BD diagnosis, as all patients were initially assessed by a physician specialized in BD and the diagnosis was confirmed by Ph.D. students with a MD or master's in psychology degree upon inclusion. Fourth, by including first-degree relatives, we provide insight to features possibly preceding BD.

Limitations

Several limitations must be considered when evaluating our study. First, the HC population was recruited amongst blood donors from the Blood Bank at Rigshospitalet, Copenhagen. This population may be selected for persons healthier than the general population in

Denmark (Golding et al. 2013). Second, the sample size of the UR group was modest, so interpretation of our findings in UR should be made with caution. Third, our measure of alcohol the preceding month prior to inclusion may not be representative in patients with BD, as many patients have had a substantial overuse of alcohol preceding initiation of treatment at The Clinic of Affective Disorders, where they at the first visit were recommended alcohol abstinence for 4–12 weeks. As a result, we decided to not adjust for alcohol. Fourth, self-reported physical activity tends to be overreported and the IPAQ has in the last years been under scrutiny for not obtaining the required validity when comparing to objective measures of activity (Lee et al. 2011). However, we would expect this influencing all three groups; hence, the actual level of activity may be lower for all participants. Fifth, the PSQI does not include oversleeping, even though there are ongoing discussions as to whether it can be detrimental (Cappuccio et al. 2010; Gallicchio and Kalesan 2009; Kurina et al. 2013). Sixth, the cross-sectional nature of the design does not allow for studying possible temporal associations between the variables and the self-reported assessment rely on one time point, only. Finally, the present results are based on self-reported sleep questionnaires and not objectively measured sleep patterns, e.g. using telemonitoring devices which is recommended in future studies.

Conclusion

Patients with BD in full or partial remission reported more sleep disturbances and less moderate and vigorous physical activity than their UR and HC. The sleep disturbances and lower activity levels were associated with subsyndromal affective symptoms pointing towards the clinical importance of obtaining full remission in BD. The unaffected first-degree relatives reported sleep latency problems which may possibly be a risk marker of BD and they also used more time on moderate to vigorous physical activity. In the ongoing longitudinal BIO study, we will obtain further knowledge about sleep disturbances and patterns of physical activity preceding BD.

Acknowledgements

A special thanks to all the participants in the study for their valuable contribution and the clinicians at Copenhagen Affective Disorder Clinic, Copenhagen University Hospital, Denmark. Also, we wish to acknowledge the BIO-team for assisting in recruiting participants.

Authors' contributions

MV and LVK conceived and designed study. LVK and MV obtained the funding. LVK applied for the Data and the Ethical permissions. KC, SS, SM, KOS recruited the patients and runned the study together with the BIO group. MV, KC and NK undertook the data extraction and the statistical analyses. NK, KC and MV drafted the manuscript drafts. All authors had substantial contributions to the design, analysis, and interpretation, and participated in manuscript drafting. All authors read and approved the final manuscript.

Author details

[1] Copenhagen Affective Disorders Research Centre (CADIC), Psychiatric Center Copenhagen, Department O, 6243, Rigshospitalet, Blegdamsvej 9, 2100 Copenhagen, Denmark. [2] Faculty of Health and Medical Sciences, University of Copenhagen, Copenhagen, Denmark. [3] Psychiatric Research Unit, Psychiatric Centre North Zealand, Hillerød, Denmark.

References

Aguib Y, Al Suwaidi J. The Copenhagen city heart study (Osterbroundersogelsen). Glob Cardiol Sci Pract. 2015;2015(3):33.

Andersen LB, Schnohr P, Schroll M, Hein HO. All-cause mortality associated with physical activity during leisure time, work, sports, and cycling to work. Arch Intern Med. 2000;160(11):1621–8.

Baldessarini RJ, Tondo L, Baethge CJ, Lepri B, Bratti IM. Effects of treatment latency on response to maintenance treatment in manic-depressive disorders. Bipolar Disord. 2007;9(4):386–93.

Bender RE, Alloy LB. Life stress and kindling in bipolar disorder: review of the evidence and integration with emerging biopsychosocial theories. Clin Psychol Rev. 2011;31(3):383–98.

Berk M, Post R, Ratheesh A, Gliddon E, Singh A, Vieta E, et al. Staging in bipolar disorder: from theoretical framework to clinical utility. World Psychiatry. 2017;16(3):236–44.

Buysse DJ, Reynolds CF 3rd, Monk TH, Berman SR, Kupfer DJ. The Pittsburgh Sleep Quality Index: a new instrument for psychiatric practice and research. Psychiatry Res. 1989;28(2):193–213.

Buysse DJ, Rush AJ, Reynolds CF 3rd. Clinical management of insomnia disorder. JAMA. 2017;318(20):1973–4.

Cappuccio FP, D'Elia L, Strazzullo P, Miller MA. Sleep duration and all-cause mortality: a systematic review and meta-analysis of prospective studies. Sleep. 2010;33(5):585–92.

Coello K, Kjaerstad HL, Stanislaus S, Melbye S, Faurholt-Jepsen M, Miskowiak KW, et al. Thirty-year cardiovascular risk score in patients with newly diagnosed bipolar disorder and their unaffected first-degree relatives. Aust N Z J Psychiatry. 2019;53(7):651–62.

Correll CU, Solmi M, Veronese N, Bortolato B, Rosson S, Santonastaso P, et al. Prevalence, incidence and mortality from cardiovascular disease in patients with pooled and specific severe mental illness: a large-scale meta-analysis of 3,211,768 patients and 113,383,368 controls. World Psychiatry. 2017;16(2):163–80.

Craddock N, Sklar P. Genetics of bipolar disorder. Lancet. 2013;381(9878):1654–62.

Craig CL, Marshall AL, Sjostrom M, Bauman AE, Booth ML, Ainsworth BE, et al. International physical activity questionnaire: 12-country reliability and validity. Med Sci Sports Exerc. 2003;35(8):1381–95.

Dagani J, Signorini G, Nielssen O, Bani M, Pastore A, Girolamo G, et al. Meta-analysis of the interval between the onset and management of bipolar disorder. Can J Psychiatry. 2017;62(4):247–58.

Duffy A, Jones S, Goodday S, Bentall R. Candidate risks indicators for bipolar disorder: early intervention opportunities in high-risk youth. Int J Neuropsychopharmacol. 2015. https://doi.org/10.1093/ijnp/pyv071.

Evans DL, Charney DS, Lewis L, Golden RN, Gorman JM, Krishnan KR, et al. Mood disorders in the medically ill: scientific review and recommendations. Biol Psychiatry. 2005;58(3):175–89.

Gallicchio L, Kalesan B. Sleep duration and mortality: a systematic review and meta-analysis. J Sleep Res. 2009;18(2):148–58.

Gold AK, Sylvia LG. The role of sleep in bipolar disorder. Nat Sci Sleep. 2016;8:207–14.

Golding J, Northstone K, Miller LL, Davey Smith G, Pembrey M. Differences between blood donors and a population sample: implications for case–control studies. Int J Epidemiol. 2013;42(4):1145–56.

Goldstein BI, Carnethon MR, Matthews KA, McIntyre RS, Miller GE, Raghuveer G, et al. Major depressive disorder and bipolar disorder predispose youth to accelerated atherosclerosis and early cardiovascular disease: a scientific statement from the American Heart Association. Circulation. 2015;132(10):965–86.

Hamilton M. A rating scale for depression. J Neurol Neurosurg Psychiatry. 1960;23:56–62.
IPAQ Group. Guidelines for data processing and analysis of the international physical activity questionnaire (IPAQ)—short and long forms. [Internet]. The Group; 2005. https://www.researchgate.net/file.PostFileLoader.html?id=5641f4c36143250eac8b45b7&assetKey=AS%3A294237418606593%401447163075131 [cited Feb 2018].
Kantomaa MT, Tikanmaki M, Kankaanpaa A, Vaarasmaki M, Sipola-Leppanen M, Ekelund U, et al. Accelerometer-measured physical activity and sedentary time differ according to education level in young adults. PLoS ONE. 2016;11(7):e0158902.
Kapczinski F, Dias VV, Kauer-Sant'Anna M, Frey BN, Grassi-Oliveira R, Colom F, et al. Clinical implications of a staging model for bipolar disorders. Expert Rev Neurother. 2009;9(7):957–66.
Kapczinski F, Magalhaes PV, Balanza-Martinez V, Dias VV, Frangou S, Gama CS, et al. Staging systems in bipolar disorder: an International Society for Bipolar Disorders Task Force Report. Acta Psychiatr Scand. 2014;130:354–63.
Keskin N, Tamam L, Ozpoyraz N. Assessment of sleep quality in bipolar euthymic patients. Compr Psychiatry. 2018;80:116–25.
Kessing LV, Andersen PK. Evidence for clinical progression of unipolar and bipolar disorders. Acta Psychiatr Scand. 2017;135(1):51–64.
Kessing LV, Hansen HV, Christensen EM, Dam H, Gluud C, Wetterslev J, et al. Do young adults with bipolar disorder benefit from early intervention? J Affect Disord. 2014;152–154:403–8.
Kessing LV, Munkholm K, Faurholt-Jepsen M, Miskowiak KW, Nielsen LB, Frikke-Schmidt R, et al. The Bipolar Illness Onset study: research protocol for the BIO cohort study. BMJ Open. 2017;7(6):e015462.
Kilbourne AM, Rofey DL, McCarthy JF, Post EP, Welsh D, Blow FC. Nutrition and exercise behavior among patients with bipolar disorder. Bipolar Disord. 2007;9(5):443–52.
Kodama S, Saito K, Tanaka S, Maki M, Yachi Y, Asumi M, et al. Cardiorespiratory fitness as a quantitative predictor of all-cause mortality and cardiovascular events in healthy men and women: a meta-analysis. JAMA. 2009;301(19):2024–35.
Kurina LM, McClintock MK, Chen JH, Waite LJ, Thisted RA, Lauderdale DS. Sleep duration and all-cause mortality: a critical review of measurement and associations. Ann Epidemiol. 2013;23(6):361–70.
Lear SA, Hu W, Rangarajan S, Gasevic D, Leong D, Iqbal R, et al. The effect of physical activity on mortality and cardiovascular disease in 130 000 people from 17 high-income, middle-income, and low-income countries: the PURE study. Lancet. 2017;390(10113):2643–54.
Lee PH, Macfarlane DJ, Lam TH, Stewart SM. Validity of the International physical activity questionnaire short form (IPAQ-SF): a systematic review. Int J Behav Nutr Phys Act. 2011;8:115.
Levenson JC, Axelson DA, Merranko J, Angulo M, Goldstein TR, Mullin BC, et al. Differences in sleep disturbances among offspring of parents with and without bipolar disorder: association with conversion to bipolar disorder. Bipolar Disord. 2015;17(8):836–48.
McGuffin P, Rijsdijk F, Andrew M, Sham P, Katz R, Cardno A. The heritability of bipolar affective disorder and the genetic relationship to unipolar depression. Arch Gen Psychiatry. 2003;60(5):497–502.
Melo MC, Garcia RF, Linhares Neto VB, Sa MB, de Mesquita LM, de Araujo CF, et al. Sleep and circadian alterations in people at risk for bipolar disorder: a systematic review. J Psychiatr Res. 2016a;83:211–9.
Melo MC, Daher Ede F, Albuquerque SG, de Bruin VM. Exercise in bipolar patients: a systematic review. J Affect Disord. 2016b;198:32–8.
Mesman E, Nolen WA, Reichart CG, Wals M, Hillegers MH. The Dutch bipolar offspring study: 12-year follow-up. Am J Psychiatry. 2013;170(5):542–9.
Pancheri C, Verdolini N, Pacchiarotti I, Samalin L, Delle Chiaie R, Biondi M, et al. A systematic review on sleep alterations anticipating the onset of bipolar disorder. Eur Psychiatry. 2019;58:45–53.
Pedersen CB, Mors O, Bertelsen A, Waltoft BL, Agerbo E, McGrath JJ, et al. A comprehensive nationwide study of the incidence rate and lifetime risk for treated mental disorders. JAMA Psychiatry. 2014;71(5):573–81.
Piercy KL, Troiano RP, Ballard RM, Carlson SA, Fulton JE, Galuska DA, et al. The physical activity guidelines for Americans. JAMA. 2018;320(19):2020–8.
Post RM, Luckenbaugh DA, Leverich GS, Altshuler LL, Frye MA, Suppes T, et al. Incidence of childhood-onset bipolar illness in the USA and Europe. Br J Psychiatry. 2008;192(2):150–1.
Ritter PS, Hofler M, Wittchen HU, Lieb R, Bauer M, Pfennig A, et al. Disturbed sleep as risk factor for the subsequent onset of bipolar disorder—data from a 10-year prospective-longitudinal study among adolescents and young adults. J Psychiatr Res. 2015;68:76–82.
Rosa AR, Magalhaes PV, Czepielewski L, Sulzbach MV, Goi PD, Vieta E, et al. Clinical staging in bipolar disorder: focus on cognition and functioning. J Clin Psychiatry. 2014;75(5):e450–6.
Shapero BG, Weiss RB, Burke TA, Boland EM, Abramson LY, Alloy LB. Kindling of life stress in bipolar disorder: effects of early adversity. Behav Ther. 2017;48(3):322–34.
Takaesu Y. Circadian rhythm in bipolar disorder: a review of the literature. Psychiatry Clin Neurosci. 2018;72:673–82.
Vancampfort D, Firth J, Schuch F, Rosenbaum S, De Hert M, Mugisha J, et al. Physical activity and sedentary behavior in people with bipolar disorder: a systematic review and meta-analysis. J Affect Disord. 2016;201:145–52.
Vancampfort D, Firth J, Schuch FB, Rosenbaum S, Mugisha J, Hallgren M, et al. Sedentary behavior and physical activity levels in people with schizophrenia, bipolar disorder and major depressive disorder: a global systematic review and meta-analysis. World Psychiatry. 2017;16(3):308–15.
Verkooijen S, van Bergen AH, Knapen SE, Vreeker A, Abramovic L, Pagani L, et al. An actigraphy study investigating sleep in bipolar I patients, unaffected siblings and controls. J Affect Disord. 2017;208:248–54.
Wing JK, Babor T, Brugha T, Burke J, Cooper JE, Giel R, et al. SCAN. Schedules for clinical assessment in neuropsychiatry. Arch Gen Psychiatry. 1990;47(6):589–93.
World Health Organization. International Classification of Diseases, 10th Revision (ICD-10), Genova, Schweitzerland. 2005.
Yin J, Jin X, Shan Z, Li S, Huang H, Li P, et al. Relationship of sleep duration with all-cause mortality and cardiovascular events: a systematic review and dose-response meta-analysis of prospective cohort studies. J Am Heart Assoc. 2017;6(9):e005947.
Young RC, Biggs JT, Ziegler VE, Meyer DA. A rating scale for mania: reliability, validity and sensitivity. Br J Psychiatry. 1978;133:429–35.

13

Antidepressant efficacy of low-frequency repetitive transcranial magnetic stimulation in antidepressant-nonresponding bipolar depression: a single-blind randomized sham-controlled trial

Arthur D. P. Mak[1*], Sebastiaan F. W. Neggers[2], Owen N. W. Leung[1], Winnie C. W. Chu[3], Jenny Y. M. Ho[1], Idy W. Y. Chou[1], Sandra S. M. Chan[1], Linda C. W. Lam[1] and Sing Lee[1]

Abstract

Background: To examine the antidepressant efficacy and response predictors of R-DLPFC-LF rTMS for antidepressant-nonresponding BD.

Methods: We conducted a single-blind randomized sham-controlled trial for 54 (28 sham, 26 active) patients with antidepressant-nonresponding BD (baseline MADRS $\geq$ 20). Patients received 15 daily sessions of active or sham neuronavigated rTMS (Figure-of-8 coil, five 1 Hz 60 s 110% RMT trains). Outcome measures included depressive response ($\geq$ 50% MADRS reduction, CGI $\leq$ 2) and remission (MADRS < 7, CGI = 1) rates, treatment emergent hypo/mania (YMRS), depressive and anxiety symptoms (HAM-A).

Results: 48 patients (25 sham, 23 active) completed treatment, with 3 drop-outs each in active and sham groups. Active rTMS did not produce superior response or remission rates at endpoint or 6 or 12 weeks (ps > 0.05). There was no significant group * time interaction (ps > 0.05) in a multivariate ANOVA with MADRS, HAMA and YMRS as dependent variables. Exploratory analysis found MADRS improvement to be moderated by baseline anxiety (p = 0.02) and melancholia (p = 0.03) at week 3, and depressive onset at weeks 6 (p = 0.03) and 12 (p = 0.04). In subjects with below-mean anxiety (HAMA < 20.7, n = 24), MADRS improvement from active rTMS was superior to sham at week 3 (ITT, t = 2.49, p = 0.04, Cohen's d = 1.05). No seizures were observed. Groups did not differ in treatment-emergent hypomania (p = 0.1).

Limitations: Larger sample size might be needed to power subgroup analyses. Moderation analyses were exploratory. Single-blind design. Unblinding before follow-up assessments due to ethical reasons.

Conclusions: 1-Hz 110% RMT (5 × 60 s trains) **R**-DLPFC-LF rTMS was not effective for antidepressant non-responding BD but may be further investigated at increased dosage and/or in BD patients with low anxiety.

Trial registration CCRB Clinical Trials Registry, CUHK, CUHK_CCT00440. Registered 04 December 2014, https://www2.ccrb.cuhk.edu.hk/registry/public/279

*Correspondence: arthurdpmak@cuhk.edu.hk
[1] Department of Psychiatry, The Chinese University of Hong Kong, G/F Multicentre, Tai Po Hospital, Tai Po, Hong Kong, SAR, China
Full list of author information is available at the end of the article

Keywords: Bipolar disorder, Depression, Transcranial magnetic stimulation, Randomized controlled trial

Background

Depressive episodes dominate the illness course of Bipolar Disorder (Judd et al. 2005), which is a disabling condition with significant suicide risk that affects approximately 4% of the population (Kessler et al. 2005; Zarate et al. 2000; Goldstein et al. 2012). Treatment resistance is also common in bipolar depression—40% for 8 weeks of quetiapine and even less favorable in other first-line options such as lithium lamotrigine, olanzapine or olanzapine–fluoxetine combination (De Fruyt et al. 2012; Sidor and Macqueen 2011; Geddes et al. 2009), and unlike for unipolar depression, antidepressants commonly lead to non-response, rapid cycling and precipitating manic switches (Fela-Thomas et al. 2018; Viktorin et al. 2014).

Repetitive transcranial magnetic stimulation (rTMS) has recently gained recognition as an effective treatment for bipolar depression, with left-DLPFC high frequency (L-DLPFC-HF) rTMS obtaining FDA approval for bipolar depression (Neuronetics 2020). Earlier research, however, suggested that right-DLPFC low frequency (R-DLPFC-LF) rTMS may have comparable antidepressant efficacy for Major Depressive Disorder (Chen et al. 2013; Cao et al. 2018; Dell'Osso et al. 2015; Eche et al. 2012), but obtainable in shorter treatment time (4–9 min versus 30 min in L-HF) (Eche et al. 2012; Dell'Osso et al. 2009), with reduced discomfort at site of stimulation (Kaur et al. 2019) and a practically non-existent risk of seizure-induction (Sun et al. 2012; Theodore et al. 2002). Antidepressant efficacy of R-DLPFC-LF rTMS for bipolar depression has only received preliminary support mainly from open-label and active comparison non-inferiority trials, (Dell'Osso et al. 2009, 2015; Pallanti et al. 2014; Fitzgerald et al. 2006; Dell'osso and Altamura 2009). The only randomized sham-controlled trial (RCT) done so far, failed to demonstrate significant benefit of R-DLPFC-LF or L-DLPFC-HF rTMS over sham control (Hu et al. 2016) possibly attributable to a small sample size (L-HF on 12 subjects, R-LF on 13 subjects and 13 receiving sham). The effectiveness of R-DLPFC-LF rTMS for bipolar depression therefore needs to be examined in a larger sample. On the other hand, response to rTMS in depressive states is heterogeneous (Fitzgerald et al. 2016), with widely varied response rates from 42 to 75% (Dell'Osso et al. 2009; Pallanti et al. 2014; Fitzgerald et al. 2006; Hu et al. 2016; Kazemi et al. 2016), influenced by clinical factors such as depressive severity (Fitzgerald et al. 2016; Trevizol et al. 2002), anxiety (Trevizol et al. 2002; Brakemeier et al. 2007), medication use (Harel et al. 2011), and course variables (Fitzgerald et al. 2016). It would therefore be of interest to examine determinants of response, and identify potential subgroups of bipolar depressed patients that would show a superior response to R-DLFPC-LF rTMS.

In view of the above, we conducted a randomized single-blind sham-controlled study that examined the antidepressant efficacy of 3-week augmentative neuronavigated 1-Hz R-DLFPC-LF rTMS in 64 adults with antidepressant non-responding bipolar depression. We also performed moderation analysis to examine the influence of baseline clinical parameters, including depressive (Fitzgerald et al. 2016; Trevizol et al. 2002) and anxiety severity (Trevizol et al. 2002; Brakemeier et al. 2007), medication use (Harel et al. 2011), melancholic vs. atypical features, and course variables (Fitzgerald et al. 2016), on clinical response to the rTMS regime.

Methods

Study design

This study is a randomized, sham-controlled, single-blind trial of 3-week augmentative neuro-navigated 1-Hz R-DLPFC rTMS for antidepressant non-responding bipolar depression with post-treatment follow up assessments up to 12 weeks from treatment endpoint.

Subjects

We recruited and randomized 64 right-handed patients aged 18 to 65 who met DSM-5 criteria for bipolar I or II disorder with a current major depressive episode (MDE) that showed no response to at least one previous adequate antidepressant trial (defined as having $\leq$25% reduction of MADRS following full or best tolerated dose of an antidepressant drug [bupropion or SSRI apart from paroxetine, commensurate with 3rd-line treatment recommendations in CANMAT 2013 guidelines (Yatham et al. 2013) for at least 6 weeks] in addition to at least one mood stabilizer (lithium, sodium valproate or lamotrigine). Only subjects with at least moderately severe depressive symptoms (Montgomery-Åsberg Depression Rating Scale [MADRS] $\geq$20) at treatment commencement were included in the analysis. The patients and their responsible psychiatrists were advised to avoid alterations to psychiatric medication and report whenever such alterations were necessitated. Patients with organic brain syndromes, current psychotic symptoms, mental retardation, substance use in recent 3 months, suicidal ideation or attempt in past month, obsessive–compulsive disorder, post-traumatic stress disorders, eating disorders, metallic implants, current pregnancy, unstable cardiac disease, personal or known 1st degree relatives' history of seizures were excluded. None of the participants had previously received rTMS nor had record of non-response to electroconvulsive therapy.

Randomization and blinding

64 subjects were randomly allocated to the active intervention or sham control group on a 1:1 ratio using a random allocation sequence obtained from a computer-generated list of random numbers in blocks of 10 by a statistician with no other involvement in the study. The allocation was concealed from patients and the researchers responsible for data collection and analysis, but not the TMS therapists. The TMS therapists was forbidden from disclosing the randomized allocation status to the participants. Participants were unblinded on the day of their final treatment session after progress evaluation. Those in the sham control group were offered the option of receiving active TMS treatment, where recommended by their responsible psychiatrists, after treatment unblinding. Where open-label active TMS treatment commenced within the follow-up assessment period, all subsequent assessment data were excluded in per-protocol (PP) analysis and imputed with last observation carried forward method in intention-to-treat (ITT) analysis.

Neuronavigation

Prior to treatment, subjects underwent a structural brain MRI using a Philips 3.0-T whole-body scanner (Achieva TX, Philips Healthcare, Best, the Netherlands). Whole brain anatomical datasets were acquired with a T1-weighted sequence (repetition time (TR)/echo time (TE): 7.6/3.5 ms, field of view 230 mm, 250 contiguous slices, 0.6 mm thickness, reconstruction matrix 224 × 224). The datasets were installed on a neuro-navigation software (Brainsight 2 Neuronavigator for TMS, Rogue Research Inc. 2007) to guide coil placement over the right dorsolateral prefrontal cortex (RDLPFC) (MNI X, Y, Z [SD] = 35.71 [5.81], 44.63 [8.72], 31 [8.08]), corresponding to areas between 9 and 46 (middle third of the middle frontal gyrus and most rostral portion of inferior frontal gyrus) in the original Brodmann Map.

TMS parameters

70 mm Magstim figure-of-eight coil was hand-held in place guided by neuronavigation, tangential to the scalp with the handle pointing back and away from the midline at 45°.

TMS treatment were delivered using Magstim Super Rapid 2 with a 70 mm figure-of-eight coil. The coil was held tangential to the scalp with the handle pointing back and away from the midline at 45°. Treatment parameters were based on Dell'Osso's single-arm study (Dell'Osso et al. 2009). During each session, subjects were given 300 pulses of stimulation at 1 Hz divided into 5 trains of 60 stimuli, each train separated from the next by a one-minute pause. Subjects received 15 sessions over week-days of 3 consecutive weeks, with a total of 4500 stimuli over the full intervention course. rTMS was delivered at 110% of subjects' resting motor threshold, defined as the minimum magnetic intensity required to elicit 5 motor evoked potentials (50 μV), as measured using a Brainsight EMG amplifier, out of 10 consecutive stimuli in the abductor pollicis brevis.

Neuronavigation, positioning, protocol of treatment for the sham treatment group, including weekly determination of resting motor threshold, were identical to that in the treatment group, except that sham treatment was delivered with a Magstim sham coil, essentially an inactive figure-of-eight coil which looked identical and produced sounds mimicking the frequency and loudness of the active coil.

Diagnostic and symptomatic evaluation

Diagnoses were obtained using the validated Chinese-bilingual version of the Structured Clinical Interview for DSM Mental Disorders (SCID–C/B) (So et al. 2003) by trained research assistants under supervision of an experienced academic psychiatrist (AM). The severity of depressive, anxiety and manic symptoms were evaluated respectively using Montgomery-Åsberg Depression Rating Scale (MADRS) (Montgomery and Asberg 1979), Hamilton Anxiety Rating Scale (HAMA) (Hamilton 1958) and Young Mania Rating Scale (YMRS) (Young et al. 1978). Subjects were also evaluated using Clinical Global Impression Scale (CGI) (Guy 1976) to reflect global clinical severity. Symptom severity was evaluated before the first treatment session (week 0), after the last treatment session (week 3), and at two post-treatment follow-ups three (week 6) and 6 weeks (week 12) after the last treatment session.

Data analysis

In the 64 randomised subjects, 6 allocated to the active arm and 4 in the sham arm had MADRS score dropped below 20 by treatment commencement and became ineligible. Intention-to-treat analysis included the 54 participants with MADRS ≥ 20 and entered randomized treatment phase (26 active rTMS, 28 sham rTMS). Missing data (treatment termination, follow-up assessments conducted after the start of open-label active treatment, interview decline) were removed in per protocol analysis (see Additional file 1: Fig. S1), and imputed with last observation carried forward in ITT analysis (see Additional file 2: Fig. S2).

The primary outcome measure was clinical response (defined as $\geq 50\%$ reduction in MADRS score and CGI ≤ 2) in depressive symptoms at treatment endpoint. Secondary outcome measures included changes in depressive, anxiety and manic symptom severity, endpoint remission rate (defined as MADRS < 7 and CGI $= 1$), sustained response and remission rates at weeks 6 and 12, and treatment-emergent hypomanic or manic episodes by treatment endpoint.

Differences in response and remission rates were compared between the active intervention and sham control groups were using the Fisher's exact test.

Multivariate repeated measures ANOVA was used as a global test to identify any between-group differences in depressive, anxiety and hypomanic symptoms over time while limiting the joint error rate. Univariate ANOVAs were also performed separately for depressive, anxiety and hypomanic symptoms to gauge their respective effect sizes. Time contrasts (each assessment timepoint contrasted with the subsequent) were also applied to identify when group differences emerge.

As an explorative analysis, moderation analysis was performed to identify if antidepressant effect depended upon demographic (age, sex, education level) and clinical variables (baseline MADRS, HAMA, YMRS, bipolar subtype (I vs. II), age of first depressive onset, years since depressive onset, length of current depressive episode, melancholic, atypical and rapid cycling specifier lifetime and current number of comorbid mental disorders) at each of the timepoints. The moderation effects of antidepressants and antipsychotics use at baseline were also tested on MADRS change at week 3, but not at follow-up assessments in the absence of data on post-treatment medication changes. As the explorative moderation analysis is aimed at identifying potential response predictors from a broad range of 16 candidate variables, correction for multiple comparison was not applied at this stage.

Significant moderators were then used to stratify the sample (with/without the characteristic for binary variables, above/below average for continuous variables). In each of the resultant subgroups, Holms–Bonferroni corrected t-tests were conducted to compare the level of MADRS improvement in active versus sham treatment.

All statistical analyses were conducted with Python 3.8. Results with two-sided p values lower than 0.05 were considered significant.

Results

26 subjects from active and 28 subjects from sham treatment groups were included in ITT analysis. Subjects were on average 40 (SD 11.45) years old, 67% were female, over half (59%) received post-secondary education. Most of the subjects were of bipolar II (85.2%, n = 46 vs. bipolar I 14.8%, n = 8), with no significant difference between treatment and sham groups ($p = 1.0$). All subjects were at least moderately depressed (MADRS ≥ 20). The two groups did not differ in baseline psychopharmacological profile or any demographic, symptom or course variables ($p > 0.05$) (see Table 1).

23 and 25 subjects in the active and sham treatment arms, respectively, completed 3 weeks of study treatment. Treatment was terminated for 3 subjects from each group in the first week of study treatment. 2 subjects from the active group were terminated due to erratic drug use, and one reported suicidal ideation that was not disclosed prior to recruitment screening, and was then referred for emergency clinical care. Two subjects from the sham group withdrew citing scheduling difficulties and one withdrew stating intention to seek alternative treatment.

Main results

In multivariate ANOVAs with MADRS, HAMA and YMRS as dependent variables, time × group effects were insignificant for both ITT ($F[9, 44] = 1.36$, $p = 0.23$, $\eta p2 = 0.22$) and PP ($F[9, 31] = 1.52$, $p = 0.19$, $\eta_p^2 = 0.31$) analyses (see Table 3).

In univariate MADRS analysis, the time × group effect was insignificant and with small effect size (ITT: $F[3, 156] = 1.07$, $p = 0.37$, $\eta p2 = 0.02$, PP: $F[3, 117] = 1.1$, $p = 0.35$, $\eta p2 = 0.03$) (see Table 3). The only timepoint where MADRS improvement from baseline was higher in active group (ITT 8.34 [SD 6.71], PP 9.43 [7.63]) than in sham (ITT 6.71 [8.28], PP 7.52 [8.41]) was week 3 (see Fig. 1), but the group * time effect was insignificant (Baseline—week 3 contrast ITT: $F[1, 52] = 0.56$, $p = 0.46$, $\eta p2 = 0.01$ PP: $F[1, 39] = 0.61$, $p = 0.44$, $\eta p2 = 0.02$) (see Table 3).

Response and remission

Response rates did not differ significantly between the two groups at week 3 (ITT—active 12% vs. sham 11%; PP—active 13% vs. sham 12%) or at week 6 or 12 follow ups (ITT—active 8% vs. sham 7%; PP—active 9% vs. sham 9–11%). One subject receiving active intervention (ITT 4%, PP 4%) and none from sham group remitted at week 3. Remission was sustained upon week 12 (active vs. sham $p > 0.05$) (see Table 2).

Exploratory moderation analyses and subgroup analyses

Exploratory moderation analysis showed that week 3 improvement in depression (MADRS) was moderated by baseline anxiety (interaction $p = 0.02$) (see Fig. 2a) and melancholic features (interaction $p = 0.03$) (see Fig. 2b). No significant moderation effect on week 3 depressive symptoms was found from other clinical variables such

Table 1 Demographic and clinical variables

	ITT				PP			
	Sham n=28	Treatment n=26	t/chi^2	p	Sham n=25	Treatment n=23	t/chi^2	p
Age, mean (SD)	39.4 (11.3)	40.7 (11.4)	−0.4	0.69	40.0 (11.4)	39.7 (11.6)	0.09	0.93
Sex, male n (%)	10 (36)	8 (31)	0.01	0.92	9 (36)	8 (35)	0.05	0.83
Education, n (%)			–	0.70			–	0.5
Primary or below	1 (4)	1 (4)			1 (4)	1 (4)		
Secondary	12 (43)	8 (31)			12 (48)	7 (30)		
Post-secondary	15 (54)	17 (65)			12 (48)	15 (65)		
Bipolar disorder subtype, n (%)			–	1			–	1
Type 1	4 (14)	4(15)			4 (16)	4 (17)		
Type 2	24 (86)	22 (85)			21 (84)	19 (83)		
Baseline MADRS, mean (SD)	27.0 (5.1)	27.5 (5.2)	−0.41	0.68	26.2 (3.8)	26.8 (4.9)	−0.48	0.63
Baseline HAM-A, mean (SD)	20.5 (7.0)	21.0 (10.3)	−0.19	0.85	21.0 (7.1)	20.0 (10.4)	0.38	0.71
Baseline YMRS mean (SD)	1.0 (1.9)	2.3 (3.2)	−1.83	0.07	1.1 (2.0)	1.7 (2.4)	−0.82	0.42
Melancholic specifier, n (%)	18 (64)	17 (65)	0.04	0.84	16 (64)	14 (61)	0.01	0.94
Atypical specifier, n (%)	6 (21)	13 (50)	3.65	0.06	6 (24)	11 (48)	2.02	0.16
Rapid cycling specifier, n (%)	13 (46)	17 (65)	1.27	0.26	12 (48)	15 (65)	0.83	0.36
Onset	23.5 (8.4)	23.9 (9.0)	−0.18	0.86	23.7 (8.5)	23.7 (8.8)	−0.02	0.98
Years since onset	15.9 (8.9)	17.6 (9.5)	−0.69	0.5	16.3 (8.8)	17.0 (9.7)	−0.23	0.82
On antidepressant at baseline, n (%)	19 (68)	19 (73)	0.01	0.9	17 (68)	17 (74)	0.02	0.9
On antipsychotic at baseline, n (%)	24 (86)	20 (77)	–	0.49	22 (88)	19 (83)		0.7
Number of comorbid disorders (lifetime)	1.9 (1.3)	2.3 (1.2)	−0.99	0.33	2.0 (1.3)	2.3 (1.2)	−0.83	0.41
(Current)	1.5 (0.9)	2.0 (1.1)	−1.85	0.07	1.6 (0.9)	2.0 (1.1)	−1.52	0.14

ITT intention-to-treat, *PP* per-protocol, *MADRS* Montgomery–Åsberg Depression Rating Scale, *HAMA* Hamilton Anxiety Rating Scale, *YMRS* Young Mania Rating Scale

as baseline antidepressant use, bipolar subtype or age of depressive onset. Subgroup analysis then proceeded with subjects stratified by baseline anxiety score, and found significantly greater MADRS improvement in active compared to sham group in those with below-mean (HAM-A = 20.7, n = 24) baseline anxiety ($t = -2.49$, Holms-Bonferroni corrected $p = 0.04$, Cohen's $d = 1.05$) (see Fig. 2a). No significant active-sham difference in MADRS change was found in the sub-groups stratified by baseline melancholic features (see Fig. 2b).

At week 6 and 12, age of depressive onset (week 6 and 12 interaction ps = 0.03, 0.04) (see Fig. 2c, d) moderated MADRS improvement in ITT analysis. This moderation effect was also significant in PP analysis at week 6 but not 12 (interaction $p = 0.04$) (see Fig. 3). None of the subgroup analyses stratified by age of onset showed significant group*time interaction at week 6 or 12. No significant moderation effect on week 6 or 12 depressive symptoms were found with any other clinical variables.

Secondary outcomes—anxiety and manic symptoms

There were weak time*group interactions for anxiety (ITT: $F[3, 156] = 2.8$, $p = 0.04$, $\eta p2 = 0.05$; PP: $F[3, 117] = 3.14$, $p = 0.03$, $\eta p2 = 0.08$) and hypomanic symptoms (PP: $F[3, 117] = 3.39$, $p = 0.02$, $\eta p2 = 0.08$) in univariate ANOVA that were not significant in the multivariate analysis (see Table 3).

The interaction in anxiety symptoms emerged after the end of treatment—whereas anxiety symptoms continued to decrease in sham, it rebounded in active treatment (week 3–6 contrast ITT: $F[1, 52] = 5.73$, $p = 0.02$, $\eta p2 = 0.1$, PP: $F[1, 39] = 6.49$, $p = 0.02$, $\eta p2 = 0.14$). No other contrasts were significant (see Table 3).

The interaction in hypomanic symptoms emerged between the two post-treatment follow-ups (week 6–12 contrast)—hypomanic symptoms decreased in active treatment group but increased in sham treatment group (ITT: $F[1, 52] = 6.41$, $p = 0.01$, $\eta p2 = 0.11$; PP: $F[1, 39] = 6.56$, $p = 0.01$, $\eta p2 = 0.14$). No other contrasts were significant (see Table 3).

There was no report of any treatment-emergent seizures or other serious adverse events. The rate of treatment-emergent hypomania did not differ significantly between active intervention (ITT 31%, PP30%) and sham control (ITT 11%, PP12%) groups, (Fisher's exact test: ITT $p = 0.1$, PP $p = 0.16$) (Table 2) and active treatment

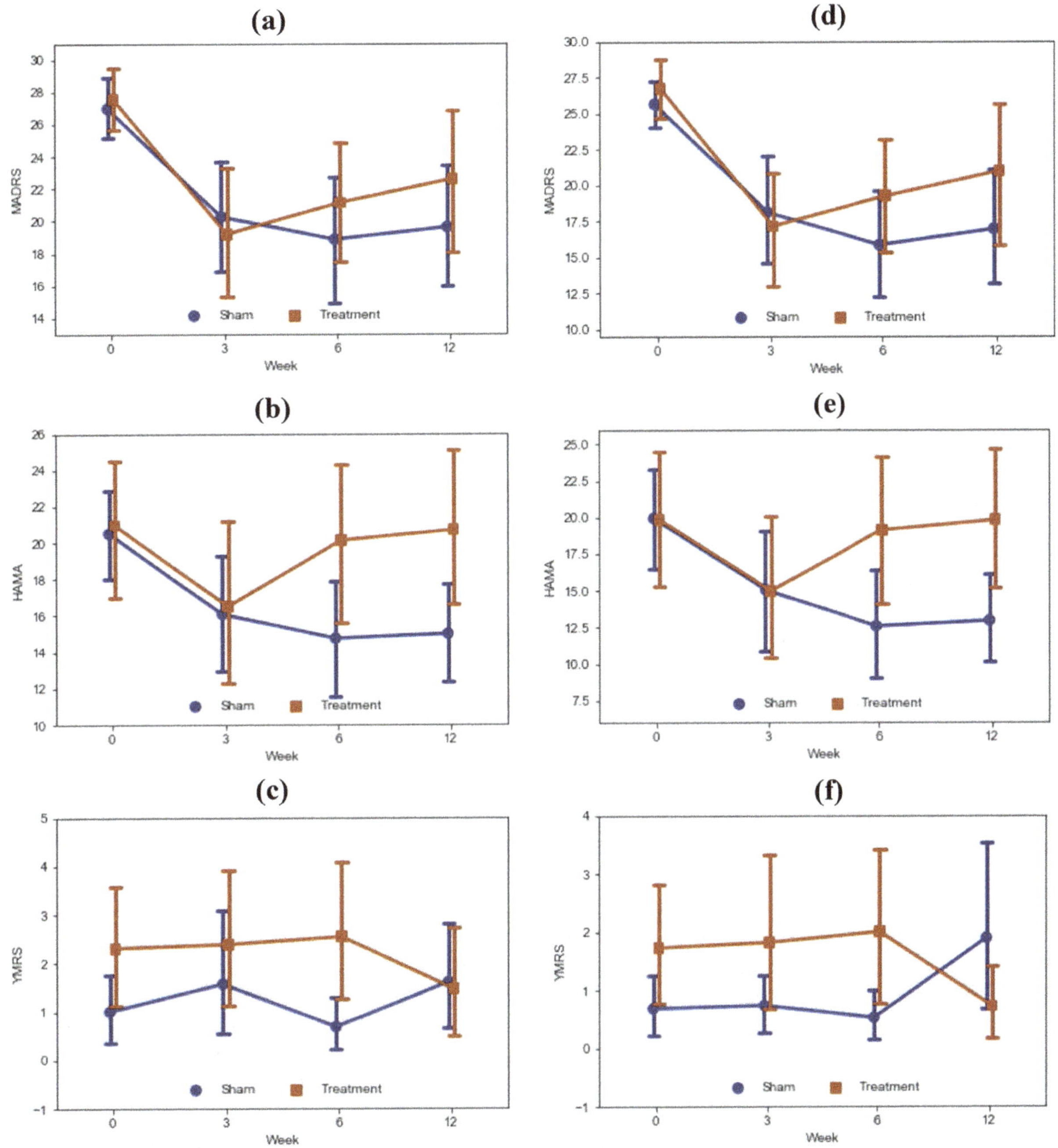

Fig. 1 Marginal means of MADRS, YMRS and HAMA across assessment timepoints. *MADRS* Montgomery–Åsberg Depression Rating Scale, *HAMA* Hamilton Anxiety Rating Scale, *YMRS* Young Mania Rating Scale. **a–c** Intention-to-treat. **d–f** Per-protocol

was not associated with significantly increased YMRS between any time points (see Table 3).

Discussion

In this randomized sham rTMS-controlled, single-blind study, we did not observe significant antidepressant effect from 1 Hz R-DLPFC rTMS for antidepressant-nonresponding bipolar depressed patients, but observed a significant antidepressant effect in those with low baseline anxiety.

The additional improvement in depressive symptoms in active versus in sham intervention at week 3 was small (ITT 1.64 point difference). The small effect size (ηp2 ITT = 0.01) means that a much larger sample (n = 134 per arm) would be required to detect a significant effect. This was far larger than the sample size used in the present study, which was estimated a priori based on single-arm

Table 2 Fisher's exact test of response and remission rates and treatment-emergent manic/hypomanic episodes

	ITT[a]			PP[b]		
	Sham	Active	p	Sham	Active	p
Response[c]						
Week 3	3 (11)	3 (12)	1	3 (12)	3 (13)	1
Sustained at week 6	2 (7)	2 (8)	1	2 (9)	2 (9)	1
Sustained at week 12	2 (7)	2 (8)	1	2 (11)	2 (9)	1
Remission[d]						
Week 3	0 (0)	1 (4)	0.48	0 (0)	1 (4)	0.48
Sustained at week 6	0 (0)	1 (4)	0.48	0 (0)	1 (4)	1
Sustained at week 12	0 (0)	1 (4)	0.48	0 (0)	1 (5)	1
Manic or hypomanic episodes by week 4	3 (11)	8 (31)	0.095	3 (12)	7 (30)	0.16

[a] Sham n = 28, treatment n = 26

[b] Sham n at week 3, 6 and 12 = 25, 23, 19; treatment n at week 3, 6 and 12 = 23, 23, 22

[c] Response defined as 50% reduction in MADRS from baseline and CGI ≤ 2

[d] Remission defined as MADRS < 7 and CGI = 1

data (55% response rate, versus 12–13% obtained in the present study), when no controlled comparison was available (Dell'Osso et al. 2009). The negative results from another, even smaller randomized controlled trial (n = 13 per arm) (Hu et al. 2016) of L-DLPFC or R-DLPFC rTMS on bipolar II depression (Hu et al. 2016) is therefore not surprising.

The response and remission rates were lower than those previously reported (42–75% response; 13–40% remission) (Dell'Osso et al. 2009; Pallanti et al. 2014; Fitzgerald et al. 2006; Hu et al. 2016; Kazemi et al. 2016). The discrepancy is unlikely attributable to differences in sample characteristics since this sample did not differ vastly in age, depressive severity or treatment resistance compared to those in previous studies (Dell'Osso et al. 2009; Pallanti et al. 2014; Fitzgerald et al. 2006; Hu et al. 2016; Kazemi et al. 2016). As expected by the study design for recruiting antidepressant-nonresponding bipolar depressed patients, a rather high proportion of (70%) patients in our sample received concurrent antidepressant treatment, whereas 23% (Kazemi et al. 2016) to 91% of patients from previous R-DLPFC-LF rTMS studies (Dell'Osso et al. 2009) received antidepressant treatment. In lieu of clear evidence on the impact of concurrent antidepressant drug use on rTMS effectiveness, it is difficult to assess if this was relevant in explaining the low response and remission rates found in this study. Instead, the discrepancies may reflect the more stringent response and remission criteria with the addition of CGI improvements in addition to changes in depressive symptom score (Dell'Osso et al. 2009; Pallanti et al. 2014; Fitzgerald et al. 2006; Hu et al. 2016; Kazemi et al. 2016), and the lower stimulation dosage compared to new stimulation protocols that have been found to have good effectiveness and tolerability profiles since this study has started—eg., with 5 additional rTMS sessions, or more pulses per session (total 420–1500), and shorter wait time between trains (Pallanti et al. 2014; Hu et al. 2016; Kazemi et al. 2016). Future studies should examine the effectiveness of R-DLPFC-LF rTMS regimes with either higher stimulation intensity, number of pulse per sessions or total number of sessions.

Nonetheless, we did observe a significant antidepressant effect from R-DLPFC-LF rTMS in low-anxiety bipolar depressed patients. Greater antidepressant effect in patients with low anxiety has been observed for L-DLPFC-HF rTMS (Trevizol et al. 2002; Brakemeier et al. 2007) and antidepressant drug (Fava et al. 2008; Saghafi et al. 2007). Effect size (Cohen's d = 10.5) was large, and the level of improvement (mean 10.8 point MADRS reduction) appeared clinically meaningful, especially given previous non-response to antidepressant drugs which was required for enrolment in this study. The results at hand suggest that the present protocol could be beneficial to bipolar depressed patients with mild (HAM-A ≤ 17) and potentially some of the patients with mild to moderate (HAM-A 18–24) anxiety (Hamilton 1958). The insignificant moderation results at week 6 and 12 may either suggest that baseline anxiety did not influence maintenance of effect from rTMS, or the lack of sustained treatment effect from the current regime. Future studies exploring R-DLPFC-LF rTMS may consider increasing number of treatment sessions, treatment strength, or incorporating maintenance rTMS (Richieri et al. 2013).

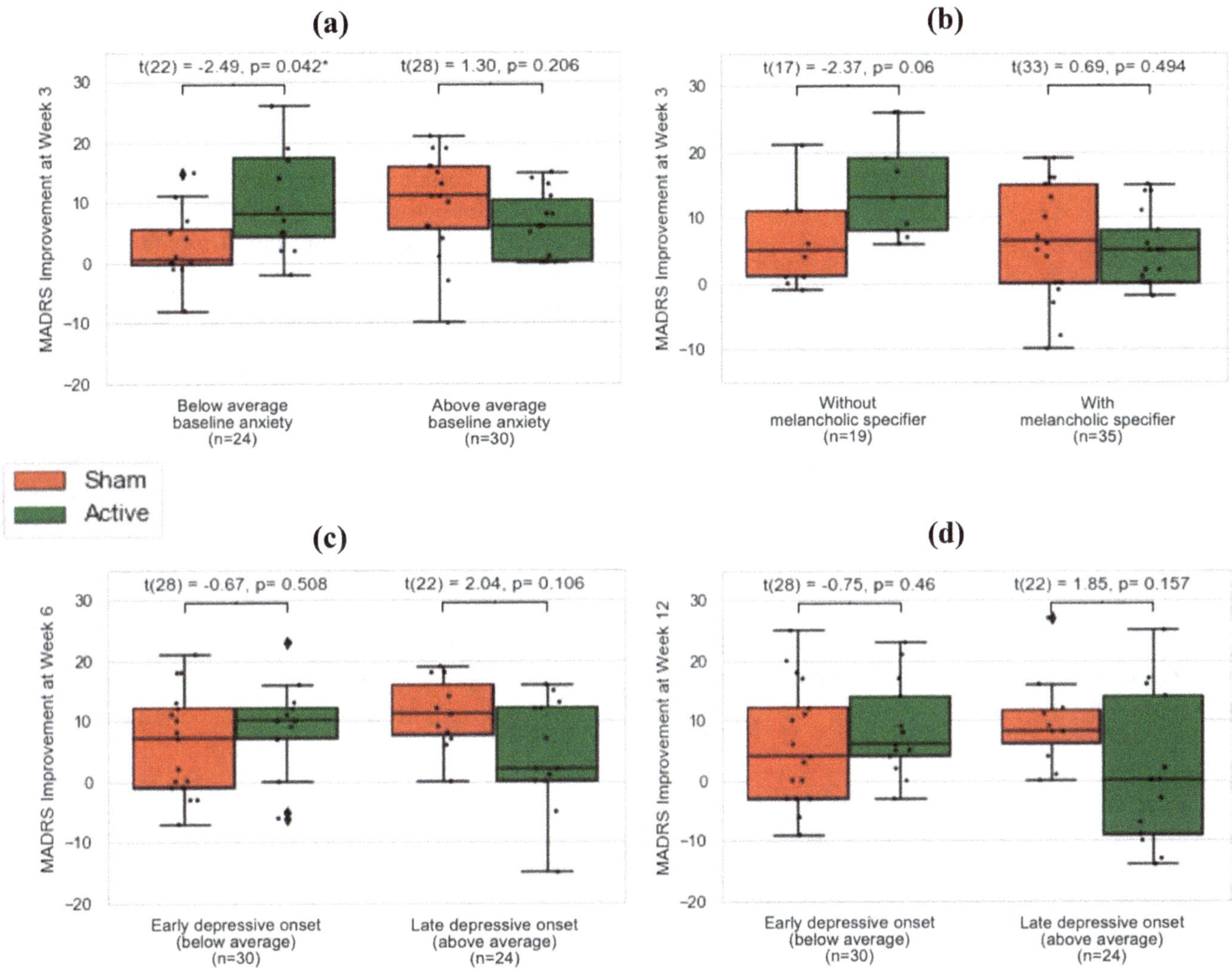

Fig. 2 Variables interacting with MADRS improvements in intention-to-treat analysis. MADRS, Montgomery–Åsberg Depression Rating Scale; *$p < 0.05$. **a** Baseline anxiety * treatment group interaction at week 3: $\beta = -0.62$ 95% CI (−1.14–0.10), $p = 0.02$. **b** Melancholic specifier * group interaction at week 3: $\beta = -9.83$ 95% CI (−18.46–1.20), $p = 0.03$. **c** Onset * group interaction at week 6: $\beta = -0.58$ 95% CI (−1.09–0.07), $p = 0.03$. **d** Onset * group interaction at week 12: $\beta = -0.66$ 95% CI (−1.29–0.03), $p = 0.04$. *Significant at $p < 0.05$

In contrast to previous rTMS studies, response to R-DLPFC-LF rTMS in the present study was not influenced by baseline depressive severity or length of current episode (Fitzgerald et al. 2016). This could be related to this narrower range of depressive severity resulting from the exclusion of actively suicidal or psychotic patients who were likely more depressed (Melhem et al. 2019; Gaudiano et al. 2009). In Hong Kong, these patients would have been treated in in-patient settings where rTMS is unavailable. We observed non-melancholic depression to predict greater acute improvement in depressive symptoms, which stood in contrast to clinical trials of antidepressant drugs and electroconvulsive therapy where melancholic depression predicted superior response (Brown 2007). Previous rTMS studies have identified individual symptoms, cognitive vs. somatic symptoms, guilt, severity of sleep disruption and somatic anxiety as predictors of rTMS response (Poleszczyk et al. 2018), but few examined the effect of melancholic vs. atypical subtypes of depression. It has also remained unclear if certain common features of melancholia or atypicality, such as vegetative (or reversed) symptoms or psychomotor retardation would predict rTMS response in the way they would for ECT and antidepressant treatment. The effect of, and changes in these clinical phenomena should be further examined with more refined measures in future rTMS studies, incorporating imaging and electro-physiological investigations to examine the neurobiological mechanisms of these treatment modalities.

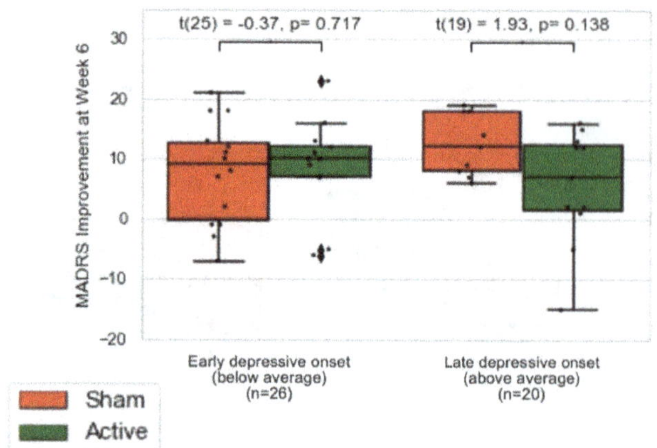

Fig. 3 Variables interacting with MADRS improvements in per-protocol analysis. *MADRS* Montgomery–Åsberg Depression Rating Scale. Onset * group interaction: β = − 0.66 95% CI (− 1.28–0.04), p = 0.04

Nonetheless, we found R-DLPFC-LF rTMS to be safe, as reported in previous studies (Dell'Osso et al. 2009; Pallanti et al. 2014; Fitzgerald et al. 2006; Hu et al. 2016). There was no report of seizures or significant increase in manic symptoms or episodes.

Our study has several limitations. Firstly, a larger sample size may have been required to not only reveal between-group effects, but also adequately power identification of predictors and subsequent subgroup analyses. In fact, even though a stringent correction method was applied when splitting the sample for subgroup analysis, the moderation analyses used to highlight likely response predictors were itself uncorrected, and their results should thus be considered preliminary, at most highlighting potential candidate predictors for further study. Secondly, although bipolar subtype was not found to moderate clinical response, it should be noted that bipolar I only constituted 14.8% of this sample. Since subjects were recruited irrespective of bipolar subtype, and that both subtypes are associated with similar extents of depressive morbidity (Judd et al. 2005), this may reflect the more common occurrence of bipolar II than bipolar I (Merikangas et al. 2007) especially in specialist clinic settings (Akiskal et al. 2000). Nonetheless, findings in this study may have limited generalizability to bipolar I patients, and the association of bipolar subtype and response to R-DLPFC-LF rTMS should be examined in further studies. Thirdly, inherent limitations of the rTMS system used (Magstim) necessitated a single-blind

Table 3 ANOVA time * group interaction effects

	ITT				PP			
	F	df	Sig	ηp2	F	df	Sig	ηp2
ANOVA across all time points								
Multivariate								
MADRS, HAMA, YMRS	1.36	9, 44	0.23	0.22	1.52	9, 31	0.19	0.31
Univariate								
MADRS	1.07	3, 43.77	0.37	0.02	1.1	3, 52.75	0.35	0.03
HAMA	2.8	3, 116.39	0.04*	0.05	3.14	3, 157.54	0.03*	0.08
YMRS	1.99	2.57, 11.41	0.13[a]	0.04	3.39	3, 14.66	0.02*	0.08
Time contrasts (each time point contrasted to the subsequent)								
MADRS								
Baseline vs. week 3	0.56	1, 52	0.46	0.01	0.61	1, 39	0.44	0.02
Week 3 vs. week 6	1.8	1, 52	0.19	0.03	2.02	1, 39	0.16	0.05
Week 6 vs. week 12	0.09	1, 52	0.77	0	0.04	1, 39	0.85	0
HAMA								
Baseline vs. week 3	0	1, 52	0.99	0	0	1, 39	1	0
Week 3 vs. week 6	5.73	1, 52	0.02*	0.1	6.49	1, 39	0.02*	0.14
Week 6 vs. week 12	0.02	1, 52	0.89	0	0.01	1, 39	0.92	0
YMRS								
Baseline vs. week 3	0.32	1, 52	0.57	0.01	0	1, 39	0.96	0
Week 3 vs. week 6	1.09	1, 52	0.3	0.02	0.16	1, 39	0.7	0
Week 6 vs. week 12	6.41	1, 52	0.01*	0.11	6.56	1, 39	0.01*	0.14

ITT intention-to-treat, *PP* per-protocol, *MADRS* Montgomery–Åsberg Depression Rating Scale, *HAMA* Hamilton Anxiety Rating Scale, *YMRS* Young Mania Rating Scale

*p < 0.05

[a] Sphericity not assumed, Greenhouse–Geisser test used instead

design, which may not have the fidelity of allocation concealment of a double-blind design. Fourthly, although patients were explicitly advised to maintain their psychotropic regime throughout the rTMS trial, record of drug adherence required self-report and some patients may still have reduced medication dosage after experiencing antidepressant effects from rTMS, as various factors, including subjective recovery or improvement has been reported as reasons for treatment non-adherence (Arvilommi et al. 2014; Montes et al. 2013). Lastly, unblinding at week 3 may have influenced subsequent adjustments to psychotropic regimes with impact on mood change. Although we lack data to substantiate this speculation, it is plausible that more subjects from the sham group may have begun antidepressant drug after unblinding, which would be consistent with the sham group's more sustained improvements at week 6–12 in antidepressant moderation analysis.

Conclusions

R-DLPFC-LF rTMS was found to have a good safety and tolerability profile, but did not significantly reduce depressive symptoms in antidepressant-nonresponding bipolar depressed patients in general at the current dosage, although our preliminary findings suggested potential effectiveness in patients with low anxiety. Further sufficiently powered studies will be needed to examine if R-DLPFC-LF rTMS at a higher dosage is effective for bipolar depression, especially with low anxiety, where it may then become a viable alternative to conventional L-DLPFC-HF rTMS given the shorter treatment time and reduced discomfort.

Abbreviations

BD: Bipolar depression; R-DLPFC-LF: Right-DLPFC low frequency; L-DLPFC-HF: Left-DLPFC high frequency; MADRS: Montgomery–Asberg Depression Rating Scale; YMRS: Young Mania Rating Scale; HAMA: Hamilton Anxiety Rating Scale; CGI: Clinical Global Impression Scale; PP: Per-protocol; ITT: Intention-to-treat; RDLPFC: Right dorsolateral prefrontal cortex; SCID: Structured Clinical Interview for DSM Mental Disorders.

Supplementary Information

Additional file 1: Figure S1. Subject flowchart per protocol.

Additional file 2: Figure S2. Subject flowchart per intention-to-treat.

Acknowledgements

The authors would like to thank the participants for their generous support to this study.

Authors' contributions

AM: conceptualization, funding acquisition, investigation, methodology, writing—original draft; writing—review and editing. NSFW: writing—review and editing. OL: project administration, investigation, formal analysis, writing—original draft, approval of final article. WC: validation; visualization, writing—review and editing. YH: data curation, project administration. IC: data curation, software. SC: resources, writing—review and editing. LL: resources, writing—review and editing. SL: resources, supervision, writing—review and editing. All authors read and approved the final manuscript.

Author details

[1]Department of Psychiatry, The Chinese University of Hong Kong, G/F Multicentre, Tai Po Hospital, Tai Po, Hong Kong, SAR, China. [2]Department of Psychiatry, Brain Center Rudolf Magnus, University Medical Center Utrecht, Utrecht, The Netherlands. [3]Department of Imaging and Interventional Radiology, The Chinese University of Hong Kong, Hong Kong, SAR, China.

References

Akiskal HS, Bourgeois ML, Angst J, Post R, Moller H, Hirschfeld R. Re-evaluating the prevalence of and diagnostic composition within the broad clinical spectrum of bipolar disorders. J Affect Disord. 2000;59(Suppl 1):S5–30.

Arvilommi P, Suominen K, Mantere O, Leppamaki S, Valtonen H, Isometsa E. Predictors of adherence to psychopharmacological and psychosocial treatment in bipolar I or II disorders—an 18-month prospective study. J Affect Disord. 2014;155:110–7.

Brakemeier EL, Luborzewski A, Danker-Hopfe H, Kathmann N, Bajbouj M. Positive predictors for antidepressive response to prefrontal repetitive transcranial magnetic stimulation (rTMS). J Psychiatr Res. 2007;41(5):395–403.

Brown WA. Treatment response in melancholia. Acta Psychiatr Scand Suppl. 2007;115(433):125–9.

Cao X, Deng C, Su X, Guo Y. Response and remission rates following high-frequency vs. low-frequency repetitive transcranial magnetic stimulation (rTMS) over right DLPFC for treating major depressive disorder (MDD): a meta-analysis of randomized, double-blind trials. Front Psychiatry. 2018;9:413.

Chen J, Zhou C, Wu B, Wang Y, Li Q, Wei Y, et al. Left versus right repetitive transcranial magnetic stimulation in treating major depression: a meta-analysis of randomised controlled trials. Psychiatry Res. 2013;210(3):1260–4.

De Fruyt J, Deschepper E, Audenaert K, Constant E, Floris M, Pitchot W, et al. Second generation antipsychotics in the treatment of bipolar depression: a systematic review and meta-analysis. J Psychopharmacol. 2012;26(5):603–17.

Dell'osso B, Altamura AC. Augmentative transcranial magnetic stimulation (TMS) combined with brain navigation in drug-resistant rapid cycling bipolar depression: a case report of acute and maintenance efficacy. World J Biol Psychiatry. 2009;10(42):673–6.

Dell'Osso B, Mundo E, D'Urso N, Pozzoli S, Buoli M, Ciabatti M, et al. Augmentative repetitive navigated transcranial magnetic stimulation (rTMS) in drug-resistant bipolar depression. Bipolar Disord. 2009;11(1):76–81.

Dell'Osso B, Oldani L, Camuri G, Dobrea C, Cremaschi L, Benatti B, et al. Augmentative repetitive transcranial magnetic stimulation (rTMS) in the acute treatment of poor responder depressed patients: a comparison study between high and low frequency stimulation. Eur Psychiatry. 2015;30(2):271–6.

Eche J, Mondino M, Haesebaert F, Saoud M, Poulet E, Brunelin J. Low- vs high-frequency repetitive transcranial magnetic stimulation as an add-on treatment for refractory depression. Front Psychiatry. 2012;3:13.

Fava M, Rush AJ, Alpert J. Difference in treatment outcome in outpatients with anxious versus nonanxious depres sion: a STAR*D report. Am J Psychiatry. 2008;165:342–51.

Fela-Thomas AL, Olotu OS, Esan O. Risk of manic switch with antidepressants use in patients with bipolar disorder in a Nigerian neuropsychiatric hospital. S Afr J Psychiatr. 2018;24(1):1–6.

Fitzgerald PB, Huntsman S, Gunewardene R, Kulkarni J, Daskalakis ZJ. A randomized trial of low-frequency right-prefrontal-cortex transcranial magnetic stimulation as augmentation in treatment-resistant major depression. Int J Neuropsychopharmacol. 2006;9(6):655–66.

Fitzgerald PB, Hoy KE, Anderson RJ, Daskalakis ZJ. A study of the pattern of response to rTMS treatment in depression. Depress Anxiety. 2016;33(8):746–53.

Gaudiano BA, Dalrymple KL, Zimmerman M. Prevalence and clinical characteristics of psychotic versus nonpsychotic major depression in a general psychiatric outpatient clinic. Depress Anxiety. 2009;26(1):54–64.

Geddes JR, Calabrese JR, Goodwin GM. Lamotrigine for treatment of bipolar depression: independent meta-analysis and meta-regression of individual patient data from five randomised trials. Br J Psychiatry. 2009;194(1):4–9.

Goldstein TR, Ha W, Axelson DA, Goldstein BI, Liao F, Gill MK, et al. Predictors of prospectively examined suicide attempts among youth with bipolar disorder. Arch Gen Psychiatry. 2012;69(11):1113–22.

Guy W. ECDEU assessment manual for psychopharmacology. Rockville: U.S. Dept. of Health, Education, and Welfare, Public Health Service, Alcohol, Drug Abuse, and Mental Health Administration, National Institute of Mental Health, Psychopharmacology Research Branch, Division of Extramural Research Programs; 1976.

Hamilton M. The assessment of anxiety states by rating. Br J Med Psychol. 1958;32:50–5.

Harel EV, Zangen A, Roth Y, Reti I, Braw Y, Levkovitz Y. H-coil repetitive transcranial magnetic stimulation for the treatment of bipolar depression: an add-on, safety and feasibility study. World J Biol Psychiatry. 2011;12(2):119–26.

Hu SH, Lai JB, Xu DR, Qi HL, Peterson BS, Bao AM, et al. Efficacy of repetitive transcranial magnetic stimulation with quetiapine in treating bipolar II depression: a randomized, double-blinded, control study. Sci Rep. 2016;6:30537.

Judd LL, Akiskal HS, Schettler PJ, Endicott J, Leon AC, Solomon DA, et al. Psychosocial disability in the course of bipolar I and II disorders: a prospective, comparative, longitudinal study. Arch Gen Psychiatry. 2005;62(12):1322–30.

Kaur M, Michael JA, Fitzgibbon BM, Hoy KE, Fitzgerald PB. Low-frequency rTMS is better tolerated than high-frequency rTMS in healthy people: empirical evidence from a single session study. J Psychiatr Res. 2019;113:79–82.

Kazemi R, Rostami R, Khomami S, Horacek J, Brunovsky M, Novak T, et al. Electrophysiological correlates of bilateral and unilateral repetitive transcranial magnetic stimulation in patients with bipolar depression. Psychiatry Res. 2016;240:364–75.

Kessler RC, Demler O, Frank RG, Olfson M, Pincus HA, Walters EE, et al. Prevalence and treatment of mental disorders, 1990 to 2003. N Engl J Med. 2005;352(24):2515–23.

Melhem NM, Porta G, Oquendo MA, Zelazny J, Keilp JG, Iyengar S, et al. Severity and variability of depression symptoms predicting suicide attempt in high-risk individuals. JAMA Psychiatry. 2019;76(6):603–13.

Merikangas KR, Akiskal HS, Angst J, Greenberg PE, Hirschfeld RM, Petukhova M, et al. Lifetime and 12-month prevalence of bipolar spectrum disorder in the national comorbidity survey replication. Arch Gen Psychiatry. 2007;64(5):543–52.

Montes JM, Maurino J, de Dios C, Medina E. Suboptimal treatment adherence in bipolar disorder: impact on clinical outcomes and functioning. Patient Prefer Adherence. 2013;7:89–94.

Montgomery SA, Asberg M. A new depression scale designed to be sensitive to change. Br J Psychiatry. 1979;134:382–9.

Neuronetics I. FDA Grants NeuroStar® advanced therapy system breakthrough device designation to treat bipolar depression ir.neuronetics.com. 2020. http://ir.neuronetics.com/news-releases/news-release-details/fda-grants-neurostarr-advanced-therapy-system-breakthrough/.

Pallanti S, Grassi G, Antonini S, Quercioli L, Salvadori E, Hollander E. rTMS in resistant mixed states: an exploratory study. J Affect Disord. 2014;157:66–71.

Poleszczyk A, Rakowicz M, Parnowski T, Antczak J, Swiecicki L. Are there clinical and neurophysiologic predictive factors for a positive response to HF-rTMS in patients with treatment-resistant depression? Psychiatry Res. 2018;264:175–81.

Richieri R, Guedj E, Michel P, Loundou A, Auquier P, Lancon C, et al. Maintenance transcranial magnetic stimulation reduces depression relapse: a propensity-adjusted analysis. J Affect Disord. 2013;151(1):129–35.

Saghafi R, Brown C, Butters MA, Cyranowski J, Dew MA, Frank E, et al. Predicting 6-week treatment response to escitalopram pharmacotherapy in late-life major depressive disorder. Int J Geriatr Psychiatry. 2007;22(11):1141–6.

Sidor MM, Macqueen GM. Antidepressants for the acute treatment of bipolar depression: a systematic review and meta-analysis. J Clin Psychiatry. 2011;72(2):156–67.

So E, Kam I, Leung CM, Chung D, Liu Z, Fong S. The Chinese–bilingual SCID-I/P project: stage 1—reliability for mood disorders and schizophrenia. Hong Kong J Psychiatry. 2003;13:7–18.

Sun W, Mao W, Meng X, Wang D, Qiao L, Tao W, et al. Low-frequency repetitive transcranial magnetic stimulation for the treatment of refractory partial epilepsy: a controlled clinical study. Epilepsia. 2012;53(10):1782–9.

Theodore WH, Hunter K, Chen R, Vega-Bermudez F, Boroojerdi B, Reeves-Tyer P, et al. Transcranial magnetic stimulation for the treatment of seizures: a controlled study. Neurology. 2002;59(4):560–2.

Trevizol AP, Downar J, Vila-Rodriguez F, Thorpe KE, Daskalakis ZJ, Blumberger DM. Predictors of remission after repetitive transcranial magnetic stimulation for the treatment of major depressive disorder: an analysis from the randomised non-inferiority THREE-D trial. EClinicalMedicine. 2020;22:100349.

Viktorin A, Lichtenstein P, Thase ME, Larsson H, Lundholm C, Magnusson PK, et al. The risk of switch to mania in patients with bipolar disorder during treatment with an antidepressant alone and in combination with a mood stabilizer. Am J Psychiatry. 2014;171(10):1067–73.

Yatham LN, Kennedy SH, Parikh SV, Schaffer A, Beaulieu S, Alda M, et al. Canadian network for mood and anxiety treatments (CANMAT) and international society for bipolar disorders (ISBD) collaborative update of CANMAT guidelines for the management of patients with bipolar disorder: update 2013. Bipolar Disord. 2013;15(1):1–44.

Young RC, Biggs JT, Ziegler VE, Meyer DA. A rating scale for mania: reliability, validity and sensitivity. Br J Psychiatry. 1978;133:429–35.

Zarate CA Jr, Tohen M, Land M, Cavanagh S. Functional impairment and cognition in bipolar disorder. Psychiatry Q. 2000;71(4):309–29.

14

Psychological therapy for mood instability within bipolar spectrum disorder: a randomised, controlled feasibility trial of a dialectical behaviour therapy-informed approach (the ThrIVe-B programme)

Kim Wright*, Alyson L. Dodd, Fiona C. Warren, Antonieta Medina-Lara, Barnaby Dunn, Julie Harvey, Mahmood Javaid, Steven H. Jones, Christabel Owens, Rod S. Taylor, Deborah Duncan, Alexandra Newbold, Shelley Norman, Faith Warner and Thomas R. Lynch

Abstract

Background: A subgroup of those with bipolar spectrum disorders experience ongoing mood fluctuations outside of full episodes. We conducted a randomised, controlled feasibility study of a Dialectical Behavioural Therapy-informed approach for bipolar mood fluctuations (Therapy for Inter-episode mood Variability in Bipolar [ThrIVe-B]). Our study aimed to examine the feasibility and acceptability of a future definitive trial evaluating the clinical and cost effectiveness of the ThrIVe-B programme. Participants were required to meet diagnostic criteria for a bipolar spectrum disorder and report frequent mood swings outside of acute episodes. They were randomised to treatment as usual (control arm) or the ThrIVe-B intervention plus treatment as usual (intervention arm). Follow-up points were at 3, 6, 9 and 15 months after baseline, with 9 months as the primary end point. To evaluate feasibility and acceptability we examined recruitment and retention rates, completion rates for study measures, adverse events and feedback from participants on their experience of study participation and therapy.

Results: Of the target 48 participants, 43 were recruited (22 in the intervention arm; 21 in the control arm), with a recruitment rate of 3.9 participants per month. At 9 months 74% of participants engaged in research follow-up assessment, exceeding the pre-specified criterion of 60%. There were no serious concerns about the safety of the research procedures or the intervention. On one of the four candidate primary outcome measures, the 95% CI for the between-group mean difference score excluded the null effect and included the minimal clinically important difference, favouring the intervention arm, whilst on no measure was there evidence of deterioration in the intervention arm relative to the control arm. Attendance of the intervention (50% attending at least half of the mandatory sessions) was below the pre-specified continuation criterion of 60%, and qualitative feedback from participants indicated areas that may have hampered or facilitated engagement.

Conclusions: It is broadly feasible to conduct a trial of this design within the population of people with frequent bipolar mood swings. Changes should be made to the therapy to increase uptake, such as simplifying content and considering individual rather than group delivery.

*Correspondence: K.A.Wright@ex.ac.uk
Washington Singer Labs., University of Exeter Department of Psychology, Perry Road, Exeter EX4 4QG, UK

Trial registration ISRCTN: ISRCTN54234300. Registered 14th July 2017, http://www.isrctn.com/ISRCTN54234300

Keywords: Bipolar disorder, Dialectical behavior therapy

Background

Within bipolar spectrum disorders, ongoing instability of mood (henceforth referred to as bipolar mood instability [BPMI]) is characteristic of Cyclothymic Disorder, yet can also be experienced by individuals with Bipolar disorder I or II outside of acute episodes of mania or depression (Bonsall et al. 2012). BPMI may be an important target for intervention in its own right: as well as Cyclothymic Disorder being a risk factor for future episodes of mania and depression (Akiskal et al. 1977), BPMI between episodes is associated with increased psychiatric comorbidity, reduced psychosocial functioning and lower self-reported quality of life (Faurholt-Jepsen et al. 2019; Henry et al. 2008; Gershon and Eidelman 2015; Strejilevich et al. 2013).

Trials of medication for Bipolar disorders rarely target BPMI specifically and consequently there is no generally accepted pharmacological treatment strategy for this aspect of the condition. Similarly, trials of psychological therapies for Bipolar disorders have tended to focus upon treating acute depression or reducing risk of relapse rather than reducing mood instability. Whilst a small number of studies have tested psychological interventions for Cyclothymic Disorder or given consideration to BPMI within Bipolar disorder (Fava et al. 2011; Hales et al. 2018; Totterdell and Kellett 2008; Totterdell et al. 2012), none of these have tested an intervention specifically developed for BPMI across the Bipolar Spectrum. Here we report a randomised controlled feasibility study of such an approach.

Our approach is informed by Dialectical Behaviour Therapy (Linehan 1993) which was originally developed for another patient group with ongoing instability of mood, those with a diagnosis of Emotional Unstable Personality Disorder (EUPD). DBT teaches skills both in acceptance of situations and emotional responses, and in selection of adaptive behavioural responses to emotional and situational triggers, and has been found to be effective in EUPD (Cristea et al. 2017). Whilst versions of DBT have been explored within those with Bipolar disorder in an open trial and two pilot randomised controlled trials (Goldstein et al. 2007, 2015; Dijk et al. 2013) none of these have specifically targeted those experiencing BPMI.

To address this gap we developed the ThrIVe-B programme (Therapy for Inter-episode mood Variability in Bipolar) as a bespoke approach for those with BPMI. In this approach participants are invited to reflect upon their behavioural response to extreme mood and activation states day-to-day, modifying this where necessary, congruent with evidence that unhelpful behavioural response to mood is associated with bipolar symptom exacerbation (Lam et al. 2001; Palmier-Claus et al. 2016). In DBT this is achieved by building mindful awareness skills and through giving participants a framework through which to appraise their emotional responses and to develop alternative ways of relating to and managing these. In ThrIVe-B we further developed this process with respect to hypomanic and depressive feelings. ThrIVe-B also attended to triggers of mood dysregulation: circadian rhythm disruption has been found to precede the onset of Bipolar episodes (Takaesu 2018) whilst social support appears to be associated with a more favourable course of symptoms (Cohen et al. 2004; Johnson et al. 1999) therefore we utilised elements of DBT that promote stable routine and interpersonal problem-solving and communication, and developed elements around mobilising social support.

Initial evaluation of the ThrIVe-B programme in an uncontrolled feasibility study (N=12) (Wright et al. 2020) found it to be acceptable to recipients: 75% completed therapy. Consistent with potential for clinical benefit, reliable improvement in depression, anxiety and general mental health symptoms was observed in least half the participants, with very few instances of reliable deterioration on any measure. Participant feedback supported this, and congruent with the key putative mechanism of change, participants described gaining the ability to step back from intense feelings and make better choices. There were no trial-related serious adverse events or concerns about therapy safety.

To resolve uncertainties in the design and delivery of a future efficacy trial, the present study was a randomised, controlled feasibility study across two sites (Devon and Cumbria). Our objectives were to: (i) establish recruitment pathways and trial teams in two sites; (ii) establish the number of participants initially identified, approached, consented, randomised and completed; (iii) establish the acceptability and experience of the trial process to participants, including randomisation and completion of outcome measures; (iv) further assess the acceptability of the treatment via qualitative interviews and, based on input from trial participants and clinicians, to further refine and develop the treatment manual and the procedures for training, supervising and assessing the competence of trial therapists; (v) assess the performance of selected candidate primary outcome measures for a future definitive trial with respect to level of acceptability to participants and participant-perceived relevance and value; (vi) measure data completeness at follow-up, SD of the likely primary outcome measure, and describe the variability of the comparator condition, treatment as usual (TAU), across individuals and sites; (vii) pilot a measure of resource use and to assess the feasibility and acceptability of candidate health outcome measures for economic evaluations; and (viii) identify, measure and cost the resources used and needed to deliver the intervention.

We also aimed to evaluate whether the following continuation criteria were met prior to planning a future definitive trial: (i) trial participation does not lead to serious negative consequences (unexpected serious adverse reaction) for participants; (ii) any serious concerns about the acceptability and feasibility of the trial procedures can be rectified prior to a full trial; (iii) follow-up data at 9 months are available for at least 60% of participants; (iv) at least 60% of patients in the intervention group complete treatment (attend at least 50% of possible sessions).

Method

Trial design

We conducted a feasibility study with a two-arm, randomised, parallel, controlled trial design. Participants were randomised in a 1:1 ratio to TAU only (control arm) or TAU plus the ThrIVe-B programme (intervention arm). Outcome measures were administered at baseline and at 3, 6, 9 and 15 months after randomisation. The primary end point was predetermined to be at 9 months. The full trial protocol is reported elsewhere (Wright et al. 2018).

A panel of individuals with lived experience of mood disorders advised on study design and delivery throughout the trial.

Participants

Participants were required to be aged 18 years or older, with a diagnosis of BD (I, II, other specified BD) or Cyclothymic Disorder, according to the criteria in the Diagnostic and Statistical Manual of Mental Disorders, Fifth Edition (DSM-V) (American Psychiatric Association 2013), and to have a period of at least 2 days during which symptom criteria for hypomania/mania were met. They were required to have current BPMI, defined as either meeting DSM-V criteria 1 and 2 for Cyclothymic Disorder, or having a score of at least 1.3 [the mean for individuals with Bipolar disorder in previous research (Henry et al. 2008)] on the bipolar subscale of the short form of the Affective Lability Scale (ALS) (Oliver and Simons 2004). Participants had to be willing to engage in psychological therapy that focusses primarily on ongoing mood instability and its consequences, and be willing and able to attend scheduled group therapy sessions. Sufficient competency in English to be able to complete study measures without the need for translation was required, as was registration with a primary care physician in the study catchment area. Exclusion criteria included current substance dependence, other ongoing psychological therapy for BD at study entry, lack of capacity to consent to treatment or research participation, and acute mania or depression (DSM-V). Participants engaging in frequent, significant self-harming behaviour, at high risk of suicide, or posing a significant risk to other group members were not eligible. Initially patients receiving ongoing, co-ordinated care in secondary mental health services were excluded from participation because the ThriVe-B programme was aimed at those at the interface between primary and secondary care, however this criterion was removed at month 9 of the 11 month recruitment phase to facilitate recruitment.

Participants were recruited from two sites in the United Kingdom, Cumbria and Devon. Both are relatively rural however Cumbria has a population density less than half that of Devon's. Recruitment was via primary care services, secondary care mental health services and self-referral. Following an expression of interest, participants providing written agreement to be contacted by the study team were sent information about the study and invited to attend a baseline eligibility assessment interview. Those not referred from secondary care (and thus who had not recently participated in a specialist Psychiatric assessment) completed a telephone screening interview prior to the eligibility assessment to increase the likelihood that those invited for a time-consuming face-to-face assessment would be eligible. At the eligibility assessment written, informed consent was sought, eligibility criteria were checked and baseline measures completed.

Planned sample size

On the basis of our previous work (Wright et al. 2020) we estimated an attrition rate of 17% with respect to the 9 month primary end point. A sample of 48 would allow estimation of this level of attrition for a future definitive trial with a precision of $\pm$15% with 95% certainty. The 48 participants (24 per arm) would represent recruitment to three ThrIVe-B groups at full capacity (8 per group: 2 in Devon and 1 in Cumbria).

Intervention

The intervention (ThrIVe-B) was delivered in addition to TAU. The content of the ThrIVe-B programme is described in detail in the logic model in Additional file 1. In brief, modules covered Mindful Awareness,

Day to Day Mood Regulation. Tolerating Intense Moods, and Wise Relationships The programme consisted of 15 weekly group meetings and up to eight individual sessions of up to 45 min held either face-to-face or by telephone, according to participant preference for modality, number and duration. All participants were expected to attend the initial and final individual meeting. There was a group "booster" session 3 months after the final group meeting, and midway through the programme participants were offered a "supporters" session which friends or family could attend. To help generalisation of learning, participants were given a folder of written materials. In addition we used a custom-built smartphone application ('ThrIVe-B app') to prompt participants to use skills at times of extreme mood, between therapy sessions. The app asked participants to rate their mood from −10 to +10 each day between 0 and 10 times, with number of ratings per day determined by the user. Users specified 'high' and 'low' mood thresholds and when these were surpassed, users saw a feedback screen containing advisory messages they had pre-programmed either alone or with therapist support, which could contain techniques from the therapy programme (see Additional file 2). A version of this app, with reduced functionality, was also used to monitor mood stability over 7-day periods at baseline and at follow-up for all participants.

Therapy was delivered by four qualified mental health professionals with previous specialist training in cognitive behavioural therapy and related approaches (two therapists per group). A 5 day bespoke, face-to-face training programme was provided by the main author of the ThrIVe-B therapy protocol, which covered background information about Bipolar disorder, the therapeutic stance within DBT-informed approaches, therapy components, and skills in group facilitation. Weekly supervision occurred throughout therapy delivery. Before each group session participants completed the Beck Depression Inventory (Beck et al. 1961) and Altman Scale for Rating Mania (Altman et al. 1997).

Participants in the TAU arm received their usual NHS care, with no stipulation from the trial regarding the minimum constituents of this. In addition, in order that the two arms were broadly equivalent in time spent using the app between assessment points, those in the TAU arm were invited to use it for mood monitoring only (no additional therapeutic functionality) between months 3 and 9. As per the intervention arm, participants could set number of alerts per day from 0 to 10. Other than the experimental intervention no treatments were withheld.

Outcomes

Primary outcome measures. Numbers of patients identified, approached, consented, randomised and completed were used to assess feasibility, as was participant attrition from the trial and from treatment. Acceptability was assessed by questionnaires at baseline, 9 month follow-up and on ineligibility or withdrawal from the study. Items with quantitative ratings at 9 month follow-up were rated on a five point scale and asked about acceptability and satisfaction (anchored from "not at all" to "extremely") and likelihood of recommending the trial to eligible friends and family. To assess patient valuation of outcomes, at the 9-month follow-up point participants were asked to rank the four candidate outcome measures (see below) and a measure of anxiety symptoms, the Generalised Anxiety Disorder 7-item scale (GAD-7) (Spitzer et al. 2006) in order of priority, in terms of where they would most want to see change following psychological treatment. Participants were also asked to estimate the smallest change on each measure that would feel meaningful.

A subset of 14 participants from both sites took part in a semi-structured interview exploring their experiences of the research study and therapy in more detail. Referring clinicians were asked for their views of the therapy and research process using a brief survey form, and ThrIVe-B therapists took part in an interview about their experiences and views of the therapy, training and supervision.

Adherence to treatment was measured in terms of number of therapy sessions attended; because some individual sessions were optional, "possible sessions" (continuation rule 4) was defined as all 15 group sessions, booster session and initial and final individual sessions (18 sessions in total).

The ThrIVe-B app was used to gather data on momentary mood in order to assess mood stability. All participants were invited to use the app for 1 week at baseline and at 9-month follow-up, to give comparable 1 week periods of mood stability data that did not overlap with periods of therapeutic app use. Mood stability measured by the ThrIVe-B app is a potential secondary outcome in a definitive trial, therefore we tested the feasibility and acceptability of gathering these data, as indicated by completion rates and participant feedback.

Secondary outcome measures. The following were candidate primary outcome measures for a future definitive trial and were completed at baseline and all follow-up points: the Patient Health Questionnaire 9-item scale (PHQ-9) (Spitzer et al. 1999) which measures depressive symptoms; the short-form Affective Lability Scale; the Bipolar Recovery Questionnaire (BRQ) (Jones et al. 2013); and the brief Quality of Life in Bipolar disorder scale (QoL-BD) (Michalak et al. 2010). Participants also completed the GAD-7. At baseline, 9 and 15 months, the Bech Mania Rating Scale (BMRS) (Bech et al. 1978), the

Hamilton Depression Rating Scale (HDRS) (Hamilton 1986) (both observer-rated), and the Brief Adherence Rating Scale for medication adherence (BARS) (Byerly et al. 2008) were completed, as was relevant sections of the Structured Clinical Interview for DSM-V (First et al. 2014). This was used both to assess eligibility criteria, and to identify affective episodes during the follow-up period.

To assess feasibility of health outcome measures for a future cost-effectiveness analysis was assessed with two measures: the EuroQoL 5-dimension 3-level (EQ-5D-3L) (Oppe and Devlin 2007),[1] and the 36-item Short Form Health Survey (SF-36) (Garratt et al. 1993), these were administered at baseline and follow-up points. In addition, participants were asked to complete a resource use questionnaire (last 6 months or since last assessment point) for assessing the feasibility of collecting accurate health and social service use. Finally information on resource use and costs of delivering the ThrIVE-B programme were also collected.

Quantitative process measurement

Measurement of putative mechanisms of change was included in order to inform measurement in a definitive trial. These were completed at baseline and all follow-up points. We included measures of impulsive behavioural response to high and low mood (Positive and Negative Urgency, Premeditation, Perseverance, Sensation-Seeking impulsive behaviour scales [UPPS-P] (Cyders et al. 2007); Behavioral Activation in Depression Scale [BADS] (Kanter et al. 2007)) as this is a key process that ThrIVe-B aims to disrupt. In DBT this is achieved in part by building mindful awareness skills, hence we measured this using the Kentucky Inventory of Mindfulness Skills (KIMS) (Baer et al. 2004). We assessed social rhythm stability using the adapted Social Rhythm Metric (SRM) (Monk et al. 1990) and emotional problem solving using the Means-Ends Problem Solving task (MEPS: baseline, 9 and 15 months only) (Kehrer and Linehan 1996).

The schedule for administration of study measures is shown in Additional file 3.

Procedure

Prior to conducting the trial ethical approval was obtained from the National Research Ethics Service (Ref: 219816) and local departmental research ethics committees. Assessments were face to face, by telephone, by post or online, dependent upon participant preference. In-person contact was required at baseline and at months 9 and 15 in order to complete the interview-based measures. At 9 months the questionnaire on experiences of the study was completed and a subset of participants completed the semi-structured interview.

Randomisation, concealment of allocation, and blinding

Participants were randomised on a 1:1 ratio, with minimisation by trial site and medication status (any medication for Bipolar disorder prescribed: yes/no). To ensure concealment, eligible participants were randomised via a validated password website hosted by Exeter Clinical Trials Unit. The first ten participants were allocated using simple randomisation; the remainder were allocated using the minimisation procedure, maintaining a stochastic element to the algorithm to allow concealment. Participants were randomised prior to the start of each therapy group, and informed by an unblinded researcher.

Researchers conducting follow-up assessments were blind to allocation and participants were reminded of this at each follow-up contact. All unblindings were recorded and where possible, researchers who remained blinded to that participant's status conducted future follow-up assessments. All statistical analyses were performed by a statistician using groups indicated by an anonymised code.

Statistical and economic methods

The primary analyses were performed after 9-month follow-up. Further analyses were performed after the final 15-month follow-up. No interim analyses were conducted. All analyses were on an intention-to-treat basis; included outcomes were reported according to randomised allocation, regardless of the treatment actually received. No attempts to address missing data, such as multiple imputation, were made. The economic analysis took the NHS and social care perspective.

At 9-month follow-up only, an inferential analysis was performed for continuous outcomes only, reporting the relevant 95% CI for the between-group mean difference (intervention minus TAU), but no p value. Inferential analyses included the randomisation covariates of site and baseline medication status.

Qualitative analysis

Qualitative interviews and written responses on the feedback questionnaires were analysed using a framework approach (Ritchie and Spencer 2002). A preliminary set of a priori themes was drawn up, based on interview/questionnaire questions (e.g. expectations of therapy; most helpful aspects; unhelpful aspects). Data were entered onto a spreadsheet, creating a matrix of rows (participants) and columns (themes) and populating it with summarised responses. During the process,

[1] The National Institute of Health and Clinical Excellence preferred health-related quality of life measure in adults for economic evaluations is EQ-5D. This study used the 3-level instead of the 5-level version stated in the original protocol.

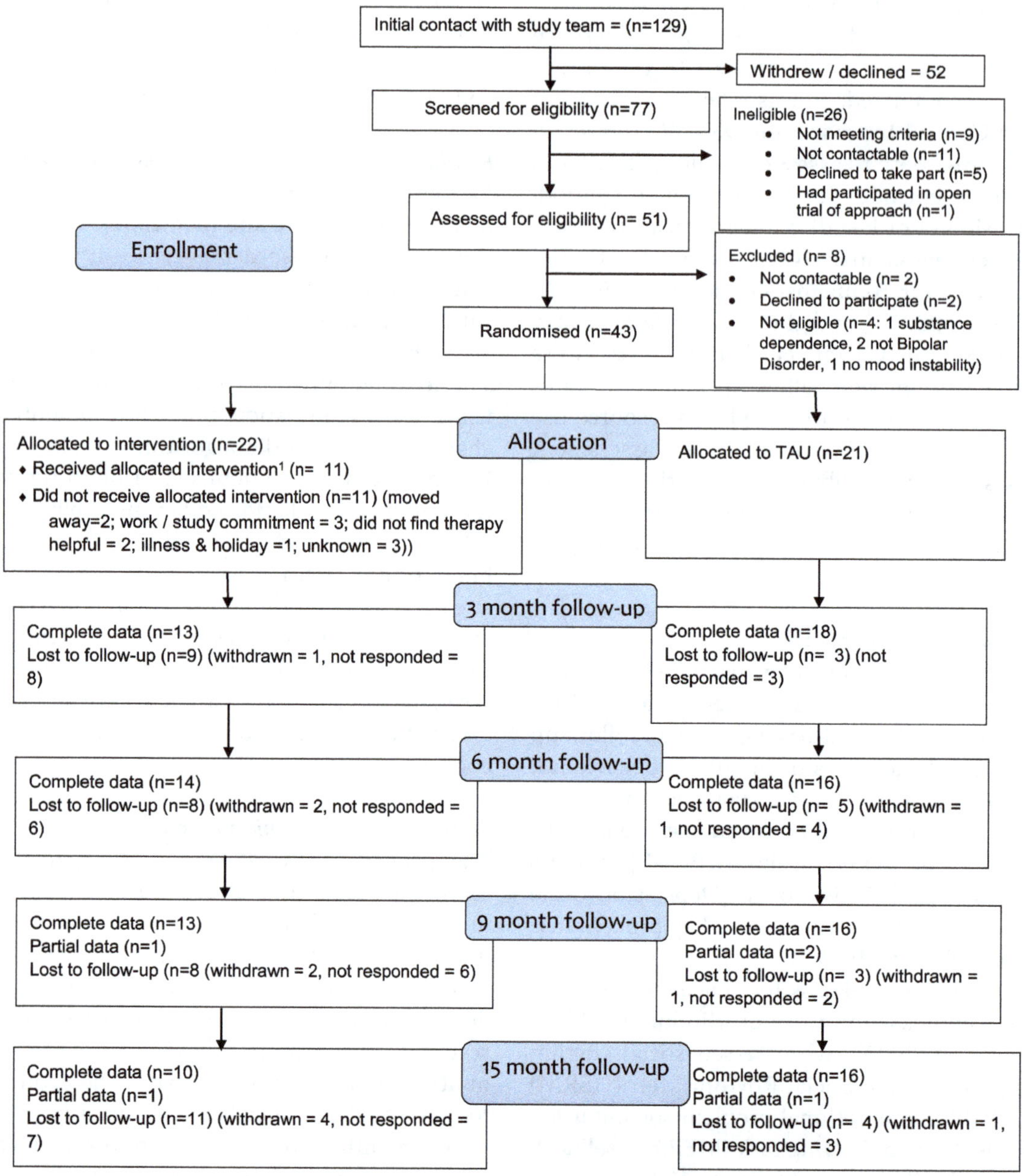

Note. [1]did not receive the allocated intervention = did not attend at least 50% of mandatory therapy sessions.

Fig. 1 CONSORT diagram of trial recruitment and retention

higher-order themes and sub-themes were inductively generated. These were then tabulated, with exemplary quotes and analytic notes, and visually mapped to explore relationships between them.

Results

Feasibility outcomes

Recruitment and participant flow

Recruitment took place over an 11 month period between August 2017 and July 2018, with follow-up ending in October 2019 after the final piece of data had been collected.

Recruitment and retention outcomes are shown in Fig. 1. Of 129 individuals who had initial contact with the research team, 77 (60%) were contactable for and completed the screening telephone call. Following this, 9 did not meet criteria, 11 were not contactable afterwards, 5 declined to participate and 1 had already received a previous version of the approach. A total of 51 potential participants were assessed for eligibility. Following this, four were not eligible, two were not contactable and two declined to participate. Of the 43 people randomised 22 were allocated to the intervention arm and 21 to the TAU arm. Recruitment was above target at one site (Devon: 32 planned, 34 actual) and below at the other (Cumbria: 16 planned, 9 actual), resulting in an overall number slightly below our original target (43/48).

The overall randomisation rate for the study was 3.9 participants per month. Within the two sites, this was 3.8 per month in Devon (34 participants over 9 months) and 1.3 per month in Cumbria (nine participants over 7 months).

Of those randomised 33 (77%) were informed about the study by their GP, 5 (12%) through contact with local mental health services, 4 (9%) through media and social media campaigns and 1 (2%) unknown.

Of those randomised to the intervention arm, 8 were allocated to the first Devon group, 9 to the second, and 5 to the group in Cumbria.

Table 1 Demographic and clinical characteristics of trial participants

	ThrIVe-B (n = 22)	Treatment as usual (n = 21)	Total (N = 43)
Gender; n (%)			
Female	14 (64)	9 (43)	23 (53)
Male	8 (36)	12 (57)	20 (47)
Age in years			
Mean (SD)	43.6 (13.0)	49.3 (14.5)	46.4 (13.9)
Median [min, max]	43 [20, 68]	51 [24, 75]	44 [20, 75]
Ethnic group; n (%)			
White	22 (100)	20 (95)	42 (98)
Asian	0 (0)	1 (5)	1 (2)
Prescribed medication for			
Bipolar disorder; n (%)	19 (86)	19 (90)	38 (88)
Mood stabiliser	14 (63)	12 (57)	26 (61)
Antipsychotic	10 (46)	14 (67)	24 (56)
Antidepressant	7 (32)	8 (38)	15 (35)
Site; n (%)			
Devon	17 (77)	17 (81)	34 (79)
Cumbria	5 (23)	4 (19)	9 (21)
In ongoing secondary care; n (%)			
Yes	2 (9)	4 (19)	6 (14)
No	20 (91)	17 (81)	37 (86)
Age of depression onset[a]; mean (SD), n; median [min, max]	19.4 (12.6), 19 16 [6, 58]	18.7 (8.4), 20 18 [6, 44]	19.1 (10.5), 39 18 [6, 58]
Age of mania onset; mean (SD), n; median [min, max]	21.1 (7.9), 15 20 [10, 35]	16.5 (5.7), 17 18 [6, 25]	18.7 (7.1), 32 18 [6, 35]
Bipolar I disorder; n (%)	19 (86)	18 (86)	37 (86)
Bipolar II disorder; n (%)	3 (14)	3 (14)	6 (14)

[a] Minimum age set to 6 years

Baseline data

The demographic and clinical characteristics of the sample are given in Table 1. Of 43 participants, 23 (53%) were female, with a median age of 44 years (range 20 to 75 years). The majority of participants met research diagnostic criteria for Bipolar I disorder with the remainder meeting criteria for Bipolar II disorder. In terms of characterising the usual psychiatric care for our sample, of the 40 participants providing detailed information on this for the 6 months prior to study entry, 19 (48%) had contact with a Community Mental Health Team, 1 (3%) reported a psychiatric admission, 10 (25%) reported contact with crisis services and 18 (45%) reported contact with a therapist, counsellor or psychologist. The majority of the sample (38/43: 88%) were prescribed medication for Bipolar disorder at study entry, and most participants were seen in primary care only for their mental health care.

At study entry participants reported mean depression and anxiety levels in the moderate range, and low levels of current mania symptoms (Table 2). Mean quality of life (QoL.BD) and sense of personal recovery (BRQ) scores for the sample were below but within one SD of those reported in the literature for individuals with Bipolar disorder (Bech et al. 1978; Hamilton 1986).

Trial and therapy retention of participants

We distinguish between research follow-up attrition and therapy attrition, as it was possible for participants to complete therapy and then opt not to complete research follow-up assessments, and vice-versa.

At 9-month follow-up 74% of participants (14 in intervention arm and 18 in TAU arm; 24 [71%] in the Devon site and 8 [89%] in the Cumbria site) provided at least partial follow-up data; 11/43 (26%; 95% CI 14 to 41%) were lost to follow up. Five participants withdrew in the period between randomisation and final follow-up (four in the intervention arm; one in the TAU arm); none were withdrawn by the research team. Figure 1 shows the number of participants returning data at each follow-up point.

Of the 22 participants allocated to receive the intervention, 17 attended at least three sessions (in other words, attended beyond the first individual and first

Table 2 Scores on candidate outcome and process measures at baseline and follow-up

Outcome[b]	Baseline		3-month follow-up		6-month follow-up		9-month follow-up			15-month follow-up		SMC (Med, range)
	ThrIVe-B	TAU	ThrIVe-B	TAU	ThrIVe-B	TAU	ThrIVe-B	TAU	ThrIVe-B–TAU[c] (95% CI)	ThrIVe-B	TAU	
PHQ-9[a]	15.5 (6.6) n=21	12.9 (5.2) n=20	10.4 (5.4) n=12	11.4 (6.1) n=16	10.6 (5.6) n=14	12.3 (7.7) n=17	10.3 (6.5) n=12	9.8 (4.9) n=17	− 0.2 (− 4.6; 4.2)	10.7 (7.2) n=11	8.9 (5.5) n=17	2 (0–20) n=20
BRQ[a]	2036 (342) n=19	1923 (369) n=16	1969 (503) n=13	1988 (416) n=17	1951 (493) n=11	1927 (427) n=14	2124 (327) n=13	1886 (404) n=16	349 (107; 591)	2238 (483) n=9	1929 (350) n=16	447 (2–1903) n=19
QoL-BD[a]	33.2 (7.5) n=20	36.6 (6.8) n=20	34.2 (9.7) n=13	34.0 (7.9) n=17	34.1 (8.3) n=14	34.1 (9.6) n=17	35.1 (8.3) n=14	34.0 (10.7) n=17	2.4 (− 5.2; 9.9)	35.0 (10.7) n=10	34.5 (9.8) n=16	4 (0–38) n=20
ALS total[a]	37.3 (6.1) n=22	31.5 (13.1) n=21	23.8 (13.3) n=13	27.2 (11.7) n=15	24.9 (8.1) n=14	27.0 (12.0) n=17	26.0 (13.5) n=14	23.5 (12.2) n=17	− 1.6 (− 8.4; 5.3)	26.6 (15.2) n=10	21.6 (11.1) n=16	5 (0–37) n=21
ALS depression-elation subscale	17.5 (3.3) n=22	14.9 (6.7) n=21	10.2 (6.0) n=13	12.9 (5.7) n=15	10.8 (5.4) n=14	13.3 (5.8) n=17	12.8 (6.8) n=13	12.2 (5.5) n=17	− 1.5 (− 4.6; 1.6)	13.1 (7.1) n=10	11.1 (5.7) n=16	–
GAD-7	11.2 (4.7) n=19	10.4 (5.1) n=20	11.3(4.9) n=13	9.2 (5) n=17	11.5 (5.1) n=14	8.1 (4.6) n=17	9.3 (5.4) n=14	7.5 (5.9) n=17	1.4 (− 2.9; 5.6)	7.8 (4.5) n=10	8.7 (7.3) n=16	2 (0–11) n=20
HDRS	12.8 (8.1) n=22	6.6 (4.2) n=19	NR	NR	NR	NR	8.5 (4.8) n=13	9.5 (5.8) n=16	− 2.6 (− 7.6; 2.3)	8.2 (7.8) n=11	6.1 (3.0) n=17	–
Mean SRM	5.1 (2.9) n=17	4.6 (2.1) n=17	5.6 (0.8) n=11	5.5 (2.8) n=14	3.9 (2.0) n=10	3.6 (2.1) n=12	5.5 (1.9) n=11	4.9 (1.0) n=10	0.5 (− 1.5; 2.5)	5.0 (1.2) n=8	5.5 (0.8) n=13	–
BMRS	1.8 (2.4) n=21	1.7 (1.8) n=21	NR	NR	NR	NR	1.8 (3.2) n=13	1.9 (2.5) n=17	0.4 (− 1.6; 2.4)	1.8 (3.6) n=11	1.0 (1.8) n=17	–
BARS	2.8 (0.7) n=18	2.9 (0.5) n=19	NR	NR	NR	NR	3.8 (0.8) n=10	3.9 (0.4) n=15	0.0 (− 0.5; 0.5)	3.9 (0.2) n=8	3.8 (0.8) n=14	–
MEPS	3.1 (2.4) n=21	3.4 (2.2) n=19	NR	NR	NR	NR	3.7 (2.6) n=11	2.6 (1.2) n=16	1.6 (− 0.1; 3.3)	4.1 (2.6) n=11	2.6 (1.4) n=17	–
UPPS-P	160.9 (23.8) n=20	164.3 (25.0) n=19	158.6 (23.3) n=13	152.8 (23.0) n=17	156.8 (22.5) n=13	158.1 (21.9) n=17	149.5 (25.7) n=14	153.5 (21.8) n=17	− 6.7 (− 16.0; 2.6)	147.5 (28.7) n=10	154.3 (24.8) n=16	–
BADS	71.4 (23.4) n=20	78.5 (26.5) n=19	81.9 (24.5) n=13	73.5 (25.1) n=16	74.5 (33.1) n=12	72.9 (27.4) n=16	80.2 (21.5) n=14	75.1 (33.1) n=17	7.4 (− 13.3; 28.2)	85.6 (30.3) n=10	76.6 (30.6) n=16	–
KIMS total	114.5 (19.1) n=20	114.8 (21.3) n=20	117.2 (22.7) n=12	117.1 (24.7) n=17	116.2 (24.2) n=13	116.3 (21.9) n=16	125.4 (22.9) n=14	117.9 (25.9) n=16	13.1 (4.9; 21.3)	128.1 (21.3) n=10	115.4 (25.7) n=16	–

TAU = Treatment as usual arm; ThrIVe-B = intervention arm; PHQ-9 = Patient Health Questionnaire; BRQ = Bipolar Recovery Questionnaire; QoL-BD = brief Quality of Life in Bipolar Disorder Scale; GAD-7 = Generalised Anxiety Disorder; HDS = Hamilton Depression Rating Scale; SRM = Social Rhythm Metric; BMRS = Bech Mania Rating Scale; BARS = Brief Adherence Rating Scale; MEPS = Means-Ends Problem-Solving task; UPPS-P = Positive and Negative Urgency, Premeditation, Perseverance, Sensation-Seeking impulsive behaviour scales; BADS = Behavioural Activation in Depression Scale; KIMS = Kentucky Inventory of Mindfulness Scale; SMC = smallest meaningful change according to participant report

[a] Candidate primary outcome measure

[b] Outcomes are reported as mean (SD) unless otherwise stated

[c] Between group mean difference adjusted for site, baseline use of bipolar disorder medications and baseline score

group session).[2] Of the remaining five, two moved out of the area at the start of the intervention period, one had a competing commitment, one decided the intervention was not suited to them, and one did not attend for reasons unknown. Of the original 22 participants, 11 (50%) completed treatment, defined as attending at least half the 18 "mandatory" sessions. In terms of group attendance per session this ranged from 1 to 8.

Data completion for the smartphone app was low: at baseline, 16 participants provided data for at least 7 days (mean days 10.7, SD 15.5). Between months 3 and 9, 10 participants (6 intervention, 4 TAU) used the app at least once; at 9 months 3 TAU participants used the app at least once (no participants in the intervention group used the app at 9 months).

Acceptability

Quantitative acceptability data were available from 17 participants (8 in the therapy arm, 9 in the TAU arm) at 9 months. Of these, 16 found the research process at least moderately acceptable, with 14/17 at least moderately satisfied. Of the eight participants in the therapy arm who responded, seven rated therapy as "very" or "extremely" acceptable, and were at least "moderately" satisfied with therapy; one found therapy "slightly" acceptable/satisfactory.

Qualitative acceptability data were synthesised from four sources: acceptability surveys at 9 month follow-up (n = 17), qualitative interviews at 9 month follow-up (n = 14, 8 in therapy arm), surveys of participant experience after the baseline assessment (n = 19) and surveys of those who declined to take part or were not eligible (n = 9).

Making a contribution to society, learning more, and having the chance to access a new therapy emerged as key motives for participation. With regard to the experience of being involved, some participants found the volume of measures challenging; participants also highlighted how important it was that the measures felt relevant to them. Having a positive relationship with the research team was seen as important and was associated with a positive experience of interviews. Participants in the control group expressed some disappointment at not being offered therapy, whilst appreciating of the need for a control group in trials. Barriers to taking part in the study included cost of travel and childcare, and the level of commitment required. The smartphone app was used as part of both the research and therapy aspect of the study. Interruption of activities due to the alerts and direction of attention to negative feelings whilst making mood ratings were seen as downsides and several suggestions were made for improvement. Some participants reported technical issues with the app which may have contributed to low rates of data return.

Analysis of qualitative feedback on the therapy itself (n = 8 interviews, n = 8 surveys) was organised under three main themes: interpersonal aspects of therapy (subdivided into group process and therapist style); therapy content and delivery modes, and where/how the therapy helped. A summary of themes and sub-themes with exemplar quotes is given in Additional file 4.

Participants valued the closed nature of the group (that the same group of people met each session) and the mutual support it generated, although some struggled with particular group dynamics. Both the group and the therapist were instrumental in enabling participants to feel held and understood, which was key to a positive therapeutic experience. Therapist personality and style was seen as very important; authenticity was particularly valued and helped participants to feel that the material was coming from a person rather than from a textbook: "Yeah, [therapist] would give examples from her life which you felt were very genuine ... it felt very genuine, and I could get on with that" (201: 4,6). The amount of information delivered was seen to be high; some found this problematic and were worried about overload, but reported that it was helped by the use of multiple modes of delivery and tools for repeating and retaining information, such as handouts and booster sessions. Participants noted the importance of feeling that the material was relevant and tailored to them, and that it was offered at the right time of life. Participants noted several areas of benefit from the therapy, including greater understanding of the self, including re-evaluation of the self in a more positive or accepting way; greater understanding between the self and others; changes in behavioural responses to moods (even if the mood did not change), and broadening their range of activities.

Local clinicians (n = 8) saw DBT-informed therapy as appropriate for the client group, similarly the length of treatment and point of delivery in the care pathway. Clinicians queried whether a group based approach could be delivered and accessed successfully in the health service, as patients might initially be put off by the prospect of a group-based approach, and whether extreme mood states might interfere with group work. Feedback from therapists (n = 4) revealed overall high satisfaction with the techniques and materials, and with the potential to help this patient group, but there was also a sense of having a great deal of information to communicate to patients.

With regard to rankings of personal importance of the candidate primary outcome measures and GAD-7, the

[2] One participant in the TAU arm unintentionally received one session of ThrIVe-B content. They remained in the study.

Table 3 Health states utility value scores at baseline and follow-up

Outcome[a]	Baseline		3-month follow-up		6-month follow-up		9-month follow-up			15-month follow-up	
	ThrIVe-B	TAU	ThrIVe-B	TAU	ThrIVe-B	TAU	ThrIVe-B	TAU	ThrIVe-B–TAU[b] (95% CI)	ThrIVe-B	TAU
EQ-5D-3L	0.52 (0.30) [− 0.18, 1] n=20		0.65 (0.25) [0.08, 1] n=13	0.59 (0.36) [− 0.18, 0.85] n=14	0.51 (0.31) [− 0.02, 1] n=14	0.65 (0.33) [− 0.18, 1] n=16	0.63 (0.29) [0.08, 1] n=14	0.63 (0.35) [− 0.08, 1] n=17	0.15 (− 0.12, 0.41) n=28	0.64 (0.31) [0.08, 1] n=10	0.57 (0.35) [− 0.02, 1] n=16
SF-36	0.58 (0.15) [0.26, 0.85] n=20	0.64 (0.11) [0.46, 0.86] n=20	0.63 (0.12) [0.39, 0.81] n=13	0.63 (0.12) [0.40, 0.81] n=17	0.63 (0.10) [0.50, 0.86] n=14	0.64 (0.13) [0.40, 0.86] n=17	0.64 (0.14) [0.37, 0.88] n=13	0.60 (0.13) [0.32, 0.88] n=16	0.11 (0.01, 0.20) n=29	0.65 (0.12) [0.43, 0.85] n=10	0.62 (0.11) [0.45 0.88] n=15

[a] Outcomes are reported as mean (SD) [range] unless otherwise stated

[b] Adjusted for site, base use of bipolar disorder medication and baseline score

mean rankings were highest for the BRQ and ALS and lowest for the PHQ9. The GAD7 was ranked number 1 by the greatest proportion of participants (8/30: 27%), followed by the BRQ and ALS (both 7: 23%). The median smallest meaningful change values for each of the five measures are given in Table 2: for each measure, values given by participants were widely distributed. This may represent genuine lack of consensus but may also suggest that further refinement of the process of obtaining smallest meaningful change values is required in this population.

Study and therapy safety

Over the study period there were 48 adverse events (8 prior to randomisation, 19 in the therapy arm and 18 in the TAU arm post randomisation). These included 32 instances related to risk of suicide or self-harm (including enactment of study risk protocol following reports of suicidal ideation, and any reported acts of self-harm or towards ending one's life), six reports of distress during or after study procedures, eight physical health events requiring treatment and two psychiatric admissions. Five were serious adverse events, none of which were unexpected. It was judged that trial procedures (completion of questionnaires) may possibly have contributed to one of these events (low mood culminating in admission to hospital); the other serious adverse events were judged unrelated to the trial.

Candidate primary clinical outcomes

Mean scores on candidate primary and secondary outcome measures at follow-up are given in Table 2. At 9 months, the between group mean difference for BRQ was 349 (95% CI 107 to 591), with the intervention arm scoring higher (indicating greater personal recovery). The 95% CI included the minimum clinically important difference score of 200 found by the measure developers (Jones, personal communication), and excluded the null treatment effect. For the PHQ-9, there was minimal between group difference (− 0.2 (95% CI − 4.6 to 4.2)); the between-group differences for the ALS (− 1.6 (95% CI − 8.4 to 5.3) and QoL.BD (2.4 (95% CI − 5.2 to 9.9)) favoured the intervention arm but for all three measures the 95% CIs included the null treatment effect.

At 9-month follow-up, the between group mean difference for the Kentucky Inventory of Mindfulness Skills was 13.1 (95% CI 4.9 to 21.3), indicating higher self-reported mindfulness skills in the intervention group, with the 95% CI excluding the null treatment effect. The remaining nine secondary outcomes all yielded a 95% CI that included the null treatment effect.

Completion rates were similar between EQ-5D-3L and SF-36 measures, but lower for the resource use measure. Table 3 displays aggregated data for the health states utility values derived from the EQ-5D-3L and the SF-36. At 9-months, the arms differed significantly with respect to SF-36 utility scores (0.11; 95% CI 0.01–0.20), favouring in the intervention arm. At 9 months no significant difference between arms was observed in health care resource use (Additional files 5 and 6). The cost of providing the ThrIVE-B intervention per participant was £806.29 (Additional file 7).

Discussion

This randomised, controlled feasibility trial is the first to focus specifically upon people with ongoing mood instability within Bipolar Spectrum Disorders, and represents an important step in the development and testing of a novel psychological intervention for this population. In accordance with the study aims, we established recruitment pathways and trial teams in two sites and gathered information on patient recruitment and attrition rates. The overall rate of randomisation of 3.9 participants per month supports the feasibility of a larger trial, recruiting across a longer period and across multiple sites. This could be maximised by learning from experiences in the current trial, where one site recruited more successfully than the other. In particular, rural sites face greater challenges than do more urban ones when aiming to fill a therapy group with patients who have a relatively low-prevalence condition. In this study we initially sought to recruit patients from primary care only; whilst this was the case for the majority of participants, a small number were in secondary care. Setting out to work with a larger number of GP practices per site, selecting sites with a track record of primary care mental health recruitment and including a generally publicised self-referral option should be a priority for future studies in this population.

All four candidate primary outcome measures were seen as similarly valuable by participants and had similar rates of completion: on this basis any of these could be suitable as a primary outcome measure in future trials. Based on participant feedback about key areas of perceived change, it may be appropriate to select two primary outcome measures, one reflecting mood variability and another functioning or recovery. Rates of completion were similar across health economics measures.

Continuation criterion one (no unexpected serious adverse reactions to the therapy or research procedures) was met. Completion rate of measures met continuation criterion three (follow up data at 9 months are available from at least 60% of participants), with no evidence of greater attrition in the control arm. Nevertheless some participants in both arms reported finding the self-report measures onerous; this could potentially be improved by reducing the number of measures, using a more sophisticated online data collection platform, and making more use of participant payment. Whilst participants reported many positive aspects of the therapy, overall therapy attendance rates were numerically lower than the previous open trial (Wright et al. 2020), which may be the result of the imprecision inherent in estimates derived from small samples, but may also request variation in ease of recruitment in this multi-site trial. Nevertheless, as they were also below those specified a-priori in continuation rule four (at least 60% of patients complete at least 50% of sessions) improvement of the therapy content and delivery is required. Using a one-to-one rather than group-based method of delivery would increase accessibility to patients due to flexibility in scheduling and the potential to conduct sessions by telephone when patients are unable to attend in person. Feedback from participants suggested that whilst there were some benefits of group-based delivery, therapist factors played a significant role in successful engagement with the therapy content, thus supporting the feasibility of one-to-one delivery. Responding to feedback from participants about the high level of information provided and the importance of material being personally tailored, future iterations should focus on simplifying the therapy content and working out how to best tailor it to participants' situations and stage in life.

The study was not designed to test efficacy thus conclusions about the effects of the therapy cannot be drawn from the outcome data, however from the pattern of results there was no strong indication of a detrimental effect of therapy, and where there were significant differences between groups these favoured the therapy arm.

As an assessment of feasibility, a limitation of the current study is that qualitative feedback about the therapy and trial procedures was not gathered from all participants, with fewer than half the original sample completing the acceptability survey at 9 months. In particular, it is possible that those returning written feedback or participating in interviews may be those with a more positive view of the study.

Following modifications to the therapy protocol, further feasibility testing will be necessary to establish whether these result in increased therapy attendance, before progressing to a definitive trial of the approach.

In conclusion it is broadly feasible to conduct a trial of this design within the population of people with frequent bipolar mood swings; our findings suggest several areas of improvement that could be made to enhance recruitment and retention and to increase therapy accessibility and acceptability.

Supplementary Information

Additional file 1. Logic model for ThrIVe-B programme.

Additional file 2. Screenshots displaying elements of the ThrIVe-B App.

Additional file 3. Table displaying administration schedule for study measures.

Additional file 4. Table of themes relating to the intervention, arising from qualitative analysis of interview transcripts (n = 8) and feedback surveys (n = 8).

Additional file 5. Table displaying intervention costing.

Additional file 6. Table displaying unit cost of services.

Additional file 7. Table displaying cost of services by participant (average number of contacts).

Acknowledgements

The authors are grateful to the staff of the Research and Development Teams in Devon Partnership NHS Trust and Cumbria Partnership NHS Foundation Trust for their assistance with the management and conduct of the research, and secondary mental health community team staff in these Trusts for assistance with recruitment. We also thank the South West and North East and North Cumbria Clinical Research Networks for their help with recruitment. Exeter Clinical Trials Unit provided assistance with randomisation and database construction and management; Michaela Sibsey and Emily Gurr assisted with data entry and Michaela Sibsey and Faraz Mirza assisted with the analysis of qualitative data. The authors are grateful to Sally Parkin and Chris Lodge for their assistance with the conduct of the study and the dissemination of findings, and the study therapists Joanna Mackenzie, Anna Turner, Geraldine Ash and Karen Bell for delivering the intervention. We thank all the study participants for giving up their time to take part.

Authors' contributions

KW, TL, FCW, AML, AD, SJ, CO, RT, BD and JH contributed to the design of the study. Data were collected by AN, SN, DD and FW, and analysed by FCW and AML; analysis of qualitative data was overseen by CO and KW. The smartphone application was designed by KW and MJ and built by MJ. The manuscript was drafted by KW with contributions from the other authors where appropriate. All authors read and approved the final manuscript.

References

Akiskal HS, Djenderedjian AH, Rosenthal RH, Khani MK. Cyclothymic disorder: validating criteria for inclusion in the bipolar affective group. Am J Psychiatry. 1977;134:1227–33.

Altman EG, Hedeker D, Peterson JL, Davis JM. The Altman self-rating mania scale. Biol Psychiatry. 1997;42(10):948–55.

American Psychiatric Association. Diagnostic and statistical manual of mental disorders. 5th ed. Washington, DC: Publisher; 2013.

Baer RA, Smith GT, Allen KB. Assessment of mindfulness by self-report: The Kentucky Inventory of Mindfulness Skills. Assessment. 2004;11(3):191–206.

Bech P, Rafaelsen OJ, Kramp P, Bolwig TG. The mania rating scale: scale construction and inter-observer agreement. Neuropharmacology. 1978;17:430–1.

Beck AT, Ward CH, Mendelson M, Mock J, Erbaugh J. An inventory for measuring depression. Arch Gen Psychiatry. 1961;4:561–71.

Bonsall MB, Wallace-Hadrill SM, Geddes JR, Goodwin GM, Holmes EA. Nonlinear time-series approaches in characterizing mood stability and mood instability in bipolar disorder. Proc R Soc b Biol Sci. 2012;279(1730):916–24.

Byerly MJ, Nakonezny PA, Rush AJ. The Brief Adherence Rating Scale (BARS) validated against electronic monitoring in assessing the antipsychotic medication adherence of outpatients with schizophrenia and schizoaf-

fective disorder. Schizophr Res. 2008;100(1–3):60–9.
Cohen AN, Hammen C, Henry RM, Daley SE. Effects of stress and social support on recurrence in bipolar disorder. J Affect Disord. 2004;82(1):143–7.
Cristea IA, Gentili C, Cotet CD, Palomba D, Barbui C, Cuijpers P. Efficacy of psychotherapies for borderline personality disorder: a systematic review and meta-analysis. JAMA Psychiat. 2017;74(4):319–28.
Cyders MA, Smith GT, Spillane NS, Fischer S, Annus AM, Peterson C. Integration of impulsivity and positive mood to predict risky behavior: development and validation of a measure of positive urgency. Psychol Assess. 2007;19(1):107.
Faurholt-Jepsen M, Frost M, Busk J, Christensen EM, Bardram JE, Vinberg M, Kessing LV. Is smartphone-based mood instability associated with stress, quality of life, and functioning in bipolar disorder? Bipolar Disord. 2019;21(7):611–20.
Fava GA, Rafanelli C, Tomba E, Guidi J, Grandi S. The sequential combination of cognitive behavioral treatment and well-being therapy in cyclothymic disorder. Psychother Psychosom. 2011;80(3):136–43.
First MB, Williams JB, Karg RS, Spitzer RL. Structured clinical interview for DSM-5 disorders—research version (SCID-5-RV). Arlington: American Psychiatric Association; 2014.
Garratt AM, Ruta DA, Abdalla MI, Buckingham JK, Russell IT. The SF36 health survey questionnaire: an outcome measure suitable for routine use within the NHS? BMJ. 1993;306(6890):1440–4.
Gershon A, Eidelman P. Inter-episode affective intensity and instability: predictors of depression and functional impairment in bipolar disorder. J Behav Ther Exp Psychiatry. 2015;46:14–8.
Goldstein TR, Axelson DA, Birmaher B, Brent DA. Dialectical behavior therapy for adolescents with bipolar disorder: a 1-year open trial. J Am Acad Child Adolesc Psychiatry. 2007;46(7):820–30.
Goldstein TR, Fersch-Podrat RK, Rivera M, Axelson DA, Merranko J, Yu H, Brent DA, Birmaher B. Dialectical behavior therapy for adolescents with bipolar disorder: results from a pilot randomized trial. J Am Acad Child Adolesc Psychiatry. 2015;25(2):140–9.
Hales SA, Di Simplicio M, Iyadurai L, Blackwell SE, Young K, Fairburn CG, Geddes JR, Goodwin GM, Holmes EA. Imagery-focused cognitive therapy (ImCT) for mood instability and anxiety in a small sample of patients with bipolar disorder: a pilot clinical audit. Behav Cogn Psychother. 2018;46(6):706–25.
Hamilton M. The Hamilton rating scale for depression. In: Assessment of depression. Berlin: Springer; 1986. 143–52 p.
Henry C, Van den Bulke D, Bellivier F, Roy I, Swendsen J, M'Baïlara K, Siever LJ, Leboyer M. Affective lability and affect intensity as core dimensions of bipolar disorders during euthymic period. Psychiatry Res. 2008;159(1–2):1–6.
Johnson SL, Winett CA, Meyer B, Greenhouse WJ, Miller I. Social support and the course of bipolar disorder. J Abnorm Psychol. 1999;108(4):558.
Jones S, Mulligan LD, Higginson S, Dunn G, Morrison AP. The bipolar recovery questionnaire: psychometric properties of a quantitative measure of recovery experiences in bipolar disorder. J Affect Disord. 2013;147(1–3):34–43.
Kanter JW, Mulick PS, Busch AM, Berlin KS, Martell CR. The behavioral activation for depression scale (BADS): psychometric properties and factor structure. J Psychopathol Behav Assess. 2007;29(3):191.
Kehrer CA, Linehan MM. Interpersonal and emotional problem solving skills and parasuicide among women with borderline personality disorder. J Personal Disord. 1996;10(2):153–63.
Lam D, Wong G, Sham P. Prodromes, coping strategies and course of illness in bipolar affective disorder—a naturalistic study. Psychol Med. 2001;31(8):1397.
Linehan MM. Diagnosis and treatment of mental disorders. Cognitive-behavioral treatment of borderline personality disorder. New York: Guilford Press; 1993.
Michalak EE, Murray G, CREST. BD. Development of the QoL. BD: a disorder-specific scale to assess quality of life in bipolar disorder. Bipolar Disord. 2010;12(7):727–40.
Monk TK, Flaherty JF, Frank E, Hoskinson K, Kupfer DJ. The social rhythm metric: an instrument to quantify the daily rhythms of life. J Nerv Ment Dis. 1990;178:120–6.
Oliver MN, Simons JS. The affective lability scales: development of a short-form measure. Personal Individ Diff. 2004;37(6):1279–88.
Oppe M, Devlin NJ. EQ-5D value sets: inventory, comparative review and user guide. Berlin: Springer; 2007.
Palmier-Claus JE, Dodd A, Tai S, Emsley R, Mansell W. Appraisals to affect: testing the integrative cognitive model of bipolar disorder. Br J Clin Psychol. 2016;55(3):225–35.
Ritchie J, Spencer L. Qualitative data analysis for applied policy research. In: The qualitative researcher's companion, vol. 573. 2002; pp. 305–29.
Spitzer RL, Kroenke K, Williams JB, Patient Health Questionnaire Primary Care Study Group. Validation and utility of a self-report version of PRIME-MD: the PHQ primary care study. JAMA. 1999;282(18):1737–44.
Spitzer RL, Kroenke K, Williams JB, Löwe B. A brief measure for assessing generalized anxiety disorder: the GAD-7. Arch Intern Med. 2006;166(10):1092–7.
Strejilevich SA, Martino DJ, Murru A, Teitelbaum J, Fassi G, Marengo E, Igoa A, Colom F. Mood instability and functional recovery in bipolar disorders. Acta Psychiatr Scand. 2013;128(3):194–202.
Takaesu Y. Circadian rhythm in bipolar disorder: a review of the literature. Psychiatry Clin Neurosci. 2018;72(9):673–82.
Totterdell P, Kellett S. Restructuring mood in cyclothymia using cognitive behavior therapy: an intensive time-sampling study. J Clin Psychol. 2008;64(4):501–18.
Totterdell P, Kellett S, Mansell W. Cognitive behavioural therapy for cyclothymia: cognitive regulatory control as a mediator of mood change. Behav Cogn Psychother. 2012;40(4):412.
Van Dijk S, Jeffrey J, Katz MR. A randomized, controlled, pilot study of dialectical behavior therapy skills in a psychoeducational group for individuals with bipolar disorder. J Affect Disord. 2013;145(3):386–93.
Wright K, Dodd A, Warren FC, Medina-Lara A, Taylor R, Jones S, Owens C, Javaid M, Dunn B, Harvey JE, Newbold A. The clinical and cost effectiveness of adapted dialectical behaviour therapy (DBT) for bipolar mood instability in primary care (ThrIVe-B programme): a feasibility study. Trials. 2018;19(1):560.
Wright K, Palmer G, Javaid M, Mostazir M, Lynch T. Psychological therapy for mood instability within bipolar spectrum disorder: a single-arm feasibility study of a dialectical behaviour therapy-informed approach. Pilot Feasibility Stud. 2020;6:1–2.

15

How to make online mood-monitoring in bipolar patients a success? A qualitative exploration of requirements

B. Geerling[1,2*], S. M. Kelders[2,3], R. W. Kupka[4], A. W. M. M. Stevens[1] and E. T. Bohlmeijer[2]

Abstract

Background: The Life-Chart Method (LCM) is an effective self-management treatment option in bipolar disorder (BD). There is insufficient knowledge about the consumers' needs and desires for an e-monitoring solution. The first step towards a new mood monitoring application is an extended inventory among consumers and professionals.

Methods: The aim of the current study was: to identify opinions about online mood monitoring of patients with BD and professionals and to identify preferences on design, technical features and options facilitating optimal use and implementation of online mood monitoring. This study used a qualitative design with focus-groups. Participants were recruited among patients and care providers. Three focus-groups were held with eight consumers and five professionals.

Results: The focus-group meetings reveal a shared consciousness of the importance of using the Life-Chart Method for online mood monitoring. There is a need for personalization, adjustability, a strict privacy concept, an adjustable graphic report, and a link to early intervention strategies in the design. Due to the fact that this is a qualitative study with a relative small number of participants, so it remains unclear whether the results are fully generalizable. We can't rule out a selection bias.

Conclusions: This study demonstrates the importance of involving stakeholders in identifying a smartphone-based mood charting applications' requirements. Personalization, adjustability, privacy, an adjustable graphic report, and a direct link to early intervention strategies are necessary requirements for a successful design. The results of this value specification are included in the follow-up of this project.

Keywords: Bipolar disorder, Monitoring, Focus-group, Digital, Life Chart

Background

Bipolar disorder (BD) is a severe mental illness characterized by recurrent manic, hypomanic, and depressive episodes alternating with euthymic periods. The illness often manifests in adolescence and young adulthood (Goodwin and Jamison 2012; Kupka et al. 2008). It is estimated that BD types I and II occur in 2% of the world's population and that another 2% has a form of subthreshold BD (Geddes and Miklowitz 2013). In the Netherlands, the prevalence of BD in adults is 1.3% (de Graaf et al. 2010).

Monitoring of mood is an important element in self-management and treatment of BD. The prospective Life Chart Method (LCM) has been validated for daily mood monitoring (Denicoff et al. 2002). It provides a graphic representation of mood fluctuations above (hypo/mania) and below (depression) a euthymic baseline. Current medication, comorbid symptoms, hours of sleep, and significant life events are also reported. The primary purpose is to gain insight into the course of the illness and early signs of relapse. Daily monitoring facilitates early

*Correspondence: b.geerling@dimence.nl; b.geerling@utwente.nl
[1] Dimence Mental Health Institute, Centre for Bipolar Disorder, SCBS Bipolaire Stoonissen, Pikeursbaan 3, 7411 GT Deventer, The Netherlands
Full list of author information is available at the end of the article

recognition and intervention, thereby improving personal functioning (Gershon and Eidelman 2015).

Despite these advantages, the use of the LCM can be a regular confrontation with the illness (van Bendegem et al. 2014a). Some patients use the LCM only when early signs of relapse occur and not consistently (van Bendegem et al. 2014b). Draisma et al. (2015) found that 35% of the participants had missing LCM-data during a 1-year follow-up (Draisma et al. 2015). When data are reported retrospectively, there is a considerable risk of recall bias, especially when patients complete batches of daily ratings at a single time (Stone et al. 2003; Whybrow et al. 2003).

Carefully choosing the right moment to introduce self-monitoring in the treatment and tailoring to the potential user is a critical success factor (Lysaker et al. 2014; van Bendegem et al. 2014b). In their study van Bendegem et al. (2014a) plea for further customization and personalization to optimize motivation and compliance.

Redesigning the LCM from a paper and pencil method (P&P) into a digital instrument may facilitate daily compliance (Malik et al. 2012). Over the past decades, several electronic mood monitoring systems have been developed and assessed (Faurholt-Jepsen et al. 2016; Matthews et al. 2008; Saunders et al. 2017). In some studies, digital monitoring aimed to improve compliance (e.g. by sending reminders or increasing user-friendliness) (Lieberman et al. 2010; Matthews et al. 2008). Other studies are focused on detecting differences between P&P and digital monitoring in depressive and manic symptoms (Bauer et al. 2004; Bopp et al. 2010; Depp et al. 2012; Faurholt-Jepsen et al. 2014; Schärer et al. 2002; Whybrow et al. 2003). In a systematic review, Faurholt-Jepsen et al. (2016) concluded that electronic self-monitoring of mood appears to be a reliable measure of mood in depression but not in mania (Faurholt-Jepsen et al. 2016). This finding is in contrast to the validation study of the Life Chart Method. Denicoff et al. (2000) found that the LCM ratings have a strong correlation to the Yong Mania Rating Scale and the Global Clinical Impression BD (Denicoff et al. 2000; Young et al. 1978, 2004).

A qualitative study demonstrated that e-mood monitoring could lead to a better understanding of BD, increase insights into illness, and change behaviours towards more effective self-management strategies (Saunders et al. 2017). The participants also mentioned the possibility of being too preoccupied with monitoring as a potential risk of e-mood monitoring; in addition, the participants highly appreciated the option of personalizing the monitoring system to their insights (Saunders et al. 2017). Van den Heuvel et al. (2018) found that patients had better insight into the factors that contribute to mood instability or mood episodes when they used digital monitoring (van den Heuvel et al. 2018). This underlines that electronic longitudinal mood monitoring can lead to a better impression of the course of mood fluctuations in BD (McKnight et al. 2017).

Although several studies have described patients' experiences (including the benefits and their doubts) and measured satisfaction or user experience after development (Faurholt-Jepsen et al. 2019; Saunders et al. 2017; van den Heuvel et al. 2018), only a few studies had involved patients and professionals in (or before) the development of an online monitoring tool (e.g. Goodday et al. 2020). The current study aims to explore patients' and professionals' opinions about online mood monitoring ('must-haves' and 'don'ts') before developing a digital version of the widely used LCM. To the best of our knowledge, our study is the first and only study in (online) mood monitoring in bipolar disorder that involved consumers and professionals during the development process, which included the contextual inquiry, value specification, and the design of the application. The development process of interventions is described in several studies (e.g. van Gemert-Pijnen et al. 2011).

Method

Design

A qualitative design was used to identify and characterize the opinions about and needs ('must-haves' and 'don'ts') of relevant stakeholders (patients and professionals) of online monitoring. Three focus-group meetings (FGMs) were held. FGMs are an efficient way of gathering information on how people express their ideas on a construct (Polit and Beck 2015). FGMs are chosen as part of a qualitative design to gather participants' narratives, generate experiences and opinions, and stimulate discussion on peers' opinions (Gray 2014; Green and Thorogood 2018). To get a broad perspective on online mood monitoring in the Netherlands, the target group was defined as patients, professionals, and developers/researchers. This approach is also known as an patient-centered digital health design (Birnbaum et al. 2015) and is an example of an initiative with enables more engaged research participation.

We designed the study to conform to holistic development principles, as stated in the CeHRes roadmap (Centre for e-Health Research and Disease management, van Gemert-Pijnen et al. 2011). This study covers the first two steps of the model, which are contextual inquiry and value specification. The CeHRes endeavours to facilitate a continuing process of evaluation and participation of all stakeholders.

Ethical approval for the study was obtained from the University of Twente (Utwente; 18067) and the scientific board of Dimence, the mental health centre where the research was conducted.

Participants

The inclusion criteria to participate in the focus-group were: (1) patients with BD I or professionals who were treating BD or developers and researchers, (2) in possession of a smartphone, and (3) the willingness to travel to attend FGM. In the recruitment of our sample, we aimed to get a maximum variation sample to get a wide range of dimensions and a maximum variation among the participants of the FG. Therefore we use several recruitment options.

The professionals in the focus-group came from various disciplines (psychiatrists, psychiatric nurses, and psychologists). The professionals were recruited from the Dutch national knowledge institute for BD (Kenniscentrum Bipolaire Stoornissen, KenBiS), a chapter of the International Society for Bipolar Disorders (ISBD). Recruitment took place during a lecture at one of the periodic meetings of KenBiS and via leaflets.

Participating patients were recruited in an outpatient clinic and the national advocacy group (plusminus) in order to represent patients from different regions in the Netherlands and avoid potential selection bias. All the participants received treatment for BD I or II, but the treatment approaches could differ from each other due to the selection method. An announcement with a call for participation was posted in the magazine of the advocacy group. The researchers (BG and SK) were not involved in the participants' treatment to avoid selection bias. Patients were asked if they were euthymic at the start of the FGM, although no specific questionnaire was conducted to established mood.

All participants signed an informed consent form, in which they also agreed on audio recordings during the focus-groups. Thirteen participants (eight patients and five professionals) participated in one or more FGM.

Procedure and materials

We used the data from a previous study that aimed to gain insights from patients with BD about reasons to use, continue, or discontinue health-related apps in supporting self-management to operationalize topics for the FGM held in September and October 2018. In three semi-structured, 2-h meetings, the following topics were discussed; experiences with monitoring, technology and monitoring, the requirements of a monitoring app, and a monitoring app that can provide users with their needs. The participants were informed about the topics before the FGM. After the brief introduction of the focus-group (FG), participants were asked to write down the pros, cons and wishes on post-it memos collected on flip-charts. These statements comprised the basic assumptions used to start the discussion about the different opinions. The agreements and disagreements were summarised, and in the following FG, the members were asked again to find a preference until consensus was reached. In doing that, we gained insight into how the participants valued the current methods that give information for developing the digital version of the LC. The conversations were recorded and transcribed, and they were then followed by a consensus check. After each session, a report was made and sent to the participants for validation and comments to increase objectivity (member checking).

For the goal of mood monitoring we used the definition for the LCM as described by Denicoff et al. (2000): "*The LCM allows for the daily assessment of mood and episode severity based on the degree of mood associated functional impairment*" (Denicoff et al. 2000). The results gain insight in the course of the mood episodes and is used within the relation patient—professional to established proper treatment options.

Data analysis

The discussion and consensus rounds were transcribed and analyzed by deductive coding.

Open coding, via ATLAS.ti, is used to process the data. Concepts of a 'consensus document' were discussed in the second and third meeting and finally, after the last meeting established.

Results

Participants

We recruited 17 participants (11 patients with BD and six mental health professionals). Three patients and one professional withdrew before the start of the study for various reasons, like not being available at the time of the FGM or having a current mood episode. One psychiatrist, one psychologist, two nurse specialists, and one psychiatric nurse represent the professionals. There was a balanced representation in the sample across age (16–24 years one person = 7.7%; 25–40 years four persons = 30.8%; 41–55 years five persons = 38.5%; and 56–70 years three persons = 23%), gender (53.8% female) and residence (rural 46.2%, urban 53.8%). In education (high school, 23%; higher professional education, 61.5%; university, 15.5%), the distribution was less balanced. Although preferences didn't seem to differ between subgroups (e.g. age or education).

Emerging themes FGM

The FGM were structured in five themes or categories; positive and negative experiences with monitoring, positive and negative aspects of technology and monitoring, and requirements for a monitoring app. The topics that the FG members initially brought forward (by post-it memos) are placed within these categories and summarized in Table 1. Topics that came forward from the FGM are outlined in Table 2.

Experiences (positive and negative) with mood monitoring

First, we discussed the positive and negative aspects of monitoring. The Life Chart Method (LCM) was often mentioned as a monitoring tool, and some remarks refer primarily to the LCM. These valuable remarks were placed in the broad concept of mood monitoring to avoid 'tunnel vision' on the LCM in the FG's early stage.

The following positive experiences were mentioned: 'providing insight', 'guiding in self-management' and 'insight into the course of the illness over a more extended period/historical overview'. These items refer to the utility and necessity of the monitoring. Not only insight into the course of the illness was mentioned but also factors that can influence the mood (e.g., medication and sleep). Monitoring can also give direction about how to handle when early signs of relapse do occur.

> *'Provides a good insight into the course of bipolar disorder' (participant 1).*
> *'Provides insight into the combination of sleep, mood*

Table 1 Overview results focus group

Topic	Code	Times initially mentioned
Positive experiences with monitoring	Provides insight	4×
	Gives direction	3×
	Insight into the course of the illness	2×
Negative experiences with monitoring	Stressful	3×
	Confrontation with the disease	3×
	Lack of privacy	2×
Positive aspects of technology and monitoring	Getting more insight	3×
	More overview options	2×
	Possibility to use notifications	4×
	Better availability	2×
	More secure	1×
Negative aspects of technology and monitoring	Need for a device	2×
	Privacy	2×
	Focus on illness	2×
	Provoke the use of the telephone	2×
Requirements for a monitoring app	**Freedom of choice** Possibility to add text/photos/videos Monitor temporary items Adding own parameters Adjustable notifications Free wording	8×
	User-friendliness No unnecessarily features Linking possibilities (e.g., RRP) Compatibility with other devices Notifications Clear design Easy to operate	5×
	Trustworthiness Clear privacy statement No hidden data extraction Reliable supplier Clear access protocol with the logging option	4×
	Goal-setting Personal feedback Increase of self-management Self-regulation	3×
	Remaining Based on the LCM	3×

Table 2 Additional topics

Additional topics after discussion in the FGM				
Requirements for a monitoring app				
Freedom of choice	**User-friendliness**	**Trustworthiness**	**Goal-setting**	**Remaining**
• Handle algorithms • Monitor temporary items • Choose words that apply to the user • Flexibility • Add text, photos, videos or music • Scroll function to zoom in or out on the graphic of the LC • Diary function	• Exactly meet the users' demands • Connect with different applications • Multiple-use (phone, tablet, pc) • No daily login	• Clear privacy statement • Clear who has access to the data • Clear who can watch the LC	• Supporting in the regulation of the users • Personalized feedback	• No compulsory use • No linking with other social media

and events' (participant 6).

'Provides quick insight, but must be used with the relapse prevention plan' (participant 11).

On the opposite, participants mentioned several negative experiences or aspects of mood monitoring. Mood monitoring can be experienced as a stressful task that 'has to be' accomplished daily, especially in the early stage of the illness. Monitoring is also seen as a confrontation with the illness that can even induce self-stigma. When used in treatment, monitoring can also be *'experienced as a violation of privacy'* since caregivers can wander through personal data.

'Being involved with the disease every day by the LC can eventually become compulsive' (participant 6).

'It's [monitoring] not always necessary can lead to panic reactions' (participant 4).

'You may also be displeased [because of the monitoring, you are too focused on the disease]' (participant 2).

What could technology mean to improve monitoring?

Secondly, the use of technology as a possible solution was discussed (both potentially positive and negative). As positive aspects, the participants came forward with several expected benefits of online mood monitoring, like *'get more insight'* in the monitoring and that there will be *'more overview options'*. The FGM expect better availability when the monitoring is always in reach (on mobile devices), the possibility to zoom in and out on the long-term course, the option to *'use notifications'*, and the data to be shared with their caregivers. All the aspects mentioned above contribute to better insight; the FGM didn't expect significant changes in mood monitoring base principles.

Also mentioned was; the *'possibility of getting feedback'*, the idea that it fits in the modern technological age, that the users have *'more control'* and, because of having a personal account, *'better privacy'* is guaranteed. The participants partly related their expectations to their experiences with online applications that support their P&P mood monitoring;

'I discovered when I did the monitoring on my desktop (in Excel, I had made a program for it) that it was easier to fill in the LC because I am sitting daily behind the desktop computer' (participant 6).

'I used notifications from another app to remember me to fill in the paper and pencil LCM'—(participant 11).

On the other hand, the participants named different possible negative aspects of online mood monitoring. The need for a device is conditional. The participants are concerned about privacy issues; access to the data has to be limited to patients, caregivers and researchers. Online mood monitoring can lead to a focus on the illness, according to the FGM.

The FG concerns are divided into two themes; technical aspect of mobile phone use and the 'side effects' of mobile phone use. The *'problems in operating the app'* and the *'incompatibility with other devices'* are mentioned as possible technical barriers. The complex operation required to use an app can reduce the motivation to use the app. The same is expected to occur when the app is not compatible with other devices (e.g., desktops). Also, *'too many functionalities'* is mentioned as a possible barrier; people can get lost in all kinds of functionalities that distract them from mood monitoring's main goal. The second theme, 'side effects', concerns a technical application that can *'provoke the use of the mobile phone'* (too much). Even users are *'unwillingly switch to social media'*, especially when they are in a (hypo) manic mood episode.

> *'I don't want any interaction with other people, like on social media, because I'm afraid of what I would say when I am manic or depressed.' (participant 4).*
> *'One of the disadvantages is that you always, it could be out of power or broken (the mobile device BG); with the booklet (paper and pencil LCM), you do not have that problem.' (participant 1).*

(Technological) requirements

To establish perceptions of an online mood monitoring application's essential elements, we discussed possible features and how they can tribute to compliance. The identified features can be classified into four categories: *freedom of choice, user-friendliness, trustworthiness* and *goal-setting*. The participants unanimously stressed that the LCM principles must be leading in developing the online mood monitoring application.

Freedom of choice seems to be one of the most important topics (8× mentioned). This topic comprises the following aspects: the application must *'exactly meet the users' demands'*, the possibility to *'handle algorithms'*, although that may also be a bit threatening, like 'Big Brother'. A clear wish to be able to *'monitor temporary items'* and that you can *'choose the words that apply to you'* in the monitoring. *'Flexibility'*, in addition to a fixed basis, is considered highly desirable. Also, the possibility *'to add text, photos, videos or even music fragments'* was mentioned. If there are elements in the app that are personally 'indispensable' for you, using the app makes it more natural (for example, a link with calendar appointments).

The following items were mentioned in the FGM about *user-friendliness*: the desires to use the app on *'multiple applications'* and to *'combine different applications'* are also widely shared (e.g. the combination of the LC with relapse prevention plan, wellness recovery plan or mindfulness app), possibly with a link to the personal health file (PGD) or the electronic patient records (EPD).

The *trustworthiness* of the application is the third subcategory. The app must have a *'clear privacy statement'* and a reliable company that markets the application. It must be clear *'who has access to the LC's data'* and *'who can watch the data'*. When others view data, one can receive messages (logging).

Finally, *goal setting* could be identified as an important topic. *'Goalsetting in self-management'* and the importance of being able to *'regulate yourself'* seems essential. Also, *'personalized feedback'* is a motivational option to achieve monitoring goalsetting and increase compliance. In summary, the following quotes show the most important requirements as mentioned by the participants:

> *'I would like to see a kind of scroll function that you zoom in or out on the graphic of the LC; I think that would be absolutely fantastic'—(participant 1).*
> *'I would like to have a kind of diary function in the app so that I can see my appointments with the clinician, and even can monitor of the visit is worsened or improve my mood'—Participant 2*
> *'The opportunity to load up a video or audio recordings on moments that I being Euthymic so that, when I'm depressed, I can play like a kind of mantra... It could be everything; even a barking dog can you remember at good times.'—(participant 11).*
> *'Clear graph, the possibility to add notes, the option to add extra data, medication to be filled in per day, the possibility to add additional data (on or off), clarity about data exchange, applicable to multiple devices. No more functions than necessary, no chat function, no hidden data exchange.'—(participant 6).*
> *'User-friendly, using LC indicators, additional options for monitoring, sending reminders every day (to be set up), giving positive feedback.'—(participant 8).*
> *'Easy to operate, customizable, different variables, combined with a plan, in addition to having it monitored, being able to turn off notifications. No compulsory use.'—(participant 10).*

Based on the results of the FGM, the first concept of functionalities of the app was made.

The consensus within the FG

In the last meeting, the definitive consensus was achieved on how the monitoring application should be working. In developing an online mood-monitoring application, the LCM principles should be the priority. Adjustability and personalization are vital components to start and maintain the use of the application. Privacy must be strictly described, and the patients should own the data.

The consensus statement is shown in Table 3.

Discussion

The aim of the current study was twofold: to identify opinions about online mood monitoring of patients with BD and professionals and to identify preferences on design, technical features, and options facilitating optimal use and implementation of online mood monitoring.

Regarding the first aim, the results showed a shared consciousness of the importance of using the LCM, but only when it's appropriate in the context of patient's treatment and recovery process. These findings are consistent

Table 3 Consensus monitoring

Consensus agreed on elements for online monitoring
• A basis in which all elements of the Life-Chart method are included:
o Functions in this part are not adjustable
o Notifications for monitoring are adjustable
• Graphic display of the course of mood:
o In weeks, months and years
o Possibility to adjust different parameters and to switch on/off or to combine in the graphics (for example, the parameters sleep and mood)
o The graphics display is adjustable (like zoom in and out)
• Additional options to adjust the app to personal circumstances and preferences:
o Possibility to add text/photos/music/link to the Life-Chart
o Possibility to add own parameters like substance use or work duration
o Possibility to receive personalized feedback
o Possibility of personalizing with photos
• Provide a link with the relapse prevention plan or with WRAP
• Adjustable notifications
• Quick to fill in for daily use
• Useable on all devices
• Guarantee for privacy:
o Distinctness about data storage,
o No access to the personal data by ICT-company or others who are not involved with the treatment of the patient
o The patient who is monitoring is the owner of the collected data and is the only one who can add others (like professionals) to his/her chart
• NO link with other social media to prevent uploading of personal data from the LC during an episode
• NO 'forced' monitoring; this will reduce the motivation for mood monitoring
• NO log in for daily use (only at the start of using the application)

with previous studies in which both patients and professionals underscored the importance of the LCM (van Bendegem et al. 2014a, b). Lysaker et al. (2014) claims that, when not carefully integrated into the patient's recovery process, the LCM can be contra-productive and can even lead to self-stigma and low self-esteem levels (Lysaker et al. 2007; Lysaker et al. 2014). The FG members in our study mentioned similar experiences, such as the daily confrontation with the disease that eventually can lead to self-stigma and over-focus on the disease. This underlines the necessity for flexibility. Not only flexibility in the application of the LCM (in with stage of the treatment of BD it is applied) is an important requirement for successful monitoring, but also personalization of the use of the LCM.

Regarding the second aim, our results confirm the importance of tailoring and personalization in digital monitoring tools (Saunders et al. 2017; Valenza et al. 2014). First, customization can be used in a way that patients are able to add text or photos. Also, adjustability can be integrated by using own parameters such as alcohol consumption or notifications. The FGM underlines the importance of adding (temporary) monitoring items that can influence the course of the BD, such as removal, unemployment, marriage and family extension. In BD, life events can lead to mood episodes (Koenders et al. 2014). Therefore, it can support monitoring life events more closely, even during long(er) euthymic episodes. Another aspect is the possibility to link to other self-management tools, such as a relapse prevention plan (RPP). Interventions from the RPP should appear when (mild) depression or (mild) mania is rated in the monitoring application. Such a link seems to be conditional for our participants to use online monitoring tools, which indicates the importance of personalization. In a phenomenological study of the use of the RRP, Daggenvoorde et al. (2013) found that it can be difficult for patients to put early signs of relapse into concrete prevention actions (Daggenvoorde et al. 2013). Especially in longer euthymic episodes, the RPP can be drawn to the background for some patients and can't be applied effectively (Murray et al. 2011). If concrete early interventions, when indicated, directly appear in the monitoring application, we expect that it is easier to perform those early interventions. This pleads for integrating the RPP in the online monitoring tool to improve early interventions and improve self-control. Moreover, our results underline the importance of tailoring and personalization in a digital monitoring tool.

Besides the importance of personalization, online monitoring provides the possibility for patients and professionals to share the monitoring data at any time. Although data security has to be guaranteed, the FG members label this possibility as useful. When digital monitoring is shared with professionals, there is enhanced communication between patients and clinicians. This could lead to a better understanding of factors that influence mood (van den Heuvel et al. 2018; McKnight et al. 2017). The concerns about privacy focus on the data exchange, access to the data and in addition who can exactly can see the life-chart. Vendors should add a proper, transparent statement about data collection and view (Motti and Caine 2015). This seems conditionally for a successful implementation of an online mood monitoring system.

The results also yielded some important concerns about online monitoring. Connection with social media platforms is seen as one of the risks by the FG. The participants fear posting anything during depressed episodes and more so during (hypo)manic episodes that they will subsequently regret during euthymic episodes. Although in some papers the benefits of social media on mental health have been discussed (O'reilly et al. 2019; Välimäki et al. 2016). Naslund and Aschbrenner (2019) discovered that in a cohort of people with severe mental illness (37% with bipolar disorder), about one-third expressed concerns about privacy risks similar to our findings. The concerns are related to using social media, addressing fears of stigma, the impact on personal relationships, and facing hostility (Naslund and Aschbrenner 2019). In the FGM, the members reveal similar concerns. Therefore, it is essential to be careful in including features in applications, such as social media links, that may harm the target group.

Although health applications are widely available and a majority (90%) of patients are interested in digital interventions (Ranney et al. 2012). Only a minority of patients are actually using that kind of interventions cause of various reasons. Patients do use interventions when it fits in their needs (Lupton 2013). Like many developing groups, we held focus-group sessions to determine content and (Rosen et al. 2015). By using the model of the CeHRes, in with participation throughout the whole development process is one of the preconditions of the model, we tried to bridge the gap between the needs of end-users (patients and professionals) and the development of a new E-monitoring tool, that enables us to create a patient-centred digital health tool (Birnbaum et al. 2015; Gemert-Pijnen et al. 2011).

In sum, we argue that the results provide a number of important prerequisites for developing a mood-monitoring app that is in line with the target group's needs. In this process, we followed the steps of the CeHRes (van Gemert-Pijnen et al. 2011). A development process using the CeHRes roadmap, can 'clarify areas that would otherwise remain unanswered, unclear, or unknown' (van Gemert-Pijnen et al. 2011). We believe that we have succeeded to clarify this in our study, especially possibilities for personalisation, adjustability and need for integration of self-management tools in the daily monitoring.

Limitations

The study has some limitations. The first is a potential selection bias in the recruitment of professionals. They were voluntarily recruited in the Dutch chapter (KenBiS) of the International Society of Bipolar Disorders (ISBD) network. It is conceivable that the professionals who are interested in the topic of online monitoring have come forward to participate in this research and are overrepresented. The same applies to the consumers; they were partly recruited in one outpatient clinic and partly in the Dutch advocacy network 'plusminus'. That may raise a question: do the participants represent the overall target group? We think that our study sufficiently represents the target group in combining advocacy members and patients treated in an outpatient clinic. In our sample both extensive app users and users with less experience with apps were participating. This increases the chance that the findings are a balanced representation of patient experiences and opinions. Another limitation is that the FG members involved in this study were mainly highly educated, which implicates a potential higher level of digital skills and a more positive attitude towards new digital applications. A recent study found that low levels of education can be linked to meagre digital skills, low use of the internet, and anxiety for new digital developments (Vasilescu et al. 2020). It is recommended to involve more patients with lower levels of education when developing mood-monitoring devices. Although we argued that the FG mix of patients and professionals was beneficial, we cannot rule out the possibility that other participants influence the FG members' opinions. We tried to avoid this bias through an individual member check after every meeting and the individual opinions' inventory before the discussion started. Finally, the present study is mainly a qualitative study with a relatively small number of participants, so it remains unclear whether the results are fully generalizable.

We didn't explore the possibilities of auto-tracking and returning objective measures of symptoms options by devices.

Despite these shortcomings, we believe that the findings give a relevant overview of consumers' and professionals' thoughts and opinions on the topic of online mood monitoring in BD.

Conclusion and practical implications

This study demonstrates the importance of involving stakeholders when identifying the requirements of a smartphone-based mood-charting application. We found a shared consciousness of the importance of using the Life-Chart Method as a leading principle for online mood monitoring. The design of online mood monitoring devices needs to include personalization, adjustability, strict privacy, an adjustable graphic report, and a direct link to early intervention strategies.

The value specifications are included in the follow-up of this project. Consumers and professionals will also be involved in the design and operationalization phases of the development of an online monitoring app. Our findings imply that any newly created application needs the careful integration of persuasive technology to increase adherence. This thorough approach is necessary for developing a monitoring app that stimulates sufficient compliance among people with BD. In the next step of the development of online mood monitoring, we suggest that consumers and professionals shine their light on the subject of passive sensing or EBT related tasks like activity levels, or objective sleep.

Abbreviations

BD: Bipolar disorder; CeHRes: Centre for e-Health Research and disease management; EPD: Electronic Patients Records (Dutch); FG: Focus Group; FGM: Focus Group Meeting(s); KenBiS: Kenniscentrum Bipolaire Stoornissen (Dutch national knowledge institute for BD); LCM: Life Chart Method; P&P: Paper & pencil; RPP: Relapse prevention plan.

Acknowledgements

Not applicable.

Authors' contributions

BG and SK analysed and interpreted the Focus group data regarding the online monitoring of BD. BG is the first author and corresponding author. SK and EB did the first edit, AS and RK did the second round of editing. All authors read and approved the final manuscript.

Author details

[1]Dimence Mental Health Institute, Centre for Bipolar Disorder, SCBS Bipolaire Stoonissen, Pikeursbaan 3, 7411 GT Deventer, The Netherlands. [2]Department of Psychology, Health and Technology, Centre for eHealth and Wellbeing Research, University of Twente, Enschede, The Netherlands. [3]Optentia Research Focus Area, North-West University, Vanderbijlpark, South Africa. [4]Department Psychiatry, Amsterdam Public Health Research Institute, Amsterdam UMC, Vrije Universiteit, Amsterdam, The Netherlands.

References

Bauer M, Grof P, Gyulai L, Rasgon N, Glenn T, Whybrow PC. Using technology to improve longitudinal studies: self-reporting with Chrono record in bipolar disorder. Bipolar Disord. 2004. https://doi.org/10.1046/j.1399-5618.2003.00085.x.

Birnbaum F, Lewis D, Rosen RK, Ranney ML. Patient engagement and the design of digital health. Acad Emerg Med. 2015;22(6):754. https://doi.org/10.1111/acem.12692.

Bopp JM, Miklowitz DJ, Goodwin GM, Stevens W, Rendell JM, Geddes JR. The longitudinal course of bipolar disorder as revealed through weekly text messaging: a feasibility study. Bipolar Disord. 2010;12(3):327–34. https://doi.org/10.1111/j.1399-5618.2010.00807.x

Daggenvoorde TH, Goossens PJJ, Gamel CJ. Regained control: a phenomenological study of the use of a relapse prevention plan by patients with a bipolar disorder. Perspect Psychiatr Care. 2013;49(4):235–42. https://doi.org/10.1111/ppc.12009.

de Graaf R, ten Have M, van Dorsselaer S. De psychische gezondheid van de Nederlandse bevolking. Utrecht: Trimbos instituut; 2010. https://doi.org/10.1007/s00127-010-0334-8.

Denicoff KD, Leverich GS, Nolen WA, Rush AJ, McElroy SL, Keck PE, Suppes T, Altshuler LL, Kupka R, Frye MA, Hatef J, Brotman MA, Post RM. Validation of the prospective NIMH-life-chart method (NIMH-LCM(TM)-p) for longitudinal assessment of bipolar illness. Psychol Med. 2000;30(6):1391–7. https://doi.org/10.1017/S0033291799002810.

Denicoff KD, Ali SO, Sollinger AB, Smith-Jackson EE, Leverich GS, Post RM. Utility of the daily prospective National Institute of Mental Health Life-Chart Method (NIMH-LCM-P) ratings in clinical trials of bipolar disorder. Depress Anxiety. 2002. https://doi.org/10.1002/da.1078.

Depp CA, Kim DH, Vergel De Dios L, Wang V, Ceglowski J. A pilot study of mood ratings captured by mobile phone versus paper-and-pencil mood charts in bipolar disorder. J Dual Diagn. 2012. https://doi.org/10.1080/15504263.2012.723318.

Draisma S, Van Zaane J, Smit JH. Data quality indicators for daily life chart methodology: prospective self-ratings of bipolar disorder and alcohol use. BMC Res Notes. 2015. https://doi.org/10.1186/s13104-015-1436-x.

Faurholt-Jepsen M, Vinberg M, Frost M, Christensen EM, Bardram J, Kessing LV. Daily electronic monitoring of subjective and objective measures of illness activity in bipolar disorder using smartphones-the MONARCA II trial protocol: a randomized controlled single-blind parallel-group trial. BMC Psychiatry. 2014;14(1):1–2.

Faurholt-Jepsen M, Munkholm K, Frost M, Bardram JE, Kessing LV. Electronic self-monitoring of mood using IT platforms in adult patients with bipolar disorder: a systematic review of the validity and evidence. BMC Psychiatry. 2016. https://doi.org/10.1186/s12888-016-0713-0.

Faurholt-Jepsen M, Torri E, Cobo J, Yazdanyar D, Palao D, Cardoner N, Andreatta O, Mayora O, Kessing LV. Smartphone-based self-monitoring in bipolar disorder: evaluation of usability and feasibility of two systems. Int J Bipolar Disord. 2019;7(1):1–11. https://doi.org/10.1186/s40345-018-0134-8.

Geddes JR, Miklowitz DJ. Treatment of bipolar disorder. Lancet. 2013. https://doi.org/10.1016/S0140-6736(13)60857-0.

Gershon A, Eidelman P. Inter-episode affective intensity and instability: predictors of depression and functional impairment in bipolar disorder. J Behav Ther Exp Psychiatry. 2015. https://doi.org/10.1016/j.jbtep.2014.07.005.

Goodday SM, Atkinson L, Goodwin G, Saunders K, South M, Mackay C, Denis M, Hinds C, Attenburrow MJ, Davies J, Welch J, Stevens W, Mansfield K, Suvilehto J, Geddes J. The true colours remote symptom monitoring system: a decade of evolution. J Med Int Res. 2020;22(1):e15188. https://doi.org/10.2196/15188.

Goodwin F, Jamison KR. Manic-depressive illness: bipolar disorders and recurrent depression. J Ecol. 2012. https://doi.org/10.1111/j.1365-2745.2011.01925.x.

Gray DE. Doing research in the real world. 3rd ed. London: SAGE; 2014.

Green J, Thorogood N. Qualitative methods for health research. London: SAGE; 2018.

Koenders MA, Giltay EJ, Spijker AT, Hoencamp E, Spinhoven P, Elzinga BM. Stressful life events in bipolar i and II disorder: cause or consequence of mood symptoms? J Affect Disord. 2014. https://doi.org/10.1016/j.jad.2014.02.036.

Kupka RW, Knoppert-van der Klein E, Nolen WA. Handboek Bipolaire Stoornissen. Uitgeverij De Tijdstroom; 2008.

Lieberman DZ, Kelly TF, Douglas L, Goodwin FK. A randomized comparison of online and paper mood charts for people with bipolar disorder. J Affect Disord. 2010. https://doi.org/10.1016/j.jad.2009.10.019.

Lupton D. The digitally engaged patient: self-monitoring and self-care in the digital health era. Soc Theory Health. 2013;11(3):256–70. https://doi.org/10.1057/sth.2013.10.

Lysaker PH, James AV, Leonhardt BL. Life chart methodology: risks associated with failing to assess patient preferences and the sources of poor insight for patients with bipolar disorder. J Am Psychiatr Nurses Assoc. 2014. https://doi.org/10.1177/1078390314562248.

Lysaker PH, Roe D, Yanos PT (2007) Toward understanding the insight paradox: Internalized stigma moderates the association between insight and social functioning, hope and self-Esteem among people with schizophre-

Malik A, Goodwin GM, Holmes EA. Contemporary approaches to frequent mood monitoring in bipolar disorder. J Exp Psychopathol. 2012. https://doi.org/10.5127/jep.014311.

Matthews M, Doherty G, Sharry J, Fitzpatrick C. Mobile phone mood charting for adolescents. Br J Guid Couns. 2008. https://doi.org/10.1080/03069880801926400.

McKnight RF, Bilderbeck AC, Miklowitz DJ, Hinds C, Goodwin GM, Geddes JR. Longitudinal mood monitoring in bipolar disorder: course of illness as revealed through a short messaging service. J Affect Disord. 2017. https://doi.org/10.1016/j.jad.2017.07.029.

Motti VG, Caine K. Users' privacy concerns about wearables: impact of form factor, sensors and type of data collected. In: Lecture notes in computer science (including subseries lecture notes in artificial intelligence and lecture notes in bioinformatics). 2015;8976. https://doi.org/10.1007/978-3-662-48051-9_17.

Murray G, Suto M, Hole R, Hale S, Amari E, Michalak EE. Self-management strat egies used by "high functioning" individuals with bipolar disorder: from research to clinical practice. Clin Psychol Psychother. 2011;18(2):95–109. https://doi.org/10.1002/cpp.710.

Naslund JA, Aschbrenner KA. Risks to privacy with use of social media: understanding the views of social media users with serious mental illness. Psychiatr Serv. 2019. https://doi.org/10.1176/appi.ps.201800520.

O'reilly M, Dogra N, Hughes J, Reilly P, George R, Whiteman N. Potential of social media in promoting mental health in adolescents. Health Promot Int. 2019. https://doi.org/10.1093/heapro/day056.

Polit DF, Beck CT. Nursing research: generating and assessing evidence for nursing practice. 10th ed. Philadelphia: Wolters Kluwer Health; 2015.

Ranney ML, Choo EK, Wang Y, Baum A, Clark MA, Mello MJ. Emergency department patients' preferences for technology-based behavioral interventions. Ann Emerg Med. 2012;60(2):218–27. https://doi.org/10.1016/j.annemergmed.2012.02.026.

Rosen RK, Ranney ML, Boyer EW (2015) Formative research for Mhealth HIV adherence: the iHAART app. In: Proceedings of the annual Hawaii international conference on system sciences, 2015-March. p. 2778–85. https://doi.org/10.1109/HICSS.2015.336.

Saunders KEA, Bilderbeck AC, Panchal P, Atkinson LZ, Geddes JR, Goodwin GM. Experiences of remote mood and activity monitoring in bipolar disorder: a qualitative study. Eur Psychiatry. 2017. https://doi.org/10.1016/j.eurpsy.2016.11.005.

Schärer LO, Hartweg V, Valerius G, Graf M, Hoern M, Biedermann C, Walser S, Boensch A, Dittmann S, Forsthoff A, Hummel B, Grunze H, Walden J. Life charts on a palmtop computer: first results of a feasibility study with an electronic diary for bipolar patients. Bipolar Disord. 2002. https://doi.org/10.1034/j.1399-5618.4.s1.51.x.

Stone AA, Shiffman S, Schwartz JE, Broderick JE, Hufford MR. Patient compliance with paper and electronic diaries. Control Clin Trials. 2003. https://doi.org/10.1016/S0197-2456(02)00320-3.

Valenza G, Lanatà A, Paradiso R, Scilingo EP. Advanced technology meets mental health: how smartphones, textile electronics, and signal processing can serve mental health monitoring, diagnosis, and treatment. IEEE Pulse. 2014. https://doi.org/10.1109/MPUL.2014.2309582.

Välimäki M, Athanasopoulou C, Lahti M, Adams CE. Effectiveness of social media interventions for people with schizophrenia: a systematic review and meta-analysis. J Med Internet Res. 2016. https://doi.org/10.2196/jmir.5385.

van Bendegem MA, van den Heuvel SCGH, Kramer LJ, Goossens PJJ. Attitudes of patients with bipolar disorder toward the life chart methodology: a phenomenological study. J Am Psychiatr Nurses Assoc. 2014a. https://doi.org/10.1177/1078390314558420

van Bendegem MA, van den Heuvel SCGH, Kramer LJ, Goossens PJJ. Attitudes of patients with bipolar disorder toward the life chart methodology: a phenomenological study. J Am Psychiatr Nurses Assoc. 2014b;20(6):376–85. https://doi.org/10.1177/1078390314558420.

van Gemert-Pijnen JEWC, Nijland N, van Limburg M, Ossebaard HC, Kelders SM, Eysenbach G, Seydel ER. A holistic framework to improve the uptake and impact of eHealth technologies. J Med Internet Res. 2011;13(4):e111. https://doi.org/10.2196/jmir.1672.

van den Heuvel SCGH, Meije D, Regeer EJ, Sinnema H, Riemersma RF, Kupka RW. The user experiences and clinical outcomes of an online personal health record to support self-management of bipolar disorder: a pretest–posttest pilot study. J Affect Disord. 2018. https://doi.org/10.1016/j.jad.2018.05.069.

Vasilescu MD, Serban AC, Dimian GC, Aceleanu MI, Picatoste X. Digital divide, skills and perceptions on digitalisation in the European Union—towards a smart labour market. PLoS ONE. 2020;15(4): e0232032. https://doi.org/10.1371/journal.pone.0232032.

Whybrow PC, Grof P, Gyulai L, Rasgon N, Glenn T, Bauer M. The electronic assessment of the longitudinal course of bipolar disorder: the ChronoRecord software. Pharmacopsychiatry. 2003;36(S3):244–9.

Young RC, Biggs JT, Ziegler VE, Meyer DA. A rating scale for mania: reliability, validity and sensitivity. Br J Psychiatry. 1978. https://doi.org/10.1192/bjp.133.5.429.

Young RC, Biggs JT, Ziegler VE, Meyer DA. Young mania rating scale. In: Handbook of Psychiatric Measures. Washington,DC: American Psychiatric Association; 2000:540-54

16

Recommendations for the use of long-term experience sampling in bipolar disorder care: a qualitative study of patient and clinician experiences

Fionneke M. Bos[1,2*], Evelien Snippe[2], Richard Bruggeman[1], Bennard Doornbos[3], Marieke Wichers[2] and Lian van der Krieke[1,2]

Abstract

Background: Self-monitoring has been shown to improve the self-management and treatment of patients with bipolar disorder. However, current self-monitoring methods are limited to once-daily retrospectively assessed mood, which may not suit the rapid mood fluctuations in bipolar disorder. The experience sampling method (ESM), which assesses mood in real-time several times a day, may overcome these limitations. This study set out to assess the experiences of patients and clinicians with the addition of ESM monitoring, real-time alerts, and personalized feedback to clinical care. Participants were twenty patients with bipolar disorder type I/II and their clinicians. For four months, patients completed five ESM assessments per day on mood, symptoms, and activities. Weekly symptom questionnaires alerted patients and clinicians to potential episodes. After the monitoring, a personalized feedback report based on the patient's data was discussed between patient and clinician. Three months later, patient and clinician were both interviewed.

Results: Thematic analysis of the transcripts resulted in four themes: perceived effects of the monitoring, alerts, and feedback, and recommendations for implementation of ESM. ESM was perceived as helping patients to cope better with their disorder by increasing awareness, offering new insights, and encouraging life style adjustments. ESM was further believed to facilitate communication between patient and clinician and to lead to new treatment directions. However, high assessment burden and pre-occupation with negative mood and having a disorder were also described. Patients and clinicians advocated for increased personalization and embedding of ESM in care.

Conclusions: This study demonstrates that long-term ESM monitoring, alerts, and personalized feedback are perceived as beneficial to the treatment and self-management of patients with bipolar disorder. Future research should further test the clinical utility of ESM. Clinically relevant feedback and technology need to be developed to enable personalized integration of ESM in clinical care.

Keywords: Experience sampling method, Ecological momentary assessment, Bipolar disorder, Self-monitoring, Implementation, Personalized feedback, Qualitative research

*Correspondence: f.m.bos01@umcg.nl
[1] Rob Giel Research Center, University of Groningen, University Medical Center Groningen, PO Box 30.001, 9700 RB Groningen, The Netherlands
Full list of author information is available at the end of the article

Background

Bipolar disorder is a severe and often lifelong affective disorder, involving depressive and (hypo)manic episodes, and is associated with tremendous burden for patients (Pini et al. 2005; Michalak et al. 2006). Many patients look for ways to successfully live and cope with the impact of the disorder (Lean et al. 2019; Murray et al. 2011). An important strategy to bolster self-management is to self-monitor mood, for example with the NIMH prospective Life-Chart (Leverich and Post 1993; Schärer et al. 2015), ChronoRecord (Bauer et al. 2004), smartphone applications, or rudimentary paper-based methods (Murnane et al. 2016). Indeed, research has suggested that self-monitoring may increase illness insight and self-management, by helping patients to make lifestyle adjustments and facilitate communication with clinicians (Murnane et al. 2016; Bilderbeck et al. 2014). However, existing methods such as the Life-Chart or ChronoRecord have two potential limitations. First, patients have to summarize their symptoms, experiences, and level of functioning into a *single* rating of their overall mood, which might not accurately capture the highly frequent and disparate mood swings patients experience throughout the day (Murnane et al. 2016). Second, the ratings are completed *retrospectively* over the previous 24 h, which may lead to inaccurate information due to mood biases (Reis et al. 2012).

The experience sampling method (ESM) is an ecologically valid self-monitoring method that may overcome these shortcomings. Although originally developed for research (Myin-Germeys et al. 2018), ESM has been advocated as a tool to promote self-management and resilience for patients in mental health care (Os et al. 2017; Bos et al. 2019; Wichers et al. 2011). With ESM, patients monitor their daily experiences, moods, and symptoms on their smartphones several times a day (see Fig. 1) (Larson and Csikszentmihalyi 1983). ESM differs from more commonly used self-monitoring methods in that multiple distinct micro-level aspects of mood (e.g., feeling cheerful/down versus manic/depressed) are assessed prospectively, as they occur in daily life. Therefore, ESM may better match patient experiences, and

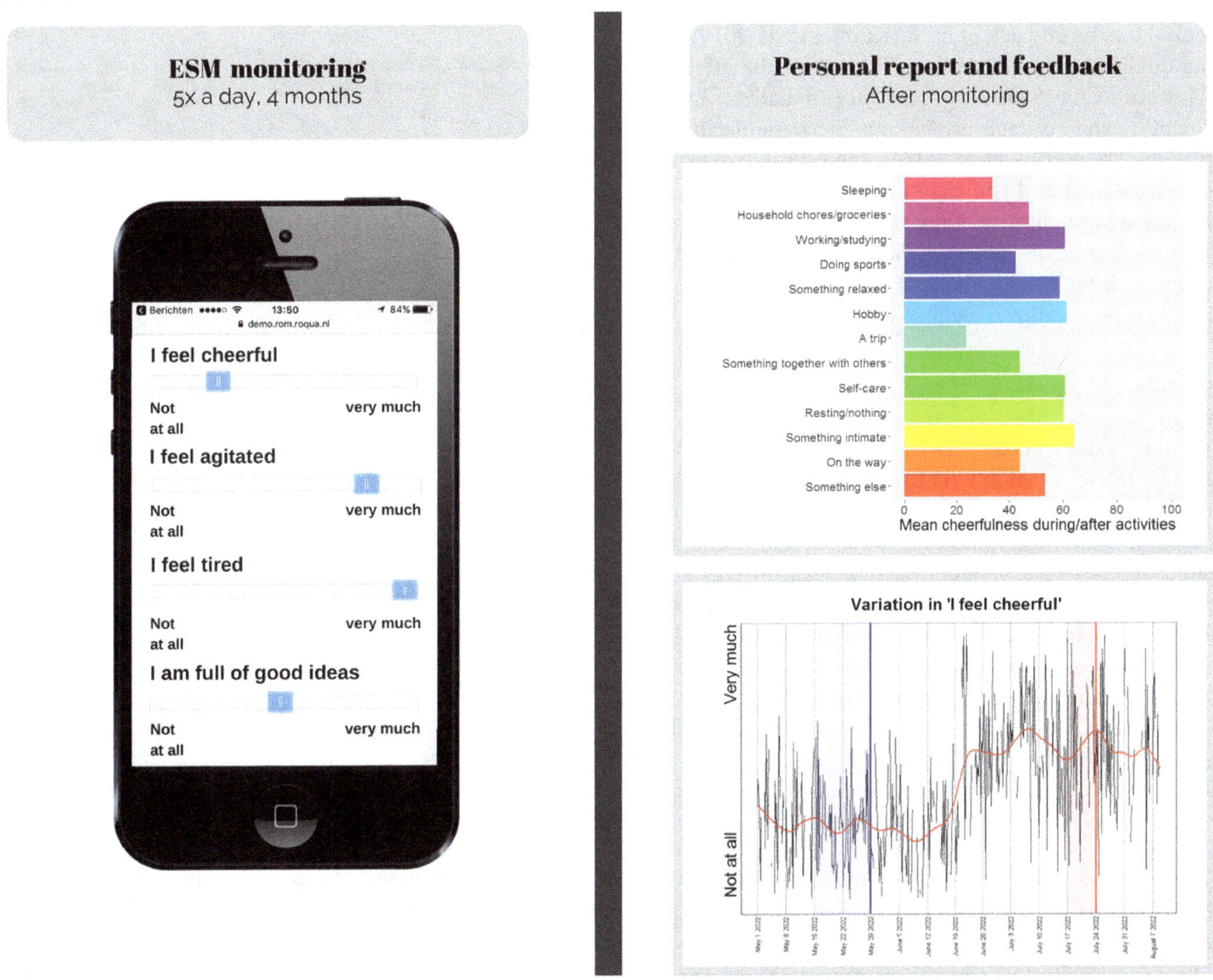

Fig. 1 Visual representation of the ESM monitoring and simulated examples of personalized feedback given to participants

may capture mood fluctuations more accurately (Reis et al. 2012). The detailed ESM data that patients gather can be used to generate personalized feedback on mood variability or associations between mood and lifestyle, or alert patients to impending manic or depressive episodes.

Importantly, patients and clinicians recognize the potential of ESM for clinical care while also noting the possibility of high assessment burden and symptom worsening (Bos et al. 2019). Still, little is known about how patients and clinicians actually experience the addition of ESM to clinical care. This is a crucial first step that will inform on future academic and practical innovations that are currently (technologically) unavailable but will need to be developed for clinical usage. Until now, qualitative studies have focused on feasibility and tolerability (Wenze et al. 2014), evaluating only short-term (1–2 weeks) or low-intensity (1–2 assessments daily) ESM (Wenze et al. 2016; Tsanas et al. 2016), whereas long-term ESM (e.g., several months) may better fit the prolonged nature of bipolar disorder treatments. Furthermore, although personalized feedback seems to be essential for the efficacy of ESM (Kramer et al. 2014), previous qualitative work has been limited to the effects of ESM monitoring (Saunders et al. 2017). Finally, if ESM is to facilitate shared decision making and patient-clinician communication (Bos et al. 2019), the combined experiences of patients and clinicians are needed.

The present qualitative study will therefore comprehensively assess patients' and clinicians' experiences with the addition of intensive long-term ESM monitoring, episode alerts, and personalized feedback to clinical care.

Methods

Participants

Reporting is done according to the Standards for Reporting Qualitative Research (O'Brien et al. 2014). Participants are twenty patients with bipolar disorder type I or type II receiving treatment, and six clinicians who treated at least two patients participating in this study (see Table 1). Included patients met the following criteria: (1) ≥ 18 years of age, (2) diagnosed with and currently in treatment for bipolar disorder type I/II, and (3) demonstrate high occurrence of episodes (at least 2) in the previous year. Clinicians were selected based on their interest in using ESM in treatment.

Recruitment took place at two Dutch tertiary care institutions between May 2016 and July 2017. Six clinicians invited their patients to participate in the study until the intended cap of twenty participants was reached. After patients signed up, researchers telephoned them to provide more information. Interested patients were invited to the research facility, where the study was explained in detail.

Table 1 Baseline demographic and clinical characteristics of patients (N = 20) and clinicians (N = 6)

Characteristic	Patients	Clinicians
Gender (N)		
Male	4	5
Female	16	1
Age (N)		
20–35 years	9	0
36–50 years	8	3
51–65 years	3	3
Education level (N)		
Higher education	9	
Secondary education	5	
Secondary vocational education	3	
Pre-vocational education	3	
Years in treatment or years of experience as clinician (*M, SD*)	10.6 (8.8)	16.4 (10.3)
Years since bipolar disorder diagnosis (*M, SD*)	6.4 (6.3)	
Bipolar disorder diagnosis (N)	9	
Bipolar disorder type I	11	
Bipolar disorder type II		
Comorbid diagnoses (N)	12	
No comorbid Axis I/II disorder	1	
Attention Deficit/Hyperactivity Disorder	1	
Autism Spectrum Disorder	1	
Sleep disorder	1	
Alcohol/drug dependence	6	
Personality disorder		
Medication use (N)	2	
None	1	
Amphetamine	10	
Anti-epileptic	10	
Atypical antipsychotic	9	
Benzodiazepine	2	
Thyreomimetica	5	
Lithium	3	
Monoamine oxidase inhibitor	4	
Selective serotonin reuptake inhibitor	1	
Tricyclic antidepressant		
Profession (N)		
Psychiatrist		3
Psychologist		1
Psychiatric nurse		2
Experience with technology in treatment (N)		
None		2
A little experience		4
A lot of experience		0

Note. ESM = experience sampling methodology; M = mean; N = number; SD = standard deviation

Clinicians referred 28 patients to the study. Two patients were unreachable. Six patients declined participation during the first telephone call, expecting that study participation and the focus on mood would be too burdensome. This left a total of twenty patients that started and finished the study, of which eighteen were interviewed until data saturation was reached. All participants signed informed consent. The University Medical Center Groningen medical ethics committee approved of the study (201501161).

Study design

The goal of this project was twofold: to examine whether ESM data can be used to detect early warning signals for mania and depression, and to qualitatively assess experiences with adding ESM to bipolar disorder treatment. The study design was developed to meet both goals.

ESM. Patients received five ESM prompts per day for at least four consecutive months. Every three hours (time-contingent schedule), patients received a text message containing a link to the ESM assessment on their smartphone. The assessments were securely administered and stored via RoQua (https://www.roqua.nl) in patients' personal health records (see Additional file 1). Patients chose their own start and end time and had one hour to complete each assessment (which took approximately 1–2 min to complete). No reminder prompts were given. Researchers contacted patients after the first three days of monitoring and if compliance was low (Baxter and Hunton 2011), if they preferred regular contact, or if the weekly questionnaires (see below) indicated a manic or depressive episode. No financial compensation was offered to participants.

Bipolar symptoms

Patients weekly completed the Dutch versions of the Altman Self-Rating Mania Scale (ASRM) (Altman et al. 2001, 1997) and the Quick Inventory for Depressive Symptomatology (QIDS) (Rush et al. 2003; Bernstein et al. 2010). Both the patient and the clinician were e-mailed when scores exceeded cut-offs indicating potential manic (ASRM $\geq$ 5) (Miller et al. 2009) or depressive (QIDS $\geq$ 10) (Rush et al. 2003) episodes.

ESM items

The questionnaire consisted of 26 Dutch items pertaining to mood (e.g., cheerful, down), symptoms of bipolar disorder (e.g., racing thoughts, feeling inadequate), sleep, and activities (see Additional file 1). These items were based on previous ESM research (Knapen 2019; Krieke et al. 2016; Tyler et al. 2015) and interviews with three patients and a clinician on relevant constructs for people with bipolar disorder. Further, patients formulated one personal item they believed might be insightful to them. Most items were answered on visual analogue scales ranging from 0 ("not at all") to 100 ("very much"). Patients further had the option to write down anything in a comment field.

Compliance

Two patients were part of a pilot and therefore completed three instead of four months of the study. The eighteen other patients all completed at least four months of monitoring with an average of 18 weeks (*range* = 16–32). Near study end, all patients were offered to continue the monitoring for their own benefit (without receiving feedback), which two did for an additional 4 and 14 weeks. Average compliance (number of completed assessments divided by the number of assessments participants received) was 76% (491 assessments, *SD* = 137.8).

ESM feedback

Within one month after the end of the ESM monitoring, researcher FB constructed a personal feedback report (see Additional files 1, 2). This report contained information on (1) variation in mood and symptoms in general and related to time of day and activities, (2) frequency of activities, (3) occurrence of episodes in association with ESM items, (4) sleeping patterns, (5) personal questions, and (6) comment field entries. The feedback session took place on average 68 days (*SD* = 33.0) after the monitoring period had ended. Clinicians explained the feedback, asked patients to interpret unexpected findings, and helped them formulate conclusions. All clinicians were briefed beforehand on the interpretation of the ESM feedback and researcher FB was present to provide explanations if necessary. If new questions arose (in five cases), the researcher ran additional analyses and e-mailed the results to both patient and clinician.

Interviews

Follow-up interviews were held with 18 patients and 6 clinicians and took place at the research facility between April 2017 and March 2018. The interviews were planned three months after the feedback session (*M* = 107 days, *SD* = 21.5) and had an average duration of 46.8 min. Participants were explained the goal of the interview: to learn more about their experiences with adding ESM to clinical care. The interview started with the open question how participants reflected on their experiences with ESM. After fully exploring their first responses to this question, a semi-structured interview guide was used to ask open questions on (1) experiences with the ESM monitoring, the alerts, and the report and feedback session, (2) potential insights gained, (3) potential behavioral changes made, and (4) the utility of ESM for clinical care. Further, person-specific questions were asked using field notes made during the monitoring phase and the feedback session. All interviews were audio-recorded and transcribed verbatim. Interviews were conducted by FB (M.Sc., female, PhD-student) and ES (Ph.D., female, postdoctoral researcher), both trained in qualitative interviewing and analysis. At the time of the interview, all participants knew FB from the introduction and follow-up calls.

Qualitative data analysis

To understand patients' and clinicians' experiences with adding ESM to clinical care, thematic analysis was applied on the transcripts by FB, LK, and ES according to the Qualitative analysis Guide of Leuven (Casterle et al. 2012). Field notes and observations were analyzed to understand the effects of ESM monitoring while it took place.

First, transcripts were summarized in conceptual interview schemes and narrative reports to gain a holistic understanding of participants' experiences. Based on subthemes identified in the data (e.g., awareness), a concept code list was constructed. This code list was then used to code the transcripts in Atlas.TI (version 8), creating new codes when previously unidentified themes were encountered. The codes were then grouped in four central themes, which were verified against all transcripts and discussed with all authors. Participants were invited to provide feedback on a summary of the themes.

Results

Thematic analysis resulted in four themes (see Fig. 2): (1) effects of ESM monitoring, (2) effects of the weekly symptom questionnaires and alerts, (3) effects of the personal report and feedback session, and (4) recommendations on the use of ESM in clinical practice. For each aspect of ESM, patients and clinicians described perceived positive and negative effects, and effects on treatment they attributed to ESM. See Tables 2 and 3 for illustrative quotes related to the themes.

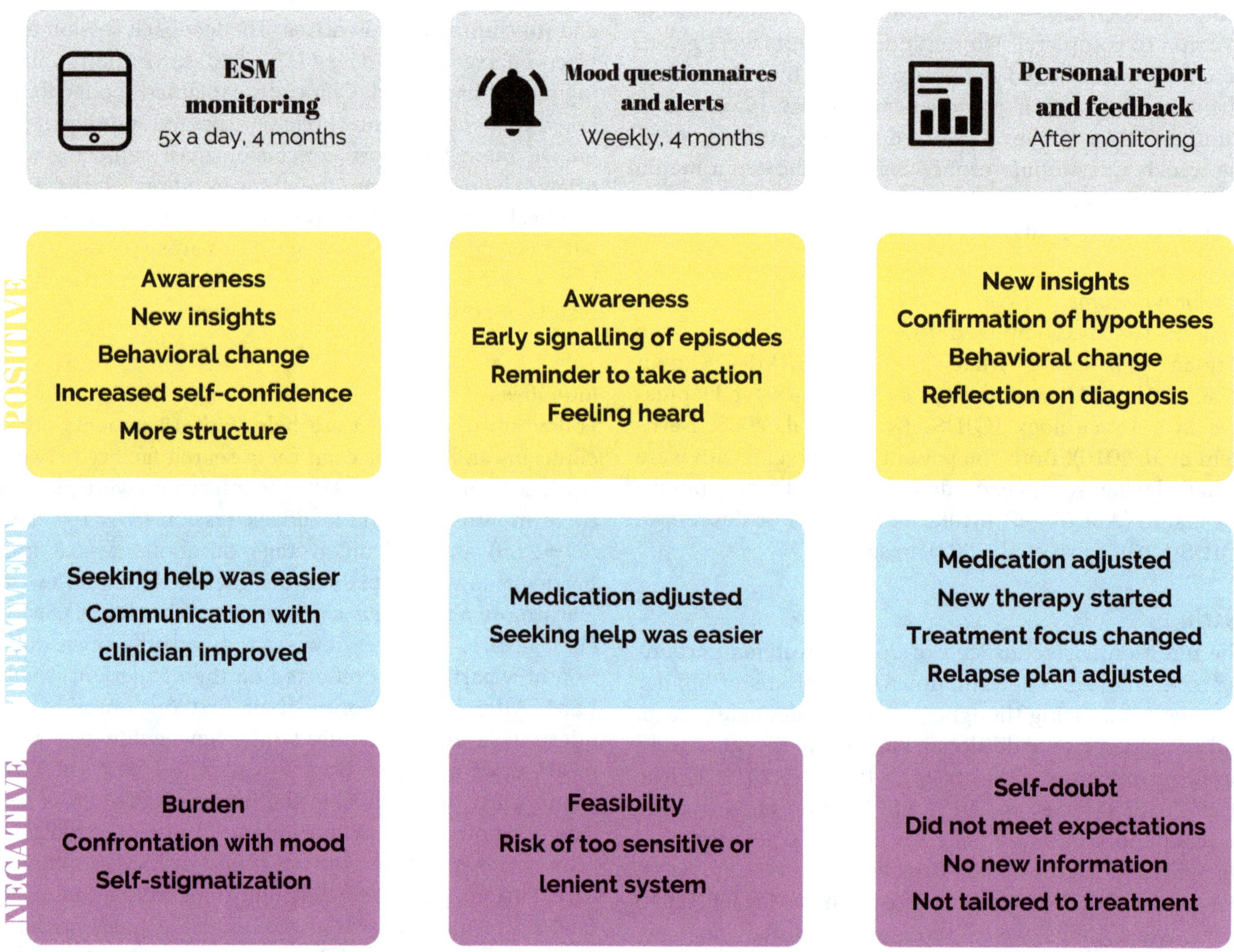

Fig. 2 Schematic overview of the main findings of the first three themes: perceived effects of ESM monitoring, the weekly questionnaires (ASRM/QIDS) and alerts, and the personal report and feedback session

Table 2 Quotes related to theme 1 (effects of monitoring) and theme 2 (effects of weekly questionnaires and alerts)

Quote patients	Quote clinicians
Theme 1: effects of monitoring	
ID13: During the monitoring period I have mentioned this several times, but what really surprised me and helped me a lot was the compartmentalization in those five parts a day. That really was a revelation that I had never heard before in mental health care. Nobody had divided it in small pieces of three hours. Previously, I only had the Life Chart, once every 24 h. A big yes, or a big no, or a big wow or a big 'bleh'. And now, something unpleasant could happen, and it would make sense that it makes me feel bad, or hyper, or sad. That will maybe last a part of three hours, but then my mood is... [...] So this is what I learned from the monitoring, and I don't know if this was the intended effect of the study. But what I learned is to look at myself much more objectively, and much more relaxed. (female patient in her forties)	ID22: Yes, that they become much more aware of factors influencing their mood. And that really differs across persons. That's one thing. Or the fact that they become much more aware of their vulnerability in developing mood swings. An important part of treatment is about accepting that you are chronically instable. Some people keep wanting a sort of stable phase or that everything will be okay again, will return to how it was before. And that of course doesn't always work out like that. And this [ESM] holds up some sort of mirror for them, of course. (male psychiatrist in his thirties)
ID2: In the period that I filled in the assessments, I experienced several times that I answered that I hadn't been outside, for example, during a week I was at my mothers' place sitting around and being depressed. And then I had to answer three times that I hadn't yet been outside, and no, I didn't feel that well. You know, like that, and then I thought, well, okay I'll just go. That happened multiple times I think. (female patient in her twenties)	ID25: Yes, this really helps, you get to the point much more easily, and can give better targeted lifestyle advice. If they haven't already developed those insights themselves. That is what I believe to be the advantage of self-monitoring and assignments you can do at home, outside our conversations here in the clinic: that you can adapt your own behavior and make healthy choices, so that is a nice side effect of this study, I think. (male psychiatric nurse in his fifties)
ID17: Especially when the assessments come at an inconvenient moment. I find that very stressful. That is mostly the problem. The questions were completed in no time, but just, when I was in the car for example, a text comes, and I keep thinking, "I should not forget, I should not forget". That's it. No, the amount of work itself was not that much. (female patient in her forties)	ID24: On the Life Chart you can indicate that you score this or that, on average. A lot of people will then say that the actual situation is very different. So the micro-level is much more fine-grained. The danger is, though, that if people feel very bad, because their relationship has ended or I don't know, that they will immediately think that they have a depression. That the micro-level overshadows the macro-level. (male psychiatrist in his sixties)
ID8: By continually confronting you with it, you keep getting reminded of the fact you're doing badly. Or badly... Sad, that you're feeling sad. So then I found it hard to look at it another way. Because normally, I do that, I try to do things differently and find distraction and everything. But when I looked for distractions, I got a new assessment, making me think, "damn, I am indeed doing very badly". And that's what I found really annoying, or really annoying... I didn't like that. (female patient in her thirties)	ID23: Well, if there are people who keep getting hung up on it and keep feeling sad as a result, then I find that a negative consequence. But still, if that is the case, it suggests to me that we [patient and clinician] have to work on that. So in that sense, it can be helpful. (male psychiatrist in his forties)
ID15: Now I'm doing well, and I complete the Life Chart every morning. And then, for the rest of the day, I don't have to think about my having bipolar disorder. Because then I know that I'm okay, I don't have to pay attention to anything. But if you have to complete a questionnaire five times a day, then you really get confronted five times a day that you have that disorder. Throughout the day, you keep being confronted with 'you have a disorder'. (female patient in her fifties)	Interviewer: Was the burden too much? Weighing it against what patients gained from it? ID23: Maybe. Maybe it was too much, but you don't know that beforehand. That's why I think: you have to try. And self-management is a major step. So to invest a good amount of energy into that, because you have a severe disorder, you can invest a lot of energy into that, and then it is actually helpful to have something like this available to see if it gives you more insight. So in hindsight, yes it might have been burdensome, but I find that a bit too easy. Although, if you start using it now as a tool in clinical practice, then it might have to be toned down just a little. (male psychiatrist in his forties)
Theme 2: effects of weekly questionnaires and alerts	
ID14: I had expected that, when feeling more manic, or hypomanic, I would really find the questionnaire stupid. That's what I expected, but that happened actually right near the end of the ESM monitoring period, that I noticed "something is happening and I don't really trust it". And you also notified me of elevated things. And at that moment, that was actually really nice. Like, I really have to take step back. I feel fantastic, that's not it, but I hadn't realized yet that the scores were high until I saw it in the questionnaires. And then I could admit it more easily to myself, that maybe I had to take a step back. I will e-mail [clinician]. That was a really good experience that really helped me. Like: if I see it coming beforehand one way or another, because usually I notice it too late, then I experience everything less intense. (female patient in her twenties)	ID22: Well, I was really busy then, and then I also got those alerts and I thought: "do I have to do something with this as well?" That felt a bit as a responsibility, in a way. Whereas I always believe, you know, people really have to reach out themselves. That's what you teach them, that we don't take it all over and take care of them. So you really need to make clear agreements beforehand, like "what are we going to do when I see this?" And now, it just happened. I think it is something you can use in your treatment, but then you really have to discuss with patients, "what will we do, do you want me to reach out, or not? You get the alerts, do you appreciate that or not?" I think that is a good opportunity, but you have to think about this really well." (male psychiatrist in his thirties)

Table 2 (continued)

Quote patients	Quote clinicians
ID7: That I was not alone or let go in this. Because on the one hand, I am really inclined to go my own way and withdraw myself, really disregard everything and everyone. But back then I would consistently complete the questionnaires. And well, that by doing so I was not and could not be invisible. And actually, I like that. Because the withdrawing that I do, I actually don't want to do that. And then it helps if somewhere a graph shows: "this woman is not doing well. And I will e-mail her." (female patient in her fifties)	

Effects of ESM monitoring

Positive effects

First, almost all patients described increased awareness of their mood and symptoms, behavior, wellbeing, factors influencing mood, and positive aspects in their lives. Many patients contrasted the Life-Chart with ESM and highlighted the benefits of dividing their mood into multiple distinct components (e.g., agitated, easily distracted, racing thoughts) rather than focusing on mania or depression as a whole, making it easier to judge their mood and the likelihood of impending episodes. Several patients described heightened mood awareness even after the monitoring period was over. Clinicians confirmed seeing heightened awareness in their patients. Both patients and clinicians found this one of the most helpful aspects of ESM monitoring.

Second, many patients described gaining new insights on the impact of their behavior, activities, events, and time of day on their mood, which their clinicians confirmed. Other patients realized that their mood could also act independently of their behavior or context, which made mood swings easier to accept. Two patients learned that their mood fluctuated much more during the day than expected. Two other patients learned they had trouble recognizing their emotions, and felt that this improved during the monitoring period. One patient learned that her job was too heavy for her. One clinician gained new insights into his patients' coping strategies. Many patients and clinicians indicated that ESM monitoring helped patients discover these insights by themselves, thereby firmly consolidating them.

Third, more than half of the patients made concrete behavioral changes to influence mood and symptoms (e.g., becoming more active when feeling depressed, or slowing down when experiencing (hypo)mania). Clinicians confirmed this observation. Several patients continued monitoring their mood in a diary or the Life-Chart. One patient felt she could safely experiment with the strict behavioral rules she had learned during years of therapy and investigated the effects with the ESM monitoring. One patient described that the monitoring led to more meaningful conversations with her environment about what it means to have bipolar disorder.

Finally, a few patients described gaining more self-confidence in rating their mood and becoming more structured due to the steady rhythm of the assessments each day.

Effects on treatment

Some patients felt that the threshold to seek help was lowered, and that their increased awareness helped in the communication with their clinician.

Negative effects

Patients attributed several negative effects to the ESM monitoring. First, although many patients noted that the assessments were quick and easy to complete, most patients found five assessments per day burdensome because they felt disturbed in daily activities. Some felt they constantly kept (the possibility of) assessments in their minds and felt guilty or irritated when missing them. Nonetheless, most patients indicated that the benefits of the monitoring outweighed the burden, which aligned with the impression of their clinicians.

Secondly, approximately half of the patients felt negatively influenced by the frequent confrontation with their moods and symptoms, especially when already feeling depressed or (hypo)manic. When feeling depressed, several patients described that this confrontation made them feel restless, emotional, or irritated, and made them worry about their wellbeing. Alternatively, when experiencing (hypo)mania, several patients felt too busy and wanted to avoid reflection when feeling good. Of those describing a negative response, around half added that the confrontation actually helped them to become aware of their mood and either accept it, act upon it, or put it into perspective. The other half believed the assessments impaired their usual coping strategy, seeking distraction. Several clinicians agreed that confrontation might be difficult for patients, although increased awareness might mobilize patients into action.

Finally, a few patients felt that the assessments were a constant reminder of their diagnosis, the "unhealthy" part of themselves. They described that each assessment reminded them that they monitored themselves because of their bipolar disorder. In this way, ESM monitoring was perceived as self-stigmatizing, which two clinicians also warned against.

Effects of the weekly questionnaires and alerts

Positive effects

First, several patients described that the alerts made them more aware of their mood and events of the past week, and possible ways to cope when mood worsened. For one patient, the alerts signaled a hypomanic state before realizing it herself, allowing her to get early treatment for the first time. Several others found that the alerts confirmed what they or their environment already suspected, which helped coax them into action. Second, many patients felt supported by the idea that someone (here, the researcher) would inform them of elevated symptoms. They described feeling heard and less alone.

Effects on treatment

For one patient, medication was occasionally adjusted upon receiving alerts. Several other patients found it easier to seek help and contacted their clinician. Clinicians differed in whether they contacted patients themselves or let patients seek contact and argued that this might differ across patients. The rationale given for not contacting patients was that recognizing and acting upon episodes are important treatment goals, and patients should be encouraged to seek help themselves. As such, several clinicians emphasized the need for making clear agreements with patients on who contacts whom in case of elevated scores. Clinicians also questioned the feasibility of acting upon alerts if sent for their entire caseload.

Negative effects

Patients did not describe negative effects. Two patients were curious of (but not bothered by) the timing of the alerts; they either received alerts when feeling well, or did not receive alerts when they signaled episodes themselves (e.g., QIDS score exceeded cut-off but for less than three weeks). Some clinicians suggested that a too sensitive alert system could lead to panic or demotivate patients.

Effects of the personal report and feedback session

Many patients and clinicians were positively surprised by the amounts of data collected by patients. The report was described as 'mapping yourself', and 'a personal history on a very small scale'. Many patients reread the report at home or showed it to close family or friends.

Positive effects

First, many patients described that the report helped them in gaining new insights on (1) the association between mood, behavior, sleep, and activities, (2) the presence or duration of emotions, (3) the benefits of healthy life style adjustments, (4) warning signals for manic or depressive episodes, and (5) the frequency and duration of behaviors and activities. Two patients used the personal report to specifically test ideas about themselves or their life style (e.g., effects of soft drugs on mood), which they saw confirmed. Many patients explicitly mentioned that the report was a more accurate, objective, and detailed reflection of their wellbeing during the monitoring period than their own account, which they described to be often discolored by present mood. Although clinicians did not describe new insights themselves, they believed that the report had been insightful to patients.

Second, several patients attributed lasting behavioral changes to the report. Two patients noticed the effects of sleep on their wellbeing, and started slowing down and cancelling appointments when they slept badly. Others learned how activities affected their mood, and started doing positive activities more often, even when feeling depressed. Finally, one patient concluded from the report that feeling tense preceded depressive episodes, and started taking medication when noticing tension. At the time of the interview, this had occurred several times, and she felt that this strategy had made the episodes less intense. Many patients felt that the graphs objectively showed the benefits of certain behavioral changes in their own data, making it easier to accept and act on these insights. The visual nature of the report further helped some patients to 'get out of their head'.

Finally, the personal report made several patients reflect on their diagnosis: some described that it was helpful to once again realize and accept the impact of the disorder, which was also described by two clinicians. Although a few other patients had hoped that the report would give rise to a different diagnosis, they found it a helpful reminder that sometimes, they could feel bad for no apparent reason.

Table 3 Quotes related to theme 3 (effects of personal report and feedback session) and theme 4 (recommendations on the use of ESM in clinical practice)

Quote patients	Quote clinicians
Theme 3: effects of personal report	
ID2: Actually, last week a lot of people asked me to go here or go there, and I told them, "actually I'm not feeling so well, I'm not sure." And they started saying, "what does it matter, if you're already sick you should come anyway and be sick tomorrow". And then I thought, "no, I'm not doing this because I know how this will go, then it will happen that day and again and again the next days and before you know it, I'm really not doing well and that will have its effect on others as well." So in that way it worked maybe, a sort of small life lessons. Interviewer: Is that something that the report taught you, or? ID2: Well, to see that on paper, that really worked, those large mood swings. That you really have some sort of reflective moment. This is what happened then, and in that sense I think unconsciously shaped the way I think, I think. (female patient in her twenties)	ID25: For example, for one client, you later explicitly investigated sleeping, tiredness. After using cannabis, for example, the night before. Well, those very specific data coming out of the study are very helpful. Because I can have a very strong intuition that something is the case, but now we have it on paper, it is confirmed. Because she herself has supplied the data that shed a light on the situation. And there were more explicit outcomes: hours of sleep, energy, that's what we discussed, that's helpful to integrate in relapse prevention plans. (male psychiatric nurse in his fifties)
ID15: Now I know immediately that when I really start to worry and feel tense, it is the beginning of a depressive episode. If it lasts for about a week, I know that it is the start of a depressive episode, and I start taking medications, and I don't sink so deeply. Interviewer: Does this help? ID15: Yes, because I start taking my medications sooner. Because usually it takes a week or three before they start working, and then I notice a bit sooner that the tension starts to disappear. Normally I am really tense first and I no longer want anything at all, and because the medications take a while to start working, you reach the point that nothing works anymore, that you really have to fight to keep doing your daily activities. Now I get there on time, because I've already started taking my medications. So I don't sink so deeply anymore. (female patient in her fifties)	
ID14: Ah yes, I couldn't do anything with it [personal report]. But that maybe also has something to do with my expectations. I don't know what I'd expected. Probably I'd expected that I… that something about myself I didn't … That's what I'd hoped, maybe. I'd hoped that something would come out that would help. A piece of the puzzle. You know. You really want that it does something big. And it mostly was a confirmation of everything I already knew. And that is okay, but that is not what I'd hoped. Nice that I know myself better than I thought, I liked that, that there were no surprises. But I also thought, "and what now, now I have this, and what should I do?" So it didn't help me as much. (female patient in her twenties)	ID23: If you look at the results, it really is so hard to interpret them. It's still much more complicated than you had hoped beforehand. On the one hand, it's a lot of data and I like graphs and such, I think they're nice, you have a sort of overview, and well, about activities and such, it is solid. But what comes out as predictors disappoints me. Such that I think: it's not so unequivocal or it's not so easy to predict. Especially for people who are so instable in their mood, then the story gets even more unclear. (male psychiatrist in his forties)
Theme 4: recommendations for the use of ESM in clinical practice	
ID5: Like I'm saying, if you're young you're really inclined to go against everything. If somebody says something, you won't accept it, whereas if you've experienced it yourself, then you just know, you can't go around it. You see, without such a study it can take years before you've been through all that or have experienced a relapse or episode. And that's such a pity. Whereas if you can demonstrate such small changes with this study, they don't have to experience it all themselves. That they don't experience all the very heavy consequences, but see the small changes in themselves, which they have filled out themselves. (female patient in her forties)	ID25: I would really try to develop it tailored to the situation of the patient. And maybe link it to the relapse prevention plan. And it would be even better to also link it to the Life Chart method, for example. Or a sort of mood app, right? I mean, those exist, but are usually not so comprehensive. This way, you have all the information that you could use in treatment, and you have the aspect of self-management that can directly, in that moment, be adapted or stimulated even. (male psychiatric nurse in his fifties)
ID10: During therapy or something, it [ESM] might also be very easy. Then the system could directly inform your clinician, rather than bringing a copy yourself, so to speak. That they [the clinicians] could directly, if you give your consent, have insight in the data. And yes, the system doesn't lie. You can show that you have filled it out, at those moments. (male patient in his twenties)	ID26: The difficulty remains that this is a self-report measure, so people indicate their own visions on their problems. There are people, if you ask them a number between 1 and 10 to indicate their stress level, who will say a 10 with a very calm demeanor. Or the other way around, sitting there like this [raising arms to indicate high stress level] saying, it's a 5. An app like this [ESM] will have it wrong too, people are not so good at judging themselves. So you always have to be aware that it is not a science, in fact it is their vision on their problems. (female psychologist in her forties)

Effects on treatment

Five patients and their clinicians made changes in treatment that they attributed to the personal report. One patient started emotion regulation therapy based on her typed entries. For one patient, the relapse prevention plan was adjusted based on new insights in the personal report. For another patient, the focus of treatment shifted, because the report had shown that the previous focus was no longer relevant. Yet another patient was referred to a psychologist. Finally, medication was adjusted for one patient. Several other patients and clinicians mentioned that the report provided them with a helpful framework to discuss the course of treatment and the patient-clinician relationship. Several patients and clinicians had planned to adjust the relapse plan or refer the patient, but had not yet started the process.

Negative effects

A few negative effects were described. Some patients were apprehensive of the feedback session, thinking that the results might have implications for their diagnosis or treatment. One patient, whose data showed large mood fluctuations, started doubting her diagnosis and ability to judge her mood: contrary to her own experiences, she had inadvertently understood from the report that she had experienced no manic episodes.

Although many patients and clinicians mostly reflected positively on the personal report, they were also somewhat disappointed by it. Many had high expectations, believing the report would suggest novel directions for treatment, indicate a different diagnosis, or provide the missing piece of the puzzle to help patients cope better with their complaints. They felt that the descriptive nature of the report did not meet their need for unambiguous conclusions. Some clinicians noted that so many factors appeared to influence mood and symptoms, that it was hard to find clear patterns in ESM data, especially because most patients showed erratic mood fluctuations. Some patients felt that the report only confirmed what they already knew or had learned during the monitoring period, or were unhappy that the monitoring took place during an unrepresentative period (e.g., during holidays or stable periods). A few patients further found the graphs difficult to understand.

Several clinicians added that the report was difficult to tie to treatment goals, and that it might have been more effective to discuss the feedback more frequently than just at the end of the monitoring period. Finally, two clinicians warned that ESM results could falsely suggest a hard truth, while ESM data supposedly only shows the patient's vision on their complaints. They stressed the need for clinicians to explain this to patients.

Recommendations for the use of ESM in clinical care

Based on their experiences with ESM, patients and clinicians reflected on the use of ESM in clinical care.

For whom and when

Many patients and clinicians would especially recommend ESM for young, recently diagnosed people, for whom the insights yielded by ESM are still new. Clinicians also proposed patients in long-term care who keep having trouble and need a fresh perspective. Some patients and clinicians would refrain from ESM during (1) highly unstable or bad periods, because ESM could be too confrontational, (2) prolonged (depressive) periods without change, (3) good periods, when patients do not want to worry about their diagnosis, and 4) periods when there is insufficient suffering to motivate patients for ESM. Indeed, all but two patients opted not to continue the monitoring after four months, when they believed to have gained sufficient insights and additional data gathering was no longer necessary for the personal report. Several clinicians would not recommend ESM to patients already very pre-occupied with their disorder.

Goals

The majority of patients and clinicians advocated that ESM be tailored to the patient's situation and treatment goal. Many patients would consider doing ESM again when (1) symptoms increase, (2) specific hypotheses arise, (3) starting new medications or treatments, or (4) they want to monitor for episodes. Clinicians highlighted the potential of providing alerts and advice in case of elevated ESM scores, to train patients in recognizing mood changes and getting help on time. Two clinicians deemed ESM more reliable and insightful than commonly used methods like paper-and-pencil registration or the Life-Chart (5).

ESM monitoring

Many patients and clinicians would have preferred the possibility to personalize the content, frequency, and duration of the ESM diary to better fit the patient's situation and treatment goal. Furthermore, many patients and clinicians liked the combination between micro-level ESM and macro-level symptom questionnaires.

Data access

Many patients and clinicians suggested discussing ESM feedback at every treatment session, to keep the feedback relevant and the patient motivated. Some patients would have liked to examine the feedback in between sessions.

Others found an overview feedback report after several months more relevant. Some patients suggested that patients should be offered the choice to share their data with their clinicians, whereas most patients assumed that all data is automatically available to both themselves and their clinician.

Report

On top of the information included in the report, several patients and clinicians would like to have seen (1) effects of starting or stopping medication or treatment, (2) effects of life style adjustments, (3) testing of specific hypotheses, (4) decisions on diagnosis, or (5) simple explanations of the data analysis.

Clinician role

All patients and clinicians saw an important role for the clinician in the process of ESM, especially in discussing the personal feedback. Many patients preferred this clinician to be someone they know well and see frequently. Patients and clinicians further emphasized that clinicians should learn how to interpret ESM feedback and should believe in the potential of ESM. Patients and clinicians suggested the feedback session is successful if the clinician (1) invests time to agree on the goal, content, and interpretation of ESM, (2) facilitates conversation on the meaning of the results, (3) teaches patients how to interpret ESM feedback, (4) is conscious of potential negative effects, and (5) makes clear agreements on what to do in case of elevated scores.

Discussion

The present qualitative study examined how patients with bipolar disorder and their clinicians experienced the addition of long-term ESM (i.e., 4 months, 5 assessments daily), episode alerts, and personalized feedback to clinical care. Confirming other qualitative work (Saunders et al. 2017), most patients and clinicians reported that ESM monitoring and personalized feedback helped patients to cope better with their disorder by increasing awareness, offering new insights, and encouraging life style adjustments. In addition, as has been described as the promise of ESM (Murnane et al. 2016; Bos et al. 2019; Saunders et al. 2017), the monitoring and alerts were perceived as facilitating communication between patient and clinician. A relatively small group perceived the personalized feedback as helpful in informing treatment directions. As such, the present study is the first to demonstrate that long-term ESM is perceived to be a helpful tool for patients with bipolar disorder and their clinicians.

The present qualitative findings warrant further quantitative research to confirm both the positive and negative effects of adding ESM to bipolar disorder treatment. Potential beneficial effects of ESM should be weighed against the considerable burden and the risk of negative effects reported by several patients, namely the confrontation with (negative) mood and pre-occupation with having a disorder. Indeed, even though quantitative studies often report high compliance rates (Vachon et al. 2019), qualitative work consistently demonstrates that patients and clinicians can be apprehensive of these effects (Bos et al. 2019; Saunders et al. 2017). For some patients, this may be sufficient reason not to participate in ESM. ESM seems to carry the risk of making a small yet significant group of patients hyperaware of their mood, especially during mood episodes (Genugten et al. 2020; Conner and Reid 2012), thereby cutting off adaptive coping strategies such as seeking distraction (Schermer 2009). Therefore, when implementing ESM, clinicians have to be aware of potential negative effects and discuss them with patients, whereas researchers have to ensure that ESM assessments minimize mood reactivity (Myin-Germeys 2012).

Notable was the finding that the descriptive nature of the personal feedback report disappointed patients and clinicians, who had hoped for more clear-cut advice on diagnosis and ways to improve well-being. Statistical analyses currently under development show promise in summarizing complex ESM data by predicting diagnosis (Perez Arribas et al. 2018), forecasting episodes (Smit et al. 2019), or testing associations (Snippe et al. 2016). These techniques could also inform on a personalized alert system that optimizes both sensitivity and specificity. However, these analyses are still relatively new and need empirical testing before they can be implemented in individual patients (Wichers et al. 2019; Faurholt-Jepsen et al. 2018). A recent study reported that, even when the same data was used, different analytical approaches led to highly disparate clinical advice across research groups (Bastiaansen et al. 2020). Indeed, patients in our sample attributed high credibility to scientific data even when it contradicted their own beliefs. These results urge researchers to further develop valid models. Until they become available, researchers should carefully manage expectations of patients and clinicians on the possibilities of ESM feedback.

In the present study, the ESM diary, alerts, and personalized feedback were standardized and minimally embedded in clinical care. However, patients and clinicians indicated a desire for more personalization and integration in care, as these ESM components can be expected to differ across people, and even vary within patients, based on current treatment goals and the patient situation

(Bos et al. 2019). This is further exemplified by the finding that only 2 out of 20 patients continued monitoring when feedback and embedding in care were no longer provided. For the academic field, this means considerable effort needs to be invested into developing the necessary technology for the integration of personalized ESM in clinical care. This translation from research to practice is often overlooked (Os et al. 2013; Fisher and Boswell 2016) but imperative for its usability. Integration requires a user-friendly interface that helps patients and clinicians to construct a personalized and scientifically valid ESM diary, sets sensitive alerts if needed, and provides them with automatically available personalized feedback. Such an endeavor necessitates intensive collaboration between researchers, patients, clinicians, and software developers. Currently, our research team is developing such a tool termed PETRA (PErsonalized Treatment by Real-Time Assessment, https://www.petrapsy.nl/en/).

Finally, if ESM should become available to clinical care, the question remains if, when, and how ESM can be useful and feasible for any given patient. For example, the low-intensity yearlong self-monitoring with the Life-Chart (Leverich and Post 1993) or ChronoRecord (Bauer et al. 2004) might suffice for some, whereas for others, the high-intensity and detailed ESM might better fit their needs. The sampling schedule will greatly depend on the intended goal of the self-monitoring: e.g., enhancing self-management, tracking treatment effects, or informing diagnostics. Therefore, many participants recommended involving both patient and clinician equally in all decisions regarding ESM: the goal and desirability of ESM, potential negative effects and burden, the ESM diary content and schedule, clinician involvement, and ESM feedback interpretation. Reaching agreement on these points beforehand is essential for enhancing patient self-management and empowerment through self-monitoring technology (Schermer 2009). Based on their experiences, we have formulated crucial issues for patients and clinicians to discuss together when considering using ESM (see Table 4). These discussion points can help in deciding if and how to use ESM in treatment.

Table 4 Practical discussion points for clinicians and patients to consider before starting ESM in treatment, based on the findings of the present study

1: Determine rationale of ESM	
Desirability of ESM	**Do both patient and clinician agree that ESM is helpful and doable?**
Goal of ESM	What do patient and clinician hope to gain from ESM? How does it fit into the patients' current treatment goals?
2: Manage expectations	
Risk of negative effects	Are patient or clinician apprehensive of any negative effects (e.g., mood worsening, pre-occupation with disorder)? What can the patient do if these occur?
Burden	Is it okay if patients' occasionally miss assessments, and how often?
Feedback	What can patient and clinician expect to learn from the ESM feedback, and what not?
3: Determine the ESM protocol	
Feasibility of the monitoring	What frequency and duration of assessments is necessary to meet the goal and remain feasible for both patient and clinician?
Content of the assessments	What should the ESM diary include to meet the goal?
Need for weekly mood questionnaires	Is weekly monitoring for episodes necessary?
Desirability of alerts to patient and/or clinician	Do patient and clinician want to be informed of elevated scores?
4: Determine level of involvement of clinician	
Data access	What data is the clinician allowed to examine and how often?
Degree of contact through ESM	Does the patient contact the clinician in case of elevated scores or alerts, or vice versa? What happens if patients indicate elevated scores?
5: Facilitate interpretation of personalized feedback	
Frequency of feedback	How often is the personalized feedback discussed?
Content of feedback	Which data are discussed? Is it necessary to discuss all the feedback every session, or only parts of it?
Interpretation of feedback	Can the clinician help the patient to read the graphs? How do both interpret the feedback, and are there meaningful differences therein?
6: Evaluate regularly	
Usefulness and feasibility of ESM	Does the current ESM protocol still meet its intended goal or does it needs to be adapted? Is it still feasible for the patient?
Negative effects	Have any negative effects of ESM occurred and (how) can the patient cope with them?

Strengths of our study include the prolonged ESM monitoring period, which so far has not been reported elsewhere, and our in-depth exploration of patients' and clinicians' experiences with all aspects of ESM (long-term monitoring, alerts, and personalized feedback). Their suggestions can inform future academic and clinical endeavors on the utility of ESM and patients and clinicians willing to experiment with ESM.

A limitation of this study is its convenience sample: 80% of included patients were women, relatively few clinicians were included, and participants were selected (in part) on their interest in self-monitoring. Given our sample of convenience, as well as the fast-moving field and the diversity in healthcare systems, generalizations to other settings should be done cautiously. Additionally, any positive or negative effects that patients and clinicians attributed to ESM could be due to other causes unknown to them. Finally, clinicians were less involved during the monitoring period, which limited integration of ESM in treatment.

Conclusions

This study provides demonstrates that long-term ESM monitoring, alerts, and personalized feedback are perceived as beneficial to the treatment and self-management of patients with bipolar disorder. To optimize clinical utility of ESM, our results suggest that future research should prioritize the development of clinically relevant data analyses and the necessary technology to enable personalized integration of ESM in clinical care. Furthermore, we recommend intensive collaboration between patient and clinician to ensure ESM fits the patient's situation and treatment goals. This way, ESM has the potential improve clinical care.

Supplementary information

Additional file 1. ESM items, data security, and example of feedback report.

Additional file 2. R code for the feedback report.

Acknowledgements

We thank all patients and clinicians who have shared their data, thoughts, and ideas with us, the clinicians at GGZ Drenthe and the University Center Psychiatry Groningen for their help with the recruitment of patients, and S. van der Tuin for helping with the data collection.

Authors' contributions

Authorship roles: All authors were involved in the design of the study. FB collected the experience sampling data and performed the qualitative interviews, with help from ES. The qualitative data was analyzed by FB with the supervision of ES and LK. FB wrote the first draft of the article, after which all co-authors critically revised the article. All authors read and approved the final manuscript.

Author details

[1] Rob Giel Research Center, University of Groningen, University Medical Center Groningen, PO Box 30.001, 9700 RB Groningen, The Netherlands. [2] Interdisciplinary Center Psychopathology and Emotion Regulation (ICPE), University of Groningen, University Medical Center Groningen, Groningen, The Netherlands. [3] Department of Specialized Training, Psychiatric Hospital Mental Health Services Drenthe, Outpatient Clinics, Assen, The Netherlands.

References

Altman EG, Hedeker D, Peterson JL, Davis JM. The Altman self-rating mania scale. Biol Psychiatry. 1997;42(10):948.

Altman E, Hedeker D, Peterson JL, Davis JM. A comparative evaluation of three self-rating scales for acute mania. BiolPsychiatry. 2001;50(6):468.

Bastiaansen JA, Kunkels YK, Blaauw FJ, Boker SM, Ceulemans E, Chen M, et al. Time to get personal? The impact of researchers choices on the selection of treatment targets using the experience sampling methodology. J Psychosom Res. 2020;89:110211.

Bauer M, Grof P, Gyulai L, Rasgon N, Glenn T, Whybrow PC. Using technology to improve longitudinal studies: self-reporting with ChronoRecord in bipolar disorder. Bipolar Disord. 2004;6(1):67–74.

Baxter RJ, Hunton JE. Capturing affect via the experience sampling method: prospects for accounting information systems researchers. Int J Account Inform Syst. 2011;12(2):90–8.

Bernstein IH, Rush AJ, Suppes T, Kyotoku Y, Warden D. The Quick Inventory of Depressive Symptomatology (clinician and self-report versions) in patients with bipolar disorder. CNS Spectr. 2010;15(6):367–73.

Bilderbeck AC, Saunders KE, Price J, Goodwin GM. Psychiatric assessment of mood instability: qualitative study of patient experience. Br J Psychiatry. 2014;204(3):234–9.

Bos FM, Snippe E, Bruggeman R, Wichers M, van der Krieke L. Insights of patients and clinicians on the promise of the experience sampling method for psychiatric care. Psychiatr Serv. 2019. https://doi.org/10.1176/appi.ps.201900050.

Conner TS, Reid KA. Effects of intensive mobile happiness reporting in daily life. Soc Psychol Person Sci. 2012;3(3):315–23.

de Casterle BD, Gastmans C, Bryon E, Denier Y. QUAGOL: A guide for qualitative data analysis. Int J Nurs Stud. 2012;49(3):360.

Faurholt-Jepsen M, Bauer M, Kessing LV. Smartphone-based objective monitoring in bipolar disorder: status and considerations. Int J Bipolar Dis. 2018;6(1):1–7.

Fisher AJ, Boswell JF. Enhancing the personalization of psychotherapy with dynamic assessment and modeling. Assessment. 2016;23(4):496.

Knapen SE. Rhythm & Blues: Chronobiology in the Pathophysiology and Treatment of Mood Disorders. Groningen: Rijksuniversiteit; 2019.

Kramer I, Simons CJP, Hartmann JA, Menne-Lothmann C, Viechtbauer W, Peeters F, et al. A therapeutic application of the experience sampling method in the treatment of depression: a randomized controlled trial. World Psychiatry. 2014;13(1):68.

Larson R, Csikszentmihalyi M. The experience sampling method. New Directions for Methodology of Social & Behavioral Science. 1983.

Lean M, Fornells-Ambrojo M, Milton A, Lloyd-Evans B, Harrison-Stewart B, Yesufu-Udechuku A, et al. Self-management interventions for people with severe mental illness: systematic review and meta-analysis. Br J Psychiatry. 2019;214(5):260–8.

Leverich GS, Post RM. The NIMH life chart manual for recurrent affective illness: The LCM. NIMH Monograph. 1993.

Michalak EE, Yatham LN, Kolesar S, Lam RW. Bipolar disorder and quality of life: a patient-centered perspective. Qual Life Res. 2006;15(1):25–37.

Miller CJ, Johnson SL, Eisner L. Assessment tools for adult bipolar disorder. Clin Psychol Sci Pract. 2009;16(2):188–201.

Murnane EL, Cosley D, Chang P, Guha S, Frank E, Gay G, et al. Self-monitoring practices, attitudes, and needs of individuals with bipolar disorder: implications for the design of technologies to manage mental health. J Am Med Inform Assoc. 2016;23(3):477–84.

Murray G, Suto M, Hole R, Hale S, Amari E, Michalak EE, et al. Self-management strategies used by 'high functioning' individuals with bipolar disorder: from research to clinical practice. Clin Psychol Psychother. 2011;18(2):95–109.

Myin-Germeys I. Psychiatry. In: Mehl MR, Conner TS, editors. Handbook of research methods for studying daily life. New York, NY: Guilford Press; 2012. p. 636.

Myin-Germeys I, Kasanova Z, Vaessen T, Vachon H, Kirtley O, Viechtbauer W, et al. Experience sampling methodology in mental health research: new insights and technical developments. World Psychiatry. 2018;17(2):123–32.

O'Brien BC, Harris IB, Beckman TJ, Reed DA, Cook DA. Standards for reporting qualitative research: a synthesis of recommendations. Acad Med. 2014;89(9):1245.

Perez Arribas I, Goodwin GM, Geddes JR, Lyons T, Saunders KE. A signature-based machine learning model for distinguishing bipolar disorder and borderline personality disorder. Transl Psychiatry. 2018;8(1):1–7.

Pini S, de Queiroz V, Pagnin D, Pezawas L, Angst J, Cassano GB, et al. Prevalence and burden of bipolar disorders in European countries. Eur Neuropsychopharmacol. 2005;15(4):425–34.

Reis HT. Why researchers should think "real-world": A conceptual rationale. In: Mehl MR, Conner TS, editors. Handbook of Research Methods for Studying Daily Life. New York: Guilford Press; 2012. p. 3.

Rush AJ, Trivedi MH, Ibrahim HM, Carmody TJ, Arnow B, Klein DN, et al. The 16-item Quick Inventory of Depressive Symptomatology (QIDS), clinician rating (QIDS-C), and self-report (QIDS-SR): A psychometric evaluation in patients with chronic major depression. BiolPsychiatry. 2003;54(5):573.

Saunders KE, Bilderbeck AC, Panchal P, Atkinson LZ, Geddes J, Goodwin GM. Experiences of remote mood and activity monitoring in bipolar disorder: a qualitative study. Eur Psychiatry. 2017;41:115–21.

Schärer LO, Krienke UJ, Graf S-M, Meltzer K, Langosch JM. Validation of life-charts documented with the personal life-chart app–a self-monitoring tool for bipolar disorder. BMC Psychiatry. 2015;15(1):1–7.

Schermer M. Telecare and self-management: opportunity to change the paradigm? J Med Ethics. 2009;35(11):688.

Smit AC, Snippe E, Wichers M. Increasing restlessness signals impending increase in depressive symptoms more than 2 months before it happens in individual patients. Psychother Psychosom. 2019;88(4):249.

Snippe E, Simons CJP, Hartmann JA, Menne-Lothmann C, Kramer I, Booij SH, et al. Change in daily life behaviors and depression: within-person and between-person associations. Health Psychol. 2016;35(5):433.

Tsanas A, Saunders K, Bilderbeck A, Palmius N, Osipov M, Clifford G, et al. Daily longitudinal self-monitoring of mood variability in bipolar disorder and borderline personality disorder. J Affect Disord. 2016;205:225–33.

Tyler E, Jones S, Black N, Carter L-A, Barrowclough C. The relationship between bipolar disorder and cannabis use in daily life: an experience sampling study. PLoS ONE. 2015;10:3.

Vachon H, Viechtbauer W, Rintala A, Myin-Germeys I. Compliance and retention with the experience sampling method over the continuum of severe mental disorders: meta-analysis and recommendations. J Med Internet Res. 2019;21(12):e14475.

van der Krieke L, Jeronimus BF, Blaauw FJ, Wanders RBK, Emerencia AC, Schenk HM, et al. HowNutsAreTheDutch ((HoeGekIsNL): A crowdsourcing study of mental symptoms and strengths. Int J Methods Psychiatr Res. 2016;25(2):123.

van Genugten CR, Schuurmans J, Lamers F, Riese H, Penninx BW, Schoevers RA, et al. Experienced burden of and adherence to smartphone-based ecological momentary assessment in persons with affective disorders. J Clin Med. 2020;9(2):322.

van Os J, Delespaul P, Wigman J, Myin-Germeys I, Wichers M. Beyond DSM and ICD: introducing "precision diagnosis" for psychiatry using momentary assessment technology. World Psychiatry. 2013;12(2):113.

van Os J, Verhagen S, Marsman A, Peeters F, Bak M, Marcelis M, et al. The experience sampling method as an mHealth tool to support self-monitoring, self-insight, and personalized health care in clinical practice. DepressAnxiety. 2017;34(6):481.

Wenze SJ, Armey MF, Miller IW. Feasibility and acceptability of a mobile intervention to improve treatment adherence in bipolar disorder: a pilot study. Behav Modif. 2014;38(4):497–515.

Wenze SJ, Armey MF, Weinstock LM, Gaudiano BA, Miller IW. An open trial of a smartphone-assisted, adjunctive intervention to improve treatment adherence in bipolar disorder. J Psychiatr Practice. 2016;22(6):492.

Wichers M, Simons CJP, Kramer IMA, Hartmann JA, Lothmann C, Myin-Germeys I, et al. Momentary assessment technology as a tool to help patients with depression help themselves. Acta Psychiatr Scand. 2011;124(4):262.

Wichers M, Snippe E, Riese H, Bos FM. The network approach to depression: Hype or Holy Grail? Gedragstherapie. 2019;52(1):43–68.

17

The effects of vagus nerve stimulation on the course and outcomes of patients with bipolar disorder in a treatment-resistant depressive episode: a 5-year prospective registry

R. Hamish McAllister-Williams[1,2*], Soraia Sousa[1,2], Arun Kumar[3], Teresa Greco[3], Mark T. Bunker[3], Scott T. Aaronson[4], Charles R. Conway[5] and A. John Rush[6,7,8]

Abstract

Background: To compare illness characteristics, treatment history, response and durability, and suicidality scores over a 5-year period in patients with treatment-resistant bipolar depression participating in a prospective, multicenter, open-label registry and receiving Vagus Nerve Stimulation Therapy (VNS Therapy) plus treatment-as-usual (VNS + TAU) or TAU alone.

Methods: Response was defined as ≥ 50% decrease from baseline Montgomery–Åsberg Depression Rating Scale (MADRS) total score at 3, 6, 9, or 12 months post-baseline. Response was retained while MADRS score remained ≥ 40% lower than baseline. Time-to-events was estimated using Kaplan–Meier (KM) analysis and compared using log-rank test. Suicidality was assessed using the MADRS Item 10 score.

Results: At baseline (entry into registry), the VNS + TAU group (N = 97) had more episodes of depression, psychiatric hospitalizations, lifetime suicide attempts and higher suicidality score, more severe symptoms (based on MADRS and other scales), and higher rate of prior electroconvulsive therapy than TAU group (N = 59). Lifetime use of medications was similar between the groups (a mean of 9) and was consistent with the severe treatment-resistant nature of their depression. Over 5 years, 63% (61/97) in VNS + TAU had an initial response compared with 39% (23/59) in TAU. The time-to-initial response was significantly quicker for VNS + TAU than for TAU ($p < 0.03$). Among responders in the first year after implant, the KM estimate of the median time-to-relapse from initial response was 15.2 vs 7.6 months for VNS + TAU compared with TAU (difference was not statistically significant). The mean reduction in suicidality score across the study visits was significantly greater in the VNS + TAU than in the TAU group ($p < 0.001$).

Conclusions: The patients who received VNS + TAU included in this analysis had severe bipolar depression that had proved extremely difficult to treat. The TAU comparator group were similar though had slightly less severe illnesses on some measures and had less history of suicide attempts. Treatment with VNS + TAU was associated with a higher likelihood of attaining a response compared to TAU alone. VNS + TAU was also associated with a significantly greater mean reduction in suicidality.

*Correspondence: hamish.mcallister-williams@ncl.ac.uk
[1] Northern Centre for Mood Disorders, Newcastle University, Newcastle upon Tyne, UK
Full list of author information is available at the end of the article

Limitations: In this registry study, participants were not randomized to the study treatment group, VNS Therapy stimulation parameters were not controlled, and there was a high attrition rate over 5 years.

Trial registration ClinicalTrials.gov NCT00320372. Registered 3 May 2006, https://clinicaltrials.gov/ct2/show/NCT00320372 (retrospectively registered)

Keywords: Bipolar disorder, Depression, Vagus Nerve Stimulation Therapy, VNS TRD registry, Response, Suicidality, Treatment-resistant depression

Background

Patients with bipolar disorder are symptomatic about 50% of the time, the vast majority of which is depression (Judd et al. 2002, 2003). However, treatment options for bipolar depression are limited. For example, the UK National Institute for Health and Social Care (NICE) guidelines for the management of bipolar depression list just 3 treatments that are supported by replicated randomized controlled trials: lamotrigine, quetiapine, and olanzapine (with or without fluoxetine) (National Institute for Health and Care Excellence 2014). Since publication of the NICE guidelines, additional evidence has emerged from randomized controlled trials supporting the efficacy of lurasidone for the acute treatment of bipolar depression (Loebel et al. 2014a, b). This limited number of treatment options for bipolar depression is further compromised as quetiapine and olanzapine are often poorly tolerated due to weight gain and sedation (Calabrese et al. 2005; Tohen et al. 2003).

The clinical challenge of managing bipolar depression is further illustrated by observations of high rates of antidepressant usage (Kessing et al. 2016; Yoon et al. 2018) despite evidence of questionable efficacy (National Institute for Health and Care Excellence 2014; Sidor and Macqueen 2011). The implication is that many patients suffer from treatment-resistant bipolar depression (TRBD). The prevalence of TRBD is unknown due to a lack of a consensus definition (Hidalgo-Mazzei et al. 2019). However, it is known that about 50% and 30% of depressed bipolar patients remain depressed at 6 and 12 months, respectively, following initiation of antidepressant treatment; and the lack of treatment effects is due to non-response, intolerance, or non-acceptance of treatment (Kupfer et al. 2000). As a result, TRBD is the major contributor to the enormous burden of disease associated with bipolar disorder (Ferrari et al. 2016).

Given the significant unmet need with regards to the management of bipolar depression, it is important that alternative treatment options for patients with TRBD are explored. One potential option is Vagus Nerve Stimulation Therapy (VNS Therapy).

VNS Therapy has primarily been examined in unipolar treatment-resistant depression (TRD). The largest data set supporting its use in TRD is a 5-year VNS TRD registry of nearly 500 participants (representing both unipolar and bipolar TRD) who received adjunctive VNS Therapy plus treatment-as-usual (VNS + TAU). In this registry, the VNS-implanted TRD participants were compared with 300 other TRD participants with similar clinical presentations who received only TAU (Aaronson et al. 2017). It is important to note that the participants included in the registry were not randomized to VNS + TAU or TAU. Rather, treatment was determined by a participant's choice and availability of VNS Therapy.

The data from the VNS TRD registry revealed that the adjunctive VNS Therapy group had significantly higher 5-year cumulative response (67.6% vs 40.9%) and remission (43.3% vs 25.7%) rates compared to the TRD patients who received TAU alone (Aaronson et al. 2017). Additionally, VNS + TAU led to a more durable response as the time-to-relapse from initial response for responders in the first year was 10.1 months versus 7.3 months for participants receiving TAU alone (Kumar et al. 2019). Safety assessment in the registry also found a greater reduction in suicidality in participants receiving VNS + TAU compared to TAU alone (Aaronson et al. 2017).

Nierenberg and colleagues have previously described the outcomes of 25 patients with TRBD who were included in acute and long-term early studies of VNS Therapy for the treatment of depression (Nierenberg et al. 2008). The authors reported that the antidepressant efficacy outcomes for these TRBD patients were similar to the unipolar TRD patients.

Benefit of VNS Therapy in patients with bipolar disorder is also supported by a published case series that included 5 patients who demonstrated sustained improvement in depressive symptoms and a lack of manic episodes during the follow-up period; and 3 of these patients were followed for about 5 years (Oldani et al. 2015).

In this report—using the 5-year VNS TRD registry discussed above—we examine the pre-treatment clinical characteristics and the clinical outcomes in a subgroup of TRD patients with TRBD comparing VNS + TAU versus TAU alone based on the following areas of interest:

I. Illness characteristics and previous treatments received prior to inclusion in the registry
II. Cumulative depressive symptom response (defined by ≥ 50% reduction in Montgomery–Åsberg Depression Rating Scale [MADRS]) over the 5-year registry observation period
III. Duration of response (defined a priori as maintenance of ≥ 40% reduction from baseline MADRS)
IV. Change in suicidality score over the 5-year registry observation period

Methods

Study population

Analysis of the 5-year VNS TRD registry data set described here included 156 participants with bipolar disorder (both bipolar I and II disorders): n = 97 received VNS + TAU and n = 59 received TAU. To be eligible to participate in the VNS TRD Registry, participants had to be over 18 years of age, experiencing an active major depressive episode of 2 years or longer in duration (either unipolar or bipolar), or had a history of at least 3 major depressive episodes, including the current depressive episode, and a history of inadequate response to 4 or more adequate antidepressant treatments (dosage per Physicians' Desk Reference labeling for a minimum of 4 weeks), which could include electroconvulsive therapy (ECT). Participants could not have a history of a psychotic disorder or rapid-cycling bipolar disorder, or psychotic features in the present major depressive episode. A more detailed list of study entry criteria can be found elsewhere (Aaronson et al. 2017; Olin et al. 2012). ClinicalTrials.gov Identifier: NCT00320372.

Study treatment

Before enrollment into the VNS TRD Registry, participants could select the treatment group of their choice (ie, TAU or VNS + TAU). The exception to this were those VNS + TAU subjects who entered the registry via rollover from a previous flexible dose-finding VNS trial (Aaronson et al. 2013). Some participants could be assigned to receive the alternate treatment by the site for various reasons, including availability of surgical implantation at a site, number of allocated slots for implantation, or failure to qualify for insurance reimbursement or VNS Therapy implantation. Device implantation surgery and related medical care were covered either by a participant's insurance policy or from personal funds.

Assessments

The assessment of the registry participants included in this analysis has been detailed elsewhere (Aaronson et al. 2017). Participants in the VNS + TAU group underwent implantation during Visit 2 (baseline). Post-baseline follow-up visits for all participants were conducted at 3, 6, 9, 12, 18, 24, 30, 36, 42, 48, 54, and 60 months. The primary measure of depression for this registry was the MADRS (Carmody et al. 2006) which was administered by central blinded raters. Other psychiatric outcome measures were the Quick Inventory of Depressive Symptomatology–Self Report (QIDS-SR) (Trivedi et al. 2004; Rush et al. 2003) and the Clinical Global Impression (CGI) scale (Guy 1976).

Statistical analysis

The intent-to-treat (ITT) population included 195 registry participants with bipolar disorder (n = 134 VNS + TAU; n = 61 TAU) defined as those who completed their baseline visit, received their respective treatment, and completed at least one post-baseline assessment. To ensure consistent VNS Therapy dose and follow-up schedule, the analysis sample excluded individuals who were "crossed over" from VNS Therapy treatment in the previously reported flexible dose study (n = 37) since most of these participants had consistent follow-up data for only 1 year (Aaronson et al. 2013). In addition, we excluded participants who had a baseline MADRS score < 10 indicating that they were already remitted from their major depressive episode (Zimmerman et al. 2004); this excluded n = 2 from the TAU group. The remaining 156 TRBD patients comprised of N = 97 receiving VNS + TAU and N = 59 receiving TAU and were included in the analysis described here. Note that participants who were crossed over to another treatment group during the study were censored at the last visit before cross-over.

Time-to-initial response was defined as the time from baseline to the first visit when there was reduction in MADRS score of ≥ 50% compared to baseline. A probability of time-to-initial response was estimated using Kaplan–Meier (KM) method. KM probability estimates were calculated for the time-to-event with 95% confidence intervals at 3, 6, 9, and 12 months. Time-to-event curves for the 2 treatment groups were compared using Log-rank test. A Cox proportional-hazard model was used to estimate the hazard ratio (and 95% confidence interval) of the instantaneous chance of a participant having an event in the VNS + TAU group compared to the TAU group at any given time during follow-up.

Given the different proportion of participants with bipolar I or II disorder between the VNS + TAU and TAU groups, a second Cox proportional-hazard model was used to evaluate the time-to-first response, adjusting for the effects of bipolar diagnosis and interaction between treatment and bipolar diagnosis.

Persistence of response was defined as an ongoing reduction in MADRS score of ≥ 40% after an antidepressant response was recorded (reduction of baseline MADRS of $\geq 50\%$). Persistence of response was calculated for all study participants who had an initial response in the first year of study treatment. Participants were categorized in subgroups by the visit when the initial response occurred. A KM analysis was performed to compare the retention of response in VNS + TAU and TAU alone in a time-to-event analysis framework.

Participants were considered severely suicidal if they had a score of ≥ 4 on MADRS Item 10. The percentage who were still severely suicidal was calculated for each post-baseline visit. Similarly, the percentage who were non-severely suicidal at baseline who became severely suicidal was calculated for each post-baseline visit. Average change in suicidality score for VNS + TAU and TAU on MADRS Item 10 is presented for each post-baseline visit.

If there were 1 or 2 consecutive missing data, then the data was imputed with the average of the 2 adjacent non-missing data. No imputation was done for 3 or more consecutive missing data points. After imputation, participants were censored at the last visit with non-missing data for all the analysis. Thus, there were a total of 412 visits with data for TAU group and 856 visits with data for VNS + TAU group in the censored data set. Imputation for a single missed data point in the censored data set was done for 32 visits (32/412 [7.8%]) of the available data for TAU group and for 59 visits (59/856 [6.9%]) of the available data for VNS + TAU group. Imputation for 2 consecutive missing data points was done for 14 visits (14/412 [3.4%]) of the available data for TAU group and for 28 visits (28/856 [3.3%]) of the available data for VNS + TAU group. Overall, there were 46 imputed data (46/412 [11.2%]) of available data in TAU group and 87 imputed data (87/856 [10.2%]) of all available data) in VNS + TAU group.

This imputation method has desirable properties as detailed in Kumar et al. (2019). The data set has a regular response pattern (when defined as reduction of MADRS score of $\geq 50\%$), ie, the same response at the adjacent visits around one missing data: 78.1% for TAU and 62.7% for VNS + TAU, and around 2 consecutive missing data items: 100% for TAU and 78.1% for VNS + TAU. Thus, occurrence of initial or second response could have been altered due to imputation only for 1.7% of the censored data for the TAU group and 3.3% of censored data in the VNS + TAU group. Similarly, the censored data set provided a regular response pattern (when defined as reduction of MADRS score of $\geq 40\%$) around 1 missing data: 71.9% for TAU and 57.6% for VNS + TAU and around 2 consecutive missing data: 100% for TAU and 78.6% for VNS + TAU. Thus, prolongation of the response maintenance could have occurred in only 2.2% of the censored data in the TAU group and 3.6% of the censored data in the VNS + TAU group. Given this small percentage of data that could have an altered response pattern due to imputation, it was concluded that the imputation method would work well for this data set and that it could not have altered the result substantially in favor of any treatment group.

Results

Sample demographics and illness characteristics

Table 1 summarizes demographic information and baseline clinical characteristics for the analysis sample.

The age at onset of depressive symptoms (around 19–20 years of age) and age at initial diagnosis of an episode of depression (around 8 years later) were similar between the groups. Overall, there were significantly higher proportion of participants with a bipolar I diagnosis in the VNS + TAU group (n = 65 [67.0%] vs n = 28 [47.5%]) and lower rate of those with a bipolar II diagnosis (32 [33.0%] vs 31 [52.5%]) compared with the TAU group (Chi-squared test for homogeneity, $p = 0.0158$). The VNS + TAU group had experienced more episodes of lifetime depressive episodes than the TAU group, though this was not statistically significant. Moreover, the VNS + TAU group had a history of more psychiatric hospitalizations within the 5 years prior to entering the registry and had more lifetime suicide attempts. Further, the VNS + TAU subjects had greater depressive symptomology as assessed by the MADRS, QIDS-SR, and CGI. Additionally, the VNS + TAU group scored significantly higher on the suicidality item of the MADRS Item 10.

Treatment histories are presented in Table 2. There was a very similar distribution of lifetime use of medications. The mean number of lifetime antidepressant treatment courses was approximately 9, with a maximum of 14 in both treatment groups. All study participants had received antidepressants in the past or present, and selective serotonin reuptake inhibitors (SSRIs) and serotonin and norepinephrine reuptake inhibitors (SNRIs) were the most frequently prescribed antidepressant medication classes. With regard to medications specifically recommended in guidelines for bipolar depression (National Institute for Health and Care Excellence 2014), lamotrigine was the drug most commonly prescribed, followed by quetiapine. About half of the VNS + TAU group had taken lithium or sodium valproate, slightly more than seen in the TAU group. Just over half of the VNS + TAU group had prior ECT treatment, with a smaller number in the TAU group (54% vs 39%). Most participants had received psychological therapies, with a lifetime frequency of individual therapy being above 80% in both groups.

Table 1 Demographic and baseline clinical characteristics

	VNS+TAU (N=97)	TAU (N=59)	*P**
Mean age ± SD (years)	47.0 ± 10.2	47.8 ± 10.6	0.65
Female, n (%)	72 (74.2%)	47 (79.7%)	0.56
White, n (%)	93 (95.9%)	56 (94.9%)	1
Mean age ± SD at initial onset of depressive symptoms (years)	20.0 ± 11.5	18.9 ± 9.2	0.51
Mean age ± SD at initial diagnosis of depression (years)	26.9 ± 10.6	27.9 ± 11.6	0.59
Lifetime number of diagnosed depressive episode	20.7 ± 29.2	13.7 ± 23.2	0.10
Psychiatric hospitalizations within the 5 years prior to registry enrollment	3.6 ± 5.4	1.5 ± 2.1	<0.001
Lifetime suicide attempts	2.7 ± 4.8	1.5 ± 2.9	0.05
DSM-IV-TR primary diagnosis, n (%)			
Bipolar I disorder, currently moderately severe major depressive episode	19 (19.6%)	18 (30.6%)	0.17
Bipolar I disorder, currently severe major depressive episode	46 (47.4%)	10 (16.9%)	<0.001
Bipolar II disorder, currently depressed	32 (33.0%)	31 (52.5%)	0.025
Baseline scores, n (%)			
Montgomery–Åsberg Depression Rating Scale	33.7 ± 7.3	29.7 ± 5.9	<0.001
Clinical Global Impression—Severity	5.2 ± 0.8	4.7 ± 0.7	<0.001
Quick Inventory of Depressive Symptomatology-Self Report	18.4 ± 4.9	15.9 ± 5.2	0.004
Suicidality-based on MADRS Item 10	2.7 ± 1.4	2.0 ± 1.2	0.003

SD standard deviation

* P-values are from two-sided t-test for comparing means assuming unequal variance or z-test for comparing proportions

Table 2 Lifetime treatment histories

	VNS+TAU (N=97)	TAU (N=59)
Number of treatment courses*		
Mean	9.2	9.0
Maximum	14	14
Minimum	3	4
Antidepressants, n (%)	97 (100%)	59 (100%)
Bupropion	71 (73%)	38 (64%)
Selective serotonin reuptake inhibitors (SSRIs)	88 (91%)	50 (85%)
Serotonin and norepinephrine reuptake inhibitors (SNRIs)	78 (80%)	48 (81%)
Other	68 (70%)	35 (59%)
Antipsychotics, anticonvulsants, and other medications, n (%)		
Lamotrigine	62 (64%)	44 (75%)
Quetiapine	56 (58%)	35 (59%)
Olanzapine	37 (38%)	24 (24%)
Olanzapine + fluoxetine	5 (5%)	6 (10%)
Lithium	53 (55%)	25 (42%)
Sodium valproate	54 (56%)	20 (34%)
Electroconvulsive therapy, n (%)	53 (54%)	23 (39%)
Psychological therapies, n (%)		
Cognitive behavioral therapy (CBT)	44 (45%)	23 (39%)
Individual therapy	83 (86%)	48 (81%)

* A course of treatment was defined as at least a 4-week continuous period in which a patient used one or more treatments for their depression. A new course of treatment started each time a drug was added or dropped. Courses of treatment were classified as electroconvulsive therapy, monotherapy, combination therapies, augmentation therapies, or other psychiatric treatments

Cumulative response rates

Over the 5-year observation period, 61 of 97 (63%) in the VNS + TAU group had an initial response (defined as ≥ 50% reduction in MADRS from baseline) compared to 23 of 59 (39%) of participants in the TAU group. The KM plot in Fig. 1 shows that time-to-initial response was significantly shorter for VNS + TAU than for TAU alone (p = 0.03 for log-rank test). The estimated cumulative probability for the time-to-initial response was higher for the VNS + TAU group as compared to the TAU group over most of the follow-up period. Median time-to-initial response was 13.7 month (Q1 = 5, Q3 = 37.7) for VNS + TAU group compared to 42.1 months (Q1 = 8.3, Q3 = not estimable) for TAU group. Hazard ratio for time-to-initial response for VNS + TAU compared to TAU was 1.7 (95% CI 1, 2.7) meaning a larger chance for a participant in the VNS + TAU group to get an initial response compared to a participant in the TAU group at any given time during the follow-up, though the hazard ratio was not statistically significant.

The Cox proportional-hazard model on time-to-first response adjusting for the effects of bipolar diagnosis and the correspondent interaction, confirmed the benefit of VNS + TAU in reducing the time-to-first response (HR = 1.6; 95% CI 0.98, 2.7) and VNS + TAU showed trends of effectiveness in both sub-populations (HR = 2.1 in bipolar I and HR = 1.3 in bipolar II, even if a significant treatment effect of VNS + TAU vs TAU was seen just in the participants with bipolar I (95% CI 1.0, 4.3) (Table 3). This may in part be driven by the smaller number of patients with bipolar II vs bipolar I disorder (n = 59 vs n = 97) and the low rate of responses in the bipolar II subgroup (n = 17 vs n = 14 for the VNS + TAU and TAU groups, respectively). Due to the low rate, it was also not possible to estimate the 95% confidence intervals in KM analysis for the median time-to-first response in the bipolar II patients (Table 4).

Duration of response

Maintenance of response was defined a priori as maintenance of ≥ 40% reduction from baseline MADRS

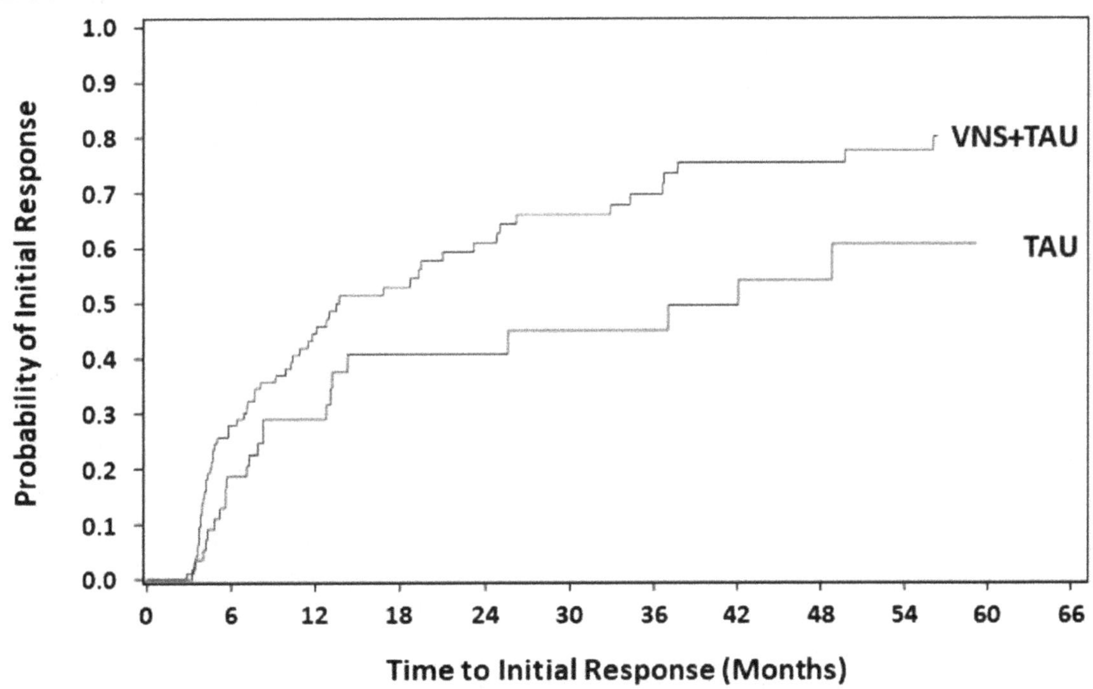

Participants with available response data by visit (month, m)

Treatment group	0 m	6 m	12 m	18 m	24 m	30 m	36 m	42 m	48 m	54 m	60 m
VNS+TAU	97	65	42	31	23	19	16	12	11	9	7
TAU	59	43	27	16	14	13	12	11	8	6	3

Fig. 1 Kaplan–Meier plot for time-to-initial response based on MADRS score

Table 3 Cox proportional-hazards model examining effect of bipolar diagnosis on the time-to-first response

Effect	Hazard ratio	95% CI lower limit	95% CI upper limit	p-value
VNS + TAU vs TAU	1.6	0.98	2.7	0.06
Bipolar II vs bipolar I	0.96	0.6	1.6	0.9
VNS vs TAU in bipolar I	2.1	1.0	4.3	0.04
VNS vs TAU in bipolar II	1.3	0.6	2.6	0.5

and assessed in those who showed a response in the first year of follow-up. In the VNS + TAU group, 46 of the 61 responders (75.4%) responded in the first year; and in the TAU group, 19 of the 23 responders (82.6%) responded in the first year. Numbers are small and hence comparisons between the 2 groups may not be robust.

A KM analysis of the data estimated that the median time-to-relapse from initial response in the first year was 15.2 months (Q1 = 6.7, Q3 = 25.4) for the VNS + TAU group compared with 7.6 months (Q1 = 3.4, Q3 = 14.7) for the TAU group. The hazard ratio for relapse after the initial response was 0.7 (95% CI 0.3, 1.4) in favor of VNS, though this was not statistically significant. In terms of actual data, it was possible to examine maintenance of response 6 months after initial response in participants who demonstrated an initial response at the 3-, 6-, or 12-month study visits. Of these, 30/39 (76.9%) in the VNS + TAU group were maintaining a response 6 months later, compared with 10/18 (55.6%) in the TAU group. There was limited data to examine maintenance of response 12 months after initial response since this was only available for those who showed an initial response at the 6- or 12-month visits. However, again, the proportion maintaining a response was numerically higher in the VNS + TAU compared with TAU group (6/13 [46.1%] vs 3/11 [27.3%], respectively).

Suicidality

A total of 33 (33/97; 34%) in the VNS + TAU group and 8 (8/59; 14%) in the TAU group were severely suicidal at baseline based on MADRS (a score ≥ 4 on MADRS Item 10 corresponding to the responses "probably better off dead" and "active preparations for suicide"). Notably, the mean reduction in suicidality score across the study visits was significantly greater in the VNS + TAU than in the TAU group (P < 0.001 as per F-test) (Fig. 2).

In each treatment group, the percentage who became severely suicidal post-baseline was less than 15% (Table 5) and the difference between the treatment groups was not statistically significant.

Discussion

Given the frequency of TRBD and its impact on patients with bipolar disorder, it is important to consider all possible treatment options. This post-hoc analysis suggests that in a non-randomized study following the outcomes of patients with TRBD for up to 5 years, the addition of VNS Therapy to TAU had significantly greater cumulative response rates, faster onset of antidepressant response, and the responses were longer in duration than in participants receiving TAU alone. Critically, VNS + TAU was also associated with a significantly greater reduction in suicidal ideation compared with TAU alone, despite the VNS + TAU group being more severely depressed at baseline and with high ratings of suicidality. These findings are consistent with the observations made in a much larger group of patients with unipolar or bipolar depression (Aaronson et al. 2017). They are also consistent with a previous post-hoc analysis of 25 patients with TRBD who made up 11% of a larger TRD population who received VNS Therapy alongside TAU in a sham-controlled acute study with long-term open-label follow-up (Nierenberg et al. 2008). The only other study of the safety and efficacy of VNS Therapy in bipolar disorder is a 1-year pilot study of VNS Therapy in 9 patients with rapid cycling bipolar disorder that did not have a comparator group (Marangell et al. 2008).

These findings suggest that VNS Therapy may be effective in patients with very significant difficult to treat

Table 4 Kaplan–Meier estimates for time-to-first response, months

	First quartile (95% CI)	Median (95% CI)	Third quartile (95% CI)
Bipolar 1			
VNS + TAU	5.8 (4.1, 7.7)	13 (7.7, 23.2)	36.6 (23.2, NE)
TAU	13.1 (4, 37)	37 (13.1, NE)	NE (37, NE)
Bipolar 2			
VNS + TAU	4.7 (3.7, 10.4)	19.5 (9.2, NE)	NE (24.8, NE)
TAU	7.9 (4.3, 13.2)	14.3 (8.3, NE)	NE (48.8, NE)

CI confidence interval, *NE* not estimable

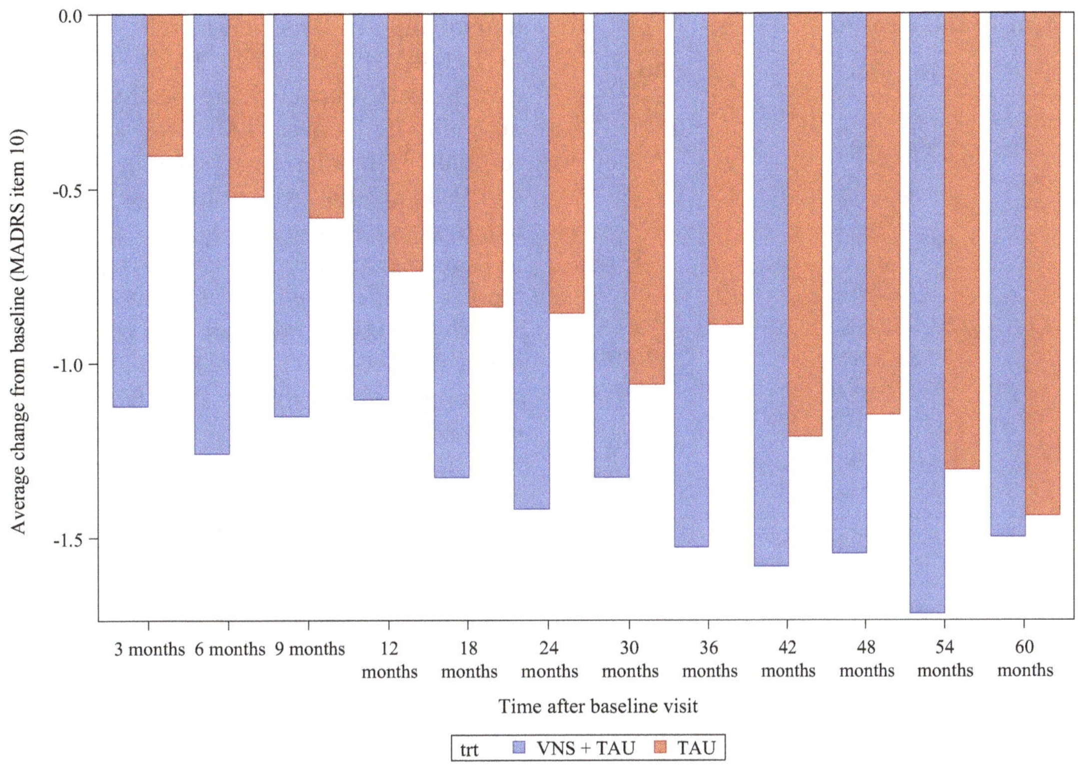

Patients with available suicidality data on MADRS item 10 by visit

trt	3m	6m	9m	12m	18m	24m	30m	36m	42m	48m	54m	60m
VNS + TAU	89	77	66	67	61	62	52	53	48	44	32	40
TAU	52	46	36	34	25	21	16	18	19	20	13	16

Fig. 2 Mean change in suicidality score from baseline based on MADRS Item 10

depression in the context of bipolar disorder. Those treated with VNS Therapy had an average of 20.7 lifetime episodes of depression, 3.6 psychiatric hospitalizations in the previous 5 years, and 2.7 lifetime suicide attempts. They had received an average of 9 mediation treatment courses over their lifetime and all had received an antidepressant, despite the lack of evidence that these are efficacious in patients with bipolar disorder (Sidor and Macqueen 2011; Young et al. 2010). The vast majority had also received psychotherapy, and about half (54%) had been treated with ECT. Importantly, despite the VNS + TAU participants having considerably more severe depressive histories (statistically significantly more severe depressive symptomology and greater suicidal ideation at baseline prior to treatment), the VNS + TAU group demonstrated superior antidepressant outcomes.

The magnitude of the effect on cumulative response rates with VNS + TAU versus TAU was slightly larger than that seen in patients with unipolar depression in the original analysis of this data set (Aaronson et al. 2017). However, the assessment of the impact of VNS Therapy on durability of response in this current analysis is not as great as that seen in the unipolar patients studied as part of this registry (Kumar et al. 2019). This is perhaps not surprising given that bipolar disorder is more recurrent than unipolar disorder (Angst et al. 2003). While there was no significant difference in durability of response between the VNS + TAU and TAU groups in this analysis, numerically the participants receiving VNS + TAU did better. The lack of significant findings with regards to durability of response may have in part arisen due to the small numbers of patients included in the analysis, particularly at later visit time points, and the relative infrequency of assessment of mood symptoms. Given the importance of prophylaxis in a recurrent disorder such as bipolar disorder, further research investigating the prophylactic efficacy of VNS Therapy is indicated, including in

Table 5 Change in suicidal rating from non-severe to severe based on MADRS Item 10

Visit months	VNS+TAU	TAU
3	3/57 (5.3%)	3/44 (6.8%)
6	2/49 (4.1%)	4/40 (10%)
9	1/43 (2.3%)	2/32 (6.3%)
12	6/44 (13.6%)	2/28 (7.1%)
18	1/39 (2.6%)	1/22 (4.5%)
24	0/36 (0%)	0/19 (0%)
30	1/29 (3.4%)	0/14 (0%)
36	1/30 (3.3%)	0/16 (0%)
42	1/28 (3.6%)	1/15 (6.7%)
48	2/27 (7.4%)	1/18 (5.6%)
54	1/18 (5.6%)	1/10 (10%)
60	2/23 (8.7%)	0/14 (0%)

The numerator denotes the number of participants who had a non-severe suicidal rating at baseline (score < 4) and developed a severe suicidal rating (score ≥ 4) at a post-baseline visit based on MADRS Item 10. The denominator denotes the number of participants who had a non-severe suicidal rating at baseline and attended a post-baseline visit

patients with rapid cycling, utilizing frequent assessments of symptoms.

Previous analyses in a mixed, but predominantly unipolar TRD population, have suggested a reduction in rates of suicide and all-cause mortality associated with VNS treatment (Aaronson et al. 2017; Feldman et al. 2013). The significant reductions in suicidality seen in this post-hoc analysis of patients with TRBD treated with VNS Therapy suggests that such findings might be expected in a larger population of individuals with TRBD, though further research is required. Similarly, it is important to further explore whether the cost effectiveness of VNS Therapy, observed in mixed TRD populations (predominantly unipolar depression), will also be observed in TRBD patients (Feldman et al. 2013).

VNS Therapy is generally well tolerated as revealed in a meta-analysis of over 1000 patients with either unipolar or bipolar depression (Berry et al. 2013). Data regarding the impact of adverse effects of medication was not available in the specific sub-sample of bipolar patients reported here. However, in the complete sample of unipolar and bipolar patients in the registry study (Aaronson et al. 2017), medication adverse effects were assessed using the frequency, intensity, and burden of side effects rating (FIBSER) scale (Wisniewski et al. 2006). Based on this scale, the patients in the VNS+TAU group reported higher scores for frequency, severity, and burden of side effects at baseline, but at the 12 and 24 months timepoints, there were no significant differences between the groups (data available on request).

There was a significant difference in the proportion of bipolar I participants in the two groups (67% in TAU+VNS vs 47% in TAU) and it is possible that this, in part, impacted the results. A significant effect of VNS+TAU over TAU was seen for time-to-first response in bipolar I participants (HR=2.1; 95% CI 1, 4.3). This was not evident in those with bipolar II disorder, though the event rate was such that it is not possible to draw meaningful conclusions regarding a bipolar I vs bipolar II difference in the effectiveness of VNS Therapy added to TAU. In addition, this registry study unfortunately did not collect formal ratings of manic symptoms, so it is not possible to infer the effects of VNS Therapy on elevated mood. A previous 12-month follow-up study of VNS Therapy that included 20 patients with bipolar disorder assessed manic symptoms (Rush et al. 2005). Two of the participants developed brief mild manic episodes that lasted 1 to 2 weeks, and there were two short periods of sub-syndromal hypomanic symptoms (about 1 to 3 days), during the first 3 months of treatment with VNS Therapy. One participant (with a baseline diagnosis of unipolar disorder) developed a manic episode during the subsequent 9 months of treatment with VNS Therapy. Additional data are required to address whether there are potential differential effects between bipolar I vs II and the effect of VNS Therapy on hypomanic/manic symptoms, and such data will hopefully become available following completion of the current ongoing RECOVER randomized trial in the USA and the RESTORE-LIFE registry in Europe.

The study had several additional limitations. Participants were not randomized to the treatment groups, and when VNS Therapy was an available treatment option, there appeared to be a tendency for the treatment to be utilized in patients with bipolar disorder who had a significant degree of pharmacological non-response (or intolerance) and who had a higher rate of ECT treatment history (54%). This rate of ECT usage is similar to that seen in the unipolar patients included in the registry (61%) who received VNS. In addition, there was no sham VNS for the "TAU" group. Therefore, it is not possible to conclude with high certainty that all the effects observed are exclusively related to treatment with adjunctive VNS Therapy. The higher baseline MADRS score in the VNS+TAU compared with TAU group might also mean that regression to the mean may have played a larger role in the VNS+TAU group. In this effectiveness trial, medications and all other treatments, such as TMS and ECT, could change during treatment for either treatment group. Furthermore, study participants and clinicians were knowledgeable about the care being given. However, the off-site central raters collecting the MADRS data were blind to both treatment group and the overall clinical status of the study participants. The population examined limits generalizability, though it is of course reasonably representative of participants suffering from a significant degree of difficult to treat depression in the context of bipolar disorder. Suicidality was not assessed using a specific suicidality scale, but rather a single item in the MADRS. Finally, in this 5-year longitudinal study, the participant attrition over time limits our ability to address with significant sample sizes some of the questions that are posed.

Conclusions

VNS Therapy as an adjunctive treatment to TAU was more effective than TAU alone in reducing depressive symptomatology, and led to a greater reduction in suicidal ideation, and, on average, a more rapid antidepressant response. Further, the antidepressant effects observed in the VNS + TAU group vis-à-vis TAU were likely more durable. Together, these findings support previously observed findings that adjunctive VNS is an efficacious antidepressant treatment in very severe, treatment-resistant bipolar depression.

Abbreviations

CGI: Clinical Global Impression; ECT: Electroconvulsive therapy; ITT: Intent-to-treat; KM: Kaplan–Meier; MADRS: Montgomery–Åsberg Depression Rating Scale; QIDS-SR: Quick Inventory of Depressive Symptomatology–Self Report; TAU: Treatment-as-usual; TRBD: Treatment-resistant bipolar depression; TRD: Treatment-resistant depression; VNS Therapy: Vagus Nerve Stimulation Therapy.

Acknowledgements

The authors would like to thank the patients who participated in the VNS TRD Registry, as well as the principal investigators and study staff. The authors thank Karishma Manzur, Ph.D. of Lenimen Consulting, Inc. for providing medical writing support, which was funded by LivaNova PLC.

Authors' contributions

RHM-W, MTB, STA, CRC, and AJR participated in the design of the study. SS analyzed the past treatments received by the study participants. AK and TG performed the statistical analysis. AJR and RHM-W drafted the manuscript. All authors contributed to the data interpretation and contributed to the revisions of the manuscript. All authors read and approved the final manuscript.

Competing interests

Dr. McAllister-Williams has received speaker honorarium fees, fees for consultancy, and/or support for research from AstraZeneca, Bristol Myers-Squibb, Compass Inc., Cyberonics, Eli Lilly, Ferrer, GlaxoSmithKline, Janssen, Janssen-Cilag, LivaNova PLC, Lundbeck, MagStim, Merck Sharp & Dohme, myTomorrows, Otsuka, Pfizer, Pulse, Roche, Servier, SPIMACO, Sunovian, Syntropharma, Wyeth, American Center for Psychiatry & Neurology in the United Arab Emirates, British Association for Psychopharmacology, European College of Neuropsychopharmacology, International Society for Affective Disorders, OCM Comunicaziona s.n.c., Qatar International Mental Health Conference, UK Medical Research Council, and Wiley; grant support from National Institute for Health Research Efficacy and Mechanism Evaluation Panel and Health Technology Assessment Panel; and non-financial support from COMPASS Pathways. Dr. Sousa has no competing interests to disclose. Dr. Kumar is a former employee of LivaNova USA PLC. Dr. Greco is an employee of LivaNova PLC. Dr Bunker is a former employee and a current consultant of LivaNova USA PLC. Dr. Aaronson has received consulting fees from Genomind, LivaNova PLC, Alkermes, and Neuronetics; research support from Neuronetics; and speaker honorarium fees from Neurocrine, Otsuka, and Sunovion. Dr. Conway has received research support from Bristol-Myers Squibb, the Stanley Medical Research Institute, the National Institute of Mental Health, NeoSync, Cyberonics, Taylor Family Institute for Innovative Psychiatric Research, The American Foundation for Suicide Prevention, Assurex Health Inc., August Busch IV Foundation, and Barnes-Jewish Hospital Foundation; and he is currently serving as a research consultant to LivaNova PLC. Dr. Rush has received consulting fees from Akili Interactive Labs, Inc., Brain Resource, Compass Inc., Curbstone Consultant LLC., Emmes Corp., Holmusk, Inc., LivaNova PLC, Johnson and Johnson (Janssen), and MindLinc; speaking fees from LivaNova PLC; and royalties from Guilford Press and the University of Texas Southwestern Medical Center Dallas, TX (for the Inventory of Depressive Symptoms and its derivatives); and he is also named co-inventor on 2 patents: US Patent No. 7,795,033: Methods to Predict the Outcome of Treatment with Antidepressant Medication (Inventors: McMahon FJ, Laje G, Manji H, Rush AJ, Paddock S, Wilson AS) and US Patent No. 7,906,283: Methods to Identify Patients at Risk of Developing Adverse Events During Treatment with Antidepressant Medication (Inventors: McMahon FJ, Laje G, Manji H, Rush AJ, Paddock S).

Author details

[1] Northern Centre for Mood Disorders, Newcastle University, Newcastle upon Tyne, UK. [2] Regional Affective Disorders Service, Cumbria, Northumberland Tyne and Wear NHS Foundation Trust, Newcastle upon Tyne, UK. [3] LivaNova USA PLC, Houston, TX, USA. [4] Department of Clinical Research, Sheppard Pratt Health System, Baltimore, MD, USA. [5] Department of Psychiatry, Washington University School of Medicine in St. Louis, St. Louis, MO, USA. [6] Duke-National University of Singapore, Singapore, Singapore. [7] Department of Psychiatry and Behavioral Sciences, Duke University School of Medicine, Durham, NC, USA. [8] Department of Psychiatry, Health Sciences Center, Texas Tech University Permian Basin, Midland, TX, USA.

References

Aaronson ST, Carpenter LL, Conway CR, Reimherr FW, Lisanby SH, Schwartz TL, et al. Vagus nerve stimulation therapy randomized to different amounts of electrical charge for treatment-resistant depression: acute and chronic effects. Brain Stimul. 2013;6(4):631–40.

Aaronson ST, Sears P, Ruvuna F, Bunker M, Conway CR, Dougherty DD, et al. A 5-year observational study of patients with treatment-resistant depression treated with vagus nerve stimulation or treatment as usual: comparison of response, remission, and suicidality. Am J Psychiatry. 2017;174(7):640–8.

Angst J, Gamma A, Sellaro R, Lavori PW, Zhang H. Recurrence of bipolar disorders and major depression. A life-long perspective. Eur Arch Psychiatry Clin Neurosci. 2003;253(5):236–40.

Berry SM, Broglio K, Bunker M, Jayewardene A, Olin B, Rush AJ. A patient-level meta-analysis of studies evaluating vagus nerve stimulation therapy for treatment-resistant depression. Med Devices. 2013;6:17–35.

Calabrese JR, Keck PE Jr, Macfadden W, Minkwitz M, Ketter TA, Weisler RH, et al. A randomized, double-blind, placebo-controlled trial of quetiapine in the treatment of bipolar I or II depression. Am J Psychiatry. 2005;162(7):1351–60.

Carmody TJ, Rush AJ, Bernstein I, Warden D, Brannan S, Burnham D, et al. The Montgomery Asberg and the Hamilton ratings of depression: a comparison of measures. Eur Neuropsychopharmacol. 2006;16(8):601–11.

Feldman RL, Dunner DL, Muller JS, Stone DA. Medicare patient experience with vagus nerve stimulation for treatment-resistant depression. J Med Econ. 2013;16(1):62–74.

Ferrari AJ, Stockings E, Khoo JP, Erskine HE, Degenhardt L, Vos T, et al. The prevalence and burden of bipolar disorder: findings from the Global Burden of Disease Study 2013. Bipolar Disord. 2016;18(5):440–50.

Guy W. ECDEU Assessment manual for psychopharmacology. Rockville: US Department of Health, Education, and Welfare; 1976.

Hidalgo-Mazzei D, Berk M, Cipriani A, Cleare AJ, Florio AD, Dietch D, et al. Treatment-resistant and multi-therapy-resistant criteria for bipolar depression: consensus definition. Br J Psychiatry. 2019;214(1):27–35.

Judd LL, Akiskal HS, Schettler PJ, Endicott J, Maser J, Solomon DA, et al. The long-term natural history of the weekly symptomatic status of bipolar I disorder. Arch Gen Psychiatry. 2002;59(6):530–7.
Judd LL, Akiskal HS, Schettler PJ, Coryell W, Endicott J, Maser JD, et al. A prospective investigation of the natural history of the long-term weekly symptomatic status of bipolar II disorder. Arch Gen Psychiatry. 2003;60(3):261–9.
Kessing LV, Vradi E, Andersen PK. Nationwide and population-based prescription patterns in bipolar disorder. Bipolar Disord. 2016;18(2):174–82.
Kumar A, Bunker MT, Aaronson ST, Conway CR, Rothschild AJ, Mordenti G, et al. Durability of symptomatic responses obtained with adjunctive vagus nerve stimulation in treatment-resistant depression. Neuropsychiatr Dis Treat. 2019;15:457–68.
Kupfer DJ, Frank E, Grochocinski VJ, Luther JF, Houck PR, Swartz HA, et al. Stabilization in the treatment of mania, depression and mixed states. Acta Neuropsychiatr. 2000;12(3):110–4.
Loebel A, Cucchiaro J, Silva R, Kroger H, Hsu J, Sarma K, et al. Lurasidone monotherapy in the treatment of bipolar I depression: a randomized, double-blind, placebo-controlled study. Am J Psychiatry. 2014a;171(2):160–8.
Loebel A, Cucchiaro J, Silva R, Kroger H, Sarma K, Xu J, et al. Lurasidone as adjunctive therapy with lithium or valproate for the treatment of bipolar I depression: a randomized, double-blind, placebo-controlled study. Am J Psychiatry. 2014b;171(2):169–77.
Marangell LB, Suppes T, Zboyan HA, Prashad SJ, Fischer G, Snow D, et al. A 1-year pilot study of vagus nerve stimulation in treatment-resistant rapid-cycling bipolar disorder. J Clin Psychiatry. 2008;69(2):183–9.
National Institute for Health and Care Excellence. Bipolar disorder: assessment and management. Clinical guideline [CG185]. 2014. https://www.nice.org.uk/guidance/cg185.
Nierenberg AA, Alpert JE, Gardner-Schuster EE, Seay S, Mischoulon D. Vagus nerve stimulation: 2-year outcomes for bipolar versus unipolar treatment-resistant depression. Biol Psychiatry. 2008;64(6):455–60.
Oldani L, Dell'Osso B, Altamura AC. Long-term effects of vagus nerve stimulation in treatment-resistant depression: a 5-year follow up case series. Brain Stimul. 2015;8(6):1229–300.
Olin B, Jayewardene AK, Bunker M, Moreno F. Mortality and suicide risk in treatment-resistant depression: an observational study of the long-term impact of intervention. PLoS ONE. 2012;7(10):e48002.
Rush AJ, Trivedi MH, Ibrahim HM, Carmody TJ, Arnow B, Klein DN, et al. The 16-item quick inventory of depressive symptomatology (QIDS), clinician rating (QIDS-C), and self-report (QIDS-SR): a psychometric evaluation in patients with chronic major depression. Biol Psychiatry. 2003;54(5):573–83.
Rush AJ, Sackeim HA, Marangell LB, George MS, Brannan SK, Davis SM, et al. Effects of 12 months of vagus nerve stimulation in treatment-resistant depression: a naturalistic study. Biol Psychiatry. 2005;58(5):355–63.
Sidor MM, Macqueen GM. Antidepressants for the acute treatment of bipolar depression: a systematic review and meta-analysis. J Clin Psychiatry. 2011;72(2):156–67.
Tohen M, Vieta E, Calabrese J, Ketter TA, Sachs G, Bowden C, et al. Efficacy of olanzapine and olanzapine-fluoxetine combination in the treatment of bipolar I depression. Arch Gen Psychiatry. 2003;60(11):1079–88.
Trivedi MH, Rush AJ, Ibrahim HM, Carmody TJ, Biggs MM, Suppes T, et al. The Inventory of Depressive Symptomatology, Clinician Rating (IDS-C) and Self-Report (IDS-SR), and the Quick Inventory of Depressive Symptomatology, Clinician Rating (QIDS-C) and Self-Report (QIDS-SR) in public sector patients with mood disorders: a psychometric evaluation. Psychol Med. 2004;34(1):73–82.
Wisniewski SR, Rush AJ, Balasubramani GK, Trivedi MH, Nierenberg AA, Investigators S. Self-rated global measure of the frequency, intensity, and burden of side effects. J Psychiatr Pract. 2006;12(2):71–9.
Yoon W, Shon SH, Hong Y, Joo YH, Lee JS. Antidepressant prescription patterns in bipolar disorder: a nationwide, Register-based Study in Korea. J Korean Med Sci. 2018;33(46):e290.
Young AH, McElroy SL, Bauer M, Philips N, Chang W, Olausson B, et al. A double-blind, placebo-controlled study of quetiapine and lithium monotherapy in adults in the acute phase of bipolar depression (EMBOLDEN I). J Clin Psychiatry. 2010;71(2):150–62.
Zimmerman M, Posternak MA, Chelminski I. Defining remission on the Montgomery–Asberg depression rating scale. J Clin Psychiatry. 2004;65(2):163–8.

18

Role of child maltreatment and gender for bipolar symptoms in young adults

Ida S. Haussleiter[1,2†], Eva Neumann[1*†], Sandra Lorek[1], Bianca Ueberberg[1] and Georg Juckel[2]

Abstract

Background: Child maltreatment has been shown to be associated with a wide range of mental disorders, including bipolar disorders. In this 2-year follow-up study, recollections of emotional, physical and sexual abuse were related to bipolar symptoms, namely depressive, hypomanic and manic symptoms.

Methods: The sample consists of 134 students who took part at five measurement times within the 2-year period. Data were collected with self-report scales.

Results: The results show that recollections of abuse, particularly emotional abuse, were associated with more severe depressive symptoms; this finding, however, only applied to women. Hypomanic and manic symptoms were not associated with recollections of abuse. For hypomanic symptoms, however, a significant decrease over the 2 years was observed.

Conclusions: The findings of this study suggest that recollections of abusive experiences in childhood combined with female gender increase the risk for depression, whereas hypomanic and manic states are probably better predicted by other factors, such as current life circumstances.

Keywords: Bipolar disorder, Depression, Child maltreatment, Emotional abuse, Gender

Background

Child maltreatment is defined as harmful behavior of significant others towards a child. Apart from forms that take place among peers (e.g., bullying in school), many children suffer from traumatic events caused by adult persons who are supposed to care for the child but fail to fulfill this role. Such misbehavior is differentiated by active and passive forms (abuse and neglect) and by the personal domain affected (emotional, physical and sexual) (Bernstein et al. 2003).

A growing body of evidence shows that child maltreatment is closely associated with mental diseases. Such evidence has been provided, inter alia, for depressive, anxiety, eating, somatoform, substance abuse and personality disorders (for reviews, see: Carr et al. 2013; Kessler et al. 2010; Vachon et al. 2015).

In recent times, the role of child maltreatment for bipolar disorders has also been explored, showing that these adverse experiences are rather common among patients diagnosed with such disorders. In two studies on bipolar disorders, about half of the patients (51% and 54%) reported experiences of abuse and neglect in childhood (Garno et al. 2005; Leboyer et al. 2007). A further analysis in the study by Garno et al. (2005), differentiating between subtypes of child maltreatment, revealed that emotional abuse is the type of trauma most frequently reported by bipolar patients, with a prevalence rate of 37%, followed by physical abuse (24%), emotional neglect (24%), sexual abuse (21%) and physical neglect (12%).

Childhood trauma is associated with the severity and course of bipolar disorders. It has been shown repeatedly that experiences of abuse and neglect in bipolar patients are associated with an earlier onset of the disease, stronger suicidal tendencies (including an elevated

*Correspondence: eva.neumann@ruhr-uni-bochum.de
†Ida S. Haussleiter and Eva Neumann contributed equally to this work
[1] Research Institute for Mental Health, Ruhr-University Bochum, LWL-University Hospital Bochum, Alexandrinenstr. 1, 44791 Bochum, Germany
Full list of author information is available at the end of the article

risk for suicide attempts) and more substance abuse (Aas et al. 2016; Daruy-Filho et al. 2011; Etain et al. 2008; Maniglio 2013). Further results point to associations of child maltreatment with a higher number of episodes, rapid cycling, more severe symptoms and an increased likelihood of comorbid mental disorders and psychotic symptoms; these results, however, were not found consistently.

Child maltreatment also seems to be associated with the mental health status between episodes, in times of remission. Etain et al. (2008) found positive correlations between a global score of child maltreatment and two scales for the measurement of emotional instability in a sample of euthymic bipolar patients. A more refined analysis revealed that these correlations were mainly based on strong associations of emotional abuse with emotional instability.

As Alloy et al. (2005) point out, most studies on the associations of bipolar disorders with stressful life events (including childhood trauma) do not distinguish between the types of episodes that are the constituting elements of this disorder. According to the DSM-5 (American Psychiatric Association 2013), bipolar disorders comprise depressive, hypomanic and manic episodes, which occur alternately; the occurrence of one manic episode, however, already justifies the diagnosis of a bipolar disorder. It is possible that depressive, hypomanic, and manic states are associated with child maltreatment in different ways. The differences might be quantitative (i.e., the strength of correlations might differ between the three types of episodes) and qualitative (i.e., the three types might be associated with different subtypes of child maltreatment). Because of the lack of studies considering these possible differences, it is unclear how far depressive, hypomanic and manic states are equally related to adverse childhood experiences.

Unipolar depression, however, has found attention in empirical studies on the role of childhood maltreatment for adult psychopathology. There is compelling evidence that depression is correlated with retrospective assessments of child abuse and neglect, indicating that participants who report such experiences show more severe symptoms of depression than participants who report not being affected by such traumas (Goodman and Brand 2009). Studies based on the differentiation of the five subtypes of child maltreatment have further revealed that emotional traumas are of particular relevance (e.g., Carvalho Fernando et al. 2014; Chapman et al. 2004; Martins et al. 2014; Neumann 2017; Spertus et al. 2003). In all of these studies, emotional abuse alone or both emotional abuse and neglect have been shown to be most strongly correlated with depression in adult life. In a recent review on this topic, Nelson et al. (2017) stated that emotional neglect is the type of childhood trauma most frequently reported by patients diagnosed with a depressive disorder. Furthermore, they found all five subtypes of child maltreatment to be associated with an increased risk for developing a depressive disorder; this risk, however, was highest for patients who reported emotional abuse and/or neglect.

In summary, empirical findings on the role of childhood trauma for depression are numerous and clear; hypomania and mania, however, have rarely been explored in this regard. In one of the rare studies in which depression, hypomania and mania were regarded separately, participants with experiences of physical and/or sexual abuse were shown to score higher on a depression scale, whereas only marginal differences emerged on scales for the measurement of hypomania and mania (Schudlich et al. 2015). Emotional abuse and neglect were not considered in this study.

The present study aims to further clarify the associations of child maltreatment with bipolar symptoms. More specifically, recollections of emotional, physical and sexual abuse in childhood are related to depressive, hypomanic, manic and overall bipolar symptoms. Based on prior findings on depression, it is expected that this variable shows strong associations with emotional abuse in particular. Because of the lack of studies on the associations of hypomania and mania with child maltreatment, reasonable hypotheses on these associations are hard to find; these associations are therefore investigated in an exploratory way.

Moreover, time effects are explored. Wittchen et al. (2003) note that little is known about the natural course of bipolar disorders not only in patient samples, but also in community samples which might include individuals with bipolar symptoms who do not receive psychiatric treatment. According to Wittchen et al. longitudinal studies with such individuals could provide insight into time and age effects of bipolar disorders. The present study addresses this research gap. The sample consists of individuals who were not diagnosed with a mental disorder. The study has a longitudinal design; there were five measurement times within a period of 2 years. This procedure allows exploration of whether depressive, hypomanic, manic and overall bipolar symptoms change with the passing of time. Both increases and decreases in the severity of these symptoms are conceivable.

Methods

Sample

The present study is part of a large longitudinal research project on prodromal symptoms of bipolar disorders conducted at the LWL University Clinic of the Ruhr-University Bochum since 2014. The participants of this study were recruited at the Ruhr-University and a link to the study homepage was sent to the 42,718 enrolled students via email. A total of 2968 students agreed to participate and fulfilled the inclusion criteria: age 18–40 years, confirmation that they were not diagnosed with a mental disease and digital signing of the informed consent form. There were five measurement times at intervals of 6 months over a period of 2 years. At the first measurement time 2329 participants provided complete data sets but only 134 participants completely filled out the questionnaires at all five measurement times. These 134 data sets were analyzed in the present study.

The sample consists of 48 men (36%) and 86 women (64%). At the first measurement time they had a mean age of 24.64 years (SD=4.08, range=18–37), 48 (36%) were singles, 74 (55%) had a romantic partner without being married, 11 (8%) were married and 1 (1%) was divorced. As expected in a student sample, the majority of 127 participants (95%) did not (yet) have children.

Measures

All data were collected with the following self-report scales.

Retrospective measurement of child maltreatment

Recollections of child maltreatment were measured with three items developed by Haussleiter et al. (2018). The items refer to experiences of emotional, physical, and sexual abuse and are worded as follows:

- Have you been abused emotionally in your childhood?
- Have you been abused physically in your childhood?
- Did you have unwanted and/or stressful sexual experiences in your childhood?

The items are responded in a yes/no answer format. Thus, they allow differentiation between participants with and without recollections of traumatic experiences in the three areas.

Beck Depression Inventory II (BDI)

The BDI is a 21-item self-report measure for the assessment of severity of depression (Beck et al. 1996, German version by Hautzinger et al. 2009). The items describe the criteria of a depressive episode according to the fourth edition of the *Diagnostic and Statistical Manual for Mental Disorders* (DSM-IV). Each item consists of four statements, coded 0–3, that indicate a range of non-agreement to agreement with the respective symptom. Respondents are instructed to mark the answer option that best describes their mental state in the current week. The BDI score is computed by summing up all the answers. Total scores of 20 or more indicate a depressive episode that is at least moderate.

The BDI showed excellent internal consistency in this study (Cronbach's alpha for the five measurement times: .93, .92, .92, .93, .92).

Hypomania Checklist 32 (HCL)

The HCL serves as a measure of hypomanic symptoms and is available in different languages, including English and German (Angst et al. 2005). The items describe experiences and behaviors that are typical of hypomanic episodes. Respondents are instructed to recall a period of their life in which they were in a good mood, and to assess whether the symptoms described in the items applied to them during that period by selecting a yes or no answer for each item. The number of items answered with a yes is the total score. Scores of 14 or more indicate hypomanic conditions.

The internal consistency of the HCL was satisfactory to good in this study (Cronbach's alpha for the five measurement times: .73, .82, .85, .87, .87).

Altman Self-Rating Mania Scale (ASRM)

The presence and severity of manic symptoms were assessed with the ASRM (Altman et al. 1997; German version by Bräunig et al. 1996). The five items of the scale refer to the last week and are answered on a five-point Likert scale from 0 to 4. Total scores of 5 or more indicate clinically relevant manic states.

The internal consistency of the ASRM was satisfactory to good in the present study, taking into account that the scale consists of only five items (Cronbach's alpha for the five measurement times: .67, .68, .80, 73, .81).

Bochumer Screeningbogen Bipolar (BSB)

The BSB is a German self-report scale for the measurement of bipolar symptoms (Zeschel et al. 2013). The 17 items of this measure describe (hypo)manic (e.g., physical agitation, racing thoughts), depressive (e.g., depressed mood, physical exhaustion) and general symptoms (e.g., anxiety, emotional instability). Respondents are instructed to assess the severity of these symptoms on a five-point Likert scale from 0 to 4 with respect to the last week, the last month and a lifetime. In this study, the BSB total score referring to the last month is considered in the analysis. A cut-off-score of 22 is proposed for the distinction between clinically not relevant and relevant bipolar conditions (Haussleiter et al. 2018).

The BSB showed good internal consistency in the present study (Cronbach's alpha for the five measurement times: .80, .82, .83, .85, .86).

Results

In the first step of the analysis, tests on normal distribution were conducted. Kolmogorov–Smirnov tests show that the total scores of the BDI, HCL, ASRM and BSB significantly deviate ($p < .001$) from the normal distribution at all five measurement times. For this reason, the data were analyzed using non-parametric tests.

To find out whether the participants of this study were a representative sample from the initial pool of participants, differences between dropouts ($n = 2195$) and non-dropouts ($n = 134$) with regard to child abuse and depressive, hypomanic, manic and overall bipolar symptoms assessed at the first measurement time were tested. Chi square tests showed that the non-dropouts did not differ significantly in the frequencies of emotional, physical and sexual abuse from the participants who dropped out of the study (emotional abuse: $\chi^2(1) = 2.29$, n.s.; physical abuse: $\chi^2(1) = 0.23$, n.s.; sexual abuse: $\chi^2(1) = 1.52$, n.s.). Differences between the BDI, HCL, ASRM and BSB scores at time 1 were tested with Mann–Whitney U tests. There were no significant differences with regard to the BDI ($z = -1.52$, n.s.), HCL ($z = -1.31$, n.s.) and ASRM ($z = -1.04$), but the non-dropouts scored slightly lower on the BSB (dropouts: median = 14.00; non-dropouts: median = 12.50; $z = -2.31$, $p < .05$). In summary, the differences between dropouts and non-dropouts can be considered marginal.

Table 1 shows the distribution of childhood trauma among the 134 participants of this study. There are gender differences in the frequencies of emotional and sexual abuse, with women being affected more often than men. Chi square tests reveal that the difference is significant for sexual abuse, whereas only a non-significant trend ($p < .10$) is shown for emotional abuse.

Next, the course of depressive, hypomanic, manic and overall bipolar symptoms was analyzed. As can be seen from Table 2, the scores for the HCL and BSB decrease from the first to the last measurement time. Friedman tests show that these decreases are significant. For the BDI and ASRM scores no significant changes are observed from the first to the last measurement time.

To explore whether bipolar symptoms vary with gender and childhood trauma, differences between men and women and between participants with and without experiences of emotional, physical and sexual abuse in the BDI, HCL, ASRM and BSB scores were tested with Mann–Whitney U tests. Table 3 shows the results.

Depressive symptoms, in particular, show clear differences between the groups. Men and women differ significantly in the BDI scores at four of the five measurement times, with women scoring higher on that scale. Significant differences also occur with regard to all three types of child abuse. Participants who report experiences of emotional, physical and sexual abuse score higher on the BDI at all five measurement times than participants without such experiences.

In contrast, hypomanic and manic symptoms do not vary considerably with gender and childhood trauma. With few exceptions, the Mann–Whitney U tests do

Table 1 Distribution of childhood trauma

Type of trauma	Total		Male		Female		$\chi^2(1)$
	No	Yes	No	Yes	No	Yes	
	n (%)	*n (%)*	*n (%)*	*n (%)*	*n (%)*	*n (%)*	
Emotional abuse	119 (89)	15 (11)	46 (96)	2 (4)	73 (85)	13 (15)	3.72
Physical abuse	122 (91)	12 (9)	44 (92)	4 (8)	78 (91)	8 (9)	0.04
Sexual abuse	121 (90)	13 (10)	47 (98)	1 (2)	74 (86)	12 (16)	4.95*

*p < .05

Table 2 Course of depressive, hypomanic, manic and overall bipolar symptoms from Time 1 to Time 5

	Time 1 *Mdn*	Time 2 *Mdn*	Time 3 *Mdn*	Time 4 *Mdn*	Time 5 *Mdn*	χ^2 (4)
BDI	8	8	8	6	6	8.75
HCL	16	15	14	13	12	73.93***
ASRM	2	2	2	2	1	9.43
BSB	12.5	11	11	10	8	50.23***

BDI Beck Depression Inventory, *HCL* Hypomania Checklist, *ASRM* Altman Self-Rating Mania Scale, *BSB* Bochumer Screeningbogen Bipolar, *Mdn* median, ***p < .001

Table 3 Differences in depressive, hypomanic, manic and overall bipolar symptoms depending on gender and childhood trauma

	Gender			Emotional abuse			Physical abuse			Sexual abuse		
	Male *Mdn*	Female *Mdn*	*z*	No *Mdn*	Yes *Mdn*	*z*	No *Mdn*	Yes *Mdn*	*z*	No *Mdn*	Yes *Mdn*	*z*
Depressive symptoms												
BDI 1	5	9	−2.36*	7	23	−4.81***	8	14	−2.17*	8	17	−2.49*
BDI 2	5	8	−2.51*	7	17	−3.53***	7	16	−3.03**	7	17	−2.54*
BDI 3	4	9	−2.91**	7	17	−4.06***	7	17	−2.24*	7	21	−3.03**
BDI 4	5	8	−2.44*	5	14	−3.07**	6	17	−1.99*	6	14	−2.17*
BDI 5	6	6	−0.99	5	13	−3.87***	6	15	−2.82**	6	19	−3.35**
Hypomanic symptoms												
HCL 1	16	16	−0.36	16	17	−1.23	16	17	−1.33	16	18	−2.08*
HCL 2	15	15	−0.33	15	17	−0.62	15	18	−1.18	15	17	−1.96
HCL 3	14	14	−0.12	14	15	−1.98*	14	16	−0.49	14	15	−1.40
HCL 4	13	13	−0.05	13	16	−1.03	13	18	−1.48	13	17	−2.24*
HCL 5	12	12	−0.03	12	16	−1.05	12	17	−1.33	12	17	−2.01*
Manic symptoms												
ASRM 1	2	2	−0.96	2	2	−1.19	2	2	−0.46	2	2	−0.16
ASRM 2	2	2	−0.14	2	3	−0.97	2	3	−0.38	2	2	−0.29
ASRM 3	2	2	−1.19	2	5	−1.97*	2	3	−0.69	2	2	−1.75
ASRM 4	2	1	−0.14	2	3	−1.39	2	3	−1.37	2	3	−1.41
ASRM 5	2	1	−1.89	1	1	−0.21	1	0	−0.84	1	0	−2.06*
Overall bipolar symptoms												
BSB 1	10	14	−2.22*	12	21	−3.85***	12	17.5	−1.14	12	15	−1.85
BSB 2	10	11	−1.25	10	17	−2.99**	10.5	12.5	−0.25	11	11	−0.65
BSB 3	9	12	−1.93	11	22	−3.54***	11	12.5	−0.54	11	18	−2.29*
BSB 4	8	12	−2.55*	9	20	−3.36**	10	11	−1.36	10	14	−2.12*
BSB 5	8	8	−0.81	8	17	−3.55***	8	7.5	−1.02	8	12	−1.85

BDI Beck Depression Inventory, *HCL* Hypomania Checklist, *ASRM* Altman Self-Rating Mania Scale, *BSB* Bochumer Screeningbogen Bipolar, *Mdn* median, $^{*}p<.05$, $^{**}p<.01$, $^{***}p<.001$

not show significant group differences for the HCL and ASRM scores.

With regard to overall bipolar symptoms, gender differences also appear as minor, as there are no significant differences between men and women at three of the five measurement times. While participants with and without experiences of physical and sexual abuse do not differ significantly in the BSB scores in most cases, there are clear differences between emotionally abused and not abused participants, with emotionally abused participants scoring higher on the BSB at all five measurement times.

The strong relations of depressive symptoms with gender and childhood trauma that were found in the foregoing analysis were further explored. With respect to emotional and physical abuse, four groups were compared with each other, having gender as one grouping variable and the statement of being affected or not affected by the respective trauma as the other. (This analysis was not conducted for sexual abuse because the group of men with recollections of sexual abuse consisted of only one person.) The median values of depressive symptoms in the four groups are shown in Figs. 1 and 2. With only one exception, women with experiences of emotional and/or physical abuse have the highest BDI scores of all groups. Kruskal–Wallis tests show that the differences between the four groups are significant in all cases (emotional abuse: BDI 1: χ^2 (3) = 25.87, $p<.001$; BDI 2: χ^2 (3) = 17.02, $p<.01$; BDI 3: χ^2 (3) = 21.89, $p<.001$; BDI 4: χ^2 (3) = 14.04, $p<.01$; BDI 5: χ^2 (3) = 15.27, $p<.01$; physical abuse: BDI 1: χ^2 (3) = 12.08, $p<.01$; BDI 2: χ^2 (3) = 15.11, $p<.01$; BDI 3: χ^2 (3) = 13.68, $p<.01$; BDI 4: χ^2 (3) = 9.75, $p<.05$; BDI 5: χ^2 (3) = 8.80, $p<.05$).

Discussion

This study shows that subclinical conditions of bipolar symptoms are associated with recollections of child maltreatment in specific ways. While hypomanic and manic symptoms do not differ depending on recollections of

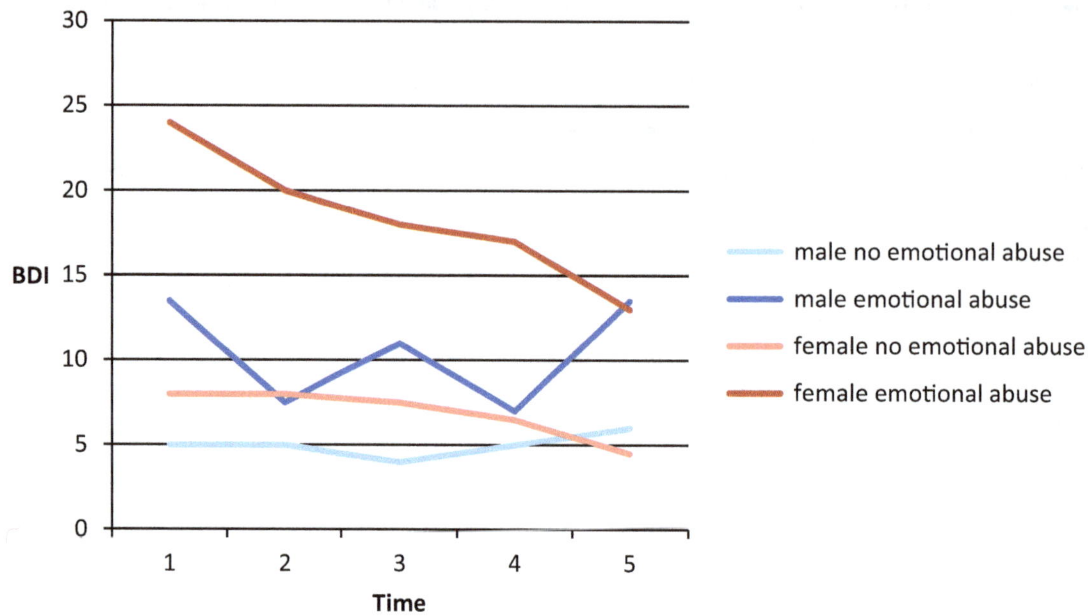

Fig. 1 Course of depressive symptoms from Time 1 to Time 5 for men and women with and without experiences of emotional abuse. *BDI* Beck Depression Inventory

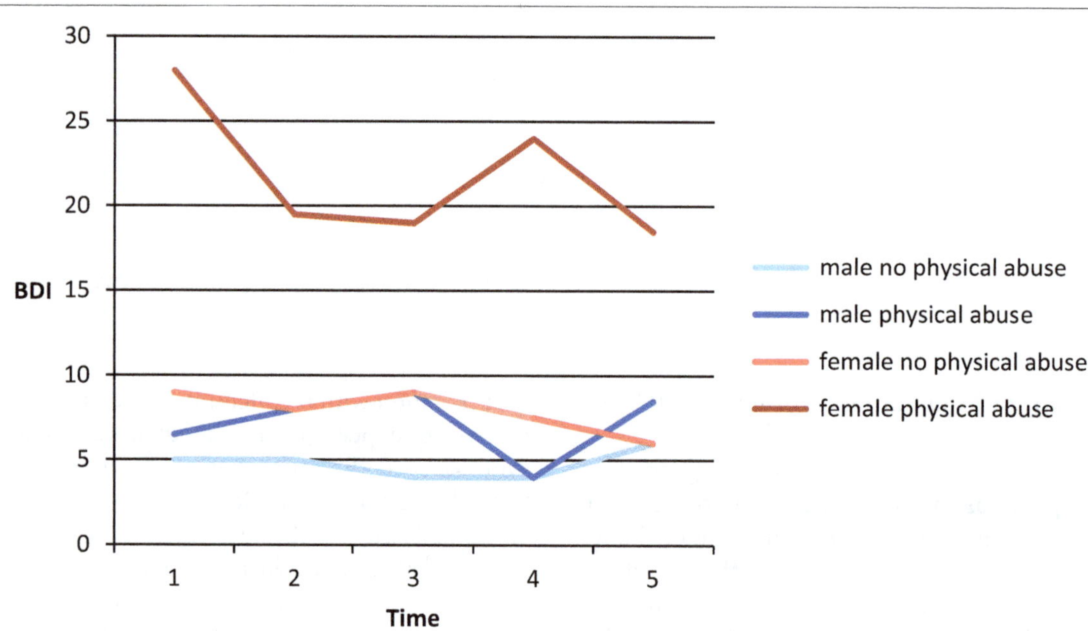

Fig. 2 Course of depressive symptoms from Time 1 to Time 5 for men and women with and without experiences of physical abuse. *BDI* Beck Depression Inventory

abuse, depressive symptoms are clearly higher among participants who report abusive experiences. This difference was found for all three types of child maltreatment considered in this study (i.e., emotional, physical and sexual abuse) but the strongest effect appeared with regard to emotional abuse. Reports of emotional abuse in childhood were associated with high depression scores. This result corresponds to former studies on the relations of child maltreatment with depression in adult life.

Further analysis revealed that experiences of abuse cannot be regarded solely as risk factors for depressive symptoms in adult life. When gender was included in the analyses, it became apparent that only women who report experiences of abuse score higher on the depression scale. Men scored as low on the depression scale as women without recollections of abuse. Thus, in this study experiences of abuse combined with female gender appear as a risk pattern for depression in adult life, whereas male gender seems to be a protective factor, independent of the presence or absence of recollections of abuse. The moderating effect of gender with respect to the detrimental effects of abuse is a new finding that needs support in future studies.

These associations, however, were only shown for emotional and physical abuse and could not be analyzed with regard to sexual abuse due to the small number of men in the sample who reported being affected by this trauma. The associations of depressive symptoms, sexual abuse and gender therefore need further clarification.

Hypomanic and manic symptoms appeared unaffected by child maltreatment, but for hypomanic symptoms an interesting time effect emerged because they showed a significant decrease over the 2 years of measurement. It is probable that this result reflects an age effect. At the beginning of this study, the participants were young adults in their early 20 s. During the following two years they probably became more mature and it is likely, for example, that their emotional stability increased. This maturing process might have diminished the tendency to go through phases of intense and changing feelings and high activity that are typical of hypomanic states. The effect of time that was found in this study suggests that subclinical conditions of hypomania become less frequent and less pronounced with increasing age. This assumption is supported by findings from a large transcultural study in which significant decreases with age in the HCL scores were consistently found in 12 different countries (Angst et al. 2010).

Manic symptoms were not related to recollections of child maltreatment and nor did they show a time or age effect. Thus, in this study no psychosocial factors could be identified that are associated with this mental state. A possible explanation for this finding is that manic symptoms are not related to past experiences in childhood but to current interpersonal experiences. It might be informative to explore associations of manic symptoms with close relationships in adult life, for example by relating them to the attachment dimension "anxiety", which stands for intense worries and a strong desire for attention and care in romantic relationships (Neumann et al. 2007). Attachment anxiety has been shown to be associated with many mental disorders (Mikulincer and Shaver 2016) and might also be correlated with mania, particularly as these two constructs are both characterized by strong inadequate feelings and overreacting behavior.

Limitations

This study has several limitations. First, child maltreatment was assessed with three single items for the measurement of emotional, physical and sexual abuse. This short measure was used for economic reasons; the set of questionnaires should not be too long in this online survey. Even though the measure is quite simple, there is some evidence that the three items led to reliable results. Iffland et al. (2013) used the Childhood Trauma Questionnaire (CTQ) by Bernstein et al. (2003) in a large representative sample from the German population ($N=2500$). The prevalence rates found in this study (emotional abuse: 10%; physical abuse: 12%; sexual abuse: 6%) are close to the rates of the present study (emotional abuse: 11%; physical abuse: 9%; sexual abuse: 10%). Furthermore, Iffland et al. also found a higher frequency of sexual abuse among women. Although these similarities suggest that child abuse was measured adequately in this study, the use of a multi-item scale such as the CTQ should be preferred in future studies.

Second, the measurement of child maltreatment was retrospective. The validity of retrospective measures is a controversial issue and has been discussed intensely. Hardt and Rutter (2004) recommend handling retrospective data with skepticism because of several limitations of this approach. For example, there are findings showing that documented occurrences of sexual abuse in childhood are not reported in adulthood by many persons concerned, particularly men. This phenomenon might have played a role in this study; it is striking, in any case, that only one man reported sexual abuse in childhood. Because of the retrospective nature of the data on child maltreatment, the findings of this study need support from data obtained in childhood.

Third, there was a substantial loss of participants from the first to the last measurement. Only 6% of the initial sample provided complete data sets for each measurement time and it is assumed that these participants differ from those who dropped out of the study; they are probably more reliable and better organized. This personality structure might rely on good mental health and little stress in childhood or in present life. Thus, it cannot be ruled out that the sample of this study is not representative for student populations; it is possible that it mainly consists of healthy persons from low-risk environments.

Fourth, in line with the foregoing arguments, the participants were not diagnosed with a bipolar disorder and the median scores for depressive, hypomanic, manic and overall bipolar symptoms were below the cut-off scores for clinically relevant levels. These results were to be expected, because the participants of this study were students, not patients, who had to confirm that they were not diagnosed with a mental disorder.

It would be interesting to explore whether the findings of this study can be replicated in clinical samples of patients with a bipolar disorder.

Conclusions

In this study the constituent elements of bipolar disorders, depressive, hypomanic and manic symptoms, were explored separately with regard to their relations with recollections of child abuse. This differentiated analysis revealed that only depressive symptoms are associated with child abuse, especially with emotional abuse. However, this result was only found for women, which might indicate that child abuse is a risk factor for depression in adulthood for women but not for men. Hypomanic symptoms were not related to recollections of abuse but showed an effect of time, suggesting that hypomanic states become less strong and less frequent with increasing age. Manic symptoms did not show any associations with the psychosocial factors considered in this study; this mental state is probably determined more by other factors such as current life stressors.

Acknowledgements
We acknowledge support by the DFG Open Access Publication Funds of the Ruhr-University Bochum.

Authors' contributions
ISH designed the study and supervised its implementation, EN analyzed the data and drafted the manuscript and SL collected the data. All authors read and approved the final manuscript.

Author details
[1] Research Institute for Mental Health, Ruhr-University Bochum, LWL-University Hospital Bochum, Alexandrinenstr. 1, 44791 Bochum, Germany. [2] Department of Psychiatry, Ruhr-University Bochum, LWL-University Hospital Bochum, Bochum, Germany.

References

Aas M, Henry C, Andreassen OA, Bellivier F, Melle I, Etain B. The role of childhood trauma in bipolar disorders. Int J Bipolar Disord. 2016;4:2.

Alloy LB, Abramson LY, Urosevic S, Walshaw PD, Nusslock R, Neeren AM. The psychosocial context of bipolar disorder: environmental, cognitive, and developmental risk factors. Clin Psychol Rev. 2005;25:1043–75.

Altman EG, Hedeker D, Peterson JL, Davis JM. The Altman Self-Rating Mania Scale. Biol Psychiat. 1997;42:948–55.

American Psychiatric Association. Diagnostic and Statistical Manual of Mental Disorders (DSM-5). Washington, DC: APA; 2013.

Angst J, Adolfsson R, Benazzi F, Gamma A, Hantouche E, Meyer TD, et al. The HCL-32: towards a self-assessment tool for hypomanic symptoms in outpatients. J Affect Disord. 2005;88:217–33.

Angst J, Meyer TD, Adolfsson R, Skeppar P, Carta M, Benazzi F, et al. Hypomania: a transcultural perspective. World Psychiatry. 2010;9:41–9.

Beck AT, Steer RA, Brown GK. Manual for the Beck Depression Inventory-II. San Antonio: Psychological Corporation; 1996.

Bernstein DP, Stein JA, Newcomb MD, Walker E, Pogge D, Ahluvalia T, et al. Development and validation of a brief screening version of the Childhood Trauma Questionnaire. Child Abuse Neglect. 2003;27:169–90.

Bräunig P, Shugar G, Krüger S. An investigation of the Self-Report Manic Inventory as a diagnostic and severity scale for mania. Compr Psychiat. 1996;37:52–5.

Carr CP, Martins CM, Stingel AM, Lemgruber VB, Juruena MF. The role of early life stress in adult psychiatric disorders: a systematic review according to childhood trauma subtypes. J Nerv Ment Dis. 2013;201:1007–20.

Carvalho Fernando S, Beblo T, Schlosser N, Terfehr K, Otte C, Löwe B, et al. The impact of self-reported childhood trauma on emotion regulation in borderline personality disorder and major depression. J Trauma Dissociation. 2014;15:384–401.

Chapman DP, Whitfield CL, Felitti VJ, Dube SR, Edwards VJ, Anda RF. Adverse childhood experiences and the risk of depressive disorders in adulthood. J Affect Disord. 2004;82:217–25.

Daruy-Filho L, Brietzke E, Lafer B, Grassi-Oliveira R. Childhood maltreatment and clinical outcomes of bipolar disorder. Acta Psychiatr Scand. 2011;124:427–34.

Etain B, Henry C, Bellivier F, Mathieu F, Leboyer M. Beyond genetics: childhood affective trauma in bipolar disorder. Bipolar Disord. 2008;10:867–76.

Garno JL, Goldberg JF, Ramirez PM, Ritzler BA. Impact of childhood abuse on the clinical course of bipolar disorder. Br J Psychiatry. 2005;186:121–5.

Goodman SH, Brand SR. Depression and early adverse experiences. In: Gotlib IH, Hammen CL, editors. Handbook of Depression. New York: Guilford Press; 2009. p. 249–74.

Hardt J, Rutter M. Validity of adult retrospective reports of adverse childhood experiences: review of the evidence. J Child Psychol Psychiat. 2004;45:260–73.

Haussleiter IS, Lorek S, Zeschel E, Mattausch S, Meyers M, Juckel G. At-risk symptoms of bipolar disorder in a university student cohort. Psychiat Res. 2018;265:324–33.

Hautzinger M, Keller F, Kühner C. BDI-II. Beck-Depressions-Inventar. 2nd ed. Frankfurt: Pearson Assessment; 2009.

Iffland B, Brähler E, Neuner F, Häuser W, Glaesmer H. Frequency of child maltreatment in a representative sample of the German population. BMC Public Health. 2013;13:980.

Kessler RC, McLaughlin KA, Green JG, Gruber MJ, Sampson NA, Zaslavsky AM, et al. Childhood adversities and adult psychopathology in the WHO World Mental Health Surveys. Br J Psychiatry. 2010;197:378–85.

Leboyer M, Etain B, Mathieu F, Henry C, Jamain S, Bellivier F. Childhood affective trauma in bipolar affective disorder: Rc6. Bipolar Disord. 2007;9:9–10.

Maniglio R. The impact of child sexual abuse on the course of bipolar disorder: a systematic review. Bipolar Disord. 2013;15:341–58.

Martins CM, Von Werne Baes C, Tofoli SM, Juruena MF. Emotional abuse in childhood is a differential factor for the development of depression in adults. J Nerv Ment Dis. 2014;202:774–82.

Mikulincer M, Shaver PR. Attachment in adulthood: structure, dynamics, and change. New York: Guilford; 2016.

Nelson J, Klumparendt A, Doebler P, Ehring T. Childhood maltreatment and characteristics of adult depression: meta-analysis. Br J Psychiatry. 2017;210:96–104.

Neumann E. Recollections of emotional abuse and neglect in childhood as risk factors for depressive disorders and the need for psychotherapy in adult life. J Nerv Ment Dis. 2017;205:873–8.

Neumann E, Rohmann E, Bierhoff HW. Development and validation of scales for measuring avoidance and anxiety in romantic relationships—The Bochum Adult Attachment Questionnaire. Diagnostica. 2007;53:33–47.

Schudlich TDR, Youngstrom EA, Martinez M, KogosYoungstrom J, Scovil K, Ross J, et al. Physical and sexual abuse and early-onset bipolar disorder in youths receiving outpatient services: frequent, but not specific. J Abnorm Child Psychol. 2015;43:453–63.

Spertus IL, Yehuda R, Wong CM, Halligan S, Seremetis SV. Childhood emotional abuse and neglect as predictors of psychological and physical symptoms in women presenting to a primary care practice. Child Abuse Neglect. 2003;27:1247–58.

Vachon DD, Krueger RF, Rogosch FA, Cicchetti D. Assessment of the harmful psychiatric and behavioral effects of different forms of child maltreatment. JAMA Psychiatry. 2015;72:1135–42.

Wittchen HU, Mühlig S, Pezawas L. Natural course and burden of bipolar disorders. Int J Neuropsychoph. 2003;6:145–54.

Zeschel E, Correll CU, Haussleiter IS, Krüger-Özgürdal S, Leopold K, Pfennig A, et al. The bipolar disorder prodrome revisited: is there a symptomatic pattern? J Affect Disord. 2013;151:551–60.

19

Predicting the risk and timing of major mood disorder in offspring of bipolar parents: exploring the utility of a neural network approach

Alysha Cooper[1], Julie Horrocks[1], Sarah Goodday[2,3], Charles Keown-Stoneman[4] and Anne Duffy[2,5*]

Abstract

Background: Bipolar disorder onset peaks over early adulthood and confirmed family history is a robust risk factor. However, penetrance within families varies and most children of bipolar parents will not develop the illness. Individualized risk prediction would be helpful for identifying those young people most at risk and to inform targeted intervention. Using prospectively collected data from the Canadian Flourish High-risk Offspring cohort study available in routine practice, we explored the use of a neural network, known as the Partial Logistic Artificial Neural Network (PLANN) to predict the time to diagnosis of major mood disorders in 1, 3 and 5-year intervals.

Results: Overall, for predictive performance, PLANN outperformed the more traditional discrete survival model for 3-year and 5-year predictions. PLANN was better able to discriminate or rank individuals based on their risk of developing a major mood disorder, better able to predict the probability of developing a major mood disorder and better able to identify individuals who would be diagnosed in future time intervals. The average AUC achieved by PLANN for 5-year prediction was 0.74, which indicates good discrimination.

Conclusions: This evaluation of PLANN is a useful step in the investigation of using neural networks as tools in the prediction of mood disorders in at-risk individuals and the potential that neural networks have in this field. Future research is needed to replicate these findings in a separate high-risk offspring sample.

Keywords: Bipolar spectrum, Major mood disorder, Prediction, Neural network, Longitudinal, High-risk offspring

Background

Bipolar disorder affects an estimated 2.5% of the population, with higher prevalence for spectrum conditions (Merikangas et al. 2007). The onset peaks in late adolescence and early adulthood (Manchia et al. 2008); however, delayed recognition and misdiagnosis remains a challenge. Untreated illness is associated with substantial morbidity and mortality early in the course (Kessing et al. 2015), and therefore timely and accurate diagnosis is critical to facilitate prompt treatment.

Bipolar disorder runs in families, and therefore the children of bipolar parents are an identifiable high-risk group ideally suited for risk prediction studies (Duffy et al. 2017). Family studies have shown that bipolar-related mood disorders segregating in families includes major depressive disorder, bipolar I, II and schizoaffective bipolar disorder (Smoller and Finn 2003; McMahon et al. 2010; Craddock and Sklar 2013). The penetrance and spectrum of phenotypes vary between families and according to the subtype of bipolar illness. Longitudinal prospective studies of high-risk offspring have provided

*Correspondence: anne.duffy@queensu.ca
[2] Department of Psychiatry, University of Oxford, Oxford, UK
Full list of author information is available at the end of the article

strong evidence that the illness often debuts with depressive episodes years before any hypomanic or manic episodes (Duffy et al. 2019).

While key risk factors for the development of bipolar disorder have been identified such as parental age of onset and clinical course, early adversity, and antecedent clinically significant symptoms (Preisig et al. 2016; Duffy et al. 2016), translatable risk prediction tools for clinicians do not exist or are in the early stages of development. For example, to our knowledge there has only been one published individualized risk calculator based on data from the BIOS longitudinal study of children of bipolar parents (Hafeman et al. 2017), which is yet to be replicated on an independent sample of familial at-risk offspring.

For studying events that occur over time, specialized modelling techniques that accommodate censoring are required (Allison 2010; Collett 2015). At the time the data analysis is conducted, not all individuals will necessarily have experienced the event of interest (bipolar-related mood disorders), and methods of survival analysis have been developed to accommodate these "censored" individuals, without introducing bias. In a longitudinal study, information on exposures and symptoms that might affect the risk of experiencing the outcome is collected repeatedly over time. Specialized techniques are necessary to include these repeatedly measured time-varying predictors in the analysis, while ensuring that only those exposures which occur before the outcome event are counted as possibly affecting the outcome. These techniques allow us to include the most up-to-date information collected on exposures, study the effect of symptoms that may not be present at baseline but develop during the course of follow-up, and ensure that the timing of the exposures in relation to the event of interest is taken into account. The latter is important as risk may be increased immediately after the exposure onset compared to later in time. Also, these techniques allow us to include numerical covariates that change over time, such as cumulative number of exposures at each timepoint. The Cox model (Cox 1972) and the discrete survival model (Efron 1988) are two such techniques from statistical survival analysis.

Recently, the use of neural networks has become increasingly popular in research for risk prediction (Charati et al. 2018; Wunnava et al. 2019; Li et al. 2017; LaFaro et al. 2015). An advantage of neural networks is that they do not rely on assumptions such as the distribution of the response variable or proportional hazards. Furthermore, they automatically accommodate non-linear relationships between the response and exposure variables (Biganzoli et al. 1998; Bourquin et al. 1997). Thus, rather than the researcher having to postulate a complicated, possibly non-linear model, the neural network can just "learn" the relationship with minimal direction from the researcher.

The purpose of this article is to explore the use of a neural network known as Partial Logistic Artificial Neural Network (PLANN) (Biganzoli et al. 1998), to predict the time to diagnosis of bipolar-related major mood disorders in the offspring of parents with confirmed bipolar disorder. For context, we compare PLANN to the more traditional discrete survival model. Both approaches accommodate censoring and time-varying predictors. The models are compared using several measures that assess the accuracy of the predictions. The prediction of which offspring are at greater risk of major mood disorder over time is important for clinical researchers, as it may allow for more proactive monitoring and prevention.

Methods

Study design

For this study, we used the data collected as part of the ongoing Canadian longitudinal high-risk offspring study described in detail elsewhere (Duffy et al. 2014, 2019). The study design is a dynamic, prospective cohort study. Briefly, original study families were identified through parents with bipolar I disorder confirmed by SADS-L interview and blind consensus review of all available clinical information. Subsequently, pedigrees were expanded and included first degree relatives of the original probands, who themselves were affected with bipolar-related major mood disorders (bipolar I, II, recurrent major depression). Agreeable offspring ages 5–25 years were enrolled and completed face to face research interviews following KSADS-PL format and study measures at baseline and then followed-up prospectively on average annually. This study has been reviewed for ethical compliance by the Ottawa Independent Research Ethics Board and the Queen's University Health Science Research Ethics Board.

Characteristics of participants and variables

In this analysis, we included 304 high-risk offspring from the Canadian high-risk cohort. The final data analysis was based on 292 high-risk individuals with no missing data for the predictors of interest. The outcome was defined as a DSM-IV diagnosis of bipolar-related major mood disorder including: bipolar disorder (Bipolar I, II, NOS), major depressive disorder and/or schizoaffective disorder based on semi-structured KSADS-PL format interviews and blind consensus review based on all available clinical and research material. Participants who did not have a diagnosis of major mood disorder before their last follow-up visit were considered censored at their last visit.

We limited variables in the model to those that would be relevant and routinely collected by clinicians in an office setting. Time-fixed predictors included sex at birth, parental response to lithium prophylaxis, parental age of onset of bipolar diagnosis, and childhood physical/sexual abuse. Time-varying predictors included the absence or presence at a given age of antecedent clinically significant symptoms and non-mood disorders (occurring prior to the outcome). In addition, the cumulative number of antecedent major and minor mood episodes at each age (occurring prior to the outcome) were included as time-varying predictors. Clinically significant activation (hypomanic), depressive, anxiety symptoms falling short of diagnostic criteria, as well as substance misuse and sleep problems were quantified based on clinical research interview and previously published consensus criteria (Duffy et al. 2019) (see Additional file 1). Childhood physical and sexual abuse was determined in offspring 13 years of age and older using the Childhood experiences of care and Abuse Scale (Bifulco et al. 2005), Note that only information up until time of diagnosis of major mood disorder or last follow-up visit was used in constructing the time-varying predictors. The time scale for both models was age of participant. In all analyses, covariates were lagged by one time interval in order to reduce the risk of reverse-causality and to enable predictions in the future time interval.

Statistical analysis

PLANN and the discrete survival model are similar in many respects. Both approaches can accommodate time-fixed and time-varying predictors and use the same data setup (see Additional file 1). Both approaches predict the probability that an individual will experience the outcome within a given time frame, conditional on the individual not yet having experienced the outcome. However, the internal calculations performed to make the predictions are different (see Additional file 1), resulting in different values for the predicted probabilities. The discrete survival model assumes that odds are proportional at each time point and that the relationship between the hazard (risk) of the event and covariates is linear on the logistic scale, whereas PLANN makes no such assumptions (Allison 2010; Biganzoli et al. 1998). Details of the two models are included in the Additional file 1.

Models were evaluated using several assessment measures. The time-dependent c-index (Antolini et al. 2005) was used to quantify how well the model can rank individuals on their time to developing the outcome. The area under the receiver operating curve (AUC) is often used as a measure of the model's ability to discriminate low and high-risk individuals (Zhou et al. 2011). Both the c-index and AUC range between 0 and 1, with 1 being best and a value greater than 0.5 being better than chance. The Brier score (Graf et al. 1999) measures the difference between the predicted probability of the event not occurring by a given follow-up time and the observed status of the individual at that time. The Brier score ranges between 0 and 1, with lower scores being better, 0 indicating perfect calibration and 0.25 indicating a non-informative model that is no better than chance. Common measures of prediction performance were used including accuracy, sensitivity, specificity, and positive predictive value. We used tenfold stratified cross-validation (see Additional file 1) to evaluate the predictive performance of the two models over 1-year, 3-year, and 5-year time intervals. For percentages, 95% confidence intervals were calculated as $100 \times (p \pm 1.96 \times \text{sqrt}(p \times (1-p)/n))$ where p is the observed proportion and n is the sample size. For means m, 95% confidence intervals were calculated as $m \pm 1.96 \times (sd/\text{sqrt}(n))$ where sd is the standard deviation.

Results

Table 1 presents the observed percent or means (and 95% confidence intervals) of the predictor variables included in the analyses. About 41% of participants were male. The mean age (at the time of the outcome event or censoring) was 21 years, and the mean age of parental onset was about 25 years. Childhood abuse was reported by 10% of offspring, while 38% were missing information on this variable as result of not being age appropriate for the measure or not yet completing the measure on next research visit. For the time-varying predictors, reported percentages/means are for disorders/episodes experienced before the outcome event or censoring. Over 41% of individuals had at least one clinically significant subthreshold symptom presentation, with the most prevalent being subthreshold anxiety at 15.4%. The most prevalent disorder was anxiety disorder at close to 30%.

Out of the 292 individuals included in the analysis, 112 (38.4%) developed a major mood disorder by their last follow-up visit, while 180 (61.6%) did not and were censored. As shown in the right-hand column of Table 1, proportionately fewer males experienced the outcome than were present in the full sample (31% versus 41%), and those who experienced the outcome were slightly younger on average (19.6 versus 21.0 years). More of those diagnosed with a major mood disorder experienced substance use, anxiety, and subthreshold activation and depression than in the full at-risk offspring sample.

Model comparisons

Table 2 compares PLANN and the discrete survival model in terms of the assessment measures, averaged across time intervals and using tenfold cross-validation, for 1-, 3- and 5-year predictions. Recall that for the Brier score, lower is better, while for the c-index and

Table 1 Percent observed or mean of all variables included as covariates in the models and 95% confidence intervals for the percent or mean, for full sample (n = 292) and individuals with the outcome (n = 112)

Variable	Full sample (n = 292)		Individuals with outcome (n = 112)	
	n (%) or mean	[95% CI]	n (%) or mean	[95% CI]
Time-fixed				
Sex (male)	121 (41.4)	[35.8, 47.1]	35 (31.3)	[22.6, 39.9]
Age (at outcome or censoring)	21.0	[20.2, 21.9]	19.6	[18.6, 20.6]
Parental lithium response	129 (44.2)	[38.5, 49.9]	47 (42.0)	[32.8, 51.1]
Parental onset age	25.4	[24.4, 26.5]	25.5	[23.7, 27.4]
Physical/sexual abuse				
Yes	30 (10.3)	[6.1, 13.8]	14 (12.5)	[6.3, 18.7]
Missing[a]	111 (38.0)	[32.4, 43.6]	32 (28.6)	[20.2, 37.0]
Time-Varying				
Disorders				
Subthreshold[b] activation	29 (9.9)	[6.5, 13.4]	19 (17.0)	[10.0, 23.9]
Subthreshold depression	31 (10.6)	[7.1, 14.2]	17 (15.2)	[8.5, 21.6]
Subthreshold sleep	9 (3.1)	[1.1, 5.1]	2 (1.8)	[0.0, 4.2]
Subthreshold substance use	36 (12.3)	[8.6, 16.1]	13 (11.6)	[5.6, 17.6]
Subthreshold anxiety	45 (15.4)	[11.3, 19.6]	17 (15.2)	[8.5, 21.9]
Substance use	51 (17.5)	[13.1, 21.8]	29 (25.9)	[17.7, 34.0]
Sleep	54 (18.5)	[14.0, 23.0]	18 (16.1)	[9.2, 22.9]
Anxiety	87 (29.8)	[24.5, 35.0]	39 (34.8)	[26.0, 43.7]
Neurodevelopmental	33 (11.3)	[7.7, 14.9]	12 (10.7)	[5.0, 16.5]
Number of episodes				
Major mood	0.2	[0.1, 0.3]	0.2	0.1, 0.3]
Minor mood	0.2	[0.1, 0.3]	0.1	[0.0, 0.2]

[a] Missing refers to having not completed the measure either due to not being age appropriate to complete or not yet completing the measure; [b]see Additional file 1 for definitions of subthreshold conditions

Table 2 Comparison of the evaluation metrics for PLANN and the discrete survival model with 1-year, 3-year and 5-year predictions

	One-year		Three-year		Five-year	
	PLANN	survival	PLANN	survival	PLANN	survival
Mean Brier Score[a]	0.177	0.180	0.182	0.188	0.179	0.190
C-index	0.633	0.556	0.549	0.513	0.590	0.520
Mean AUC(SD)[b]	0.633 (0.170)	0.740 (0.144)	0.708 (0.123)	0.655 (0.124)	0.745 (0.076)	0.669 (0.063)

[a] The mean Brier score is the average Brier score across 15, 20, and 25 years

[b] The mean AUC is the average AUC across the time intervals measured

AUC, higher is better. PLANN outperformed the discrete survival model on the Brier score which measures the difference between observed and predicted values. The c-index indicates how well the model ranks individuals in terms of their event times. PLANN outperformed the discrete survival model at all three interval lengths. On mean AUC, PLANN outperformed the discrete survival model in 3-year and 5-year predictions, but the opposite is true in 1-year predictions. PLANN does better at 5-year predictions than at 1- or 3-year predictions according to mean AUC. The 5-year mean AUC for PLANN was 0.74.

Table 3 shows mean accuracy, specificity, sensitivity, and positive predictive value (PPV), for 1-year, 3-year, and 5-year predictions for the two models, where the mean is taken across time intervals and tenfold cross-validation was used (see Additional file 1 for more details). For 1-year prediction, PLANN outperformed the discrete survival model with higher sensitivity, specificity, and PPV when the optimal threshold was used. However, for

Table 3 Mean accuracy, specificity, sensitivity, and positive predictive value (PPV) across time intervals and 10 CV-folds for 1-year, 3-year, and 5-year predictions for PLANN and the discrete survival model

Model	Threshold	Accuracy	Specificity	Sensitivity	PPV
One year					
PLANN[a]					
	0.05	0.751	0.762	0.272	0.064
	0.10	0.948	0.986	0.019	0.051
	0.15	–	–	–	–
	0.20	–	–	–	–
	Optimal[b]	0.681	0.683	0.488	0.081
Survival					
	0.05	0.772	0.783	0.360	0.073
	0.10	0.895	0.924	0.186	0.100
	0.15	0.927	0.960	0.128	0.133
	0.20	0.940	0.976	0.083	0.160
	Optimal[b]	0.556	0.560	0.383	0.043
Three year					
PLANN					
	0.05	0.269	0.186	0.822	0.107
	0.10	0.588	0.583	0.443	0.111
	0.15	0.762	0.808	0.257	0.167
	0.20	0.818	0.899	0.096	0.143
	Optimal[b]	0.591	0.591	0.506	0.134
Survival					
	0.05	0.270	0.181	0.791	0.101
	0.10	0.533	0.513	0.483	0.111
	0.15	0.760	0.813	0.218	0.125
	0.20	0.841	0.919	0.128	0.134
	Optimal[b]	0.572	0.582	0.474	0.130
Five year					
PLANN					
	0.05	0.222	0.070	0.934	0.162
	0.10	0.425	0.335	0.709	0.169
	0.15	0.582	0.546	0.565	0.210
	0.20	0.687	0.722	0.360	0.213
	0.607	0.617	0.577	0.230	0.607
Survival					
	0.05	0.264	0.116	0.893	0.161
	0.10	0.410	0.300	0.662	0.143
	0.15	0.548	0.511	0.508	0.160
	0.20	0.709	0.738	0.420	0.238
	Optimal[b]	0.601	0.615	0.515	0.224

[a] One-year predictions made by PLANN were all below 0.15 and therefore, thresholds of 0.15 or greater could not be evaluated for accuracy metrics

[b] The Optimal rows present the average accuracy metrics across time intervals when the optimal threshold of each time interval is used (see Additional file 1)

3- and 5-year predictions, PLANN and the discrete survival model gave similar results for the optimal thresholds. A trade-off between specificity and sensitivity was demonstrated for both models across all prediction intervals when examining performance across different thresholds. With lower thresholds, sensitivity is high and specificity is low, whereas the opposite was true for higher thresholds. Optimal thresholds achieve a balance between sensitivity and specificity.

Finally, it was of interest to assess whether the models could distinguish between three individuals in the test set selected based on their observed diagnosis and censoring time. The individual in the test set with the earliest diagnosis time was considered the 'earlier-onset' individual, the individual with the median diagnosis time was considered the 'mid-onset' individual and the individual with the highest censoring time (longest survival time) was the 'no onset' individual. The 'earlier-onset' individual experienced a major mood disorder at 11.64 years, the 'mid-onset' individual was diagnosed at 19.85 years and the 'no onset' individual was censored at 39.79 years. For these three individuals, the predicted survival curves were plotted for 1 year, 3 year and 5-year predictions made by PLANN (Fig. 1). PLANN predicted that the 'earlier-onset' individual had the lowest survival probability over time.

When making 1-year predictions of major mood disorder, PLANN could predict that the 'mid-onset' individual had a lower survival probability than the 'no onset' individual. However, PLANN had more difficulty distinguishing between the 'mid-onset' and 'no onset' individuals when three and five-year predictions were made. For these individuals, the predicted survival curves were additionally plotted for the discrete survival model with one-year predictions, three-year predictions and five-year predictions. As seen in Fig. 2, the discrete survival model predicted that the 'earlier-onset' individual had a higher probability of diagnosis (i.e. lower survival probability) over time compared to the 'mid-onset' and 'no onset' individuals. However, for 1-year, 3-year and 5-year predictions, the discrete survival model predicted that the 'mid-onset' individual had a higher probability of not being diagnosed than the 'no onset' individual. These findings further demonstrate that PLANN outperforms the discrete survival model in discrimination of higher-risk versus lower-risk offspring.

Discussion

In this study we explored the potential utility of using Partial Logistic Artificial Neural Network (PLANN), an extension of discrete survival analysis, to predict time to diagnosis of major mood disorder at 1, 3 and 5 years into the future in a well-characterized prospectively followed cohort of high-risk individuals identified based on a parent with bipolar disorder. We limited fixed and time-varying covariates in the model to data that would be routinely collected and available in clinical

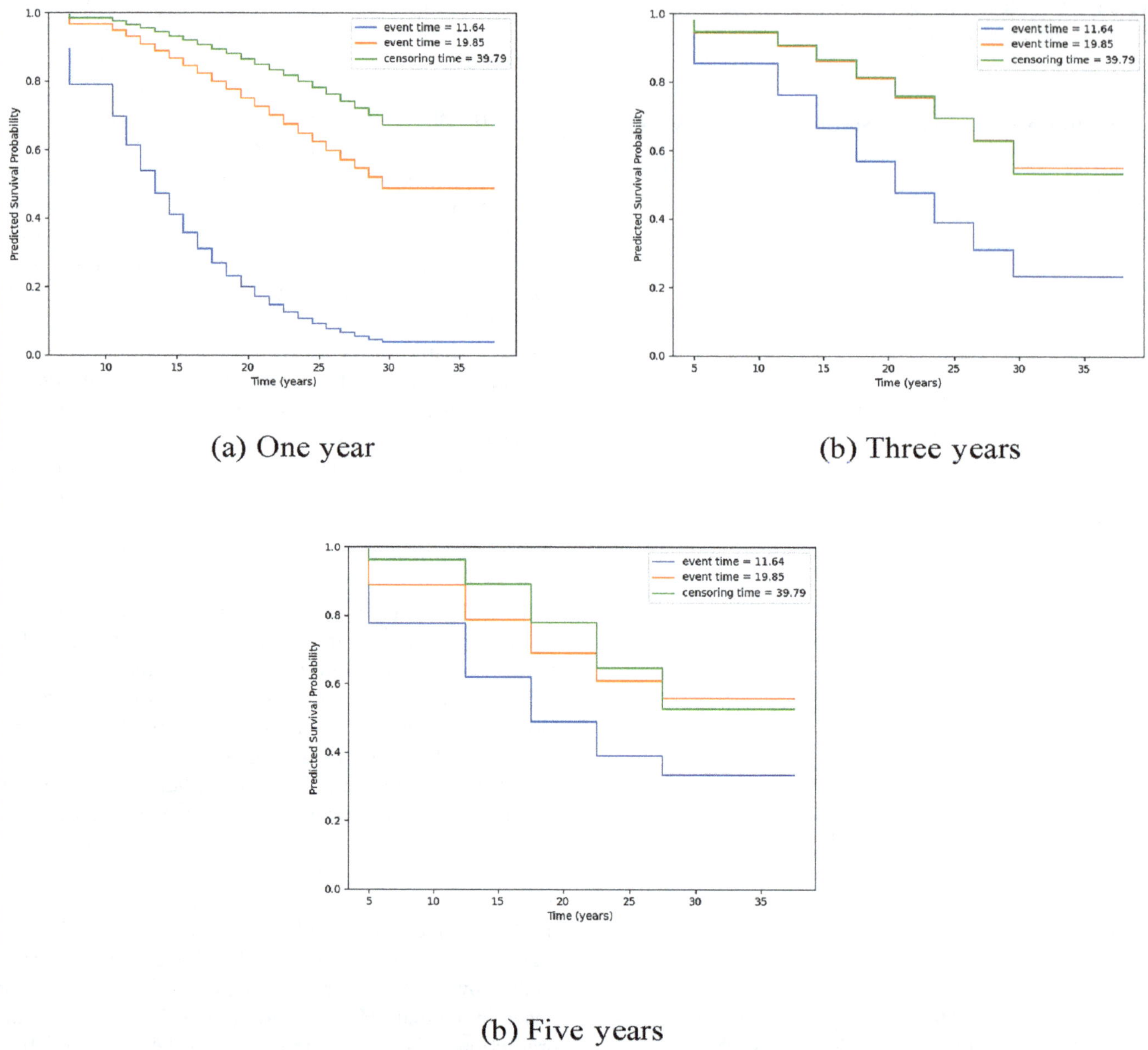

Fig. 1 Predicted survival curves for 'earlier-onset', 'mid-onset' and 'no onset' individuals in test set of single fold for PLANN with (**a**) 1 year, **b** 3 year and (**c**) 5-year predictions. Legend: blue line indicates high-risk offspring with earlier-onset, orange line indicates mid-onset and green line indicates no-onset of bipolar-related major mood disorder over observation time

practice (i.e., sex, age, childhood abuse, subthreshold antecedent clinically significant symptoms and lifetime antecedent non-mood diagnoses). We included major depressive disorder as part of the bipolar-related major mood disorders given (i) major depression is considered part of the bipolar spectrum in genetic studies (McMahon et al. 2010; McGuffin et al. 2003; Coleman et al. 2020) and (ii) bipolar disorder typically debuts as major depression in high-risk offspring of bipolar parents (Duffy et al. 2017; Mesman et al. 2013).

PLANN was compared to the more traditional discrete survival model to assess whether the use of a neural network provides any benefit over a traditional statistical modeling approach. While PLANN and the logistic model have common advantages, such as enabling the incorporation of time-varying covariates due to the use of discrete time intervals, both models also have distinct advantages over one another. The logistic model allows for the interpretation of the effect of covariates on the discrete hazard and the evaluation of whether or not the

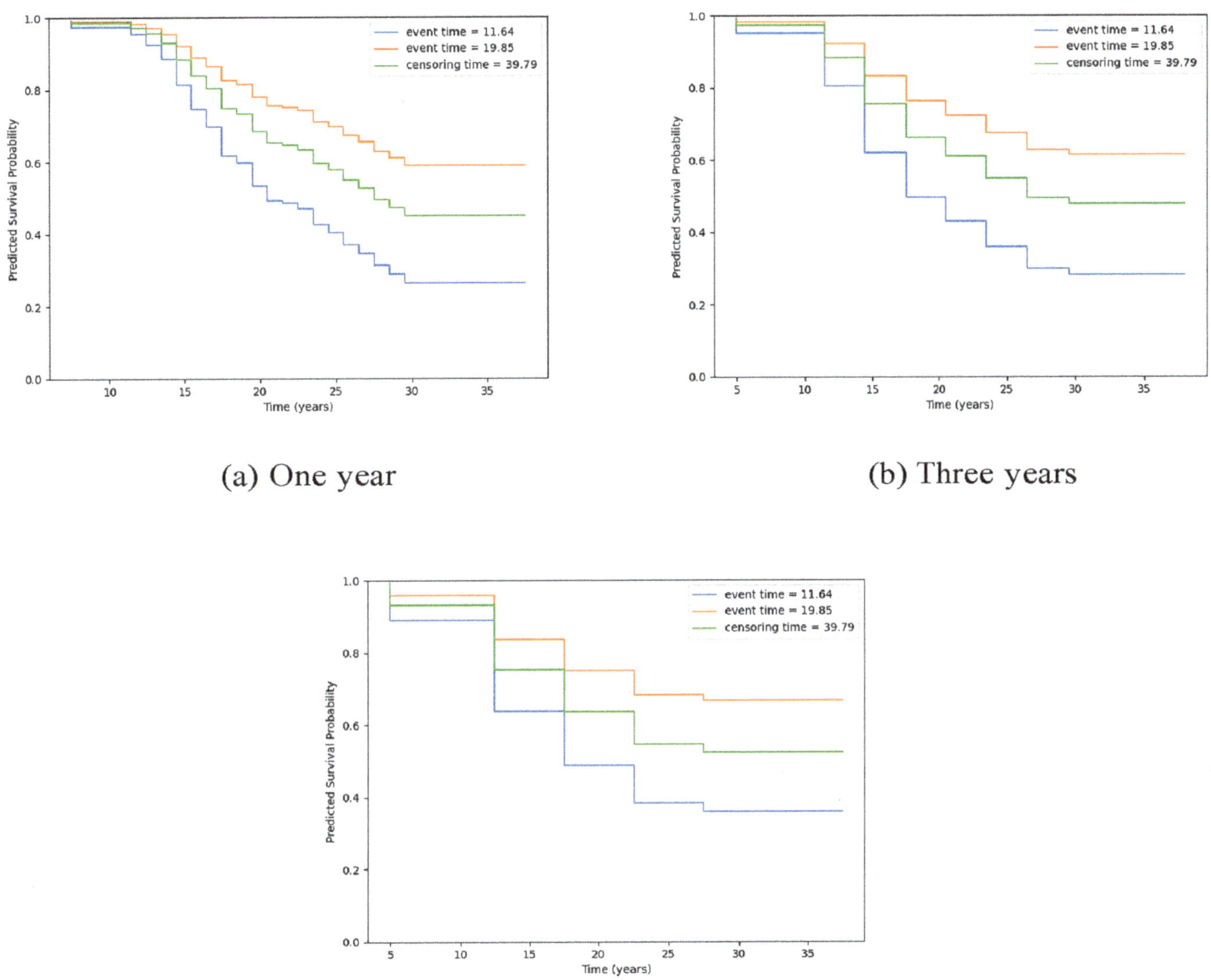

(a) One year

(b) Three years

(c) Five years

Fig. 2 Predicted survival curves for 'earlier-onset', 'mid-onset' and 'no onset' individuals in test set of single fold for the discrete survival model with (**a**) 1 year, **b** 3 year and (**c**) 5 year predictions. Legend: blue line indicates high-risk offspring with earlier-onset, orange line indicates mid-onset and green line indicates no-onset of bipolar-related major mood disorder over observation time

covariates have a significant effect on the discrete hazard, although this was not pursued here. On the other hand, PLANN makes fewer assumptions about the relationship between the outcome and covariates and has the ability to automatically detect non-linear relationships in the data. The latter point is important, as for example, mood instability has been found to follow non-linear patterns (Bonsall et al. 2012). A drawback of PLANN, and machine learning models in general, is that they are computationally intensive, requiring high-performance computer clusters and many days of computation, whereas discrete survival models take only a few seconds to fit.

Overall, for predictive performance, PLANN outperformed the logistic model for 3-year and 5-year predictions. PLANN was better able to discriminate or rank individuals based on their risk of developing major mood disorder (i.e., higher time-dependent c-indices) and better able to predict the probability of developing major mood disorder (i.e., lower Brier scores). The results were mixed for 1-year predictions, with the discrete survival model outperforming PLANN for AUC. For five-year predictions, the average AUC from PLANN was 0.74, which indicates that the model shows good discrimination between high and low risk individuals. This value is comparable to (Hafeman et al. 2017) who achieved an AUC of 0.76 for 5-year predictions.

Prediction was superior in the 3 and 5-year models compared to the 1-year models, as evidenced by higher AUC, sensitivity and positive predictive values. This is not surprising, as relatively few events occurred in specific 1-year intervals, compared to three or 5 year intervals (see Additional file 1: Tables S2 and S3). Also, it is intuitively more difficult to predict that an event will occur in a 1-year interval, than to say it will happen sometime over the next 5 years.

Individualized risk prediction has important implications for research and clinical practice. By identifying from among individuals at familial risk those most likely to develop illness, an ultra-high risk group can be identified that can inform research into the determinants of illness onset and prevention. Moreover, this ultra-high risk group would be suitable and would likely benefit from prospective surveillance and low-risk intervention and psychoeducation targeting sleep hygiene, healthy coping and stress reduction, healthy lifestyle and diet and avoidance of alcohol misuse and drug use. Our risk prediction approach of using PLANN to predict onset of bipolar-related major mood disorder differs from other published risk calculators such as (Hafeman et al. 2017), which used a "baseline re-setting" Cox proportional hazards model. Both the Cox model and PLANN allow the inclusion of covariates measured at baseline and at follow-up visits and neither method requires an assumption about the distribution of the outcome variable. However, unlike the Cox model, PLANN does not require a proportional hazards assumption. In addition, we only included model variables in PLANN that would be available in routine practice.

Strengths and limitations

Strengths include the carefully assessed parental diagnoses based on longitudinal clinical observations confirming the risk status in the offspring, the measurement of diagnosis in high-risk offspring through semi-structured research clinical assessments and blind consensus reviews. However, the following limitations relevant to this analysis are worth noting. The sample size is small, particularly for neural networks, which typically require sample sizes in the thousands; it is notoriously difficult to make predictions in medicine, due to lack of relevant variables (Lawless 2010) and thus additional breadth of data (e.g., genetic data, behavioural data) may improve predictions.

Conclusion

This evaluation of PLANN is a useful step in the investigation of using neural networks as tools in the prediction of diagnosis of mood disorders for at-risk individuals and demonstrated the potential that neural networks have in this field. PLANN performed better than the traditional discrete time survival model in predicting the development of major mood disorders in high-risk individuals. Future research replicating these approaches in different samples with the inclusion of additional data will help inform the further utility of risk prediction models to aid in research and clinical decision making in individuals at familial risk of developing bipolar-related mood disorders.

Abbreviations

BD: Bipolar Disorder; CECA: Childhood experience of care and abuse; DSM: Diagnostic and Statistical Manual for Mental Disorders; K-SADS–PL: Kiddie Schedule for Affective Disorders–Present and Lifetime; PLANN: Partial Logistic Artificial Neural Network; SADS-L: Schedule for Affective Disorders-Lifetime.

Supplementary Information

Additional file 1: Table S1. Example of discrete survival data for hypothetical scenario with sex and blood pressure as covariates. **Figure S1.** Feed-forward neural network with one hidden layer. **Table S2.** PLANN one-, three-, five-year prediction assessments showing optimal threshold, accuracy, specificity (spec), sensitivity (sens), positive predictive value (PPV), total number of individuals in the risk set (n) and total number of events observed within each time interval, determined using tenfold cross-validation. **Table S3.** Discrete survival model one-, three-, five-year prediction assessments showing optimal threshold, accuracy, specificity (spec), sensitivity (sens), positive predictive value (PPV), total number of individuals in the risk set(n) and total number of events observed within each time interval, determined using tenfold cross-validation. **Table S4.** Number of subthreshold diagnoses for individuals in the full sample, individuals who experienced the major mood disorder outcome (diagnosis of BP, MDD and/or schizoaffective disorder), and individuals who did not experience the outcome.

Acknowledgements

The authors acknowledge the unprecedented commitment to research excellence and clinical care made by Dr Paul Grof who assessed and clinically treated many of the affected parents and adult offspring in this research. Without his dedication and attention to detail this work would not be possible. We also acknowledge the excellent technical assistance of Elizabeth Tetzlaff who prepared and vetted the database for this analysis.

Authors' contributions

JH, AC designed the analysis with input from CK-S, SG and AD. AD is the PI of the high-risk study and contributed with SG to data collection. AC supervised by JH carried out the data analysis and discussed results and interpretation with the other authors listed. AC and JH drafted the manuscript and AD, CK-S and SG edited and revised iterative drafts. All authors read and approved the final manuscript.

Author details

[1]Department of Mathematics and Statistics, University of Guelph, Guelph, ON, Canada. [2]Department of Psychiatry, University of Oxford, Oxford, UK. [3]4YouandMe, Seattle, USA. [4]Dalla Lana School of Public Health, University of Toronto, Toronto, ON, Canada. [5]Department of Psychiatry, Queen's University, Kingston, ON, Canada.

References

Allison PD. Survival analysis using SAS: a practical guide. Cary: Sas Institute; 2010.

Antolini L, Boracchi P, Biganzoli E. A time-dependent discrimination index for survival data. Stat Med. 2005;24(24):3927–44.

Bifulco A, Bernazzani O, Moran PM, Jacobs C. The childhood experience of care and abuse questionnaire (CECA. Q): validation in a community series. Br J Clin Psychol. 2005;44(4):563–81.

Biganzoli E, Boracchi P, Mariani L, Marubini E. Feed forward neural networks for the analysis of censored survival data: a partial logistic regression approach. Stat Med. 1998;17(10):1169–86.

Bonsall MB, Wallace-Hadrill SMA, Geddes JR, Goodwin GM, Holmes EA. Nonlinear time-series approaches in characterizing mood stability and mood instability in bipolar disorder. Proc R Soc b Biol Sci. 2012;279(1730):916–24.

Bourquin J, Schmidli H, van Hoogevest P, Leuenberger H. Basic concepts of artificial neural networks (ANN) modeling in the application to pharmaceutical development. Pharm Dev Technol. 1997;2(2):95–109.

Charati JY, Janbabaei G, Alipour N, Mohammadi S, Gholiabad SG, Fendereski A. Survival prediction of gastric cancer patients by Artificial Neural Network model. Gastroenterol Hepatol Bed to Bench. 2018;11(2):110.

Coleman JRI, Gaspar HA, Bryois J, Bipolar Disorder Working Group of the Psychiatric Genomics Consortium, Major Depressive Disorder Working Group of the Psychiatric Genomics Consortium, Breen G. The Genetics of the Mood Disorder Spectrum: Genome-wide Association Analyses of More Than 185,000 Cases and 439,000 Controls. Biol Psychiatry. 2020;88(2):169–84.

Collett D. Modelling survival data in medical research. Boca Raton: CRC Press; 2015.

Cox DR. Regression models and life-tables. J R Stat Soc Ser B (methodol). 1972;34(2):187–202.

Craddock N, Sklar P. Genetics of bipolar disorder. Lancet. 2013;381(9878):1654–62.

Duffy A, Horrocks J, Doucette S, Keown-Stoneman C, McCloskey S, Grof P. The developmental trajectory of bipolar disorder. Br J Psychiatry. 2014;204(2):122–8.

Duffy A, Jones S, Goodday S, Bentall R. Candidate risks indicators for bipolar disorder: early intervention opportunities in high-risk youth. Int J Neuropsychopharmacol. 2016;19(1):pyy071.

Duffy A, Vandeleur C, Heffer N, Preisig M. The clinical trajectory of emerging bipolar disorder among the high-risk offspring of bipolar parents: current understanding and future considerations. Int J Bipolar Disord. 2017;5(1):37.

Duffy A, Goodday S, Keown-Stoneman C, Grof P. The emergent course of bipolar disorder: observations over two decades from the Canadian high-risk offspring cohort. Am J Psychiatry. 2019;176(9):720–9.

Efron B. Logistic regression, survival analysis, and the Kaplan-Meier curve. J Am Stat Assoc. 1988;83(402):414–25.

Graf E, Schmoor C, Sauerbrei W, Schumacher M. Assessment and comparison of prognostic classification schemes for survival data. Stat Med. 1999;18(17–18):2529–45.

Hafeman DM, Merranko J, Goldstein TR, Axelson D, Goldstein BI, Monk K, et al. Assessment of a person-level risk calculator to predict new-onset bipolar spectrum disorder in youth at familial risk. JAMA Psychiat. 2017;74(8):841–7.

Kessing LV, Vradi E, McIntyre RS, Andersen PK. Causes of decreased life expectancy over the life span in bipolar disorder. J Affect Disord. 2015;180:142–7.

LaFaro RJ, Pothula S, Kubal KP, Inchiosa ME, Pothula VM, Yuan SC, et al. Neural network prediction of ICU length of stay following cardiac surgery based on pre incision variables. PLoS One. 2015;10(12):e0145395.

Lawless JF, Yuan Y. Estimation of prediction error for survival models. Stat Med. 2010;29(2):262–74.

Li H, Luo M, Zheng J, Luo J, Zeng R, Feng N, et al. An artificial neural network prediction model of congenital heart disease based on risk factors: a hospital-based case-control study. Medicine. 2017;96(6):e6090.

Manchia M, Lampus S, Chillotti C, Sardu C, Ardau R, Severino G, et al. Age at onset in Sardinian bipolar I patients: evidence for three subgroups. Bipolar Disord. 2008;10(3):443–6.

McGuffin P, Rijsdijk F, Andrew M, Sham P, Katz R, Cardno A. The heritability of bipolar affective disorder and the genetic relationship to unipolar depression. Arch Gen Psychiatry. 2003;60(5):497–502.

McMahon FJ, Akula N, Schulze TG, Muglia P, Tozzi F, Detera-Wadleigh SD, et al. Meta-analysis of genome-wide association data identifies a risk locus for major mood disorders on 3p21. 1. Nat Genetics. 2010;42(2):128.

Merikangas KR, Akiskal HS, Angst J, Greenberg PE, Hirschfeld RMA, Petukhova M, et al. Lifetime and 12-month prevalence of bipolar spectrum disorder in the National Comorbidity Survey replication. Arch Gen Psychiatry. 2007;64(5):543–52.

Mesman E, Nolen WA, Reichart CG, Wals M, Hillegers MHJ. The Dutch bipolar offspring study: 12-year follow-up. Am J Psychiatry. 2013;170(5):542–9.

Preisig M, Strippoli M-PF, Castelao E, Merikangas KR, Gholam-Rezaee M, Marquet P, et al. The specificity of the familial aggregation of early-onset bipolar disorder: a controlled 10-year follow-up study of offspring of parents with mood disorders. J Affect Disord. 2016;190:26–33.

Smoller JW, Finn CT. Family, twin, and adoption studies of bipolar disorder. In: American Journal of Medical Genetics Part C: Seminars in Medical Genetics. Wiley Online Library; 2003. p. 48–58.

Wunnava S, Qin BIX, Kakar T, Sen C, Rundensteiner EA, Kong X. Adverse drug event detection from electronic health records using hierarchical recurrent neural networks with dual-level embedding. Drug Saf. 2019;42(1):113–22.

Zhou X-H, Obuchowski NA, McClish DK. Measures of Diagnostic Accuracy. In: Statistical Methods in Diagnostic Medicine. Wiley; 2011. p. 13–55. https://doi.org/10.1002/9780470906514.ch2

20

New vision on the mental problems of Vincent van Gogh; results from a bottom-up approach using (semi-)structured diagnostic interviews

Willem A. Nolen[1*], Erwin van Meekeren[2], Piet Voskuil[3] and Willem van Tilburg[4]

Abstract

Background: On July 29, 1890 at the age of 37 years, the Dutch painter Vincent van Gogh died from the consequences of a suicide attempt with a gun 2 days earlier. Since then many medical and psychological theories were suggested about what had happened to Van Gogh.

Aim: To present an overview of the history of the mental problems of Van Gogh and the most likely diagnoses.

Method: (Semi-)structured diagnostic interviews were applied to three art historians who are very familiar with Van Gogh from his correspondence and other sources as well as a neuropsychiatric examination to evaluate whether the symptoms might be explained by a medical condition.

Results: Several previously suggested diagnoses could be excluded as being highly unlikely, while other diagnoses could be classified as more of less likely.

Conclusion: Most likely Van Gogh suffered from comorbid illnesses. Since young adulthood, he likely developed a (probably bipolar) mood disorder in combination with (traits of) a borderline personality disorder as underlying vulnerability. This likely worsened through an alcohol use disorder combined with malnutrition, which then led, in combination with rising psychosocial tensions, to a crisis in which he cut off his ear. Thereafter, he likely developed two deliriums probably related to alcohol withdrawal, followed by a worsening with severe depressive episodes (of which at least one with psychotic features) from which he did not fully recover, finally leading to his suicide. As additional comorbidity, focal (temporal lobe) epilepsy cannot be excluded.

Keywords: Vincent van Gogh, Bipolar disorder, Psychotic depression, Borderline personality disorder, Alcohol use disorder, Delirium, Focal epilepsy

Background

On July 29, 1890 at the age of 37 years, the Dutch painter Vincent van Gogh died from the consequences of a suicide attempt with a gun 2 days earlier. Suicidal behaviour usually is the result of a history with mental problems. Although in Van Gogh's case the beginning of this his tory is not easy to determine, a critical period in his life started when he cut off his left ear followed by three con secutive hospitalizations in Arles between December 1888 and May 1889, and subsequently a transfer to the asylum of Saint-Rémy-de-Provence in May 1889, where he arrived having "absolutely no will, hardly any desires

*Correspondence: w.a.nolen@planet.nl
[1] Department of Psychiatry, University Medical Center Groningen, University of Groningen, Hanzeplein 1, 9713 GZ Groningen, The Netherlands
Full list of author information is available at the end of the article

or none" [776].[1] He stayed in Saint-Rémy for a full year but did not fully recover, and also a move to Auvers-sur-Oise did not bring the relief he wished. That his existence at that time appeared "attacked at the very root" [898] was possibly the reason for his suicide.

Van Gogh himself initially did not understand what was wrong with him. He wrote about a "mental or nervous fever or madness, I do not know quite what to say or how to name it" [739], and initially—possibly to reassure himself, his friends and family—also of "a simple artist's bout of craziness" [732]. However, Van Gogh's own doctors came to various diagnoses. Felix Rey, his doctor in Arles, called his first crisis when he cut off his ear "a transient over-excitement" [728] and blamed it on his lifestyle with much alcohol, coffee, tobacco and poor food, while Rey's chief Jules Urpar noticed "an attack of acute mania with generalized delirium" [772, note 2]. When the episodes returned Rey further suggested epilepsy as the cause [776], which was confirmed by Théophile Peyron, his doctor in Saint-Rémy: "attacks of epilepsy, separated by long intervals" [772, note 2]. Subsequently, after his death a comprehensive discussion arose not only on the above but also on many other suggested diagnoses and theories about what had happened to Van Gogh (Bakker et al. 2016). And finally, Van Gogh's extensive correspondence further inspired the discussion.

In this paper we will try to contribute to a better understanding of the psychopathology of Vincent van Gogh. Many of the previously suggested diagnoses resulted from a 'top-down approach', i.e. were based on the assumption that Van Gogh suffered from a specific illness based on arguments pro that illness in his letters and other sources without taking into account other information making that illness unlikely. In contrast, we used a 'bottom-up approach' by applying (semi-)structured interviews to assess all mental symptoms ever reported by Van Gogh in his letters or as found in other sources. Thus, we aimed to explore all possible diagnoses, in order to exclude (very) unlikely illnesses and leaving other illnesses as more or less likely in the case of Van Gogh.

Methods

General considerations

For our study we used several diagnostic approaches. However, before applying these, we had to realize whether it would be allowed to make a diagnosis without having Van Gogh interviewed and examined in person. In fact, the medical code of ethics is generally very cautious about this point (APA Calls for End to 'Armchair' Psychiatry 2020). Nevertheless, in this case we think that we can not only exclude several of the previously suggested diagnoses with certainty, but also be more or less sure about other parts of the diagnostic process. This is based on the fact that we have access to his extensive correspondence containing 902 letters, of which 820 were written by him to his brother Theo and other relatives. In these letters he described what he was experiencing in his life, including his mental problems, although it must also be realized that Van Gogh did not write his letters for his doctors, but for his brother Theo and other relatives, to inform, or to reassure them.

Diagnostic assessments

In a first step we profited from the knowledge of three art historians very familiar with Van Gogh as a person, from his correspondence as well as from several other sources. To 'use this knowledge' we interviewed them with three diagnostic assessments. The first was the 'Structured Clinical Interview for DSM-IV' (SCID-IV)[2] applied by one of the authors (WAN) (First et al. 2002). The SCID scoring system was slightly modified: any possible symptom ever reported in his life in the sources was scored as 'certainly not', 'possibly', 'probably' or 'certainly' present or as 'unclear'. In a next step we searched the whole correspondence for citations that could confirm the responses of the art historians to the SCID-IV. We present the most clear citations in the historical overview of Van Gogh's mental problems.

The same art historians were interviewed by another author (EVM) using four questionnaires on personality disorders [the 'Self Test Viersprong' (https://www.devie rsprong.nl/wp-content/uploads/); the 'McLean Screening Instrument for Borderline Personality Disorder' (MSI-BPD) (Zanarini et al. 2003); the 'General Assessment of Personality Disorders' (GAPD) (Hentschel and Livesley 2013); and the 'Personality Inventory for DSM-5' (PID 5)] (Thimm et al. 2016) about the existence of possible personality pathology while focussing on his life before the ear incident. The answers to these questionnaires were then scored by two independent experienced diagnosticians (T. Ingenhoven, psychiatrist and H. Berghuis, clinical psychologist), who were unfamiliar with the origins of the investigation and the identity of the 'patient', i.e. Van Gogh.

Finally, the same art historians were questioned by another author (PV) for a neuropsychiatric examination to evaluate whether the symptoms might be explained by a medical condition, i e. epilepsy.

[1] The numbers between brackets refer to the letters in Van Gogh's correspondence: Jansen L, Luijten H, Bakker N (eds.), Vincent van Gogh. The Letters, The Hague 2009, yearly updated, http://vangoghletters.org/vg/.

[2] At the time of the interview the SCID-5 was not yet translated into Dutch.

Historical overview of the mental problems of Van Gogh

Already from his early adulthood Van Gogh experiences mental problems. His father writes "he always has the inclination to melancholy" [102; note 53]. At about 20 years old (1873–1875, living in London) he is often gloomy, withdraws himself from other people, is focused on religious issues, and—partly because of these behaviours—he loses his job as an art dealer. In the years 1875–1877 (Paris), he shows a strict ascetic attitude, combined with an unhealthy lifestyle. In 1877–1878 (Amsterdam) he writes "My head is sometimes numb and is often burning hot, and my thoughts are confused" [117] and he mentions "indescribably strong feeling of fear" [141]. He also injures himself "Last night I used the cudgel again" (Mendes Da Costa 2020). In 1880 (Borinage) he describes himself as "a man of passions, capable of and liable to do rather foolish things for which I sometimes feel rather sorry. I do often find myself speaking or acting somewhat too quickly when it would be better to wait more patiently" [155]. He behaves so strange that his father suggests him to go the psychiatric asylum of Geel which Van Gogh refuses [185, 186]. Shortly thereafter he regains his artistic activities. Late 1881 (Etten) he writes several letters which in comparison with the rest of his correspondence, are remarkably long and also rather incoherent [180–190].

In 1882–1883 (The Hague) he feels "as though one is bound hand and foot, lying in a deep, dark pit, powerless to do anything" [203] and reports fear and sorrow which "cannot but make one agitated and nervous in speech and manner" [221]. Moreover, he mentions that he doesn't enjoy company, and that dealing with people, talking to them, is often painful and difficult [244]. Nevertheless, he remains active with drawing and painting.

Late 1883 (Drenthe) he "is overcome by a feeling of great anxiety, dejection and even despair, too much to express". Next (Nuenen) he senses a "procrastination and hesitancy in everything, which paralyzes my own passion and energy like a leaden atmosphere" [410]. A few months later (1884) he is working "from early till late" and being "absorbed in the moment", in a letter also containing 10 poems [430]. He remains very active for several months, but finally he writes "I've worked really hard recently; I believe, in conjunction with other agitation, even overworked. At least I'm in a sad mood, and all these things have affected me to such an extent that I have many days when I'm relatively powerless. I can't eat and I can't sleep, that's to say not enough, and that makes one weak" [463]. In this period he leaves the church and becomes engaged in inappropriate love affairs which also leads to a further disturbed relationship with his parents.

In 1885 Van Gogh moves to Antwerp and after a few months to Paris (1886–1887), where he goes to live with Theo, which means that he temporarily stops writing letters. In Paris, he has "the most impossible and highly unsuitable love affairs from which, as a rule, I emerge only with shame and disgrace" [574] combined with (probably) substantial alcohol use and heavy smoking [603].

In 1888 Van Gogh moves to Arles where initially he is very active "in a fury of work" [592] and experiences a "rage to paint orchards [which] won't last forever" [594]. However, a month later he reports " It's not in black that I see the future, but I see it bristling with many difficulties, and at times I wonder if these won't be stronger than I am", and "I was so worn out and ill that I didn't feel I had the strength to go and live on my own" [602, 608]. He continues drinking and smoking "the only thing that comforts and distracts—in my case—as in others, is to stun oneself by taking a stiff drink or smoking very heavily" [635]; also to find relief "If the storm within roars too loudly, I drink a glass too many to stun myself. It's being crazy, compared with what one ought to be" [645]. He has days being active with painting, but also days feeling "thoroughly discouraged" and "My life is restless and anxious" [672]. Furthermore, he reports a changed sleeping pattern: "For 3 nights I stayed up to paint, going to bed during the day. It often seems to me that the night is much more alive and richly coloured than the day" [676]. Additionally, he realizes the alternating pattern of his mental problems: "I have a terrible clarity of mind at times, when nature is so lovely these days, and then I'm no longer aware of myself and the painting comes to me as if in a dream. I am indeed somewhat fearful that that will have its reaction in melancholy when the bad season comes" [687].

In October 1888 Gauguin joins Van Gogh in Arles. Initially, their collaboration is fruitful, but soon tensions arise. Already after 6 weeks Gauguin expresses the idea to leave as he "can absolutely not live side by side without trouble, as a result of incompatibility of temperament, and both he and I need tranquillity for our work" [724, note 1]. In the night of December 22 Gauguin decides to leave. This leads to a crisis in which Van Gogh directs the aggression towards himself. On the evening of December 23, he cuts off his left ear and gives it away to a woman in a brothel.

Alarmed police finds him the next morning at home suffering from blood loss, and he is admitted to the local hospital. Two days later (December 26) he becomes so confused that he is put in isolation: "My thoughts sailed over many seas. I even dreamed of the Dutch ghost ship and the Horla, and it seems that I sang then" [739]. Afterwards he has only vague memories. He also has vivid visual images: "I again saw each room in the house at Zundert, each path, each plant in the garden, the views round about, the fields, the neighbours, the cemetery, the church, our kitchen garden behind—right up to the magpies' nest in a tall acacia in the cemetery" [741] and also "unbearable hallucinations", anxiety and nightmares [743]. Another 7 days later (January 2, 1889), he is recovered and discharged from the hospital on January 7. At that time, he thinks not much is wrong, but afterwards he has the feeling that he has been ill: "What can you say, I have moments when I'm twisted by enthusiasm or madness or prophecy like a Greek oracle on her tripod" [745]. He resumes his activities but within a month it goes wrong again.

On February 7, he is re-admitted with apparently similar symptoms and again placed in isolation. In a report, on request of the Chief of Police, doctor Albert Delon writes "I found this man in a state of extreme excitement suffering from a true delirium, only momentarily recognizing the people around him", and he hears hallucinations [747, note 1]. It is unclear whether he was drinking alcohol again between his first and second admission. Again his hospital stay is short, and on February 17 he goes back to work. However, there are complaints from a group of 30 residents about nuisance and inappropriate behaviour, e.g. touching women and making obscene remarks (The Arles Petition 1889). This results in the third and this time involuntary admission on February 27. Whether he is confused or just angry by the complaints about his behaviour and that he is placed in isolation, remains unclear [750]. Afterwards, he also mentions "terrible fits of anxiety sometimes without any apparent cause" [764].

Mid-March he has almost recovered and goes back to home although he continues to eat and sleep in the hospital while feeling uncertain about the future: "It will, I hope, suffice to say that I feel decidedly incapable of starting to take a new studio again and living there alone". In addition, he expresses concerns about his alcohol use [760]. Looking back to what happened in the previous months, he mentions four (?) "big crises in which I hadn't the slightest idea of what I said, wanted, did", while he can't precisely describe what it is like: "there are terrible fits of anxiety sometimes—without any apparent cause—or then again a feeling of emptiness and fatigue in the mind. I consider the whole rather as a simple accident, no doubt a large part of it is my fault, and from time to time I have fits of melancholy and terrible feelings of guilt" [764]. He agrees with the suggestion of his doctor and Theo to agree to a voluntary admission in the asylum in Saint-Rémy on May 8, 1889 where he will stay for a year, experiencing four episodes/crises. The first episode lasts longer (from mid-July to late August 1889) than the previous three crises in Arles. He complains about a "disturbed mind" and is "absolutely distraught, as in Arles, just as much if not worse". [797] He also shows bizarre behaviour: "It appears that I grab dirt from the ground and eat it, although my memories of these bad moments are vague" [797]. When looking back to this period he writes: "I feel cowardly in the face of anguish and suffering—more cowardly than is justified", recognizing that the crises "tend to take an absurd religious turn" and mentioning "I reproach myself for my cowardice" [801]. He also he paints himself in a recently to Van Gogh attributed self-portrait (Fig. 1) (Van Tilborgh et al. 2020).

Fig. 1 Self-portrait (August 1890), Nasjonalmuseet, Oslo, Norway

Late December 1889 follows a short crisis lasting 1 week with "great discouragement" [836] while his guard Poulet observes that he swallows paint what is interpreted by his doctor Peyron as an attempt to poison himself [833, note 2]. On January 21, 1890, 2 days after a visit to Arles, he is again seized by an attack lasting about a week. According to his doctor Peyron "He is incapable at present of any kind of work, and only responds with incoherent words when asked questions" [846, note 2]. A few days after having received a letter from Theo announcing that he has become a father, Van Gogh congratulates him: "It does me more good and gives me more pleasure" and it "contributes a great deal to making me forget these last few days when I was ill, then I no longer know where I am and my mind wanders" [850].

However, a prolonged and severe episode again follows from February to April 1890, where he is "totally dazed".

[857], "not able to read or write" and "ill at its worst" "[864]. Disappointed that he has not recovered in Saint-Rémy he then takes the decision to leave for the North [863, 865]. In May 1890 he moves to the rural Auvers-sur-Oise near Paris. However, he was again unable to make a lasting recovery and finally he shoots himself in the breast on July 27 1890, ending his life 2 days later (Van Tilborgh and Meedendorp 2013).

Results

In the following paragraphs we present of the findings of the diagnostic assessments and our interpretations. For more extensive information see Additional file 1: Tables S1–S11.

Psychotic disorder?

It is certain that Van Gogh suffered from at least three episodes with psychotic symptoms (Additional file 1: Table S3). The first two, in December 1888 (after the ear incident) and in February 1889, were short (lasting only a few days) and consisted of vivid hallucinations, with afterwards partial amnesia (indicating a decrease of consciousness) and cognitive dysfunction. According to the SCID-IV these two psychotic episodes appear to have been a delirium. The third episode occurred in July–August 1889 in Saint-Rémy, when there were apparent religious delusions, but this time no hallucinations. He was also severely depressed with self-reproach, his thinking was possibly delayed, he exhibited bizarre behaviour (swallowing paint) and his memory of it was vague. The neurologist/epileptologist among the authors (PV) assumes that this memory disturbance indicates a decrease of consciousness, while the psychiatrists (WN, EVM and WVT) are of the opinion that is can be explained by a severe depression with psychotic features. Regarding the other three crises in Saint-Rémy it is unclear whether he was psychotic and/or had a decreased consciousness.

After Van Gogh's death one of the first suggested diagnoses (1922) was schizophrenia (Jaspers 1922). However, with the current understanding of this disorder, this seems unlikely as van Gogh never exhibited psychotic symptoms before the ear incident at the age of 35, and also not during the intervals between his psychotic episodes in the last 15 months of his life. Moreover, there is no indication that he suffered from negative symptoms such as diminished emotional expression or avolition. This makes the diagnosis schizophrenia highly unlikely.

Another suggestion was cycloid psychosis, characterized by confusion states, psychotic symptoms, mood swings, anxiety and psychomotor disturbances (Leonhard 1988). Nowadays, cycloid psychosis is defined by the occurrence of recurrent short psychotic episodes with delusions, hallucinations, incoherence or disorganized behaviour which cannot be explained by a major mood disorder, schizophrenia, a general medical condition or associated substance abuse (Fusar-Poli et al. 2016). Although this diagnosis can be considered in Van Gogh's case, it has common features with other explanations, like a mood disorder or a personality disorder. In our opinion, these alternative explanations make cycloid psychosis as primary diagnosis unlikely.

Fig. 2 Still life: Café table with absinthe (February/March 1887), Van Gogh Museum, Amsterdam, The Netherlands

Unhealthy lifestyle?

Definitely since 1886, but possibly earlier, Van Gogh drank very much alcohol, and he tried to reduce it in Arles, but without success, indicating that he was dependent on alcohol. Besides wine, he also drank absinthe which at that time contained 50 to 70% alcohol (Fig. 2). In addition, there are many indications of malnutrition and poor sleeping habits, if not exhaustion. Those who consume large amounts of alcohol in combination with malnutrition, run the risk of brain function impairment including mental problems. Moreover, abrupt stopping with excessive alcohol consumption can lead to withdrawal phenomena, including a delirium. Therefore, it is likely that at least the first brief psychosis in Arles on the days after the ear incident during which he likely stopped drinking abruptly, was actually an alcohol withdrawal delirium. Only later on in Saint-Rémy, when he was forced to minimize or even stop drinking, he probably succeeded in it and he also did not have further withdrawal problems.

Mood disorder?

In many letters Van Gogh reported depressive symptoms (Additional file 1: Table S2). From 1874 (London) up to the ear incident (1988), he almost certainly suffered from several depressive episodes. Moreover, in Saint-Rémy he had at least two major depressive episodes (July–August 1889 and February-April 1890), with also psychotic features in the first episode (discussed above), and with severe distress and disfunction in both episodes. He also reported manic symptoms, possibly during his stay in London, very likely in the Borinage, and in his 1st year in Arles. There were also periods with a decreased need for sleep and high, increased activity; whether he also showed social disfunction in these periods is not fully clear.

Since the 1930s it has been suggested that van Gogh suffered from bipolar disorder (Rose and Mannheim 1938; Jamison 1993). Although Van Gogh showed mood swings and according to his brother Theo was as if he consisted of two conflicting personalities "the one marvellously gifted, sensitive and gentle, and the other self-loving and unfeeling" [FR b908], the question remains whether the diagnostic threshold of a manic episode with social disfunction has ever been exceeded at some point in its life, meaning that his episodes with manic symptoms were only hypomanic episodes. Thus, it is likely that van Gogh suffered from a bipolar disorder, and if not bipolar 1 disorder then probably bipolar 2 disorder. Nevertheless, it must also be considered that his mood symptoms were part of a personality disorder.

Personality disorder?

Van Gogh was unstable in his personal relationships, starting with his father and from then on with many other people in the different places where he lived. Even with his so beloved brother Theo there sometimes were tensions, especially during their time living together in Paris (1886) and on the subject of how he should behave towards their father. Early on he exhibited solitary behaviour, while he also had a great need to meet the Christian duties of charity. He idealized family life, but he failed to marry and to found a family himself despite he had several, although problematic, love affairs. Living with family or artists was the only alternative, but in both respects he was no ideal partner. As from 1880 (Borinage) he showed self-neglect and from 1886 (Paris) also self-destructive behaviour (drinking too much alcohol combined with malnutrition), self-mutilation [the ear incident (1888) and possible self-poisoning (1889)] and ultimately (1890) he committed a suicide attempt that resulted in his death. This raises the question whether these mental problems were part of a personality disorder and more specific a borderline personality disorder—as suggested by several authors since 1996 (Mehlum 1996; Van Meekeren 2000; Van Meekeren 2004)—with a persistent pattern of instability of interpersonal relationships, the self-image and emotions, and marked impulsivity, often combined with self-destructive behaviour such as suicidal behaviour or self-mutilation.

The conclusions of the consulted diagnosticians who scored the four personality disorder questionnaires, were 'clear suggestions for a personality disorder' (Additional file 1: Table S6–S8). All questionnaires contain strong indications for a personality disorder, while the combination of the different traits convincingly indicate a severe borderline personality disorder, given the score of 8 on the MSI-BPD and that all DSM-5 criteria are fulfilled. There are also traits of an obsessive–compulsive personality disorder, however not in the compulsive, controlling sense but in the sense of a perseverative, rigid perfectionism.

Somatic disorder?

Over the years, several somatic diagnoses have been suggested, such as Meniere's disease (Arenberg et al. 1990; Martin 2011), (neuro)syphilis (the disease that Theo died from a half year after Vincent) (Yamey 2003), acute intermittent porphyria (AIP) exacerbated by drinking absinthe containing thujone (Loftus and Arnold 1991), and various forms of intoxications including carbon monoxide poisoning.

All these suggestions are considered highly unlikely. The sources give no reason to think that he was suffering from Meniere's disease. While syphilis occurred frequently in Van Gogh's time and was well known, none of his doctors made this diagnosis, even not after they treated him for gonorrhoea. As an extremely rare autosomal genetic condition AIP is unlikely as none (even later) family members is known with this disease. In addition, thujone intoxication was rejected, first by the unlikeness that he suffered from AIP, and second by the fact that absinthe at Van Gogh's time contained a very low concentration of thujone (Bonkovsky et al. 1992). Carbon monoxide poisoning due to gas lamps in his home in Arles is also unlikely as there are no other reports of (possible) carbon monoxide poisoning in Arles (Van Slooten 2020).

Epilepsy?

The outcome of the neuropsychiatric interview is discussed in Additional file 1: Table S9–S11. When Van Gogh's doctors concluded that he had epilepsy, they probably meant 'épilepsie larvée mental' (Morel 1860). This form of epilepsy is also called 'masked epilepsy', wherein a patient does not have classical seizures, but a paroxysmal behaviour disorder based on epileptic activity in the deeper brain structures. This diagnosis is nowadays called temporal lobe epilepsy or recently focal epilepsy with focal onset seizures, resulting in a highly variable expression of anxiety, delusions and hallucinations, depending on the affected part of the mesial temporal network (Blumer 2002).

A possible explanation of such encephalopathic aetiology from the end of 1888 is then found in `Van Gogh's lifestyle with alcohol abuse, malnutrition, poor sleep and mental exhaustion. However, without further examination by electroencephalographic and imaging techniques (not available in his time) the probability of epilepsy is difficult to quantify. Therefore, focal (temporal lobe) epilepsy as comorbidity to the above discussed psychotic disorders, mood disorders and personality disorders, cannot be excluded and deserves at least to be considered (Additional file 1: Table S11) (Voskuil 2013; Voskuil 2020).

Fig. 3 Still life: Drawing board, pipe, onions and sealing-wax (January 1889), Kröller-Müller Museum, Otterloo, The Netherlands

Discussion and conclusions

As far as we know this study is the first in which (semi-) structured diagnostic interviews assessing all possible mental symptoms, were applied in a historic person to make a psychiatric diagnosis posthumously. We think this 'bottom-up approach' is valid in the case of Vincent van Gogh as he has reported so many mental symptoms in his extensive correspondence. Furthermore, our findings are supported by medical reports of the doctors who have treated him. Thus, we consider our findings as rather robust. However, we also want to repeat that Van Gogh did not write his letters for his doctors and that we have not interviewed and examined Van Gogh in person.

Our main conclusion is that in the case of Vincent van Gogh no single disorder can explain all his mental problems throughout his life, but that he most likely suffered from several comorbid disorders. Starting at young adulthood (i.e. long before the ear incident in December 1988), he frequently reported mental problems and had difficulties in relating with people. He also was regularly depressed, had probably periods with manic symptoms, drank much alcohol and did not take enough care of himself at several occasions. Overlooking this period, it seems appropriate to conclude that Van Gogh showed—in today's terminology—identity and attachment problems and/or personality problems, more specifically with borderline features. Depending on the evaluation whether or not there was an enduring pattern with impairment, he had a personality disorder or traits thereof. In addition, there appeared to be an evolving mood disorder, more particularly recurrent depressive episodes probably in the course of a bipolar disorder.

As of the end of 1888, his mental and somatic health deteriorated, preceded by an increase of alcohol consumption since 1986 combined with malnutrition (Fig. 3), resulting in the ear incident. Subsequently, there were three successive crises. In two of these crises (December 1888–February 1889) he showed features of a delirium, possibly after abrupt stopping with alcohol. After his move to Saint-Rémy (May 1889), his mood disorder got worse with several severe depressive episodes of which the first one (July–August 1889) most likely was a psychotic depressive episode. Another theoretical explanation of (part of) the symptomatology after December 1888 is focal (temporal lobe) epilepsy, either as co-morbidity or as an alternative—i.e. differential—diagnosis.

Especially the worsening of his alcohol use since 1886 appears relevant, as this seems to be part of the reason—besides conflicting strong characters with different opinions on life and art—why Gauguin decided to leave Arles as well as why Van Gogh could develop a delirium after he abruptly stopped drinking. Moreover, it can theoretically explain the development of focal (temporal lobe) epilepsy. In addition, there were several other psychosocial factors that played a role: concerns about the continuation of the financial support by Theo and maybe also about his brother's health, the imminent failure of creating a family or instead a brotherhood of painters, and finally his lack of success as a painter (he sold just one painting).

Fig. 4 Tree roots (July 1890), Van Gogh Museum, Amsterdam, The Netherlands

Despite all these problems which contributed to his illnesses, we however also would like to stress that Van Gogh was not only a great and very influential painter but also an intelligent man with an enormous willpower, resilience and perseverance. He must have had a strong constitution. He was able to arouse compassion, himself having compassion with the less fortunate. And he was a passionate man with a strong temperament. Over the years he kept on painting, also during most difficult periods in his life. Only during the most severe psychotic episodes he temporarily stopped working, but in intervals with less symptoms he was able to paint. Only in a few paintings a relationship with his mental state is evident, e.g. in the 'Oslo self-portrait' (Fig. 1) painted at the end of his psychotic depressed episode in July–August 1889 (Van Tilborgh et al. 2020). Regarding the unfinished 'Tree roots' (Fig. 4) from July 1890, Van Gogh's last work and painted on the morning before he shot himself, the question is whether he depicted there his struggle for life. Art historians think it is unlikely, "food for biographers and another story" (Maes and Van Tilborgh 2012).

Supplementary information

Additional file 1: Table S1. Overview of scores on relevant items of the SCID-IV: Screening module. **Table S2.** Overview of scores on relevant items of the SCID-IV: Module mood disorders. **Table S3.** Overview of scores on relevant items of the SCID-IV: Module psychotic disorders. **Table S4.** Overview of scores on relevant items of the SCID-IV: Module anxiety disorders. **Table S5.** Overview of scores on relevant items of the SCID-IV: Module substance use disorders. **Table S6.** Conclusions from questionnaires on personality disorders. **Table S7.** Scores on the General Assessment of Personality Disorders (GAPD). **Table S8.** Scores on the individual items of the Personality Inventory for DSM-5 (PID-5). **Table S9.** Neuropsychiatric history of Van Gogh. **Table S10.** Neuropsychiatric family history of Van Gogh. **Table S11.** Arguments pro and contra epilepsy as a possible diagnosis in Van Gogh's case.

Authors' contributions

WN, EvM and PV made substantial contributions to the conception and design of the work; and the acquisition, analysis, and interpretation of data; and has drafted the work and substantively revised it. WvT made substantial contributions to the interpretation of data. And all authors approved the submitted version (and any substantially modified version that involves the author's contribution to the study); and has agreed both to be personally accountable for the author's own contributions and to ensure that questions related to the accuracy or integrity of any part of the work, even ones in which the author was not personally involved, are appropriately investigated, resolved, and the resolution documented in the literature. All authors read and approved the final manuscript.

Author details

[1] Department of Psychiatry, University Medical Center Groningen, University of Groningen, Hanzeplein 1, 9713 GZ Groningen, The Netherlands. [2] BuurtzorgT, Oeverwallaan 130, 2498 BK The Hague, The Netherlands. [3] Torendreef 14, 4851 BH Ulvenhout, The Netherlands. [4] Department of Psychiatry, Amsterdam University Medical Centers, Vrije Universiteit, De Boelelaan 1117, 1081 HV Amsterdam, The Netherlands.

References

APA Calls for End to 'Armchair' Psychiatry; 2020. https://www.psychiatry.org/newsroom/news-releases/apa-calls-for-end-to-armchair-psychiatry. Accessed 10 Feb 2020.

Arenberg IK, Countryman LF, Bernstein LH, Shambaugh GE. Van Gogh had Meniere's disease and not epilepsy. JAMA. 1990;264:491–3.

Bakker N, Van Tilborgh L, Prins L, Meedendorp T. On the verge of insanity; Van Gogh and his illness. Amsterdam: Van Gogh Museum; 2016.

Blumer D. The illness of Vincent van Gogh. Am J Psychiatry. 2002;159:519–26.

Bonkovsky HL, Cable EE, Cable JW, Donohue SE, White EC, Greene YJ, Lambrecht RW, Srivastava KK, Arnold WN. Porphyrogenic properties of the terpenes camphor, pinene, and thujone (with a note on historic implications for absinthe and the illness of Vincent van Gogh). Biochem Pharmacol. 1992;43:2359–68.

First MB, Gibbon M, Williams JBW. Structured clinical interview for DSM-IV-TR axis I disorders, research version, patient edition (SCID-I/P). New York: Biometrics Research, New York State Psychiatric Institute; 2002.

Fusar-Poli P, Cappucciati M, Bonoldi I, Hui LM, Rutigliano G, Stahl DR, Borgwardt S, Politi P, Mishara AL, Lawrie SM, Carpenter WT Jr, McGuire PK. Prognosis of brief psychotic episodes: a meta-analysis. JAMA Psychiatry. 2016;73:211–20.

Hentschel AG, Livesley WJ. The General Assessment of Personality Disorder (GAPD): factor structure, incremental validity of self-pathology, and relations to DSM-IV personality disorders. J Pers Assess. 2013;95:479–85.

https://www.deviersprong.nl/wp-content/uploads/2016/06/LPFS-BF-2.0-English.pdf. Accessed 24 Apr 2020.

Jamison KR. Touched with fire: manic-depressive illness and the artistic temperament. New York: Free Press; 1993.

Jaspers K. Strindberg und van Gogh, Versuch einer pathographischen Analyse unter vergleichender Heranziehung von Swedenborg und Hölderlin. Bern: Bircher; 1922.

Leonhard K. Bedeutende Persönlichkeiten in ihren psychische Krankheiten. Berlin: Ullstein Mosby; 1988, 2. Aufl, S 216–234.

Loftus LS, Arnold WN. Vincent van Gogh's illness: acute intermittent porphyria? BMJ. 1991;303(6817):1589–91.

Maes B, Van Tilborgh L. Van Gogh's tree roots. In: Van Tilborgh L, editor. Van Gogh: New Findings (Van Gogh Studies 4). Zwolle: WBooks/Van Gogh Museum; 2012. p. 54–71.

Martin C. Did Van Gogh have Ménière's disease? Eur Ann Otorhinolaryngol Head Neck Dis. 2011;128:205–9.

Mehlum L. Suicidal process and suicidal motives. Suicide illustrated by the art, life and illness of Vincent van Gogh. Tidsskr Nor Laegeforen. 1996;116:1095–101 **(Norwegian)**.

Mendes Da Costa M. Personal memories of Vincent van Gogh during his stay at Amsterdam. Letter to Het Algemeen Handelsblad. Amsterdam; December 2 1910; 2020. http://www.webexhibits.org/vangogh/letter/6/etc-122a.htm. Accessed 10 Feb 2020.

Morel BA. D'une forme de délire, suite d'une surexcitation nerveuse se rattachant à une variete non encore décrite d'épilepsie (épilepsie larvée). Gazette hanbdomadaire de médecine et de chirurgie. 1860;7:773–5.

Rose M, Mannheim MJ. Vincent van Gogh im Spiegel seiner Handschrift. Basel: S Karger; 1938.

The Arles Petition. Petition signed by 30 citizens of Arles, requesting commitment of Vincent van Gogh, shortly before February 27, Archives communales d'Arles; 1889.

Thimm JC, Jordan S, Bach B. The Personality Inventory for DSM-5 Short Form (PID-5-SF): psychometric properties and association with big five traits and pathological beliefs in a Norwegian population. BMC Psychol. 2016;4:61.

Van Meekeren E. Psychiatric case history of Vincent van Gogh. Ned Tijdschr Geneeskd. 2000;144:2509–14 **(Dutch)**.

Van Meekeren E. Vincent van Gogh, Life and psychiatric history. Benecke: Amsterdam; 2004.

Van Slooten R. Van Gogh and the gas madness; 2020. https://lapostexaminer.com/van-gogh-and-the-gas-madness/2015/09/26. Accessed 20 Feb 2020.

Van Tilborgh L, Meedendorp T. The life and death of Vincent van Gogh. Burlington Mag. 2013;155:456–62.

Van Tilborgh L, Meedendorp T, Pilz K. Van Gogh as mentally ill: his contested Oslo self-portrait. Burlington Mag. 2020;162:88–101.

Voskuil P. Diagnosing Vincent van Gogh, an expedition from the sources to the present "mer à boire". Epilepsy Behav. 2013;28:177–80.

Voskuil P. Vincent van Gogh and his illness. A reflection on a posthumous diagnostic exercise. Epilepsy Behav. 2020;111:107258.

Yamey G. Pox: genius, Madness, and the Mysteries of Syphilis. BMJ. 2003;327:1173.

Zanarini MC, Vujanovic AA, Parachini EA, Boulanger JL, Frankenburg FR, Hennen J. A screening measure for BPD: the McLean Screening Instrument for Borderline Personality Disorder (MSI-BPD). J Pers Disord. 2003;17:568–73.

21

Long-term outcome of postpartum psychosis: a prospective clinical cohort study in 106 women

Anna-Sophie Rommel[1*], Nina Maren Molenaar[1,3], Janneke Gilden[3], Steven A. Kushner[1,2,3], Nicola J. Westerbeek[3], Astrid M. Kamperman[3] and Veerle Bergink[1,2,3]

Abstract

Objective: We aimed to investigate the outcome of postpartum psychosis over a four-year follow-up, and to identify potential clinical markers of mood/psychotic episodes outside of the postpartum period.

Methods: One hundred and six women with a diagnosis of first-onset mania or psychosis during the postpartum period were included in this prospective longitudinal study. Women were categorized into either (1) recurrence of non-postpartum mood/psychotic episodes or (2) mania/psychosis limited to the postpartum period. We summarize the longitudinal course of the illness per group. We used a logistic regression model to identify clinical predictors of recurrence of mood/psychotic episodes outside of the postpartum period.

Results: Over two thirds of the women included in this study did not have major psychiatric episodes outside of the postpartum period during follow-up. The overall recurrence rate of mood/psychotic episodes outside the postpartum period was ~ 32%. Of these women, most transitioned to a bipolar disorder diagnosis. None of the women fulfilled diagnostic criteria for schizophrenia or schizophreniform disorder. No clinical markers significantly predicted recurrence outside of the postpartum period.

Conclusions: For the majority of women with first-onset postpartum psychosis, the risk of illness was limited to the period after childbirth. For the remaining women, postpartum psychosis was part of a mood/psychotic disorder with severe non-postpartum recurrence, mainly in the bipolar spectrum. No clinical predictors for risk of severe episodes outside the postpartum period emerged. Our findings add to previous evidence suggesting a fundamental link between postpartum psychosis and bipolar disorder, which may represent two distinct diagnoses within the same spectrum.

Keywords: Postpartum psychosis, Bipolar disorder, Longitudinal follow-up, Course of illness, Clinical predictors

Background

Postpartum psychosis is an umbrella term for postpartum mania, psychosis, psychotic depression and a mixed affective state, occurring shortly after childbirth (Bergink et al. 2011; Kapfhammer et al. 2014; Osborne 2018). Postpartum psychosis is the most severe form of childbirth-related psychiatric disorders and has an incidence of ~ 0.3 to 0.6 per 1000 births (Bergink et al. 2011,2015a; Kapfhammer et al. 2014; Meltzer-Brody et al. 2018). Women with postpartum psychosis may initially present with mood fluctuations, insomnia and obsessive concerns about the baby, followed by severe mood symptoms, and sometimes disorganized behavior, delusions and hallucinations (Bergink et al. 2011; Kamperman et al. 2017; Brockington et al. 1981; Boyce and Barriball 2010; Sit

*Correspondence: anna.rommel@mssm.edu
[1] Department of Psychiatry, Icahn School of Medicine at Mount Sinai, Icahn (East) Building Floor 4 Room 34, 1425 Madison Ave, New York, NY 10029, USA
Full list of author information is available at the end of the article

et al. 2006). The presence of severe mood symptoms differentiates postpartum psychosis from psychosis outside of the postpartum period (Bergink et al. 2016). Postpartum psychosis is, therefore, a misnomer. Since psychotic symptoms in the postpartum period occur mostly within the setting of affective lability, the disorder is a bipolar-related mood disorder rather than a primary psychotic disorder (Meltzer-Brody et al. 2018; Bergink et al. 2015a).

Due to the high relative risk for suicide and infanticide, early recognition and adequate treatment of postpartum psychosis is crucial (Bergink et al. 2011; Wisner et al. 1994). With adequate treatment, nearly all women with postpartum psychosis achieve full remission (Bergink et al. 2015b), and a large proportion of patients achieve good functional recovery (Burgerhout et al. 2017). For some women, postpartum psychosis is part of a severe, often life-long, psychiatric disorder (Bergink et al. 2016; Munk-Olsen et al. 2012; Chaudron and Pies 2003; Nager et al. 2013). For other women, the vulnerability is limited to the postpartum period (Bergink et al. 2016; Wesseloo et al. 2016).

Despite the widespread use of the term 'postpartum psychosis', this diagnosis is not recognized in current classification systems, including the International Classification of Diseases, Tenth Revision (ICD-10) and the Diagnostic and Statistical Manual of Mental Disorders, Fifth Edition (DSM-5) (Florio et al. 2016). Instead, the majority of women with postpartum psychosis receive a DSM-5 diagnosis of bipolar disorder, because they present with prominent manic or mixed affective episodes. Yet, according to our recent meta-analysis, 43.5% of women with postpartum psychosis have no manic or psychotic recurrence outside the postpartum period over a mean follow-up of 16 years (Gilden et al. 2020), suggesting that a diagnosis of bipolar disorder might not always be warranted. It is important to note that most studies included in the meta-analysis were performed in the 1970s and 1980s, limiting the generalizability of the results. Further research is needed to reproduce these numbers in the current treatment setting. In addition, to improve long-term prognosis, it is pertinent to identify those women who may develop severe mood episodes outside the postpartum period.

Currently, little is known about which women are specifically at risk for recurrence outside the postpartum period. Previous studies identified being single/unmarried (Terp et al. 1999), a personal or family history of psychiatric disorders and older age (Blackmore et al. 2013) as potential risk factors for future recurrence after first onset postpartum psychosis (Kapfhammer et al. 2014; Benvenuti et al. 1992). However, these studies were small and conducted retrospectively. Consequently, this prospective longitudinal study was designed to investigate recurrence in 106 women with postpartum psychosis over a four-year period. We further aimed to identify potential clinical markers of a psychiatric disorder with mood or psychotic episodes outside of the postpartum period.

Methods

Study setting and procedure

The study was approved by the International Review Board of the Erasmus Medical Centre (Rotterdam, The Netherlands). All patients provided written informed consent. The study was performed on the Mother-Baby Unit (MBU), a five-bed inpatient unit that specializes in the care of patients with severe psychopathology in the postpartum period, located in the Department of Psychiatry in the Erasmus Medical Centre (Erasmus MC) in Rotterdam, The Netherlands. On the MBU, women are admitted with their babies, who stay in a fully staffed nursery adjoining the unit (Bergink et al. 2011). Every patient admitted to the MBU between May 2005 and December 2016 was screened for study inclusion (N = 315).

Participants

We included patients with a diagnosis of first-onset mania or psychosis during the postpartum period, who were aged between 18 and 45 years. 'Postpartum psychosis' was operationalized as any of the following DSM-IV diagnoses and requiring the specifier 'onset postpartum': manic episode, mixed episode, depressive disorder with psychotic features, psychotic disorder not otherwise specified (NOS) or brief psychotic disorder, as assessed with the Structured Clinical Interview for DSM (SCID). Patients were excluded if they had a chronic psychotic disorder, mania, or psychosis with onset during pregnancy or > 12 weeks postpartum, a history of psychosis or mania outside the postpartum period, or drug abuse.

A total of 315 women were admitted to the MBU between May 2005 and December 2016. One hundred thirty-seven of these patients received a diagnosis of postpartum psychosis. Of these, 14 women had a prior postpartum psychiatric episode but no episodes of mania or psychosis at other times. Of the 137 women, four patients declined participation. In addition, 21 women were excluded: 18 women were excluded because they had a history of mania or psychosis outside the postpartum period, one woman was excluded because of postpartum drug abuse, one woman was excluded because her symptom onset was > 12 weeks postpartum, one woman was excluded because her symptoms started during pregnancy. Accordingly, 112 patients fulfilled the criteria for first-onset postpartum psychosis. Five patients were lost to follow-up (4.5%) and one patient (0.9%) was lost to suicide (baseline and clinical characteristics of these women can be found in Additional file 1: Table A1). In this study, we therefore included 106 women admitted to the MBU between 2005 and 2016. None of the women were breastfeeding during their MBU admission.

Symptomatology and clinical course of the initial episode

Patients were diagnosed by a clinician using the Structured Clinical Interview for DSM (SCID-1/P research version) (First et al. 1999). The SCID is a semi-structured interview guide for making diagnoses according to the diagnostic criteria published in the American Psychiatric Association's Diagnostic and Statistical Manual for Mental Disorders (DSM). Previous hypomanic and manic episodes were also registered using the SCID. We further assessed demographics, psychiatric history, and family history of psychiatric illness (Table 1) (for more detail, see 12).

Phenomenology of the initial episode was assessed using the Bipolar Affective Disorder Dimension Scale (BADDS) (Craddock et al. 2004). The BADDS comprises four dimensions which provide a quantitative measure of psychopathology in each of four domains: (1) Manic-like episodes (the Mania dimension, M), (2) Depression-like episodes (the Depression dimension, D), (3) Psychotic symptomatology (the Psychosis dimension, P) and (4) the relationship (congruence of content and timing) between psychotic features (if present) and mood episodes (the Incongruence dimension, I). Each dimension provides a composite measure that takes both severity and frequency of relevant psychopathology into account. The dimensions are rated using integers in the range 0–100, with higher scores indicating more clinically important psychopathology—typically a mix of severity and frequency/duration.

Treatment regimen

Because clinical presentation, family history, and the longitudinal illness course overlap markedly with those of bipolar disorder, postpartum psychosis is generally considered a bipolar spectrum illness and not a primary psychotic disorder (Sit et al. 2006; Chaudron and Pies 2003; Jones and Craddock 2002). In the absence of formal guidelines, treatment in clinical practice is typically based on the most prominent symptom dimensions. Benzodiazepines are used for insomnia and agitation, antipsychotics and mood stabilizers for psychotic and manic symptoms, and antidepressants for depressive symptoms.

During admission, women with a first-onset postpartum psychosis were treated according to a standardized treatment algorithm, as described previously (Bergink et al. 2015b). The first step in treatment involves benzodiazepines at bedtime for three days (step 1). The purpose of starting with an initial period of benzodiazepine monotherapy is to evaluate whether restoration of sleep results in clinical remission of manic and psychotic symptoms, as sleep loss has been considered an important etiological factor in postpartum psychosis (Sharma and Mazmanian 2003). For patients whose manic or psychotic symptoms persist after a few days of benzodiazepine monotherapy, the next recommended step involves antipsychotic medication (step 2). Although the efficacy of antipsychotics in the absence of mood stabilizers has been described in only three case reports, antipsychotics are frequently used worldwide as first-line treatment for patients with postpartum psychosis and mania (Doucet et al. 2011). Furthermore, antipsychotics are often considered the preferred pharmacological treatment option for acute mania outside the postpartum period (Cipriani et al. 2011). Our primary recommendation for antipsychotic treatment was haloperidol at 2–6 mg/day. Patients who experienced side effects were switched to an atypical antipsychotic. A subset of patients who had already been treated with an antipsychotic before admission (e.g., by acute services) were continued on the same antipsychotic they received before admission. If there was no significant clinical response after 2 weeks, adjunctive lithium was initiated (step 3). One small open-label study and a case report have suggested that the combination of lithium and antipsychotics is more effective than antipsychotic monotherapy in patients with postpartum psychosis (Targum et al. 1979; Silbermann et al. 1975). Furthermore, studies have demonstrated efficacy of lithium in the prevention of postpartum psychosis (Stewart et al. 1991; Cohen et al. 1995; Austin 1992; Bergink et al. 2012). Lithium dosing was achieved based on plasma level (target, 0.8–1.0 mmol/L).

After complete remission of symptoms, all women were advised to taper benzodiazepines to discontinuation. Women receiving antipsychotic monotherapy were advised to continue this treatment as maintenance therapy until nine months postpartum. Women who achieved clinical remission using both antipsychotics and lithium were advised to gradually taper off antipsychotic treatment, with maintenance lithium monotherapy until nine months postpartum. Lithium dosing for relapse prevention was achieved based on plasma level (target, 0.6–0.8 mmol/L).

Longitudinal course of the illness

Four years postpartum, women were re-evaluated using the SCID (First et al. 1999). Women were not seen in between hospital discharge and follow-up for the purposes of this study. Recurrence was defined as the occurrence of any depression, (hypo)mania, psychosis or mixed state episode fulfilling DSM-IV criteria, admission

Table 1 Demographics and clinical characteristics of women with non-postpartum recurrence during follow-up and of women with no recurrence outside the postpartum period during follow-up

	Non-postpartum recurrence n=34		No recurrence outside the postpartum period n=72		p-value
Baseline characteristics at time of initial episode					
Age in years	Mean=31.0	SD=4.8	Mean=31.9	SD=4.9	0.351
Country of origin (n)					
Netherlands	79.4%	27	94.4%	68	0.018
Other	20.6%	7	5.6%	4	
Marital status (n)					
Married or in relationship	100.0%	34	91.6%	66	0.217
Not in relationship	-	-	4.2%	3	
Missing	-	-	4.2%	3	
Education (n)					
No education	3.0%	1	–	–	0.521
Primary school	–	–	1.4%	1	
Secondary school	14.7%	5	9.7%	7	
Vocational training	29.4%	10	30.6%	22	
Higher education	52.9%	18	58.3%	42	
Parity (n)					
1	79.4%	27	79.2%	57	0.343
2	11.8%	4	16.7%	12	
≥3	8.8%	3	2.8%	2	
Missing	–	–	1.4%	1	
Psychiatric history before postpartum episode (n)					
None	55.9%	19	76.4%	55	0.210
Postpartum depression	8.8%	3	2.8%	2	
Postpartum psychosis/mania (not at other times)	8.8%	3	5.6%	4	
Depression	20.6%	7	9.7%	7	
Anxiety	5.9%	2	2.8%	2	
Hypomania	–	–	2.8%	2	
Family history of psychiatric disorders† (n)					
None	47.1%	16	34.7%	25	0.238
1st degree relative with depression or anxiety	41.2%	14	36.1%	26	0.616
1st degree relative with postpartum psychiatric episode	2.9%	1	13.9%	10	0.085
1st degree relative with bipolar disorder	8.8%	3	13.9%	10	0.444
Missing	2.9%	1	4.2%	3	0.745
Length of initial hospital admission in days	Mean=59.6	SD=25.6	Mean=57.3	SD=31.2	0.700
Phenomenology initial episode (n)					
Manic with and without psychotic features	58.8%	20	61.1%	44	0.533
Psychotic only	17.7%	6	12.5%	9	
Depressed-psychotic	5.8%	2	13.9%	10	
Manic-depressed (mixed)	17.7%	6	12.5%	9	
Relation between mood and psychotic symptoms (n)					
Presence of mood-incongruent psychotic symptoms	67.6%	23	62.5%	45	0.611
>50% of time psychotic during initial episodes	52.9%	18	47.2%	34	0.596
First rank psychotic symptoms‡	8.8%	3	6.9%	5	0.730
DSM-IV diagnosis at baseline					
Bipolar I disorder	82.3%	28	77.8%	56	0.600
Bipolar II disorder	2.9%	1	1.4%	1	0.597
Major Depressive Disorder with Psychotic Features	2.9%	1	11.1%	8	0.159

Table 1 (continued)

	Non-postpartum recurrence n=34		No recurrence outside the postpartum period n=72		p-value
Mood disorders NOS	8.8%	3	9.7%	7	0.883
Lithium treatment during admission (n)					
No	20.6%	7	25.0%	18	0.617
Yes	79.4%	27	75.0%	54	
Antipsychotics treatment during admission (n)					
No	14.7%	5	18.1%	13	0.668
Yes	85.3%	29	81.1%	59	
Follow-up					
Length of follow-up period in months	Mean=46.3	SD=20.3	Mean=44.5	SD=8.8	0.543
Subsequent pregnancies (n)					
No	64.7%	22	58.3%	42	0.464
Yes	32.3%	11	40.3%	29	
Missing	3.0%	1	1.4%	1	
Recurrence period (n)					
Postpartum only	–	–	3.0	2	<0.001
Non-postpartum only	90.9%	30	-	-	
Postpartum and non-postpartum	9.1%	3	–	–	
Recurrence phenomenology (n)					
No recurrence	–	–	97.2%	70	<0.001
Hypo(mania)	42.4%	13	–		
Depression/Anxiety	33.3%	11	2.8*%	2*	
Psychotic episode without affective components	15.2%	5	–	–	
Schizoaffective disorder	9.1%	4	–	–	
DSM-IV diagnosis at follow-up					
Bipolar I Disorder	38.2%	13	4.2%	3	<0.001
Major Depressive Disorder	14.7%	5	16.7%	12	0.794
Anxiety/Panic Disorder	11.8%	4	2.8%	2	0.063
Brief Psychotic Disorder	11.8%	4	-	-	<0.001
Psychotic Disorder NOS	2.9%	1	-	-	<0.001
Schizoaffective Disorder	11.8%	4	–	–	<0.001
Mood Disorder NOS	2.9%	1	–	–	<0.001
Cyclothymic Disorder	2.9%	1	–	–	<0.001
Observation of other suspected mental condition (V71.09)	2.9%	1	75%	54	<0.001
Lithium stop in follow-up period (n)					
No	61.8%	21	45.8%	33	0.126
Yes	38.2%	13	54.2%	39	
Recurrence *within 6 months after* lithium stop (n)					
No	23.5%	8	–	–	<0.001
Yes	14.7%	5	–	–	
Lithium treatment at follow-up (n)					
No	38.2%	13	61.1%	44	0.027
Yes	61.8%	21	38.9%	28	
Antipsychotics treatment at follow-up (n)					
No	76.5%	26	94.4%	68	0.006
Yes	23.5%	8	5.6%	4	
Still in treatment at follow-up (n)					

Table 1 (continued)

	Non-postpartum recurrence n=34		No recurrence outside the postpartum period n=72		p-value
No	20.6%	7	68.0%	49	< 0.001
Yes	76.5%	26	30.6%	22	
Missing	2.9%	1	1.4%	1	

The table presents percentages and numbers of participants, unless stated

† Percentages may exceed 100% because these categories are not mutually exclusive

‡ The set of psychotic symptoms recognized as having special weight in the diagnosis of schizophrenia and schizoaffective disorder

*Recurrence in the postpartum period

to hospital or a restart of medication. All women with a recurrence were asked retrospectively about the timing of their episode, including whether this was in relation to a subsequent pregnancy. Additionally, we collected information on the timing of tapering or stopping medication if applicable. The patient's medical records were consulted to validate the information.

Based on information collected at follow-up, women were categorized into one of two groups: (1) women with recurrence of non-postpartum mood or psychotic episodes within the follow-up period, or (2) women with mania/psychosis in the postpartum period and no mood or psychotic episodes outside the postpartum period during follow-up (vulnerability to affective psychosis only after childbirth).

Statistical analysis

We summarize the longitudinal course of the illness per in Table 1. Differences between the two groups in terms of baseline demographic and clinical characteristics were assessed using Chi-squared and t-tests were appropriate (Table 1). A Kaplan–Meier Survival Curve of recurrence rates within the four-year follow-up period after first-onset postpartum psychosis was plotted. Additionally, we used a binomial logistic regression model to identify clinical predictors of postpartum psychosis group (recurrence of non-postpartum mood or psychotic episodes vs. mania/psychosis in the postpartum period only). Potential predictors of recurrence were based on the literature included admission length, maternal age, phenomenology of the index episode, and family history of psychiatric illness (Kapfhammer et al. 2014; Blackmore et al. 2013; Benvenuti et al. 1992). To improve power in the family history variable, depression and anxiety were combined into the category 'depression or anxiety' and postpartum depression and postpartum psychosis were combined into the category 'postpartum psychiatric episode'. Mania/psychosis in the postpartum period only and psychiatric disorder with non-postpartum episodes were coded as 0 and 1 respectively. Results are presented in the form of odds ratios. All statistical analyses were performed using Stata/MP 15 (StataCorp 2017). Lastly, we explored whether the set of psychotic symptoms recognized as having special weight in the diagnosis of schizophrenia and schizoaffective disorder (thought echo, insertion, withdrawal, or broadcasting; passivity experiences; hallucinatory voices giving running commentary, discussing subject in third person, or originating in some part of the body; bizarre delusions; catatonia) was a precursor for a diagnosis within the psychotic disorder spectrum.

Results

Follow-up

Seventy-two women (67.9%) did not experience recurrence during the four-year follow-up. Two women (1.9%) experienced a recurrence exclusively following later pregnancies. Both of these women subsequently received a diagnosis of depression at follow-up (Table 1).

Thirty-four women (32.1%) experienced at least one additional episode outside of the postpartum period during follow-up. The median time to recurrence during follow-up in women with episodes outside of the postpartum period was 20.3 months (interquartile range IQR: 10.4–29.6) following initial hospitalization (Fig. 1). Of the thirty-four women who had at least one episode outside of the postpartum period, 14 experienced an episode of (hypo)mania (13.2% of the overall sample), 11 experienced a depressive/anxiety episode (10.4% of the overall sample), and nine experienced a psychotic episode with or without affective components (8.5% of the overall sample) within the follow-up period.

Medication use

The majority of patients were treated with lithium (76.4%) and antipsychotics (83.0%) during their MBU admission. Over the course of the follow-up period, most women were able to successfully taper lithium: out of the

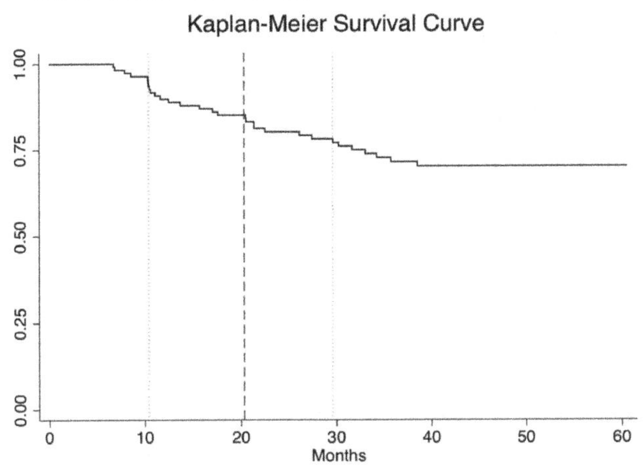

Fig. 1 Kaplan–Meier Survival Curve of recurrence rates within the four-year follow-up period after first-onset postpartum psychosis. Median time to recurrence is represented by a dashed line, the interquartile range is represented by dotted lines

52 women who stopped lithium, five relapsed within six months of discontinuation (Table 1).

Potential predictors of relapse

To identify potential clinical predictors of recurrence of non-postpartum mood or psychotic episodes, we carried out a logistic regression. We did not find significant predictors of recurrence outside the postpartum period (Table 2).

Psychotic symptoms

Eight women (7.5%) in this cohort experienced first rank psychotic symptoms during their postpartum psychosis as measured by the BADDS. These include one or more of the schizophrenia-like symptoms, including thought insertion, withdrawal or broadcasting, passivity experiences, hallucinatory voices giving running commentary, discussing subject in third person and bizarre delusions. Of these eight women, five experienced no recurrence, while two women experienced (hypo)mania within the first year after their initial episode. One woman experienced depressive episodes both during a subsequent postpartum episode, as well as outside the postpartum period. None of the women with first-rank psychotic symptoms met criteria for a schizophrenia spectrum illness, including schizophreniform, schizophrenia, and schizoaffective disorder, during follow-up.

Discussion

In this prospective longitudinal study, we investigated the long-term outcome of 106 women with postpartum psychosis over a four-year period. Over two thirds of the women included in this study did not have psychiatric episodes outside the postpartum period during follow-up. For the remaining subset of women (~ 32%), postpartum psychosis was part of a psychiatric disorder with a more disabling disease course and broader window of recurrence vulnerability, both in and outside of the postpartum period. This recurrence rate for mood or psychotic episodes outside the postpartum period is lower than the recurrence rate we recently reported in our meta-analysis (56.5%) (Gilden et al. 2020).

The differences between this study and our recent meta-analysis (Gilden et al. 2020) may be due to the differences in the follow-up period, which was four years in this study but ranged from 11 to 26 years in the meta-analysis. It is conceivable that recurrence rates increase with longer follow-up periods. The relatively lower relapse rates may also be attributed to preventive follow-up, including continued medication use, and specialized health care for these women in the current treatment setting (Bergink et al. 2011).

Table 2 Logistic regression analysis of the clinical predictors for recurrence of non-postpartum mood or psychotic episodes within the follow-up period

		ß	z	p	OR	OR 95% CI
Admission length		0.001	0.07	0.943	1.00	0.98; 1.02
Age		– 0.06	– 1.16	0.245	0.94	0.86; 1.04
Phenomenology at admission	Psychotic only	0.46	0.74	0.460	1.59	0.47; 5.42
	Depressed-psychotic	– 0.48	– 0.55	0.580	0.61	0.11; 3.47
	Manic with and without psychotic features	0.55	0.81	0.418	1.74	0.46; 6.61
Family history	Postpartum episode	– 1.65	– 1.50	0.133	0.20	0.02; 1.65
	Depression or Anxiety	0.17	0.36	0.717	1.18	0.48; 2.94
	Bipolar disorder	– 0.70	-0.94	0.345	0.50	0.12; 2.12
Lithium treatment of initial episode		0.21	0.35	0.727	1.24	0.37; 4.11
Antipsychotic treatment initial episode		0.26	0.42	0.677	1.30	0.38; 4.42

Of the 34 women with a recurrence, 14 experienced an episode of (hypo)mania (13.2% of the overall sample), 11 experienced a depressive/anxiety episode (10.4% of the overall sample), and nine experienced a psychotic episode with or without affective components (8.5% of the overall sample) within the follow-up period. Of the nine women who experienced a psychotic episode, four women met diagnostic criteria for schizoaffective disorder, four women met diagnostic criteria for brief psychotic disorder, and one met diagnostic criteria for psychotic disorder not otherwise specified. None of these women fulfilled diagnostic criteria for schizophrenia or schizophreniform disorder. Currently, the DSM-5 does not recognize postpartum psychosis (including psychotic, manic, psychotic depressed, or mixed episodes) as a distinct disease category (Kamperman et al. 2017). Women with psychotic symptoms without an affective component are currently diagnosed as either psychosis not otherwise specified, brief psychotic disorder or schizophreniform disorder, if schizophrenia-like symptoms are present. A primary diagnosis within the psychotic DSM may not be accurate.

The majority of women with postpartum psychosis have prominent manic or mixed affective features (Kamperman et al. 2017). Based on current best practice, these women are, therefore, diagnosed with bipolar disorder at the time of their first-onset postpartum psychosis. However, the fact that over 67% of our sample (and 43.5% in our recent meta-analysis (Gilden et al. 2020)) had no depressive, manic or psychotic recurrence outside the postpartum period raises questions about the validity of this approach. The diagnosis 'bipolar disorder' suggests a vulnerability to mood episodes at all times, not only during the postpartum period. Consequently, we believe a diagnosis of bipolar disorder should only be given following severe mood episodes outside of the postpartum period, either mania or depression. For women with vulnerability for episodes limited to the postpartum period, a distinct classification within the bipolar spectrum would be more accurate and reduce stigma.

To investigate predictive factors of episodes outside of the postpartum period, we assessed the association between various clinical and demographic characteristics with recurrence outcome. Unlike previous retrospective studies (Sit et al. 2006; Terp et al. 1999; Blackmore et al. 2013), we did not find that the length of the disease episode or a woman's age were significantly associated with higher risk for developing a more severe psychiatric disorder with non-postpartum episodes. This may be due to our standardized treatment algorithm, as well as the lack of variance in maternal age in our sample. Moreover, phenomenology of the index episode was also not predictive of the disease course, but this may be attributed to a lack of statistical power. The risk of recurrence for women with mania (both with or without psychotic symptoms) or psychosis without affective symptoms was very similar. Surprisingly, a schizophrenia-like presentation was neither predictive of recurrence, nor of receiving a schizoaffective diagnosis during follow-up. In line with prior longitudinal studies (Kapfhammer et al. 2014; Terp et al. 1999; Benvenuti et al. 1992; Kirpinar et al. 1999; Rohde and Marneros 1993; Schöpf and Rust 1994; Videbech and Gouliaev 1995), we found that the vast majority of non-postpartum episodes during follow-up occurred within the bipolar spectrum. In our cohort, none of the women received a diagnosis of schizophrenia during follow-up, similar to most prior studies, except Kirpinar et al. (Kirpinar et al. 1999), who found a relationship between postpartum psychosis and a diagnosis of schizophrenia during follow-up.

Understanding who is at risk of a mood or psychotic disorder during follow-up, and whose vulnerability is limited to the postpartum period, is particularly important in guiding treatment decisions including long-term pharmacotherapy. Unfortunately, no biomarkers are currently available to help guide these decisions. In clinical practice, this means that long-term monitoring is warranted for everyone with postpartum psychosis. Another reason for long-term monitoring are the high suicide rates during follow-up, reported by other studies (Kapfhammer et al. 2014; Schöpf and Rust 1994; Videbech and Gouliaev 1995).

Our findings must be interpreted in light of a number of limitations. Firstly, our sample size was relatively small. Nevertheless, this is the largest prospective longitudinal study of women with postpartum psychosis to date. Secondly, this is a naturalistic study, rather than a randomized control trial, in which patients' preferences may have influenced treatment decisions. Due to the low incidence of postpartum psychosis, a randomized control trial for its treatment would be challenging, and no such trial has been published (Bergink et al. 2016). Lastly, our cohort was recruited from a single, inpatient site in the Netherlands. Patients were more highly educated and more likely to be partnered/married than the general population, potentially limiting the generalizability of our findings.

Conclusion

In this prospective longitudinal study of first-onset postpartum psychosis, we investigated the long-term outcomes of 106 women with postpartum psychosis over a four-year follow-up. We found that for the majority of women with first-onset postpartum psychosis, the risk of illness was limited to the period after childbirth. For the remaining women, postpartum psychosis was part of a mood or psychotic disorder with severe non-postpartum recurrence, mainly in the bipolar spectrum. No clinical predictors of a woman's risk of severe episodes outside the postpartum period were found. Our findings add to previous evidence suggesting a fundamental link between postpartum psychosis and bipolar disorder, which may represent two distinct diagnoses within the same spectrum.

Abbreviations
95%CI: 95% Confidence interval; BADDS: Bipolar Affective Disorder Dimension Scale; D: BADDS Depression dimension; M: BADDS Mania dimension; P: BADDS Psychosis dimension; DSM: Diagnostic and Statistical Manual of Mental Disorders; Erasmus MC: Erasmus Medical Centre; ICD-10: International Classification of Diseases, Tenth Revision; IQR: Interquartile range; MBU: Mother-Baby Unit; mmol/L: Millimoles per liter; NOS: Not otherwise specified; OR: Odds ratio; SCID: Structured Clinical Interview for DSM.

Supplementary Information

Additional file 1: Table A1. Baseline and clinical characteristics of the women lost to follow-up.

Acknowledgements
We thank Dr. Kathelijne Koorengevel for the clinical care of these patients.

Authors' contributions
Rommel: Conceptualization, Methodology, Formal analysis, Writing—Original Draft and Review & Editing, Visualization: Molenaar: Conceptualization, Writing—Review & Editing; Gilden: Conceptualization, Methodology, Investigation, Writing—Review & Editing; Kushner: Writing—Review & Editing; Westerbeek: Investigation, Data Curation, Project administration, Writing—Review & Editing; Kamperman: Conceptualization, Methodology, Writing—Review & Editing; Bergink: Conceptualization, Methodology, Project administration, Supervision, Writing—Review & Editing.

Author details
[1]Department of Psychiatry, Icahn School of Medicine at Mount Sinai, Icahn (East) Building Floor 4 Room 34, 1425 Madison Ave, New York, NY 10029, USA. [2]Department of Obstetrics, Gynecology and Reproductive Science, Icahn School of Medicine at Mount Sinai, New York, NY, USA. [3]Department of Psychiatry, Erasmus Medical Center Rotterdam, Rotterdam, The Netherlands.

References
Austin M. Puerperal affective psychosis: is there a case for lithium prophylaxis? Br J Psychiatry. 1992;161:692–4.

Benvenuti P, Cabras PL, Servi P, Rosseti S, Marchetti G, Pazzagli A. Puerperal psychoses: a clinical case study with follow-up. J Affect Disord. 1992;26:25–30.

Bergink V, Lambregtse-van Den Berg MP, Koorengevel KM, Kupka R, Kushner SA. First-onset psychosis occurring in the postpartum period: a prospective cohort study. J Clin Psychiatry. 2011;72:1531–7.

Bergink V, Bouvy PF, Vervoort JSP, Koorengevel KM, Steegers EAP, Kushner SA. Prevention of postpartum psychosis and mania in women at high risk. Am J Psychiatry. 2012;169:609–15.

Bergink V, Boyce P, Munk-Olsen T. Postpartum psychosis: a valuable misnomer. Aust N Z J Psychiatry. 2015a;49:102–3.

Bergink V, Burgerhout KM, Koorengevel KM, Kamperman AM, Hoogendijk WJ, Lambregtse-Van Den Berg MP, Kushner SA. Treatment of psychosis and mania in the postpartum period. Am J Psychiatry. 2015b;172:115–23.

Bergink V, Rasgon N, Wisner KL. Postpartum psychosis: Madness, mania, and melancholia in motherhood. Am J Psychiatry. 2016;173:1179–88.

Blackmore ER, Rubinow DR, O'Connor TG, Liu X, Tang W, Craddock N, Jones I. Reproductive outcomes and risk of subsequent illness in women diagnosed with postpartum psychosis. Bipolar Disord. 2013;15:394–404.

Boyce P, Barriball E. Puerperal psychosis. Arch Womens Ment Health. 2010;13:45–7.

Brockington IF, Cernik KF, Schofield EM, Downing AR, Francis AF, Keelan C. Puerperal psychosis: phenomena and diagnosis. Arch Gen Psychiatry. 1981;38:829–33.

Burgerhout KM, Kamperman AM, Roza SJ, Lambregtse-Van Den Berg MP, Koorengevel KM, Hoogendijk WJG, Kushner SA, Bergink V. Functional recovery after postpartum psychosis: a prospective longitudinal study. J Clin Psychiatry. 2017;78:122–8.

Chaudron LH, Pies RW. The Relationship between postpartum psychosis and bipolar disorder: a review. J Clin Psychiatry. 2003;64:1284–92.

Cipriani A, Barbui C, Salanti G, Rendell J, Brown R, Stockton S, Purgato M, Spineli L, Goodwin G, Geddes J. Comparative efficacy and acceptability of antimanic drugs in acute mania: a multiple-treatments meta-analysis. Lancet (london, England). 2011;378:1306–15.

Cohen LS, Sichel DA, Robertson LM, Heckscher E, Rosenbaum JF. Postpartum prophylaxis for women with bipolar disorder. Am J Psychiatry. 1995;152:1641–5.

Craddock N, Jones I, Kirov G, Jones L. The Bipolar Affective Disorder Dimension Scale (BADDS)—a dimensional scale for rating lifetime psychopathology in Bipolar spectrum disorders. BMC Psychiatry. 2004;4:19.

Di Florio A, Munk-Olsen T, Bergink V. The birth of a psychiatric orphan disorder: postpartum psychosis. The Lancet Psychiatry. 2016;3:502.

Doucet S, Jones I, Letourneau N, Dennis C, Blackmore E. Interventions for the prevention and treatment of postpartum psychosis: a systematic review. Arch Womens Ment Health. 2011;14:89–98.

First MB, Gibbon M, Williams J. Structured clinical interview for DSM IV axis I disorders, patient edition (Nederlandse versie). Swets & Zeitlinger BV; 1999

Gilden J, Kamperman AM, Munk-Olsen T, Hoogendijk WJG, Kushner SA, Bergink V. Long-term outcomes of postpartum psychosis: a systematic review and meta-analysis. J Clin Psychiatry. 2020. https://doi.org/10.4088/JCP.19r12906.

Jones I, Craddock N. Do puerperal psychotic episodes identify a more familial subtype of bipolar disorder? Results of a family history study. Psychiatr Genet. 2002;12:177–80.

Kamperman AM, Veldman-Hoek MJ, Wesseloo R, Robertson Blackmore E, Bergink V. Phenotypical characteristics of postpartum psychosis: a clinical cohort study. Bipolar Disord. 2017;19:450–7.

Kapfhammer HP, Reininghaus EZ, Fitz W, Lange P. Clinical course of Illness in women with early onset puerperal psychosis: a 12-year follow-up study. J Clin Psychiatry. 2014;75:1096–104.

Kirpinar I, Coşkun I, Çayköylü A, Anaç S, Özer H. First-case postpartum psychoses in Eastern Turkey: a clinical case and follow-up study. Acta Psychiatr Scand. 1999;100:199–204.

Meltzer-Brody S, Howard LM, Bergink V, Vigod S, Jones I, Munk-Olsen T, Honikman S, Milgrom J. Postpartum psychiatric disorders. Nat Rev Dis Prim. 2018;4:1–18.

Munk-Olsen T, Laursen TM, Meltzer-Brody S, Mortensen PB, Jones I. Psychiatric disorders with postpartum onset: possible early manifestations of bipolar affective disorders. Arch Gen Psychiatry. 2012;69:428–34.

Nager A, Szulkin R, Johansson SE, Johansson LM, Sundquist K. High lifelong relapse rate of psychiatric disorders among women with postpartum psychosis. Nord J Psychiatry. 2013;67:53–8.

Osborne LM. Recognizing and managing postpartum psychosis: a clinical guide for obstetric providers. Obstet Gynecol Clin North Am. 2018;45:455–68.

Rohde A, Marneros A. Postpartum psychoses: onset and long-term course. Psychopathology. 1993;26:203–9.

Schöpf J, Rust B. Follow-up and family study of postpartum psychoses Part I: overview. Eur Arch Psychiatry Clin Neurosci. 1994;244:101–11.

Sharma V, Mazmanian D. Sleep loss and postpartum psychosis. Bipolar Disord. 2003;5:98–105.

Silbermann RM, Beenen F, de Jong H. Clinical treatment of post partum delirium with perfenazine and lithium carbonate. Psychopathology. 1975;8:314–26.
Sit D, Rothschild AJ, Wisner KL. A review of postpartum psychosis. J Women's Heal. 2006;15:352–68.
StataCorp. Stata Statistical Software: Release 15. 2017
Stewart DE, Klompenhouwer JL, Kendell RE, Van HAM. Prophylactic lithium in puerperal psychosis: the experience of three centres. Br J Psychiatry. 1991;158:393–7.
Targum S, Davenport Y, Webster M. Postpartum mania in bipolar manic-depressive patients withdrawn from lithium carbonate. J Nerv Ment Dis. 1979;167:572–4.
Terp IM, Engholm G, Meller H, Mortensed PB, Møller H, Mortensen PB, Meller H, Mortensed PB. A follow-up study of postpartum psychoses: prognosis and risk factors for readmission. Acta Psychiatr Scand. 1999;100:40–6.
Videbech P, Gouliaev G. First admission with puerperal psychosis: 7–14 years of follow-up. Acta Psychiatr Scand. 1995;91:167–73.
Wesseloo R, Kamperman AM, Munk-Olsen T, Pop VJM, Kushner SA, Bergink V. Risk of postpartum relapse in bipolar disorder and postpartum psychosis: a systematic review and meta-analysis. Am J Psychiatry. 2016;173:117–27.
Wisner KL, Peindl K, Hanusa BH. Symptomatology of affective and psychotic llnesses related to childbearing. J Affect Disord. 1994;30:77–87.

Permissions

All chapters in this book were first published by Springer; hereby published with permission under the Creative Commons Attribution License or equivalent. Every chapter published in this book has been scrutinized by our experts. Their significance has been extensively debated. The topics covered herein carry significant findings which will fuel the growth of the discipline. They may even be implemented as practical applications or may be referred to as a beginning point for another development.

The contributors of this book come from diverse backgrounds, making this book a truly international effort. This book will bring forth new frontiers with its revolutionizing research information and detailed analysis of the nascent developments around the world.

We would like to thank all the contributing authors for lending their expertise to make the book truly unique. They have played a crucial role in the development of this book. Without their invaluable contributions this book wouldn't have been possible. They have made vital efforts to compile up to date information on the varied aspects of this subject to make this book a valuable addition to the collection of many professionals and students.

This book was conceptualized with the vision of imparting up-to-date information and advanced data in this field. To ensure the same, a matchless editorial board was set up. Every individual on the board went through rigorous rounds of assessment to prove their worth. After which they invested a large part of their time researching and compiling the most relevant data for our readers.

The editorial board has been involved in producing this book since its inception. They have spent rigorous hours researching and exploring the diverse topics which have resulted in the successful publishing of this book. They have passed on their knowledge of decades through this book. To expedite this challenging task, the publisher supported the team at every step. A small team of assistant editors was also appointed to further simplify the editing procedure and attain best results for the readers.

Apart from the editorial board, the designing team has also invested a significant amount of their time in understanding the subject and creating the most relevant covers. They scrutinized every image to scout for the most suitable representation of the subject and create an appropriate cover for the book.

The publishing team has been an ardent support to the editorial, designing and production team. Their endless efforts to recruit the best for this project, has resulted in the accomplishment of this book. They are a veteran in the field of academics and their pool of knowledge is as vast as their experience in printing. Their expertise and guidance has proved useful at every step. Their uncompromising quality standards have made this book an exceptional effort. Their encouragement from time to time has been an inspiration for everyone.

The publisher and the editorial board hope that this book will prove to be a valuable piece of knowledge for researchers, students, practitioners and scholars across the globe.

List of Contributors

Ann-Kristin Evers, Julia Veeh and Andreas Reif
Department of Psychiatry, Psychosomatic Medicine and Psychotherapy, University Hospital Frankfurt, Goethe University, Heinrich-Hoffmann-Str. 10, 60528 Frankfurt am Main, Germany

Rhiannon McNeill and Sarah Kittel-Schneider
Department of Psychiatry, Psychosomatic Medicine and Psychotherapy, University Hospital Frankfurt, Goethe University, Frankfurt Am Main, Germany
Department of Psychiatry, Psychosomatic Medicine and Psychotherapy, University Hospital, University of Würzburg, Margarete-Hoppel-Platz 1, 97080 Würzburg, Germany

Michael Gitlin
Department of Psychiatry, Geffen School of Medicine at UCLA, Los Angeles, USA

Gin S. Malhi
CADE Clinic, Department of Psychiatry, Royal North Shore Hospital, St Leonards, USA
Discipline of Psychiatry, Faculty of Medicine and Health, The University of Sydney, Sydney, Australia

Marin Veldic and Balwinder Singh
Department of Psychiatry, University Hospital, Universidad Autonoma de Nuevo Leon, Monterrey, Mexico

Alfredo B. Cuellar-Barboza and Mark A. Frye
Department of Psychiatry, University Hospital, Universidad Autonoma de Nuevo Leon, Monterrey, Mexico
Department of Psychiatry and Psychology, Mayo Clinic, 200 First Street SW, Rochester, MN 55905, USA

Simon Kung, Nicolas A. Nunez, Alejandra Cabello-Arreola, Hannah K. Betcher and Katherine M. Moore
Department of Psychiatry and Psychology, Mayo Clinic, 200 First Street SW, Rochester, MN 55905, USA

Susan L. McElroy and Francisco Romo-Nava
Lindner Center of HOPE and Department of Psychiatry, University of Cincinnati, Cincinnati, OH, USA

N, Brandon J. Coombes and Stacey J. Winham
Department of Health Sciences Research, Mayo Clinic, Rochester, USA

Joanna M. Biernacka
Department of Psychiatry, University Hospital, Universidad Autonoma de Nuevo Leon, Monterrey, Mexico
Department of Health Sciences Research, Mayo Clinic, Rochester, USA

Miguel Prieto
Department of Psychiatry, Universidad de los Andes, Santiago, Chile.

Gregor Hasler
Psychiatry Research Unit, Fribourg Network for Mental Health (RFSM), University of Fribourg, Chemin du Cardinal-Journet 3, 1752 Villars-sur-Glane, Switzerland

Riccardo Guglielmo
Psychiatry Research Unit, Fribourg Network for Mental Health (RFSM), University of Fribourg, Chemin du Cardinal-Journet 3, 1752 Villars-sur-Glane, Switzerland
Department of Neuroscience, Institute of Psychiatry, Catholic University Medical School, Largo Francesco Vito 1, 00168 Rome, Italy

Kamilla Woznica Miskowiak
Copenhagen Affective Disorder Research Centre (CADIC), Psychiatric Centre Copenhagen, Copenhagen University Hospital, Rigshospitalet, Copenhagen, Denmark

Margrethe Collier Høegh, Ingrid Melle, Beathe Haatveit, Stine Holmstul Olsen, Idun B. Huflåtten and Trine Vik Lagerberg
CoE NORMENT, Norwegian Centre for Mental Disorders Research, Division of Mental Health and Addiction, University of Oslo and Oslo University Hospital, Building 49, Ullevål sykehus, Nydalen, PO Box 4956, 0424 Oslo, Norway

Sofie R. Aminoff
CoE NORMENT, Norwegian Centre for Mental Disorders Research, Division of Mental Health and Addiction, University of Oslo and Oslo University Hospital, Building 49, Ullevål sykehus, Nydalen, PO Box 4956, 0424 Oslo, Norway
Division of Mental Health and Addiction, Oslo University Hospital, Oslo, Norway

Torill Ueland
CoE NORMENT, Norwegian Centre for Mental Disorders Research, Division of Mental Health and Addiction, University of Oslo and Oslo University Hospital, Building 49, Ullevål sykehus, Nydalen, PO Box 4956, 0424 Oslo, Norway
Department of Psychology, University of Oslo, Oslo, Norway

Tobias Kallehauge, Ann-Eva Christensen and Maria Rodrigo-Domingo
Psychiatry, Aalborg University Hospital, Aalborg, Denmark

Rasmus W. Licht and René Ernst Nielsen
Psychiatry, Aalborg University Hospital, Aalborg, Denmark
Department of Clinical Medicine, Aalborg University, Aalborg, Denmark

Christoph U. Correll
Department of Psychiatry, The Zucker Hillside Hospital, Northwell Health, 75-59 263rd Street, Glen Oaks, New York City, NY, USA
Department of Psychiatry and Molecular Medicine, Donald and Barbara Zucker School of Medicine at Hofstra/Northwell, Hempstead, NY, USA
Center for Psychiatric Neuroscience, The Feinstein Institute for Medical Research, Manhasset, NY, USA
Department of Child and Adolescent Psychiatry, Charité Universitätsmedizin, Berlin, Germany

Mathilde Frahm Laursen
Psychiatry, Aalborg University Hospital, Aalborg, Denmark
Department of Clinical Medicine, Aalborg University, Aalborg, Denmark
Unit for Psychiatric Research, Department of Psychiatry, Aalborg University Hospital, Mølleparkvej 10, 9000 Aalborg, Denmark

Jinyoung Lee, Ji Hyun Baek, Dongbin Lee, Sung Woo Ahn, Yong Chun Bahk and Kyung Sue Hong
Department of Psychiatry, Sungkyunkwan University School of Medicine, Samsung Medical Center, Seoul, Republic of Korea

So-Yung Yang
Department of Psychiatry, Sungkyunkwan University School of Medicine, Samsung Medical Center, Seoul, Republic of Korea
Department of Psychiatry, National Health Insurance Service, Ilsan Hospital,Goyang-si, Republic of Korea

Yujin Choi
Center for Clinical Research, Samsung Biomedical Research Institute, Seoul, Republic of Korea

Martin Sköld, Erik Joas, Mathias Kardell and Erik Pålsson
Department of Psychiatry and Neurochemistry, Institute of Neuroscience and Physiology, Sahlgrenska Academy, University of Gothenburg, Blå Stråket 15, 413 45 Gothenburg, Sweden

Sindre Rolstad
Department of Psychology, Faculty of Social Science, University of Gothenburg, Gothenburg, Sweden

Guy M. Goodwin
Department of Psychiatry, University of Oxford, Oxford, UK

Mikael Landén
Department of Psychiatry and Neurochemistry, Institute of Neuroscience and Physiology, Sahlgrenska Academy, University of Gothenburg, Blå Stråket 15, 413 45 Gothenburg, Sweden
Department of Medical Epidemiology and Biostatistics, Karolinska Institutet, Stockholm, Sweden

Xin Qi, Yan Wen, Ping Li, Chujun Liang, Bolun Cheng, Mei Ma, Shiqiang Cheng, Lu Zhang, Li Liu, Om Prakash Kafle and Feng Zhang
Key Laboratory of Trace Elements and Endemic Diseases of National Health and Family Planning Commission, School of Public Health, Health Science Center, Xi'an Jiaotong University, No. 76 Yan Ta West Road, Xi'an 710061, People's Republic of China

Catherine V. Barnes-Scheufler, Caroline Passow, Viola Oertel and Silke Matura
Department of Psychiatry, Psychosomatic Medicine and Psychotherapy, University Hospital Frankfurt, Goethe University, Heinrich-Hoffmann-Str. 10, 60528 Frankfurt am Main, Germany

Lara Rösler
Department of Psychiatry, Psychosomatic Medicine and Psychotherapy, University Hospital Frankfurt, Goethe University, Heinrich-Hoffmann-Str. 10, 60528 Frankfurt am Main, Germany
Netherlands Institute for Neuroscience, Amsterdam, The Netherlands

Jutta S. Mayer
Department of Child and Adolescent Psychiatry, Psychosomatics and Psychotherapy, University Hospital Frankfurt, Goethe University, Frankfurt am Main, Germany

Robert A. Bittner
Department of Psychiatry, Psychosomatic Medicine and Psychotherapy, University Hospital Frankfurt, Goethe University, Heinrich-Hoffmann-Str. 10, 60528 Frankfurt am Main, Germany
Ernst Strüngmann Institute for Neuroscience (ESI) in Cooperation with Max Planck Society, Frankfurt am Main, Germany

Jan Scott
Institute of Neuroscience, Newcastle University, Newcastle upon Tyne, UK
Université de Paris, Paris, France

Florence Vorspan, Frank Bellivier and Bruno Etain
Université de Paris, Paris, France
AP-HP, Département de Psychiatrie et de Médecine Addictologique, GH Saint-Louis-Lariboisière-Fernand-Widal, DMU Neurosciences Tête et Cou, Paris, France
Inserm UMRS 1144, Université de Paris, Paris, France

Josephine Loftus
Centre Expert Trouble Bipolaire, Hospital Princesse Grace Monaco, Monaco

Nikolaj Folke la Cour Karottki, Klara Coello, Sharleny Stanislaus, Sigurd Melbye, Hanne Lie Kjærstad and Kimie Stefanie Ormstrup Sletved
Copenhagen Affective Disorders Research Centre (CADIC), Psychiatric Center Copenhagen, Department O, 6243, Rigshospitalet, Blegdamsvej 9, 2100 Copenhagen, Denmark

Lars Vedel Kessing
Copenhagen Affective Disorders Research Centre (CADIC), Psychiatric Center Copenhagen, Department O, 6243, Rigshospitalet, Blegdamsvej 9, 2100 Copenhagen, Denmark
Faculty of Health and Medical Sciences, University of Copenhagen, Copenhagen, Denmark

Maj Vinberg
Copenhagen Affective Disorders Research Centre (CADIC), Psychiatric Center Copenhagen, Department O, 6243, Rigshospitalet, Blegdamsvej 9, 2100 Copenhagen, Denmark
Faculty of Health and Medical Sciences, University of Copenhagen, Copenhagen, Denmark
Psychiatric Research Unit, Psychiatric Centre North Zealand, Hillerød, Denmark

Arthur D. P. Mak, Owen N. W. Leung, Jenny Y. M. Ho, Idy W. Y. Chou, Sandra S. M. Chan, Linda C. W. Lam and Sing Lee
Department of Psychiatry, The Chinese University of Hong Kong, G/F Multicentre, Tai Po Hospital, Tai Po, Hong Kong, SAR, China

Sebastiaan F. W. Neggers
Department of Psychiatry, Brain Center Rudolf Magnus, University Medical Center Utrecht, Utrecht, The Netherlands

Winnie C. W. Chu
Department of Imaging and Interventional Radiology, The Chinese University of Hong Kong, Hong Kong, SAR, China

Kim Wright, Alyson L. Dodd, Fiona C. Warren, Antonieta Medina-Lara, Barnaby Dunn, Julie Harvey, Mahmood Javaid, Steven H. Jones, Christabel Owens, Rod S. Taylor, Deborah Duncan, Alexandra Newbold, Shelley Norman, Faith Warner and Thomas R. Lynch
Washington Singer Labs, University of Exeter Department of Psychology, Perry Road, Exeter EX4 4QG, UK

A. W. M. M. Stevens
Dimence Mental Health Institute, Centre for Bipolar Disorder, SCBS Bipolaire Stoonissen, Pikeursbaan 3, 7411 GT Deventer, The Netherlands

B. Geerling
Dimence Mental Health Institute, Centre for Bipolar Disorder, SCBS Bipolaire Stoonissen, Pikeursbaan 3, 7411 GT Deventer, The Netherlands
Department of Psychology, Health and Technology, Centre for eHealth and Wellbeing Research, University of Twente, Enschede, The Netherlands

T. Bohlmeijer
Department of Psychology, Health and Technology, Centre for eHealth and Wellbeing Research, University of Twente, Enschede, The Netherlands

S. M. Kelders
Department of Psychology, Health and Technology, Centre for eHealth and Wellbeing Research, University of Twente, Enschede, The Netherlands
Optentia Research Focus Area, North-West University, Vanderbijlpark, South Africa

R. W. Kupka
Department Psychiatry, Amsterdam Public Health Research Institute, Amsterdam UMC, Vrije Universiteit, Amsterdam, The Netherlands

Richard Bruggeman
Rob Giel Research Center, University of Groningen, University Medical Center Groningen, PO Box 30.001, 9700 RB Groningen, The Netherlands

Fionneke M. Bos and Lian van der Krieke
Rob Giel Research Center, University of Groningen, University Medical Center Groningen, PO Box 30.001, 9700 RB Groningen, The Netherlands
Interdisciplinary Center Psychopathology and Emotion Regulation (ICPE), University of Groningen, University Medical Center Groningen, Groningen, The Netherlands

Evelien Snippe and Marieke Wichers
Interdisciplinary Center Psychopathology and Emotion Regulation (ICPE), University of Groningen, University Medical Center Groningen, Groningen, The Netherlands

Bennard Doornbos
Department of Specialized Training, Psychiatric Hospital Mental Health Services Drenthe, Outpatient Clinics, Assen, The Netherlands

R. Hamish McAllister-Williams and Soraia Sousa
Northern Centre for Mood Disorders, Newcastle University, Newcastle upon Tyne, UK
Regional Affective Disorders Service, Cumbria, Northumberland Tyne and Wear NHS Foundation Trust, Newcastle upon Tyne, UK

Arun Kumar, Teresa Greco and Mark T. Bunker
LivaNova USA PLC, Houston, TX, USA

Scott T. Aaronson
Department of Clinical Research, Sheppard Pratt Health System, Baltimore, MD, USA

Charles R. Conway
Department of Psychiatry, Washington University School of Medicine in St. Louis, St. Louis, MO, USA

A. John Rush
Duke-National University of Singapore, Singapore, Singapore
Department of Psychiatry and Behavioral Sciences, Duke University School of Medicine, Durham, NC, USA
Department of Psychiatry, Health Sciences Center, Texas Tech University Permian Basin, Midland, TX, USA

Eva Neumann, Sandra Lorek and Bianca Ueberberg
Research Institute for Mental Health, Ruhr-University Bochum, LWL-University Hospital Bochum, Alexandrinenstr. 1, 44791 Bochum, Germany

Ida S. Haussleiter
Research Institute for Mental Health, Ruhr-University Bochum, LWL-University Hospital Bochum, Alexandrinenstr. 1, 44791 Bochum, Germany
Department of Psychiatry, Ruhr-University Bochum, LWL-University Hospital Bochum, Bochum, Germany.

Georg Juckel
Department of Psychiatry, Ruhr-University Bochum, LWL-University Hospital Bochum, Bochum, Germany.

Alysha Cooper and Julie Horrocks
Department of Mathematics and Statistics, University of Guelph, Guelph, ON, Canada

Sarah Goodday
Department of Psychiatry, University of Oxford, Oxford, UK
4YouandMe, Seattle, USA

Charles Keown-Stoneman
Dalla Lana School of Public Health, University of Toronto, Toronto, ON, Canada

Anne Duffy
Department of Psychiatry, University of Oxford, Oxford, UK
Department of Psychiatry, Queen's University, Kingston,ON, Canada

Willem A. Nolen
Department of Psychiatry, University Medical Center Groningen, University of Groningen, Hanzeplein 1, 9713 GZ Groningen, The Netherlands

Erwin van Meekeren
BuurtzorgT, Oeverwallaan 130, 2498 BK The Hague, The Netherlands

Piet Voskuil
Torendreef 14, 4851 BH Ulvenhout, The Netherlands

Willem van Tilburg
Department of Psychiatry, Amsterdam University Medical Centers, Vrije Universiteit, De Boelelaan 1117, 1081 HV Amsterdam, The Netherlands

Anna-Sophie Rommel
Department of Psychiatry, Icahn School of Medicine at Mount Sinai, Icahn (East) Building Floor 4 Room 34, 1425 Madison Ave, New York, NY 10029, USA

Steven A. Kushner and Veerle Bergink
Department of Psychiatry, Icahn School of Medicine at Mount Sinai, Icahn (East) Building Floor 4 Room 34, 1425 Madison Ave, New York, NY 10029, USA
Department of Obstetrics, Gynecology and Reproductive Science, Icahn School of Medicine at Mount Sinai, New York, NY, USA
Department of Psychiatry, Erasmus Medical Center Rotterdam, Rotterdam, The Netherlands

Nina Maren Molenaar
Department of Psychiatry, Icahn School of Medicine at Mount Sinai, Icahn (East) Building Floor 4 Room 34, 1425 Madison Ave, New York, NY 10029, USA
Department of Psychiatry, Erasmus Medical Center Rotterdam, Rotterdam, The Netherlands

Nicola J. Westerbeek, Astrid M. Kamperman and Janneke Gilden
Department of Psychiatry, Erasmus Medical Center Rotterdam, Rotterdam, The Netherlands

Index

www.ingramcontent.com/pod-product-compliance
Lightning Source LLC
LaVergne TN
LVHW082153200926
848484LV00008B/2151

* 9 7 9 8 8 8 7 4 0 0 1 3 6 *